ECONOMIC ANALYSIS

FOURTH EDITION

VOLUME I

MICROECONOMICS

ECONOMIC ANALYSIS

FOURTH EDITION

VOLUME I

MICROECONOMICS

KENNETH E. BOULDING

PROFESSOR OF ECONOMICS, UNIVERSITY OF MICHIGAN

Harper & Row, Publishers

NEW YORK

ECONOMIC ANALYSIS, Fourth Edition—Volume I: *Microeconomics* / Copyright © 1966 by Kenneth E. Boulding. Printed in the United States of America. All rights reserved. No part of this book may be used or reproduced in any manner whatsoever without written permission except in the case of brief quotations embodied in critical articles and reviews. For information address Harper & Row, Publishers, Incorporated, 49 East 33rd Street, New York 16, N.Y. 10016

Library of Congress Catalog Card Number: 66-10054

H-Q

TO THE MEMORY OF

Elizabeth Ann Boulding

(1880–1961)

CONTENTS

LIST OF FIGURES

LIST OF TABLES

PREFACE TO THE FIRST EDITION

The purpose of this book is twofold. It is intended as a text from which the student can learn and the teacher can teach the methods and results of economic analysis. It also seeks to be a contribution to the development and systematization of the body of economic analysis itself. These purposes are not separate. The task of presenting a systematic, orderly, and accurate account of economic analysis is identical with the task of preparing the material for teaching. It must be emphasized, however, that the purpose of this work is not primarily to entertain the student, or to enable him to regurgitate appropriate material into examination books, or to learn a few pat phrases, or to indoctrinate him with an abstract discipline which he will never use. Economics is like photography in this respect, that underexposure is less desirable than no exposure at all; and it is to be feared that too many half-exposed students are produced by our institutions of higher learning. The picture of economics held in their minds is a blurred and confused one, and what they have learned is not sufficiently accurate to serve as a tool for the analysis of practical problems. It is hoped that the student who survives this book will at least have come to regard economic analysis as a discipline useful in the interpretation and solution of numerous problems of life and thought, and will be able to add its methods to the cutting tools of his mind. Hence this is a work for the serious student, and not for the course-taster.

Economics presents a peculiar problem of exposition in that its various parts are much more closely related than is the case in many studies. Unless the student catches some vision of the whole great globe of analysis, therefore, he is likely to miss the significance of each part that he studies. It is the experience of most economists that on first approaching the subject it seems to be a hopeless confusion of unrelated principles. After a certain period of study, however, it may happen that the student experiences an illumination, often quite sudden, of the true nature and relationships of the subject, and from that time forth every part that he studies falls into its proper place and the subject is seen as a closely integrated whole. For this reason I have divided the work into two parts,

xix

each of which contains about enough material for a half-year's course of study. In the first part I have endeavored to range over the whole field of economic analysis, using the simplest possible weapons of analysis, so that the student may obtain a rough outline of the whole picture. In this part, therefore, I treat the concepts of demand and supply curves as self-evident, without discussing the marginal analysis which underlies them. With the concepts of demand and supply as the principal instruments of analysis, I outline the main principles of price determination and of distribution. In this part also I consider the theory of money, banking, international trade, and the business cycle, still confining myself to the tools of demand and supply.

In the second part I give in detail the marginal analysis underlying the demand and supply curves, including the theory of the individual firm, of consumption, of imperfect competition and monopoly, together with a discussion of the theory of capital. With the foundation laid in Part I the student will be able to integrate this more difficult material into his studies as he goes along. In this part I have followed the practice of segregating the more difficult material into separate chapters. Hence this part can be studied on two levels: the student can go through it on an elementary level, or he can take the more advanced material in his stride.

The arrangement of this work thus is not according to subject matter, as usually seems to be the case, but according to the methods of analysis used. The old fourfold division—production, consumption, distribution, and exchange—has almost completely disappeared. Instead we have a twofold division: into the part of the analysis which can be conducted with the aid of the demand and supply concepts, and the part that requires the concepts of the marginal analysis. A surprising amount can be accomplished with the aid of demand and supply analysis alone. Determination of prices, the elementary theory of distribution and exchange, the elementary theory of money, international trade, and the business cycle can be discussed without once using the word "marginal." Therefore, this word so full of torment for the beginner does not occur in Part I. In Part II all this analysis can be elaborated; demand curves can be derived from utility or from production functions, supply curves from cost curves, and the whole theory of the individual firm can be worked out. A possible defect in this method is that the theory of monopoly and imperfect competition must be postponed to Part II. Nevertheless, there are sound reasons for this; a student who is introduced to the modern theory of the market and the individual firm before he receives a thorough grounding in supply and demand analysis is often inclined to lose sight of the broad principles governing the whole economy through his absorption with the study of special cases. The conclusions of the analysis of perfect competition are modified, but not superseded, by the introduction of more complex and realistic assumptions; and the student will perceive more clearly the implications of these modifications if he knows what they modify.

The method of this work, therefore, is somewhat new; it may be called the "implemental" method, as it seeks to classify the various topics of analysis according to the analytical tools or implements used. It is thus hoped that the student will come to regard these tools as instruments, not as playthings. To this end I have introduced a system of discussion of practical problems which has, I believe, some claim to novelty. Instead of having one volume on "principles" and another volume on "problems," as is usually the case, and where all too frequently the "problems" have little or nothing to do with the "principles," I have integrated principles and problems throughout. That is, after each theoretical section in which the student has been introduced to a tool of analysis, there will be found a section dealing with those practical problems to which the tools thus far acquired can be applied. For example, after the chapter on the determination of prices in a competitive market, I discuss immediately the practical problems of organized competitive markets, such as the foreign exchange market, the capital market, and the commodity markets. After the section on normal demand and supply curves I have two chapters of problems which may be solved with the aid of these concepts, and so through the book.

In selecting these problems I have sought to choose those which provide the best illustrations of the principles involved, rather than those whose interest centers merely in their topicality. It is my belief that a work on principles should compete with neither the popular magazines nor the encyclopedias. Consequently I have not endeavored to write a compendium to current economic problems, for the reason that by the time the student has to face economic problems those of today may no longer be current. It seems to me more important to give the student a training which will fit him to understand the problems of the world of his maturity rather than of his youth. Consequently it is more important to give him a rigorous training in methods of analysis than to prime him with personable current opinions. It also seems to me that it is unwise to crowd a principles course with masses of factual material in special studies —labor, marketing, etc.—merely for the sake of giving the work an air of factuality. The place for such factual studies is later in the student's career, when he has acquired the techniques for interpreting the monstrous riddle of the factual material.

No advanced mathematical knowledge is required for this work. A knowledge of plane geometry will carry the student through all except the advanced chapters in Part II. Even in these chapters a nodding acquaintance with solid figures is all that is required. Any material involving algebra or the calculus is carefully segregated in appendices.

K. E. B.

Hamilton, New York
March, 1941

PREFACE TO THE FOURTH EDITION

It is now ten years since the appearance of *Economic Analysis,* Third Edition, and it is not surprising, therefore, in the light of what has happened in this interval, that the Fourth Edition should involve a substantial rewriting and rearrangement of the work. It has been divided into two volumes. The first volume, the present work, is entitled *Microeconomics.* It is divided into two parts. Part I is entitled *Elementary Price Theory,* and Part II *The Theory of Economic Behavior.* The second volume is entitled *Macroeconomics.*

The first six chapters of Volume I, though they draw upon some material in the first three chapters of *Economic Analysis,* Third Edition, are mainly new work. One of the principles that have guided the organization of *Economic Analysis* through its various editions has been to try to develop as much of economics as possible with simple apparatus before going on to more complex techniques. In this way the student is presented right at the start with the concept of Economic Analysis as a rounded whole, in which every part depends on every other. The first six chapters of Volume I, then, represent an attempt to develop the major principles of economics with the aid of an extremely simple model of a two-commodity economy. This is a model which derives a great deal from Adam Smith's famous example of "the nation of hunters" producing only beaver and deer. It has surprised me, and it may surprise the reader, how much of the essential body of economic thought can be developed within this very simple framework.

We then go on to the theory of Supply and Demand in Chapters 7–14. This section is essentially a revision of Chapters 4–12 of *Economic Analysis,* Third Edition. There has been a good deal of rewriting, however, especially in the later chapters, and much of Chapter 14 is essentially new. In this edition I have laid a great deal more stress throughout on the importance of dynamic factors and dynamic theory. This is not to say that equilibrium analysis and comparative statics are neglected, for indeed the student must master these techniques if he is to understand economic life. Nevertheless, equilibrium theory must always be regarded as a steppingstone to that wider understanding of economic processes that are involved in dynamics.

Some of the interests, both of myself and of the economics profession, that have grown in strength in the last ten years are reflected in this revision. There is a great deal more stress, for instance, on problems of economic development than there was in the earlier editions. I have also made more use in certain places of techniques derived from linear programming, even though I do not regard these as representing a fundamental change in principle. Throughout this edition, I have also laid much more stress on general equilibrium and on the setting of particular equilibrium models within the framework of the whole economy.

In Part I, I have tried to set forth in a reasonably small space what I regard as the bare essentials of economics. I would regard it as particularly suitable for the student who is not going on with economics but who wants some kind of guide to the complexities of economic life. It is also an essential groundwork for the more detailed and complex analysis of Part II.

Volume I, Part II, represents perhaps the most radical departure from the earlier editions, even though it still contains a good deal of the old material. There has been hardly any other area of economics in which greater progress has been made in the last ten years than in the theory of economic behavior and economic organization. This part is based on Parts III and IV of the Third Edition, but it has been extensively rewritten and a great deal of new material has been included. The first two chapters are essentially new, and represent a dynamic approach to the theory of economic organization and behavior which was not represented in earlier editions. The marginal analysis is now seen as a useful special case of a much more general theory, even though the techniques of marginal analysis still remain central in the discussion of economic behavior. Techniques derived from linear programming are now used to make some theoretical contributions, even though no new matter of principle is introduced by them. A new instrument of analysis, the events table, which was only implicit in earlier editions, is now developed as an important tool. I believe that in so putting the marginal analysis in a dynamic setting, the student should come to appreciate its value as well as its limitations.

Part II requires the reading of Part I or some reasonable substitute as a prerequisite. The student should not tackle it unless he is already familiar with the elementary theory of supply and demand and the idea of a general equilibrium of the price system.

KENNETH E. BOULDING

Ann Arbor, Michigan
September, 1965

PART I

Elementary
Price Theory

CHAPTER 1

THE TASK AND METHODS
OF ECONOMIC ANALYSIS

WHAT IS ECONOMIC ANALYSIS?

A distinguished economist,[1] on being asked to define the subject matter of his science, once replied, "Economics is what economists do." There is truth in the parry, for the boundaries of any branch of study are seldom quite clear, and topics which it contains at one time may be excluded at another. Consequently, any short definition of the boundaries of economic analysis is unavoidably inadequate. To define it as "a study of mankind in the ordinary business of life"[2] is surely too broad. To define it as the study of material wealth is too narrow. To define it as the study of human valuation and choice is again probably too wide, and to define it as the study of that part of human activity subject to the measuring rod of money is again too narrow.

Economic Phenomena

Nevertheless, we are all aware of a broad class of facts which may be described as *economic*. There are, for instance, four types of human activity which readily fall into such a category: *production, consumption, utilization,* and *exchange.* Acts of transforming raw materials and labor into products, or acts of transporting products to places where they are wanted are clearly matters of interest to the economist. Similarly, acts of consumption—the burning of coal, the wearing of clothes, the eating of foods—are of interest to the economist, as presumably all commodities are ultimately destined to be consumed. Commodities are utilized as well as consumed; the satisfaction we gain from using clothes, houses, furni-

[1] Jacob Viner.
[2] Alfred Marshall, *Principles of Economics,* 8th ed., London, 1922, p. 1.

3

ture, and so on, has nothing to do with the incidental fact that they are gradually being worn out or consumed. Finally, acts of exchange probably constitute by far the greater part of the phenomena subject to economic investigation.

Indeed, it is hardly too much to say that the study of exchange comprises nine-tenths of the economist's domain. The purchase and sale of a commodity or a security is easily recognized as an exchange in which usually one form of property—money—is given in exchange for some other form of property. It is perhaps less generally recognized, but nevertheless easily perceived, that the hiring of labor, the leasing of houses or land, and even the borrowing or lending of money are also acts of exchange. When labor is employed, hours of labor are exchanged for money, and the wage of labor is the price of the commodity bought and sold in this transaction. When property is leased, the services of the property are bought and sold for money, and rent is the price of these services. When money is borrowed, in the immediate present money is given by the lender in exchange for a "security," i.e., for a promise on the part of the borrower to pay money in the future. If we consider the borrowing and repayment as part of the same transaction, it appears as an exchange of present money against future money.

Economic Quantities

In all the events noted above, certain quantities or magnitudes appear, and those also are a principal object of economic inquiry. Economists do not merely note idly that there is production, consumption, and exchange; they concern themselves with the quantities produced, consumed, and exchanged. The output, consumption, and accumulated stocks of wheat; the price of butter; the wages of bricklayers; the rent of apartments; the interest on bank loans; the tax on tobacco; the tariff on cloth —all such quantities are of interest to the economist. These things we call *economic quantities*. Their collection is the task of economic statistics and economic history, and their interpretation is the principal task of economic analysis.

Economic Organisms

A third object of economic analysis is found in the organizations and institutions which direct economic activity. Who produces, who consumes, who exchanges? All acts are of course acts of individuals, but frequently individuals act on behalf of some organization. A housewife buys for a family, a purchasing agent for an orphanage, a buyer for a department store. A manager lends for a bank, a personnel director hires for a corporation, an official borrows for a government. These organizations or institutions, on whose behalf their agents buy and sell, borrow and lend, hire and fire, are *economic organisms*. They have a being and patterns of behavior independent in some degree of the persons who direct them. They have personalities, even if they are not persons, and decisions are made on their behalf. The study of their behavior therefore constitutes another important part of economic analysis.

The Task of Interpretation

We have now indicated the broad field of fact within which economic analysis functions. We have yet to define the specific task of economic analysis itself. The purpose of any analytical treatment of material is to provide a body of principles according to which facts can be selected and interpreted. The complaint is frequently heard that people want "facts" not "theories." The complaint may be justified in protest against theories which have no basis in fact, but usually it arises from a misunderstanding of the true relationships of facts and theories. Theories without facts may be barren, but facts without theories are meaningless. It is only theory—i.e., a body of principles—which enables us to approach the bewildering complexity and chaos of fact, select the facts significant for our purposes, and interpret that significance. Indeed, it is hardly too much to claim that without a theory to interpret it there is no such thing as a fact at all. It is a fact, for instance, that Oliver Cromwell had a wart on his nose. But what constitutes this fact? To the chemist it is a certain conglomeration of atoms and molecules. To the physicist it is a dizzy mass of unpredictably excitable electrons. To the biologist it is a certain impropriety in the behavior of cells. To the psychologist it may be the key to the interpretation of Cromwell's character and a fact of overwhelming importance. The historian may consider it an insignificant detail or an important causative factor, according to whether he follows economic or psychological interpretations of history. To the economist the wart may be of negligible importance unless Cromwell were prepared to pay a good round sum for its removal. What, then, *is* the fact about the wart? It may be any or all of the above, depending on the particular scheme of interpretation into which it is placed.

The Selection of Facts of Economic Significance

It should now be evident that any fact contains a great deal more than any single field of inquiry requires. The first task of economic analysis, therefore, is to select from economic events and facts those elements which are significant in relation to the general scheme of economic analysis itself. Consider, for instance, an event such as an exchange. Lest we forget the origins of economics as the science of household management, let us take as our illustration the purchase of two pounds of butter by a house-wife, Mrs. Jones, for $1.60, at a definite moment in history. The example is humble, but the event is representative of transactions everywhere, whether on the floor of the stock exchange, in the sanctum of the bank, or in the mart of merchandise.

Facts in an Act of Exchange

RELEVANT FACTS. When Mrs. Jones buys her two pounds of butter, then, we observe first that there are two persons participating in the event, the buyer and the seller. We observe also that there are two physical ob-jects involved. One is the butter, which passes from the possession of the storekeeper to Mrs. Jones. The other is the $1.60, which passes from the possession of Mrs. Jones to the storekeeper. An exchange, therefore, con-sists of two reciprocal transfers of ownership. At least three economic quantities are involved in the event: the quantity of butter (two pounds), the quantity of money ($1.60), and the *ratio* of these quantities, $1.60 for two pounds, or, what is the same thing, 80 cents per pound. The ratio of the quantities exchanged is the *price,* or exchange ratio. In transactions involving money and a commodity it is usually expressed as the price per unit of commodity and is equal to the quantity of money exchanged, divided by the quantity of commodity exchanged. Eighty cents per pound, therefore, is the price of butter. We have now selected, from this event, the aspects which most concern the economist. Other aspects of the event are relevant to him principally because of the bearing they exercise on the three quantities mentioned above. Thus the pleasant smile and win-ning manner of the storekeeper or the attractiveness or location of the store may be important for the economist, but their importance arises principally because they may help to explain why the price of butter in one store differs from the price in another.

IRRELEVANT FACTS. In describing this apparently simple event, how-ever, the economist has already abstracted from reality the portions which interest him most, and even in simple description he is dealing not with mere facts but with selected facts. There are innumerable other facts about the event which interest other people. The public health officer may be most interested in the chemical and bacteriological composition of the butter, the artist may be most interested in the pictorial possibilities of the scene, the novelist may be most interested in the emotions of the participants, the numismatist may be most interested in the exact inscrip-tions on the coins transmitted from one hand to the other, the linguist may be most interested in the exact words spoken, the costumier may be most interested in the clothes worn, and the store cat may be most in-terested in the aroma of fish in Mrs. Jones' shopping bag. All these things are facts about the event we are describing, and it is evident that we have by no means exhausted the list. Indeed, to describe the simplest event completely would require volumes of words and months of investigation. Those, therefore, who cry, "Give me facts, not theories," must beware lest their request be taken too seriously. Taken literally it could be answered only by such a flood of irrelevancy as to obliterate the facts completely. The very concept of relevancy implies the existence of theory, for all facts are relevant only in relation to some body of principles.

Economic Analysis as the Interpretation of Economic Quantities

We see by the above illustration that the most significant aspects of any economic event, for the economist, are the economic quantities concerned in it. The greater part of economic analysis, indeed, is concerned with investigating the nature of economic quantities, the relationships existing between them, and the forces which determine them. In describing the above event we selected as a fact significant for the economist that the price of butter was 80 cents per pound. A major task of economic analysis is to explain *why* the price of butter is 80 cents per pound and, of course, why all prices, wages, incomes, interest rates, and other economic quantities are what they are. Its task, therefore, is not primarily one of description, although the mass of recorded fact provides much of its raw material. Description is particularly the task of the historian and the statistician, although it must not be thought that history or statistics consist merely in the recording of fact. History and statistics themselves need principles of interpretation, and it is one task of economic analysis to help provide these principles. The student must not expect to find in these volumes a complete discussion of all the economic phenomena throughout history, or even the problems of that small part of history called today. Such studies are the discourses of economics; economic analysis is its grammar. It consists of a body of general principles and of a discipline of logic which may be applied to the interpretation of all economic problems, past or present. Although it has been developed largely with reference to a free capitalistic society and consequently is particularly concerned with the problems of market societies, it rests on a broad foundation in the theory of human behavior, and its most fundamental propositions can be applied to all conditions of mankind.

Economics and Welfare

Up to this point we have defined the main task of economic analysis as the explanation of the magnitudes of economic quantities. The student will find also that the main part of this, as of most other works on the subject, is concerned with the theory of the determination of prices, wages, interest rates, incomes, and the like. He may well inquire, therefore, in the midst of so much mathematics, whether the first task of economics is not the investigation of wealth, or welfare. Some economists have endeavored to restrict the boundaries of the science to the investigation of those quantities which are numerically measurable. Well-being, under such a restriction, would not be part of economics at all. Lionel Robbins, for instance, in defining economics as "the science which studies human behavior as a relationship between ends and scarce means which have alternative uses,"[3] seems to deprive economics of the right to study welfare, for welfare is an "end" in itself. Nevertheless, economists have always been interested in problems of wealth and welfare. Adam Smith, founder of the science, bravely called his masterpiece *An Inquiry into the Nature and Causes of the Wealth of Nations;* and though it may be argued that the most important part of his work deals not with wealth at all but with the equilibrium of prices, nevertheless he not only concerns himself with wealth but openly advocates certain measures, such as free trade, which he believes will lead to an increase in wealth. His lineal successors—Mill, Marshall, Pigou, and the modern welfare economists—likewise concern themselves with problems of wealth and welfare. It is evident, therefore, that whether or not the study of welfare is within the province of economic analysis, it is certainly adjacent.

Prices and Satisfaction

Indeed, it is impossible to explain even the determination of prices without some reference to the concept of well-being. In attempting to define the quantity of any commodity we are constantly forced to recognize that commodities are wanted not for their own sakes but for the sake of some satisfaction derived from their use or consumption. The moment any idea of "quality" enters into our discussion of the nature of commodities we are involved immediately in a discussion of the well-being, or satisfactions, which commodities create. There is no satisfactory test of quality except the test of intelligent preference. If, out of a proper experience of each kind, Mrs. Jones chooses butter A instead of butter B, when the price of both is the same number of cents per pound, we can assume that for Mrs. Jones butter A has the higher quality. For someone else, however, butter B might have the higher quality. Chemical and physical standards of quality are important, but they can never be wholly satisfactory, if only because quality is ultimately not a material property but a psychological property.

[3] *Essay on the Nature and Significance of Economic Science,* 2nd. ed., New York, St. Martin's Press, p. 16.

The Limitations of Economics

It is impossible, then, to exclude problems of welfare, of wants, and their satisfaction from the subject matter of economics. Nevertheless, these problems are of peculiar difficulty, and I have therefore reserved them as far as possible to Part II. Even then the propositions which emerge from our analysis may seem to the student vague and unsatisfactory. But it is well to realize that economic analysis alone does not provide the ultimate answers to what is right or wrong in individual or political conduct, and gives no magic formula by which schemes for the betterment of mankind are to be tested. It is not, for instance, the business of the economist as such to decide whether large armaments are necessary, whether a marriage is successful, a religion efficacious, or even whether a law is wise. The attention of the economist is directed principally to the area in which values can be measured in numerical terms, and consequently he cannot claim jurisdiction over the great region of valuation where such imponderable realities as friendship, patriotism, sincerity, and loyalty are assessed. In all political questions such imponderable valuations are of vital importance, and economic analysis is an important witness, but is not the sole judge.

This is not to say, of course, that the economist denies validity to the imponderables. He recognizes them and, indeed, uses them in explaining the magnitude of the ponderables. It is impossible to explain differences in wages, for instance, without reference to imponderables such as danger, enjoyment of work, pleasantness of associations, loyalty to employers, and so on. Nor is it proper to draw a sharp line between ponderable and imponderable values, between gain and glory. The concepts of economic analysis—concepts, for instance, of choice, of exchange, and of price—apply to the imponderable values as much as to the ponderables, though of course in a less measurable fashion. Every man has his price, even if that price be in some exceptional cases infinite. Glory may be purchased by the sacrifice of ease, just as guns may be purchased by the sacrifice of butter. Love and loyalty are treasuries which may be exhausted by too many claims, as many nations have found to their cost. We will probably exert ourselves more to rescue a friend than to rescue a stranger. The propositions of economics, therefore, though quantitatively applicable only where valuations can be expressed in numerical terms, extend wherever choices are made, be they between butter and eggs or between good and evil. But the economist studies the choices; he does not judge them, except in so far as they are made without proper knowledge of the possible alternatives. His main responsibility to the statesman or to the reformer is to show clearly the nature of the choice to be made, particularly in its quantitative aspects. The responsibility for the choice itself, however, always rests with the individual who makes it. Whether there are absolute standards by which choices themselves may be valued is an interesting question. But it is not one that can be answered by the methods of economic analysis.

THE METHODS OF ECONOMIC ANALYSIS

We now have a rough idea of the questions to be answered. We must next inquire by what methods the answers are to be found. It is clear at the outset that the experimental method, so fruitful in the natural sciences, is of strictly limited application in the social sciences. The experimental method consists essentially in bringing about certain preconceived events in a highly simplified environment. The chemist, for instance, studies a reaction by bringing his chemicals together in a controlled environment with known impurities or with none. An experiment, therefore, is an event or series of events in which only relevant elements are present, or in which, at least, the irrelevant elements are known. It is possible occasionally to perform controlled experiments in the social sciences. For example, the effect of a milk diet on school children can be determined by observing two groups of children, similar in all respects except diet. One group may be given a diet which includes extra quantities of milk, the other may receive a regular diet, and the differences in progress can then with some security be attributed to the milk. Experiment in economics, however, is of limited importance. It is impossible, for instance, to determine the effect of high interest rates on the conduct of businessmen by dividing them into two groups and subjecting one group to a high rate of interest and the other group to a low rate.

The Statistical Method

In these circumstances we are forced back on two other methods of gaining knowledge. The first of these is the statistical method. The second we may call the method of *intellectual experiment*. The statistical method is in a sense a substitute for the method of controlled experiment—a poor substitute, but the best we have. We cannot, as we have just seen, divide people into two groups in order to find their exact reaction to various changes. What we can do, however, is to observe similar groups of people at different times and under different circumstances, and then record both the difference in the circumstances and the difference in the behavior which we may expect the circumstances to effect. Then we may *tentatively* suppose that the change in circumstances caused the change in behavior.

ITS LIMITATIONS. It is important to realize, however, that statistical information can only give us propositions whose truth is more or less probable; it can never give us certainty. Statistics, for instance, tell us that in the years when the price of sugar has in fact been high, the consumption of sugar has in fact been low. From this statement it may seem that we can jump straight to the important proposition that *if* the price of sugar is high, *then* the consumption *must* be small. This conclusion (which is, of course, the generalization at which we really want to arrive) does not inevitably follow from the historic, statistical facts. It may be that things other than the price of sugar affect its consumption, and that it was these other things which made the consumption low in the years when the price of sugar happened to be high.

STATISTICS VS. EXPERIMENT.   This illustrates the difference between the statistical method and the experimental method. In an experiment we can actually keep out of our test tubes the other things in which we are not for the moment interested, but in statistical work either we have to take the other things specifically into account—which, of course, makes the problems more difficult—or we must hope that the other things remain constant, or nearly so, during the period of years under investigation. The most dangerous fallacy in statistical investigation is that of assuming that if two things have been observed together in a few instances, they *must* of necessity be causally connected. Because two young people are constantly found in each other's company, it does not follow in the least that they cannot be separated. The same holds true of two statistical series.

The Method of Intellectual Experiment

We shall return later to the uses of the statistical method in economics. For the most part, however, we shall be using the method of intellectual experimentation in this study. The essential *problem* of economic analysis is, as we have seen, to study the nature and the relationships of the various economic quantities—prices, wages, and the like. The actual world of economic quantities and relationships, however, is almost unbearably complicated. It is impossible to follow through immediately, without considerable training, all the ramified economic effects of even the simplest event. Under these circumstances what we do is to postulate, in our own minds, economic systems which are simpler than reality but more easy to grasp. We then work out the relationships involved in these simplified systems and, by introducing more and more complex assumptions, finally work up to the consideration of reality itself.

ANALOGY WITH MATHEMATICS.   This method is similar in a great many respects to the method of pure mathematics. In mathematics we start with some very simple propositions to which we can give assent without any difficulty, e.g., that a straight line cuts each of two parallel straight lines at the same angle. Starting from these propositions we can train ourselves by processes of proof to perceive more complicated propositions which we could not otherwise see, as, for instance, that the sum of the three angles of a triangle is equal to two right angles. Similarly, in so-called pure economics we also start from simple assumptions and deduce from them conclusions which *necessarily* follow. The propositions of pure economics, therefore, are all *hypothetical* propositions; that is to say, they all take the form, "*If* A and B and C are true, *then* X and Y and Z will be true."

NON-EUCLIDIAN ECONOMICS. In this sense it would be quite possible to build up any desired system of economics, depending on the initial assumptions taken. Just as it is possible to have non-Euclidian geometries in mathematics—that is, geometries whose fundamental axioms do not correspond to the facts of our ordinary experience—so there can be non-Euclidian systems of economic relationships in economics whose fundamental axioms do not correspond to the facts of our experience. In ordinary economics we assume that an enterprise wishes to make as great profits as it can. There is nothing to prevent our assuming, however, that firms wish to make fixed profits, or that they wish to make the value of the product as great as they can, or that they wish to make their average cost of production as small as they can. By assuming these different things, we shall of course get different conclusions, but the same method of analysis applies to them all. Naturally, however, we are more interested in those assumptions which correspond most closely to reality as we know it, i.e., to the system in which we live. But it is important to realize that the method of economic analysis is not confined to one particular system. Indeed, perhaps economic analysis can make contributions to the study of noncapitalist economic systems quite as significant as those it makes to the study of capitalism.

The Method of Simulation

The development of electronic computers has permitted an important extension of the method of intellectual experiment sometimes called the method of *simulation*. Very complex systems of relationships can be programmed on a computer and the course of the system through time can be observed. In this way systems which begin to approach the complexity of actual economic systems can be simulated and their properties observed. This is likely to be an increasingly important method of research in all sciences in the future.

Economic Analysis as a Map of Reality

The method of economic analysis, then, is to start with very simple assumptions concerning human behavior, then to discover what consequences would follow for the economic system as a whole if these assumptions were true. In this way we can build up a picture of a *simplified* economic system. Having mastered this simple picture, we can then proceed to bring it into closer relation to real life by introducing qualifications of our original assumptions and seeing how they affect the picture as we see it. But never do we come to real life, however closely we may approach it, for reality is always more complex than the economist's picture of it. This fact frequently makes students feel that economic analysis is unrealistic, because the world with which it deals seems to be so much simpler than the real world. To think this, however, is to misunderstand the whole nature of economics. Economic analysis is not a perfect picture of economic life; it is a *map* of it. Just as we do not expect a map to show every tree, every house, and every blade of grass in a landscape, so we should not expect economic analysis to take into account every detail and quirk of real economic behavior. A map that is too detailed is not much use as a map. This is not to say, of course, that all the economic maps have been good maps, for many of them have falsified even the broad outlines of reality. But it is a map that we are looking for, and not a detailed portrait. Consequently, we should not look to economic analysis for intimate details as to how to run a business or a bank, any more than we should expect to find in it the technical details of manufacture or mining. It is not even the business of the economist to give detailed advice to the statesman. His business is to take the system which the businessman, the banker, the worker, and even the statesman see only in part and visualize it as a whole, even though in seeing the whole he inevitably misses some of the detail.

QUESTIONS AND EXERCISES

1. A knowledge of ballistics (the theory of moving balls) would not necessarily help a tennis player, although he constantly practices by a kind of instinct the principles laid down therein. Does the same apply to the relations between economic analysis and the practice of business? If so, is this any argument against studying either ballistics or economics?
2. Is a *price* a sum of money?
3. Suppose the price of chocolate was 5 cents per bar. Suppose now that the manufacturer made the bar bigger but still charged only 5 cents per bar. Would you say that the price of chocolate had fallen? Now suppose that instead of making the bar bigger the manufacturer made it *better* (i.e., made it taste better) and again charged only 5 cents per bar. Has the price of chocolate fallen now?
4. If a Cadillac costs twice as much as a Ford, does that mean that there is twice as much automobile in a Cadillac as there is in a Ford? If this were true, would the prices of all cars really be the same?

5. Write out formal definitions, in your own words, of the following terms: economic analysis; price; economic quantities; exchange; experiment.

6. Which of the following would you classify as economic quantities? (a) The average wage. (b) The number of senators in Congress. (c) The salary of the President of the United States. (d) The price of eggs. (e) The number of days in a month. (f) The number of unemployed workers. (g) The basic rate of income tax. (h) The number of pages in this book.

7. The physical sciences are commonly supposed to be more successful than the social sciences. Why?

CHAPTER 2

EXCHANGE AS THE ORGANIZER
OF SPECIALIZATION

We may now define economics tentatively as the study of how society is organized through acts of exchange. The next step is to look more carefully at the act of exchange, itself, and to ask how this act operates as an organizer of society.

THE NATURE OF EXCHANGE

Figure 1 symbolizes the essential economic abstraction of the act of exchange. It always involves at least two *parties,* here called A and B.

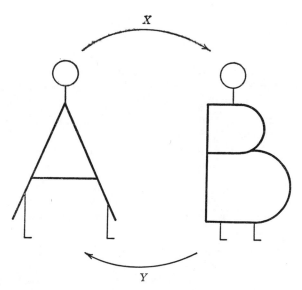

Fig. 1. A picture of Exchange

15

It involves at least two exchangeables, or commodities, X and Y. One exchangeable, say X, goes from A to B, and the other, Y, from B to A. The ratio of the amount of X to the amount of Y is the *ratio of exchange.* This may be expressed with equal validity as the ratio of the amount of Y to the amount of X. If X is 25 apples and Y is 100 nuts, the ratio of exchange can be expressed either as 4 nuts per apple (100 nuts divided by 25 apples) or ¼ apple per nut (25 apples divided by 100 nuts). Where one of the exchangeables is money the ratio of exchange is usually expressed as a *price,* which is the ratio of the amount of money to the amount of the other exchangeable. If X is 80 cents and Y is 4 apples, the price is 20 cents per apple, (80 cents divided by 4 apples).

Exchange always originates in an *offer to exchange,* which may be either tacit and simply understood or quite specific. I do not generally exchange with the man sitting next to me in a subway, because neither of us is offering to exchange. If, however, a man sets up a store and puts out goods with price tags on them he is in effect offering to exchange the goods for money to all comers. In its most general form exchange begins with an offer or conditional promise on the part of one party: "You do something good for me and I will do something good for you." If the offer is accepted by someone who has the power to do the "something good" suggested, the exchange is consummated and, as we shall see more clearly later, both parties presumably benefit.

Who Exchanges? Economic Organisms

Exchanges can be classified according to the nature of the parties to the exchange. When Mrs. Jones buys the two pounds of butter, the answer to the question *Who* exchanges? would seem to be simple: Mrs. Jones on the one hand and the storekeeper on the other. But the matter is not so simple as that. Perhaps Mrs. Jones is buying for her family, or perhaps she runs a boardinghouse and wants the butter for her paying guests. The storekeeper also may not be acting merely in his personal capacity. He may be acting as a representative, who is selling not for himself but for the store. This is obviously true if the storekeeper is an employee. It is also true even when the storekeeper is an independent grocer working for himself, for his activities as a private individual must be distinguished from his activities as a seller of commodities over the counter. It should now be clear that exchanging, i.e., buying and selling, is something done not only by individuals in a private capacity. It is usually done, in fact, by individuals who *represent* some institution or organization, such as a family, a church, an orphanage, a bank, a corporation, or a government. These organizations on behalf of which people enter into exchange we call *economic organisms.* It is convenient to extend this concept to include people who buy and sell in their individual capacity, representing themselves. Thus an economic organism is simply another name for a party to an exchange. The party however is never simply a person but always a person taking a role in an economic organism.

Types of Economic Organism

Let us now return to Mrs. Jones. She buys butter in her capacity as a housewife, not in order to sell it again but in order to consume it. The butter finds its ultimate end and goal on the table of the Jones family. When the storekeeper originally bought the butter, however, he bought it not for his own use but in order to sell it again. Moreover, we may suppose that he sold the butter to Mrs. Jones for a price somewhat higher than the price he paid for it. The difference between the two prices represents something else which he has sold to Mrs. Jones—his *services* as a retailer, which he did not buy from anyone else. It seems here as if there are three fairly distinct classes of economic organisms.

INTERMEDIARIES. These are organizations which buy in order to sell again, or sell in order to buy again, or which buy in order to produce something to sell. The *firm* is the most typical economic organization of this kind. However, governments, churches, and most other social organizations fall in this category for some purposes.

ULTIMATE DEMANDERS. These, like Mrs. Jones, buy things not to sell again but to enjoy or to consume. The family is the most important class of ultimate demanders, but other organizations like orphanages, monasteries, and even governments may be put in this class.

ORIGINAL SUPPLIERS. These are organisms which sell what they have not previously bought but have produced themselves. If Mr. Jones hires himself out as a barber, his income comes from the sale of services which he has produced himself. In some cases the commodity sold by an original supplier is sold directly, as when a worker sells his labor. In other cases the commodity is sold indirectly, as when an independent storekeeper "sells" his services by selling goods at a price higher than the price he paid for them.

Individuals Have More Than One Capacity

Every individual who has to spend money in the purchase of commodities for consumption is an ultimate demander. Every individual who receives a money income not derived from gift or charity is also an original supplier in the sense used above. We obtain our personal income by selling something we have not previously bought, such as the services of our bodies or the services of other property we own. Many individuals act as representatives of intermediaries and also as ultimate demanders or original suppliers. A farmer, for instance, will buy food for his cattle as a representative of his business. In this case it is the "firm" rather than the farmer which makes the exchange. He will buy food for himself and his family in his capacity as an ultimate demander. He will supply labor, and may supply land, to his farm in his capacity as an original supplier. In practice, he may not keep separate accounts for these three capacities. In principle, however, we must keep the distinction clear between the accounts of the farm as a business and the accounts of the farmer as a supplier of labor or land to the farm, and as a demander.

Types of Exchange

We can now distinguish several types of exchange, according to the types of economic organism participating in them. First, there are exchanges between ultimate demanders, as when two boys swap marbles for stamps in the schoolyard, or when Mrs. Jones exchanges some of her surplus butter with Mrs. Smith next door for some of Mrs. Smith's surplus bread. These exchanges are not very important. Indeed, they can only be regarded as accidental, for if Mrs. Jones bought her butter with the *intention* of selling it to Mrs. Smith she would be acting as a firm and not as an ultimate demander at all.

The most important exchanges are those between intermediaries, those between intermediaries and ultimate demanders, and those between intermediaries and original suppliers. When the storekeeper buys butter from a wholesaler, there is an exchange between firms. When Mrs. Jones buys butter from the store, there is an exchange between a firm and an ultimate demander. When the store buys the services of a clerk, there is an exchange between a firm and an original supplier. In the great majority of cases a firm, or a series of firms, acts as an intermediary between the original supplier and the ultimate demander, though sometimes these exchange directly without an intermediary.

What Is Exchanged?

This brings us to our next question: *What* is exchanged? Again the answer might seem to be simple, but again it proves to be more complicated than it looks at first sight. In the vast majority of exchanges the objects exchanged are physical goods or services on the one side, and money—dollars and cents—on the other side. An exchange in which both the things exchanged are physical goods or services is called a *barter* exchange. This is occasionally found in the schoolyard or across the garden wall, but it is not important except in primitive society. About the only important examples of barter exchanges in the modern world are those involved in sharecropping, in which the landowner exchanges the services of land for a part of the crop, and those in certain international agreements where there is direct bartering—for instance, of Egyptian cotton for Russian machinery.

A Commodity as a Bundle of Services

To return to our original example. Mrs. Jones, who has just bought her two pounds of butter, now has $1.60 *less* than she had before, and two pounds of butter *more* than she had before, while the storekeeper has $1.60 more than he had before, and two pounds of butter less. But the storekeeper has presumably bought the butter from someone else —a wholesaler, let us say, for $1.20. What he has *really* sold Mrs. Jones, then, is $1.20 worth of wholesale butter plus 40 cents' worth of his own retailing services. But of course the wholesaler did not make the butter; he bought it, say, from a creamery for 80 cents, and spent 20 cents for transport and 20 cents for his own expenses. So what Mrs. Jones has bought is evidently 80 cents' worth of butter-at-the-creamery, plus 20 cents' worth of transport service, plus 20 cents' worth of wholesaler service, plus 40 cents' worth of retailer service. But do we even stop there? The creamery perhaps paid the farmer 70 cents for milk, and paid 10 cents for manufacturing. The farmer, in producing the milk, spent perhaps 25 cents for feed, 10 cents for his cows, 15 cents for hired labor, and 20 cents for his own labor. It seems, therefore, that what Mrs. Jones has *really* bought is not merely $1.60 worth of butter, but 40 cents' worth of retailing, 20 cents' worth of wholesaling, 20 cents' worth of transport, 10 cents' worth of buttermaking, 25 cents' worth of cattle feed, 10 cents' worth of depreciation of cows, 15 cents' worth of hired farm labor, and 20 cents' worth of farmer's labor. Mrs. Jones would indeed be surprised to learn that all this—and more—was wrapped up in that innocent package of butter. However, a moment's reflection will show us that, in one sense at least, what we are really buying when we buy any commodity is a little bit of the services of all the retailers, wholesalers, transport workers, stevedores, processors, farmers, miners, and whatnot that have gone to make it up, together with the services of all the land and equipment they have used, and of all the managers who have organized them. Some of these services may have been performed at the moment of purchase, some a few days before, some weeks, some even years or decades before.

We can look at the same phenomenon in another way. Consider, not the butter, but the $1.60. Who gets the $1.60? In the first instance, of course, it goes to the storekeeper, but it does not all stay with him. He keeps 40 cents of it to pay for the services he has performed, and passes on $1.20 to the wholesaler, who in turn keeps his share and passes the rest on to the transporter, and so back to the creamery, the farmer, the farm laborer, the landlord, and all the other people involved.

All Exchanges Seen as Exchange of Services for Services

Even now we have not finished. Where did the $1.60 *come from?* Where did Mrs. Jones get it? The answer may be, of course, from her husband. But still the question remains, how did Mr. Jones get the $1.60? Perhaps he earned it by selling his services as a barber. Our simple exchange, therefore, of $1.60 for two pounds of butter seems to have been resolved into an exchange of $1.60 worth of haircutting against $1.60 worth of a remarkable collection of services of all kinds of original suppliers, ranging from retailers to landowners. Thus it seems that all exchanges are in a sense "barter" exchanges between original suppliers, effected through the intermediary of firms of all descriptions, through the operations of the peculiar stuff known as *money,* and through the production of goods.

Money as a Veil

This was what the older economists meant when they spoke of money as a "veil" that hid the real operations of the economic system. The too rigorous adoption of this point of view led them to neglect the very important effects which money itself has on the economic system. Nevertheless, the concept of a *barter system* is useful in avoiding certain crude fallacies which are frequently adopted by those unversed in thinking about society. We must get a picture of the economic order as a system in which each individual exchanges his services, or the services of things he owns, for the services of other people or of the things they own, even though these services may not be direct but may be wrapped up in the parcels that we call *goods.*

SPECIALIZATION

Specialization as a Prerequisite of Exchange

This brings us to another very important proposition concerning exchange. It is clear that no exchange could take place if everyone had, or made, the same things. If there were only one commodity—say, butter —there would be no exchange, for obviously it would be silly to exchange butter for butter. It is possible to imagine a society in which each family owns a plot of land on which they raise all their own food, make all their own clothes, dig or cut all their own fuel, and entertain themselves with their own songs. In such a society, where each family lived like the Swiss Family Robinson, there would be no exchange in the ordinary sense of the term. There would be for each family a choice of alternatives in production, in many ways analogous to exchange. They might, for instance, have to give up building a house in order to find the time to build a boat, and we might perhaps say that the house they might have had is in a sense "exchanged" for the boat which they in fact make. But exchange in the sense of a transaction between two parties always implies a difference in the possessions or abilities of the parties concerned. Unless different individuals possess different things, the exchange of goods is impossible, or at least futile. Unless different individuals perform different tasks, the exchange of services is impossible.

This doing of different things is called *specialization*, and it plays a very important part in economic development. Instead of each sitting under his own vine and his own fig tree, caring for all his own wants by himself, as soon as there is anything we can call society at all, one man will begin to grow vines and another to grow figs, and they will exchange wine for figs. Even in savage societies there are specialized crafts—the tentmaker, the fisherman, the hunter, the weaver. In complex societies there are thousands of different occupations—some 200,-000 in the United States alone! Each one of these occupations means that somebody is devoting the bulk of his available time to a single form of service and exchanging that service, or its products, for the products or services of innumerable other people. One proposition should now be clear: Exchange cannot take place unless there is specialization, for there would be nothing to exchange; but specialization without exchange would be useless, for the tailor would starve and the farmer go naked. *Exchange without specialization is impossible; specialization without exchange is silly.* This is a proposition the importance of which extends far beyond the field usually covered by economics; it applies, for instance, to the question of specialization in knowledge and discovery. If specialization in the sciences is carried to the point where exchange of ideas becomes impossible—where each man is so specialized that he can understand only himself—then specialization has become silly. We need middlemen in the sciences to perfect the system of exchange of ideas as much as we need them in economic life to facilitate the exchange of goods and services.

The Importance of Middlemen

This proposition can be used immediately to explode a common fallacy —that middlemen, or distributors, are *unproductive*. This fallacy is current in agricultural circles; the farmer frequently feels that he is the *real* producer because he produces the physical commodity, and consequently he feels that the middlemen and distributors are parasites. But it is no use for the farmer to produce milk if he cannot exchange that milk for other things. Milk-on-the-farm is a different commodity from milk-on-the-doorstep, and the people who get the milk from the farm to the doorstep—and, indeed, the housewife who gets the milk from the doorstep to the pudding—are just as much producers as is the man who gets it from the udder to the bottle. Circumstances may arise, of course, in which middlemen are too well paid for the services they render, but this does not mean that these services are inherently valueless.

Why Do People Exchange? Because Both Parties Benefit

There remains the third question: *Why* do people exchange? The answer is simple: because people want to exchange—that is, of course, if there is no compulsion present. Ruling out difficult cases like the payment of taxes or the granting of forced loans where the exchange is not free, we can formulate the proposition that no exchange will take place unless both parties to it feel, at the time, that they will benefit from it. Unless Mrs. Jones feels that she wants two pounds of butter more than she wants $1.60, and unless the storekeeper feels that he wants $1.60 more than he wants two pounds of butter, the exchange will not take place. Even if one party thinks he will benefit and the other party does not, there will be no exchange, for though an offer may be made it will be refused. An exchange, therefore, is not so much an equality (two pounds of butter = $1.60) as *two inequalities*. Mrs. Jones thinks two pounds of butter are worth more to her than $1.60, and the storekeeper thinks that $1.60 is worth more to him than two pounds of butter.[1]

How Can Both Parties Benefit? Because of Differences in Valuation

The question at once arises: How can this be? How is it possible for something to be *worth more* to one person than to another? We shall find the answer in a proposition which forms one of the primary axioms of economic analysis. Stated in a rather crude, nonmathematical form

---

[1] This proposition may seem almost too obvious to be worth stating, but it is surprising what trouble has been caused in economic thought by the failure to realize its truth. Thus Karl Marx argued that, as an exchange is an equation (e.g., $1.60 = 2 lbs. butter), the two things that are equal must have a common attribute. If a pound of apples is equal to a pound of oranges, we mean that they are equal in respect to some attribute common to both—in this case, weight. If, then, $1.60 is equal to two pounds of butter in *value*, there must be some attribute, common to them both, which gives them their value. The common attribute, he decided, was labor. This error, which runs through the whole "classical" school of economics, might have been avoided had there been a more adequate interpretation of the phenomenon of exchange.

it is as follows: The more of anything we have (under the condition that the quantities of all the other things we have remain the same), the less we want more of it.[2] If we had only two ounces of sugar a week, we should greatly welcome an extra ounce. If, however, we had a hundred ounces of sugar a week, an extra ounce would make very little difference to us. The more sugar we have, the less we want an extra ounce of it. The less sugar we have, the more we want an extra ounce of it. This again is an obvious truth, once it is stated. Again, the failure to understand it causes trouble and confusion.

Fallacy of Intrinsic Value

Popular economic discussion often assumes that things have an intrinsic worth. As soon as we perceive the truth of the above proposition, however, it becomes clear that what a thing is worth to us depends on how much of it we have, and that therefore the worth is not anything *in* a commodity. It is not a physical property of an object like weight or volume, but is simply how we feel about it. Things are valuable because somebody thinks they are, and for no other reason whatever. This is true, as we shall see, even of gold—a commodity which people are inclined to think has an *intrinsic value*. Gold, like everything else, is valuable only because people think it is.

Exchange Possible, Even Among Those With Identical Tastes, Where Quantities Possessed Differ

We can now see how exchange can be possible, even between people who have identical tastes. Suppose Mrs. Jones has laid in a great deal of butter, and Mrs. Smith next door has laid in a great deal of bread, and all the shops are shut. Then we may imagine Mrs. Jones knocking at the Smiths' back door and asking, "Will you give me a loaf of bread for a pound of butter?" Mrs. Smith replies that she would be delighted. Because Mrs. Jones has a lot of butter, the loss of a pound does not mean a great deal to her. Because she does not have very much bread, an extra loaf of bread *does* mean a good deal to her. So she is willing to give up a pound of butter, which she does not want very much, for a loaf of bread, which she wants rather more. Mrs. Smith is in the opposite situation. Because she has so little butter, an extra pound means a great deal to her. Because she has so much bread, one loaf less means very little. Consequently, she also is glad to make the exchange, and to give up the loaf she wants little for the butter she wants more.

[2] This is the principle which usually goes under the name of the "law of diminishing marginal utility." As, however, the mathematical discussion of this problem presents some difficulty, it will be reserved for Part II, especially Chapters 24 and 27.

We thus see how, even if Mrs. Jones and Mrs. Smith were identical in their *tastes* regarding bread and butter, they might still find exchange desirable if they possessed at the start different quantities of the things to be exchanged.

How Specialization Gives Rise to Exchange

There should now be no difficulty in seeing exactly why exchange takes place in economic life generally. Because each individual is specialized, if there were no exchange he would have a large quantity of the thing in which he specializes. The farmer's barns would burst with corn, the tailor's shelves be stuffed with suits. Because, therefore, we each have a relatively large quantity of the things in which we specialize, we are eager to get rid of them in exchange for the other things we do not have, just as Mrs. Jones was eager to get rid of some of the butter of which she had plenty for the bread of which she had little. A dairy farmer and a baker are perpetually in the position of Mrs. Jones and Mrs. Smith, for one has a continual surplus of butter, the other a continual surplus of bread. This does not mean, of course, that we must exchange everything we have, for neither exchange nor specialization is usually carried to the extreme. The dairy farmer will keep some butter for his own use; the baker will keep some bread. Exchange will stop when either of the parties feels that the loss involved in giving up a little more of what he has is just balanced by the gain involved in getting a little more of the thing received in exchange. Mrs. Jones will be willing to go on exchanging butter for bread as long as she feels that an extra loaf of bread is worth more to her than the butter she gives for it. As she goes on exchanging she finds her stock of butter dwindling and her stock of bread increasing. This means that extra butter means more to her and extra bread less, so the moment will soon arrive when the additional bread ceases to mean more to her than the relinquished butter. At that moment she will say to Mrs. Smith (unless, of course, Mrs. Smith has anticipated her), "Thank you, I think that's all I want now," and the exchange will stop.

But Why Do We Specialize?

Thus, if we have specialization, we shall also have exchange. We have not yet answered the question: Why do we have specialization? Why do we bother with this extraordinarily complex system of exchange? Why do we not each cultivate our own garden and provide for our own wants directly by our own labor? Such is largely the case in primitive society. Even in the feudal period each village grew its own food, brewed its own drinks, made its own clothes, and built its own houses. Today, even our breakfast table is loaded with products from all over the world, and many of the things that our grandparents did for themselves are now done for us by other people. Mother no longer cuts father's hair, and she sends out his suits to the cleaners.

BECAUSE SPECIALIZATION MAKES US RICHER. A general answer to this question is, of course, that by specialization and exchange of the specialized products we can satisfy our wants better than if we all lived like Robinson Crusoe. Popular recognition of the principle can be seen in the proverb, "Jack of all trades and master of none." If there are two castaways on a desert island instead of one, specialization will soon begin. Each will find there are certain tasks in which he excels, and each will specialize in these tasks and perform them for both. One may be more successful at fishing than the other; he will catch enough fish for both. The other may be more successful in building huts; he will build huts for both. Thus they will both have more fish and better huts than if each tried to catch fish and build a hut for his own use. Exactly the same principle applies in a more complex form to any society. If we all lived like Robinson Crusoe we should all be extremely poor. It is only because we have this complex system of specialization and exchange that we can enjoy the conveniences and luxuries of modern life.

Two Kinds of Specialization

1. OF PRODUCTS. Specialization takes two forms: the specialization of *products,* which we may call external specialization, and the specialization of *processes*, which we may call internal specialization. We could imagine a society in which each man specialized in making a given product and also performed all the processes necessary for its production. Even today that is approximately true of some occupations. A farmer, for instance, often performs almost all the operations connected with the production of his products: he raises seed, sows it, cultivates the soil, reaps his crop, stores it, feeds it to his cows, milks his cows, and bottles their milk. Such external specialization is the first to arise, and this in itself, of course, is sufficient to bring about exchange.

2. OF PROCESSES. In modern industrial society, however, another kind of specialization is important, in which a man confines himself not merely to the production of a single product but to a single *operation* in that production. The automobile industry is a good example of this internal specialization. Each worker in an automobile plant performs a single, simple task and consequently becomes highly proficient at it. By *mass production* in this way we can produce a great many more automobiles than we could if one man tried to perform all

the operations necessary in their production. Internal specialization still involves exchange, but the thing exchanged is not a product the individual makes but a service he renders. Mr. Smith, who works in the automobile factory, exchanges, in effect, with society at large a certain quantity of his service of screwing bolts for the food, clothing, and other consumables he buys with his wages.

The Principle of the Best Alternative

The general principle governing exchange and specialization may be called the *principle of the best alternative*. It may be stated roughly thus: In his endeavor to obtain the commodities he desires, an individual has two possible alternatives. He can either produce the commodities for himself directly, or he can produce some other commodity and exchange it for what he wants. Which alternative he will choose will depend on which is the easier way of getting the commodity he wants, for it is the easier way that he will follow. How we define which is the easier way will not usually depend on monetary considerations alone but will involve an estimate of the total advantages and disadvantages of each alternative. Thus it may be the best alternative for a man to go fishing—even though he could buy fish for much less than he can catch them—because his enjoyment of fishing is included in the total advantages.

Exchange Is Indirect Production

It is important to realize that exchange is an *alternative way* of producing something. If I want a suit of clothes I can either buy the cloth and make the suit myself or I can earn money (by performing some services for society) and pay a tailor to make the suit for me. The first would be direct production; the second would be production through exchange. Instead of spending my time and energies on making a suit myself, I would do something else with my time and energies and exchange that something else through the mechanism of money, for the suit I want. If I am an indifferent tailor, I may find that by working for a hundred hours I could make myself a rather unsatisfactory suit of clothes. However, by working for a hundred hours at the occupation in which I am skilled—say, haircutting—I could earn perhaps $120 with which I could pay a tailor to make me *two* suits of clothes of much better cut and quality than I could make myself. In this case it is obvious that production through exchange is much more effective than direct production. On the other hand, I would be unlikely to go to a dentist to have my teeth cleaned every morning, even though he might clean them more quickly and more efficiently than I could myself, because I would feel that to take the time and earn the money with which to pay the dentist I would have to put in more time and effort than is necessary to clean my teeth for myself.

The Principle of Comparative Advantage

In this connection it is important to notice that specialization and exchange will take place even in the case of an individual who could produce the commodity obtained in exchange more efficiently than the person from whom he obtains it. For instance, a doctor who is an excellent gardener may very well prefer to employ a hired man who as a gardener is inferior to himself, because thereby he can devote more time to his medical practice. Suppose that the doctor could keep his garden in good shape by working for one hour a day, and that the hired man took three hours to do the same amount of gardening. If the hired man was paid $1 an hour and the doctor earned $10 an hour, it might still pay the doctor to work at his profession for the hour which he otherwise might have spent in the garden, and to pay the hired man $3 for his three hours of work. In that case, by working at his profession instead of in the garden the doctor would gain $7. To put the same problem in another way: the doctor could do his gardening in an hour if he worked at it directly. By working at his profession, however, for eighteen minutes, he will have earned enough to pay for three hours of the hired man's time. Consequently he can do his gardening in eighteen minutes by staying in his office, as against the hour it would take him if he were out in the garden! In this particular case the situation may be complicated by the fact that the doctor may like gardening for its own sake. But this complication does not affect the fundamental principle. If the doctor is fond of gardening he may prefer an hour of direct gardening to eighteen minutes of indirect gardening, but it remains true that for him medical practice may be an indirect method of horticulture.

Extent of Specialization Depends on the Extent of the Market

There is one more proposition to state concerning specialization and exchange. It is that the *extent of specialization* depends on the ease with which things can be exchanged or, as it has been phrased, by the *extent of the market*.[3] The main things affecting the ease with which things are exchanged are, first, the density of the human population and, second, the ease or difficulty of transportation. Obviously, if large numbers of people are closely packed together, and if the means of transportation of commodities and of persons are good, it will be easier

[3] Adam Smith, *The Wealth of Nations* Modern Library ed., Book 1, chapter 3.

to make exchanges than it would be among a widely scattered population separated by high mountains and deserts. Robinson Crusoe does not specialize, only because the means of transportation between him and the outside world do not exist. In a remote mountain village where transportation is difficult and the population is small, specialization will not be carried on as far as it is in a great city like New York. We should not expect to find economists, opticians, gem cutters, or patent lawyers in a mountain community in Tennessee. We should expect to find them in New York City. A highly specialized occupation can exist only where its products are available to a large number of people, for the average quantity of the product taken by any individual is small. An eye specialist, for instance, might find a comfortable practice in a community of 100,000 people when he would be idle most of the time in a community of 5,000.

Specialization and Transportation

Any improvement in the means of communication will, therefore, probably result in an extension of the degree of specialization and in the volume of exchanges. The great cities of the present day owe their existence to the development of a world system of transportation. London and New York, for instance, could not exist unless they could draw food supplies from all over the world, and unless they could send products all over the world in return. Even Robinson Crusoe would probably begin to specialize in the production and export of coconuts if communications were established between his island and the outside world.

EXCHANGE, PRODUCTION, AND CONSUMPTION

We should now have a mental picture or *model* of the economic system in which exchange is related to production and consumption. Production consists in the creation of goods (valuable objects) and adds to the stocks of these goods. Consumption consists in the destruction of these goods and subtracts from the total stock of goods. Some consumption is unintended, as when a house burns down. The rest is intended consumption, as when we eat a dinner. If production exceeds consumption, the total stock of goods increases. The total stock of exchangeables consists of the stock of goods plus certain other things, such as money, bonds, stocks, securities of various kinds, and so on. Some things which are valuable are not exchangeable, by law or by custom. Thus in a slave society persons (slaves) are valuable and are bought and sold. In a free society persons cannot be bought and sold; they are not exchangeables, but they are still valuable; each man is his own slave and derives income from the sale of his own services which, if he were a slave, would accrue to his master. In exchange, the stock or part of the stock of exchangeables is circulated among owners; nothing is produced or consumed in the act of exchange itself. Nevertheless, exchange enormously facilitates production and consumption, and without it, as we have seen, production and consumption would be confined to what the unspecialized household could produce. It is the possibility of exchange that creates *specialized* production and hence enormously increases the total output of society.

Production as Similar to Exchange

From the point of view of an intermediary, such as a manufacturing firm, production has much the same effect as exchange. Thus suppose a flour miller starts his day with certain stocks of wheat, machinery and equipment, and money. During the day he hires workers and uses his equipment to grind wheat into flour; he ends the day with less wheat, less money, slightly depreciated equipment, but more flour. In effect he has exchanged wheat, money, and equipment for flour, and from the point of view of his assets the result is much the same as if he had exchanged wheat, money, and equipment directly with some other party for flour. If he had done this, however, the total quantities of wheat, flour, and so on in the whole system would not have changed. Production, however, may be thought of as a kind of *exchange with nature*; as a result of the day's activity there is now more flour and less wheat in the system, though—and the importance of this will be made clear later—there is no less money. Furthermore the flour will presumably have more value than the wheat and other assets used up in its production; there is *value added* in the course of production which comes from the original suppliers.

Production and Alternative Cost in the Crusoe Economy

Even for Robinson Crusoe, production has aspects which are much like exchange, even though he has no other party with which to exchange except nature. If he devotes his time and energy to catching fish he cannot at the same time catch rabbits. By producing fish he gives up producing rabbits; if with the time and energy he devotes to catching 10 fish he could have caught 2 rabbits, then in a sense he has *exchanged* 2 rabbits for 10 fish. The ratio, called the *alternative cost ratio*, is a very important quantity in the economic system, as we shall see in Chapter 3. It applies to any economic system, no matter how complicated, for if resources are limited, increasing the production of one thing by x may force us to decrease the production of something else by y. The ratio

x/y is, as it were, an exchange ratio in production, and we should not be surprised to find later that it is closely related to exchange ratios in the market.

Exchange and Income

The opportunities for exchange and the ratios of exchange in these opportunities are an important factor in determining the income of persons, families, groups, or nations. Real income may be defined as the total amount of goods and services coming in to the person or group. Real income consists of two parts: goods and services produced directly by the person or group, and goods and services obtained by exchange of other things which are produced. The total income then depends on the proportions of resources devoted to direct production and to production for exchange, and on the ratio of exchange between the goods given up and the goods received. This latter quantity is often called the *terms of trade*. The *better* the terms of trade, that is, the more goods obtained for one unit of goods given up, the greater the income will be.

The Income Formula

A simple formula will illustrate the point. Suppose L is the total resources of a person or group, and that the total is divided into L_h devoted to direct production at home of goods and services used or consumed directly, and L_e, to production for exchange. Suppose now that p_h is the productivity of resources devoted to direct production, so that the total quantity of goods produced is $L_h p_h$. Now let p_e be the productivity in producing for exchange, so that $L_e p_e$ is the total amount of goods produced for *export*—that is, to be exchanged. Then if T is the terms of trade, the total amount of goods purchased by these exports will be $L_e p_e T$, and total real income, Y, is given by the formula

$$Y = L_h p_h + L_e p_e T$$

We are neglecting here the difficult problems of measurement when many different kinds of goods and services have to be added up together; this problem will be considered in Volume II: *Macroeconomics*, Chapter 2. The formula shows roughly, however, that income will be increased if either p_h, p_e, or T rises—that is, the two major sources of rising income are an improvement in productivity and an improvement in the terms of trade. It also shows that, if $p_e T$ is greater than p_h, it will pay to shift resources from home to export production, and if $p_e T$ is less than p_h, or $p_e/p_h < T$, it will pay to shift resources from export to home production. The implications of this proposition are important, and will be examined later.

QUESTIONS AND EXERCISES

1. Some economists have argued that since nothing was *created* in an act of exchange (as exchange merely means a change in ownership of commodities already in existence), exchange could not add to wealth. Do you think this is correct? If not, how would you answer this argument?
2. State and prove at least five propositions concerning exchange and specialization.
3. What is meant by the statement that an exchange in which money is one (or both) of the things exchanged is not a *complete* exchange? What is a complete exchange?
4. The three types of parties to exchange—intermediaries, original suppliers, and ultimate demanders—form six different pairs, representing six type of exchange. Name these pairs, and give two examples of each type of exchange.
5. Why do some people shave themselves, while some have themselves shaved by a barber?
6. Does the wealth of a person affect the proportion of real income obtained by exchange, i.e., would you expect a wealthy person to do more or less for himself than a poor person?
7. Would you expect to find that a greater proportion of things made are sold (exchanged) in a wealthy society than in a poor one?
8. Danish butter producers in normal times eat very little butter. They use margarine to spread on their bread although they produce some of the best butter in the world. Is this stupid behavior? Or is there a good reason for it?
9. Discuss the effect of improvements in transportation on the geographic distribution of human activity.
10. The following table shows certain items in a manufacturer's stock at the beginning and end of a day.

| | Amount in Stock | |
Item	9 A.M.	5 P.M.
Raw material	100 tons	90 tons
Finished goods	10 tons	11 tons
Cash	$20,000	$18,000

Outline a number of various happenings during the day which might account for these changes.

11. A country has only two commodities, wheat and bicycles. For purposes of calculating real income we always assume 1 bicycle=30 bushels of wheat. It has a labor force of 1,000,000 men, with 400,000 producing wheat and 600,-000 producing bicycles. In a year, 1 man can produce 10 bicycles or 500 bushels of wheat. It exports 4,000,000 bicycles a year in return for 160,000,000 bushels of wheat. What is its real income, measured in bushels? Determine

its real income under the following separate changes: (a) a shift of 100,000 men from producing wheat to producing bicycles; (b) an increase in the export of bicycles to 5,000,000 on the old terms. Repeat (a) and (b), assuming a change in the terms of trade from 40 bushels per bicycle to 60 bushels per bicycle. Comment on your results. What distribution of the labor force and amount of export would make real income the greatest under the old and under the new terms of trade? Would it make any difference if we measured real income in terms of bicycles rather than in terms of bushels?

CHAPTER 3

SOME APPLICATIONS OF THE ELEMENTARY THEORY OF EXCHANGE

ECONOMIC CONFLICT

Community of Interest in Exchange

One important practical application of the principles of the last chapter is to discussion of the problem of economic *conflict*. Is there any possibility of conflict arising in exchange? How are people's interests affected by the act of exchange or by the quantities arising from it? We have seen that an exchange cannot take place unless both parties gain, or at least think they gain. There is evidently, therefore, a certain community of interest in exchange. This in itself is an important conclusion, for it is commonly believed that in trade—especially in international trade—one party must gain and the other party must lose. But if one party to a prospective exchange thinks he will lose by it, he will not enter into the exchange at all. This is true even in an exchange which is commonly regarded as an occasion for conflict—the exchange of labor for money between employers and employed. Even here there is a community of interest in the exchange in the sense that, unless both parties believe themselves to be benefited, the exchange will not take place. A wage bargain cannot be struck, in the absence of coercion, unless the employer prefers buying the labor to buying any of the other things for which he could spend the money, and unless the worker prefers to spend his time working for a wage rather than in any other way.

Conflict of Interest About the Ratio of Exchange: Range of Mutual Benefit

But this is not the whole of the matter. There may be a community of interest in the *fact* of exchange. There is always a conflict of interest, except in some rare cases, about the *ratio* of exchange—i.e., about the *price*, the terms on which the things are exchanged. Generally speak-

ing, in any given exchange there is a certain range of prices within which
the exchange will take place but outside of which one of the parties will
feel that he does not benefit by the exchange. To return to our friends
Mrs. Jones and the storekeeper. There must be some price for butter
above which Mrs. Jones will not buy; suppose it is $1 per pound. At any
price below $1 Mrs. Jones will buy that particular two pounds of butter,
but at any price above it she will not. There is also some price for butter
below which the storekeeper will not think it worth his while to sell;
at any price below, say, 25 cents per pound he will prefer to keep the
butter in his shop, or keep it for his own use. Consequently, at a price
below 25 cents or above $1 per pound this particular transaction cannot
take place. At any price between 25 cents and $1 per pound the trans-
action may take place, as both parties feel they benefit. We may represent this situation diagramatically as in Fig. 2. The line *AB* represents

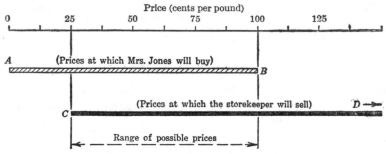

Fig. 2.   The Range of Mutual Benefit

the prices at which Mrs. Jones is willing to buy the two pounds of butter
in question; the line *CD* represents the prices at which the storekeeper is
willing to sell. Only at those prices where the lines overlap, between
C and *B,* is an exchange possible, for only at those prices will both
parties feel that they gain. The *amount by which* the parties to the
exchange feel that they gain depends, however, upon exactly *where* the
price falls within this range. If the price is $1 a pound, Mrs. Jones will
feel that she barely gains anything by the exchange, and the storekeeper
will gain much more than the minimum which would induce him to
make the exchange. If the price is 25 cents a pound, Mrs. Jones will
gain greatly by the exchange while the storekeeper will feel it is only
just worth while making. Clearly, the nearer the price is to 25 cents a
pound, the more will Mrs. Jones gain by the exchange, and the less will
the storekeeper gain. The nearer the price is to $1 a pound, the more the
storekeeper will gain and the less Mrs. Jones will gain. Mrs. Jones,
therefore, who is buying, wants the price to be as low as possible, and the
storekeeper, who is selling, wants it to be as high as possible.

Most Economic Conflicts Are of This Type. This principle applies to any exchange whatever and accounts for a large part of the real conflict of interest in economic life. Thus in the exchange between employers and employed, even though both benefit, the worker will benefit more if the wage is high, the employer more if the wage is low. In the exchange of the products of any one industry—say, farming—the producer wants a high price, the consumer wants a low price, even though over a wide range of prices, the farmer prefers to sell his crops rather than to try to spend his time making manufactured goods at home, and the industrial population prefers to sell its products rather than to try to grow its food in its own back yards.

Vertical and Horizontal Conflicts

Just as we classified exchanges according to the character of the exchangers involved, so we can classify conflicts in exchange. Corresponding to exchanges between firms and original suppliers, especially workers, we have what is usually called the "class" conflict—the conflict, for instance, between the working class, interested in high wages, and the employing class, interested in low wages. Corresponding to exchanges between original suppliers and ultimate demanders are what may be called *vertical* conflicts of interest. Thus all the people concerned with coal mining—miners, operators, owners—have a common interest in maintaining a high price for coal, as compared with all people not in the mining industry, who have a common interest in keeping the price of coal low. These vertical, or group, conflicts may be in practice much more important than the *horizontal*, or class, conflicts. Very few acts or lines of policy will affect wages or profits as a whole, but it is easy to organize lines of action which will affect particular prices, particular wages, or particular profits. The organization of monopolies is one of the principal weapons of this group conflict.

Tariffs as an Example. Tariff policy is also intimately bound up with group conflict. A duty on the import of shoes may improve the lot of people in the shoe industry, as it may, at least for a time, enable them to raise the price at which they can sell shoes. An increase in the price of shoes, however, will injure all the people who buy shoes. Here is a clear conflict of interest between a *group* in society—all those concerned with making shoes—and those outside the group. The groups are frequently well organized and able to exercise political pressure, but the people outside the group, i.e., everybody else, are not organized—everybody being nobody in particular! Consequently, a great deal of legislation is passed which makes us on the whole poorer because it makes a small group richer. The effect on the small group is obvious, and the small group is organized to exert pressure on legislatures. The effect on the rest of us is diffuse and not always immediately apparent, and so does not influence lawmakers as it should.

THE DETERMINATION OF PRICE

Higgling and Bargaining

We have seen that in most acts of exchange there is a certain *range* of prices within which the exchange may take place. The question naturally arises: What determines the exact position of the price within this range? In our example we supposed the price of butter to be 80 cents a pound, although we saw that even if it were as high as $1 or as low as 25 cents the exchange would still take place. Why, then, should not the price of butter be 90, or 50, or 40 cents a pound instead of 80? The rest of this book is little more than an attempt to answer this question. However, there are one or two things we may say about it now. One answer is of course that the price may be decided by *higgling* and *bargaining*.

Mrs. Jones might come into the shop, see the two pounds of butter nicely wrapped on the counter, and say to the storekeeper, "That's a nice package of butter you have there; I'll give you 80 cents for it." Now the storekeeper would be willing, if necessary, to sell the butter for 80 cents (i.e., 40 cents a pound), but of course he would like to get more for it if he could. So, suspecting that Mrs. Jones would give more for it if pressed, he might say, "I'm sorry, Mrs. Jones, but I couldn't think of selling it under $2 this morning." Mrs. Jones' reply might be, "Don't be absurd; I'll give you $1.20 for it," and the storekeeper again might say, "Well, I'll come down to $1.80, but no further." Mrs. Jones might answer, "A dollar fifty is absolutely the limit," and the storekeeper might follow with, "I could let you have it for $1.70 and no less." Then Mrs. Jones might say, "Let's split the difference and call it $1.60," and the storekeeper would say, "Done!" A few things are sold in this way, even in Western countries—antiques and rugs, for instance. In Oriental countries a great many more things are sold thus; and although to us it may sound ridiculous to higgle for butter in the manner described above, in some countries even ordinary day-to-day purchases are made in this way. Even two or three hundred years ago the practice of higgling was much commoner in Western countries.

Collective Bargaining

Perhaps the most important example of higgling today is that known as *collective bargaining,* the name given to the process of deciding a price between *organized* groups of buyers and sellers. It is found when a trade union bargains with an employer's association or even with a single employer. In this case the trade union is selling a certain commodity—the labor of its members—which the employers are buying. The object of the collective bargain is to set a price which will prevail in all purchases of labor of the type in question. Collective bargaining is also to be found between producers of raw materials and the users of those raw materials. In the milk industry, for example, we frequently find collective bargaining between the organized farmers who sell milk and the organized distributors who buy it. In this case also the purpose of the bargain is to determine the price at which all the individual sales shall be made. The opposite of collective bargaining is, of course, individual bargaining, in which each individual buyer or seller makes his own arrangements as to the price and the other terms on which the transaction shall be made.

CONDITIONS OF SETTLEMENT OF A COLLECTIVE BARGAIN. The process of higgling just outlined is essentially similar to what occurs when collective bargains are made. It may happen that the highest price at which one party will buy is less than the lowest price at which the other party will sell. Under those conditions no bargain will be effected and there will be a strike, or else a breakdown of collective bargaining altogether. If the highest wage that an employer would pay were $2.60 an hour, and if the lowest wage that a trade union would accept were $2.80 an hour, it is clear that no settlement would be reached. Either there would be no exchange at all (i.e., a strike) or the men would go behind the back of the trade union and make individual bargains with the employer. If the men remained loyal to the union, the strike would go on until one or other of the parties changed its mind about its extreme price. In this case the strike might go on until either the employer raised the highest wage that he was willing to pay to $2.80 an hour or more, or the union lowered the lowest wage at which the men were willing to work to $2.60 an hour or less—or, of course, until both made a corresponding shift.

The Custom of the Fixed Price

We see, therefore, that higgling forms an important part of our method of determining prices. Nevertheless, in most of our ordinary transactions higgling plays no part. Naturally we ask, "Why is this?" One possible answer is: custom. It is customary for most sellers to set a fixed price at which they are willing to sell, to make that price known beforehand publicly so that all potential buyers know it, and then to allow the buyers to take advantage of the price or not, as they wish. Thus custom originated partly as a result of a moral feeling against the appearance of lying and cheating which is always present in higgling. The early Quakers, for instance, in the seventeenth century set fixed prices for their goods and refused to higgle about prices, for they felt that to ask a price at first which was higher than the price they expected to receive was untruthful. But the spread of the custom was undoubtedly due to the fact that higgling is for most people a troublesome waste of time. People preferred to deal with storekeepers who did not higgle but set a fixed price at which the customer could buy or not as he pleased. Gradually, therefore, the custom became almost universal, so much so in fact that we now seldom realize how comparatively recent the habit is in our society.

Many Buyers and Sellers

As a general rule, the custom of the fixed or *quoted* price can flourish only where there is a large number of buyers or sellers. Higgling is a method of determining prices most frequently used where there is only one buyer and one seller in the market, or where, as in the case of collective bargaining, there is an organized group of buyers facing an organized group of sellers. However, a seller who is faced with a large number of potential buyers and repeats his transactions frequently with different buyers is likely to quote a price without higgling. In quoting his price the seller takes account of the prospective volume of sales at the price quoted, and in that sense the buyers assist in determining the price. The buyers' part is not, however, the active part of higgling but the passive part of deciding how much to buy at the set price. This is the situation usually found in retailing, and frequently in manufacturing.

In other markets, notably in the market for standardized agricultural commodities like wheat or cotton, the price is quoted by the buyer. In this case the seller has the option to sell or not to sell at the price quoted, and this power of the sellers again plays a decisive part in determining the price the buyers will quote. It will be observed that where the custom of a fixed price prevails, it is generally the middleman who quotes the price. The demander at one end of the chain and the supplier at the other end have the power merely to take or to leave the exchange offered by the middleman, be he retailer or wholesale merchant. This does not mean, however, that the middleman has arbitrary power over prices. If he offers to buy at a price which is "too low," not enough people will offer to sell to him. If he offers to sell at a price which is "too high," not enough people will offer to buy from him. The power of the buyers to refuse to buy, or of the sellers to refuse to sell, is therefore the real factor which determines the price fixed by the middleman.

Auction Sales

An interesting example of a situation in which we have many buyers and a single seller is the auction sale. This is a method of determining prices commonly used in the sale of objects which cannot be standardized, such as cattle, vegetables, wool, or household goods and equipment. In the ordinary type of auction an article is put up for sale by the auctioneer —suppose it is a cow at a cattle auction. The auctioneer then invites bids from the people who have come to the auction. He may start at $30; someone in the crowd nods to show that he is willing to buy at that price. Someone else, however, thinks the cow is worth (to him) more than $30; he bids $35, someone else bids $40, and so on until no further bids are received. The cow then goes to the person who has made the last—and therefore the highest—bid.

DETERMINATION OF PRICE IN AN AUCTION. It should not be difficult to formulate a principle by which the price is determined in such a sale. The price of any article sold will be the next price above the greatest price which the second most eager buyer will give. This principle may sound a little strange at first, but it should be grasped easily. For any given article put up for sale the buyers can be ranged in the order of their eagerness to buy—their eagerness to buy being measured by the greatest price they are willing to pay for the article. Thus one buyer might be willing to buy the cow at any price below $30, another at any price below $35, another at any price below $40, and so on up the scale until we get to the most eager buyers of all—one who will buy it at any price below, say, $50, and another who will buy it at any price below $60. As the bidding goes on and as the price rises gradually, all the less eager buyers drop out until the price is $50, when only the two most eager buyers are left. At the next price rise—say, to $55, if it is the convention to raise the bids by five dollars at a time—the second most eager buyer, who will buy below $50 but not above, drops out, leaving only the most eager buyer, to whom the cow is sold. Notice, however, that the price is not necessarily the *greatest* which the most eager buyer would be willing to pay; in this case he would have been willing to pay $60, but in fact has to pay only $55, for that is the price which knocks out his nearest competitor.

THE DUTCH AUCTION. An interesting variant of the auction is the Dutch auction in which the bids come down from a high price instead of rising from a low price. Cheap-Jacks at fairs sometimes use this method. Department stores occasionally use what is essentially a variant of it by reducing the price of certain goods by so much each day. In Holland this method of auction is used extensively in the sale of agricultural commodities. As there organized, it has the advantage of dispensing with the services of an auctioneer. The buyers sit at desks facing a dial, like a clock, on which prices are indicated instead of hours. The sale is begun by starting the hand of the clock at some price well above what is expected. Every few moments the hands move to another and lower price.

At each buyer's desk there is a button which will stop the clock when pressed. When the hands move down to a price he wishes to pay, the buyer presses the button and so stops the clock. In this case we may expect the button to be pushed by the most eager buyer at a price which is just about the highest he is willing to pay, for the most eager buyer does not know what prices the other buyers are willing to give. He does not know, indeed, until he stops the clock, that he is in fact the most eager buyer, for each buyer fears someone may slip in ahead of him. Thus we might suppose in this case that each buyer has in his mind a price at which he will bid; one will bid at $60, another at $50, another at $48, and so on. Suppose the clock starts at $80, and ticks away—$80, $75, $70, $65—and still nothing happens. Then at $60 the most eager buyer pushes the button. He gets the cow; the others do not. The most eager buyer does not wait till the price falls to $55, because he is afraid some other buyer will get in first.

SMALL RANGE OF PRICE IN AN AUCTION.   In both these cases there is an interesting fact. Although in an exchange between *two* bargainers the price can lie within a certain range, the actual price depending only on the relative bargaining skill or bluffing powers of the two bargainers, in this case, where we have a large number of buyers, the price appears to be quite definite. There is no range over which it may vary, or at most only a small range between the highest prices of the most eager and the second most eager buyers. This is an important result of quite general application. Wherever we have a large number either of buyers or of sellers, or of both, the price will be quite definite—or, as we say, *determinate*—in spite of the fact that there may be, as in the auction, no custom of charging a fixed price.

International Trade

Another important application of the theory of exchange is to problems of international trade. What we have done so far—little as it is—will enable us to clear from our minds a good many of the illusions that cling to this topic. We have seen that for society as a whole exchange is essentially the exchange of goods and services for other goods and services. Money is only an intermediary in the *swapping* of the specialized services of suppliers. This is as true of international trade as it is of domestic trade, and realization of that fact will at least enable us to avoid the spectacular error in the remark (which may be attributed to any politician whom you dislike), "When we buy from abroad we get the goods but the foreigner gets the money; when we buy at home we have the goods and have the money too."

RESULT OF A PURCHASE FROM ABROAD.   It is, of course, quite true that the initial result of a purchase from abroad—let us say, of an English bicycle by an American—is that some American owns a bicycle he did not have before and has, say, $80 less than he did before, while some Englishman owns one bicycle less and $80 more than he had before. But this, as we can readily see, is not the end of the matter. We are now sufficiently trained in economics to inquire, "What does the Englishman do with the $80?" The answer is, generally speaking, "The same as an American would do with $80." He may, of course, eat it, or put it in a stocking, or burn it, or lose it. These things, however, are unlikely. What we should expect him to do is spend it. If he spent it on buying a sewing machine from America, obviously, in an international sense, the exchange is complete. The English bicycle has been bought with an American sewing machine, and money has merely played the part of a go-between in the transaction. Actually, the situation is likely to be much more complicated. The Englishman may spend the $80, or its equivalent in English money, on buying an English sewing machine; but then we still have to ask, "What will the English sewing machine seller do with the $80?" Perhaps he will buy coffee with it from Brazil, and then the Brazilian may buy a machine from America. Sooner or later, the money will come back to roost; sooner or later, it will buy American goods. In the absence of borrowing or lending, the only way to buy goods or services is with other goods and services; and this applies to international trade as much as to trade in general. In other words, over a long period of time, imports can be bought only with exports. As we shall see, there are a good many exceptions and qualifications that modify this statement; but if we hang on to it now, it will at least save us from falling into gross misunderstandings about the nature of international trade.

ECONOMIC DEVELOPMENT

Even with the very elementary concepts of the theory of exchange we can throw a lot of light on a problem which has attracted a great deal of attention in recent years, that of economic development. By this we mean simply the process by which a nation, or a region, or for that matter even a family continues to get richer over a long period of time. The usual measure of riches in this sense is real income per head of the population. There are objections to this measure, to be discussed later, but it is at least a useful first approximation and for the moment we can accept it. Certainly when per capita real income in some countries doubles every twenty or thirty years, while in some other countries it remains stationary at low levels, we can be pretty sure that some process is going on in the one group which is not going on in the other.

The Per Capita Income Formula

The *income formula* developed in the previous chapter can easily be modified to yield a formula for real per capita income, y. Let P be the total population of a country divided between the labor force, L, and those not in the labor force, L_n, and let L be further divided into those producing for domestic consumption, L_d, and those producing for export, L_e; then $P = L_n + L_d + L_e$. If then p_d is the productivity of labor in the domestic consumption industry, p_e is the productivity of labor in the export industry, and T is the terms of trade (imports per unit of exports), then $L_e p_e$ is the volume of export goods produced, $L_e p_e T$ is the volume of imports obtained for them, total income $Y = L_d p_d + L_e p_e T + G$, where G is the amount of gifts or pure transfers. Per capita income is then given by

$$y = \frac{L_d p_d + L_e p_e T + G}{L_n + L_d + L_e} \tag{1}$$

In spite of the difficulties of measurement involved, this is a most instructive formula. It shows, for instance, that per capita income will rise if there is a rise in the productivity of labor, (p_d or p_e), and if there is an improvement in the terms of trade (T increases), and if there is a diminution in the nonworking part of the population, L_n, for this must increase either L_d or L_e, or both.

If now we ask what are the sources of long continuous rise in per capita income, the answer is clear that it can only be due to a long continuous rise in the productivity of labor—in p_d, p_e, or both. T may rise for a time, but it cannot rise for long, and a rise is likely to be followed by a fall; no nation or group can expect constantly to increase the imports it can get for a unit of exports over a long period. Similarly a shift from the nonworking population into the labor force cannot go on for very long, for there is a limit to the decline of the nonworking population imposed by the necessity of keeping children and young people in school and older people in retirement. Similarly G, which may represent foreign aid or public assistance—or if negative, taxes or tribute—cannot be expected to grow indefinitely even though it can increase per capita income for a time. Only a growth in p_d and p_e can be expected to persist for very long, and this is the only ultimate source of economic development.

Causes of Rise in Productivity

The causes of a rise in productivity are complex and are by no means to be found wholly within the exchange economy. Nevertheless the development of exchange and the specialization it permits and encourages play an important role. Adam Smith in a remarkable passage[1] indicates three ways in which the "division of labour," as he calls it, increases productivity. The first is the increase of skill and dexterity as people apply themselves to a single trade. The second is less important but still worth mentioning: the saving of time lost in passing from one occupation to another. The third is the most important of all, the development of machines which "facilitate and abridge labour." Here again exchange and specialization facilitate the process. Some machines are invented or improved by the workmen who use them. A more important source of improvement comes when there are specialized makers of machines who have a strong incentive to improve them. A third—and in the long run the most important source of improvement— comes from what Adam Smith calls "philosophers," that is, scientists, and one should also include engineers, whose specialized business it is to increase our knowledge and improve its application. As science develops, specialization takes place within science itself, with a still further increase in the "quantity of science." Thus exchange and specializing set up a continual, interacting set of processes by which productivity is continually increased, and the increase of productivity permits more and more specialized resources to be devoted to that increase. This process can be arrested by the folly of governments or accelerated by their wisdom; it can be checked by the dead hand of custom or the weight of tradition, or encouraged by the development of favorable subcultures within a society. A large part of its dynamic, however, arises out of the sheer organizing power of exchange which operates, as Adam Smith also said, as an "invisible hand" working for constant improvement of productivity. This is not to say that the exchange system is *sufficient* to meet all social needs. Many things we do not leave solely to private exchange, such as defense, education, or even economic development itself. Sometimes, as we shall see, the exchange system develops pathological conditions and breaks down in unemployment and depression. Nevertheless, when it works in the direction of well-being, it is indeed a natural force, not to be shunned but to be used wisely. How to use it wisely is one of the main practical skills which should be augmented by economic analysis.

QUESTIONS AND EXERCISES

1. An important distinction is often made between money income and real income. From what you now know of the nature of exchange, what do you think that distinction would be?

[1] Adam Smith, *The Wealth of Nations*, Modern Library Edition, book 1, chapter 1, pp. 7–10.

2. "Everybody wants a low price for the thing he buys and a high price for the thing he sells." How does this principle apply to (a) trade union activity, (b) a tariff legislation, (c) complaints about the "cost of living"?

3. Construct formal definitions of the following expressions: (a) international trade, (b) a tariff, (c) collective bargaining, (d) sale by auction, (e) economic conflict.

4. "The more eager people are to buy anything, the higher will be its price." Illustrate the operation of this principle with reference to (a) sale by auction, (b) sale by higgling (or collective bargaining).

5. "Economic conflict is only apparent when there is a small number of buyers and sellers." Do you agree? If so, would you say that collective bargaining increases economic conflict?

6. The statement "When we buy from abroad we get the goods but the foreigner gets the money; when we buy at home we have the goods and have the money too" is a half truth. Try to state the same idea in a way that is (a) wholly false, (b) wholly true.

7. Consider a country with only two commodities, wheat and bicycles. Its population is divided into those not working, L_n, those producing wheat L_w with productivity p_w, and those producing bicycles L_b with productivity p_b. Of the bicycles produced, X are exported for wheat with terms of trade T bushels of wheat per bicycle. Bicycles not exported $(L_b p_b - X)$ are valued for purposes of calculating real income at S bushels of wheat per bicycle: real income is all reduced to wheat as a measure. Show that per capita real income is

$$y = \frac{L_w p_w + XT + (L_b p_b - X)S}{L_n + L_w + L_b}$$

Calculate y for values of the other variables as shown in the table below.

	L_w	L_b	L_n	p_w	p_b	X	T	S
							Bushels per	Bushels per
				Bushels	Bicycles	Bicycles	per	per
	(millions of people)			per Man	per Man	(millions)	Bicycle	Bicycle
1.	4	2	4	500	10	10	50	40
2.	5	2	3	500	10	10	50	40
3.	5	1	4	500	10	10	50	40
4.	4	2	4	500	10	10	50	60
5.	5	1	4	500	10	10	50	60
6.	4	2	4	500	10	10	100	40
7.	4	2	4	1000	10	10	50	40
8.	4	2	4	500	20	10	50	40
9.	4	2	4	500	10	20	50	40

In the light of these results comment on the effectiveness of various means of trying to increase per capita income.

AN ELEMENTARY MODEL OF
THE PRICE SYSTEM

We have seen in a rough way how exchange acts to organize men into specialized occupations and industries, and how it operates to promote economic development. We must now pursue this theme further and show how the whole system of exchange opportunities, and the price system which describes and defines these opportunities, help to organize economic activity. To do this we must first build up a more elaborate model or concept of what the economic system looks like.

COMMODITY, QUANTITY, AND PRICE SETS

The Commodity Set

The first concept is that of a *commodity set,* or list of commodities. In practice this is a very long list—there are indeed hundreds of thousands, if not millions, of different commodities in an advanced society. For some purposes we can group these into aggregates and talk, for instance, of agricultural commodities or metal goods or furniture. Theoretically, however, there is no reason the list should not be as long as we wish. Corresponding to each commodity there will be a segment of economic activity concerned with producing the output of the commodity; such a segment is frequently called an industry, though here again the boundaries which define an industry can be as broad or as narrow as suits our immediate purpose. For some purposes we may wish to regard agriculture as a single industry, for other purposes we may wish to consider the production of early potatoes or Delicious apples as a single industry. Some commodities are an output of one industry and an input of another—wheat is an output of wheat farming, an input of flour milling. Sometimes, therefore, we shall be referring to all the operations that go to

45

make a final product, in which therefore the bread industry will include retail stores selling bread, trucks delivering it, bakeries baking it, flour mills making flour, farmers growing wheat, and so on. Sometimes we shall refer to a smaller segment. We can always fix our definitions however so that, corresponding to each commodity in our list, there is an industry.

The Market Price Set

Then corresponding to each commodity in our list there is also a market price. The whole list of prices is the *market price set*. Each price represents an exchange opportunity. If the price of wheat is $2.00 per bushel, this means that people with wheat can exchange it for dollars, or people with dollars can exchange them for wheat, at that price ratio. For the moment we shall assume that each price represents an unlimited opportunity to buy or sell as much as anyone wants to do. As we shall see, this is not always or even often quite true, but this modification will be introduced later. The concept of a price, as we saw earlier, involves the ability to measure the quantity of commodity—something we frequently have to do rather arbitrarily. Once we make a convention and stick to it, however, this should cause little difficulty.

Quantity Sets

Corresponding to each commodity in our list there will also be certain commodity *quantities* which are relevant to the system. There will be a set of *stocks* of the various commodities, a stock being the total quantity which exists at a moment of time. There will also be certain flow quantities which are important. Over a period of time a certain quantity will be produced, and a certain quantity will be consumed; we have therefore, corresponding to the commodity set, a set of production or output figures and a set of consumption figures. The excess of production over consumption in a period, as we have seen, is the amount of addition to stocks in that period. If consumption exceeds production there is a subtraction from stocks.

The Normal Advantage Price Set

Still another set of quantities which goes along with the commodity and market price sets is a set of hypothetical prices at which the pursuit of each industry, profession, and occupation is normally advantageous— that is, neither abnormally advantageous nor abnormally disadvantageous. This may be called the *normal advantage price set*. There may be some doubt about whether such a set of hypothetical prices exists, but its existence can be shown to be at least plausible. We saw in the previous chapter that a rise in the terms of trade of a person or group raised its real income. A rise in the price of one commodity—say, shoes—with all other prices remaining constant, is equivalent to a rise in the terms of trade of the shoe industry. Shoe producers can now get more other things for every pair of shoes they produce and sell. A rise in the price of shoes, therefore, relative to other things, makes the shoe industry more advantageous to be in, and a fall in the price of shoes makes it less advantageous. We can suppose then that there is some price of shoes at which the advantages of the shoe industry will be "just about right" compared with other industries, and that if the market price of shoes is higher than that the shoe industry will be unusually advantageous, while if the market price is lower than that the industry will be unusually disadvantageous. The greater the excess of the market price over the normal advantage price, the greater the advantages of the industry. I have used the word advantage rather than profitability because it refers not merely to profits in the narrow sense, but also to all the net advantages derived from pursuing the production of a particular commodity. If the price of shoes is high the income of the whole industry will be large, and this is likely to be reflected in high wages as well as high profits.

Description of the State of an Economic System

We can now summarize the condition or state of an economic system at a moment and during a subsequent interval of time, in a table such as Table 1a.

TABLE 1a. STATE OF AN ECONOMIC SYSTEM IN A GIVEN PERIOD

(1) Commodity (industry)	(2) Market Price	(3) Initial Stock of Commodity	(4) Production of Commodity	(5) Consumption of Commodity	(6) Normal Advantage Price
Shoes	$10 per pair	20 million pairs	40 million pairs	45 million pairs	$12 per pair
Ships	$10,000,000 per ship	1,000 ships	100 ships	80 ships	$9,000,000 per ship
Sealing wax	10¢ per ounce	1,000 ounces	5,000 ounces	5,000 ounces	10¢ per ounce

We have to imagine the list extended to millions of commodities. Column 1 is the commodity or industry set, column 2, the market price set, column 3, the set of initial stocks (that is, stocks at the beginning of the period). Column 4 is the production quantity set, column 5, the consumption quantity set, and column 6, the normal advantage set. From these sets we can immediately derive three others, shown in Table 1b.

TABLE 1b.

(1) Commodity (industry)	(7) Increase in Stock	(8) Final Stock	(9) Advantage Index
Shoes	−5 million pairs	15 million pairs	−$2 per pair
Ships	+20 ships	1,020 ships	+$1,000,000 per ship
Sealing wax	0	1,000 ounces	0

Column 7 is the set of increase of stocks, and is obtained by subtracting the consumption figure of column 5 from the production figure of column 4. A negative item indicates a decrease in stocks, or an excess of consumption over production. Column 8, final stocks, shows the total stock of the commodity at the end of the period, and is equal to the initial stock, column 3, plus the increase or minus the decrease (column 3 + column 7). Column 9 is the market price less the normal advantage price (column 2 − column 6). If the market price is just equal to the normal advantage price the advantages of the industry are normal, by definition: the excess of market over normal advantage price measures the degree to which the industry is abnormally advantageous.[1]

Is the Market Price Set Arbitrary?

Table 1 now enables us to describe many of the important elements of a particular state of an economic system in a given period. The crucial question of price theory is whether it *matters* what prices are in the market price set. We could substitute another set of numbers for the ones given in column 2 of the table; if we do, however, all the other columns except perhaps 3 and 6 will change. If this should not matter to anyone, then the price set can be arbitrary—one set of prices is just as good as another. It is obvious immediately, however, that the price set cannot be arbitrary in this sense, that it does matter to someone, indeed to almost everyone, and that one set of prices is not just as good as another. It matters, for instance, if some industries are more advantageous

---

[1] I have called this quantity the *advantage index* because it is not a direct measure of the advantages or disadvantages of the various industries. It is, however, an index of the advantages and disadvantages, in that it has the following properties: 1) It is zero if the advantages are "normal," positive if the industry is abnormally advantageous, negative if it is less than normally advantageous. (2) For any one industry a rise in the index always means a rise in advantages, even though we cannot say how much.

than others. It matters also if stocks of some commodities are rising and of others are falling. The people to whom these things matter will do something in response to their discontents, and among the things which they can do is to change market prices. The machinery by which this is done will be the subject of later chapters.

Disequilibrium States of the System: Changing Stocks

Even at this stage, however, we can see that the situation portrayed in Table 1 could not endure for very long. Stocks of shoes, for instance, are declining at the rate of 5 million a year—using year as a convenient name for the period of time considered. This cannot go on for more than four years or the total stock will be wholly exhausted. One reaction to that is almost certain to be a rise in the price of shoes. There are people who need to own stocks of shoes—retailers, wholesalers, and so on. If their stocks are declining these people will tend to bid up the price; or manfacturers, noticing that stocks of shoes are low, may decide to raise their prices. If the price of shoes rises consumers are likely to buy less, producers are likely to produce more, and the gap between production and consumption will close. As the price of shoes rises, furthermore, the gap between the market price and the normal advantage price will close also. Similarly, the price of ships in Table 1 is likely to be unstable, though not under the same pressures as the price of shoes. If the conditions indicated in Table 1 persist for long, however, the stock of ships will continue to increase and this eventually will produce a pressure to reduce the price. Suppose then that the pressures eventually produce a situation described in Table 2.

Equilibrium State of the System

Here no further pressures arise to change the market price set. The consumption of each commodity is equal to its production, and all industries are equally advantageous, so there is no inducement to shift production from one commodity to another. Under these circumstances the price structure will be in dynamic equilibrium; Monday's price set creates conditions which simply reproduce it on Tuesday and on subsequent days.

EQUILIBRIUM AND DISEQUILIBRIUM

The Meaning of Equilibrium

The word *equilibrium* will recur very frequently, and consequently it may be advisable to pause for a moment and examine what it means.

TABLE 2.   EQUILIBRIUM STATE OF AN ECONOMIC SYSTEM

(1) Commodity (industry)	(2) Market Price	(3) Initial Stock of Commodity	(4) Production of Commodity	(5) Consumption of Commodity
Shoes	$12 per pair	20 million pairs	43 million pairs	43 million pairs
Ships	$9,000,000 per ship	1,000 ships	90 ships	90 ships
Sealing wax	10¢ per ounce	1,000 ounces	5,000 ounces	5,000 ounces

The word comes from two Latin words meaning an equal balance. Anything is in equilibrium when the forces acting on it are such that it has no tendency to change its condition. A book at rest on a desk is in equilibrium relative to its surroundings, for it has no tendency to change its position. On the other hand, a book falling through the air is not in equilibrium; the forces acting upon it do not balance, and therefore it changes its position. Similarly in economic life we say that any quantity— e.g., a price—is in equilibrium if there are no net forces acting upon it, on balance, tending to change it one way or another.

The Equilibrium Price and the Actual Price

The equilibrium price set is very rarely, if ever, the actual price set existing at a given instant of time. A price may exist—i.e., there may be transactions taking place at a certain ratio of exchange—and yet there may be forces operating in the market which tend to bring about a change in that price. In the same way a book falling through the air could be photographed at any moment and we should see that it had a definite position—say, four feet above the floor. This would not be an equilibrium position, however, because the book would be moving away from it. The equilibrium position would be on the floor below. Thus we are *never* likely to reach the equilibrium price set, and in fact no actual price is ever an equilibrium price. Before the forces which would bring together the actual and the equilibrium prices have had time to work themselves out, it is almost inevitable that the circumstances will have changed, and with them the equilibrium price. The pursuit of the equilibrium price by the actual price is rather like the activity of a dog chasing a rabbit. The position of the rabbit at any one moment is the *equilibrium* position of the dog, for that is the spot where the dog wants to be, the spot toward which all the forces acting on the dog are driving him. Nevertheless, the dog may never reach the rabbit because by the time he has reached the rabbit's original position the rabbit is no longer

TABLE 2 *(Continued)*

(6) Normal Advantage Price	(7) Increase in Stock	(8) Final Stock	(9) Advantage Index
$12 per pair	0	20 million pairs	0
$9,000,000 per ship	0	1,000 ships	0
10¢ per ounce	0	1,000 ounces	0

there, and the dog starts off to a new "equilibrium position." In much the same way the actual price at any moment may be moving toward an equilibrium price which itself changes as the actual price approaches it. But the fact that the equilibrium price may not be the actual price does not mean it is not important. The rabbit in the above illustration is absolutely necessary for the explanation of the dog's behavior, even if it is never caught.

General Equilibrium

A situation such as is shown in Table 2, when *all* commodities are included in column 1, is known as *general* equilibrium. With a system as complex as this it is almost impossible to prove beyond all doubt that a general equilibrium set of prices exists, and still more difficult to prove that it is stable. The complexity of the problem can be appreciated if we calculate how many different price sets there might be. Suppose we had a million commodities, and each of these had only three different prices. The number of possible prices is much larger than three, but this is the least we can assume if we want to investigate the result of prices rising, falling, or staying the same. Even with this restriction the number[2] of possible price sets is $3^{1,000,000}$. This is a very large number, much larger than the biggest "astronomical" number we can imagine. It has about 477,000 digits in it. Writing it down at the rate of one digit per second would take about five and a half days, twenty-four hours a day. If we imagine a 3" x 5" card for each price set, and then imagine the whole astronomical universe, 2 billion light years in diameter, filled with these cards, we could not cram more than 10^{82} cards into it, a number which we could write down in less than a minute and a half, and which is a

---

[2] For one commodity there are three possibilities; for each of these there are three further possibilities for a second commodity, or 3^2; for each of these 9, three more for a third commodity, making 3^3 or 27, and so on, so that with n commodities there are 3^n price sets possible.

negligible fraction of the total number of combinations of prices. One would think that with this number of cards there must surely be one which is the equilibrium price set. Even if we could find it, however, we could not be sure that the system moved towards it, and it may well be that a system of this kind moves in a circular path around the point of equilibrium.

The Price System as a Computer

Nevertheless the miracle of the price system is that it does in fact seem constantly to move towards an equilibrium, and that even after a massive disturbance such as a war or a great inflation, the set of relative prices is not greatly changed. We shall find, for instance, that butter is about ten (or five, or twenty) times the price of bread per pound, but not a thousand times, nor a tenth of the price of bread, even after great disturbances. Furthermore where there are changes in relative prices we can generally explain them with reference to a shift in the equilibrium set. We may think of the price system as a vast computer, which continually selects those price sets which are closer to equilibrium and rejects those which are further away, simply through the operation of the decisions of millions of people.

We might well despair of analyzing a system so complex as this were it not that it possesses one very important property; its essential characteristics can be described by means of *models* of systems which contain only a few variables. Increasing the number of variables in our models increases our knowledge of the properties of the larger system, but at a rapidly decreasing rate. The whole method used in this book is based on that proposition. We begin by investigating the properties of economic systems with a small number of variables; once we have explored these simple systems we shall find that we can introduce some new properties by increasing the number of variables, but that each new variable adds less and less to our knowledge. Thus many of the essential properties of a price system can be explored with a model with only two commodities; extending this to three commodities opens up further important, but less essential properties, going to four commodities adds much less, and so on. We need never go to a million commodities in our analysis, even though this is the degree of complexity of the real world.

THE TWO-COMMODITY MODEL

Deer and Beaver

Let us begin our exploration, then, with a model of a very simple economy in which there are only two commodities. In this we may follow

Adam Smith, who says "If, among a nation of hunters, for example, it usually costs twice the labor to kill a beaver which it does to kill a deer, one beaver should naturally exchange for or be worth two deer."[3] The model here is that of a village producing two commodities, deer and beaver, and we suppose some kind of market place where the deer hunters bring deer which they exchange for beaver brought by the beaver hunters. It is presumably easy for deer hunters to become beaver hunters, and vice versa. A certain, unspecified amount of labor produces either 2 deer or 1 beaver. The *alternative production cost* is then 2 deer per beaver, or ½ beaver per deer.

Why then, should 1 beaver exchange for 2 deer in the market place? As in many problems of this sort the answer is found by asking what would happen if the ratio of exchange in the market place were *not* 1 beaver to 2 deer. Suppose, for instance, 1 beaver in the market place exchanged for 3 deer. Deer hunters would soon discover that with the same amount of effort which got them 2 deer in the woods they could get 1 beaver in the woods, which would then yield them 3 deer in the market place. Under these circumstances the deer "industry" would rapidly decline and the beaver "industry" correspondingly increase. Soon the number of beaver coming into the market place would increase, and the number of deer would diminish. The price of beaver would fall (deer per beaver) and, what is the same thing, the price of deer (beaver per deer) would rise.[4] When the price of beaver dropped to 2 deer per beaver in the market place, it would no longer pay to transfer from the deer to the beaver industry; the decline in the number of deer coming to the market would cease, as would the rise in the number of beaver, and the price would remain stable. Similarly, if the price in the market were 1 beaver to 1 deer, hunters would transfer from beaver to deer, for the effort which got 1 beaver in the woods would get 2 deer, which could be exchanged for 2 beaver in the market place. This would soon increase the number of deer, and diminish the number of beaver coming to market until the price of beaver rose to 2 deer per beaver. We clearly have a stable equilibrium at a price of 2 deer per beaver, and this is the *normal advantage price,* as well as the alternative production cost, for at this price there is no tendency to shift from the production of one commodity into the other; both occupations are normally advantageous.

---

[3] Adam Smith, *The Wealth of Nations,* Modern Library Edition, book 1, chapter VI, p. 47. A word of warning is in order here: whenever Adam Smith says "naturally," this means his insightful mind has skipped over several stages in the argument which he has not bothered to make explicit. This often gets him, and economic thought, into serious trouble.

[4] In this simple system the price of deer is the reciprocal of the price of beaver.

The Production Opportunity Boundary

The facts of Adam Smith's little story can be set out in another way which will be useful later on. His little nation of hunters will have a given labor force, say, of 100 men who can produce 5 beaver or 10 deer per man in a given period. They can then produce 500 beaver, if they all work at getting beaver. If they all work at getting deer they would produce 1000 deer. Any combination between these two, such as 300 beaver plus 400 deer would also be open to them. In Fig. 3 we measure the number of deer produced horizontally from the "longitude" of point *O*, and the number of beaver vertically from the "latitude" of point *O*. Any point in the field represents a conceivable combination of quan-

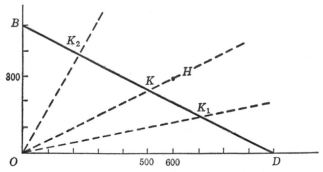

Fig. 3.   The Two-Commodity Economy: Constant Cost

tities of deer and beaver. The line *BD* however, where *B* represents 500 beaver and 0 deer, and *D* represents 1000 deer and 0 beaver, is a *production opportunity boundary;* with the limited resources of the society no combination to the right of or above this line is attainable. Thus the point *H*, representing 300 beaver and 600 deer, is beyond the capacity of this society. Points to the left of and below the line *BD* are attainable, but represent less than full employment of resources. If we assume full employment, all possible combinations are on the boundary between *B* and *D*.

Relative Outputs: Dependence on Demand

The slope of the line *BD*, which in this case is constant throughout, is the *alternative production cost* of deer in terms of beaver; giving up one beaver in the woods enables us to get two more deer. This is the same concept developed for the Crusoe economy on page 29. If the alternative cost is constant, that is, independent of the quantities produced, the production opportunity boundary will be a straight line, as in Fig. 3. We need more information, however, before we can tell *where* on the line the equilibrium combination of outputs will be found. It may be at a point such as K_1, where a lot of deer and few beaver are produced, or it may be at K_2, where a lot of beaver and few deer are produced, or it may be at any other point. Where the equilibrium point will settle depends on the structure of *demand*. If, in our nation of hunters, deer meat and deer skins are highly esteemed whereas beaver is not, the equilibrium point will be found toward D at, say, K_1. If by contrast beaver are much esteemed and deer are not, the equilibrium will be found toward B at, say, K_2. If the two commodities are held in about equal esteem the equilibrium will be at some intermediate point such as K. Furthermore, a shift in demand toward beaver and away from deer will move the equilibrium point toward B; a contrary shift will move it toward D.

The Demand Proportion Line

We need at this point a simple way of describing the demand structure. The simplest way is to suppose that the two commodities are wanted in a certain equilibrium *proportion*. If the actual proportion of outputs differs from this then the commodity being produced in excess will have a price in the market below the alternative cost, and its production will decline; while the output of the commodity in deficient production will likewise expand until the proportion of outputs corresponds to the demand proportion. In Fig. 3 the demand proportion can be represented by a *demand proportion line* such as OH drawn straight from the origin, O. Where this line cuts the production opportunity line at K is, then, the position of equilibrium of the whole system. We shall see in Chapter 5 that this method of describing demand has some defects and involves some rather special assumptions about the nature of demand, but the simplicity of the method makes it attractive as a first approximation, and we shall find later that the modifications we may have to make can be quite small.

Increasing Alternative Cost

We can now relax the assumption that the alternative cost is independent of the quantities produced. In our nation of hunters we are likely to find a production opportunity boundary of a shape shown in Fig. 4. Here the opportunity cost of deer rises as the output of deer increases; the curve gets steeper as we move toward D, indicating that giving up one beaver gives us less and less deer as more deer and less beaver are produced. Similarly the opportunity cost of beaver rises as we go from D toward B; the slope of the curve declines, indicating that giving up a deer gives us less and less beaver. The reasonableness of this assumption can be seen if we consider the conditions under which deer and beaver are hunted. Suppose for instance that demand shifts toward deer, so that the output of deer increases and that of beaver declines. It will become harder to get deer, as hunters have to go farther afield; it will become easier to get beaver, as a small catch of beaver may be found quite near at hand. As we move toward D, beavers start building dams right

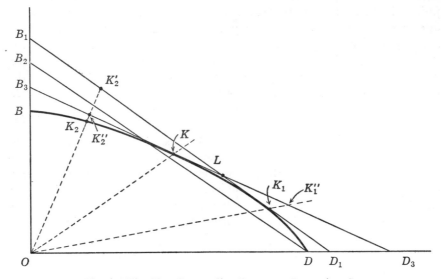

Fig. 4. The Two-Commodity Economy: Increasing Cost

on the edge of the village, deer have to be sought far in the forest. Similarly as we move toward B, beaver have to be sought far away, while deer are seen in the village streets. This condition is known as "increasing cost."

Equilibrium Price: Depends on Demand Only If Cost Is Not Constant

An important conclusion follows immediately from this analysis. It is that under conditions of constant alternative cost the equilibrium price set--in this case simply the ratio of exchange of deer for beaver, or its reciprocal—is independent of the output set or quantities produced and is therefore independent of the structure of demand. Whether we are at K, K_1, or K_2 on the line BD in Fig. 3, its slope is still the same. Where alternative cost is *not* constant, however, the equilibrium price set does depend on outputs, and therefore does depend on demand. If the demand proportion line shifts from OK_1 to OK, in Fig. 4, beaver will become relatively more expensive and deer relatively cheaper as resources are withdrawn from the deer industry and put into beaver.

MORE GENERAL MODELS

The Three-Commodity Model

Now that we have developed some of the properties of a two-commodity system it is easy to extend the analysis to a three-commodity system. Suppose we have three commodities, *A, B,* and *C.* All combinations of quantities of these commodities can be represented in a three-dimensional

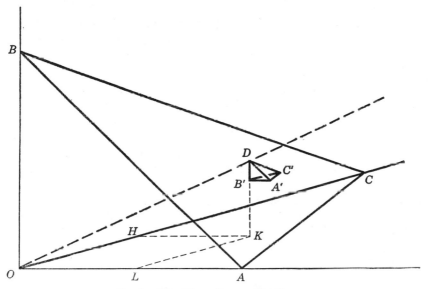

Fig. 5. The Three-Commodity Economy

figure such as Fig. 5 (drawn in rough perspective, with *OC* extending back from the plane of the paper, *OAB*). Quantity of *A* is measured parallel to *OA,* quantity of *B* parallel to *OB,* and quantity of *C* parallel to *OC.* The production opportunity line, such as *BD* of Fig. 3, now becomes a production opportunity surface, *ABC.* If alternative costs are constant, this surface is a plane. *OA* shows the amount of commodity *A* which would be produced if all the resources of the society were devoted to its production; *OB* and *OC* are the corresponding amounts for *B* and *C.* Combinations of quantities represented by points within the tetrahedron *OABC* are feasible; points beyond this are unattainable. We can now suppose a demand proportion line *OD,* which is a straight line from the origin cutting the surface *ABC* at *D.* This represents three proportions:

if we drop the perpendiculars DK, KH, and KL, HK/DK is the proportion of A to B, HK/LK is the proportion of A to C, and DK/LK is the proportion of B to C. There are only two independent ratios, as the third can be derived from the other two by dividing one into the other. As demand moves toward commodity A, OD will swing toward OA, and D toward A; and as demand moves to commodities B or C, D will similarly swing toward B or C. All possible demand proportions can therefore be represented by different positions of the line OD. The actual quantities produced and consumed will be the coordinates of D, HK of A, DK of B, LK of C.

The Price Set

At any point such as D the production opportunity surface will have three coefficients of slope, parallel to each of the three planes OAB, OAC, and OBC. These represent the three alternative cost ratios, or equilibrium prices, of the three commodities. Thus $B'A'/DB'$ (the slope of the line DA') is the amount of A which can be got per unit of B given up, $B'C'/B'A'$ (the slope of the line $B'C'$) is the amount of C which can be got by giving up a unit of A, and the ratio of these two ratios, $B'C'/DB'$ is the amount of C which can be got by giving up a unit of B. The whole equilibrium price set therefore is represented by the slopes of the opportunity surface at D. If alternative costs are all constant, as in the figure, these slopes will be the same at all points on the surface. If costs are not constant the surface ceases to be a plane and becomes a curved surface. If all costs are increasing with increased output the surface will look something like a segment of an orange. The relative price of A will rise as the equilibrium point D moves toward point A, and similarly for B and C.

General Equilibrium with n Commodities

We can now generalize the model for four, five, or any number of commodities whatever, though we cannot now draw the diagrams. For n commodities there will be a production opportunity *hypersurface of n-1* dimensions in n-space; this will be cut at a point such as D by a demand proportion line from the origin; the n slopes of the production opportunity surface yield the whole equilibrium price set, and the coordinates of the point D, the quantity set. This is as close as we can come now to a proof that there is a general equilibrium of a price system.

Effects of Trade Opportunities

It is clear that not much is added to the structural properties of this model by extending it to n commodities, so that we can continue to explore the properties of the two-commodity model with some confidence that what we discover will be generalized to *n* commodities without much difficulty. Let us return, then, to the simple linear production opportunity boundary of Fig. 3, and ask what will happen if this society comes into contact with the outside world and trade is opened up. Consider first the case of Fig. 6 (i), where traders from the outside now come to the market place and offer to trade beaver for deer, or deer for beaver, at a ratio of 3 beaver per 4 deer. More beaver can now be got per deer through "foreign trade" than can be got in the domestic woods. If the society specialized entirely in deer, going to point *D* on its production line, it can then come back up the line *DB'* by exchange. In the extreme

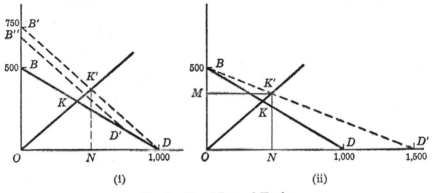

Fig. 6. The Effects of Trade

case, by devoting all its resources to producing beaver in its own woods it could get only 500; by devoting all its resources to getting deer in its own woods and trading them all it could get 750 beaver. The opportunity line *DB'* is at all points superior to *DB,* for from any point on *BD* (except *D* itself) we can move to some point on *DB'* which gives more of *both* deer and beaver than before. It is likewise superior to any opportunity line such as *DD'B"*, with *D'B"* parallel to *DB'*, which shows the opportunity boundary under partial specialization, producing some beaver but also getting some by exchanging deer for beaver in international trade. The society will specialize completely in deer, therefore, and beaver production will disappear. If *OKK'* is the demand proportion line, the equilibrium position will move from *K* to *K'*, with more deer and more beaver than before; *OD* deer will be produced, *DN* deer will be exchanged for *NK'* beaver, and *ON* deer will be retained for domestic consumption.

Figure 6 (ii) similarly shows the situation where international trade is

possible at a ratio of 3 deer to 1 beaver. Deer are now cheaper in trade
than in the domestic woods; the society will specialize wholly in beaver;
BD' is the new opportunity boundary, the equilibrium point moves from
K to K', at which OB beavers are produced, BM are traded for MK' deer,
and OM are retained for domestic consumption.

APPLICATIONS: INTERNATIONAL TRADE

Principle of the Best Alternative

The above model is simply an explicit rendering of the *principle* of the
best alternative, which we noted earlier (p. 26), and which we can now
state more exactly. In the commodity space, or set of commodity quantities, which is relevant to a person, organization, or society there will
be a number of opportunity boundaries representing different alternatives
or policies. An opportunity boundary, *A,* is said to be *superior* to another,
B, if for any point on *A* one or more points can be found on *B* which
represent more of *all* commodities than the point on *A* does. The best
alternative is that which yields the opportunity boundary which is
superior to all others. It may be visualized in the conventional diagram
as that boundary which is above and to the right of all others.

The Two-Nation Model: Principle of Comparative Advantage

The principle of the best alternative, however, is not enough to explain the structure of specialization. We must now go on to ask how
exchange opportunities can exist which give rise to the kind of specialization suggested by Fig. 6. Let us suppose that we have two nations of
hunters with different alternative costs. This is shown in Fig. 7: B_1D_1
is the production opportunity boundary for nation (i); B_2D_2 is the corresponding boundary for nation (ii). Alternative costs are 1 beaver = 2
deer in (i) and 1 beaver = 1.5 deer in (ii). Under these circumstances
trade at any ratio of exchange between these two limits, assuming no cost
of transport, will enable *both* nations to move to a superior opportunity
boundary by specialization. Thus suppose this ratio of exchange in trade
is 1 beaver = 1.6 deer. If nation (i) specializes wholly in deer, and trades
for beaver its opportunity boundary is now $D_1B'_1$; if nation (ii) specializes
in beaver and trades them for deer its opportunity boundary is now $B_2D'_2$,
parallel to $D_1B'_1$ Both nations are obviously better off as a result of
specialization and trade, because the alternative costs differed: if the alternative costs were the same in both nations trade and specialization would
not move either of them to a superior opportunity boundary. This is the
principle of comparative advantage noted on page 27. It may be stated:

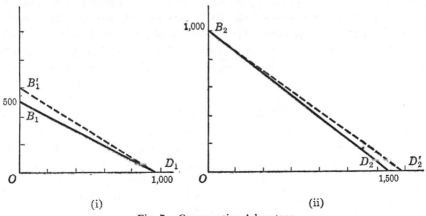

Fig. 7. Comparative Advantage

Trade and specialization are advantageous to two parties at any ratio of exchange between the alternative production cost of one party and the alternative production cost of the other.

Incomplete Specialization

A modification must now be introduced into the model of Fig. 7, because one party may not wish to continue trading up to the point which would lead to the complete specialization of the other. This is shown in Fig. 8: B_1D_1 and B_2D_2 represent the production opportunity boundaries of the two nations as before. When exchange is opened up the new boundaries are $D_1B'_1$ and $B_2D'_2$ as before, with $D_1B'_1$ drawn parallel to $B_2D'_2$. Now, however, suppose that $OK_1K'_1$ and $OK_2K'_2$ are the demand

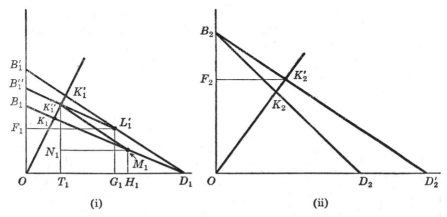

Fig. 8. Incomplete Specialization

proportion lines for the two nations. Nation (ii) will find its equilibrium at K'_2, where it specializes wholly in beaver and exchanges B_2F_2 beaver for $F_2K'_2$ deer. K'_2 is clearly superior to K_2, where it would be in the absence of trade. If nation (i) now had an unlimited exchange opportunity it would move similarly to K'_1. If nation (ii) is the only other nation, however, it cannot do this: nation (ii) is only willing to trade B_2F_2 $(=L'_1G_1)$ beaver in return for $F_2K'_2$ $(=D_1G_1)$ deer. Nation (i) therefore, if it is specializing completely in deer, can move only to the point L'_1, simply because nation (ii) does not want to trade any more at this point. With complete specialization on the part of nation (i) its opportunity boundary is $D_1L'_1F_1$, which may even be inferior at some points to its original production opportunity boundary D_1B_1. Its best alternative however is *incomplete* specialization. Suppose it produces OH_1 deer and H_1M_1 beaver, and exchanges M_1N_1 $(=F_2K'_2)$ deer for N_1K_1 $(=F_2B_2)$ beaver. It can move to point K''_1, where it has OT_1 deer and $T_1K''_1$ beaver. By a similar maneuver it could move to any point on the line $L'_1B''_1$, drawn from L'_1 parallel to B_1D_1 and generated by moving the line L'_1D_1 along B_1D_1 parallel to itself. The best alternative boundary is now $D_1L'_1B''_1$. Assuming for the present that demand proportions do not change, represented by the lines OK'_1 and OK'_2, we see that the opening up of trade moves the equilibrium from K_1 to K''_1 for nation (i), and from K_2 to K'_2 for nation (ii). This demand assumption is open to serious question in this case, but we must reserve that problem for a later chapter.

INCOMPLETE SPECIALIZATION UNDER NONCONSTANT COSTS.   Another possible case of incomplete specialization arises when alternative cost increases with output, as in Fig 4. Suppose in this case an unlimited exchange opportunity presented itself, with a ratio of exchange equal to the slope of the line B_1D_1. The best alternative is then represented by the exchange opportunity line $B_1K_1D_1$, of the proper slope, drawn to touch the production opportunity curve, which it does at K_1. If we go to complete specialization at D the resulting exchange opportunity line, DB_2 is clearly inferior at all points to D_1B_1. In this case we may note that whether the exchange opportunity is in fact used depends on the demand ratio. If in Fig. 4 the demand ratio were given by the line OK_1, the opening up of exchange would have no effect at all; the equilibrium point would remain at K_1. If, however, the demand ratio were given by OK_2 the equilibrium position would move to K'_2 under the exchange opportunity. In this case the effects of a *change* in the exchange opportunity can be quite ambiguous. Suppose, for instance, that the opportunity is still unlimited in quantity, but that the price of beaver falls and the price of deer rises. The best alternative boundary now shifts to D_3KB_3, which touches BKD at K. This *cuts* the old boundary D_1B_1 at L. Whether the change is beneficial or not now depends entirely on the structure of demand. Above and to the left of L the change is for the worse; below and to the right of L the change is for the better. If the demand proportion were OK_2 the change would be for the worse, from K'_2 to K''_2, as the price of the beaver exported has fallen. If the demand proportion were OK_1 the change would be for the better, from K_1 to K''_1 —deer are now exported, and their price has risen.

PRINCIPLE OF COMPARATIVE ADVANTAGE UNDER INCOMPLETE SPECIALIZATION. Even with incomplete specialization, the principle of comparative advantage still holds, as long as costs are constant. For as shown in Fig. 8, it will always pay each nation to trade some quantity, provided the slope of the exchange opportunity lines B'_1D_1, $M_1K''_1$, or $B_2D'_2$ (the ratio of exchange in trade) lies *between* the slopes of the two production opportunity lines, B_1D_1 and B_2D_2, or the two alternative production costs. Only if the two alternative production costs are identical can no ratio of exchange be found between them.

Absolute Advantage Irrelevant to Trade

We should note that it is not the absolute efficiency or advantage which makes trade possible. One nation may be more efficient than the other in the production of *both* deer and beaver, but this fact is simply irrelevant. As Figure 8 shows, for instance, nation (ii) may be more efficient than nation (i) in both deer and beaver, and may produce its large outputs with smaller expenditure of resources. Trade will only take place, however, if each nation is *relatively* more efficient than the other in different commodities and can specialize in and export that commodity in which it has the greatest relative efficiency, or comparative advantage.

The alternative cost ratio in each nation is itself the ratio of the efficiencies in the use of resources in each industry. Thus as one unit of resources produced 2 deer or 1 beaver in nation (i) the alternative cost would be 2 deer per beaver. If now in nation (ii) one unit of resources will produce 4 deer or 2 beaver, nation (ii) has an absolute advantage in both commodities, but its alternative cost is the same as that of nation (i)—2 deer per beaver—and no trade will result.[5]

[5] The problem of trade between two nations with nonconstant costs (nonlinear production opportunity boundaries) presents some unusual problems. Here there is no single alternative cost, and the principle of comparative advantage cannot be stated in any simple way, even though the general concept holds true. Each nation will produce those quantities at which the alternative cost *equals* the exchange ratio, as we see in Fig. 4. However, if exchange is profitable at all, then for each country the trade

The existence of costs of transport introduces a further modification into the above analysis. Suppose, for instance, that it cost 1 beaver in 10 to ship beaver, and 1 deer in 9 to ship deer between the two nations. Then there will be a difference between the market prices in the two nations sufficient to permit the commodities to bear the cost of transport both ways. If the market price in nation (ii) were 1.5 deer per beaver, 100 deer exported from nation (i) would yield $100 \times 8/9$ deer in nation (ii), which would be exchanged for $100/1.5 \times 8/9$ beaver, which when brought back to nation (i) would yield $100/1.5 \times 8/9 \times 9/10$ or 53 1/3 beaver, which is 1.875 deer exported per beaver returned. Similarly

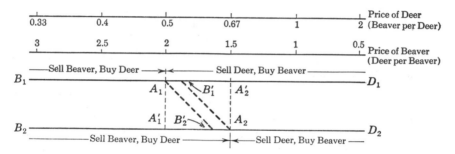

Fig. 9.   Effects of Transport Costs on Trade

if the market price in nation (i) were 2 deer per beaver, nation (ii) would only get 1.6 beaver imported for each deer exported. In the model of Fig. 7, the slopes of the exchange opportunity lines $D_1B'_1$ and D'_2B_2 would now no longer be equal, and the lines would no longer be parallel but have an angle between them which will be greater, the greater the cost of transport. This cuts down the range within which trade is mutually advantageous. Without costs of transport, as we have seen, trade will be mutually advantageous at any price between the 2 deer per beaver which is the alternative production cost in nation (i), and the 1.5 deer per beaver which is the alternative production cost in nation (ii). Now with the above costs of transport it will be profitable only between the range

---

price of its export must exceed its alternative cost on the demand proportion line. Thus in Fig. 4, if D_1B_1 is the exchange opportunity, the slope of this line at K'_2 exceeds the slope of the production opportunity line at K_2. In this rather restricted sense the principle of comparative advantage still holds. So long as the alternative cost in one nation at its point of equilibrium in isolation differs from that of the other at the similar point, trade at any ratio between these two extremes is profitable to both parties.

2 and 1.875 deer per beaver in nation (i) and the equivalent range 1.6 and 1.5 deer per beaver in nation (ii).

Figure 9, similar to Fig. 2, shows another way of looking at the same problem. The price of beaver or deer is measured along B_1D_1 for nation (i), B_2D_2 for nation (ii). A_1 is the alternative production cost for nation (i); for all points to the right of that it will pay this nation to sell deer and buy beaver; for all points to the left it will pay to sell beaver and buy deer. A_2 is the similar point for nation (ii). If these points are at the same price, no trade is possible; if they are at different prices, there will be an overlap where trade is profitable to both parties, in this case between A_1 and A'_2 (or A_2 and B'_1). If there is a cost of transport, then price A_1 in nation (i) corresponds to price B'_2 in nation (ii), and A_2 to B'_1; the range within which trade is profitable shrinks to $A_1B'_1$ in nation (i) or its equivalent, B'_2A_2 in nation (ii).

QUESTIONS AND EXERCISES

1. Which of the following items would you include in a market price set: (a) the price of eggs; (b) the wage of carpenters; (c) the rent of a farm; (d) the rate of interest; (e) the national debt; (f) the income tax schedule; (g) imports of cheese; (h) the labor force?

2. In a society which is advancing in wealth and population the stocks of most commodities will continually increase. How might this fact change the definition of an equilibrium price set? Construct an equilibrium price set as in Table 2, in which however stocks are increasing at the rate of growth appropriate to the society, say 2 percent per annum. What now happens to the normal advantage price set?

3. In Tables 1 and 2 we have assumed implicitly that the production and consumption of sealing wax was independent of the state of the other commodities. Suppose now that sealing wax is an important input in the making of shoes. How might Table 2 have to be modified to get an equilibrium for all three commodities?

4. There are many different kinds of equilibrium, and many systems in which equilibrium is an important concept. Discuss the nature and importance of equilibrium in the following systems: (a) a man riding a bicycle; (b) a book at rest on a table; (c) a pendulum; (d) a clock with an escapement; (e) a thermostat; (f) the succession of the seasons; (g) a ball rolling at constant speed; (h) a forest. Which of these do you think the equilibrium of the price system most resembles?

5. As a little exercise in astronomical and combinatorial numbers, calculate, using logarithms: (a) the number of neutrinos (the smallest particle known, 10^{-43} cm in diameter) which could be packed into the astronomical universe, assumed 4 billion light years in diameter (1 light year $= 9.4 \times 10^{12}$ km. (b) the number of possible patterns of pieces on a chess board, assuming each

square capable of 33 positions (any of 32 pieces, or empty). Note: This is larger than the number of positions possible in real chess. Why? (c) the number of possible states of the human nervous system, assuming 10^{10} neurons, each of which can assume one of two positions. Calculate how long it would take to write down each of these three numbers at the rate of 1 digit per second.

6. In a nation of hunters, suppose one man can produce either 10 beaver or 15 deer in a given period. The total labor force is 1,000. Draw up a table showing how many deer can be produced if the output of beaver is 10,000, 9,000, 8,000, etc., down to 0. Plot this production opportunity boundary on a graph. What is the alternative production cost? Repeat for a labor force of 200, 400, 600, 800, and plot the corresponding production boundaries on the same graph. Suppose now the productivity of labor in the beaver industry rises to 12 beaver. Plot the new set of production opportunity boundaries. What is now the alternative production cost?

Suppose now that the equilibrium demand proportion is 4 deer to 1 beaver. What are the equilibrium quantities of output of deer and beaver in each of the above cases?

7. Suppose a society with three commodities, *A, B,* and *C.* One man can produce either 5 of *A,* 10 of *B,* or 20 of *C.* The total labor force is 100 men. Each of the squares in the following table represents a combination of quantities of *A* (column) and *B* (row); copy this table and write in each square the greatest quantity of *C* which can be produced.

Quantity of *A*

		0	100	200	300	400	500
	0						
	200						
	400						
Quantity of *B*	600						
	800						
	000						

Make a model out of paper of the production opportunity surface, measuring *C* vertically. Draw the figure in perspective.

Repeat, on the assumption that the labor force falls to 80 men. Repeat, on the assumption that the labor force remains at 100 men, but productivity falls so that one man can now produce only 4 of *A,* 8 of *B,* or 16 of *C.*

Repeat, assuming the labor force remains at 100 men, but the productivity of labor producing *C* falls so that one man can produce either 5 of *A,* 10 of *B,* or 16 of *C.*

8. Suppose that one unit of resources in the United States could produce 1 ton of steel or 100 yards of silk, and one unit of resources in Japan could produce ¾ ton of steel or 90 yards of silk. What would be the alternative prices of steel in terms of silk in the United States and in Japan? If there were no

costs of transport would there be international trade? If so, in what range of prices (of steel in terms of silk) would trade be possible? Suppose that it cost 1 yard of silk in every 15 to transport silk from Japan to the United States, and that it cost 1 ton of steel in every 21 to transport steel from the United States to Japan. What is the range of prices within which trade would be possible?

9. A tariff is an artificial increase in the cost of transport. Suppose that in the above case there were no costs of transport. What would be the effect of the imposition of a tariff on silk by the United States equivalent to 1 yard of silk in every 10 yards imported? What would be the smallest tariff on silk that would be prohibitive—i.e., that would prevent trade altogether?

10. In the example of Exercise 8, suppose that the United States has 100 million units of resources, and Japan has 40 million units. Draw the opportunity production boundaries for the two countries on squared paper, assuming them to be linear. Suppose the equilibrium demand proportion for the United States is 2 tons of steel to 100 yards of silk, and for Japan is 15 tons of steel to 1100 yards of silk. Show that it will pay Japan to specialize completely in silk, but that the United States will not be able to specialize completely in steel (assume no other countries). What will be the equilibrium position of the whole system?

APPENDIX

THE MATHEMATICS OF MODELS

The method of this book is to develop as much theory as possible with simple tools and concepts before going on to more complex tools. In pursuit of this objective I try to make the theory accessible to students with relatively little mathematical knowledge. Many of the ideas involved, however, are mathematical in nature, and there is no reason why this should not be made explicit for the benefit of the students who have the previous mathematical training.

In this Appendix the student is introduced to the concept of an economic equilibrium model. Mathematically this consists always of a set of variables and a set of functional relations among them. These functional relations may consist either of identities, which are true by the definition of the variables, or behavioral equations, which express certain properties of the system which the model represents. In an equilibrium model we must have as many functional relations as there are unknown variables, and the solution of these relations—that is, a set of values of the variables for which *all* the relations are true—is the equilibrium position of the system.

Thus take the model of Fig. 3. The system has only two variables, q_b, the quantity of beaver produced, and q_d the quantity of deer. The production opportunity boundary is a line represented by the linear equation,

$$\frac{q_b}{K_b} + \frac{q_d}{K_d} = 1 \tag{1}$$

K_b and K_d are constants or *parameters* of this equation, and are all we need to know to define the position of the line BD in Fig 3. $K_b = OB$, the quantity of beaver produced if no deer are produced and all resources employed. Similarly $K_d = OD$, the quantity of deer produced with no beaver. The alternative production cost can be expressed either as K_b/K_d beaver gained per deer given up, or as K_d/K_b deer gained per beaver given up.

The demand proportion line OH is represented by the equation

$$q_b = nq_d \tag{2}$$

n measures the relative demand for beaver—demand is satisfied when n times as much beaver as deer are produced.

Equations (1) and (2) can then be solved to give the equilibrium values, represented by the point K in Fig. 3:

$$q_d = \frac{K_b K_d}{nK_d + K_b} = \frac{1}{\dfrac{n}{K_b} + \dfrac{1}{K_d}} \tag{3a}$$

$$q_b = \frac{nK_b K_d}{nK_d + K_b} = \frac{n}{\dfrac{n}{K_b} + \dfrac{1}{K_d}} \tag{3b}$$

Some simple properties of the system are apparent from the inspection of these equations. A rise in K_b, or K_d, or both, will raise the outputs of both commodities. A shift in demand toward beaver (a rise in n) will raise the output of beaver, lower the output of deer.

In Fig. 4 the relationship expressed by the line *BKD* is no longer linear, and the simplest possible equation for it would be a quadratic. With nonlinear simultaneous equations more than one mathematical solution is possible, but all the mathematically possible solutions may not be economically significant, for the equations have to be solved under certain constraints—for instance, that prices and quantities must be positive. Even with linear equations we must be very careful in the algebraic treatment where discontinuities are involved, as in the model of Fig. 8.

An equation, say, in two variables, defines a line in 2-space. Thus in the plane of the paper in Fig. 3 each point represents a conceivable ordered pair of quantities of deer and beaver, but only those ordered pairs of quantities which conform to equation (1) are found on the line *BD* and its extensions. An *inequality* defines a half-space, of which the corresponding equation defines the boundary. Thus the inequality

$$\frac{q_b}{K_b} + \frac{q_d}{K_d} < 1 \tag{4}$$

defines all those points in Fig. 3 which lie below and to the left of the line *BD*. Three linear inequalities are sufficient to define a triangular area; thus all points within the triangle *OBD* satisfy condition (4) above, plus the two other conditions: $q_b > 0$ and $q_d > 0$.

EXERCISES

1. Suppose R is the total resources of a society, of which R_b are devoted to beaver with an efficiency e_b, so that $q_b = R_b e_b$ and R_d are devoted to deer with efficiency e_d, so that $q_d = R_d e_d$. Derive the equation for the production opportunity line. Suppose now that $e_b = \frac{E_b}{q_b}$ and $e_d = \frac{E_d}{q_d}$: What is now the equation of the production opportunity line? What kind of curve is it? Using equation (2) as the second equation, find the formulae for the equilibrium values of q_b and q_d.

2. Demonstrate algebraically the propositions derived from Figs. 6 and 8.

CHAPTER 5

APPLICATIONS OF THE ELEMENTARY
MODEL: ECONOMIC DEVELOPMENT

In the previous chapter a model of a price or commodity system was constructed in the simplest practicable terms. In doing so it was necessary to leave out a great many important variables in real economic systems. In spite of this the elementary model is capable of many applications and extensions and throws a surprising amount of light on the working of actual economic systems.

THE COMPARATIVE STATICS OF DEVELOPMENT

Consider first some applications to the problem of economic development. Even though economic development is essentially a dynamic process, some of the properties of a developing system can be illustrated by means of what is called *comparative statics*. The method of comparative statics is one of the major methods of economic analysis, and though it has limitations it also has considerable power. It consists essentially of formulating an equilibrium model and then asking what will happen to the position of equilibrium for given changes in the parameters, that is, the constants or given conditions of the model. The set of coefficients which emerges from this inquiry, relating the change in the equilibrium variables to changes in parameters, is what we mean by the *properties* of a model. Where these properties correspond to some observed sequences in a real economy we have some confidence that our model is useful.

Effects of Improvements in Techniques

Suppose then we return to the deer and beaver nation of Fig. 3, p. 54. This is shown again in Fig. 10. Suppose B_1D_1 is the original production opportunity boundary, and K_1 the position of equilibrium of the system, with constant demand proportions given by OK_1. Suppose now there is an improvement in the technique of producing beaver, but not of producing deer. The production opportunity boundary will move to D_1B_2, as if all the resources of the society were devoted to beaver, more beaver could now be produced—OB_2 as against OB_1. The equilibrium point will move to K'_1, with more of both beaver and deer produced but still, by the initial assumption, in constant proportions. The price of beaver will fall relative to deer, as seen by the slope of D_1B_2 If there is an equal proportional increase in productivity of both deer and beaver the production opportunity line will move parallel with itself to, say, D_2B_2. The equilibrium point moves to K_2; again more of both beaver and deer are pro-

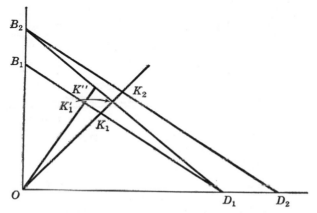

Fig. 10. Effects of Technical Improvement

duced, but the relative price remains the same: alternative cost at K_2 is the same as at K_1. It is this moving of the production opportunity line *outward* to superior positions which is the essential meaning of economic development. If development is at a uniform rate in all industries, the equilibrium price structure will be unchanged. If however development proceeds unevenly, the relative price of the commodities produced by the more rapidly developing industries will fall. In fact development always proceeds unevenly, and it always therefore results in marked changes in the relative price structure. Thus in the course of the past two hundred years in Western countries the prices of foods and manufactured goods have fallen sharply relative to the prices of personal services, education, medical care, and so on, where increases in the efficiency in the use of resources has been relatively smaller.

Variable Demand Proportions

It is now time to relax the assumption made earlier that demand proportions are constant. In the face of both changing prices and changing incomes this assumption is unrealistic, as it implies that the commodities are completely nonsubstitutable for each other, and will be taken in the same proportions at all incomes or prices. Suppose, for instance, that in Fig. 10, when the production opportunity line shifts from B_1D_1 to B_2D_2, beaver become cheaper relative to deer, and as a result the demand proportion line shifts toward beaver, say, to OK''; K'' will be the new equilibrium, with a larger proportion of beaver to deer

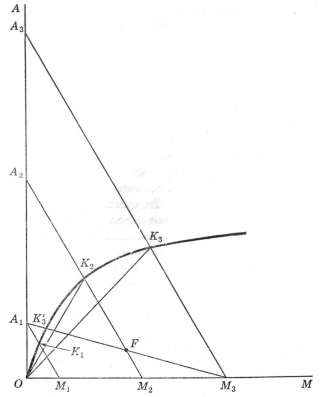

Fig. 11. Technical Improvement with Variable Demand Proportions

than before. Comparing K'' with the old equilibrium at K_1, we see that if the shift in demand proportion is large enough the improvement in the production of beaver, while it will always increase the production and consumption of beaver, may actually diminish the consumption and production of deer if the shift to beaver is sufficiently pronounced.

DEMAND PROPORTION VARYING WITH INCOME. Figure 11 shows an important case in which the demand proportion varies with income. In this case suppose OA measures agricultural commodities, and OM manufacturing output. In this case as development proceeds and income rises, with production opportunity lines moving from M_1A_1 to M_2A_2 and M_3A_3, the proportion of agricultural goods continually declines. The richer a society becomes, the lower the proportion of its income it spends on food and the like, and the higher the proportion it spends on other things. The equilibrium therefore moves from K_1, with a high proportion of agricultural goods when the society is poor, to K_3 with a low proportion of such goods. At K_3 we suppose the demand proportion curve becomes almost horizontal, indicating that further improvements in productivity, either in agriculture or in manufacturing, will be reflected almost wholly in an expansion of manufacturing, with the output of agriculture increasing very little.

BALANCED DEVELOPMENT. Figure 11 also illustrates the importance of *balanced development* in the sense of increasing productivity in all sectors of the economy. Suppose, for instance, that agriculture remained stagnant from position A_1M_1, but that efficiency in manufacturing improved to the point where the exclusive concentration of resources in manufacturing would produce AM_3, the production opportunity line being A_1M_3. We see that the equilibrium position moves only from K_1 to K'_3, a very meager improvement compared with the rise to K_3 which proportionate improvements in all industries would produce. A country which develops a high efficiency in manufacturing, but which has a low productivity in agriculture, will find that it has to keep a large proportion of its labor force in agriculture just to feed its population, and that total output of manufactures and the standard of life of the people will be low. This is, of course, assuming the absence of exchange opportunities in foreign trade.

The Construction of Production Opportunity Boundaries

Further interesting propositions can be drawn from this model if we expand it to include the construction of the production opportunity boundaries from productivity data. A useful method of construction is shown in Fig. 12. Here on the usual two-commodity field are drawn lines showing the product of various amounts of resources devoted to a single industry. Thus in Fig. 12 (i) $D_1D'_1$ shows the amount of deer (OD_1) obtained by applying one unit of resources to the deer industry, $D_2D'_2$ the amount of deer (OD_2) obtained by employing 2 units of resources, and so on: $B_1B'_1$, $B_2B'_2$ are the corresponding lines for beaver. The deer lines are drawn vertically, indicating that the amount of deer obtained is independent of the number of beaver produced and, for a similar reason, the beaver lines are drawn horizontally. The lines are equally spaced, $OD_2 = 2(OD_1)$, $OD_3 = 3(OD_1)$, and so on, indicating constant

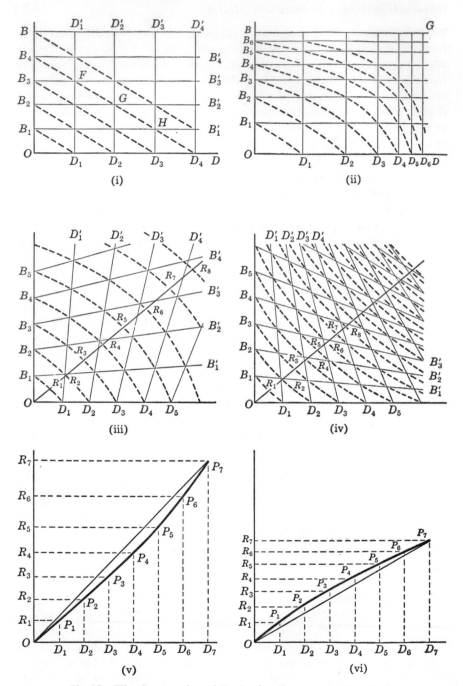

Fig. 12.   The Construction of Production Opportunity Boundaries

resources cost; a unit increment of resources applied always produces the same result. Then the lines drawn across the "northwest" to "southeast" diagonal of the cells of this diagram are the production opportunity boundaries corresponding to different total amounts of resources employed. Thus B_4 is the point showing the results of employing 4 units of resources on beaver, none on deer: F shows the results of employing 3 units on beaver, 1 on deer; G, of 2 units on beaver, 2 on deer; H, of 1 unit on beaver, 3 on deer; and, D_4 0 units on beaver, 4 on deer. All points on the line B_4D_4 therefore represent the result of dividing 4 units of resources between the beaver and the deer industries. Similarly, B_3D_3 is the production opportunity boundary corresponding to 3 units of resources, and so on. Where productivity is constant it is easy to see that the production opportunity boundaries will be straight lines.

The Results of Increasing Cost

Figure 12 (ii) shows the results of increasing cost: as we increase the output of deer, successive points—D_1, D_2 to D_6—get closer together, indicating that successive units of resources are producing successively less effect in getting more deer; and similarly for beaver. The production opportunity lines, derived in the same way as those of Fig. 12 (i), are now curves, concave to the origin, indicating increasing alternative cost. If the successive points D_1, D_2 to D_6 get farther apart, indicating decreasing resources cost with increase in the amount of resources used, the production opportunity lines will be convex to the origin, indicating decreasing alternative cost. The reader may test this by simply rotating Fig. 12 (ii) through 180° so that G becomes the origin. This phenomenon is sometimes found where larger outputs permit better organized and more internally specialized processes of production.

Complementary and Competitive Efficiencies

Figure 12 (iii) shows an interesting case in which the two commodities are complementary—that is, help each other—in production, in the sense that the product of a given amount of resources devoted to one is greater, the greater the production of the other. Thus the line $D_1D'_1$ shows the production of deer with one unit of resources employed on deer; its slant shows the production of deer will be more efficient (more deer per unit of resources), the more beaver are produced. This property also makes the production opportunity lines exhibit increasing cost. They have however a more interesting property: the interval between successive lines increases as the amount of resources increases. This means that the overall productivity of the society is increasing as the total size of the society, measured by its resources, increases. Thus if OR_8 is the demand proportion line, the equilibrium position of the society is R_1 with one unit of resources, R_2 with two units, and so on. It is clear that a movement from, say, 7 to 8 units of resources, moving the equilibrium point from R_7 to R_8 produces a larger increase in output than an increase from 1 to 2 units (R_1 to R_2). The reverse is true in Fig. 12 (ii) because of the operation of increasing cost. The reverse is also true in Fig. 12 (iv), where the two industries are competitive in efficiency, meaning that the efficiency of one declines as the output of the other expands. In Fig. 12 (iv), the individual production opportunity lines exhibit decreasing alternative cost—that is, they are convex to the origin. Their more important property, however, is that they get closer together as we move "northeast," indicating that successive unit increases of resources produce successively smaller increases in output. This is clearly a situation to be avoided in economic development; the situation of Fig. 12 (iii) is to be encouraged.

Limiting Factors in the Creation of Alternative Cost

Up to now we have been deliberately vague about what exactly constitutes the resources used to produce the commodities. Resources are in fact a heterogeneous collection of *factors of production* of many different kinds, and it does some violence to reality to assume, as we have done, that they can be measured in homogeneous units. The concept of the production opportunity boundary has the great advantage that it enables us to sidestep many difficult questions about the measurement of resources. The fundamental principle remains, however, that the boundary exists because the resources which produce commodities are limited. If resources were unlimited there would be no production boundary and no alternative cost. We could have our cakes and eat them too, and an increase in one commodity would involve no sacrifice of others. The exact nature of this limitation, however, is often quite complex. The most fundamental limitation is undoubtedly the limitation of human resources. A society has only so many people, only a certain proportion of these are active, and each person has only twenty-four hours a day to spend on any kind of activity. There are, however, other sources of limitation on production. Land areas is limited, so that land used for one crop cannot be used for another. Mineral resources are limited and may put upper boundaries on production of commodities for which they are required. Energy sources are limited, and the use of energy in the production of one community may deny energy to the production of another commodity. Information, knowledge, and intelligence are limited, so that if one industry receives an unusual portion of them, the others will be on short rations. Even courage and the willingness to take risks are limited factors, and industries may compete for them.

How Scarcity Creates Value

So long as a production opportunity boundary is significant, *scarcity* is said to exist. Only if a society prefers to operate within its production opportunity boundary is this boundary not significant, and that condition can be found only when all commodities are available to the point of satiation. Thus in Fig. 11, if A_3M_3 is the production opportunity boundary, the society may be so rich that it is satiated with all commodities at K_2 and does not proceed to the boundary at all. In that case economics would practically disappear: no choices have to be made, alternative costs are not relevant, and there is no price system, so all goods in effect are free goods. We can safely say however that no society to date, not even the richest, has even come close to that condition, and all societies therefore operate on some kind of opportunity boundary, that is, under conditions of economic scarcity. It is this scarcity, that is, the limitation the boundary imposes, which creates the necessity for a relative price system, and which creates *value*—value in this sense being merely another term for alternative cost, for the fact that the gain of one thing involves a given sacrifice of another.

Special Significance of the Human Resource

It is not only the scarcity of the human resource which creates value, but *any* source of limitation as well. This is the central fallacy of the labor theory of value, and of that Marxist theory based on it. Nevertheless the human resource is uniquely significant because the test by which we judge whether one economy is better or worse than another is the ability of the system to satisfy human wants as measured, say, by the output per unit of human resource. To measure the significant unit of human resource is a troublesome problem. The simplest measure is the individual person, in which case output per head of the total population becomes the significant measure of economic development. As a first approximation, this measure can be accepted; we cannot doubt that a society with an output per head of $2,000 worth of goods is richer than one with an output per head of $200 worth of goods. A society can increase its output of goods per head however by working people too hard, by putting into the labor force children, mothers, and old people who ought to be out of it, and so on. We must therefore admit the necessity for more refined measures of the unit of human resources, but we also have to admit that such measures are not generally available, and in what follows we shall generally take the person as the unit.

THE DYNAMICS OF DEVELOPMENTAL SEQUENCES

The main importance of comparative statics—the kind of analysis engaged in up to this point—is as a steppingstone to the study of the movements of a system through time and the succession of states or conditions of a system; this latter study is dynamics. We shall return later (Volume II: *Macroeconomics,* Chapter 8) to the study of dynamic systems in more explicit form. Even with the elementary apparatus of our two-commodity model, however, we can throw a lot of light on the essential dynamic processes of an economic system. Returning again to Fig. 11, we have seen that economic development consists in a succession of production opportunity boundaries each superior to the previous one. Thus the lines A_1M_1, A_2M_2, A_3M_3 constitute one such sequence; we may think of them as the production opportunity lines of successive dates—say, 1700, 1800, 1900. Lines A_1M_1, A_1M_3, A_3M_3 would likewise represent a developmental sequence, this time with uneven development in different industries. The sequence A_1M_3, A_2M_2 is ambiguous, as the two lines cross; above the point F this is development, below F it is retrogression.

Development from Growth in Population

The question now is what forces in society produce developmental sequences of this kind? The first answer is simple growth in population. In Fig. 12, for instance, we can consider the lines B_1D_1, B_2D_2, B_3D_3, and so on, of diagrams (i) to (iv) as a developmental sequence produced by successive equal increases of population. Consider diagram iii. Successive output positions are shown by R_1, R_2, R_3, etc. We can avoid the troublesome problem of the measurement of output when it is a mixture of different commodities (Volume II, Chapter 2) by assuming a constant demand proportion. We can then measure output by the lengths OR_1, OR_2, OR_3, etc. Thus in Fig. 12 (v) we take the line OR_1R_2 to R_7 from Fig. 12 (iii) and make it the vertical axis: the horizontal axis, OD_1D_2 to D_7 is the same, indicating successive increases of population. The line OP_1P_2 to P_7 then shows the total output for different populations; as population increases, output increases, following this line: thus for a population OD_7 output is D_7P_7. Output per head with population D_1 is D_1P_1/OD_1, or the tangent of the angle OP_1, the slope of the straight line OP_1; similarly output per head at population OD_7 is the slope of the straight line OD_7. In diagram (v) output per head is rising with increased population, as this is derived from diagram (iii) where the commodities cooperate in production. In diagram (vi), derived from (iv), exactly as (v) is from (iii), output per head declines with increased population because the commodities compete in production.

Development by Improved Technology: The Growth Industry

In the above models there is no real change in technology. Once that is put into the picture the possibility for increased per capita output improves greatly, for we can get movements like those from A_1M_1 to A_2M_2 to A_3M_3 in Fig. 11 even without a change in population. The dynamics of these systems can be fairly complex, and we shall have to postpone their analysis. Even with our present apparatus however some important conclusions emerge. The rate of increase of per capita output in a society depends on the size of what might be called the "growth industry." This may be defined as that segment of human activity which is devoted to production beyond replacement. A large amount of human activity has to be devoted to mere replacement of things and people as they get consumed, wear out, or die. A large part of agriculture and manufacturing, and even a great part of child rearing and education, are devoted essentially to keeping the stock of things, people, and knowledge constant. If this replacement activity covers the whole activity of the society, there will be no growth; each generation as it grows up will be exactly like its parents, living in the same kinds of dwelling, wearing the same kinds of clothing, eating the same kinds of food in the same quantity. Only if there is activity beyond replacement—that is, a growth industry—is there growth. The growth industry is hard to identify in practice: it may include a parent here, a teacher there, a business man, an inventor, a missionary, an official, a commissar. A part of education, most of research and development, some capital goods industries are clearly included in it. Part of the growth industry is devoted to increasing the population, and part to increasing output. Output per head will increase only if output grows faster than population. The rate of growth of per capita output therefore depends on two main factors: the proportion of resources devoted to growth, and the proportion of that devoted to increasing output.

THE STATIONARY STATE

The classical economists thought that the process of development would eventually lead to a stationary state. This is a condition where population is constant in numbers, age composition, and skill, and where stocks of capital goods are likewise constant in size and composition. People are born and die, and goods are produced and consumed, but births equal deaths and production of each good equals its consumption. Prices are stable; so is the quantity of money and of all other assets. The question as to whether interest (or profit) can exist in a stationary state is somewhat in dispute; if it exists, however, it must be stable in amount.

Most important of all, the knowledge industry in the stationary state must be only sufficient to replace the knowledge lost by aging and death, so that there is no increase in the total stock of knowledge. This all means that there is no growth industry: the whole activity of the society is devoted to simple replacement. If then a stationary state is to emerge as a result of the process of development, there must be an eventual, continued rise in the replacement activity in all sectors of the economy as the size of the economy increases.

The Subsistence Theory

Thus the model of the stationary state first implies that population growth is a function of economic variables, especially real incomes. This is the essential assumption of the classical model, associated especially with Malthus and Ricardo. If the stationary state is to be stable, in the sense that all economic processes lead toward it, it must also be assumed, at least beyond a certain point, that increase in population leads to a

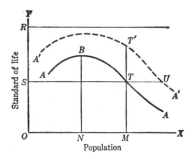

Fig. 13.   The Subsistence Theory

decline in real income per head. This is the essence of the unjustly despised *subsistence theory* of wages. The proposition that per capita incomes will be lower at larger populations, techniques and natural resources being constant, follows from the principle noted, for instance, in Fig. 12 (ii), of eventually increasing resources cost as output expands in a given environment. It is likewise an example, as we shall see later (Chapter 20), of the famous *law of diminishing returns*. Applying larger and larger quantities of labor to fixed natural resources (land) will eventually result in declining product per head.

The subsistence theory is illustrated in Fig. 13. Here the population is measured horizontally, and the per capita real income, or *standard of life,* is measured vertically. Curve *AA* shows what standard of life can be maintained at each level of population. The population at which the standard of life is a maximum (*NB*) is called the *optimum population* (*ON*).

The subsistence theory of wages of the classical economists is based on the assumption of some such curve as *AA*, plus the assumption that there is some standard of life at which the population (in particular, the working population) will just maintain itself. This standard of life is the *subsistence level*. It is not a level of physical subsistence necessarily, for, as Ricardo himself recognized, the subsistence level may be purely conventional. It depends on the degree to which low income prevents the successful rearing of children. We assume, then, that there is some standard of life below which the people will raise so few children that the population will decline and above which the people will raise so many children that the population will increase. Suppose *OS* is this standard of life. Then *ST* is the population at which this standard can be maintained. If the population is smaller than *ST* (= *OM*), it will grow, and the standard of life will decline to *OS*. If the population is larger than *ST*, it will decline, and the standard of life will rise to *OS*. The subsistence level, therefore, is an equilibrium level of the standard of life, a very long-run equilibrium, it is true, but nevertheless valid as a statement of tendency.

The Dismal Science

It is not difficult to see how this theory led to conclusions which justly earned for political economy the title of the *dismal science*. There is indeed a dismal theorem, that if the only thing that can check the growth of population is starvation and misery, then population will grow until there is enough misery and starvation to stop its growth. Furthermore, there is an even more dismal theorem, which I have called the utterly dismal theorem, which states that if only starvation and misery can check the growth of population, then any improvement in the techniques of production will have the ultimate effect of increasing the total sum of human misery, for it will merely enable a larger population to exist in misery and starvation.

In terms of Fig. 13, an improvement in production, which may be due to new techniques or to the opening up of new lands or other resources, will shift the whole curve *AA* to a position *A'A'*, indicating that at each level of population a higher standard of life can be maintained than before. If this happens with a population *OM* (= *ST*) in equilibrium at a subsistence level *MT* (= *OS*) the standard of life would of course increase from *MT* to *MT'*. But, alas, this blessing would be merely temporary. The standard of life *MT'* being above the subsistence level *MT*, the population would set itself to breeding, children would cease to expire at untimely ages, and the population would grow. As it grew, the standard of life would decline until finally the population had risen to SU and the standard of life had sunk once more to the subsistence level OS. The effect of an improvement in the productive efficiency of labor, therefore, in the absence of any change in the subsistence level, is eventually to allow a larger population to exist, but in precisely the same state of misery as before. This is the nightmare of the Reverend Mr. Malthus, and a real nightmare it is in many stages and types of society. Shelley was unjust when he remarked that he would "rather be damned with Plato and Lord Bacon, than go to Heaven with Paley and Malthus." Malthus was also a reformer, but one who saw where the only possibility of reform ultimately lay—in raising the subsistence level itself by the voluntary restriction of births.

Overpopulation and the Malthusian Trap

In many societies today, and in most societies of the past, the Malthusian nightmare is a grim reality. The disappointing results of technological development in many countries can be attributed in part to the enormous growth in population which has followed from it. Beyond a certain point in the rise of population density, land becomes a more important limiting factor than labor in determining the production opportunity boundaries. A continued rise in population then inevitably lowers the per capita food intake, which lowers human energy and has adverse effects on production in all industries. The society is then caught in a *Malthusian trap;* food production does not rise as rapidly as population, and industrial development is arrested because of the difficulty of feeding the industrial workers with the inadequate food surplus from agriculture.

The Dynamic Population Trap

Another aspect of the same trap is that a sudden reduction of infant mortality, without a corresponding reduction in the birth rate—such as happened in many tropical countries in the late 1940s as a result of anti-malaria campaigns and the use of new insecticides—greatly increases the proportion of children in the population and correspondingly diminishes the proportion of people of working age. Thus in 1955 in tropical Africa and Southeast Asia 43 percent of the population was under the age of 15; in Europe and North America this percentage was from 24 to 28. Correspondingly, in Europe and North America about 61 percent of the population was between 15 and 59, in the prime working age, whereas in the poor tropical countries only 49 to 53 percent of the people fell in this age group. If we reckon that every two children need about 1 person of working age to look after them, raise food for them, and educate them, then the percentage of the population available for other things, which might be called the *net labor force,* falls to about 29 percent for the poor tropical countries, about 48 percent for the rich, temperate zone countries. It is little wonder that the rich countries are getting richer while many poor countries are stagnating.

Population in Developed Countries

In the 1930s it looked as if a new danger threatened the Western world —that of race suicide. In many civilized countries the growth of economic consciousness, and especially of economic calculation in the planning of family size, coupled with easy methods of birth control, had brought the net reproductive ratio[1] down below 1, and it looked as if the populations would eventually die out. In terms of Fig. 13 it looked as if the subsistence level had risen, say, to $OR,$ above the maximum possible standard of life. In that case no equilibrium is possible short of zero for, no matter what the size of the population, it will not be willing to produce enough children to reproduce itself. These fears have been dissipated by the remarkable increase in birth rates and reproduction rates in the forties and fifties; in the United States, for instance, the number of births in the 1940s was about $1\frac{1}{2}$ times the number in the 1930s. In no small degree this seems to be a result of rising real income, and we therefore face the possibility that the Malthusian specter may be a real one for the developed as well as for the underdeveloped countries. In the underdeveloped countries the Malthusian pressure arises because economic calculation is not present in the production of children. Even when economic calculation is present, however, a sufficient rise in income may bring most families to the point where they can afford three or four children. In developed societies nearly all children survive, so that a fourchild family pattern may lead to a very rapid rate of population increase. Thus we may have two Malthusian problems—one in societies where people have children because they cannot afford them, and one in societies where they have them because they can. If North America continues its present rate of population increase it will reach a billion people in a mere hundred years. At this density we would have to confine ourselves to a largely vegetable diet and, unless there are striking advances in technology, our standard of life would be much lower than it is today. Even

[1] The net reproductive ratio is usually defined as the average number of surviving female children per woman of childbearing age. Assuming constant sex ratios, if the net reproductive ratio is 1, each generation as it dies off leaves a generation of equal size, and the population will settle down to stationary equilibrium. If the ratio is more than 1, population must grow as each generation more than replaces itself; if it is less than 1, population must decline as each generation fails to replace itself (see Volume II, p. 193).

if the coming biological revolution should solve the food problem through artificial foods made of rapidly growing unicellular organisms, the problem of space and amenity remain. At present rates of growth the whole world will become one continuous city in about 300 years.

The Stationary State in Capital and Knowledge

Other factors in the system besides the human resource may exhibit a *stationary state,* because at some point the effort needed to replace the depreciation and consumption of existing stocks may be so large as to prevent further resources being devoted to growth. Thus as the stock of physical capital—that is, buildings, machines, stocks of goods of all kinds—increases, the amount of current resources which must be devoted to making good the constant wear and tear likewise increases. This is

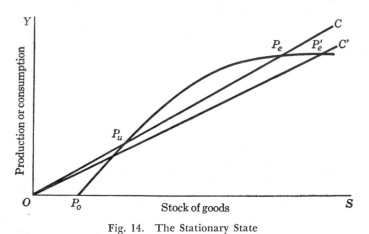

Fig. 14. The Stationary State

shown in Fig. 14, where we measure the total stock of capital along OS and its production or consumption along OY. If the durability of capital is constant, the line OC shows the annual consumption or depreciation of capital, assumed proportionate to the total stock. The production of goods may not begin until a certain stock has accumulated, OP_o, but the production curve P_oP_e rises rapidly from P_o. Then P_u is a point of unstable equilibrium; if the society does not get past it production will fall back; if it does get past it, however, every year production will exceed consumption and the total stock will increase. If, now, as in the figure, production does not increase proportionally as the stock of goods increases—perhaps because of some pressure on land or resources base—the process of growth will come to an end at a point such as P_e, which is the stable equilibrium of the stationary state.

Exactly the same figure can be used to illustrate a possible equilibrium in the quantity of knowledge. Knowledge is constantly being lost by death and, the greater the total stock, the more will be lost each year, following the curve OC. The slope of this curve will be less, the greater the average age at death. The production of knowledge likewise, perhaps beyond a certain critical point P_u, increases more rapidly than its consumption, but here again with given techniques in the production and transmission of knowledge there is likely to be declining effectiveness of additions to knowledge and an equilibrium may be reached at P_e. Many such equilibrium positions have been noted in human history: paleolithic man seems to have been in a stationary state, for instance, for tens if not hundreds of thousands of years. Even from a stationary state at P_e, an improvement in either production or consumption will set the process of growth off again. Thus suppose goods (or people) suddenly become more durable; the consumption curve shifts to OC', permitting growth to begin at P_e, and growth will continue to the new equilibrium at P_e'. A rise in the curve P_oP_e has much the same effect.

QUESTIONS AND EXERCISES

1. In Exercise 6, p. 66, suppose that instead of having a constant equilibrium demand proportion, C (beaver per deer), the demand proportion C (beaver per deer) is related to the price of beaver P (deer per beaver) in such a way that $CP = 0.375$. If the productivity of deer production remains constant at 15 deer per man, plot the equilibrium position of the system (on a figure such as Fig. 10) for productivity of beaver production of 1, 3, 5, 10, 15, 20, 30, and 50 beaver per man. Assume a 1000-man labor force. Connect these various equilibrium points by a curve. Comment on the results.

2. What would you expect to happen to the equilibrium demand proportions of the following pairs of commodities as a society increased its per capita income from low, through middle, to high levels: (a) knives and forks, (b) cereals and meat, (c) donkeys and horses, (d) street cars and automobiles, (e) margarine and butter, (f) goods and services. Draw curves to indicate.

3. In Fig. 12 (iv) the slopes of the construction lines such as $D_1D'_1$ and $B_1B'_1$ get closer together as we move "northeast" in the figure. What will happen when these lines coincide, and what would be the economic significance of this case? Is there a corresponding problem in Fig. 12 (iii)? Do we need to introduce any special assumptions to deal with this problem?

4. In the "nation of hunters" again suppose one man can produce 10 beaver or 15 deer per year, and that the labor force is 1,000 men. Suppose however that the woods around the village are limited in extent, and can produce at the very maximum 8,000 beaver or 12,000 deer. Draw the production opportunity curve, and discuss the properties of such a system, for different assumptions about demand.

CHAPTER 6

ALLOCATION AND DISTRIBUTION: THE PRINCIPLE OF EQUAL ADVANTAGE

The price set, or more generally the whole set of exchange opportunities, is deeply involved in the solution of two of the major problems of any economic system: the allocation of resources and the distribution of income.

The Allocation Problem

In any advanced economic system there exists a high degree of *specialization* of resources. That is to say, our resources—labor, land, equipment—are divided among a large number of different industries. Each industry puts out a product or a group of related products which it exchanges for the product of other industries. The allocation problem is then how do we determine *how big* each of these industries, these specialized employments of resources, shall be. How much of each commodity should be produced? How many men should be employed in each occupation? How much land should be devoted to corn? to cabbages? to skyscrapers? These are fundamental questions of economic life, and all economic systems are attempts to answer them.

The Distribution Problem

The distribution problem is how the total product of economic activity is divided among persons and groups of various kinds—industrial groups, class groups, groups classified by types of income received, national groups, and so on. How much, for instance, goes to agriculture or to manufacturing; how much goes to the richest 10 percent or the poorest 10 percent of families; how much goes in wages and salaries and how much in interest, rent, and profit?

We cannot hope to answer all these questions with the simple models we have developed up to this point, and indeed some of these are the hardest questions to answer in the whole of economics. We must be clear also that the market and the institutions of exchange and the price system are not the only mechanisms which contribute to the solution of these problems. Some allocation and some distribution is governed by gifts, grants, taxes, and allotments out of a budget or a plan. In order to separate out, however, the role of the price system in organizing both allocation and distribution, we shall assume here a model of a *market economy*. This is an economic system in which any individual is allowed to put the resources he owns to any use he thinks fit, provided he does not thereby violate the property rights of others. In such an economy there is no economic dictator who decrees that so many men shall become barbers and so many lawyers, or that so many acres of land shall be used for corn and so many for houses. Nevertheless, the interacting wills of all the individuals in such a society succeed in effecting an apportionment of resources among the various employments. The same process which allocates resources, furthermore, establishes a distribution of income consistent with each allocation.

THE PRINCIPLE OF EQUAL ADVANTAGE

The market economy is governed by a principle which we may call the *principle of equal advantage*. It may be stated thus: If the owners of any resources think these can be put to better advantage in some other use than the one in which they are employed, the resources will be transferred from the less advantageous to the more advantageous use. The process of transfer will generally have the effect of making the occupation *into* which resources have been transferred *less* advantageous than before; it will make the occupation *out of* which resources have been transferred *more* advantageous than before. As long, therefore, as there are people who believe that the resources they own, whether these be their own bodies or some other object, will yield them a greater advantage in an occupation different from that in which they are at present employed, then resources will be transferred from one occupation to another. In this statement, it should be noticed, we use the word *advantage* deliberately, for it includes both monetary and nonmonetary advantages. We do not assume that people are moved only by differences in monetary reward. Indeed, as we shall see, permanent differences in monetary rewards between different occupations may be explained by assuming that people are in fact moved by nonmonetary considerations.

Equilibrium: Advantages Equal in All Employments

A position of *equilibrium* in the distribution of economic resources means a situation in which there is no tendency for resources to move from one occupation to another, on balance. In equilibrium, that is to say, the proportion of resources devoted to the various industries does not change. In the present chapter we assume there are no restrictions on the migration of resources from one occupation to another. Under these circumstances the economic system will be in equilibrium only when the advantage derived from the employment of resources in all occupations is the same. For, if this were not so, resources would move from the occupations of low advantage to those of high advantage. This movement would raise the advantage in the former occupations and lower the advantage in the latter, until all occupations offered equal advantages. At this point there would be no incentive to a further transfer of resources, and the system would be in equilibrium.

EXAMPLE: THE GEOGRAPHIC DISTRIBUTION OF DOCTORS. We may illustrate this principle first by a simple example. How does it come about that the number of doctors in any one town is roughly proportionate to its size and wealth? How does it happen that a village of 2,000 people may have only four doctors and a town of 20,000 people may have forty? There is no authority of government which sets out to achieve this desirable result; there is no official who says to the medical students, as they come fresh from the schools, "Lo, you must go to Oskaloosa and you to Kankakee." It is the operation of the great and universal principle of equal advantage which brings the distribution about. It is evident that as a general rule the more doctors there are in any one town, the less advantageous will be the lot of each. If there are four doctors practicing in a village, the incursion of a fifth will unquestionably bring down the average remuneration of doctors in that village, unless the newcomer strikes a wholly new demand for his services. The incursion of a sixth will bring that remuneration down still further; a seventh might bring all the doctors to scraping, and an eighth to penury. On the other hand, if one doctor leaves a community, the remuneration of the others is likely to increase. There may be exceptions to this rule, but we shall not consider them now, for in the mass they will clearly be unimportant.

Consider, then, the situation of a young doctor just starting out in practice. Where is he most likely to go? To a place which is already overstaffed with doctors? Surely not. He will seek a place where doctors are relatively few, and where therefore their remuneration may be expected to be relatively high. Similarly, if a doctor residing in a place where there is a surplus of doctors hears of an opportunity in a place which has too few, he will be likely to take the opportunity, because thereby he may hope to better himself. Even in so altruistic a profession as that of medicine, therefore, it is the *advantage motive* which by its slow but persistent pressure constantly pushes doctors out of places where there are too many to make what they consider an average living, into places where they are so few that they make what is considered a better than average living. This force does not act rapidly. Indeed, for long periods we may find places which have too many doctors and places which have too few. But like the pressure of water on the rocks in a stream, even though it does not always cause change immediately, it invariably determines the direction of change when it comes. Just as we never find streams washing stones uphill, so we never find the force of advantage pushing people from occupations which they think are better into those they think are worse.

The Allocation of Resources in General

UNPROSPEROUS INDUSTRIES DECLINE. The same principle applies, in a rather more complex manner, to the distribution of resources in general. Is an industry unprosperous? That is a sign that it is too big relative to what it ought to be. Is an industry abnormally prosperous? That is a sign that it is too small relative to what it ought to be. What will happen? Resources will leave the unprosperous industry. Firms in that industry will close down, workers will be thrown out of employment or forced to accept low wages; profits and wages will be low and unemployment may be high. Consequently, the industry will decline. Those workers who can get out will do so. The workers who die off will not be replaced, for the new, young workers will not be attracted into the declining industry. Capitalists who can get their capital out of the industry will do so, and new capital will not flow in. Consequently, the output of the industry will be smaller. If the underlying conditions of demand and supply do not change, the price of the product of the industry will rise. If, then, the industry decreases in size sufficiently, its prosperity will rise until it is "normal" once more. Then the decline will cease. The industry will be in equilibrium.

PROSPEROUS INDUSTRIES GROW. Now imagine an industry which is unusually prosperous. Profits are high, wages are high, it is easy to get employment. What will be the result? Workers will be attracted into it, and new firms will enter it. Its output will increase, and therefore the price of that output will fall. The industry will become rather less prosperous. It will continue to expand until it becomes just "normally" prosperous, when it will cease to attract resources into it and will stop growing. It will then be in equilibrium.

The Adjustments of the Whole System

We must therefore picture the industries of our economic system: some declining under the shadow of adversity, some expanding under the sun of prosperity, some perhaps remaining stationary. But the expanding ones will not expand indefinitely, for the very prosperity which induced their expansion will decline as the industry grows. Likewise those which contract will not contract indefinitely, for by their very contraction they tend to rectify the situation which made them unprosperous.

Equal Advantage and Alternative Cost

The *principle of equal advantage* is the main dynamic machinery by which the set of relative market prices comes to approximate the set of relative alternative costs, as we saw in the elementary model (p. 53). If relative market prices are *not* equal to alternative costs, then occupations producing those commodities for which the market price is "high" will be unusually advantageous, and resources will shift into them from occupations for which the market price is "low." The resulting shift in relative outputs will move the market prices closer to conformity with the alternative cost ratios. When relative market prices are all equal to alternative costs, advantages in all occupations are equal, and no further movement between occupations will take place.

THE DISTRIBUTION OF INCOME

Just as the market system is not the only set of institutions which determines allocation, so it is not the only set of institutions which determines distribution in its many different forms. The price set, however, if we include in this the prices of the services of factors of production, is perhaps the most important single factor determining distribution of income in any society. We shall again therefore adopt the model of a market economy, and see how far the principle of equal advantage determines the distribution of income in it.

Let us ask first, then, what determines the total income of any individual. Suppose John Jones receives an income of $7500 in a certain year. What are the sources of this income? Suppose he has a job which brings in $5000 a year, owns two houses which bring in a net $1200 a year, and owns land which brings him $1300 a year. It is evident that his income can be divided into two parts. What he derives from the labor of his body or mind is one, and what he derives from his property is another. Evidently, owning property, provided the services of the property are valuable, entitles one to income. Indeed, if we widen our definitions sufficiently, we can see that all income is essentially derived from the ownership of property. Income from the sale of the services of mind and body is not generally regarded as income from property. Yet a little reflection will show that it is, because our own bodies are property from which we obtain income. In a slave society this fact is very evident, for there the owner of the slave receives the income which the slave earns. A slave does not obtain income any more than a cow does. Both receive maintenance, both are domestic animals, and the income they earn belongs to their owner. In a nonslave society each man owns his own body—i.e., each man is his own "slave." Consequently there is no market in bodies, only in the services of those bodies, and people do not usually think of their bodies as property. But the fact that each man owns his own body does not make that body any the less property, and does not make the income derived from it any the less income from property.

Income Determined by Amount of Property and Price of Its Services

The income of any individual, therefore, is determined by two things: the amount of property he owns and the price of the services of that property. To find the income of an individual two lists are necessary: one, a list of the property he owns, including his own body; the other, a corresponding list of the services derived in a given period of time from each item of property. The quantity of each service multiplied by its price is the income obtained from it. In the case of John Jones, the list might read as in Table 3.

TABLE 3. SOURCES OF INCOME

Property	Service in One Year	Price of Service (dollars)	Income Derived from Sale of Service (dollars)
One body	50 weeks	100 per week	5000
Two houses	12 months	50 per month per house	1200
260 acres of land	260 acre-years	5 per acre-year	1300
		Total	7500

It is evident that two things will cause John Jones to have more income. One is an increase in the amount of his property and the other is an increase in the price of the services of the property he already owns. The link between the problems of personal distribution and the price system lies, therefore, in the distribution of property.

Inequality of Personal Incomes

We can now see what factors make for greater or less equality in personal incomes. The more equal the distribution of all forms of property, the more equal will be the distribution of income, if there is a uniform price for the services of each form of property. Also, the greater the price of the services of those forms of property which are widely distributed, the more equal will be the distribution of income. A society in which property is concentrated in the hands of a few will be a society with very unequal incomes. The extreme case would be a slave system in which all the property of the society, including the bodies of the workers, belonged to a small ruling class. On the other hand, where property is widely distributed incomes will be more equal. A peasant economy in which each man owns his own farm and implements is one with a relatively equal distribution of income. An economy of great landed estates worked by landless laborers is one in which incomes are relatively unequal.

That form of property in a free society which is most widely distributed is the property each man has in his own body. An increase in the price of the services of human bodies, therefore—i.e., in wages—at the expense of the price of the services of other forms of property—i.e., rents —will usually lead to a more equal distribution of income. Even if there were no change in the distribution of property, a general rise in wages would make the poor richer, and a general fall in rents would make the rich poorer.

What Determines the Distribution of Property?

The distribution of property is the result of historical processes and accidents, and study of the laws which govern these processes belongs rather to the social historian than to the economist. The institutions of society in regard to inheritance, taxation, and the rights of property are particularly important in determining the historical trend toward concentration or dissemination of property. If primogeniture is the rule, we may expect the process of inheritance to lead to the concentration of property in the hands of a small ruling class. In that case the property of the father passes down undivided to the eldest son, and the younger sons get little. The English "squirearchy" is a good example. If, however, an inheritance is divided equally among all the children of a family, property will become more and more widely distributed and we may expect to see a system of peasant proprietorship, as in France. If the wealthy classes have few children, as each generation of inheritors arises property will become more concentrated; but if the rich have many children and squander their wealth, property will be disseminated. Revolutions, wars, taxes, and inflations disseminate the property of the old ruling classes, but may re-establish concentrations in the hands of the *nouveaux riches.*

It is difficult to make any general rules. If Aunt Jemima leaves her millions to her nephew Archibald, who marries the wealthy Rosalind and has only one son, we see wealth concentrating dangerously in the hands of Junior. If, however, Aunt Jemima leaves her millions to a home for waifs or distributes them widely among a vast host of distant and needy relatives, her demise leads to a less concentrated distribution of wealth. Before the vagaries of Aunt Jemima the economist is helpless; he can observe, but he cannot prognosticate.

Concentration or Dissemination?

The available statistical evidence is inconclusive. There is certainly no evidence of any necessary movement toward either the concentration or the dissemination of wealth. Favoring the increasing concentration of wealth are two facts: one is that the wealthy have fewer children than the poor, and the other is that the wealthy find it more easy to save out of their incomes than the poor do. It is no hardship for a rich man to save half or three-quarters of his income, but it is privation for a poor man to save a tenth of it. Nevertheless, there are also powerful forces making for the dissemination of wealth. The children of the wealthy may be few, but they are also frequently corrupted by too great fortune. The excesses and follies of a grandson may often dissipate the painfully accumulated fortune of a grandsire. All that is saved is not retained, and the greater the fortune, the greater the risk of loss. A man with thousands may conserve them carefully, but a man with millions may squander them in wild ventures, feeling that with so much he can afford to lose. The liberality of benefactors and the requisitionings of the tax gatherer alike serve to break up large fortunes. In our day the inheritance tax is perhaps the most potent force opposing the concentration of wealth, and nothing breaks down a large fortune more quickly than a rapid succession of deaths among its inheritors.

Functional Distribution as a Part of Price Theory

The economist, then, cannot make many conclusive generalizations about the distribution of property. It is otherwise when we come to consider the prices of the services of property (a problem which is sometimes given the name "functional distribution"). Here the economist is immediately at home. The wages of labor, the rents of land or of capital equipment are prices, the prices of the services of property. These prices are established in acts of exchange, different perhaps in appearance but similar in reality to the exchange of Mrs. Jones's cents for the store-keeper's butter. When a worker is employed, he gives up a certain commodity—a week's labor—and receives in return a sum of money. When a house is rented, the owner gives up a certain commodity—the use of the house for a month—and receives in return a sum of money. The principles which govern exchange and the determination of prices apply also to these exchanges and these prices. In particular, the principle of equal advantage applies as much to wages and rents as it does to other prices. The case of profits and interest, as we shall see later (Volume II: *Macroeconomics,* Chapter 6) is somewhat peculiar; nevertheless the principle of equal advantage applies here also.

Equal Advantages Explaining Differences in Reward

The question now perhaps may be asked: How can we maintain that there is a principle of equal advantage when wages, rents, and also profits and interest differ so widely from person to person and occupation to occupation, and when furthermore, there seem to be such large and irreducible differences in income among persons, groups, and nations? It is however a tribute to the power of the model that it is precisely these cases of apparent exception to the principle on which the principle itself throws the most light.

Wage Differences

Let us consider first the question of labor. Why does a garbage collector receive, let us say, only $60 per week while a film star receives $10,000 per week? This difference in monetary remuneration is one of the most striking facts about our economic system. How, the student may well ask, can we reconcile this obvious fact with any principle of equal advantage? There are two parts in the answer to this question. The first is that the monetary remuneration is not the whole of the advantages and disadvantages of an occupation. There are other advantages or disadvantages, such as the pleasantness or danger of the work, the constancy of employment, the security of income, the attractiveness of the place in which the worker must live, the agreeableness of his workfellows, and so on. Suppose that there were two occupations with the same monetary remuneration which did not have equal non-monetary advantages. If this were the case, people would move into the occupation with the greater nonmonetary advantages and out of the occupation with the smaller nonmonetary advantages, until the money wage in the first occupation was so much less than the money wage in the second that there was no temptation, on the balance, for people to move from one to the other. If two occupations, A and B, are equally easy of access, we may write:

Nonmonetary advantages of A + monetary advantages of A =
  Nonmonetary advantages of B + monetary advantages of B

and therefore in those occupations in which the nonmonetary advantages are high the monetary advantages (i.e., the wages) will tend to be correspondingly low.

Immediate Nonmonetary Advantages

Nonmonetary advantages and disadvantages are of two broad kinds. The first may be called the *immediate* advantages and disadvantages. There are some occupations which are immediately and obviously more pleasant than others. Other things being equal, therefore, we should expect these pleasant occupations to be paid less. A good example is found in the difference in the remuneration of professors and lawyers. The occupation of a teacher is, by and large, a pleasant one. He lives usually in agreeable surroundings, works among congenial associates, has a good deal of leisure, has long vacations, exercises a little brief authority over his students, and has opportunities for molding young minds. The occupation of a lawyer, although attractive to some, frequently involves work in a crowded and unpleasant environment, meticulous attention to detail, association with unsavory characters, difficult moral problems, uncertain income, and so on. We should not be surprised to find, therefore, that although the professions of university teaching and of the law require about the same amount of native ability and about the same amount of expensive education, the remuneration of a university teacher is generally less than that of a lawyer. The explanation is clear. If the monetary remuneration of these two professions were about the same, education would seem more attractive than the law. The number of professors or would-be professors would grow, either by direct transfer or by a surge of new graduates into teaching, and the number of lawyers would undergo a relative decline, again either by direct transfer or because of a drying up of the stream of young blood. Consequently, the remuneration of lawyers would increase, and that of professors diminish, until there was no longer a force making for the increase of one profession at the expense of the other.

Whole-Life Nonmonetary Advantages

The other class of nonmonetary advantages may be called the whole-life advantages. In comparing the total advantage or disadvantage of one occupation against another, not only must we consider the state of affairs during a single period of employment, we must also consider the process of education which led up to that employment and the ultimate consequences which will follow from it. This accounts very largely for the difference in remuneration between the skilled occupations and the unskilled. In order to get into a skilled trade and still more in order to get into a profession, a process of education, more or less painful and expensive, must be undertaken. This must be offset by the advantages to be enjoyed once the skill has been obtained, and it accounts for the fact that the monetary remuneration of skilled occupations is generally higher than that of unskilled occupations. Suppose, for instance, that of two equally pleasant and equally well-paid occupations, one involved a long and expensive process of training while the other could be entered without delay. It is clear that there would be nothing to attract people into the skilled occupation as against the unskilled. The numbers in the skilled occupation would decline and in the unskilled would increase; the money wage in the skilled occupation would rise and in the unskilled occupation would fall; until finally there would be sufficient difference between them to prevent any further transfer of numbers from the skilled to the unskilled trade. The difficulty and expense of training, therefore, can be likened to a wall around the occupation; there must be a sufficinet difference between the money wage inside the wall and that outside to induce enough people to go to the trouble of climbing it.

In a similar way we must assess the consequences of following any occupation. If it is dangerous, or unhealthy, or a "blind alley" occupation leading nowhere, then the wage will have to be higher than in occupations which are similar in other respects, in order to attract people over this barrier.

Nonmonetary Advantages as Explaining Differences in Money Wages

So much, then, for the first part of our answer to the question of why different occupations are paid differently. Even if everybody knew what the nonmonetary advantages and disadvantages of all occupations were, and if everybody were free to go into that occupation he knew would satisfy him best, there would still be differences in monetary reward. That is to say, a system of money wages is possible in which there are different money wages in different occupations, and yet nobody wants to move from one occupation to another even if he knows all about the relative advantages, and is free to move.

Other Sources of Wage Differences

However, there is yet another source of actual differences in monetary rewards. People may be ignorant and may move into an occupation because they think they would be better off in it, when actually as events turn out they are worse off. Also, people may be prevented by some means outside their control from moving into some occupation which they would like to enter if they could. These two factors we may label ignorance and immobility.

IGNORANCE. Ignorance in this connection has two aspects. There is the ignorance of the advantages and disadvantages of the occupation itself. Generally speaking, people are inclined to underestimate the non-monetary advantages and disadvantages when they are taking up an occupation. This is not surprising, for the money rewards are usually fairly well known, while the nonmonetary rewards are elusive, and to take them into one's calculations requires the exercise of some imagination. Consequently, in occupations with marked nonmonetary disadvantages the wage is frequently lower than it would be if people were fully aware of the circumstances. This is particularly so with dangerous occupations; for a few paltry dollars the lowly and the uneducated can easily be induced to barter their lives. The sand hog or the steeple jack may get a money wage which is greater than the average of his class, but he pays for it dearly. There is also ignorance of one's personal abilities. This usually takes the form of a persistent overestimate of one's skill, charm, and good fortune. Consequently, in occupations which require considerable personal ability for real success, and which offer glittering prizes to the successful, there is all too frequently a large penumbra of failures—larger than there would be if people at the outset had a truer estimate of their abilities and chance of fortune.

NATIVE IMMOBILITY. Immobility also has many facets. Of these, perhaps the most important is *native* ability. Skill is not merely a matter of education; it is also a matter of inherent capacity. Some occupations—notably those among the most highly paid—require a degree and kind of native capacity that is extremely rare. In these the remuneration may be very high indeed without attracting other people into the occupation—simply because the other people who might come into the occupation do not exist. This is the case with film and stage stars and with many, if not all, highly paid executives. It also accounts in part for the high remuneration of the professions, of bankers, and of people in positions of trust.

In answer to the question of why a garbage collector receives $60 per week and a Gable $10,000, we may say that anyone can become a garbage collector, but there was only one Gable. If the number of garbage collectors were so small that each one received $10,000 per week, there would be a wild rush into the garbage-collecting business, which would very rapidly bring down the remuneration of the garbage collectors. The number of Gables was so small that he in fact may have received $10,000 per week. But there was no rush of males into the Gable business, for the peculiar quality of charm he possessed was, fortunately or unfortunately, confined to him alone.

GEOGRAPHIC IMMOBILITY.   Another important fact making for occupational immobility is the difficulty most people find in changing their place of residence. Many ties bind people to the localities in which they live. A well-established habit of life, a congenial circle of friends and associates, familiar surroundings, children at school, and sometimes the ownership of a house all conspire to make it difficult to uproot a worker from one locality and transplant him to another. Consequently, when the employments of a particular region fail, it is hard to shift populations from the depressed area to one where the opportunities for employment are greater. Wide variations in the real advantages of occupations in different regions may persist, therefore, for a long time. The difficulties of depressed areas, such as, for instance, many coal-mining regions, are a case in point. Adjustment takes place, it is true. The young workers move away, leaving an even more hopeless residue behind them. But the process of adjustment is so slow that it may never catch up with the swiftly changing pattern of economic opportunity.

SPECIFICITY.   Yet another important element in the occupational immobility of resources we may call their *specificity*. Once resources have been applied to a specific use, it may be difficult or even impossible to transfer them to another. Once we have devoted some of our resources to building a shipyard, there is virtually nothing we can do with it but build ships; we cannot spin cotton with it, or build houses with it, or grow strawberries with it. Similarly, once we have devoted some of our resources to the training of a naval engineer, we shall find it hard to use him for any other purpose than for building ships; it will be difficult to use him for preaching sermons, or for weaving rugs, or even for washing dishes.

There are two ways of effecting the transfer of some specific resource from one occupation to another. First, there is the possibility of direct transfer. A factory built for one purpose may be used for another, skill acquired for one job may be carried over into another, or a tool used in one occupation may be used in another. Second, there is the possibility of indirect transfer through obsolescence and replacement. A surplus of shipyards cannot be adapted to spinning cotton, but the resources which would otherwise have been used in replacing these shipyards as they wore out can be devoted to building cotton mills and to making spinning machines. If there is a surplus of naval engineers there may be nothing else to do with them but pension them off. But the young men who are coming up can be turned toward other professions—young men who otherwise would have gone into naval engineering. Through obsolescence, therefore, and the kindly and reformative hand of death, the transfer even of the most specific resources can be achieved. This process, however, takes a long time. It may take a lifetime, or even longer, and meanwhile real differences in advantages between different occupations may persist.

ARTIFICIAL RESTRICTIONS. Finally, there are those hindrances to the mobility of resources between different occupations which may be traced to artificial restriction and regulation, whether of governments or of other organizations. We have seen that the entry of new members into any occupational group will generally have the effect of lowering the average remuneration of all the members of the group. This is no doubt why all professions and trades, at all times, feel themselves to be overcrowded: it is because if more people come into them, those already established will probably be worse off. What is more natural, therefore, than to find that those who already enjoy the benefits of a favored occupation seek to preserve those superior advantages for themselves by making it more difficult for other people to enter the occupation? So trade unions of the craft type seek to prevent the entry of too many people into the craft by imposing arduous and often unnecessary apprenticeship conditions or by demanding high membership fees. Professional associations, under the respectable guise of establishing "standards," frequently impose a long and costly ritual of education and preparation upon the neophyte. Nations favored with great natural resources and relatively small populations, with a consequently high standard of life, shut off immigration in an attempt to preserve that high standard of life against the leveling which might result from the transfer of population from the poor countries to the rich.

The principle of equal advantage in explaining differences in reward for labor also applies to use of capital and land.

Application to Capital

Practically everything we have said in explaining the differences in monetary rewards among the different occupations of labor can also be applied to explaining the differences in monetary rewards in the different occupations of capital and land. The same principle of equal advantage applies, modified by difficulties of mobility. If all the occupations of capital—i.e., if all the different ways in which money could be invested—were equally safe, equally reputable, equally convenient, and so on, we should expect the rate of profit in each to be the same. If this were not so, capital would move from the less profitable to the more profitable occupation. This movement in itself would raise profits in the less profitable and lower them in the more profitable occupation, until the profits in all occupations had come to equality. Then there would be no further tendency for capital to move from one occupation to another.

NONMONETARY ADVANTAGES. The principle is again modified by two conditions. The first is that the monetary rewards are not the only inducements which entice capital into one occupation or drive it from another. A "disreputable" occupation, like the liquor trade or the white slave trade, may persistently make high profits, if these high profits are not sufficient to tempt new investors in over the barrier of disreputability; and it is a strange paradox that the greater the disreputability of a business, the greater are its money profits likely to be. Likewise, risky occupations of capital may also make high profits, if the general temper of the people is to avoid risk. But if (as may very well have been the case in Western capitalism) the people are largely infected with the gambler's temperament, so that risk becomes a pleasure rather than a burden, then risky occupations may on the average make smaller money profits than safe occupations.

NATURAL IMMOBILITY. The second modification refers to the problem of mobility. There may be cases in which the owners of capital would like to transfer their capital from one use to another, but for some reason or other they cannot do so. This immobility of capital may exist for *natural* reasons. It may be, for instance, that a special degree of investing skill is required in some occupations, which therefore can command a higher rate of profit than normal without attracting more capital into them. It may be that capital can be employed in some occupations only in very large quantities, and that therefore any fine adjustments of the quantity of capital are not possible. This is likely to be the case in what are often called natural monopolies like railroads. A single railroad built between two places may yield profits greater than the average. Nevertheless, if another railroad were built to run alongside the first and in competition with it, the profits of both railroads might well be reduced to a point far below normal. It is the fact that we cannot have railroads in small quantities which makes this possible. If we could build half a railroad, we might find that with one and a half railroads between two places the profits would be normal, whereas with one railroad they are abnormally high and with two railroads they would be abnormally low. In this case the fact that half a railroad is actually worse than no railroad at all will prevent the influx of capital into this occupation even when the profits are above normal.

ARTIFICIAL IMMOBILITY. The difficulties in the way of moving capital from one occupation to another may also be *artificial,* i.e., created by the action of government or other authority. If the employment of capital in a particular occupation requires the use of a patent, it may thereby be confined to one particular group of persons. Governments may grant monopolies in certain occupations to favored groups and may prevent the entry of other persons into these groups by law. Or a private group may establish a monopoly through the control of some essential raw material, or through the threat of price wars, or through special favors from transportation companies, and so on. The factor of geographic mobility may also enter into the picture in the case of capital. The owners of capital may prefer to have their capital at home rather than abroad. In that case, we should expect to find a higher rate of profit on foreign than on domestic investments.

Application to Land

NONMONETARY ADVANTAGES. In applying the principle of equal advantage to the use of land, the element of immobility is so important that it has obscured the real similarity between the case of land and the case of other sources of income. But even so, if all acres of land could be equally well applied to any occupation, we would expect the remuneration of each acre to be the same, for otherwise acres would be transferred from the poorly paid to the well-paid occupations until all were rewarded equally. Why, then, do not all acres obtain the same remuneration? The answer is much the same as that to the question, "Why do not all hours of labor receive the same remuneration?" In the first place, there may be some nonmonetary advantages in the use of land. These would explain, for instance, why the owner of an estate may use some of his land for a private park and garden, even though it brings him no monetary return, or why a fox-hunting squire might prefer a tenant who paid less rent but did not object to hunting, as against one who paid more rent but did object to hunting. This element in the case of land, however, is of little importance, especially in America.

IMMOBILITY. The second part of our explanation of differences in remuneration—summed up in the word *immobility*—is of profound importance in the case of land. The principal feature of land which distinguishes it from other sources of income is its geographic immobility. An acre is where it is, and it can be nowhere else. Consequently, if the *position* of any acre results in its obtaining a large remuneration, that remuneration cannot be threatened by the influx of acres from outside. The number of acres in the entertainment business in New York is very small, and consequently the owner of each acre can obtain a very high price for the use of its services. The same principle, therefore, that explains how a film star comes to receive a salary so much greater than the meager wage of a garbage collector also explains how an acre of land on Broadway rents for an amount so remarkably in excess of the rent of an acre of northern woods. Just as there are factors which prevent garbage collectors from becoming film stars, so there is a factor which prevents acres in the Adirondacks from taking wings and flying down the Hudson Valley to Broadway. This fact is the sheer geographic immobility of land. The owner of land in the Adirondacks would no doubt *like* to employ his land in the entertainment business on Broadway. He is prevented from doing so because he can neither bring the crowds which constitute the peculiar advantage of Broadway to the Adirondacks, nor take the Adirondacks to the crowds.

SOME DYNAMIC ASPECTS OF ALLOCATION

Up to this point we have considered the allocation and distribution problems on the whole from the point of view of *comparative statics*— that is, by comparing two positions of equilibrium having different underlying determinants. There are, however, some important problems which belong to the field of dynamics proper, either because they involve cumulative and irreversible changes or because the conditions of equilibrium are disturbed so frequently and regularly that the stationary position is never reached. We shall illustrate these problems by three examples: the mining industry, agriculture, and the problem of interregional differences in wealth and income.

Mining—A Suicidal Industry

Take first the case of mining. Mining is the process of taking some form of raw material out of the earth, such as coal, oil, metals or metal ores, salt, clay, or gravel. The dominating feature of the mining industry over a long period of time is that the material once extracted from the earth is never replaced. Consequently, as all deposits of material in the earth are in the last resort limited, mining is an industry which is perpetually committing suicide. The history of a mining community will always take this form: discovery of the deposits, opening up of the deposits, boom period, settling down perhaps into a steady output; gradual exhaustion of the deposits leading to greater difficulties of extraction, a final decline, and then the extinction of the industry in that particular location. The peculiar social problems of mining communities arise very largely from this fact of impermanence. Because of it, mining communities are generally ugly, rough, flimsy, and exciting. It is evident that what is most needed in the mining industry is mobility.

Like the Arabs, miners should be able to steal silently away once the mine which gave them livelihood is exhausted. Unfortunately, this is not always the case, and the elements of immobility we have discussed make the problem of the declining mining community a particularly intractable one. The soft-coal industry is an important case in point.

Agriculture

Agriculture does not present the problem of exhaustion of resources, except in the special case of "soil mining" where the fertility of the soil is not maintained. By proper treatment the fertility of land, in the absence of climatic changes, can be maintained indefinitely. Agricultural communities are therefore likely to be more stable, more settled, less "tough," than mining communities. Nevertheless, in a progressive society agriculture presents a special problem. As a society progresses in wealth the proportion of its total resources which it needs to spend upon agriculture inevitably declines. This is because agriculture, for the most part, provides basic necessities like food and raw materials for clothing. The richer a society becomes, the less is the proportion of its resources which it must spend on these basic necessities and the greater is the proportion which it can afford to spend on luxuries—on automobiles, radios, and so on. In very poor societies almost the whole population must be engaged in agriculture, or at least in food production. In rich societies the food producer can produce enough food not only for himself and his family but for many other people besides—people who are employed in producing manufactured commodities.

Consequently, in rich societies agriculture forms a much smaller proportion of the total activity than it does in poor societies. As a society gets richer, the *relative* magnitude of agriculture—and indeed of all the industries producing basic necessities—must decline. Now, the way in which a competitive society engineers a relative decline in any industry is by making it relatively unprofitable; people are squeezed out of a declining industry by the fact that it is uncomfortable. But in a progressive society, as we have just seen, agriculture must always be declining relative to the other occupations and must always be in process of absorbing a smaller proportion of the whole of economic activity. In such a society agriculture must always be in the uncomfortable position of being "squeezed." The squeeze may be masked for some time by the fact that it is only a relative decline that is necessary. We may even find, as in the Western world of the nineteenth century, that the whole realm of economic activity is expanding so rapidly that agriculture also expands—witness the great geographic expansion of the United States. Nevertheless, in such a situation the nonagricultural occupations expand still further, and the *proportion* of resources engaged in agriculture declines.

Qualitative Decline of a Declining Industry

One further aspect of the problem of the declining industry should perhaps be mentioned—the problem of the *quality* of the resources which are likely to be left in it. When an industry is declining, it is the energetic workers and the enterprising employers who leave it and strike out for fresh industries. This leaves behind the rather less energetic and enterprising to breed the next generation. Consequently, a declining industry is likely to suffer in a qualitative as well as quantitative sense. It will lack leadership, it will run on old routines, and the quality of its personnel will be inferior, at least in some respects, to that of newer industries which can afford the pick of the brains and talent. A declining industry frequently does not adapt itself to new situations as well as it might, simply because there is greater scope elsewhere for the brains that might make this adaptation. The same may be true of a region or nation which is a source of emigrants. It is frequently the most vigorous and energetic who emigrate, leaving behind the somewhat less vigorous (or troublesome!) to reproduce the culture in succeeding generations.

Interregional Differences in Income and Wealth

A striking feature of the present world economy is the great differences in per capita wealth and income among various nations and regions. Thus in the United States per capita real income is at least thirty times what it is in some parts of Asia and Africa and, though statistical comparisons of highly different cultures are very inexact, the differences are so great by any measure that they represent almost different orders of magnitude. In part these differences are due to differences in population density and are perpetuated by both natural barriers to migration (costs of transport, upheaval, and resettlement) and by artificial barriers in the form of restrictive immigration laws. If we look at the problem as a whole, however, it is clear that the differences in regional incomes are not *mainly* due to differences in population density but to differences in *rates of economic growth*. The rich areas are those in which capital has been accumulating, techniques improving, and consequently income increasing at a faster rate than population, especially in the past two hundred years. The "poor" areas are those in which income has not been increasing, over the long pull, as fast as population has, and there are even some declining areas (of which China over the past hundred years seems to have been an example) where total income has increased more slowly than population, and so per capita income has actually declined.

TABLE 4. GROWTH SCHEDULES

Period (years)	Rate of Growth (percent per annum)				
	0	1	2	3	4
Proportional growth in					
50	1	1.649	2.718	4.482	7.389
100	1	2.718	7.389	20.08	54.60
200	1	7.389	54.60	403.4	2981.0

The extraordinary differences which may arise in relatively short periods because of differences in average rates of growth are shown in Table 4, which shows by what proportion an initial quantity will grow in 50, 100, and 200 years at steady (exponential) rates of growth from 0 to 4 percent per annum. Thus a nation or region in which the rate of growth of per capita income is 2 percent per annum will have a per capita income 54.60 times that of a stagnant region in only 200 years!

Migration and Economic Growth

Because of the enormous cumulative impact of quite small differences in rates of economic growth, the effects of migration may be quite different from what they would be in a static world in which misallocation was the principal source of differences in income. Immigration frequently stimulates the growth of per capita income in the recipient region, and emigration may even lower the rate of growth in the donor regions. Furthermore, if the population growth of a region is limited mainly by infant mortality due to malnutrition, emigration may do little to relieve the population pressure, for the adults who leave the region may release enough food to enable even more children to survive than is necessary to replace the emigrants. The region thus becomes an inexhaustible spring of emigrants!

QUESTIONS AND EXERCISES

1. For any industry we can postulate an *advantage function,* relating an index of total advantages A to the proportion of society's resources engaged in it, P. Suppose then we have a two-industry society (deer and beaver), and the advantage function for the deer industry is $A_d = 100P'_d$ and for the beaver industry is $A_b = 50P'_b$. Note that $P_d + P_b = 1$. Calculate P_d and P_b. Solve the problem graphically by drawing a line DB of unit length, each point of which represents a distribution of the total resources, so that at D, $P_d = 0$, $P_b = 1$, and at B, $P_d = 1$, $P_b = 0$. Then measure advantage vertically above the line DB, and draw the advantage functions for both industries. These will intersect at the equilibrium point. We have assumed that $A_d = 0$ when $P_d = 1$,

and that $A_b = 0$ when $P_b = 1$. What is the meaning of this assumption, and does it need to be relaxed? Is the equilibrium point in this model stable, and if so, why? Can you construct a model with an unstable equilibrium of equal advantage? Linear functions, as assumed in the above example, are very unrealistic in this case. Draw on a diagram curves which embody more realistic assumptions about the shape of these functions.

2. Some years ago the Home Owners Loan Corporation issued a statement advising workers to buy their own homes, as being the best and safest investment they could make, and on the same day the Department of Labor issued a statement warning workers against buying their own homes, as that would lead to too much immobility. Comment on this paradox, indicating which type of worker should follow the first advice and which the second.

3. Make a classified list, as exhaustive as you can, of all the factors which explain why wages are unequal in different occupations. How many of these factors can you apply to explaining why (a) the profits of capital and (b) the rents of land are different in different occupations? Are there any factors which are peculiar to capital or land?

4. "It is nonsense to suppose that higher wages are paid for unpleasant work, when a professor gets more than a street sweeper." Criticize this statement.

5. What would you expect to be the effect of the provision of free public education up to the college level on the difference between the remuneration of the white-collar worker and the ordinary laborer?

6. The birth rate in the country is usually considerably higher than that in the towns. How would this fact react upon the wages of the agricultural laborer?

7. Discuss the effects of occupational *prestige* on the differences in monetary remuneration of various classes of labor, bearing in mind that the prestige of an occupation frequently depends on the monetary reward itself, i.e., the higher the monetary reward, the greater the prestige.

8. Studies of the economic effects of education indicate that each year of formal education up to the level of the M.A. increases the probable future money income of the student by an amount which more than covers the cost of the education, but that this is not true for expenditure incurred in obtaining a Ph.D. Why, then, do people take Ph.D.'s? If the *principle of equal advantage* operated fully in regard to investment in education, what exactly would be equalized?

CHAPTER 7

THE THEORY OF MARKET PRICE
IN PERFECTLY COMPETITIVE
MARKETS

INTRODUCTION

We now move on to the construction and use of another set of tools for analyzing price systems and their impact—supply and demand func tions, and their near relations. In many respects this represents merely another way of looking at the problems we have tackled in the preceding pages. It is, however, a way of looking at things which is essential for a deeper understanding of the way in which a market economy works.

The main theme of supply and demand analysis is the relations be tween prices and quantities of commodities. These prices and quantities may be defined in different ways for different purposes. A supply curve or supply function, however, always expresses a relationship between some price and some quantity of commodity supplied, produced, or offered for sale; and a demand function similarly relates price to the quantity of commodity demanded, consumed, or offered to purchase.

Supply and demand analysis operates at two different levels, corre sponding to two different functions or jobs which the price system has to perform. The first level is the problem of market price, that is, what determines the actual price structure as it exists on a given day. The model which is most useful here is that of a pure exchange system, in which no commodities are produced or consumed, but in which constant stocks of commodities, securities, or money circulate among different owners through the process of exchange. The main function of the price set in such a model is to *clear the market,* that is, to ensure that all commodities offered for sale can find purchasers, and all commodities offered to purchase can be bought from sellers. As we shall see, this is equivalent to saying that the price set has to perform the function of persuading the owners of exchangeable assets to hold exactly the stock of each that exists in the market. This analysis of market price, and its applications, occupies this chapter and the two immediately following.

The second level of supply and demand analysis is the problem of *normal price,* which is the problem of how the price system operates to allocate resources among different industries and equate production with consumption. The normal price set is a set of hypothetical market prices equivalent to the set of alternative costs, as seen in the previous chapters. We shall see also, in later chapters, how the normal price set acts as a long-run equilibrium for the market price set, in the sense that if the market price set diverges from the normal price set, long-run forces are brought into play to move the two sets closer to each other.

THE COMPETITIVE MARKET

Some Definitions

In Chapter 3 we studied two situations in which prices may be decided—one, where two individuals or groups bargain with each other, and the other, sale by auction. We must now consider a third very important situation in which prices are decided: the *competitive market.* Many commodities are bought and sold under conditions in which each seller can find many buyers, and each buyer many sellers. The organized bourses and exchanges, such as the stock exchanges, money markets, and commodity exchanges found in the major cities of the Western world come closest to the ideal type of the competitive market, but they represent only the extreme case of a large volume of actual exchanges. The actual circumstances under which exchanges are carried out are almost infinitely varied.

A Simplified Model

As usual, however, we shall find it useful to construct a simplified model, which may not correspond to the conditions of any actual market, but which will serve as a reference point in the interpretation of actual phenomena. This is the model of a *perfectly competitive market.* It may be defined as a large number of buyers and sellers all engaged in the purchase and sale of identically similar commodities, who are in close contact one with another and who buy and sell freely among themselves. Let us examine each of these four conditions more carefully.

1. LARGE NUMBER OF BUYERS AND SELLERS.   What is meant by a *large* number of buyers and sellers? There is no definite answer in terms of numbers, of course—we cannot say that 1000 is a large number but 999 is not. It is important, however, to appreciate the significance of largeness as applied in this connection. The number of buyers and sellers must be so large in a *perfectly* competitive market that the ordinary transactions of any single one of them do not appreciably affect the conditions under which other transactions are made. Obviously, the smaller the number of sellers selling any given commodity, the greater will be the effect of the transactions of any one seller on the fortunes of the others. Where we have only two or three sellers of clothes in a community and one has a bargain sale, the fortunes of the others are pretty sure to be affected. Where, however, we have a large number of sellers selling the same thing, any increase in sales on the part of one of them will probably not affect the fortunes of any single one of the others to any great extent. If seven million farmers are all selling wheat, however much Farmer Giles increases his sales the sales of his neighbors will not be appreciably affected as a result, because the total effect is spread over such a large number of people.

2. A HOMOGENEOUS COMMODITY.   The second condition of a competitive market is that the units of commodity bought and sold by all buyers and sellers shall be identically similar. When this is the case, the commodity is described as *homogeneous*. That is to say, the commodity sold by one seller must not be different, in the mind of a buyer, from the commodity sold by any other seller. This condition is present only when the commodity is a substance of definite chemical and physical composition, such as salt, tin, or specified grades of wheat or cotton. Then the buyer—or seller—is influenced in his choice of a seller—or buyer—only by considerations of price.

3. CLOSE CONTACT OF BUYERS AND SELLERS.   A competitive market is also one in which the buyers and sellers are in close contact. This means that there must be *knowledge* on the part of each buyer and seller of the prices at which transactions are being carried on, and of the prices at which other buyers and sellers are willing to buy or sell. It means also that there must be opportunity to take advantage of that knowledge. If nobody knows what prices the automobile dealers of a certain town are charging for their cars, then these dealers do not form a perfectly competitive market. If the people in one village know that the stores in the next village sell groceries much cheaper than their own stores, but the roads are blocked so that no one can get over, then the stores of these two villages do not compete with each other.

4. No Discrimination. The fourth condition is that the buyers and sellers must buy and sell freely among themselves. This means that they must be willing to enter into transactions with all and sundry. When a buyer announces that he is willing to buy or a seller announces that he is willing to sell at a certain price, these gentlemen must be willing to buy and sell openly to *all* comers. There must be nothing of the business of taking Mr. Jones to the back of the shop and telling him that as a special favor he will be given a 10 percent cut.

Competition a Matter of Degree

It should now be clear that competition in a competitive market is a matter in which there can be degrees. A *perfectly* competitive market would presumably be one in which there was an infinite number of buyers and sellers, dealing in an absolutely homogeneous commodity, with perfect knowledge on the part of all, and with complete openness in all transactions. In an absolute sense such a market could not, of course, exist. Nevertheless, there are many commodities, especially those bought and sold on organized exchanges like the Stock Exchange or the Cotton Exchange, in which the market is perfect enough to make the conclusions derived from the study of a perfect market practically useful.

THE EQUILIBRIUM OF THE MARKET

Price as Depending on Eagerness to Buy and Sell

It seems obvious that prices are going to be concerned in some way with the *eagerness* of people to buy or sell. We have seen already that, in the case of an auction, the more eager people are to buy, the higher the price of any commodity put up for sale is likely to be. We should expect this principle to be generally true. We may formulate it by saying that the more eager people are to buy a commodity, the higher will be its price, and the more eager people are to sell a commodity, the lower will be its price. If people as a whole want a thing very badly the price will be high, for the people who do not have it will be willing to give a lot for it, and the people who have it will not be willing to let it go unless they get a good deal for it. Likewise, if people as a whole want a certain thing but little, the people who have it will be willing to let it go for a little, and the people who do not have it will not be willing to pay very much for it.

The Measurement of Eagerness

Our next task is to try to reduce these broad principles to *measurable* terms. It is all very well to talk loosely about people's eagerness to buy or sell, but we cannot be content with that. A device is necessary which will enable us to measure how eager people are to buy or sell, and to be quite accurate, for instance, about what we mean by people being *more* eager or *less* eager to buy or sell.

CAN IT BE MEASURED BY QUANTITIES OFFERED OR DEMANDED?   In order to do this we shall have to introduce a new idea into our concept of exchange. Up to now we have assumed that the quantities of goods to be exchanged were fixed, and have argued as if—to return again to our old friend, Mrs. Jones—the only possible exchange were of two pounds of butter for money, and the only question, whether the exchange took place or not. Similarly, in the case of an auction, a given article is "put up for sale" and is either sold or not sold. In any given transaction of this kind there is no question of the *quantity* of the commodity to be bought or sold. In a competitive market, however, it is evident that the question may not be merely, "Shall I buy this given commodity or shall I not?" The question is more often, "Shall I buy two pounds of butter at this price, or one pound, or half a pound, or three pounds?" The introduction of the idea that the *quantity* of a given commodity which people are willing to buy or sell may vary gives us a clue to the accurate description of the concept of *eagerness* to buy or sell. Can we measure the eagerness of people to buy or sell anything by the quantities which they are willing to buy or sell? A man who is willing to buy a large quantity of a commodity is presumably more eager to buy it than one who is willing to buy only a small quantity.

NO, BECAUSE THESE DEPEND ON THE PRICE.   However, the matter does not end there. The quantity of a commodity which people are willing to buy or sell depends, among other things, on the price of the commodity. A man may buy more hair oil *either* because there is a cut in the price of hair oil which tempts him to buy more, *or* because he has fallen in love with a girl who is particular about untidy hair, *or* because he has had a raise in pay. It is clearly going to be necessary to distinguish between these various situations, for we should not use the same word indiscriminately to describe them all. There is something about the increase in the purchases of hair oil resulting from falling in love which differs from the increase in purchases resulting from a fall in the price of hair oil. Indeed, it would probably not be stretching the meaning of words too far to say that the increase in purchases which was a result of falling in love was a *real* increase in the eagerness to buy, whereas the increase which resulted from the fall in price of the hair oil was not so much an increase in the eagerness as in the opportunity to buy.

We would not be justified, then, in taking the simple quantity which people are willing to buy or sell as a measure of their eagerness to buy or sell, for people may become willing to buy or sell larger or smaller quantities *merely* because there is a change in the price of the commodity concerned. It is not enough to say, "This man is eager to buy doughnuts, for he is willing to buy sixteen of them in a week." If the price of doughnuts were forty cents a dozen these purchases might not be at all remarkable. But if the price were a dollar apiece, the willingness to buy sixteen in a week might indicate a passion for doughnuts verging on insanity.

The Individual Market Schedule

The eagerness of any individual to buy or sell may be indicated by a *schedule* showing how much he will be willing to buy or sell at *various prices*. To make the illustration more concrete, suppose we consider the situation of a single wheat merchant, on a particular day, in the Chicago Wheat Market. He has in his possession, or at his command, a given stock of wheat—let us say 5000 bushels. He also has in his possession, or at his command, a certain sum of money—let us say $10,000. The problem is, *how much* wheat will he sell (i.e., turn into money) or how much will he buy (i.e., how much money will he turn into wheat)? Now a number of things may affect his decisions as to how much wheat to buy or sell. The weather, the crop reports, even his own state of health, may make him more or less eager to buy or sell. The problem under consideration here, however, is what determines the *price* of wheat. We must therefore concentrate our attention on the effect exercised by the price, and by the price alone, on the quantity he will buy or sell. In order to do this we must suppose all other things except the price to remain constant during the day, and inquire under these circumstances what quantities the merchant would buy or sell at various hypothetical prices. At very high prices he would probably be willing to sell a large quantity; at lower prices he would probably wish to sell less; at a still lower price he would probably wish neither to buy nor to sell, being satisfied with his present stock; at yet lower prices he would be willing to buy, and at very low prices he would buy a great deal. These facts can be expressed in the form of a schedule, or table, as in Table 5. We should read this schedule: "If the price of wheat were $1.20 a bushel, he would not be willing to buy any but would be willing to sell 5000 bushels. If the price of wheat were $1.10, he would not be willing to buy any but would be willing to sell 2000 bushels; if . . . , etc." Of course there should also be places on the schedule for other prices— $1.19, $1.18, and so on—but we leave these out for the sake of simplicity.

This schedule describes the *market function* of the individual in question. It tells us exactly how much wheat he will be willing to give or to take in exchange for money at some hypothetical prices of wheat. It also

Table 5. The Individual Market Schedule

If the Price of Wheat Were (per bushel)	He Would Be Willing To Buy (bushels)	He Would Be Willing To Sell (bushels)
$1.20	0	5,000
1.10	0	2,000
1.00	0	0
0.90	3,000	0
0.80	12,500	0

tells us how much money he would be willing to take or give for wheat at some hypothetical prices. Thus at a price of $1.20 he would be willing to take $6000 in exchange for wheat (5000 bushels at $1.20 per bushel), at a price of $1.10 he would be willing to take $2200 in exchange for wheat, and so on.

The market schedule of Table 5 can be expressed on a graph by measuring, as in Fig. 15, the price vertically above the base line *AA*

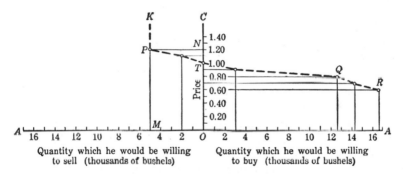

Fig. 15. The Individual Market Curve

and the quantity which would be bought or sold at each price horizontally from the axis *OC*. Quantities bought are assumed to be *positive;* following the usual mathematical convention these will be measured to the right of *OC*. Similarly, quantities sold are *negative,* and will be measured to the left of *OC*. On such a figure, therefore, any point represents a combination of a certain price with a certain quantity bought or sold. We may read the point *P,* for instance, as an expression of the fact that at a price of $1.20 per bushel, represented by *MP* (or *ON*), our marketer will wish to sell 5000 bushels of wheat, represented by *NP* (or *OM*). The point *Q* expresses the fact that at a price of $0.80 he is willing to buy 12,500 bushels—and so on for all the other points.

The Individual Market Curve

If all the points on the graph which correspond to the market schedule of Table 5 are connected by a line, *KPTQR*, we shall have a line on the graph which tells us exactly the same set of facts as the market schedule does. This is called the *market curve* of the individual marketer. In the figure the vertical section *PK* reflects the assumption that he has only 5000 bushels of wheat to sell, and the section *QR* is drawn on the assumption that he has only $10,000 to spend. If he can borrow money, or borrow wheat, as we shall see later, these assumptions must be modified. We will simplify the present analysis by assuming that only the segment *PQ* is relevant.

Market Schedule of an Eager Buyer

Every individual in the market on any particular day will have his own market curve expressing his eagerness to buy or sell. The market curves of these various individuals will not necessarily be the same; indeed, as we shall see, it is only because the market curves of various individuals are different that any transactions take place in the market at all. The question arises, therefore, how can we express the *eagerness* of people to buy or sell in terms of these market curves? What will happen, for instance, to the market curve of an individual if for some reason he becomes more eager to buy (which is the same thing, of course, as becoming less eager to sell)? This will mean that *at each price* he will be willing to buy a *greater* quantity (or sell a smaller quantity) than he did before. His market schedule, instead of being as it was in Table 5, may now be as in Table 6. At a price of $1.20, whereas before he was willing to sell 5000 bushels, now he is more cautious; he is willing to sell only 2500. At a price of $1.10, whereas previously he was willing to sell 2000 bushels, now he is not willing to sell anything. At a price of $1, whereas previously he was not willing either to buy or sell, now he is willing to buy 4000 bushels, and so on for all other prices.

TABLE 6. MARKET SCHEDULE OF AN EAGER BUYER

If the Price of Wheat Were (per bushel)	He Would Be Willing	
	To Buy	To Sell
	(bushels)	
$1.20	0	2,500
1.10	0	0
1.00	4,000	0
0.90	11,000	0
0.80	12,500	0

Market Schedule of an Eager Seller

In a similar way, if for any reason he becomes less eager to buy (or, what is exactly the same thing, more eager to sell), this means that at each price he will be willing to buy a smaller quantity (or sell a larger quantity) than he did before. His market schedule may now be as in Table 7.

TABLE 7. MARKET SCHEDULE OF AN EAGER SELLER

If the Price of Wheat Were (per bushel)	He Would Be Willing To Buy	To Sell (bushels)
$1.20	0	5,000
1.10	0	5,000
1.00	0	2,400
0.90	0	0
0.80	4,500	0
0.70	14,000	0

GRAPHIC ILLUSTRATION. The market curves corresponding to the schedules of Tables 5, 6, and 7 are shown in Fig. 16. We see immediately that an increased eagerness to buy is reflected in a rise in the market curve, and an increased eagerness to sell is reflected in a fall in the market curve. Curve $KP'T'Q'R$ is the market curve corresponding to Table 6, the eager buyer. Curve $KP_1T_1Q_1R$ is the market curve corresponding to the eager seller of Table 7. Curve $KPTQR$ corresponds to our original schedule, Table 5.

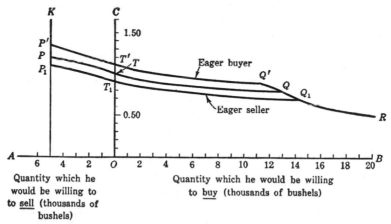

Fig. 16. Market Curves of Eager Buyers and Sellers

*Derivation of Market Demand and Market Supply Schedules from
Individual Market Schedules*

With the information given merely by the market schedules or curves
of all the individuals in the market we can now proceed to deduce what
will be the market price of the commodity and what will be the quantity
exchanged. Suppose as an example that there are five marketers. Such a
market would not of course fulfill the conditions of a perfectly competitive
market, but for the sake of simplicity of arithmetic we shall assume first a
relatively small number of buyers and sellers. The processes can easily
be extended to any number whatever. Let us suppose that the market
schedules of each one of these marketers is represented in Table 8. For
the sake of convenience we shall represent a quantity which people are
willing to buy, by a (+) sign, and a quantity which people are willing to
sell, by a (−) sign.

Mr. A is a very eager seller. He will sell something, even if the price
is as low as $0.80, and it has to fall almost to $0.70 before he will be
persuaded to buy. Mr. E, on the other hand, is a very eager buyer. Even
a price as high as $1.10 will find him still willing to buy a small quantity.
The other marketers range somewhere in between.

TABLE 8.   DERIVATION OF THE MARKET DEMAND AND SUPPLY SCHEDULES

Price (per bushel)	Quantity Which Each Marketer Would Buy (+) or Sell (−) at That Price					Demand Supply (bushels)	
	A	B	C	D	E	Demand	Supply
$1.20	−5,000	−3,000	−1,500	−1,000	− 500	0	−11,000
1.10	−3,000	−2,000	− 500	− 200	+ 100	+ 100	− 5,700
1.00	−2,000	−1,500	− 200	+ 100	+ 500	+ 600	− 3,700
0.90	−1,000	− 800	+ 200	+ 600	+1,000	+ 1,800	− 1,800
0.80	− 500	+1,000	+1,500	+2,000	+3,000	+ 7,500	− 500
0.70	+ 500	+1,500	+2,000	+3,000	+5,000	+12,000	0

THE MARKET DEMAND SCHEDULE.   The seventh and eighth columns
of the table are of great importance. The first is obtained by adding
up all the individual amounts which the marketers are willing to *buy*
at each price. Thus, at a price of $1.20 there are no buyers at all and
nothing will be bought. At a price of $1.10 Mr. E will buy 100 bushels,
but nobody else will buy. At a price of $1 Mr. E will buy 500 bushels.
Mr. D will buy 100 bushels, making 600 bushels in all. At a price of $0.90
Mr. E, Mr. D, and Mr. C are all willing to be buyers, and will buy together 1800 bushels, and so on. This schedule shows the relation between
the price of the commodity and the total quantity of that commodity

which all the people in the market will buy at each price. It is called the *market demand schedule* for the commodity.

THE MARKET SUPPLY SCHEDULE.   The last column is obtained by adding up all the separate amounts which the marketers are willing to *sell* at each price. Thus a price of $0.70 is so low that no sellers will be found. At a price of $0.80 there will be one seller, Mr. A, who will sell 500 bushels. At a price of $0.90 Mr. A and Mr. B between them will be willing to sell a total of 1,800 bushels, and so on. This schedule shows the relation between the price of the commodity and the total quantity which people are willing to *sell* at each price. It is called the *market supply schedule* of the commodity. The market demand schedule is an expression of the general willingness to buy on the part of the people in the market. The market supply schedule is an expression of the general willingness to sell.

THE EQUILIBRIUM PRICE

The Condition for an Equilibrium Price

We now come to what is perhaps the most important proposition in the whole of economic analysis, the key that unlocks the doors to a vast number of problems. Unless the price in the market is such that the quantity of the commodity which people want to buy is equal to the quantity which people want to sell, there will be a tendency for the price to change. If the market price is such that sellers in the market as a whole wish to sell more than buyers in the market wish to buy, then the price must fall. If the market price is such that buyers as a whole wish to buy more than sellers wish to sell, then the price must rise. The price at which the quantity of the commodity that the sellers wish to sell is just equal to the quantity that the buyers wish to buy is called the *equilibrium price*. It is that price which "clears the market."

AT EQUILIBRIUM PRICE ALL SELLERS CAN FIND BUYERS, AND ALL BUYERS, SELLERS.   The general significance of the equilibrium concept in an economic model was discussed on pages 49–52. We can now go on to examine the significance of the equilibrium price in our wheat market. In Table 8 this price is clearly $0.90, where the total amount that the sellers want to sell is 1800 bushels and the total amount that the buyers want to buy is also 1800 bushels. Mr. A and Mr. B sell their wheat to Mr. C, Mr. D, and Mr. E. It should be observed that we do not make any assumptions regarding the persons or the amounts involved in any individual transaction. All we assume is that all buyers can find enough sellers to fill their requirements, and all sellers can find enough buyers to fill their requirements. Perhaps in the above case Mr. A will sell to Mr.

E the whole 1000 bushels which he offers, and Mr. B may sell 200 bushels to Mr. C and 600 to Mr. D. Perhaps Mr. A will sell 500 bushels to Mr. E and 500 bushels to Mr. D, and Mr. B will sell 200 bushels to Mr. C, 100 to Mr. D, and 500 to Mr. E. Obviously, there are many possible combinations of individual transactions. It will not matter to any of the marketers which combination is finally reached, for if the price is $0.90 per bushel, everyone will be able to buy or sell the quantity he desires.

IF PRICE IS ABOVE EQUILIBRIUM PRICE, SOME SELLERS CANNOT FIND BUYERS AND WILL CUT PRICES.   Now, suppose the price at which transactions are being made in this case is not $0.90, but $1. We see from Table 8 that at this price buyers will be willing to buy only 600 bushels and sellers will want to sell 3700 bushels. It will be easy enough for the buyers to be satisfied, for they will soon find sellers to sell them all they want. But when that is done there will still be a number of sellers who have *not* sold all they want. Suppose that Mr. D and Mr. E buy the 600 bushels they want from Mr. A. That still leaves Mr. A with 1400 bushels that he would like to sell, Mr. B and Mr. C with 1500 and 200 bushels, respectively, which they would also like to sell, but for which they cannot find buyers.

What, then, is going to be the response of sellers who cannot find buyers for what they want to sell? The answer is, clearly, to *cut* their prices. Rather than not sell anything at a price of $1, or not sell as much as they wish, Messrs. A, B, and C will lower their prices in the hope of attracting buyers. As they lower their prices, the quantity they are willing to sell declines while the quantity the buyers are willing to buy increases. If they lower the price to $0.90, as we have seen, the quantity that people are willing to buy will increase to 1800 bushels, the quantity that people are willing to sell will decrease to 1800 bushels, and neither buyers nor sellers will go unsatisfied.

IF PRICE IS BELOW EQUILIBRIUM PRICE, BUYERS WILL RAISE PRICES. Similarly, if the price in the market is $0.80, buyers (B, C, D, and E) will wish to buy 7500 bushels; sellers (Mr. A) will be willing to sell only 500 bushels. After Mr. A has sold his 500 bushels, there will still be unsatisfied buyers who wish to buy a total of 7000 bushels at that price. Again, what will happen in these circumstances is that the buyers will *raise* the prices at which they are offering to buy, in the hope of attracting more from the sellers. As they raise the price, however, the quantity that they wish to buy declines, the quantity that sellers wish to sell increases, and some who were buyers before now become sellers, until we find at a price of $0.90 that the amount the sellers offer is equal to the amount the buyers wish to take, and none will go unsatisfied.

Thus, from the market schedules of the individual buyers, and from

them alone, we have been able to deduce the price at which the transactions in the market will take place, and also the volume of transactions,
i.e., the quantity bought and sold—in the case of Table 8, 1800 bushels.

GRAPHIC ILLUSTRATION. The graphic method of statement can also
be used in this case. In Fig. 17 the price is measured vertically from
the base. The quantity bought or sold is measured horizontally. We can
represent both the demand and the supply schedules of Table 8 on the
one figure. *DD′* represents the demand schedule; it is called the *market
demand curve*, and may be defined as the curve showing the relationship
between the price of a commodity and the quantity which people in the

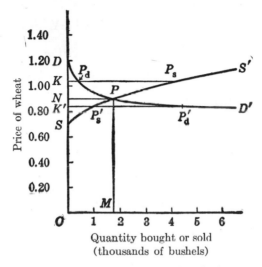

Fig. 17. Market Demand and Supply Curves

market are willing to *buy* at each price in a given period of time. The
demand curve usually slopes downward to the right with the conventional
coordinates. This indicates the fact that the higher the price, the less
will people be willing to buy, and the lower the price, the more will
they be willing to buy.[1] *SS′* represents the supply schedule of Table 8; it
is called the *market supply curve*. It may be defined as the curve showing
the relationship between the price of a commodity and the quantity which
people are willing to *sell*. On this figure it usually slopes upward to the
right, indicating the fact that at higher prices people are willing to sell
greater quantities of a commodity than they are at lower prices. The
point where these two curves intersect, *P*, shows the equilibrium price

[1] This proposition is frequently called the *law of demand*.

(MP or ON) and the quantity (NP or OM) which will be bought and sold at this price, for this is the only price at which the quantity people wish to buy is equal to the quantity people wish to sell. At any price above this—e.g., OK—the quantity people want to buy—(KP_d) is less than the quantity people want to sell (KP_s). At any price below ON— say, OK'—the quantity people want to buy ($K'P'_d$) is greater than the quantity people want to sell ($K'P'_s$). If the price is *too low,* buying is too much encouraged, selling too much discouraged. If the price is *too high,* selling is too much encouraged, buying too much discouraged.

ASSET PREFERENCES AND THE MARKET IDENTITY

The Market as an Expression of Asset Preferences

When a person buys in a market, he diminishes his stock of money and increases his stock of commodity. Similarly, when he sells he increases his stock of money and diminishes his stock of commodity. We can think of the transactions in the market as consisting essentially of rearrangements of the total stock of assets of all kinds (that is, exchangeables) among owners; the money stock shifts into the hands of sellers out of the hands of buyers, the commodity stock shifts into the hands of buyers out of the hands of sellers. This gives us a clue to the description of the preferences of the marketers in terms of the proportion of different kinds of assets which they wish to hold. Thus a buyer of commodity is obviously motivated by a desire to decrease the proportion of his assets held in the form of money and increase the proportion held in the form of commodity; the reverse would be true of a seller. The market is then *cleared* at the price at which there is no *net* desire to change the proportions of the value of different assets in the total value of all assets, for at this point everyone who wants to shift out of money into commodity can find someone else who wishes to shift out of commodity into money.

The Market Identity

In the light of this point of view of the function of market price, and with the aid of certain simplifying assumptions, a very useful identity can be derived showing what determines the market price. It is assumed that there is a given quantity of money, M "dollars," and a given physical quantity of commodity, A "bushels," present in the market in the possession of the marketers. We assume that the result of the transactions of the "day" is simply to redistribute the ownership of this money and commodity among the various marketers concerned; no new stocks either of money or of commodity are supposed to come on the market. Now let us assume that the marketers as a whole wish to hold a certain proportion, r_m, of their assets in the form of money, and a certain proportion r_a in the form of the commodity. The name *preferred liquidity ratio* may be given to r_m; if it were, say, 10 percent, or $\frac{1}{10}$, that would mean that the people in the market, on the whole, wanted to hold $\frac{1}{10}$ of the value of their total assets in the form of money. If, for instance, the total amount of money held by them was $100,000, they would not be satisfied unless the total value of their assets was $1,000,000. Similarly, r_a may be called the *preferred commodity ratio*. If the commodity is, say, wheat, a preferred wheat ratio of $\frac{1}{5}$ would mean that the market would not be satisfied unless $\frac{1}{5}$ of the value of its assets were held in the form of wheat.

Now, let the total value of all assets held by the marketers be T. The total value of the stock of commodity, A, is $p_a A$, where p_a is the money price of the commodity. Then by definition we have:

$$r_m = \frac{M}{T} \quad \text{and} \quad r_a = \frac{P_a A}{T}$$

Eliminating T between these two equations we obtain:

$$P_a = \frac{M r_a}{A r_m}$$

This may be called the *market identity*.

Significance of the Market Identity

In order to bring out the significance of this fundamental identity let us consider an arithmetical example. Suppose first a case in which there are only two kinds of assets—money and a commodity—call it wheat. Suppose there are 50 million bushels of wheat in the market and $10 million of money. Suppose also that the liquidity preference ratio is 0.2 and the commodity preference ratio 0.8. The two preference ratios in this case must add up to 1, for if there are only two kinds of assets, to say that we prefer to hold 20 percent of our assets in one form is the same as to say we prefer to hold 80 percent of our assets in the other form. Then Table 9 (p. 122) shows the condition of the market on the assumption of various prices for wheat.

It is evident that only at the price of $0.80, given by the market formula, is the total value of assets such that the ratio of money to total assets or of commodity to total assets is what the market wants. If the price were above this level, say at $1 per bushel, the value of the stock

TABLE 9. THE MARKET IDENTITY

Price of Wheat p_a	Value of Wheat p_aA ($ million)	Value of Money M	Total Value of Assets $p_aA + M$ ($ million)	r_m	r_a
$1.00	50	10	60	0.167	0.833
0.90	45	10	55	0.182	0.818
0.80	40	10	50	0.2	0.8
0.70	35	10	45	0.222	0.778
0.60	30	10	40	0.25	0.75

of wheat, and therefore the value of the total assets of the market, would be too high, relative to the quantity of money held. That is to say, there would be an excess of people in the market who felt that they held too much commodity and not enough money, and who would, therefore, be *eager sellers*. An individual, of course, increases his money holding by selling and increases his commodity holding by buying. The situation would be like the price OK in Fig. 17, and the excess of sellers would soon force down the price. Similarly, if the price were 60 cents, there would be an excess of people who wanted to increase their commodity holdings and lower their money holdings, and these *eager buyers* would force up the price. The situation would be like the price OK' in Fig. 17. Thus we see that the function of clearing the market can also be expressed in another form, and we can say that the function of price is to adjust the value of assets to those proportions which best satisfy the market. The value of assets depends on their price; a rise in the price raises and a fall lowers the total value of assets. A rise in price, therefore, lowers and a fall raises the proportion of the total value of assets held in the form of money.

QUESTIONS AND EXERCISES

1. What are the aspects of the model of the perfectly competitive market described above which justify the name *competitive* for this model? It is sometimes argued that in perfect competition there is no conflict, for any buyer can immediately escape a seller with whom he cannot agree and find another seller, and any seller likewise can find another buyer if he finds himself in conflict with his present buyer. Is there a real paradox here, or is this just a problem of semantics?

2. Would we be justified in constructing demand and supply schedules in the way we have done if (a) there were only a small number of buyers and sellers; (b) all transactions were quite private, so that no one person in the market knew what prices were being offered and taken by others in the market; (c) the commodity were of a large number of grades and qualities? If we could

construct supply and demand schedules in any of these three cases, could we still use them to determine the market price?

3. In a perfectly competitive market we have assumed that all transactions take place at the same price. What characteristics of a perfectly competitive market justify us in making this assumption?

4. How would you expect a general rise in the eagerness to sell to affect (a) the price and (b) the quantity bought and sold of a commodity sold in a perfectly competitive market? Analyze in detail, using supply and demand curves.

5. We have assumed that selling is a kind of negative buying. Would a negative price have any meaning? If so, what? What would be the meaning of the *price of money* in terms of wheat, if the price of wheat in terms of money were 90 cents per bushel?

6. Construct a market schedule from Table 1, showing what amounts of *money* the marketer in question will be willing to give or to take in exchange for wheat at various prices of wheat.

Now take the schedules of our five marketers in Table 4, and transform these similarly into market schedules for money. From these derive the demand schedule of money for wheat, showing how the amount of money which people will *accept* in exchange for wheat will vary with the price of wheat. Derive also the supply schedule of money for wheat, showing how the amount of money which people will *offer* will vary with the price of wheat. From these demand and supply schedules of money for wheat deduce (a) the equilibrium market price of wheat and (b) the amount of money that will change hands in exchange for wheat.

7. Draw the supply and demand curves of the individual marketer in Table 5.

8. Suppose a market with two commodities, A and B, one form of money, M, and no other assets. The quantity of money is $8 million, the quantity of A is 12 million bushels, and the quantity of B, 5 million tons. Let the preferred liquidity ratio, $r_m = 0.2$, the preferred commodity ratios $r_a = 0.3$, and $r_b = 0.5$. Construct tables showing the total value of assets for various prices of A and B, and show that the only prices which satisfy the above conditions are those given by the market identities.

9. Prove, by means of the market identity, that (a) a change in the quantity of money, other things being equal, will affect all prices; (b) a change in the quantity of a single commodity will affect the price of that commodity, but of no other, as long as there is no change in the preference ratios; (c) a change in the preference for one commodity, other things remaining the same, will not only affect its own price but will also affect the prices of other commodities. (Note that the sum of the preference ratios must be equal to 1.)

CHAPTER 8

SUPPLY AND DEMAND IN A COMPETITIVE MARKET

PRICES AND QUANTITIES DETERMINED BY STATES OF MIND

The concepts of supply and demand are very powerful weapons of analysis. We shall use them first to investigate the question, how do *changes* in the states of mind of the people in a market affect the price of the commodity and the quantity of it which is exchanged? We have seen that the price and the quantity of commodity exchanged in a market on a given day depend *solely*, in the first instance, on the states of mind of the people in the market, as described by their market schedules. We can therefore attribute any change in the price or the quantity sold to a change in the state of mind of the marketers. Of course these states of mind are not self-subsistent fantasies, unconnected with any other facts of the system. Indeed, a great deal of our inquiry will be spent in seeking out the underlying causes of the states of mind of people who buy and sell. But these underlying causes, such as, for instance, costs of production or the tastes of consumers, affect prices and quantities only because they affect the states of mind of people who buy and sell. The market schedules of individuals, and the demand and supply schedules which are derived from them, are merely convenient ways of describing those states of mind that are the immediate determinants of prices.

A General Increase in the Eagerness to Buy a Commodity

Let us consider the effects on the price of a commodity, and on the quantity exchanged, of a general increase in the eagerness to buy. This will be reflected by a rise in the market schedules of the individual marketers. Each marketer will now be willing to buy more, or to sell less, than he did before. Let us suppose that Table 10 shows the market schedules of the five marketers of Table 8, page 116, after there has been a general increase in the eagerness to buy or, what is the same thing, a general decrease in the eagerness to sell. Comparing this table with Table 8, we see that at each price each marketer will buy more, or sell less, than before. At $1.20, for instance, marketer A is now willing to sell only 3000 bushels, whereas previously he would have sold 5000; marketer E will actually buy 100 bushels, whereas previously he would have wished to sell 500 bushels.

LEADS TO AN INCREASE IN PRICE. What has happened to the demand and supply schedules? Table 8 shows that at a price of $1.20 a quantity

TABLE 10. MARKET SCHEDULES IN AN EAGER BUYER'S MARKET

Price (per (bushel)	Quantity Which Each Marketer Would Buy (+) or Sell (−) at That Price					Quantity De- manded (bushels)	Quan- tity Offered
	A	B	C	D	E		
$1.20	− 3,000	− 2,000	− 500	− 200	+ 100	+ 100	− 5,700
1.10	− 2,000	− 1,500	− 200	+ 100	+ 500	+ 600	− 3,700
1.00	− 1,000	− 800	+ 200	+ 600	+ 1,000	+ 1,800	− 1,800
0.90	− 500	+ 1,000	+ 1,500	+ 2,000	+ 3,000	+ 7,500	− 500
0.80	+ 500	+ 1,500	+ 2,000	+ 3,000	+ 5,000	+ 12,000	0

of 11,000 bushels will be offered for sale, but nothing will be demanded. After the change (Table 10) at this same price only 5700 bushels will be offered for sale, and 100 bushels will be demanded. The result of the change in the market schedules has been, therefore, that at each price more is demanded and less is offered than before. The equilibrium price has risen from $0.90 to $1, for $1 is now the price at which the quantity offered and the quantity demanded are equal.

NEED NOT LEAD TO ANY CHANGE IN QUANTITY EXCHANGED. In the above example, although the equilibrium price has risen, the quantity which will be exchanged at the equilibrium price has not changed. Our five marketers would exchange 1800 bushels among themselves even if each one were to become a more eager buyer. This conclusion follows because there has been a special kind of rise in the market schedules which we shall call a *pure* rise. Comparing Tables 8 and 10 we see that the "shapes" of the market schedules have not changed. Indeed, all that we have done to make Table 10 is to move the schedule of prices in Table 8 one row downward. Mr. A, for instance, in Table 8, is willing to sell 3000 bushels at $1.10. In Table 10 he sells 3000 bushels only when the price is $1.20. In Table 8 he sells 2000 bushels at $1, and in Table 10 he sells 2000 bushels only at $1.10. If we have an irregular rise in the market schedules, it does not necessarily follow that the quantity exchanged will be unaltered.

GRAPHIC ILLUSTRATION. Fig. 18 shows the effect of a pure change in the market schedules on the market supply and demand curves. As before, the price of wheat is measured vertically, and the quantity bought and sold horizontally. Then the old demand curve is *DD′*, the old supply curve is *SS′*, as in Fig. 17. After the pure rise in the market schedules the demand curve is *EE′*, the supply curve is *TT′*. These are the graphic descriptions of the demand and supply schedules of Table 10. The point of intersection of the demand and supply schedules, i.e., the point where

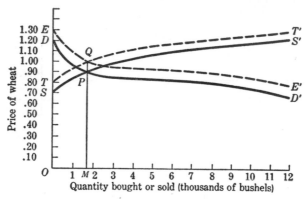

Fig. 18.   Effect of Increased Eagerness to Buy

the quantity offered and the quantity demanded are equal, has moved from *P* to *Q*. The equilibrium price has changed from *MP* to *MQ*. The quantity which will be exchanged, however, has not changed, being *OM* in both cases.

A Pure Fall in Market Schedules Causes a Fall in Price

In an exactly similar way a *pure* fall in the market schedules brings about a fall in the equilibrium price but no change in the quantity exchanged. If the situation in Table 10 were the original situation, Table 8 would represent the market schedules after a pure fall. The price would have fallen from $1 to 0.90, the quantity remaining the same at 1800 bushels. Or in Fig. 18, if *EE′*, *TT′* represented the original supply and demand curves, *DD′*, *SS′* would represent the supply and demand curves after a pure fall in the market schedules.

The Total Market Schedule

There is no harm in looking at a thing from more than one point of view, especially when the thing in question is one of the most important features of the economic landscape. We may therefore pause for a moment to look at the problem of the effect of a change in market schedules in another way. Table 11 shows the demand and supply schedules of Table 8. For each price, we have found the excess demand or the excess supply, as the case may be. The excess supply is found by subtracting the total quantity demanded by the market from the total quantity offered, where the total quantity offered is the greater. The excess demand is found by subtracting the total quantity offered from the total quantity demanded, when the total quantity demanded is the greater. Algebraically, the excess demand (+) or supply (−) is the sum of the quantity demanded (+) and the quantity offered (−).

It will be seen from Table 11 that at the equilibrium price the excess

TABLE 11.   THE TOTAL MARKET SCHEDULE

Price (per bushel)	Quantity Demanded	Quantity Offered (number of bushels)	Excess Demand (+) or Excess Supply (−)
$1.20	0	−11,000	−11,000
1.10	+ 100	− 5,700	− 5,600
1.00	+ 600	− 3,700	− 3,100
0.90	+ 1,800	− 1,800	0
0.80	+ 7,500	− 500	+ 7,000
0.70	+12,000	0	+12,000

demand (or supply) is zero. This is another way of stating the proposition that at the equilibrium price the quantity offered and the quantity demanded are equal. The schedule of excess demand or excess supply may be called the total market schedule, as it is calculated by taking the algebraic sum of the quantities in all the individual market schedules at each price.

If now there is a pure rise in all the individual market schedules there will also be a rise in the total market schedule. This is shown in Table 12, where we calculate the total market schedule corresponding to the market in Table 10.

TABLE 12.   TOTAL MARKET SCHEDULES IN AN EAGER BUYERS' MARKET

Price (per bushel)	Quantity Demanded	Quantity Supplied (number of bushels)	Excess Demand (+) or Excess Supply (−)
$1.20	+ 100	−5,700	− 5,600
1.10	+ 600	−3,700	− 3,100
1.00	+ 1,800	−1,800	0
0.90	+ 7,500	− 500	+ 7,000
0.80	+12,000	0	+12,000

GRAPHIC ILLUSTRATION. In Fig. 19 the price of wheat is measured vertically, and the quantity which will be in excess demand or supply, horizontally. Quantities in excess demand are measured to the right of the origin *O,* and quantities in excess supply, to the left of *O,* following the convention that quantities demanded are positive and quantities offered are negative. Then *MPM'* is the curve corresponding to the total market schedule of Table 11. It may be called the *total market curve.* The equilibrium price, *OP,* is found at the point *P,* where the total market curve cuts the price axis *OY.* This is the price at which the excess demand (or supply) is zero. *NQN'* is the total market curve after the rise

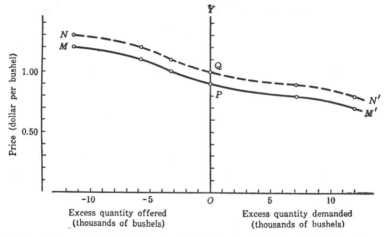

Fig. 19.   Effect on the Total Market Schedule of an Increased Eagerness to Buy

in the eagerness to buy. It corresponds to the total market schedule of Table 12. It will be seen immediately from this figure that any rise in the total market schedule causes a rise in the price, and any fall in the total market schedule causes a fall in the price. What is perhaps more important, a rise in price *can occur only* as a result of a rise in the total market schedule, and a fall in price can occur only as a result of a fall in the total market schedule. The rise or fall in the total market schedule need not, of course, be a pure rise or fall. When there is a pure rise or fall, the *shape* of the market schedule does not change; it rises or falls as a unit. In that case the quantity exchanged is not affected. But any change in the individual market schedules which results in a generally increased eagerness to buy and a generally diminished eagerness to sell, whether the changes are pure or not, will raise the price of the commodity.

What Determines the Volume of Transactions?

Let us now see if we can isolate the factor that determines the quantity exchanged—i.e., the volume of transactions. Let us first consider an extreme case in which the market schedules of all the people in the market are identical.

Table 13 shows a market in this condition. The equilibrium price

TABLE 13.   MARKET SCHEDULES IN A MARKET WHERE THERE IS NO DIVERGENCE

Price (per bushel)	Quantities Which the Various Individuals Will Buy (+) or Sell (−) (number of bushels)					Total Quantity Supplied	Total Quantity Demanded
	A	*B*	*C*	*D*	*E*		
$1.20	−1,000	−1,000	−1,000	−1,000	−1,000	5,000	0
1.10	− 600	− 600	− 600	− 600	− 600	3,000	0
1.00	− 300	− 300	− 300	− 300	− 300	1,500	0
0.90	0	0	0	0	0	0	0
0.80	200	200	200	200	200	0	1,000
0.70	400	400	400	400	400	0	2,000
0.60	700	700	700	700	700	0	3,500

in this case is $0.90, but the total quantity which will be bought and sold at this price is zero! We may illustrate this situation in Fig. 20, where *TS* is the supply curve and *TD* is the demand curve corresponding to the situation above. The demand and supply curves intersect at the point *T*, where the price is *OT* and the volume of transactions is zero.

It is evident, therefore, that there will be no transactions at all in a market where the schedules of all the marketers are identical. We can go further than this. Even if the individual market schedules are not identical, there will be no transactions if the price at which each marketer will neither buy nor sell is the same in all the schedules. Thus in Table 13, so long as at a price of $0.90 none of the marketers were willing to buy or sell even the smallest quantities, it would not matter what the offers to sell at higher prices might be, or the offers to purchase at lower prices, for there would still be no transactions.

Divergence of Attitude

That feature of a group of market schedules which gives rise to a volume of transactions we may call *divergence of attitude*. The volume of transactions depends therefore on the divergence of attitude in the market, as described by the market schedules. If the market shows a wide divergence of attitude, with one group of eager buyers and another group of eager sellers, there will be a large volume of transactions. If there is

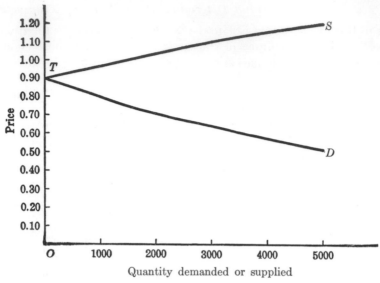

Fig. 20.   Supply and Demand in a Market Without Divergence

little divergence of attitude, if all the people in the market are about equally eager to buy and sell, there will be a small volume of transactions.

What Makes an Eager Buyer?

What creates this divergence in the market schedules? To answer that question we must first answer another: What makes any particular marketer an eager buyer or an eager seller? A marketer will be an *eager buyer*—i.e., his market curve will lie relatively high, for one of two reasons. He may have a strong *preference* for the possession of the commodity rather than for the possession of money. When a buyer buys a certain quantity of commodity, he changes the form of his possessions, for he diminishes the quantity of money which he owns and increases the quantity of commodity. If a buyer has a strong preference for the possession of the commodity, he will probably be an eager buyer. If he has a strong preference for holding his possessions in the form of money, he will probably be an eager seller. The second reason why a marketer may be an eager buyer is that he may have in his possession a relatively large sum of money and a relatively small quantity of the commodity. In that case even if his preference for holding the commodity is below the average, he may still be a relatively eager buyer; for if the quantity of commodity which he possesses is very small, he will want to buy in order to increase that quantity. On the other hand, a buyer who has a relatively large stock of the commodity and a relatively small stock of money will probably be an eager seller, for he will want to get rid of part of his stock of the commodity and so increase his stock of money, even if the price of the commodity is low.

What Makes for Divergence of Market Schedules?

1. DIVERGENCE OF PREFERENCE. We have, therefore, a strong divergence of market schedules and therefore a large volume of transactions, when there is a strong divergence of preference in the market and also when there are great differences in the quantity of the commodity possessed by people in the market. If one group of marketers has a strongly marked preference for holding their possessions in the form of wheat, and another group has a strongly marked preference for holding their possessions in the form of money, then the divergence of preference in the market will be great and the volume of transactions will also be great. There will be a large number of buyers who wish to increase their holdings of wheat, and of sellers who wish to increase their holdings of money, when the price is in equilibrium. If, on the other hand, there is not much divergence of preference in the market, if every marketer has about the same degree of preference for wheat or for money, the volume of transactions will be small.

2. DIVERGENCE IN THE QUANTITIES POSSESSED. Similarly, if there is a great divergence in the relative quantities of wheat and money held by the marketers, there is also likely to be a great divergence in the market schedules and therefore a large volume of transactions. If some marketers hold a large quantity of wheat, and some hold a small quantity, then the former will be eager sellers and the latter eager buyers; and at the equilibrium price there will be a large number of both buyers and sellers. If, however, at the equilibrium price all the marketers are pretty well satisfied with the quantities they possess, the volume of transactions will be small.

THIS IS TRUE EVEN IN ISOLATED EXCHANGES. This result is what we should expect from our preliminary study of exchange. We saw that Mrs. Jones was able to exchange her butter for Mrs. Smith's bread because there was a divergence of opinion between them about the relative value of butter and bread. The greater this divergence, the greater will be the volume of transactions between them. This divergence of opinion, again, depends on two factors. The first is the divergence of *preference* between the two ladies. If Mrs. Smith is passionately fond of butter, for which Mrs. Jones cares very little, and if Mrs. Jones is passionately fond of bread, for which Mrs. Smith cares very little, then Mrs. Jones, who has the butter, will give up a large quantity to Mrs. Smith, who has the bread. The second factor is the divergence of the *quantities possessed* by the two ladies. If Mrs. Smith possessed no butter and Mrs. Jones possessed no bread, the volume of transactions between them will be greater than if they each possessed roughly equivalent quantities of both bread and butter.

Effect on Price of an Increase in the Quantities Possessed

We can now apply our analysis to the problem of the effect of a change in the total quantities, either of the commodity or of money, which are held by the people in a market. Up to now we have assumed that the total quantity of commodity, and of money, held by all the marketers does not change in the course of the transactions of the day. All that happens is that some units of the commodity and some units of money change owners. In any actual market, however, the quantity of commodity, and even the quantity of money, held by the marketers is constantly changing. On the wheat market, for instance, wheat is continually coming into the market from the farms where it has been produced, and is continually being taken out of the market into consumption. The next step in our analysis is therefore to answer the question: What happens to the price and to the volume of transactions, when there is a change in the *total* holdings of the commodity, or of money?

We have seen that the greater the quantity of commodity held by any individual, the lower will be his market schedule—i.e., the more eager will he be to sell, and the less eager to buy. If, therefore, there is a general increase in the quantity of wheat held by people in the wheat market, there will be a general fall in market schedules and this will lead to a fall in the total market schedule and a fall in the price of wheat. Similarly, if there is a decrease in the quantity of wheat held by people in the market, there will tend to be a rise in the price of wheat.

Effect on the Volume of Transactions

What, now, will be the effect on the volume of transactions of an increase in the total quantity of wheat held? This question is not quite so easy to answer and may not admit of a definite solution. If the extra quantity of wheat comes only into the hands of marketers who are already eager sellers, there will be an increase in the divergence of the market schedules, for the market schedules of the owners of the new wheat will fall, while those of the other marketers will be unchanged. But if the new wheat comes into the hands of marketers who previously were relatively eager buyers, the fall in their market schedules will lessen the divergence of market schedules. In the first case there will be an increase, in the second case, a decrease in the volume of transactions. To put the matter in another way: It is evident that there will be some distribution of quantities of wheat in the hands of the various marketers which will lead to a zero volume of transactions, all marketers being satisfied with the amount of wheat which they possess when the price is in equilibrium. If the increased quantity of wheat falls into the hands of those marketers who already have more wheat than they want (the eager sellers), the volume of transactions will be increased, for the eager sellers will sell the new wheat, as well as the quantity which they would otherwise have sold, to the eager buyers. If however, the new wheat falls into the hands of those who have less wheat than they want (the eager buyers), it will help to satisfy their desire for wheat, and they will buy less from the eager sellers than they otherwise would have done.

Similarly, when wheat is taken out of the market, the effect will certainly be a rise in the equilibrium price. There may be either an increase or a decrease in the volume of transactions, according to which group of marketers loses the wheat.

Effect of a Change in the Quantity of Money

A change in the quantity of money possessed by the marketers will have an effect on the price opposite to the effect of a change in the quantity of the commodity. If there is an addition to the total quantity of money held in the market, the result will be a general increase in the eagerness to buy, a rise in market schedules, and a rise in the price of the commodity. If there is a decrease in the total quantity of money held in the market, there will be a fall in the price of the commodity. The effect of a change in the quantity of money on the volume of transactions again depends on how the "new" money is distributed.

Analysis by the Market Identity

The market identity (p. 121) $p_a = Mr_a/Ar_m$ summarises all these various effects on price. If there is an increase in M, with A, r_a, and r_m remaining constant, there will be an equal proportionate increase in p_a. This, we shall see later, is the foundation of the quantity theory of money. If there is an increase in A, the stock of commodity, with M, r_a, and r_m constant, there will be a proportionate decrease in the price p_a, so under these circumstances the total value of the commodity stock Ap_a will be constant. A spontaneous increase in the preference for money will lower the price, and a spontaneous increase in the preference for the commodity will raise the price. All these events, it should be noticed, may produce dynamic effects. If a rise in the price causes an expectation of a further rise, people will wish to hold commodity rather than money;

r_a will rise and r_m will fall, which will further increase the price. Under these circumstances a rise in the quantity of money or a fall in the quantity of commodity may bring about a more than proportionate rise in price. Under these circumstances it is quite possible for a fall in the physical stock of a commodity to be accompanied by a rise in the total value of that stock! This model will be explored further in Volume II: *Macroeconomics*, Chapter 4.

ARBITRAGE AND SPECULATION

There is yet another phenomenon to study in connection with the formation of prices in a competitive market. This we may name *arbitrage*. It may be defined as the process of increasing the value of one's possessions by buying a commodity at one time or place and selling it at another time or place *at a higher price*. In a sense, as we shall see, all enterprise is arbitrage; for the moment, however, we shall confine the term to the buying and reselling of some physical commodity.

Suppose, for instance, that in one corner of a wheat market transactions are going on at 90 cents per bushel while in another corner they are going on at 80 cents per bushel. It would clearly pay anyone who was aware of this to buy in the cheap market and sell in the dear market. If, for instance, a man has $1000, he can buy 1250 bushels of wheat with it in the 80-cent market. He can then take the wheat over to the 90-cent market and there exchange his 1250 bushels for $1125. His original $1000 has now grown into $1125; he has increased the value of his possessions by $125, and has made a profit of 10 cents on every bushel of wheat bought and sold. Now, however, observe what happens to the two corners of the market when our enterprising friend plunges into them. Into the cheap corner has entered an eager buyer, and the price in that corner will therefore rise. Into the dear corner has entered an eager seller, and the price in that corner will therefore fall.

Prevention of Permanent Price Differences by Arbitrage

Our friend, therefore, who is called an *arbitrageur*—has by his very act of arbitrage raised the cheap price and lowered the dear price, and so has made any subsequent act of arbitrage less profitable. The act of arbitrage itself, therefore, tends to do away with the price differences which make it possible. Nevertheless, in most markets these differences are always being recreated, and consequently arbitrageurs can make a living. It is their operations, however, which prevent any great divergence from the rule of "one price in all transactions in one market at one time."

ARBITRAGE WHEN THERE ARE COSTS OF TRANSPORT.   Where the two parts of a market are geographically separate, there may be a certain cost of transport of the commodity between the two parts. In this case the effect of arbitrage is to ensure that the difference in price between the two markets shall not appreciably differ from the cost of transport of a unit of the commodity between them. Thus, we may regard the Chicago wheat market and the Liverpool wheat market as essentially part of a single world market in wheat. Wheat normally flows from Chicago to Liverpool, and the price of wheat on the Liverpool market in normal times tends to be greater than the Chicago price by an amount equal to the average cost per bushel of transporting wheat from Chicago to Liverpool. Let us suppose that the cost of transporting wheat from Chicago to Liverpool is $0.30 per bushel. Then when the price in Chicago is $0.90 per bushel we should expect the price in Liverpool to be $1.20 per bushel. If in these circumstances the price in Liverpool was $1.15 while the price in Chicago was $0.95, it would not pay anyone to buy wheat in Chicago and ship it to Liverpool. Consequently, people on the Chicago market as a whole would be less eager to buy. Also, as wheat kept coming into the Chicago market from the wheat fields, the market would become even more eager to sell and less eager to buy, and the Chicago price would fall. At the same time, in Liverpool there would be no wheat coming in from Chicago; as the stocks of wheat fell off (because of wheat passing into consumption), the price would rise. By the time the difference between the Chicago and Liverpool prices had reached $0.30 per bushel, wheat would begin to flow again from Chicago to Liverpool.[1] The exporter-buyers would come on to the Chicago market and would prevent the price from falling further there and the importer-sellers would come on to the Liverpool market and prevent the price from rising further there. Similarly, if the difference in price between the Liverpool and Chicago markets was $0.40, it would be very profitable to buy wheat in Chicago, transport it to Liverpool, and sell it there. Consequently, there would be a rush of buyers on the Chicago market—which would raise the price there—and a rush of sellers on the Liverpool market—which would lower the price there. The price in Chicago would rise and the price in Liverpool would fall until the difference between them was again $0.30 per bushel.

ARBITRAGE MAKES FOR CONSISTENCY IN EXCHANGE RATIOS.   Arbitrage is also very important in establishing *consistency* in the exchange ratios existing among three or more markets. Suppose, for instance, to develop our example further, that in Chicago wheat is exchanged against dollars,

[1] In the "cost" of transportation we include the normal profits of the merchants and businesses concerned, so that the price differential does not have to be *more* than $0.30 per bushel in order to make it profitable to ship wheat from Chicago to Liverpool.

that in Liverpool it is exchanged against shillings, and that in New York
shillings are exchanged against dollars. Here we have three markets: the
Chicago wheat market, the Liverpool wheat market, and what we call
the foreign exchange market where dollars and shillings are exchanged.
Let us suppose, to make the arithmetic easier, that there are no costs of
transport for any of these things between the various markets. Suppose
now that in the Chicago market wheat is exchanging for $0.90 a bushel,
in the Liverpool market it is exchanging at a rate of 4 shillings to the
bushel, and in the foreign exchange market shillings are exchanging
for dollars at a rate of 4 shillings to 1 dollar. If this is the case, it
will be possible to make profits by buying wheat in Chicago for dollars,
then buying shillings with the wheat in Liverpool, and then buying dollars again with the shillings in the foreign exchange market. Thus, if I
took $900, bought 1000 bushels of wheat in Chicago, sold it for 4000 shill-
ings in Liverpool, and then sold my shillings for $1000 in the foreign
exchange market, my original $900 would have grown to $1000; I would
have made $100 profit. As long as it is possible to make profits by these
three-cornered transactions, we say that the exchange ratios are not
consistent.

Now, however, observe what this act of three-cornered arbitrage will
do. By bringing a new buyer of wheat into the Chicago market it will
raise the price of wheat there, say, to $0.95 per bushel. By bringing a
new seller of wheat into the Liverpool market it will lower the price
there, say, to 3.895 shillings per bushel. By bringing a new buyer of
dollars into the foreign exchange market it will raise the price of dollars,
say, to 4.1 shillings per dollar. With these prices it is no longer possible
to make profits by buying and selling among the markets. If I now take
$950, buy 1000 bushels of wheat with it, get 3895 shillings for my wheat
at Liverpool, and exchange my 3895 shillings for dollars at 4.1 shillings
per dollar, I will get only $950 back again; no profit. In this case also
the act of arbitrage tends to bring the ratios (i.e., the prices) in the various
markets into line again. These processes may perhaps be brought more
vividly to mind by the illustration in Fig. 21.

Speculation Is Arbitrage Through Time

The idea of arbitrage will also help us to explain another phenomenon
which many have found puzzling—the phenomenon of *speculation*. By
speculation we mean essentially the phenomenon of buying something
cheap at one *time* and selling the same thing dear at another time.
Speculation, therefore, may be defined as *arbitrage through time;* instead of buying in one place and selling in another we now buy at one
time and sell at another. Of course all buying and selling of the same

commodity, where the purchase and the sale do not occur at the same time, is in a sense speculation. Nevertheless, we can distinguish broadly between profits which are made because the same thing has different prices in different places and profits which are made because the same thing has different prices at different times. Just as there is a cost of transport of things through space so there is a cost of "transport" through time; as we have to pay charges for the transport of wheat from Chicago to Liverpool, so we have to pay charges for the transport of wheat from September to March. Holding wheat in a warehouse is essentially transporting it from one date to another; and the costs of storage, of insurance,

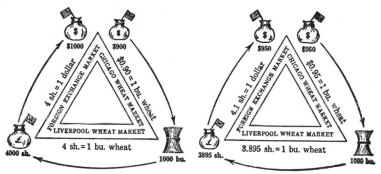

Fig. 21. Three-Cornered Arbitrage

of interest, and other charges correspond in this case to the costs of shipping, insurance, and other charges in the other. Just as in the case of space arbitrage we should usually expect it to result in an equality between the average cost of transport between two places and the difference in price between the two places, so in the case of time arbitrage we should expect, for instance, the price of wheat in September to differ from the price of wheat in March by a sum equal to the average cost of holding the wheat for that period.

EFFECT OF UNCERTAINTY OF THE FUTURE. There is, however, one fundamental difference betwen arbitrage through space and arbitrage through time. In the case of arbitrage through space the prices in the various markets are *known*. In the case of arbitrage through time the price at the present moment, or at past dates, is known, but the price at future dates cannot be known; it can only be estimated.

APPLICATION TO SEASONAL FLUCTUATIONS. In the case of seasonal fluctuations of prices the uncertainty of the future is not so great that we cannot make reasonably good estimates. Consequently, arbitrage through time operates fairly well in the case of seasonal variations. In the case of a commodity like wheat, the bulk of the world's harvest comes on the market in September. The wheat is consumed, however, at a fairly steady pace throughout the year. The greater part of the crop, therefore, has to be stored for various periods. Ideally, about a twelfth would have to be stored for one month, another twelfth for two months, and so on. But if the price of wheat at dates later than September does not exceed the price of wheat in September by at least the cost of storage, it will not pay dealers and speculators to store wheat. If, for instance, it cost 1 cent per bushel per month to store wheat, we should expect the October price to be 1 cent per bushel greater than the September price, the November price to be 2 cents per bushel greater than the September price, and so on. If the differences were greater or less than this, arbitrage through time would tend to rectify the situation. If in the above case the December price were only 2.5 cents above the September price, the owners of wheat would hold it off the market in the hope of still higher prices in January or later. This would raise the price till it stood at 3 cents above the September price. If, on the other hand, the December price stood at 4 cents above the September price, owners of wheat who otherwise would hold their wheat for later dates would be tempted to throw it on the market to gain the additional profit. This would lower the price till again it stood at 3 cents above the September price.

Generally speaking, in the case of agricultural commodities which are storable and which have a crop that comes on the market all at once, we find that the price is lowest at the time of the crop and rises gradually through the year until the next crop comes on the market. This does not always happen; in some years, for instance, the price of potatoes falls sharply even between one crop and the next. But this is always because of some misjudgment on the part of the dealers and owners of the crop.

APPLICATION TO COMMODITY SPECULATION. If we had accurate knowledge of future events the principle of arbitrage through time would apply even to fluctuations covering long periods of time. For instance, it is well known that the output of agricultural commodities varies from year to year; in some years we have a poor crop, and in other years we have a good crop. If the crop could not be stored for any length of time, of course, the whole crop would either have to be eaten or go to waste in the year in which it was produced. In a year of a large crop, therefore, we should expect to find a low price, and in a year of a small crop we should expect to find a high price. If, now, we suppose that the commodity can be stored fairly easily, it will pay speculators to buy the commodity in years when the price is low (i.e., when the crop is large) and to sell the commodity again in the years when the price is high (i.e., when the crop is small). In this way the action of speculators tends to make the price vary less from year to year. In the years of good crops they take some of the crop off the market in order to store it for a later year; this has the effect of making the price higher than it otherwise would be. In the years of poor crops the speculators bring out what they have stored and place it on the market; this has the effect of making the price lower than it otherwise would be. If speculators had perfect knowledge of the future, we would expect them to take just so much off the market in years of good crops and to put just so much on the market in years of lean crops, so that the difference in price between the good and the lean years would be just sufficient to make it worth while to store and hold the commodity between the good and the lean years. If, to take a very simple case, we knew that a good year was always followed by a lean year, and the cost of holding, say, wheat for a year was 12 cents per bushel, then we should expect the price in the good year to be 12 cents per bushel lower than the price in the lean year.

In fact, unfortunately, things do not always work themselves out in this simple way. The action of the speculators can be based only upon *estimates* of what the future is going to bring. Consequently, if these estimates are wrong—as they may well be—the result of speculation may be very different from what we have indicated here. To this problem, however, we shall return later.

QUESTIONS AND EXERCISES

1. The following table shows the individual market schedules of eight marketers, A, B, C, D, E, F, G, and H.

Price (per bu- shel)	Quantity Which Each Would Buy (+) or Sell (−) at Each Price (thousand bushels)							
	A	B	C	D	E	F	G	H
$1.20	+ 1	0	− 3	− 5	−10	−20	−25	−23
1.10	+ 4	+ 2	+ 2	0	− 3	−11	−18	−16
1.00	+ 9	+ 7	+12	+ 6	+ 5	0	− 9	− 9
0.90	+16	+11	+25	+13	+14	+10	0	− 4
0.80	+23	+16	+40	+22	+24	+16	+ 3	− 1

a. Derive and draw the market demand and market supply curves, and the total market curve for this market, and derive from them the equilibrium market price and the volume of transactions at this price. (Assume that the market is perfectly competitive.)

b. Suppose now that H drops out of the market. How would you describe this change in the situation? Draw the supply and demand curves and the total market curve for the market as it now stands, with only A, B, C, D, E, F, and G left in it, on the same diagrams on which you drew the supply and demand curves and the total market curve for the eight marketers. How would you describe the change in these curves? What difference has the removal of H made to the price and to the volume of transactions?

c. Repeat part b of this question, on the assumption that not H but A has dropped out of the market, and that therefore only marketers B to H remain.

2. Suppose each of the marketers in the example above suddenly became willing to buy or sell *double* the quantities which they had before (i.e., suppose that each of the quantity figures in the table were doubled). What would happen to:
   a. The demand and supply curves?
   b. The total market curve?
   c. The market price?
   d. The volume of transactions?

3. In Exercise 2 the change in the individual market schedules changed *both* demand and supply curves. Why? Under what circumstances could the market demand curve change without a change in the supply curve, or the market supply curve change without a change in the demand curve?

4. Would it be possible to have a pair of supply and demand curves which did not intersect anywhere? Construct a numerical system of market schedules in which this would be the case. What would be the significance of such a condition?

5. Explain in your own words exactly why you would expect the price of wheat in Liverpool to be greater than the price of wheat in Chicago.

6. During the last century important wheat fields have been developed in the southern hemisphere, in Australia and in South America. Remembering that the months of harvest in the southern hemisphere are February and March, what effect would you expect this development to have on the seasonal variation in the price of wheat, assuming that there is a competitive market and that wheat can be stored without difficulty?

7. Read the Book of Genesis, chapters 41 and 47. Discuss, with the chapters in mind, the problem of the nature, functions, and desirability of speculating in grain.

8. Suppose that no expenses were involved in holding wheat, and that knowledge of the future were perfect. In this case the action of speculators would result in the price of wheat being constant from year to year. Why, exactly? Would this mean that the *incomes* of farmers were constant from year to year also?

9. Suppose three countries, A, B, and C, with different currencies called *alphas, betas,* and *gammas.* The following table (matrix) shows the price of each currency in each country on a given day, reckoned in that country's currency.

		Country		
		A	B	C
Country	A	1	4	10
	B	0.24	1	2.7
	C	0.09	0.42	1

Each figure in this table represents the price of the currency of the country at the head of its column, in the country at the head of its row. Thus the price of betas in A is 4 alphas per beta, the price of alphas in C is 0.09 gammas per alpha.

a. Keeping the figures of row A, construct a similar matrix in which the various prices are consistent, assuming no costs of transport or exchange.

b. List all the opportunities for arbitrage in the original matrix, with the proportion of profit to original investment.

c. Suppose the cost of each transaction is now 5 percent of the original investment. What now are the opportunities for arbitrage, and the proportion of profit to investment in each?

d. What would be the least ratio of the cost of transactions to original investment which would eliminate all arbitrage from the original table?

(Hint: if a_b alphas per beta is the price of betas in A, and if b_a betas per alpha is the price of alphas in B, then if $a_b \cdot b_a \neq 1$, arbitrage is possible. Similarly if, say, $a_b \cdot b_c \cdot c_a \neq 1$, three-cornered arbitrage is possible.)

APPENDIX

A MATHEMATICAL NOTE

If the market curve for an individual is a straight line, its equation may be written in the form

$$q_i = m_i P_i - m_i p_i \qquad (1)$$

where q_i is the amount he will buy $(+)$ or sell $(-)$ at the price p_i, P_i is his *null price,* that is the price at which he will neither buy nor sell $(OT$ in Fig. 15), and m_i is his *price responsiveness*—that is, the amount by which he will increase his purchases (or decrease his sales) for a unit fall in price. If p_e is the equilibrium price, q_{ie} the equilibrium quantity which he will buy and sell, then

$$q_{ie} = m_i P_i - m_i p_e \qquad (2)$$

Summing the equations (2) for all the marketers we have

$$\Sigma q_{ie} = \Sigma P_i m_i - p_e \Sigma m_i = 0 \tag{3}$$

whence

$$p_e = \frac{\Sigma P_i m_i}{\Sigma m_i} \tag{4}$$

That is, the equilibrium price is the weighted arithmetic mean of the null prices of all the marketers, weighted by the price responsiveness of each marketer. This beautifully simple result is only strictly true if the market functions are linear. However, even if they are not linear, if we interpret m_i to mean the average price responsiveness between the null price and the equilibrium price, defined as

$$\overline{m}_i = \frac{q_e}{P_i - p_e} \tag{5}$$

Equation (4) still holds if $\overline{m}_i$ is substituted for m_i. In the nonlinear case, of course, $\overline{m}_i$ is not constant, so the formula cannot be used for calculating p_e, except by successive approximation.

To get a significant measure of "divergence" in the market we must first solve the equations for the equilibrium price, then take all those market curves which have a null price above the equilibrium price and call these the "buyers." Then summing equations (2) for the buyers alone we get

$$q_{be} = \Sigma P_{bi} m_{bi} - p_e \Sigma m_{bi} \tag{6}$$

where q_{be} is the total amount bought at the equilibrium price, P_{bi} is the null price and m_{bi} the price responsiveness of the ith buyers, so that

$$P_b = \frac{\Sigma P_{bi} m_{bi}}{\Sigma m_{bi}} \tag{7}$$

then equation (6) becomes:

$$q_{be} = (P_b - p_e) \Sigma m_{bi} \tag{8}$$

The difference between the average null price of the buyers and the equilibrium price $(P_b - p_b)$ is a good measure of divergence, and if the m_b's are constant is proportional to the quantity exchanged. Similarly it can be shown that

$$q_{se} = (P_s - p_e) \Sigma m_{si} \tag{9}$$

where q_{se} is the quantity sold, P_s is the weighted average null price of the sellers, or those with null prices below the equilibrium price, and m_{si}

is the price responsiveness of the *i*th seller. $(P_s - p_e)$ is an alternative measure of divergence: if $\Sigma m_{bi} = \Sigma m_{si}$ (that is if the total price responsiveness of the demand and supply curves is the same) then, as

$$q_{be} = -q_{se},$$
$$(P_b - p_e) = -(P_s - p_e)$$

CHAPTER 9

SOME APPLICATIONS OF THE THEORY OF MARKET PRICE

The concepts and principles of the two preceding chapters have many important applications to practical problems. Before we proceed to further forms of analysis, it will repay us to consider some important aspects of economic life to which the theory of market price can be applied.

THE FOREIGN EXCHANGES

The Meaning of National Currencies

One aspect of the world of today which many people find puzzling is the question of the foreign exchanges. With the aid of the analysis in the previous chapters this apparent mystery becomes understandable. The world is divided into a number of nations, each of which has a monetary unit of its own. The United States has its dollar, Great Britain its pound, France its franc, Germany its mark, and so on. A unit of any one of these currencies represents a tacit undertaking, on the part of the people of the countries concerned, to supply the owner with an amount of goods or services equal in value to the money he owns. If I own a dollar bill, I can go to any American who offers goods for sale to the public and obtain from him a dollar's worth of goods in exchange for the dollar. If I own a pound note, I can go to any Britisher who offers goods or services for sale to the public and obtain from him one pound's worth of his goods or services. But if I go to an American and offer him a pound note, or if I go to a Britisher and offer him a dollar bill, I will be unlikely to get goods and services in exchange. Frequently, however, we find Americans, with nothing but dollars in their possession, who wish to buy goods and services from Britishers, and who consequently must change their dollars into pounds before that can be done. An American tourist, for instance, must transform some of his dollars into pounds before he can buy British hotel services and British meals. There will also be Britishers who wish to buy goods and services from Americans, and who have to transform their pounds into dollars before this can be done. Or perhaps there are American manufacturers who have sold their goods in Britain and received pounds in return, who wish to bring these pounds home and spend them in America; they must transform them into dollars. Or there may be British manufacturers who have sold goods in America, and who wish to transform into pounds the dollars they have received.

The Foreign Exchange Market

The foreign exchange market, then, is an arrangement whereby dollars can be transformed into pounds, and pounds can be transformed into dollars. Just as the wheat market is an arrangement whereby people who have money and want wheat can meet people who have wheat and want money, so the foreign exchange market is an arrangement whereby people who have pounds and want dollars can meet people who have dollars and want pounds. The dollars and pounds in question are not, of course, necessarily dollar bills and pound notes; for the most part they consist of checks, drafts, or bills of exchange, which are *orders to pay* dollars or pounds. As we shall see later, these amount to practically the same thing as dollars or pounds in any other form, so we can neglect the form for the moment.

The Foreign Exchange Rate

The *foreign exchange rate* is the ratio of exchange in transactions taking place in the foreign exchange market. It is, in other words, the price of one currency in terms of the other. If we say that the price of wheat is 90 cents per bushel, we mean that anyone can take 90 cents to the wheat market and get a bushel of wheat in return, or anyone can take a bushel of wheat to the market and get 90 cents in return. Similarly, if the price of dollars is £0.357, or about 7 shillings per dollar in the foreign exchange market or if—what is the same thing—the price of pounds is $2.80 per pound, anyone can go to the market and find a trader there who will give him $2.80 for every pound he offers, or £0.357 for every dollar he offers.

The Foreign Exchange Market as a Competitive Market

If, then, the foreign exchange market is a competitive market, the principles which apply to the competitive market in general should apply to it. For instance, an increased desire on the part of the people in the market to get rid of dollars should cause the *price* of dollars in terms of other currencies to fall; but an increased desire to acquire dollars should cause the price of dollars to rise. We could interpret the day-to-day fluctuations in the foreign exchange rates therefore— just as we could similar fluctuations in the price of wheat—as being due to changes in the market schedules of the people who are in the market.

Application of Principle of Clearing the Market

The principle of *clearing the market* can be applied to the foreign exchange market, as to any other; the *equilibrium* ratio of exchange is that at which the quantity of each currency which the marketers wish to sell is equal to the quantity of each currency which the marketers wish to buy. In the dollar-pound market, for instance, we can postulate market schedules for each marketer showing how many dollars he will buy and sell at each price of dollars. From these market schedules we can derive the market demand and supply schedules for dollars and, from these, deduce the equilibrium price and the quantity which will be exchanged at that price. Or, as a demand for dollars is exactly the same thing as a supply of pounds, and a supply of dollars the same thing as a demand for pounds, we could deduce demand and supply schedules for pounds which would equally well give us the equilibrium price and the quantity exchanged. These principles are illustrated in Table 14. Column 1 gives the price of dollars. Just as the price of wheat in terms of pounds is the number of pounds which exchange for 1 bushel, so the price of dollars is the number of pounds which exchange for 1 dollar. Column 6 is the price of pounds—i.e., the number of dollars which will exchange for one pound. Each figure of column 6 is the reciprocal of the corresponding figure of column 1. Column 2 gives the number of dollars demanded at each price. In column 4 essentially the same set of facts is expressed in the form of the number of pounds offered for dollars at each price. The number of pounds offered at each price is equal

TABLE 14. THE EQUILIBRIUM OF THE FOREIGN EXCHANGES

1	2	3	4	5	6
Price of Dollars (£ per $)	Number of Dollars Demanded (millions)	Number of Dollars Offered (millions)	Number of Pounds Offered (millions)	Number of Pounds Demanded (millions)	Price of Pounds ($ per £)
0.333	12	8	4.00	2.66	3.00
0.345	11	9	3.79	3.10	2.90
0.357	10	10	3.57	3.57	2.80
0.370	9	11	3.33	4.07	2.70
0.385	8	12	3.08	4.62	2.60

to the number of dollars demanded at that price, multiplied by the price of dollars. If, for instance, at a price of £0.357 per dollar a man wants to buy $2.80, to get the $2.80 he must offer £1. A demand for $2.80 and an offer of £1 are therefore exactly the same thing if the ratio of exchange is $2.80 per pound. Column 3 shows the number of dollars offered at each price, column 5, the corresponding number of pounds demanded.

Demand and Supply in the Foreign Exchange Market

Columns 1 and 2 form the demand schedule for dollars, and columns 1 and 3 the supply schedule for dollars. Columns 6 and 5 form the demand schedule for pounds, columns 6 and 4 the supply schedule for pounds. The equilibrium price is clearly £0.357 per dollar, or $2.80 per pound. These supply and demand schedules give us sufficient equipment to analyze the effect of any external changes on the foreign exchanges. If for instance the number of dollars possessed by the people in the market increases, our analysis of the preceding chapter indicates that the marketers will be willing to offer more dollars, and to demand fewer, at each price. The equilibrium price of dollars will therefore fall. Likewise, if the number of dollars possessed by the marketers diminishes, the price of dollars will rise.

The Offer Ratio Equal to the Price in Equilibrium

We can, however, effect a certain simplification in the exposition of problems of the foreign exchanges if we make an assumption which is not wholly true, but not far from the truth. It is that in any given period of time there will be a certain number of pounds which are in the market "looking for dollars," and which will be offered no matter what the price; and also a certain number of dollars "looking for pounds," which will also be offered no matter what the price. The demand and supply schedules corresponding to this situation are shown in Table 15.

TABLE 15.   EQUILIBRIUM OF THE FOREIGN EXCHANGES WITH FIXED SUPPLIES

1	2	3	4	5	6
Price of Dollars (£ per $)	Number of Dollars Demanded (millions)	Number of Dollars Offered (millions)	Number of Pounds Offered (millions)	Number of Pounds Demanded (millions)	Price of Pounds ($ per £)
0.333	10.71	10	3.57	3.33	3.00
0.345	10.36	10	3.57	3.45	2.90
0.357	10.00	10	3.57	3.57	2.80
0.370	9.64	10	3.57	3.70	2.70
0.385	9.29	10	3.57	3.85	2.60

In this table there are 10 million dollars in the market looking for pounds, and 3.57 million pounds looking for dollars. In this circumstance the ratio of exchange will be equal to the ratio of the quantities of the two currencies being offered. We need merely write $10,000,000 = £3,570,000, or $2.80 = £1, to obtain the exchange ratio immediately. The ratio of the quantities of the two exchangeables offered in a market may be called the *offer ratio*. Turning to either Table 14 or Table 15, we see that at the equilibrium price, the price is equal to the offer ratio, and at no other price is this true. At £0.333 per dollar in Table 14, for instance, the offer ratio is $\dfrac{£4.00}{\$8.00}$ or £0.20 per dollar. Only at the equilibrium price is the offer ratio $\left(\dfrac{£3.57}{\$10.00}\right)$ equal to the price (£0.357 per dollar). This is a general principle and is in fact an alternative way of stating the principle of *clearing the market*.

Effect of Changes in Trade Situation on Exchange Rates

This principle gives us an easy way of telling how any particular change in the trade situation will affect the exchanges, for the foreign exchange rate will always tend to be equal to the ratio in which the two currencies are looking for each other in the market. If the rate is $3.00 to £1, there are three times as many dollars looking for pounds as there are pounds looking for dollars. All that is necessary, then, in investigating the effect of some event on the foreign exchanges, is to ask what will be the effect of this event on the number of pounds looking for dollars, on the one hand, or on the number of dollars looking for pounds, on the other hand.

EXAMPLES: 1. EUROPEAN WAR. One or two examples should make the principle clear. Suppose that Britain gets into a war and suddenly increases her purchases of munitions from the United States.[1] The purchases are made with pounds, which come into the possession of the American manufacturers. These manufacturers do not want pounds; they want dollars. Consequently, the pounds become pounds looking for dollars on the foreign exchange market. If previously in each period there were £10,000,000 and $44,000,000 looking for each other on the foreign exchange market and finding each other at a rate of £1 = $4.40, now there are £11,000,000 looking for dollars but only $44,000,000 look-

[1] The average price of a pound sterling in New York in August, 1939, was $4.623. In September, 1939, it was $4.041. This fall was not, of course, due wholly to an immediate increase of purchases made by Britain in America after the declaration of war; part of the fall may have been due to speculative anticipation of increased purchases, part to the regulative activity of the Exchange Equalization Funds.

ing for pounds, for nothing has yet happened to increase that figure. The exchange rate will therefore move to £11 = $44, or £1 = $4.00. The excess of pounds on the market has made pounds cheaper; instead of having to pay $4.40 for one we can now buy one for $4.00.

2. An International Loan. Now suppose that the British government raises a loan on Wall Street of $5,000,000. Naturally, it will want these dollars turned into pounds and will put them into the foreign exchange market with this in mind. Again, suppose that previously there were £10,000,000 looking for dollars and $40,000,000 looking for pounds. Now there are the same number of pounds looking for dollars—£10,000,-000—but as a result of the loan there are $45,000,000 looking for pounds. The exchange rate will therefore move to £1 = $4.50; i.e., the increase in the number of dollars on the market will make dollars cheaper, pounds dearer. In a similar way we can analyze the probable effects on the foreign exchanges of many other events.

The Case of More Than Two Currencies: Arbitrage

In the foregoing analysis we have assumed, in effect, that there were only two countries—the United States and Britain. In fact, of course, there are many more countries and many more currencies. Our analysis will also enable us to deal with this problem. In each market the exchange rate will be in equilibrium at that point where it is equal to the ratio of the quantities of currencies looking for each other. As between the different markets the exchange rates will be kept *consistent* by means of the operations of arbitrage. The preceding chapter showed how arbitrage made for consistency in exchange ratios between three markets —a wheat-dollar market, a wheat-pound market, and a dollar-pound market. In exactly the same way arbitrage makes for consistency in the exchange rates in, say, the dollar-pound market, the pound-yen market, and the yen-dollar market.

Suppose, for instance, that exchange rates in London, Tokyo, and New York are as follows:

London $2.70 = £1
Tokyo   £1 = Y1020
New York   Y1020 = $2.90
                  (Y352 = $1.00)

It is evident that a trader could take $2.70 in London, buy £1 with it there, take the pound to Tokyo and buy Y1020 there, then take the yen to New York and buy $2.90, thus making $0.20 on the transaction, assuming no costs of transport or exchange. These transactions in themselves, however, will change the exchange rates. Because people are throwing dollars on the London market and buying pounds there, dollars will become cheaper and pounds dearer. Similarly in Tokyo, yen will become dearer and pounds cheaper, and in New York, yen will become cheaper and dollars dearer. The final result may then be as follows:

London $2.80 = £1
Tokyo   £1 = Y1008
New York   Y1008 = $2.80
                     (Y360 = $1.00)

At these rates of exchange arbitrage is no longer profitable, for $2.80 in London becomes £1, which becomes 1008 yen in Tokyo, which becomes again $2.80 in New York. The rates therefore are consistent.

Apparent Inconsistency Due to Cost of Transport and Exchange

We have assumed in this that there are no costs of transport or of exchange. In fact, there are small costs involved in transferring funds between various markets and in making the necessary exchanges. Consequently, a certain amount of inconsistency in the exchange rates is possible without giving rise to arbitrage transactions, for unless the gross profit to be made by arbitrage is at least equal to the expenses of performing the operation, the operation will not be performed. In the first example above, for instance, if the cost of performing the operation described were $0.20 or more, there would be no arbitrage, and the rates would therefore be consistent in the sense of not being subject to change through arbitrage. Thus where there is a certain cost of operation of arbitrage, there exists a certain range of variation of the exchange rates within which arbitrage will not take place and within which, therefore, the relative exchange rates may vary freely.

EXAMPLE. To take a simple example, suppose that in New York the pound-dollar ratio is £1 = $2.80, and that in London the pound-dollar ratio is £1 = $2.85. If no expenses are involved, it would clearly be profitable to take $2.80 in New York, buy £1 with it, take the pound to London, and there change it for $2.85, making a profit of $0.05 on each $2.80 thus exchanged. These transactions would soon do away with the difference in rates. The extra dollars coming into the New York market would make dollars cheaper, moving the rate, say, to £1 = $2.82; the extra pounds coming into the London market would make pounds cheaper there, moving the rate, say, to £1 = $2.82—and arbitrage would cease. But if the cost of making these exchanges amounts to $0.05 on each $2.80 involved, it will not pay to perform the transaction unless the difference between the two exchange rates amounts to more than $0.05 for each $2.80. If, for instance, the rate in New York were £1 = $2.80

and the rate in London were £1 = $2.86, it would then pay to ship pounds from New York to London, and dollars from London to New York, even if the cost of doing this were $0.05 for each pound shipped. Similarly, if the rate in New York were £1 = $2.80 and the rate in London were £1 = $2.74, it would then pay to ship pounds from London to New York and dollars from New York to London, even if it cost $0.05 to make the shipment. The rates in London and New York, therefore, may differ in this case by as much as 5 cents in $2.80, either way, before arbitrage will occur.

THE GOLD STANDARD

Another mystery which we can now clear up is that of the gold standard. The gold standard is simply a law, passed by the legislative authority of a country like any other law, which says that some authority in the country (usually the Central Bank or the Treasury of the government itself) shall be obliged to exchange gold for the money of the country, and the money of the country for gold, at a *fixed legal rate*. Under the old free gold standard, for instance, the Bank of England was compelled by law to buy gold from anyone who offered it at a price of £4.2409 per fine ounce, and to sell it at a price of £4.2477 per fine ounce to anyone who demanded it. Similarly, the United States Treasury was compelled by law to buy and sell gold at a price of $20.67 per ounce. There are thus two essential features of a gold standard—a fixed legal price for gold, and some arrangement for making that price effective, i.e., for enabling people to buy and sell gold at that price.

Exchange Rates Fixed Between Two Gold Standard Countries

Now, when two countries are on the gold standard, the principle of arbitrage operates to make it impossible for the exchange ratio of the two currencies in the foreign exchange market to differ appreciably from the ratio of the fixed prices of these currencies in terms of gold. If (to use simple figures for the sake of the arithmetic) the United States Treasury were compelled to buy and sell gold for dollars at a rate of $35 per ounce of gold, and the Bank of England had to buy and sell gold for pounds at a rate of £12.5 per ounce of gold, the exchange rate between dollars and pounds in the foreign exchange market could not vary very much from the rate of £12.5 = $35 or £1 = $2.80. For suppose that in the foreign exchange market in any one day there are £10,000,000 looking for $30,000,000, so that the equilibrium rate is £1 = $3. At this rate a person wishing to buy pounds with dollars would not buy them in the foreign exchange market at all. By taking $2.80 to the Treasury in New York he could get 0.08 ounces of gold, and by crossing the Atlantic to London and presenting this gold to the Bank of England he could get £1 for it. Thus by using gold as an intermediary he could get his pound for $2.80 instead of having to pay $3 as he would in the foreign exchange market. This would remove dollars from the foreign exchange market until there were only $28,000,000 looking for the £10,000,000, and the rate would be $2.80 = £1.

Conversely, if we suppose that on a given day there are only $25,000,000 looking for pounds, and £10,000,000 looking for dollars, the rate in the foreign exchange market will be $2.50 = £1. But if this is the case it will pay anyone who wants dollars for his pounds to take each pound to the Bank of England, get 0.08 ounces of gold for it, ship that gold across the Atlantic to New York, and get $2.80 for it there. Thus he would get $2.80 for each pound instead of $2.50 in the foreign exchange market. But if people bought their dollars through the intermediary of gold, pounds would be removed from the foreign exchange market until the rate in the foreign exchange market was again £1 = $2.80. We should recognize this procedure as merely a special case of the principle of three-cornered arbitrage discussed earlier—a special case which arises because in the pound-gold and the dollar-gold markets the price is fixed by law.

The Gold Points

In the preceding example we assumed that there were no costs of transport of gold between the financial centers. Of course, actually there is a small cost of transport, which introduces the possibility of apparent inconsistency in the exchange rates and the gold prices. Suppose that it costs $0.02 to transport 0.08 ounces of gold across the Atlantic in either direction between New York and London. If, then, a man bought 0.08 ounce of gold with £1, shipped the gold to New York, and there bought dollars with it, he would receive a net sum of only $2.78 for his £1, for out of the $2.80 received for the gold at the United States Treasury he would have paid $0.02 for transport. Similarly, a man would have to take $2.82 in New York in order to obtain £1 in London through the intermediary of gold. Gold will not move from one center to the other, therefore, as long as the exchange rate in the market lies within the range from $2.78 to $2.82 per pound. These limits are called the *gold points*. If the price of pounds rose above $2.82 in the market, gold would begin to flow from New York to London, for it would be cheaper to buy pounds indirectly through buying gold in New York and selling it in London. This rate, therefore, is the gold export point for New York, the gold import point for London. Similarly, if the price of pounds in the market fell below $2.78, it would pay to buy dollars by shipping gold to New York. This rate is the gold import point for New York, the gold export point for London.

Significance of Monetary Standards

The international gold standard was a fairly transitory phenomenon, characteristic only of the half-century or so before 1914. Other commodities, such as silver, have frequently been used as monetary standards. Some countries in the nineteenth century had a bimetallic standard, offering to buy or sell both gold and silver at fixed prices. This tended to be unstable, for if the ratio of exchange of the two metals in world markets differed from the standard ratios, arbitrage would soon denude the bimetallic country of one metal or the other. Thus, suppose a country offered to buy and sell gold and silver at a ratio of 1 to 16, when on world markets an ounce of gold could be bought or sold for 20 ounces of silver. Traders could then profit by taking silver to the bimetallic country, getting gold for it and selling this for silver on the world market; by this means 16 ounces of silver would be exchanged for 20 ounces; if this process went on for long the bimetallic country would lose all its gold and end up with a pure silver standard.

Composite Commodity Standards

From time to time various *composite commodity standards* have been proposed which would involve the government offering to buy and sell a fixed "bundle" of commodities, or titles to commodities for a fixed sum of the national money. This would operate to stabilize the money value of the bundle in the market, for if the market value rose above the standard value it would pay traders to buy bundles from the government and sell their component commodities in the market, which would lower the market prices. If the market value of the bundle fell below the standard value, however, it would pay traders to assemble bundles in the market and sell them to the government; this would raise the market prices. The advantage of this plan is that relative prices of the various commodities in the bundle would be free to fluctuate, but their aggregate value would remain practically constant.

Stabilization of exchange rates can be accomplished without any monetary standard commodity if the monetary authorities of the two countries concerned, or even of one country, offer to buy and sell the currencies at a fixed rate of exchange. This indeed is the general mode of regulating foreign exchange rates today. If rates are fixed too high or too low the exchange control agency may be denuded of one currency or the other through the operations of arbitrage. Since World War II the International Monetary Fund has acted as coordinating agency for the stabilization of the currency exchange rates of its member countries. Unfortunately exchange control usually goes along with quantitative restrictions and quota allocations on foreign exchange which severely distort the flow of international transactions.

THE SECURITIES MARKET

From our present vantage point we can also gain some insight into the operations of another important feature of economic life—the securities market. Any market is a place where things are exchanged. The first step to the understanding of a market is to answer the question: What is exchanged in it? The things that are exchanged in the securities markets are not commodities but rights, expectations, or claims. In these transactions it may be that only a few pieces of engraved paper actually change hands. It may be, even, that the transactions consist of an exchange of abstract rights recorded only in the books of a banker or a stockbroker. These rights are of many kinds. They may, however, be divided into two broad classes, one of which we shall call securities, the other, money. As a first approximation to an understanding of the securities market we shall assume that it is an organization through which securities are exchanged for money. It is an organization whereby people who have money and want securities are enabled to meet people who have securities and want money and so effect the exchanges which both parties desire.

What Is a Security?

But what is a *security?* What do we buy when we give up money for a security? A security is a *right* to certain future benefits, when viewed from the side of its owner. It is an *obligation* to grant certain future benefits to the owner, when viewed from the side of the issuer. It would perhaps be even more accurate to describe a security as an *expectation.* The owner of the security expects to receive certain benefits in the future. The issuer of the security expects to grant certain benefits. The benefits in question usually consist of sums of money. They do not, however, have to consist of *definite* sums of money. The possessor may merely gain a right to share in residual profits, or to participate in the control of a corporation.

Kinds of Securities

1. BONDS. There are many different kinds of securities. They can be divided, however, into two broad classes—*bonds* and *stocks.* A bond is a promise, or an obligation, to pay certain definite sums at definite future

dates to the person who owns it. In the technical language of the market the word bond is usually confined to those securities which oblige the issuer to pay a series of equal annual or semiannual payments, culminating in a much larger payment known as the *redemption* of the bond. A security, for instance, which conferred on its owner the right to receive $50 on the first of January each year for the next ten years and a further payment of, say, $1000 at the end of the ten years would be a bond. For want of a better term, however, we may broaden the term bond to mean any security which consists of an obligation to pay definite sums on definite future dates. A promissory note, therefore, would be a bond in this sense, for the issuer of the note is bound to pay, let us say, a single sum of $1050 twelve months from the present date. A bank loan would be a bond of the person to whom it is issued, for he gives his promise to pay the bank a stated sum on a stated date in return for a sum of money in the present.

2. SHARES OF STOCK.   At the other extreme is a type of security known as a *share of stock*, represented in its purest form by what is known as an *ordinary* or *common share*. This is not an obligation to pay a series of definite sums at definite future dates, nor does its owner expect to receive a series of known sums in the future. It is an obligation to pay a definite share of the divided profits of a business. Consequently to its owner it represents at any one moment a series of expected future payments whose magnitude depends on the expectation which he entertains as to the future profitability of the business. A given ordinary share, therefore, may represent a different series of expected payments in the mind of each person in the market. One person may be optimistic about the future of the business. He thinks it will make large profits in the future, and so for him the ordinary share represents an expected series of large payments. Another may be equally pessimistic. For him, the same share will represent an expected series of small payments, or perhaps of no payments at all. Insofar as all future events are uncertain, all securities, whether stocks or bonds, may mean different expectations to different people. In the case of a bond, however, the expected payments are limited on one side by the contract written in the bond and on the other side by the possibility of the repudiation of this contract at some future date. If I have a bond which gives me a right to receive $50 for ten years, I shall not expect to receive more than this. I may, of course, receive less if the bond is repudiated. But the possibility of variation in the payments from an ordinary share is much greater.

3. PREFERENCE SHARES.   Midway between the bond and the ordinary share comes a class of security known as the *preference share*. This has something of the character of a bond in that it represents an obligation of the issuer to pay not more than a stated sum each year. A 7 percent

preference share with a nominal value of $100 would entitle its owner
to a maximum of $7 per year. If, however, the profits of the issuing com-
pany do not justify this payment, it does not have to be made. In this
sense it is like an ordinary share.

Other Benefits

The future benefits expected by the owner of a security may include
certain nonmonetary benefits. An ordinary share, for instance, usually
entitles its owner to a voice in the management of the issuing company. A
bond normally gives no such right, except when a company defaults on
its bonds and is reorganized. Nonmonetary benefits may be important
in determining what various people will pay for a security.

Price of Securities Determined as Any Other Price Is

What is meant by the *price* of a security? A price is a ratio of exchange;
that is, the ratio of the quantities of things exchanged in a transaction.
In order to be able to measure the price of a security in any transaction,
we must be able to measure both the quantity of the security and the
quantity of the thing given in exchange. The thing given in exchange
is almost invariably money of some kind. The barter of securities for
securities may sometimes occur, but it is rare. We can easily measure the
quantity of money as a sum of dollars. The quantity of security is
generally measured in conventional units of some nominal value—e.g.,
thousand-dollar bonds. Each of these conventional units, however, may
represent a different expectation, a different series of expected future
benefits, at various times or even in the eyes of various people at one time.

If any security is present in the market in a large number of identical
units and has a large number of buyers and sellers, it will have a competitive market. In that case its price will be determined according to
the general principles which govern such a market. Its equilibrium price
will be that at which the quantity of the security offered for sale is equal
to the quantity demanded for purchase. For any such security we can
draw demand and supply curves, as in Fig. 17, page 119, derived from
the market schedules of all the people in the market. Its equilibrium price
will then be given by the point of intersection of these demand and supply
curves. Alternatively, we could draw the total market curve for the
security, as in Fig. 19, page 128, to find the price at the point where there
was no excess demand or supply.

Why Does the Price of a Security Change?

If the price of such a security changes, it must be because of a change
in the market schedules of the people in the market, leading to a change

in the total market curve. What may cause these market schedules to change? That is to say, what may cause a change in the general eagerness to buy or sell any given security? One thing which may cause such a change is a revision in the expectations of future benefits from a security. Suppose, for instance, that it becomes generally believed in the market that a certain government is about to default on its bonds. The expected sum of future payments from these bonds becomes smaller, no matter what the face value of the obligation. As a result, people become more eager to sell them, less eager to buy them. The total market curve will fall, and with it the equilibrium price will fall. Or, to put the same matter in another way, the fact that people are now less eager to buy the bonds means that the demand for them has fallen; their demand curve has moved to the left. People are also more eager to get rid of them, so their supply has risen; their supply curve has moved to the right. We see from Fig. 18, page 126, that this means a decline in the equilibrium price.

Similarly, if there is a favorable revision of the expected future payments from a security, there will be a rise in the demand for it, a fall in the supply of it, and its price will go up. Ordinary shares are more susceptible to changes of this sort than bonds are, as revisions in the expectations of future profit of a company have to be made frequently. A rise in the price of an ordinary share may therefore mean solely that the market as a whole takes a more cheerful view of the prospects of the issuing company. A change of this kind may be called a change in the *quality* of a security. In a corresponding way, if the quality of any commodity rises, its price per unit of quantity may be expected to rise.

Changes in the Price of Fixed Expectations

Securities do not change in price merely because of changes in their quality, however. Their prices are subject to frequent fluctuations which have nothing to do with changes in their expected future payments. These are brought about by variations in the relative desire of people in the market to hold *money* as against securities. Whenever a security is bought, the buyer relinquishes a certain quantity of money and acquires an equivalent quantity of the security. The seller relinquishes a certain quantity of the security and acquires an equivalent quantity of money. A sale of securities therefore is the same thing as a purchase of money, and a purchase of securities is the same as a sale of money. A *demand* for securities is the same thing as a *supply* of money, and from the demand curve for a security we can construct a supply curve of money offered for the security which will describe exactly the same set of facts. If, for instance, at a price of $100 per unit 500 units of a security should be demanded, this means also that (100 × 500), or $50,000, will be offered in exchange for the security at that price. Similarly, a supply of a security is the same thing as a demand for money.

Equilibrium Price

The equilibrium level of the price of securities on any one day is that level, therefore, at which there is no *net* desire on the part of the people in the market to increase their holdings either of money or of securities. If at a certain price an individual wishes to buy securities, he must be dissatisfied with the distribution of his total funds between securities and money. He must feel that he has too much money and too few securities, and consequently he wishes to increase the amount of securities and to decrease the amount of money which he holds. Similarly, if an individual wishes to sell securities at that price, he must want to increase the amount of money and to decrease the amount of securities which he holds. If, now, the price of securities is such that the desire to get rid of securities and acquire money on the part of some individuals is just balanced by the desire to get rid of money and acquire securities on the part of others, there will be equilibrium. But if at the existing price there is on balance a *general* desire to increase holdings of money and to decrease holdings of securities, then the price of securities must fall.

Increased Demand for Securities or Money

The assumption in this argument, it should be noticed, is that the total quantity both of securities and of money in the possession of the marketers is fixed, so that transactions do not change this total quantity but merely change its ownership. In short periods this assumption is substantially true; over longer periods it is of course much less accurate. In short periods, then, any general increase in the desire to hold securities cannot be satisfied by an increase in the *quantity* of securities held, for the total quantity of securities is assumed to be fixed. It can be satisfied only by an increase in the money *value* of the securities held, i.e., by a rise in the price of securities. Similarly, any increase in the desire to hold money cannot be satisfied by an increase in the *quantity* of money held; it can be satisfied only by an increase in the value of the money held in terms of securities, i.e., by a fall in the price of securities.

EXAMPLE. Suppose that the people in the market on a given day possess $10,000,000 of money and 1,000,000 units of securities. Suppose that the price of securities is $50 per unit, so that the total value of the securities held is $50,000,000. Now let there be an increased desire to hold securities, which is the same thing as a desire on the part of the market as a whole to increase its holding of securities, i.e., to acquire securities. The price of securities will rise, let us say, to $60 per unit. The value of the 1,000,000 securities held will now be $60,000,000 instead of $50,000,000. The rise in the desire to hold securities has resulted in an increase in the *value*, not in the *quantity*, of the securities held. On the other hand, suppose there is an increased desire to hold money—i.e., to acquire money by selling securities—on the part of the market as a whole. The price of securities will fall, let us say, to $40 per unit. Previously the $10,000,000 of money in the market was worth 200,000 units of securities; now it is worth 250,000 units. The increased desire to hold money has resulted not in an increase in the quantity of money held but in an increase in the value of that money. This is a principle of very general importance, as we shall see later.

Effect of Increase in the Quantity of Securities or Money Held

Just as in the wheat market where an increase in the quantity of wheat held by the people in the market is likely to depress the price of wheat, so an increase in the quantity of securities held by the people in the market is likely to depress the price of securities. And again, just as an increase in the quantity of money held by people in the wheat market is likely to raise the price of wheat, so an increase in the quantity of money held by people in the stock market is likely to raise the price of securities. Both these propositions, of course, depend on the assumption that the fundamental desires to buy and sell do not change. If, for instance, the government presented $1000 in cash to each person in the stock market one morning, that in itself would have the effect of raising the price of securities. But an event so odd might conceivably scare the wits out of the very people who were the recipients of this bounty, and so increase greatly their desire to get rid of securities and to hold money in readiness to flee so crazy a country. Consequently, the net effect *might* be to lower the price of securities, though in fact this is unlikely.

THE FUTURES MARKET

One further phenomenon, often puzzling to the layman, can be explored with the aid of our analysis of the market. This is the phenomenon of the *futures* market, and the related problem of *hedging*. We have seen how in the securities market present money can be exchanged for promises to pay money in the future. So in the commodity markets money can be exchanged for promises to pay, or deliver, commodities in the future. Indeed, a promise to pay money in the future can be exchanged for a promise to deliver, say, wheat in the future. These obligations are in fact a peculiar kind of security and are known as futures. If I buy May futures in the wheat market, I have in effect bought a security consisting of the obligation of the seller to deliver to me a certain quantity of wheat next May. A future contract, then, is a kind of promissory note, the promise being to pay not money but some commodity. Usually, what is given in exchange for this promise to pay wheat is a promise to pay money. That is, a promissory note in wheat is really exchanged for a promissory note in money.

EXAMPLE. Suppose, for instance, that in December I buy 1000 bushels of May wheat at $0.90 per bushel. This is known as *buying* futures. What I have done is to exchange my promise to pay $900 to the seller next May in return for his promise to deliver to me 1000 bushels of wheat next May. If I *sell* futures—for instance, if I sell 1000 bushels of May wheat at $0.90 per bushel—I have exchanged my promise to deliver 1000 bushels of wheat next May in return for the buyer's promise to deliver $900 next May.

Speculation in Futures

The price of current wheat is called the *spot price*. This is the ratio of exchange between present wheat and present money. Suppose, now, that a dealer expects the spot price of wheat next May to be $1 per bushel, and suppose that he can buy May futures for $0.90 per bushel. In these circumstances he will think it profitable to buy May futures. He exchanges his promise to pay $900 in May for a right to receive 1000 bushels of wheat in May. When May comes around, he fulfills his part of the bargain, pays $900, receives 1000 bushels of wheat, and then sells this wheat for $1000 in the spot market. Thus he makes $100 profit on his transaction. By purchasing May futures at an earlier date he is enabled to come gathering wheat in May at a price which is lower than the spot selling price, and so he makes a profit.

If, on the other hand, the dealer expected the spot price next May to be $0.80, with May futures now selling for $0.90, he would think it profitable to *sell* May futures. He gives his promise to pay 1000 bushels of wheat in May in exchange for the promise of the buyer to pay $900 in May. If his expectation as to the spot price is correct, when May comes he will be able to buy 1000 bushels in the spot market for $800, and to deliver these bushels to the buyer of futures for $900, according to his contract. People who expect the spot price in the future to be greater than the futures price now will therefore be likely to buy futures now, and those who expect the spot price in the future to be less than the futures price now will be likely to sell futures now. Any futures transaction, therefore, is the result of a difference of opinion between the buyer and the seller. The buyer thinks the spot price in the future will be relatively high, and the seller thinks it will be relatively low.[2]

Purpose of the Futures Markets

Just as bonds on the securities market may change hands many times before the obligation which they represent is fulfilled by the original issuer, so futures, which are essentially *commodity bonds,* can also be exchanged many times before the contract which they represent is fulfilled. The professional speculator in the wheat market may seldom, if ever, handle wheat or make actual deliveries of wheat. He spends his time, and makes his income, if any, by selling and buying the futures contracts themselves. Nevertheless, these complicated arrangements serve really to organize *arbitrage through time* as a specialized function. Their purpose is to separate the function of carrying the commodity through time, i.e., of owning and storing it, from the function of bearing the *risks* of price changes. The market in futures enables the speculator to speculate on future price changes without compelling him to own and store the commodity. It also enables the owner and storer of the commodity to escape the risks of speculating on future price changes.

Hedging

The process whereby the owner and storer of a commodity escapes having to speculate on its future price is known as *hedging*. A farmer, for instance, may have 10,000 bushels of wheat in his barn in September which he does not wish to sell until May. If he merely holds the wheat until he sells it in the spot market in May, he is in effect speculating on the spot price of wheat in May. If that price is high, he will do well; if it is low, he will do badly. He can lift some of the burden of this uncertainty from his mind by selling May futures. If May futures stand at $0.90 per bushel, he can enter into a contract with a buyer of futures, binding himself to deliver 10,000 bushels of wheat in May, and binding the buyer to pay in exchange $9000 in money in May. Then no matter what the spot price is when May arrives, the farmer is certain to receive $0.90 per bushel for his wheat. The uncertainty of the future price is lifted from his mind. This does not mean, of course, that he will necessarily gain by the transaction. If in fact the spot price in May turns out to be $1, the farmer would have done better to hold his wheat and sell it in the spot market. Nevertheless, he is protected against a fall in the spot price. It should be noticed that while hedging eliminates speculation

---

[2] Insofar as futures contracts are not held to maturity, the expected trend of price of the futures contract itself, rather than the expected spot price at the time of maturity, may be the main factor affecting the market demand and supply.

from the hedger in so far as it eliminates the uncertainty of the future price, it is not altogether independent of the *profit* motive. A person hedges because he fears a fall in the future spot price more than he hopes for a rise. The holders of wheat will be much more likely to hedge when they are fairly sure of a fall in the spot price than when they are fairly sure of a rise. If, in fact, the holders of wheat were absolutely sure that the spot price in the future would be higher than the futures price now, they would not hedge.

Relation Between Spot and Futures Prices

The price of a commodity in either spot or futures contracts depends on the supply and demand curves in each case. The price of *spot* wheat, for instance, depends on the eagerness of the market to buy or sell wheat in current contracts. The price of *futures* for any month depends on the eagerness of the market to buy and sell the contracts which comprise these futures. The current spot price may be greater or less than the current futures quotation. The possibility of storing a commodity, however, sets a lower limit to the spot price relative to any given futures quotation. If the spot price is below this limit, it will pay dealers to buy the commodity in the spot market and to sell contracts to deliver the commodity in the future—i.e., to sell futures—for they will be able to make profits by holding the commodity for future delivery. The extra buyers in the spot market will bring about a rise in the spot price, and the extra sellers in the futures market will bring about a fall in the futures price, until the minimum difference is once more established. The minimum difference is fixed by the cost of carrying the commodity from the present date to the date when future delivery must be made.

Suppose, for instance, that it cost $0.10 in warehouse, insurance, interest, and other charges to carry a bushel of wheat from September to May. If the price of May futures in September was $1.11, when the spot price was $0.99, a dealer could make a profit of $0.02 per bushel by buying spot wheat in September, selling May futures in September, and holding the wheat bought in September until he had to deliver it to meet his futures contract in May. The cost of the wheat to him in May would be the cost in September, plus the carrying charge, or ($0.99 + 0.10) —$1.09 per bushel. In this case there would be a rush to buy wheat in the spot market in September which would force the spot price up, say, to at least $1. There would likewise be a corresponding rush to sell May futures in September which would force down the price of May futures to at most, say, $1.10. When the difference between the spot price and the price of May futures is less than $0.10, this particular form of arbitrage ceases.

Comparison with Arbitrage

We see, therefore, how the fact that there is a certain cost of transport of wheat from September to the following May tends to set a limit to the amount by which the May futures price can exceed the spot price in September. This limit is closely analogous to the limit on the amount by which, say, the Liverpool price of wheat exceeds the Chicago price, set by the fact that there is a certain cost of transport of wheat from Chicago to Liverpool. Holding a commodity is indeed nothing more than transporting it from one *time* to another, as the very expression *carrying* the commodity indicates. As we saw in the preceding chapter, speculation is essentially arbitrage through time, for it consists ultimately of trying to buy things when they are cheap and trying to sell them when they are dear. But there is one important difference between space arbitrage and time arbitrage. Transport in space can take place in both directions. Gold, for instance, can be transported with equal ease from New York to London or from London to New York. Hence there is both an upper and a lower limit to the variation in the price of a commodity in one center relative to that in another. The dollar price of gold in London can be neither much greater nor much less than the dollar price in New York, these limits being set by the cost of transport of gold across the Atlantic. Transport through time, however, can take place only in one direction—from the past to the future, never from the future to the past. We can take wheat from September to the following May. We can under no circumstances take it from May to the previous September. Therefore, although the cost of carrying wheat through time tends to set a limit on the fall of the spot price below the futures price, there is no upper limit set by this kind of arbitrage. If wheat is very scarce in September, but on account of good harvests in the southern hemisphere it is expected to be very plentiful in May, the spot price of wheat in September may exceed greatly the price of May futures in September. The willingness of people to buy May futures depends on what they think the spot price will be in May, not on what the spot price is in September. If the prospect of a plentiful supply of wheat in the following May induces a belief that the spot price next May will be low, the price of May futures will also be low.

Short Selling and Margin Buying in the Securities Market

A phenomenon somewhat analogous in principle, if not in mechanism, to the futures contracts in the commodity markets is also found in the securities market, where it is known as *short selling*. A speculator in the securities market sells short when he contracts to deliver stock to a buyer

at some future date at a price fixed in the present. The seller hopes that
at the future date the spot price of the stock will be less than the price at
which he has contracted to deliver it. Generally speaking, therefore,
the short seller is a *bear*—i.e., he expects the price of securities to fall.

The *bulls*—those who expect the price of securities to rise—may also
indulge in a practice somewhat analogous to the futures contract known
as *buying on margin*. This is in effect a contract to deliver *money* at a
future date in return for stock purchased in the present. The margin
buyer is one who buys stock in part with borrowed money. To borrow
money is of course to contract to deliver money at some future date.
When or before that date arrives, the buyer hopes to be able to sell his
stock at a higher price than that at which he bought. Suppose, for example, that a speculator buys 100 securities in September at a price of $80
per security. He pays the seller, let us say, $4000, and contracts to pay
him $4120 in the following March. He has in effect, though not in legal
form or conventional terminology, sold March futures in money. If
when March comes around the spot price of his securities is $90 per
unit, he can sell his 100 securities in the spot market for $9000, pay the
$4120 according to his contract, and have $4880 left. The $4000 which
he paid out in September has grown into $4880 in March, and his in-
vestment has shown a handsome profit. But if the spot price of the security
in March had been $70 per unit, he would have realized only $7000 in
March, and after fulfilling his contract to deliver $4120 he would have
had only $2880 left. His initial capital of $4000 would have shrunk,
and he would have suffered a loss.

SPECULATIVE FLUCTUATIONS

We observed in the previous chapter that speculation, in the sense of
the holding of assets in the expectation of a rise in their value, could
perform the valuable social function of arbitrage over time. We also
noted, however, that the preferences for assets of different kinds, on
which the market price structure partly depends, depend in turn on expected future prices. This introduces an element of instability and fluctuation into speculative markets which may have quite undesirable consequences. There are two main motives for holding assets, the *use* motive
and the *speculative* motive. Thus we may hold stocks of goods because
we are using them, stocks of money because we are using it currently to
make purchases, or securities because we are living on the interest or
dividends. On the other hand we may hold either goods or securities
merely because we expect to sell them later after a rise in price, or we
may hold money because we expect to buy things later at a lower price.

This speculative motive is not evil in itself, and indeed can motivate socially useful behavior. It can also however give rise to self-justifying expectations and to meaningless speculative fluctations in price.

How Expectations Justify Themselves. This phenomenon is found in all kinds of markets at times; there have been speculative land booms and even tulip booms which have eventually crashed. It is especially characteristic of the stock market, because of the predominance of the speculative motive in it. Thus, if people expect the price of securities to go up, they will become more eager to buy securities and to get rid of money, and consequently the price of securities *will rise*. The very expectation of a rise tends to bring it about. Similarly, if people expect the price of securities to fall, they will become more eager to sell securities and to acquire money, and therefore the price of securities *will fall*. This is what we mean when we say that anticipations are *self-justified*. The very fact that a certain thing is anticipated by a large number of people tends to bring it about. This accounts for the great magnitude of the ups and downs on the stock market, although there are also other causes at work.

The Bull Market

If for some reason people expect the prices of securities to rise, rise they will. Suppose now that people find in the fulfillment of their expectations justification for believing in the continuance of the rise. Then the continued belief in a future rise in prices will cause prices to rise still further. This is the phenomenon known as a *bull market*. The New York Stock Exchange between 1927 and 1929 provides a good example. Prices rise because people think they are going to rise, and people think they are going to rise because they are rising. However, prices cannot go up forever, and the time must eventually come, even in the most bullish of bull markets, when people in large numbers begin to doubt whether the rise can continue. The moment they do this, they will wish to sell securities and to acquire money, for now it is money, not securities, which is expected to appreciate in value.

The Bear Market

Now take the reverse condition. Because prices have fallen, people expect them to fall further. Hence the desire to sell securities grows as prices drop, and prices will go on dropping until people believe that they can go no further. Then when prices are so low that most people believe they cannot fall further, the drop will be checked. A new rise may then begin, and the vicious cycle starts all over again.[3]

[3] The "market identity" provides a convenient way of expressing the phenomenon of the securities market. If S is the quantity of any given security and M is the quantity

Fluctuations Due to Predominance of Speculation

Here is an example of speculation—i.e., arbitrage through time—failing utterly to perform its proper function. Instead of smoothing out the fluctuations of prices, as it does usually in the case of commodity markets, it leads to an increase in their amplitude. Whether speculation does one or the other depends mainly on the relative importance of the speculative as against the use motive among the traders. In commodity markets, on the whole, use motives predominate, with some exceptions; in security and money markets speculative motives frequently predominate.

The Flight from the Market

In the twentieth century market institutions have been unpopular and subject to political attack and have declined somewhat in importance as a result. The most spectacular example of the *flight from the market* is seen in Communist countries, where the market has been reduced to a relatively peripheral organizer of social life, and major allocational decisions are made through a centralized budget and plan. Even in the West, however, there has been a tendency to substitute government pricing and controls for the market mechanism. The decline in the futures contract is especially noticeable. In agricultural commodity markets, especially, price supports—government obligations by commodity purchase to prevent the price's fall below a certain level—have led to a decline in the importance of the futures contract. In the foreign exchange market exchange control is almost universal, and a free market in foreign exchange is a rarity. In the securities market short selling and margin buying have been curtailed by regulation, at least in the United States, though speculative movements in the stock market are still troublesome.

Much of the dissatisfaction with the free market must be attributed to the instability of prices in it. There is a real question, however, as to the extent to which governmentally supported and regulated markets can be made sensitive to changing conditions. The mere fact that the state takes over the task of price stabilization does not mean that the risks of faulty pricing are eliminated; it merely means that the losses due to faulty

---

of money in the possession of the people in the market, and if r_m is the preferred liquidity ratio and r_s the preferred security ratio, then we have, as on page 121, the price of the security, $p_s = \dfrac{M r_s}{S r_m}$. An improvement in the *quality* of a security—i.e., an optimistic change in the expectations of future receipts from it—will increase r_s and so increase p_s. An increase in liquidity preference—i.e., an increased desire to hold money—increases r_m and so diminishes p_s. An increase in M or a decrease in S, other things being equal, will increase p_s. The principle of self-justifying anticipations arises because the expectation of a rise in p_s will of itself increase r_s and so will increase p_s: if, therefore, a rise in p_s creates expectation of a further rise, the further rise is likely to take place.

pricing no longer fall on those who have made the mistaken decisions but are spread in some rather arbitrary way over many groups in society. It is a moot point whether governmental pricing may not in fact lead to errors even more costly than those of the free market.

QUESTIONS AND EXERCISES

1. Construct definitions, in your own words, for the following expressions: (a) the gold standard; (b) the foreign exchange market; (c) the securities market; (d) bonds; (e) shares; (f) the futures market.

2. Suppose British capitalists lent a sum of £50,000,000 to the government of Argentina, to build a railroad, and suppose that the Argentine government spent half that money in buying equipment from the United States and the other half in paying Argentine labor. Trace the effects of such a transaction on the ratios of exchange between (a) pounds and Argentine pesos, (b) pesos and dollars, (c) dollars and pounds. Assume that there is a free market in all these currencies and that there is no gold or other standard.

3. Suppose the British government imposed a tax on all gold coming into the country. Assuming that both Britain and the United States were on the gold standard, what difference would this tax make to the operation of the foreign exchange market?

4. In 1934 the United States Treasury raised the price at which it offers to buy and sell gold from $20.67 to $35 per ounce. What effect would you expect this *devaluation* (as it is called) to have upon (a) the price of gold in London, and (b) the dollar-pound ratio in the foreign exchange market, on the assumption that Britain is on a gold standard, or that Britain is not on a gold standard?

5. Write a short essay on speculation.

6. "The price of a security can fall for two reasons: either because people have an increased desire to hold their resources in the form of money or because people have a lessened confidence in the future of the security." Discuss and explain this statement.

7. As long as the foreign exchange market is a free competitive market the national economic systems of the various countries will move together; a stock market boom in New York will tend to bring about a similar boom in London. Why, exactly? Trace all the steps in this process.

8. What common elements are there in the phenomena of the commodity markets and of the securities markets?

9. "A supply of commodities or of securities is the same thing as a demand for money." Explain carefully what is meant by "supply" and "demand" in the above statement, and illustrate by constructing an arithmetical example.

10. In 1946 the Canadian Exchange Control raised the price at which it bought and sold United States dollars from $0.90 Canadian to $1 Canadian. In the New York market the price rose only to about $0.97. Explain this difference carefully, in terms of the fact that the Canadian Exchange Control sold strictly limited quantities of United States currency.

CHAPTER 10

THE THEORY OF NORMAL PRICE

So Far We Have Assumed No Change in the Quantities of Goods or Money Possessed by Marketers. The analysis of the three previous chapters has been confined to a market in which the total quantity of things exchanged remained constant. That is to say, we have considered literally the exchange of goods for money, or of one money for another money, or of present money for future money, or of future money for future goods. We have supposed that in all these exchanges the final result is merely a change in ownership of the things concerned. In the wheat market, for instance, we have supposed that at the beginning of a day there is so much wheat and so much money in the possession of the marketers, and that at the end of the day some of the wheat and some of the money have changed owners. We have then considered what forces determine how much wheat and how much money shall change owners, and at what prices.

Now We Must Observe the Phenomenon of Flows on and Off a Market. Even in our previous discussion, however, we have not been able to leave the matter there, for wheat comes on the market and is taken off the market. It is this phenomenon of a *flow* of a commodity on and off a market which we must now consider. Where do new stocks of a commodity come from? The answer is, from production. The farmer grows his wheat and harvests it, the miner digs his coal, the ironworker smelts his iron, and so on. All these activities continually add to the quantity of the commodity in existence. Every time a farmer harvests a bushel of wheat, he adds one bushel to the quantity of wheat owned by someone. Every time the miner raises a ton of coal, he adds one to the number of tons of coal in the possession of the owners of coal. Stocks of commodities, however, do not merely accumulate; we do not produce for the purpose of piling up monstrous piles of stuff. Out of the stocks of commodities we are continually drawing, and stocks continually disappear. Where do they go? The answer is, into consumption. We burn coal, we eat bread, we wear out clothes, buildings, roads, and all the million and one things which we possess. This drain into consumption must constantly be made good from production. Indeed, the purpose and end of production, of the creation of new stocks of commodities, is to enable us to consume— that is, to destroy these stocks of commodities in a useful and appropriate manner.

PRODUCTION, CONSUMPTION, AND STOCKS

We must get a picture of the production and consumption of any given commodity—let us say, wheat—as a process something like the flow of water into and out of a tank. The quantity of water in the tank cor-

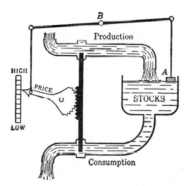

Fig. 22. How Price Regulates Production and Consumption

responds to the quantity of the commodity in existence at a moment of time—1,000,000,000 bushels of wheat, say, in the various storehouses of the world. From the production of farms wheat is constantly being added to the total stock; this corresponds to the flow of water into the tank. The flow is not of course regular, for at harvest time it is very large and at other times very small. However, we may call the rate of flow, averaged over a number of years, the *rate of production,* measured not in bushels but in *bushels per year.*

Wheat is also continually flowing out into consumption, corresponding to the flow of water out of the tank. This flow may also not be quite regular, though it will be more regular than the flow of production. The average rate of flow may be called the *rate of consumption,* measured also in bushels per year. Fig. 22 may help to visualize this process.

The Bathtub Theorem

A simple identity, which in the light of the above diagram I have somewhat frivolously called the *bathtub theorem,* relates production (P), consumption (C), and accumulation (A);

$$P = C + A \qquad (1)$$

We shall find this identity of crucial importance, not only in the theory of demand and supply, but also in (Volume II: *Macroeconomics,* Chapter 3). It can be stated also in the form;

$$A = P - C \qquad (2)$$

P is what is added to the stock; C is what is subtracted from the stock; A is the *net* addition to the stock. If consumption exceeds production, A is negative; if consumption equals production, A is zero.

The Equilibrium of Production and Consumption

There will be some level of A at which production and consumption can be said to be in *equilibrium.* This is the average level of accumulation, or the rate of increase in the stocks of a commodity, A_e, which just takes care of the need for increased stocks imposed by rising population or income. In a stationary society $A_e = 0$, in a declining society it may even be negative; even in an advancing society it will usually be a small proportion of annual production or consumption. For the sake of simplicity in exposition we will assume either that $A_e = 0$, or that we define consumption to include A_e. Then the condition for an equilibrium is that over the years the average rate of production and the average rate of consumption must be equal. If production is greater than consumption, the stock will grow continually by more than the general growth of the society requires. But a stock cannot grow forever. It is not merely that there are physical limitations on the growth of a stock of commodities, set in short periods by the capacity of warehouses. There are psychological limitations on the growth of such a stock, set by the fact that if the stock gets too large people cannot be found who are willing to own it. Our "tank" has therefore a limited capacity, and if more continually runs in than runs out, it will sooner or later be filled to overflowing. Similarly, if consumption is persistently greater than production over a given period, the stock must decline. But the stock cannot decline forever, for a limit is reached when the stock is reduced to nothing. If more runs out of a tank than runs in, the tank will empty itself until nothing remains. After that it is impossible for more to run out than runs in. Evidently, there must be some arrangement in our society whereby the rate of production of each commodity can be made equal to its rate of consumption.

THE NORMAL PRICE

In a free capitalist society this equalization of the rates of production and consumption is brought about through the effect of *prices* on these quantities. It is clear that in a general way a high price will encourage production and discourage consumption, while a low price will discourage production and encourage consumption. For each commodity, therefore, under given conditions, there must be some price which will make the rate of production and the rate of consumption equal. This price is called the *normal price*. It is not one which is necessarily present in any actual exchanges—i.e., it does not have to be the same as the *market price*. However, if the market price is such that, other conditions remaining the same, the rate of production of a commodity will be persistently above its rate of consumption, then the market price is *above* the normal price. At this price production is too much encouraged, consumption not encouraged enough, so that there is a persistent tendency for stocks to pile up. If, however, the market price is such that, other conditions remaining the same, the rate of production of a commodity is persistently *below* its rate of consumption, then the market price is below the normal price. At such a price production is too much discouraged, consumption too much encouraged, and the stocks of the commodity show a persistent tendency to decline. If the market price were equal to the normal price, however, and all other conditions remained the same, there would be no tendency on balance, over a period of years, for stocks of the commodity either to increase or to decrease, although of course there might be seasonal and other variations in short periods.

To return to our analogy of the tank, the price of a commodity may be compared to a valve regulating the flows of production and consumption, as in Fig. 22. If it is turned to high, the production flow is turned on and the consumption flow is turned off. If it is turned to low, the production flow is turned off and the consumption flow on. The normal position is that at which, in spite of seasonal or other spurts and jets, the tank over a long period shows no signs of draining away or of overflowing.

The mechanism relating the stocks and the price is illustrated in Fig. 22 by the float *A* and the bar *B;* as stocks rise, the float rises and depresses the price; as stocks fall, the float falls and raises the price. It is evident that a mechanism such as Fig. 22 is self-regulating, or *cybernetic,* the float acting as a governor. There will be some level of stocks, price, consumption, and production at which the system is in equilibrium. If stocks rise above that level, the rise in stocks will depress the price; the fall in price will shut off production and turn on consumption and so reduce stocks. A similar correction takes place if stocks fall below the equilibrium level.

Relation Between Rates of Production and Consumption and the Normal Price

In order to determine the normal price of any commodity, then, we must know what will be the rates of production and consumption at each of a series of possible prices. The table showing the rate of production at a number of hypothetical prices is called the *normal supply schedule*. The table showing the rate of consumption at a number of hypothetical prices is called the *normal demand schedule*. These schedules are illustrated in Table 16.

TABLE 16.   NORMAL SUPPLY AND DEMAND SCHEDULES

Price (per bushel)	Rate of Production (bushels per year, millions)	Rate of Consumption
$1.30	140	60
1.20	100	66
1.10	70	70
1.00	50	74
0.90	30	78
0.80	10	80

This table must be interpreted carefully. It should be read as follows: if the price of wheat were $1.30 per bushel over a considerable period of time, and if all the other factors affecting the production of wheat were to remain constant, then the production of wheat would eventually settle down to a rate of 140 million bushels a year. If the other factors affecting the consumption of wheat were to remain constant, the consumption of wheat would eventually settle down to a rate of 60 million bushels a year. So for all the other lines of the table. It is important to observe the phrase *if the other factors affecting the production (or consumption) of wheat were to remain constant*. Price is not the only thing, by a long way, which affects the production or consumption of a commodity. The prices of things which go to make it, the prices of commodities related either in production or in consumption, the temperament and tastes of the people, the incomes of the people, the techniques of production of the commodity in question and of other commodities, even the weather—all these things affect the rate of production and consumption of a commodity. Nevertheless, to separate out the effects of price, we must suppose that all these other things do not change, and then ask what happens when price alone changes. This is what we are doing in Table 16.

Determination of Normal Price

In Table 16 it is clear that the normal price is $1.10, for this is the only price at which the rate of production is equal to the rate of consumption, both amounting to 70 million bushels a year. That is, if the average market price over a number of years is $1.10, and other conditions do not change, there will be no persistent tendency for stocks of the commodity to pile up or to drain away, beyond what is needed, though they may show fluctuations from year to year.

Our next task is to consider by what mechanism the conditions affecting the normal price act upon the actual price in the market. Suppose that in the present example the market price is averaging around $1.20 over a considerable period of time. At this price the production of wheat is highly profitable, and the high price attracts many producers into the field. The rate of production settles down to 100 million bushels a year. The high price, however, acts to discourage consumption, and the rate of consumption settles down to only 66 million bushels a year. If the high price is maintained for some years, the rate of production will gradually rise and the rate of consumption will gradually fall until eventually production exceeds consumption by 34 million bushels a year. That is to say, this amount will be added each year to the total stocks of wheat. Now, as we have seen, the greater the quantity of wheat held by its owners, the less willing are they to buy it and the more willing are they to sell it. As the total stock of wheat rises, therefore, the market curves of most of the wheat marketers will fall, the total market curve will fall, and the market price will fall. So if the market price is above the normal price, it will not be long before the accumulation of stocks forces the market price down. And if the market price is below the normal price—e.g., $1 in Table 16— consumption will outrun production, the total stock of the commodity will decline, and the decline in the stock will raise the market price. The market price, therefore, constantly fluctuates about a level which is the normal price, for whenever the market price differs from the normal price a force comes into play to pull the market price back. Statistically, the "trend" value of the market price is an approximation to the normal price, for the normal price is that toward which the market price is tending.[1]

[1] It should be observed that the normal price is determined from the normal supply and normal demand relationships alone, and does not depend on the market equation

GRAPHIC ILLUSTRATION: NORMAL DEMAND AND SUPPLY CURVES. This principle can be illustrated graphically by plotting the price against the rates of production or consumption as in Fig. 23, where Table 16 is so illustrated. These curves are usually called *normal* demand and supply curves. It will be seen immediately that they appear very similar to the *market* demand and supply curves which were evolved in Chapter 7. It is important, however, to distinguish between them. Market demand and supply curves represent the relation between the possible prices on one "day" and the quantities which people will offer for sale or desire to purchase at these prices. The normal demand and supply curves refer to the relationship between possible average prices over long periods of time and the eventual rates of production and consumption which will be attained at each of those prices if other things do not change. In the case of market demand and supply curves it can seldom be assumed that the demand curve and the supply curve are *independent*. That is, any change in the market situation will nearly always affect *both* the demand *and* the supply curves, because generally speaking a market is not divided sharply into buyers and sellers but is composed of marketers any one of whom may buy or sell if the price is suited to his taste. In the case of normal demand and supply curves, however, it can often be assumed without difficulty that the curves are independent. That is, it is reasonable to suppose that there can be conditions which will change the position of the normal demand curve *without* changing the position of the normal supply curve. For instance, there might well be a decrease in the willingness of people to consume wheat, reflected in a shift to the left of the normal demand curve, which did not in any way affect the willingness of producers to produce wheat.

EQUILIBRIUM WHERE NORMAL DEMAND AND SUPPLY CURVES INTERSECT. We can interpret Fig. 23, then, as follows: *SS* is the normal supply curve and *DD* the normal demand curve. These intersect at *P*, the point where the rate of consumption is equal to the rate of production, both being equal to *OM* (= *NP*). The normal price is *MP* (= *ON*). If the average

---

relationship between stocks and price. Once the normal price has been determined, however, the normal level of stocks, W, follows from the market identity, $p = \dfrac{Mr_w}{Wr_m}$. If we rewrite this in the form $W = \dfrac{Mr_w}{pr_m}$ it will be seen that the exact relationship between W and p depends on the quantity of money and on the commodity and liquidity preferences. In the long run the commodity preference ratio, r_w, will depend mainly on the technical conditions of production, and especially on the average time interval between production and consumption; the longer this interval, the more necessary is it to hold stocks of the commodity, the greater will be the long-run value of r_w, and the larger the normal stocks of the commodity.

price over a period is greater than ON—say, ON_1—then the rate of production, N_1S_1, will be greater than the rate of consumption, N_1D_1. The difference, D_1S_1, is the rate at which stocks of the commodity are increasing. When stocks are increasing, however, the price will be forced down. But if the price is below the normal price—say, equal to ON_2—

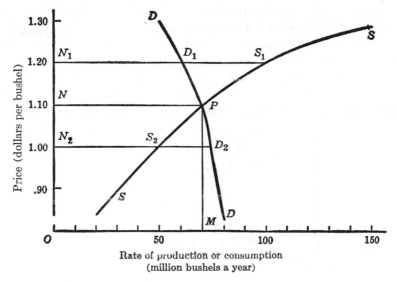

Fig. 23. Normal Demand and Supply Curves (Quantity-Dependent)

the rate of production, N_2S_2, will be less than the rate of consumption, N_2D_2. The difference, S_2D_2, is the rate at which stocks of the commodity are decreasing.

Supply Price and Demand Price

Another approach to the description of the equilibrium of normal price follows the lines laid down by Alfred Marshall.[2] In the above analysis we have treated price as the independent and quantity supplied or demanded, produced or consumed as the dependent variables. We have looked at the supply and demand curves as if they were the ends of a set of *horizontal* lines, each corresponding to the quantity produced or consumed at a given price. This is the method of Walras and Hicks.[3] It is also possible however to look at the same curves as if they were the ends

[2] Alfred Marshall, *Principles of Economics*, 8th ed., London, 1922, Book 5.

[3] Léon Walras, *Elements d'économie politique pure*, 4th ed., Lausanne, 1900. Translated by William Jaffé, *Elements of Pure Economics*, Homewood, Ill., Irwin, 1954; J. R. Hicks, *Value and Capital*, 2nd ed., New York, Oxford University Press, 1946.

of a set of *vertical* lines, each corresponding to the price at which a given quantity is produced or consumed. That is, we can regard the quantity as the independent and the price as the dependent variable. The price at which a given quantity would be supplied (or produced) is called the *supply price* of that quantity, and the price at which a given quantity would be demanded or consumed is the *demand price* of that quantity. The demand price can then be thought of as the price which will actually be obtained in the market for a given quantity; the supply price is the least price which a quantity would have to fetch in order for the production of that quantity to continue indefinitely.

THE MARSHALLIAN EQUILIBRIUM. Again it can be shown that the equilibrium position is where the supply and demand curves intersect. Suppose in Fig. 24 at the quantity OM_1, M_1D_1 is the demand price,

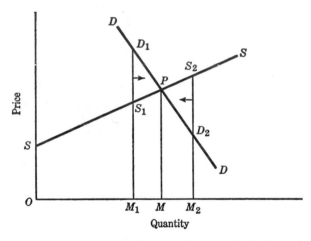

Fig. 24.   Normal Supply and Demand Curves (Price-Dependent)

which exceeds the supply price M_1S_1 by an amount S_1D_1. This means that if the rate of production is OM_1, M_1D_1 will be the price actually received, as this is the price at which the whole production can be sold, but M_1S_1 is all that is necessary to induce producers to produce this amount. The production of this particular commodity therefore will be unusually profitable, and will remain so as long as the demand price remains above the supply price. If however the production of this commodity is unusually profitable, its output will expand as new producers are attracted into the industry and as old firms expand. As the output expands, however, from OM_1 to OM the demand price falls and the supply price rises, and at OM the supply price and the demand price are equal. At this point therefore the industry is normally profitable; its output can be sold at a price which just induces the existing output to continue. Beyond the point M, at an output, say, of OM_2, the demand price M_2D_2 is below the supply price M_2S_2. This means that the industry is abnormally unprofitable, for its output is so large that it cannot be sold except at a price which is less than what would be required to make the industry normally profitable and so perpetuate the existing output. The output will therefore decline until again it reaches OM, where there is neither excess demand price nor excess supply price. The equilibrium is clearly stable.

The equilibrium positions of the price-dependent and the quantity-dependent approaches are similar, though not always identical, as we shall see later. In most simple problems the differences can be neglected. The dynamic assumptions of the two systems, however, are quite different. The quantity-dependent approach relies on the movements of price to reach equilibrium, and the price-dependent approach relies on the movements of quantity. In practice of course both may move; a disequilibrium situation may express itself both in movements of price under the impact of changing stocks, and in movements of output under the impact of changing profitability.

Effect of a Rise or a Fall in Demand

It is evident now that an increase in the willingness to produce or to consume will be reflected in our curves. An increase in the willingness to consume (called a rise in demand) means that *at each price* the rate of consumption will be greater than it was before. A *rise* in demand means, therefore, a movement of the whole demand curve to the *right*. Similarly, a fall in demand means a movement of the whole demand curve to the left, for a fall in demand indicates that *at each price* consumers are willing to consume less than before.

The effect of a rise or fall in demand, the supply curve being unchanged, is illustrated in Fig. 25. Let SS be the normal supply curve, DD

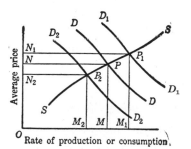

Fig. 25. A Change in Demand

the original normal demand curve. An increase in demand for the commodity in question would be indicated by a shift of the demand curve to a position such as D_1D_1. The normal price would increase from PM to P_1M_1, and the rate of production and consumption would increase from OM to OM_1. A decrease in the demand for the commodity would be indicated by a shift of the demand curve to a position such as D_2D_2. The normal price would then decrease from PM to P_2M_2 and the rate of production and consumption would decrease from OM to OM_2.

Effect of a Rise or a Fall in Supply

An exactly analogous concept is that of a rise or fall in supply, or in the willingness to produce. A rise in supply means an increase in the willingness of producers to produce, reflected in a willingness to produce more *at each price* than they did before. A rise in supply, therefore, is reflected in a shift of the whole supply curve to the right. Similarly, a fall in supply signifies a shift in the whole supply curve to the left.

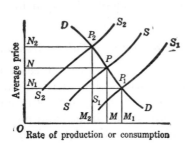

Fig. 26. A Change in Supply

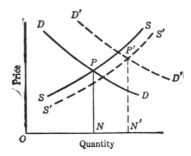

Fig. 27. A Change in Demand and Supply

The effect of a rise or fall in the supply, the demand being unchanged, is illustrated in Fig. 26. Let DD be the normal demand curve, SS the original supply curve. A rise in supply will be reflected in a shift of the supply curve from position SS to S_1S_1. The normal price will decrease from PM to P_1M_1; the rate of production or consumption will increase from OM to OM_1. A fall in supply will be reflected in a shift of the supply curve from SS to S_2S_2. The normal price will now *increase* from PM to P_2M_2; the rate of production or consumption will *decrease* from OM to OM_2.

General Method for Finding Effects of Shifting Demand or Supply

Any case involving shift in demand or supply curves, either singly or together, can be analyzed in a similar manner. To take a single example, suppose there is a large rise in demand coupled with a small rise in supply. The "original" demand and supply curves are *DD* and *SS* in Fig. 27, the "new" demand and supply curves are *D'D'* and *S'S'*. The coordinates of the point of intersection of the "old" curves, *P*, show the original price, *PN*, and the original volume of transactions at that price, *ON*. The coordinates of the point of intersection, *P'*, of the "new" curves show the "new" price, *P'N'*, and the "new" volume of transactions, *ON'*. In this case evidently a large rise in demand and a small rise in supply result in a rise in price, from *PN* to *P'N'*, and a rise in the volume of transactions, from *ON* to *ON'*. In all such problems a solution can quickly be found by comparing the coordinates of the point of intersection of the original demand and supply curves with the coordinates of the point of intersection of the new curves. This is the type of analysis known as comparative statics (see p. 70).

Changes in Demand Price and Supply Price

In the above section we have visualized changes in demand and supply as shifts in the curves to the right or to the left, indicating a change in the quantities demanded or supplied *at each price*. The same shifts in the curves, however, can be described as movements *up* or *down*, indicating changes in the demand or supply price of each quantity. Thus in Fig. 27 we see that the shift in demand from *DD* to *D'D'* is at once a shift to the right and a shift upward. It represents an increase in the quantity demanded at each price and in the demand price of each quantity. In the case of supply, we see that the shift from *SS* to *SS'* represents an increase in the quantity supplied at each price, but a *decrease* in the supply price at each quantity—that is, the shift to the right is also a shift downward. There is no inconsistency in this, for the shift of the supply curve represents an increased willingness to supply, and this can be described either as a willingness to supply more at any given price or as a willingness to supply any given quantity for less. The situation, however, is superficially confusing, and for this reason the student is advised to think of a rise in demand or supply as a movement to the right, rather than as a movement up or down.

Difficulties in Terminology

Certain confusions are apt to arise also because the terms *demand* and *supply* are often used, even by economists, in two senses. They may refer either to the whole schedule of prices and quantities—that is, to the demand or supply functions or curves—or they may be used to mean a single quantity demanded or supplied at a given price. Thus when we talk about a rise in demand or a rise in supply, we generally mean a shift in the whole curve or schedule to the right. In this sense we would say that a rise in demand causes a rise in price. Sometimes however we say (carelessly) that a fall in price causes a rise in demand. Here we mean by demand not the whole function, but the *quantity demanded.* We are thinking of a movement along a given demand curve, and not a movement in the curve itself. Similarly a large supply may simply mean that the quantity supplied happens to be large because the price is high, whereas a rise in supply means that the whole supply curve has shifted and that more will be supplied at *each* price. Confusion will be avoided if the student substitutes *demand function* or *quantity demanded* for the ambiguous term *demand,* and similar expressions for *supply.*

Description of Supply and Demand Curves

For purposes of describing the nature and properties of the supply and demand curves or functions, we need to be able to specify not only that price does affect the quantity demanded or supplied, but we also want to measure, at least roughly, *how much* a change in price affects the quantity supplied or demanded. There is a great difference between a commodity like salt, for instance, in which the rate of consumption is but little affected by the price, and a commodity like passenger travel on the railroads, in which a fall in price may result in a large increase in the quantity demanded.

THE ELASTICITY CONCEPT

In order to describe this characteristic of demand and supply relations, economists have invented the concept of *elasticity* of demand or supply. It measures the *responsiveness*[4] of the quantity demanded or supplied to changes in the price. We have already visualized the relationship between price and quantity as a causal one; a rise in price, for instance, calls forth an increase in the quantity supplied and a fall in price brings about a decrease. The elasticity measures the degree to which price is effective in calling forth or holding back the quantity. The relation between price and the quantity supplied is rather like the relation between a whistle and a dog—the louder the whistle, the faster comes the dog; raise the price and the quantity supplied increases. If the dog is responsive—in economic terminology, "elastic"—quite a small crescendo in the whistle will send him bounding along. If the dog is unresponsive, or "inelastic," we may have to whistle very loudly before he comes along at all. We need, therefore, a quantitative measure of this responsiveness of quantity to changes in price. One such measure is the elasticity.

---

[4] On p. 141 it was noted that in the case of the individual market schedule, price responsiveness could be measured by the amount by which the marketer will increase his purchases, or decrease his sales, for a unit fall in price.

The Measurement of Elasticity: Absolute Elasticity

There are two different measures of elasticity. The first may be called the *absolute* elasticity. Over a given range it may be defined as the ratio of the change in quantity to the change in price. Thus if a rise in the price of wheat from $1.20 to $1.30 per bushel reduced the rate of consumption from 66 to 60 million bushels per year, then the absolute elasticity would be $- \dfrac{66-60}{\$1.30-\$1.20}$ or $- 6$ million bushels per 10 cents per bushel. The negative sign simply indicates that price and quantity move in opposite directions. As we usually draw demand curves, with the price axis vertical and the quantity axis horizontal (an unfortunate conven-

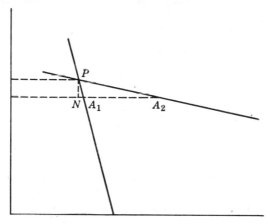

Fig. 28. Absolute Elasticity

tion, but one too firmly established to change), the absolute elasticity between two points is the reciprocal of the slope or steepness of the line joining them. Where the curve is a straight line (a linear function) the absolute elasticity is the same at all points. Where the curve is not a straight line the absolute elasticity differs over different ranges. The elasticity over a range is the *arc elasticity*. Between two points that are indistinguishably close together the elasticity is said to be the *point elasticity*. A steep curve is *inelastic*—a unit change in price produces only a small change in quantity; the quantity, that is to say, is unresponsive to changes in the price. A flat curve on the other hand is *elastic*—a unit change in price produces a large response in the form of an increase in quantity.[5] Thus in Fig. 28 PA_1 is an inelastic demand curve and PA_2 an

---

[5] Students whose wits desert them in examinations may find it helpful to remember that *I*nelastic curves look something like a letter I!

elastic curve. A unit fall in price, *PN*, causes a small increase in quantity, NA_1 in the first case and a large increase, NA_2, in the second case.

Relative Elasticity

The absolute elasticity concept is the one which is most significant in the application of supply and demand analysis to problems of comparative statics. For historical reasons, however, and because it is necessary to understand economists as well as economics, the student must also be familiar with the concept of elasticity introduced by Alfred Marshall, who invented the term. To distinguish Marshall's concept from that of absolute elasticity it may be called *relative elasticity*. Marshall[6] defined elasticity as the ratio of the proportional change in quantity (demanded or supplied) to the proportional change in price. The simplest way to visualize the meaning of the Marshallian elasticity is to define it as the percentage change in the quantity (demanded or supplied) which would result from a 1 per cent change in price.[7] If the relative elasticity of supply of a given commodity is 2.5, that means that a 1 percent increase in the price will eventually result in a 2.5 percent increase in the quantity supplied. If the relative elasticity of demand for a commodity is − 0.6, that means that a 1 percent increase in the price will eventually result in a 0.6 of 1 percent *decrease* in the quantity demanded.

Five Cases of Relative Elasticity

It is customary to distinguish five cases of relative elasticity.

1. A *perfectly elastic* demand or supply is one in which an infinitesimally small change in price will cause an infinitely large change in the quantity demanded or supplied. The elasticity, both absolute and relative, in this case is infinite.

2. A *relatively elastic* demand or supply is one in which a given change in price will produce a finite but more than proportionate change in the quantity. A supply is relatively elastic if, for instance, a doubling of the price will more than double the quantity supplied, or if a 1 percent increase in price will produce a more than 1 percent increase in the quantity supplied. The numerical value of the relative elasticity is between 1 and infinity. Algebraically, it is between + 1 and + ∞ in the case of supply, and between − 1 and − ∞, in the case of demand.

[6] Alfred Marshall, *Principles of Economics*, 8th ed., London, 1922, p. 102.

[7] This definition is open to some mathematical objections, which are treated in the Appendix to this chapter. It is, however, sufficiently accurate for all practical purposes, and it gains in clarity what it loses in accuracy.

3. *Unit relative elasticity* of demand or supply is found where a given change in price produces an equal proportionate change in the quantity. In this case, if the price doubles, the quantity supplied will double, or if the price doubles, the quantity demanded will halve. A 1 percent rise in price will produce a 1 percent rise in the quantity supplied or a 1 percent fall in the quantity demanded. The numerical value of the elasticity is 1. The algebraic value is $+1$ in the case of supply, -1 in the case of demand.

4. A *relatively inelastic* demand or supply is one in which a given change in price produces a less than proportionate change in quantity. In this case a 1 percent rise in price will bring about a less than 1 percent rise in the quantity supplied or a less than 1 percent fall in the quantity demanded. The numerical value of the elasticity is between 0 and 1. The algebraic value is between 0 and $+1$ in the case of supply and between 0 and -1 in the case of demand.

5. A *perfectly inelastic* demand or supply is one in which a change in the price produces *no change* in the quantity. The quantity demanded or supplied is completely unresponsive to changes in price. The numerical (and algebraic) value in this case is zero.

Relative and Absolute Elasticity Compared

If Δp is the change in price at the price p, and Δq is the change in quantity at the quantity q, then the absolute elasticity, e, is

$$e = \frac{\Delta q}{\Delta p} \tag{3}$$

and the relative elasticity, ϵ, is

$$\epsilon = \frac{p \Delta q}{q \Delta p} \tag{4}$$

We see immediately that the relative elasticity does not merely depend on the steepness of the curve, but that it gets larger as we move toward the price axis, smaller as we move toward the quantity axis, even when absolute elasticity is constant. Indeed, for any curve which cuts one or the other of the axes, the relative elasticity is always zero on the quantity axis ($p = o$) and infinite on the price axis ($q = o$).

Elasticity as Determining Effect of Change in Demand or Supply

With the elasticity concept we can now state two very important propositions in the comparative statics of demand and supply, roughly as follows: First, a given change in demand will affect the quantity more, and the price less, the more elastic is the supply. And second, a given change in supply will affect the quantity more, and the price less, the more elastic is the demand. These propositions will be stated more precisely in the appendix. Meanwhile they are illustrated in Figs. 29 and 30 for the five cases of relative elasticity. Thus in Fig. 29 we suppose

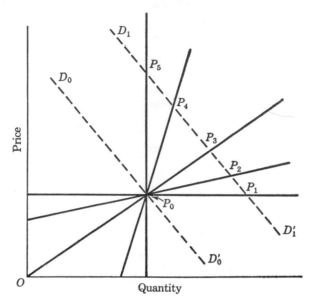

Fig. 29. Effects of Change in Demand

demand rises from $D_0D'_0$ to $D_1D'_1$. The old equilibrium is at P. Then if the supply curve, P_0P_1, is perfectly elastic, the new equilibrium is at P_1 there will be no change in price, and a large change in quantity. If the supply curve is relatively elastic, P_0P_2, the new equilibrium is at P_2, with a small rise in price, a fairly large change in quantity. If the supply curve has unit elasticity, OP_0P_3, (proof that the supply curve of unit elasticity goes through the origin, O, is given in the Appendix), there will be an equal proportionate rise in both price and quantity, from P_0 to P_3. If the supply curve, P_0P_4, is relatively inelastic, there will be a large change in price, a relatively smaller change in quantity. If the supply curve is perfectly inelastic, P_0P_5, there will be no change in quantity, and the whole result taken out in a large change in price, from P_0 to P_5.

Similarly in Fig. 30, we show a rise in supply from $S_0S'_0$ to $S_1S'_1$. With a perfectly elastic demand, P_0P_1, there is no change in price, a large change in quantity. With a relatively elastic demand, P_0P_2, there is some fall in price, but still a large change in quantity. With a unit relative elasticity of demand, as in P_0P_3, the fall in price is in the same proportion as the rise in quantity. With a relatively inelastic demand P_0P_4 there is a large fall in price, P_0 to P_4, a small change in quantity. With a perfectly inelastic demand, P_0P_5, there is no change in quantity, all the impact is in the fall in price, P_0 to P_5.

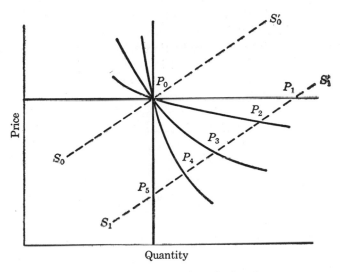

Fig. 30.   Effects of Change in Supply

FACTORS UNDERLYING DEMAND AND SUPPLY

It will not be possible to discuss fully the factors which shape the demand and supply curves until the analysis has been taken much further. Nevertheless, there are a few propositions of great importance in this connection which should be stated at this point, even if we cannot prove them formally.

The elasticity of demand for a commodity depends primarily on the extent to which *substitutes* are obtainable. If a commodity has good substitutes, a rise in its price will divert the expenditures of consumers to the substitutes, and their purchases of the original commodity will decline sharply. If its price falls, consumers who previously bought the substitutes will be attracted to the cheaper commodity, and their purchases will rise sharply. The demand will therefore tend to be elastic. If, on the other hand, a commodity has poor substitutes, consumers will be unable to respond to a rise or fall in its price, and the demand will tend to be inelastic. It is assumed that the prices of the substitutes remain the same. This assumption is necessary to the discussion of elasticity; for if the prices of substitutes change, the whole demand curve of the original commodity changes.

The elasticity of normal supply is an index of the ease or difficulty of changing the total volume of production of a commodity. Just as the elasticity of demand depends on the ease of substitution in consumption, so the elasticity of supply depends on the ease of substitution in production. If it is easy to turn resources at present engaged in other occupations into the production of a commodity, a rise in its price will result in a large increase in its production, for a good many resources will substitute the production of the high-priced commodity for their present employment. Likewise, a fall in price will cause many resources now engaged in the production of the commodity to turn to other employments, and there will be a large drop in its production. The supply is elastic. If, on the other hand, it is difficult for new resources to enter an occupation, or for resources at present employed in it to shift to other occupations, the supply will tend to be inelastic.

Changes in Demand or Supply

Changes in demand or supply are due to many factors. A rise in demand may be due to an increase in the intensity of desire for the commodity, as for ice cream in hot weather. It may also be due to an increase in the money incomes of buyers, for the more money a buyer has to spend, the more of any commodity is he likely to buy at each price. It may also be due to a rise in the prices of other commodities, and especially to a rise in the prices of close substitutes. If the price of beef rises, consumers are likely to buy more pork than before, at each price of pork. It may even be due to a fall in the price of complementary commodities the consumption of which assists the consumption of the original commodity. A fall in the price of automobiles, for instance, by increasing the purchases of automobiles, will increase the demand for tires and gasoline. In like fashion, a fall in demand may be due to a decline in the intensity of desire for the commodity, to a fall in money incomes, to a fall in the prices of substitute commodities, or to a rise in the price of complementary commodities.

An increase in supply may be due to a decline in the intensity of desire of producers for their own product. If milk producers decide to drink less milk themselves, the supply of milk will probably increase. It may also be due to a decline in the money costs of production of the commodity. If the costs of production of milk fall, more milk will be supplied at each price than before. A fall in the costs of production may take place either because of technical improvements or other economies, or because of a fall in the prices of the factors of production—e.g., a fall in wages or rents. A fall in the price of a substitute which is alternative in production may also cause the supply of a commodity to increase, for the production of the substitute will be less profitable and resources previously employed in making the substitute will turn to the now relatively high-priced commodity. Commodities may also be complementary in production, in which case the production of one assists the production of the other. Thus a by-product of cheese production, whey, is a useful raw material in the production of hogs. A rise in the output of a commodity will raise the supply of products which are complementary to its production. Thus a rise in cheese production is likely to increase the supply of hogs through the intermediary of an increased supply of whey. In like fashion a decrease in supply may be due to an increase in the desire of producers for their own product, to a rise in the costs of production, to a rise in the price of commodities substitutable in production, or to a rise in the output of commodities complementary in production.

QUESTIONS AND EXERCISES

1. From Table 16, page 172, derive an *excess consumption* curve corresponding to the excess demand curve of Chapter 8. What is the exact meaning of this curve? How can it be used to determine the normal price? Can you define the normal price in terms of this curve?
2. What will be the effect on the price and the rates of production and consumption, of the following?
   a. A rise in demand and an equal rise in supply.
   b. A rise in demand and an equal fall in supply.
   c. A large rise in demand and a small fall in supply.
   d. A small rise in demand and a large fall in supply.
3. Comment briefly on the truth or falsehood of the following statements:
   a. A rise in demand always means an increase in the elasticity of demand.
   b. If the consumption of wheat this year is greater than the consumption of wheat last year, the demand for wheat has either risen or it is inelastic.
   c. The demand for a commodity is elastic if a rise in the price causes a fall in the quantity demanded.
   d. If both the demand and the supply for a commodity were perfectly elastic, there would be no single normal price.
4. What would you expect to be the effect on the normal demand and supply curves for *milk* of the following?
   a. A decline in the birth rate.
   b. The discovery of a very superior breed of milch cow.
   c. A great rise in the price of beef.
   d. Increased taxation of the middle classes.
   Deduce the effects on the price of milk and on the rate of production and consumption of each of these four changes taken separately.

5. What do you think would be the effect of a great hurricane on the price of (a) firewood and (b) building timber?

6. Prove, with or without graphic analysis, the following propositions:

   a. A change in demand will cause no change in the price when the supply of a commodity is perfectly elastic.

   b. A change in demand will cause no change in the quantity supplied when the supply of a commodity is perfectly inelastic.

   c. A change in supply will cause no change in the price when the demand for a commodity is perfectly elastic.

   d. A change in supply will cause no change in the quantity bought when the demand for a commodity is perfectly inelastic.

   e. When the demand for a commodity is relatively inelastic, a fall in supply will increase the price and decrease the quantity supplied, but the decrease in quantity will be proportionally smaller than the increase in price.

   f. When the supply of a commodity is relatively elastic, a fall in demand will decrease both the price and the quantity supplied, but the fall in price will be proportionally smaller than the fall in quantity.

7. Discuss the following propositions:

   a. The causes which operate to produce a rise in demand will also usually operate to produce a fall in supply.

   b. Demands and supplies which are inelastic are less likely to rise or fall than those which are elastic.

8. Suppose we have a straight-line demand curve, such that when $p = 0$, $q = 9$, and when $q = 0$, $p = 18$. Calculate the relative elasticity of demand for values of $q = 0, 1, 2$ to 9, and tabulate. What is the absolute elasticity?

APPENDIX

THE MATHEMATICS OF ELASTICITY

Where the demand and supply curves are linear, with absolute elasticities constant, the comparative statics of changes in demand or supply can be stated in a simple formula. Thus, in Fig. 31, PP' is a straight-line

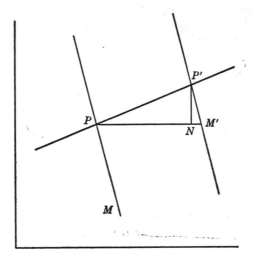

Fig. 31.   Elasticities and the Effect of a Change in Demand

supply curve, PM and $P'M'$, successive positions of a straight-line demand curve. P and P' are the successive positions of equilibrium. The increase in demand, ΔD, is measured by PM'—that is, the increase in the quantity that will be demanded at each price. The increase in output is PN; the increase in price, NP'. Then the absolute elasticity of demand, $e_d = -\dfrac{NM'}{NP'}$, and the absolute elasticity of supply, $e_s = \dfrac{PN}{NP'}$. Then we have

$$\Delta D = PM' = PN + NM' = e_s NP' - e_d NP'$$

whence the increase in price,

$$\Delta p = NP' = \frac{\Delta D}{e_s - e_d} \tag{1}$$

and the increase in quantity,

$$\Delta Q = PN = \frac{e_s \Delta D}{e_s - e_d} \tag{2}$$

Thus with ΔD and e_d given, the smaller is e_s, the larger is Δp, and the smaller is ΔQ. It is worth noting, however, that the effect of a given change in the demand curve depends on the elasticity of demand as well as of supply. The elasticity of demand, it should be observed, is negative, as an increase in price is accompanied by a *fall* in the quantity demanded.

The more elastic the demand, therefore, the larger is the numerical value of $e_s - e_d$, as e_d is a larger negative number, and therefore the smaller are *both* ΔQ and Δp. A similar formula applies to a change in supply. If Δp_r and Δq_r are the *relative* changes in price and quantity between P and P', then $\Delta q_r = \epsilon \Delta p_r$, where ϵ is the relative elasticity of supply. That is, the more elastic the supply, the greater will be the effect of a given change in demand in the relative quantity, and the less will be the effect on the relative price. Similarly it follows that the more elastic the demand, the greater the effect of a given change in supply on the relative quantity, and the less the effect on the relative price.

THE MATHEMATICS OF RELATIVE ELASTICITY

In economic literature, since Alfred Marshall introduced the concept which I have called *relative elasticity*, it is to the relative concept that the word elasticity usually refers. In many ways this is unfortunate, as for purposes of comparative statics it is the absolute, not the relative elasticities which are most significant. Marshall was apparently influenced by the desire to have a measure which would be without economic dimensions; this however is a matter of mathematical aesthetics rather than usefulness, for there are no difficulties in the use of parameters which have dimensionality if the units are specified and, indeed, we use such measures all the time. The relative elasticity concept could therefore be dispensed with entirely with very little loss, and it has caused a lot of quite unnecessary difficulty to beginning students of the subject. The more advanced student however must master this concept if he is not to be misled by the use of the term in the literature of economics.

Relative Elasticity of Supply

A simple geometrical construction will show at once whether a supply curve at any point is relatively elastic, relatively inelastic, or has unit elasticity. All that is necessary is to draw the tangent to the curve at the point in question. If this tangent passes through the origin, the supply curve at the point of tangency has unit elasticity. If the tangent cuts the vertical (price) axis, the curve is relatively elastic. If the tangent cuts the horizontal (quantity) axis, the curve is relatively inelastic. Thus Fig. 32 shows a supply curve, QPR. At point Q the elasticity of supply is greater than 1, i.e., the curve is relatively elastic, for the tangent QH cuts the price axis, OY. At point P the curve has unit elasticity of supply, for the tangent at P, OP, goes through the origin, O. At point R the elasticity of supply is less than 1, i.e., the supply is relatively inelastic, for the tangent RK cuts the quantity axis, OX.

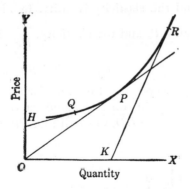

Fig. 32. Relative Elasticity of Supply

The proof of these propositions is contained in Fig. 33. PP' represents a small linear segment of a supply curve. The relative elasticity of supply, e, at point P is the *relative* increase in the quantity supplied divided by the *relative* increase in price. Draw perpendiculars PN, $P'N'$ to meet the axis OX at N and N'. Let $P'P$ be produced to meet the axis OY at H. Drop perpendiculars HK to PN, and PK' to $P'N'$. Then

$$e = \frac{\dfrac{NN'}{ON}}{\dfrac{K'P'}{NP}} = \frac{PK'}{K'P'} \cdot \frac{NP}{ON} = \frac{HK}{KP} \cdot \frac{NP}{HK} = \frac{NP}{KP}$$

for $NN' = PK'$, $ON = HK$, and by the properties of similar triangles $\dfrac{PK'}{K'P'} = \dfrac{HK}{KP}$. In Fig. 33A, where OH is positive, $\dfrac{NP}{KP}$ is greater than 1, for NP is greater than KP. In Fig. 33B, H coincides with O, and K

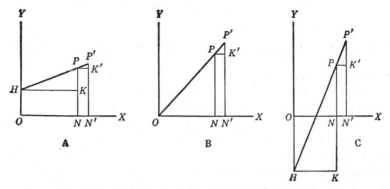

Fig. 33. Proof of Elasticity Propositions

with N. $KP = NP$, and the elasticity is unity. In Fig. 33C, OH is negative, KP is greater than NP, and the elasticity, $\dfrac{NP}{KP}$, is less than 1.

Relative Elasticity of Demand

Fig. 34 shows a simple geometrical method for finding the relative elasticity of demand at any point on a demand curve. Let PP' be a small segment of the demand curve DD, so small that PP' can be taken to be a

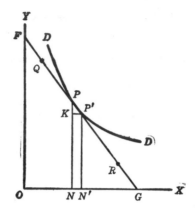

Fig. 34.   Relative Elasticity of Demand

straight line. Then the relative elasticity of demand, ϵ, is again equal to the relative change in quantity divided by the relative change in price. That is,

$$\epsilon = \frac{\dfrac{NN'}{ON}}{\dfrac{PK}{NP}} = \frac{KP'}{PK} \cdot \frac{NP}{ON} = \frac{NG}{PN} \cdot \frac{NP}{ON} = \frac{NG}{NO} = \frac{PG}{PF}$$

for $NN' = KP'$, and by the properties of similar triangles $\dfrac{KP'}{PK} = \dfrac{NG}{PN}$.

FG is the tangent to the demand curve at the point P.

To find whether a demand curve is relatively elastic or relatively inelastic at any point, P, then, we draw the tangent at that point, cutting the price axis at F and the quantity axis at G. Then if PG is longer than PF the demand is relatively elastic. If PG is shorter than PF the demand is inelastic. If PG is equal to PF the elasticity of demand is unity. A demand curve of unit elasticity throughout would be a rectangular hyperbola. We should not ordinarily expect, however, to find demand curves with constant elasticity over any considerable portion of their length. Any demand curve is bound to intercept both axis, for there must be some price, be it ever so high, at which no quantity of the commodity will be bought, and even at a zero price only a finite quantity will be bought. In such a case the demand will be relatively elastic near the price axis—i.e., at high prices—and relatively inelastic near the quantity axis— i.e., at low prices. Suppose that *FG* in Fig 34 represented a straight-line demand curve. At point *Q* the elasticity of demand is equal to $\dfrac{QG}{QF}$, and is clearly greater than 1. At point *R* the elasticity demand is $\dfrac{RG}{RF}$, and is clearly less than 1. At a point which bisects line *FG* the elasticity of demand will be unity.

The Calculus

The demand curve can be represented algebraically by a functional relationship between the price, *p*, and the quantity which people will buy at each price, *q*. Thus

$$q = F(p) \tag{1}$$

The elasticity of demand, ϵ, is given by the formula

$$\epsilon = \frac{\dfrac{dq}{q}}{\dfrac{dp}{p}} = \frac{p}{q} \cdot \frac{dq}{dp} \tag{2}$$

In the case of demand the derivative $\dfrac{dq}{dp}$ is almost invariably negative; i.e., a rise in prise brings about a fall in the quantity demanded; ϵ, therefore, is also negative.

Solving the differential equation (2) we have, as the equation of a demand curve of constant elasticity, ϵ,

$$p^{-\epsilon}q = \text{Constant} \tag{3}$$

In the case of unit elasticity of demand $\epsilon = -1$, and equation (3) becomes

$$pq = \text{Constant} \tag{4}$$

This is the equation of a rectangular hyperbola. From this equation we see immediately that when the elasticity of demand is unity the total value of what is bought *(pq)* is independent of the price or the quantity.

The supply curve can also be represented by equation (1), and the elasticity of supply by equation (2), if q now represents the quantity which people will produce or offer for sale at price p. The derivative $\dfrac{dq}{dp}$ and the elasticity e are now positive, i.e., a rise in price encourages production. The solution of equation (2) may be written:

$$q = Kp^e \tag{5}$$

This is the equation of a supply curve of constant elasticity, e. If the supply curve has unit elasticity this equation becomes

$$q = Kp \tag{6}$$

The curve is then a straight line passing through the origin.

The definition of elasticity given by formula (2) shows what is known as the *point* elasticity. The definition on page 182 defines an *arc* elasticity —i.e., an elasticity over a certain range of values of price and quantity, or over a certain arc of the demand curve. In general terms we may define the arc elasticity between the values p, q, and $p + \Delta p$, $q + \Delta q$, in any one of four possible ways:

$$
\left.
\begin{array}{l}
\text{(i)} \quad \dfrac{p}{q} \cdot \dfrac{\Delta q}{\Delta p} \\[2ex]
\text{(ii)} \quad \dfrac{p + \Delta p}{q} \cdot \dfrac{\Delta q}{\Delta p} \\[2ex]
\text{(iii)} \quad \dfrac{p}{q + \Delta q} \cdot \dfrac{\Delta q}{\Delta p} \\[2ex]
\text{(iv)} \quad \dfrac{p + \Delta p}{q + \Delta q} \cdot \dfrac{\Delta q}{\Delta p}
\end{array}
\right\} \tag{7}
$$

The ambiguity arises because we can measure a *proportional* change with reference to either the original or the final value of the variable. If, for instance, a price changes from 50 to 60, we could reckon this change as either a change of 10 on 50, or 20 percent, or a change of 10 on 60, or $16\frac{2}{3}$ percent. The smaller the absolute change, the smaller the difference between the two modes of reckoning. It does not matter very much which of the four formulas we choose. Formulas (ii) and (iii), however, have the virtue that a unit arc elasticity of demand gives a constant total value, as does a unit point elasticity. For if the elasticity in formulas (ii) and (iii) is -1, we have: $p\Delta q + q\Delta p + \Delta p\Delta q = 0$, and therefore $(p + \Delta p)(q + \Delta q) = pq$.

QUESTIONS AND EXERCISES

1. a. Prove that any demand curve which intersects the axes cannot have constant elasticity throughout.

   b. Prove that at a price so high that no quantity is bought, the demand is perfectly elastic, and that at zero price the demand is perfectly inelastic.

   c. Prove that any supply curve which is a straight line passing through the origin has unit elasticity, no matter how steep it is.

2. The following is a demand schedule:

Price:	20	30	40	50
Quantity:	100	80	60	40

   Calculate the arc elasticity in each of the three ranges of the schedule, by each of the four formulas in equation (7).

   Assume that the schedule represents a straight-line demand curve with the equation (p = price, q = quantity), $2p + q = 140$. Calculate the point elasticity from equation (2), page 193, at the intermediate points of the three ranges shown—i.e., at $p = 25$, $q = 90$; $p = 35$, $q = 70$; and $p = 45$, $q = 50$.

   Tabulate all the results for purposes of comparison.

3. Suppose we have straight-line demand and supply curves, with absolute elasticities of 1000 bushels per dollar per bushel for supply and -100 bushels per dollar per bushel for demand. Suppose now that there is a rise in demand of 1100 bushels at each price. How great will be (a) the change in price (b) the change in the quantity produced or consumed? What assumptions are made in this problem?

CHAPTER 11

APPLICATIONS OF SUPPLY AND DEMAND ANALYSIS

Relative Elasticity and Change in Total Value

The concept of relative elasticity has one significant use. The classification of demand curves into those with relative elasticity greater than,
equal to, or less than one is important in regard to the impact of changes
in price or quantity on the *total value* of the commodity produced or
consumed, or on the total revenue derived from its sale. The total
value of production (or consumption) is the quantity produced (or consumed) multiplied by the price. The total revenue from sales is likewise
the total quantity sold multiplied by the price. When the relative
elasticity of demand is numerically greater than 1, a fall in price is
associated with a more than proportionate rise in quantity. Hence a fall
in price (or a rise in quantity) is associated with a *rise* in the total value
or revenue. Thus suppose the original price and quantity were $2 per
bushel and 100 bushels. The total value or revenue would be $200.
Now suppose the price falls to $1.90 but the quantity expands in a
greater proportion—say, to 120 bushels. The rise in quantity more than
compensates for the fall in price, and total revenue rises from $200 to
$228 (1.90 × 120).

Similarly, when the relative elasticity of demand is numerically less
than 1 a fall in price is associated with a *less* than proportionate rise in
quantity, and the total value or revenue falls. If in the above example
the fall in price from $2 to $1.90 produced a rise in quantity only from
100 to 104 bushels, total revenue would *fall* from $200 to $197.60. If
the elasticity is exactly 1, a fall in price is associated with an equal
proportional rise in quantity which just compensates for the fall in
price, and total value or revenue is unaffected.

Illustration by Graphs

These principles are illustrated graphically in Fig. 35. Figure 35A shows an elastic demand curve. A fall in price from ON_1 *to* OH_1 results in an increase in the quantity bought from OM_1 to OK_1. The value of the amount purchased, or the total amount of money spent, at the price ON_1 is $N_1P_1 \times P_1M_1$, or the area $OM_1P_1N_1$. The total amount of money spent at the price OH_1 is $H_1Q_1 \times Q_1K_1$, or the area $OK_1Q_1H_1$. The latter area is clearly greater than the former.

Fig. 35B shows a demand curve of unit elasticity. As before, at a price of ON_2 the total amount spent is equal to the area $OM_2P_2N_2$, and at a price of OH_2 the total amount spent is $OK_2Q_2H_2$. In this case these two areas are equal.

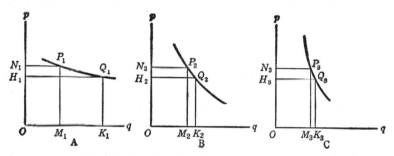

Fig. 35. Relative Elasticity and Gross Income

Fig. 35C shows a demand curve which is relatively inelastic. As before, at a price of ON_3 the total amount spent is equal to the area $OM_3P_3N_3$, and at a price of OH_3 the total amount spent is equal to $OK_3Q_3H_3$. In this case the latter area is clearly less than the former.

Practical Application

PERISHABLE CROPS. This discussion may have seemed abstract. Nevertheless, it is of the utmost importance—especially to the farmer. For it means that if the demand for his product is relatively inelastic, a good harvest with a large crop may actually bring in less money than a poor harvest with a small crop; the good harvest may be a disaster for farmers in general. This is particularly so with perishable commodities, of which the whole crop must be sold at the time of the harvest. Suppose, for instance, that Fig. 35C represented the demand for strawberries, that in one year the harvest was OM_3, and in the next year it was slightly larger—say, OK_3. If the whole harvest had to be sold, so that the supply curves were perfectly inelastic in each year, the price in the

first year would be ON_3, and in the second year OH_3. The good harvest
would have resulted in a smaller total value of the crop, and therefore
a smaller total gross income for the strawberry farmers. If the demand
for strawberries had been as represented in Fig. 35B, the total value of
the crop would have been quite independent of its quantity. If the
demand had been elastic, as in Fig. 35A, a good crop would have brought
in a greater gross return than a poor crop.

STORABLE CROPS. Crops which can be stored, such as wheat, are less
likely to have a relatively inelastic demand, for here the demand in any
one year comes not only from consumers but also from speculators.
Consequently, even though a fall in the price of wheat in any one year
may not greatly encourage consumption, it will encourage purchases by
speculators. The demand for a single year's wheat crop is therefore likely
to be relatively elastic. But even in this case the demand over, say,
ten years may be relatively inelastic.

THE STABILITY OF PRICES

Another problem on which supply and demand analysis can throw
considerable light is that of the stability of prices. We have already
seen (page 184) that a change in demand will cause a large change in
price if the supply is inelastic and a small change in price if the supply
is elastic. We also saw that a change in supply will cause a large change
in price if the demand is inelastic and a small change in price if the
demand is elastic. Now, a change in the equilibrium price can come
about only as a result of a change in demand, in supply, or in both.
It follows that the greater the elasticity of both demand and supply, the
less chance will there be of wide fluctuations in price. If both demand
and supply are highly elastic, then a change in either demand or supply,
or both, will result in only a small change in price. If demand and
supply are highly inelastic, then a change in either, or both, will result
in a large change in the price. This proposition is illustrated in Fig. 36.
Figure 36A shows the effect of a change in both demand (from DD to
$D'D'$) and supply (from SS to $S'S'$), when both demand and supply
curves are elastic. The fall in price (from PN to $P'N'$) is a small one.
Figure 36B shows the corresponding effect when both demand and supply
curves are inelastic. The fall in price in this case is clearly much larger.

Verbal Proof

It is not enough, of course, to follow the argument "on the curves."
Indeed, at this stage the reader may well be warned against thinking
too much in terms of curves themselves and not enough in terms of

what they mean. The logic of the proposition, however, is clear. In order to satisfy, let us say, an increase in demand we should expect to find an increase in the quantity supplied. If this increase can be obtained easily—that is, if a slight rise in price is sufficient to call forth a large increase in the quantity supplied, supply being elastic—there will be no need for the price to rise much. But if the increase in the quantity supplied cannot be obtained easily, supply being inelastic, the price will have to rise a good deal in order to restrict consumption and encourage production. If the supply were perfectly inelastic, so that a

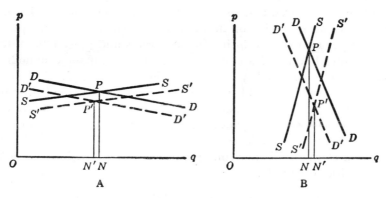

Fig. 36. The Stability of Prices

fixed quantity would be supplied no matter what the price, a rise in demand would force the price to rise to the point where the quantity demanded was the same as before.

Stability of Demand and Supply

It is evident from the above that the stability or instability of prices depends also on another factor, which we may call the *stability* of demand or of supply. A demand curve may be said to be stable if the quantity which would be bought at any given price is not much affected by changes in the factors which determine it, such as incomes, fashions, and the prices of other commodities. Similarly, a supply curve may be said to be stable if the quantity which would be supplied at each price is not much affected by changes in the factors which determine it. Commodities differ substantially in the stabilities of their demands and supplies. Necessities and conventional necessities tend to be more stable in demand than luxuries and fashion goods. Perishable consumers' goods also tend to be more stable in demand than durables.

Income Elasticity and Cross-Elasticities

No single measure of the stability of demand or supply can be given, as changes in the demand and supply curves are the result of changes in a complex and heterogeneous system of economic quantities. We can, however, define certain particular measures of stability relating the quantity demanded—price being constant—to income or to the prices of other commodities. Thus the *relative income elasticity of demand* may be defined as the percentage change in the quantity demanded which would result from a 1 percent change in money income—other quantities, prices, and the like being held constant. Similarly, the absolute income elasticity of demand is the change in the quantity demanded per unit change in income, all prices and other determinants held constant. The *relative cross-elasticity* of demand for commodity A with reference to commodity B is the percentage change in the quantity of A demanded which would result from a 1 percent change in the price of B, all other factors being held constant. Similarly, the absolute cross-elasticity of demand is the absolute change in the quantity of A demanded which would result from a unit change in the price of B, other factors held constant. Similar concepts can be developed for income and cross-elasticities of supply.

Relative Stabilities as Determining Price or Output Changes

The effect of any change in one of the other determinants of the quantities demanded or supplied, such as income, on the equilibrium price and quantity depends mainly on whether demand is more or less stable than supply with respect to the determinant in question. Thus, in Fig. 37, suppose that in each case D_0, S_0 are the demand and supply curves for some commodity when income $= I_0$; D_1, S_1 are the demand and supply curves when income $= I_1$; D_2, S_2 are the demand and supply curves when income $= I_2$, and so on. We suppose that

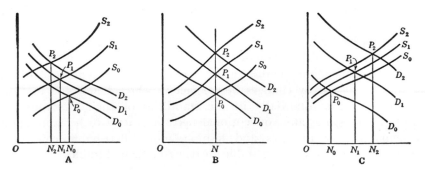

Fig. 37. Relative Stabilities of Demand and Supply

$I_0 < I_1 < I_2$. In Fig 37A we have supposed that the income elasticity (i.e., the stability with respect to income) of demand is less than that of supply. In other words, rising incomes affect the quantity supplied more than they affect the quantity demanded. In this case it is clear that rising incomes raise the price but lower the output of the commodity; at income I_0 price is $P_0 N_0$, output $O N_0$; at income I_1 price is $P_1 N_1$, output is $O N_1$, and so on. In Fig. 37C the reverse situation is shown, in which the income elasticity of demand is greater than that of supply. In this case a rise in incomes leads to a rise in the output as well as a rise in price. In Fig. 37B the income elasticities of supply and demand are equal. In this case it is evident that the effect of a rise in income is to raise the price but to leave the output unchanged. It is clear that the same type of analysis can be used to discuss the effect of changes in any other variable of the system—e.g., quantity of money, prices of other commodities. As we shall see later, this type of analysis is of great importance in the theory of money and employment.

PRICE FIXING AND STABILIZATION

Inelastic Demands Leading to Pressure for Stabilization

One of the difficulties of our present system is that many commodities, especially agricultural commodities, have rather inelastic demands and supplies, and therefore changes in the underlying conditions of demand or supply for these commodities cause quite disproportionate changes in price, with a consequent disruption of the flow of incomes. There is consequently much political pressure for a policy of stabilizing prices— especially agricultural prices—by government action. The so-called valorization schemes in tin, rubber, and coffee, the "ever normal granary" and the crop-restriction schemes of the New Deal, were all attempts to stabilize something, whether prices or incomes.

Most *stabilization* schemes in practice have also been concerned with another, and more sinister, objective than stabilization alone—that of obtaining monopoly prices and profits for their beneficiaries. Although the objective of stabilization is not necessarily inconsistent with the objective of monopoly profit, in practice the attempts to obtain monopoly profits without fulfilling the necessary conditions have frequently been responsible for the breakdown of schemes of stabilization. Indeed, a study of these schemes and their misfortunes is one of the best ways of demonstrating the necessity for economic analysis. We shall not take time to discuss the historical details. We shall, however, state some general principles.

The Failures of Price Fixing

The first principle is that any attempt to fix a price by authority, without control of either production or consumption, is doomed to failure unless, of course, the price fixed happens to be close to the price which would have been established in the unregulated market. History is strewn with the wrecks of such attempts at the fixing of prices. A government fixes prices when it passes a law forbidding any transactions in which the price is different from the one specified by the law. The result is that either the law is evaded or the transactions cease to take place— or the government is forced to interfere drastically with the production or consumption of the commodity. This is abundantly illustrated by the

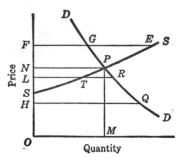

Fig. 38.   Results of Price Fixing

history of price fixing, for instance, during the World Wars. Many governments at first essayed to stop the rising price of foodstuffs by decree. What happened? In some cases commodities disappeared from the market altogether. If the price which the government fixed was below that at which the most efficient producer found that it paid to produce, then there was simply no further production.

GRAPHIC ILLUSTRATION.   This is illustrated in Fig. 38. *SS* and *DD* are the normal supply and demand curves; *ON* (=*MP*) is the normal price. Suppose the government made it illegal to sell the commodity at a price above *OH*. At this price producers would not find it worthwhile to produce anything, and although consumers would be willing to consume a quantity equal to *HQ*, this quantity would not be forthcoming and their desire would have to go unsatisfied. The commodity in this case would disappear from the market altogether, unless it was bootlegged.

Shortages

Now suppose that the legal maximum price is fixed at *OL*. At this price a certain amount, *LT*, will be produced. This is all that will be available for consumption. However, people will wish to buy more than *LT* at the price—in fact, they will want an amount equal to *LR*. What will happen? The first buyers will be satisfied. But after the early birds have bought all the available supplies there will be a number of people who would like to buy, who cannot find any of the commodity to buy, and who are prevented by law from doing the natural thing, which would be to bid up the price. The result is a *shortage*. Nothing perhaps illustrates better the function of prices in a free market than the difference between a *scarcity* and a shortage. If a commodity becomes scarcer in an unregulated market, the result is a rise in its price to the point where purchases accommodate themselves to the smaller amounts forthcoming. The commodity does not disappear from the market; stocks are always available for purchase by those who are fortunate enough to be able to afford the high price. If, however, the law prevents the price from rising to this equilibrium level, stocks disappear from the market as buyers snap them up faster than they are being replaced. Hence the commodity becomes available only at certain times, or certain places, or to certain favored people; for instance, it may come into the stores only on Fridays, or it may appear only in certain stores, or the storekeeper may keep it under the counter for his favorite customers. The rate of purchase is forced down to the rate at which the commodity is reaching the market not by the restrictive operations of high prices but by direct restrictions of one sort or another on the ability to purchase.

Rationing

Probably the most equitable method of direct restriction of purchases is *rationing*. The government issues ration coupons entitling every individual to just so much of the rationed commodity and no more. If rationing is to be successful, the total ration in any period must be about equal to the quantity coming on the market for sale. Purchases are then restricted not by the price, for at the controlled price we suppose that purchasers would wish to buy more than their ration coupons allow; the restriction of purchases is effected by the necessity of paying for the commodity not only with money but with the ration coupon as well. Thus, instead of some consumers getting all they can afford and others getting none, as in an unregulated shortage, most consumers get rather less than they would be willing to buy at existing prices but nobody needs to go completely unsatisfied. Rationing and price control are therefore a more satisfactory way of dealing with emergency scarcities, such as those created by war, than the method of allowing prices to rise freely; in the latter case the rich may bid the prices of basic necessities up to the point where they are out of reach of the poor.

Rationing, however, has difficulties of its own. Any attempt on the part of government to allocate commodities on a basis of *need* is bound to be very crude. Equal distribution is not equitable if needs are different. Consequently, once rationing is extended from commodities where needs are approximately equal, such as sugar, to more complex commodities such as gasoline, clothing, and the like, the system inevitably becomes more and more complicated, with different rations for different classes of people. The wider the field of rationing the more difficult it is to apportion successfully. Thus it is a recognized principle of food rationing that at least one basic source of calories, such as bread or potatoes, must be left uncontrolled, in order to enable individuals to adjust their caloric intake to their various individual requirements. The development of the *points* rationing system in World War II is an interesting further application of pricing principles. Consumers were given ration coupons (points) entitling them to purchase a whole range of commodities—e.g., canned goods or clothing—at "point prices" which were changed from time to time by authority as experience showed that consumption was outrunning production, or the reverse. In this case the ration coupon itself became a kind of supplementary money, and the price in terms of ration coupons rather than the money price performed the function of adjusting consumption to available supplies. The ultimate logic of such schemes would seem to be to have a special kind of money, issued to all persons equally, for the purchase of those commodities which are regarded as the basic necessities of life.

The Theory of the Black Market

An almost inevitable consequence of price control and rationing is the development of a so-called *black market*—i.e., an illegal market in which transactions take place above the legal price. Supply and demand curve analysis can throw a good deal of light on this phenomenon. The situation is illustrated in Fig. 39. *S* and *D* represent the normal supply and demand curves as they would be in the absence of any regulation. *PN* would then be the unregulated price. We now suppose that price control is imposed, and that *OR* becomes the legal maximum price. At this price only *RT* will be supplied; if buyers were free to buy without restriction at this price, they would buy *RV*. Conditions must develop, therefore, which prevent buyers from buying more than *RT*; i.e., there will be shortages or rationing. Now suppose that, as a result of the unsatisfied demand (measured by the quantity *TV*), a black market develops. We can postulate a black market supply curve, TS_B, lying to the left of the normal supply curve *TS*. As operations in the black market involve a certain cost and risk above what would be necessary in a free market, suppliers are not to be found willing to supply as much at each price in the black market as would be done in the free market; in other words, because of the higher costs, it now takes a higher price to call forth any given quantity than it did before. The higher the costs of black market operation, the steeper will TS_B rise. We can similarly postulate a black market demand curve, $T'D_b$. Even at the legal maximum price (OR) we may suppose that not all potential buyers are willing to buy in the

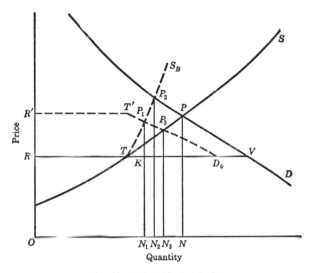

Fig. 39. The Black Market

black market, so that the quantity demanded in the black market at the price OR is not the total unsatisfied demand quantity, TV, but a smaller quantity TD_b. The higher the price, the less will be demanded in the black market, until at some price, OR', nothing will be demanded in it. Then the black market price is P_1N_1, and the quantity bought and sold in the black market is TK, RK being the total quantity in the legal and the black market combined and RT, the quantity in the legal market.

One or two interesting conclusions follow from the figure. The first is that the black market price may easily be less than the *normal* price which would have been established in a completely unregulated market, though it can be more.[1] The second is that the average price in the

[1] A. F. W. Plumtre has pointed out that the black market demand curve may rise more sharply than indicated here and cross the regular demand curve. In such a case the black market price might well be higher than the original price, See A. F. W. Plumtre, "The Theory of the Black Market: Further Considerations," *Canadian Journal of Economics and Political Science*, Vol. 13, No. 2, May 1947, p. 280.

legal and the black market together is likely to be lower than the
"normal" price, so that even if a black market develops as a result of
price control the resulting average price is less than that which would
have obtained in a perfectly free market. Only if the black market demand and supply were extremely inelastic could the reverse be the case.
The third conclusion is that the more penalties and obstructions placed
on the *buyers* in the black market and the fewer penalties placed on the
sellers, the lower the black market price is likely to be. If we suppose
that there are no penalties of any kind, legal or moral, attached to purchases in the black market, the black market demand curve will be the
same as the normal demand curve, DP_2. If at the same time there are
severe penalties on the sellers, so that the black market supply curve is
TS_B, the black market price will be high (P_2N_2). If at the other extreme
suppliers are quite unmolested and without any disabilities, the black
market supply curve will be the normal supply curve TS; if at the same
time penalties are placed on the black market buyers, so that the black
market demand curve is D_bT', the black market price will be low (P_3N_3).
The inference would seem to be that, other things being equal, it would
be better to penalize the buyers rather than the sellers in the black market
—the housewife rather than the grocer. Other things of course are not
usually equal; sellers may be more easily penalized than buyers, for
instance, and the political ease of penalizing them may more than compensate for the economic disadvantages. The results of economic analysis
must be supplemented by political analysis in any problem of practical
policy.

Fixing Prices Above Normal

At the other end of the problem we can illustrate, again with reference
to Fig. 38, what happens when some authority tries to fix a price which
is *above* the normal price. Suppose the curves on Fig. 38 represented the
supply and demand curves for coffee; suppose coffee could be sold only
by a single selling agency, and that the agency fixed the price at an
amount equal to OF. At this price the total consumption would be FG,
the total production would be FE, and stocks of coffee would pile up in
the hands of the selling agency. What, then, must the agency do? Either
it must destroy the surplus coffee or it must take steps to restrict production to an amount equal to FG—i.e., to prevent producers from supplying
as much as they wish at the price. The Brazil coffee valorization scheme
in the twenties chose to destroy coffee by dumping it into the sea.

TAXES AND TARIFFS

Another question on which supply and demand analysis can throw light is that of the effects of taxes and tariffs on particular commodities.

A Specific Tax

CONDITION BEFORE TAX IS IMPOSED.   Let us consider first the effect of a specific tax on a commodity which is produced wholly within the country imposing the tax. A specific tax is one in which a definite sum must be paid to the state on each unit of the commodity sold, no matter what the price of the commodity. Suppose, for instance, that cigarettes

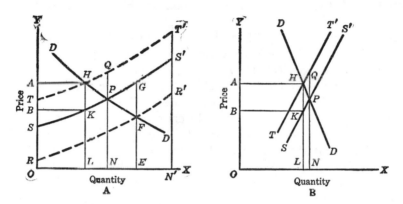

Fig. 40. Effect of Specific Taxes and Subsidies

were neither imported into nor exported from the United States, but were produced solely for the home market. In Fig. 40 the curve *DD* represents the relation between the price which the consumer pays over the counter and the quantity which consumers will buy at each price, in a given time. *SS'* represents the relation between the consumer's price and the quantity which producers and sellers would be willing to produce and sell in that same time. These curves show the situation before the tax is imposed. The price will be *NP;* the quantity produced and consumed will be *ON.*

CONDITION AFTER TAX IS IMPOSED.   Now let us suppose that a tax equal to the distance *ST* is imposed. The result is a "fall" in the supply curve *SS'*, which now moves to a position *TT'*. The significance of this movement should be noted carefully. It means that because of the tax, at any given consumer's price a smaller quantity will be supplied than before or, what is the same thing, that in order to induce suppliers to provide any given quantity, consumers must pay a higher price than formerly. Before the tax was imposed, when consumers paid a price equal to *NP,* a quantity *ON* would be forthcoming. Now consumers would have to pay a price equal to *NQ* in order to induce producers to produce a quantity *ON,* where *PQ* is equal to the tax *ST.* For when consumers pay a price, *NQ,* producers receive a net price, after they have paid the tax, of only *NP.* If, then, the paying of a tax does not in itself affect their underlying willingness to produce, a producer's price of *NP* will call forth from producers a quantity *ON* as before. As this is true for any output, the new supply curve, *TT',* will be such that at any output, *ON',* the new consumer's price needed to call forth that output, *N'T',* will exceed the old consumer's price needed to call forth that output, *N'S',* by the amount of the tax, so that *S'T'* must be equal to *ST.*

RESULT OF THE TAX. The result of the tax will therefore be to change the position of equilibrium from the point *P* to the point *H.* The output will decline from *ON* to *OL.* The price paid by the consumer will be *LH.* The net price received by the seller, after the tax has been paid, will be *LK.* When consumers have to pay *LH* they will buy only an amount equal to *OL,* and when producers receive a net price of *LK* they will produce an amount equal to *OL.* The fundamental condition of equilibrium, that the rate of production should equal the rate of consumption, is therefore observed. The result of the tax is a rise in the price to the consumer, a fall in the net price received by the producer. Unless either supply or demand is perfectly elastic the *burden* of the tax, as far as the net price paid or received is concerned, will be divided between the producer and the consumer. The consumer's price will rise, but by a smaller amount than the tax; the producer's net price will fall, but also by a smaller amount than the tax. This does not mean, however, that the real burden of the tax need be divided in this way.

RESULT OF TAX WHEN DEMAND AND SUPPLY ARE INELASTIC. The effect which the tax will have upon the *output* of the commodity will depend upon the elasticities of its demand and supply. The more *inelastic* the demand and the supply of the commodity, the smaller will be the fall in output caused by any given tax. This is illustrated in Fig. 40B, where the letters have the same significance as in Fig. 40A, but the demand and supply curves are highly inelastic. It will readily be seen from the figure that the fall in output, *LN,* in Fig. 40B is much less than in Fig. 40A. This explains why commodities with an inelastic demand or supply are best suited to taxation, for with a commodity of this type the tax will produce only a small contraction in the industry taxed, with little dislocation.

Subsidies

The effect of a specific *subsidy* or bounty, which is the direct opposite of a tax, can also be illustrated in Fig. 40. A subsidy, of course, is merely a negative tax. That is to say, instead of taking something away from the price paid by the consumer, the government adds something to that price. The net price which the producer receives will exceed the price which the consumer pays by an amount equal to the subsidy. The result of this will be that producers will supply a larger quantity at each consumer's price than before; i.e., the supply will have risen. The supply curve (Fig. 40A) will move from position *SS'* to position *RR'*, where at any output, *ON'*, the difference (*S'R'*) between the old price, *N'S'*, and the new price, *N'R'*, is equal to the amount of the subsidy. The new point of equilibrium is *F*. Under the warm sun of the subsidy, therefore, the total output will expand from *ON* to *OE;* the price paid by the consumer will fall from *NP* to *EF;* the net price received by the producer will rise from *NP* to *EG*. The difference between the consumer's price and the producer's price, *FG,* is the amount of the subsidy per unit of output. The more inelastic the demand and supply curves, the smaller will be the expansion of output. Subsidies will therefore be most effective in causing the expansion of an industry where the demand and supply curves are elastic.

An Ad Valorem Tax or Subsidy

We can also apply this analysis to the case of an ad valorem tax or subsidy. An ad valorem tax is one in which the tax paid on each unit of the commodity is not a fixed quantity but is some fixed proportion of the price of the commodity. The general sales tax is of this kind. It is a fixed percentage of the price of the commodity, so that the greater the price, the greater the amount of the tax paid. In Fig. 41, *DD'* and *SS'* are the original demand and supply curves for a commodity. *ON* is the

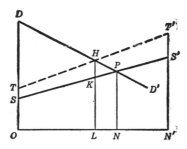

Fig. 41. Effect of an Ad Valorem Tax

output; *NP,* the price. Now suppose that a tax equal to 25 percent of the consumer's purchase price is imposed. This will mean, as before, that at any given consumer's price, producers will be willing to sell less than before, as they will receive not the price the consumer pays but this price less the tax. The supply curve, therefore, will move to the left, indicating a fall in supply, from position *SS'* to position *TT'.* To construct this new supply curve, consider first the meaning of any point *S'* on the old supply curve. It means that if consumers paid a price equal to *N'S',* producers would be willing to produce an amount equal to *ON'.* Now when the tax is imposed, a consumer's price of *N'T',* where *S'T'* = 25 percent of *N'T',* will result in a producer's price of *N'S'* as before. Consequently, after the tax is imposed, consumers will have to pay a price equal to *N'T'* in order to call forth an output of *ON'.* *T'* therefore is a point on the new supply curve. As *S'T'* is one-quarter of *N'T',* it follows that *S'T'* is one-third of *N'S'.* So in order to draw the new supply curve each price ordinate must be increased by one-third of itself.

EFFECT OF AN AD VALOREM TAX. The new point of equilibrium is *H;* the effect of the tax is to cause a decline in output from *ON* to *OL.* The consumer's price rises to *LH;* the producer's price falls to *LK.* The amount of the tax is *KH,* which is equal to 25 per cent of *LH.* The effects of an ad valorem subsidy may be analyzed in the same way.

Yield of Taxes and Expense of Subsidies

Our analysis also throws light upon the problem of the yield of commodity taxes. In Fig. 40, page 207, the total revenue produced for the government by the tax *KH* is equal to *KH* × *OL,* or the area of the rectangle *AHKB,* for this is equal to the tax per unit of commodity multiplied by the total number of units produced. It is evident from the figure that a given tax will be more productive of revenue if the demand and supply curves are inelastic than if they are elastic, for in the former case there is little shrinkage in production. The area *AHKB* is smaller in Fig. 40A than in Fig. 40B. Similarly, the expense of a subsidy will be greater, the more elastic the demand and supply curves of the commodity subsidized.

An interesting problem which can be solved if we know the demand and supply curves is that of the most productive rate of taxation. It is evident from Fig. 40A that the area *AHKB* will be small both when *KH* is small and when *KH* is large. There will be some intermediate value of *KH* at which the area *AHKB* is a maximum. This is the most productive tax rate. If the tax rate is greater than this value, the total revenue from the tax will be increased by reducing the tax—a phenomenon of not infrequent occurrence in the history of taxation. It can also be seen from the figure that the more inelastic the demand and supply, broadly speaking, the greater will be the maximum yield of a tax. It does not follow, of course, that the tax rate which gives the maximum yield is the *ideal* rate, for in evaluating the benefits of a tax the effect on the industry, as well as the revenue to the government, must be taken into consideration.

Effect of Tariffs

We can now go further and consider the effects not only of purely internal taxes but also of tariffs on specific articles. Suppose the world is divided into two countries, the United States on the one hand and the "rest" on the other. In Fig. 42A are the supply and demand curves

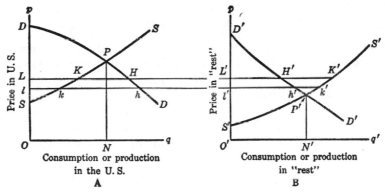

Fig. 42. Trade Between Two Countries

(*DD* and *SS*) of the commodity in question for the United States. In Fig. 42B are the supply and demand curves of the rest of the world, for the same commodity, *D'D'* and *S'S'*. It is important to see clearly what these curves mean. *DD* expresses the relation between the price which United States consumers have to pay and the quantity which they will buy at each price. *SS* expresses the relation between the price which United States producers receive and the quantity which they will be willing to produce at each price. *D'D'* expresses the relation between the price which foreign consumers have to pay and the quantity which they will be willing to buy at each price. *S'S'* represents the relation between the price which foreign producers receive and the quantity which they will be willing to produce at each price.

Conditions of Equilibrium in International Trade

We can then state the conditions of equilibrium as follows: (1) United States producers must be able to sell an amount exactly equal to what they are willing to produce. (2) Foreign producers must also be able to sell, to the United States or to foreign consumers together, an amount equal to what they are willing to produce. (3) The exports of the commodity from one country must be equal to the imports of it into the other country, for these are exactly the same thing. To say the rest exports 10,000,000 bushels to the United States is to say the United States imports 10,000,000 bushels from the rest. (4) If there are no internal taxes, the difference between the price of the commodity in the United States and the price in the rest of the world must be equal to the cost of transport per unit of commodity between them. This follows from the principle of arbitrage previously considered.

1. WITHOUT TARIFFS OR TRANSPORT COSTS. If there are no tariffs and no cost of transport, the price of the commodity in the United States will be the same as the price in the rest of the world. If this price is Ol, equal to $O'l'$, then from the curves it is evident that

lk = amount that would be produced in the United States at that price;
lh = amount that would be consumed in the United States at that price;
kh = rate at which stocks will diminish in the United States at that price,
    if there are no imports;
$l'k'$ = amount that will be produced in the rest of the world at that price;
$l'h'$ = amount that will be consumed in the rest of the world at that price;
$h'k'$ = rate at which stocks will increase in the rest of the world at that
    price, if there are no exports.

In the world as a whole, therefore, stocks will be diminishing at a rate equal to $kh - k'h'$. In this case, if the price is Ol, world stocks are evidently going to diminish; hence, as we have seen, the price must rise. It will rise to OL, where

LK = amount which will be produced in the United States;
LH = amount which will be consumed in the United States;
$L'K'$ = amount which will be produced in the rest of the world;
$L'H'$ = amount which will be consumed in the rest of the world;
$KH = K'H'$ = amount which will flow from the rest of the world to the
    United States.

At this price the United States will consume more than it produces, but the difference will be made up by imports. The rest of the world will produce more than it consumes, but the difference will be made up by exports. By moving the line lk' up and down parallel to itself we can find the place where $KH = K'H'$; this will give us the position of equilibrium.[2] It will be seen that relatively speaking the demand is

[2] A more accurate geometrical method for finding the equilibrium price is as follows: Construct the *total world* demand and supply curves by adding the quantities demanded and the quantities supplied in both "countries" at each price. The point of intersection of the world demand and supply curves gives the world equilibrium price.

smaller and the supply is greater in the country *from* which the commodity is exported than in the country *to* which the commodity is exported. This is what we should expect. We observe also that the price in the United States, *OL,* is less than it would be if there were no trade (*NP*), while the price in the rest of the world (*O'L'*) is greater than it would be if there were no trade (*N'P'*).

2. WITH TRANSPORT COSTS. Now imagine a condition in which there is a cost of transport. This is illustrated in Fig. 43. Here the curves and

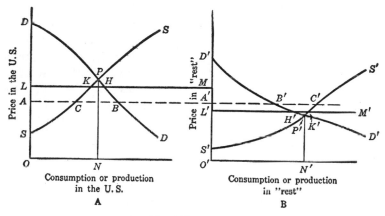

Fig. 43. Effect of a Tariff

symbols have the same meaning as in Fig. 42, except that there is now a cost of transport equal to *L'M* per unit of commodity. The price in the United States (*OL = O'M*) must now be greater than the price in the rest of the world (*O'L'*) by an amount equal to *L'M*. The equilibrium position is then the one illustrated in the figure, where *LK* and *LH* represent the production and consumption in the United States, *KH* represents the imports into the United States, *L'K'* and *L'H'* represent the production and consumption in the rest of the world, and *K'H'* represents the exports to the United States. *KH* must equal *K'H'* in equilibrium, just as in the previous case.[3]

[3] The following is a useful construction for finding the equilibrium price in this case. Let the price in the rest of the world be the *world price*. Construct demand and supply schedules for the United States in terms of the world price by subtracting the cost of transport from each U.S. supply price or demand price. Thus if the cost of transport is $3 per unit, and if at a U.S. price of $10, 100 units will be demanded, then as the U.S. price must be $3 above the world price, in this case 100 units will be demanded in the United States at a world price of $7. Adding together the quantities demanded and supplied in both the United States and the rest of the world at each world price gives us the world demand and supply schedules. The point of intersection of the world demand and supply curves, drawn from these schedules, gives the world price. The U.S. price will be higher than this by the amount of the cost of transport.

A Tariff as an Artificial Increase in Transport Costs

We can now see immediately what will be the effect of a tariff on imports (or a subsidy on exports). Suppose that originally there were no costs of transport, so that in Fig. 43 the equilibrium price in both countries was *OA,* or *O'A'.* The imports into the United States, *CB,* would be equal to the exports from the rest of the world, *B'C'.* Now suppose that the United States imposes a tariff, in the shape of a specific import tax, equal to *L'M* per unit of the commodity. *L'M* is then the *cost of transport* per unit between two countries, *OL* is the equilibrium price in the United States, *O'L'* the equilibrium price in the rest of the world. The results are evident from the figure. The volume of trade declines from *CB* (or *B'C'*) to *KH* (or *H'K'*). The price of the commodity in the United States rises from *OA* to *OL.* The price in the rest falls from *O'A'* to *O'L'.* Production in the United States rises from *AC* to *LK.* Production in the rest falls from *A'C'* to *L'K'.* Consumption in the United States falls from *AB* to *LH.* Consumption in the rest of the world rises from *A'B'* to *L'H'.*

Effects of a Tariff on Welfare

In a broad way it is evident that the interests of producers in the United States, and of consumers abroad, are affected favorably by the tariff. The interests of consumers in the United States and of producers abroad are affected unfavorably. The same result would be brought about by any increase in the cost of transport, whether due to an import tax imposed by the importing country, or to an export tax imposed by the exporting country, or to a change in the techniques of transportation. This analysis does not by itself give us sufficient information to pass judgment on any particular tariff, for it does not tell us how great are the benefits and losses involved. The very fact, however, that to discuss tariffs properly we must treat them as artificial increases in the cost of transport should make the tariff enthusiast pause. Tariffs, as Bastiat pointed out, are "negative railways." Just as railways are a device to lessen the cost of transport between two places, so tariffs are a device to increase it. A consistent advocate of tariffs, then, would at least prove his consistency if he were also prepared to advocate a return to the horse and buggy.

The Tariff and Elasticities

It should be observed that the effects of a tariff depend largely on the absolute elasticities or slopes of demand and supply in the two countries. The effect on the *price* of the commodity will be greatest in the country with the most inelastic demand and supply curves. In Fig. 43 for instance, the demand and supply curves for the United States are more inelastic than the demand and supply curves for the rest. Consequently, a relatively large rise in price in the United States, *AL,* is necessary to reduce imports to *KH,* when in the rest a relatively small fall in price, *A'L',* will reduce exports to *H'K'.* The effect on the quantities produced and consumed in the two countries will likewise depend on the elasticities of supply or demand. The more inelastic the supply curve, the smaller will be the change in the quantity produced. The more inelastic the demand curve, the smaller will be the change in the quantity consumed. If the supply of the commodity in both countries were perfectly inelastic, the imposition of a tariff would merely cut down consumption in the importing country and expand consumption in the exporting country, without affecting the volume of production at all.

Price Stabilization by Purchase and Sale Policy (Pegging)

Supply and demand analysis is useful in interpreting the effects of attempts to fix prices by a policy of purchase and sale by government or other authority. There are many examples of such policies. A monetary standard is essentially an undertaking on the part of some central authority to buy or sell the standard commodity at a fixed price in unlimited quantities. Any *pegging* operation, whether of foreign exchange rates, government bond prices, or agricultural prices, similarly involves an undertaking by some authority to buy unlimited quantities of the pegged item at the fixed price. Pegging generally involves purchase rather than sale by the authority, because the pegged price is usually above the price that would obtain in the free market.

An offer to purchase unlimited quantities at a set price represents a perfectly elastic demand for the purchased item. The effect is illustrated in Fig. 44. Suppose a law were to be passed compelling the Treasury

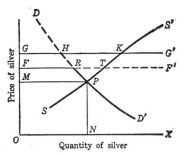

Fig. 44.   Effect of Treasury Purchases of Silver

to buy all of some commodity—say, silver—offered to it at a fixed price, *OF*. *DD'* and *SS'* represent the commercial demand and supply curves for silver. *FF'* is the Treasury demand curve. In the absence of treasury action the price will be *NP*, and the quantity put onto or taken off the market will be *MP*. Under the purchase policy, however, the demand curve becomes *DRF'*, the price rises to *OF*, a quantity *FT* is offered on the market, *FR* is taken off the market by private purchasers, and *RT* is the rate at which Treasury purchases will be made. If the Treasury price is raised to *OG*, Treasury purchases will rise to *HK*, private purchases will shrink to *GH*, and total output onto the market will rise to *GK*. Only if the Treasury price were *OM* would there be no Treasury purchases.

Assumption of Fixed Supply and Demand

In all this supply and demand analysis one word of warning must be given. We have assumed in these examples that the changes which have been considered do not alter the position of the supply and demand curves themselves. This condition must always be kept in mind, as in a great many problems it does not hold. If, for instance, the imposition of a tax on cigarettes actually made people dislike smoking because it was associated with the unpleasant act of paying taxes, we should have to modify our analysis. Again, in considering the effects of various changes, such as a tax or a tariff, through time, we must remember that the supply and demand curves are constantly changing as time goes on and conditions of tastes or of techniques change.

Difficulties in Dynamic Analysis

An even more important limitation on demand and supply analysis is apparent when we discuss the dynamics of the movements toward equilibrium, for the process of moving toward equilibrium may itself change the position of the supply and demand curves. If, for instance, a fall in price produces the expectation of a further fall, as we have seen on page 165, the demand curve itself may fall as people hold off purchases or consumption in the expectation of finding the commodity cheaper later. Similarly the supply curve may rise (move to the right) as suppliers seek to forestall the expected lower price by producing or selling now while the price is still relatively high. Thus as a price moves downward toward equilibrium from a position of excess supply (say from ON_1 in Fig. 23, page 175), the movement itself may push both supply and demand curves *downward* toward the quantity axis, and the equilibrium position itself retreats in front of the pursuing price. Similarly an upward movement of price from a position of excess demand may push the equilibrium price upward. These movements are of course only temporary; eventually the dynamic shift of the curves will slow down and the divergence between the actual and the equilibrium price will disappear. When this happens, however, the demand and supply curves themselves will revert to their normal positions and the process starts all over again, setting up what is called an *expectational* cycle. These cycles are discussed more fully later (Volume II, Chapter 8).

These dynamic effects are important in understanding the theory of price control for, in a basically inflationary situation, price control may operate not merely to suppress the symptoms and so create shortages; it may also destroy expectations of rising prices, and hence may lower the supply and demand curves themselves below where they would otherwise have been. The effect may be only temporary, and it will not be able to deal with great inflationary pressure, but it is an important element in the explanation of the success of price control, for example, in World War II.

It is evident that these modifications do not destroy the basic usefulness of supply and demand analysis. It must be used warily and with a constant sense of its limitations, but the simple equilibrium analysis always provides the base from which dynamic analysis must take its flight.

QUESTIONS AND EXERCISES

1. In our discussion, page 197, of the relation between the size of the total crop of strawberries and the price, we assumed that the supply of strawberries at the time of the harvest was perfectly inelastic. What do we mean by this? What conditions would we have to assume for this to be true? Is it likely to be absolutely true? If not, can you reframe the argument in terms of a supply curve that is not perfectly inelastic?

2. Prove that a tax on a commodity will raise the price to the consumer by the amount of the tax per unit if, and only if, the supply of the commodity is perfectly elastic.

3. Mr. Protectionist: "A tariff will not raise the price to the home consumer for, in order to sell his products, the foreigner will have to accept a lower price for himself."

    Mr. Free Trader: "On the contrary, a tariff will always raise the price which the home consumer has to pay by the amount of the tariff, for the foreign manufacturer must get his old price or he will not go on producing."

    Under what circumstances may (a) either one or (b) neither of these two statements be correct?

4. Suppose you were asked to draw up a system of duties on imports with a view to making as little change in the volume of imports or exports as you could. What kind of commodities would you choose to place the tariff on, and what kind would you leave free?

5. Suppose the Treasury was compelled to buy and sell silver at a price which was below the normal price of silver in the commercial market. What would be the effects, if any, of this policy?

6. Suppose that both Britain and the United States are on the gold standard, the price of gold in Britain being £12.5 per ounce and the price in the United States being $35 per ounce. Suppose that the cost of transport of gold across the Atlantic is $0.25 per ounce. Then show that in the foreign exchange market there will be a perfectly elastic demand for pounds at a price of $2.78 per pound, and a perfectly elastic supply of pounds at a price of $2.82 per pound. Show by means of a diagram (plotting the price of pounds against the quantity offered or demanded) that in such a case no matter what the *commercial* demand or supply of pounds, the price cannot go above $2.82 or below $2.78.

Repeat the proof in terms of the demand and supply of dollars.

7. Between 1942 and 1951 the U.S. Treasury supported the market in government bonds by buying bonds whenever the price fell below a level which would yield the rate of interest deemed appropriate. Illustrate the effects of this policy by means of supply and demand analysis.

8. Under the agricultural price support program, the Department of Agriculture found itself owning an unmanageable surplus of potatoes. In the following period price supports on potatoes were abandoned and yet potato prices were high. How do you explain these phenomena according to demand and supply analysis?

9. Suppose the following schedules represented the demand and supply schedules for a commodity in two countries, A and B.

Price (per ton)	Quantity Which Will Be Produced in A (million tons)	Quantity Which Will Be Consumed in A (million tons)	Quantity Which Will Be Produced in B (million tons)	Quantity Which Will Be Consumed in B (million tons)
$ 0	0	220	0	90
1	0	200	0	80
2	0	180	10	70
3	0	160	20	60
4	0	140	30	50
5	0	120	40	40
6	20	100	50	30
7	40	80	60	20
8	60	60	70	10
9	80	40	80	0
10	100	20	90	0
11	120	0	100	0

a. Calculate the *total* supply schedule, showing the quantities which producers of both countries together will produce at each price; also the total demand schedule, showing the quantities which consumers of both countries together will consume at each price. Draw the curves corresponding to these schedules and the four schedules of the table.

b. What would be the normal price in each country, assuming that there was no trade?

c. What would be the normal price in both countries, assuming that trade were possible without cost of transport? What would be the volume of imports and exports at this price? What would be the consumption and the production in each country, and the world totals?

d. Suppose the cost of transport were $1.50 per ton. What would then be the normal price in each country, the volume of imports and exports, of consumption and production, in each country, and the world totals? How much has world production changed because of the imposition of a cost of transport? What determines this change, if it occurs?

e. What would be the smallest specific tariff which would be prohibitive— i.e., which would cut off trade altogether—assuming that there is no cost of transport?

f. Why is the effect of an increase in the cost of transport greater on the price in B than on the price in A?

10. The price of a commodity is $1. Compare the results of (a) a specific tax of 10 cents and (b) a 10 percent ad valorem tax on the quantity produced and on the consumer's and producer's prices. Why do the results differ?

11. Suppose that e_s and e_d are the numerical values of the absolute elasticities of demand and supply for a commodity. Suppose a specific tax of T per unit is levied on the commodity. Then show that the decline in quantity, ΔQ is $\dfrac{T e_d e_s}{e_d + e_s}$. What are the formulas for the rise in the consumer's price and for the fall in the producer's price? Assume linear demand and supply functions.

12. Show that when the demand and supply functions are linear, the specific tax which maximizes the yield of the tax results in halving the quantity produced or consumed by comparison with a zero-tax situation. (Note: this proof is difficult without the calculus.)

13. Assume linear demand and supply functions, in the model of Fig. 43 or Exercise 9, of the form $q_{da} = Q_{da} + e_{da} p_a$, q_{da} being the quantity demanded in A, p_a the price, e_{da} the absolute elasticity. If t is the unit cost of transport, $p_a = p_b \pm t$. Write out the equations of this system and solve them for the unknowns; comment on the properties of the system, and on the impact of changes in the various parameters on the equilibrium position of the variables. Prove that a tariff or rise in transport costs will raise, lower, or leave unchanged the world output of a commodity, as $\dfrac{e_{sb} \gtreqless e_{db}}{e_{sa} \lesseqgtr e_{da}}$.

CHAPTER 12

FURTHER APPLICATIONS OF SUPPLY AND DEMAND ANALYSIS

THE STABILIZATION OF INCOMES

Stabilizing Price Does Not Stabilize Incomes

A more advanced problem in the theory of stabilization concerns the policy of a government which desires to stabilize not the *price* of a farm product but the *total value* of the crop. We can easily see that stabilizing the price of a crop through "time arbitrage" does not necessarily stabilize the incomes of the farmers. If the price of wheat were constant from year to year, then in a year of poor crop the gross incomes of wheat farmers would be low, and in a year of good crop the gross incomes of wheat farmers would be high.

Gross Incomes Constant Only if Elasticity of Demand Is Unity

If, now, the relative elasticity of demand for the wheat crop of each year were unity, this would mean that no matter what the size of the crop, the gross incomes of the wheat producers (i.e., the total value of the crop) would be constant. In years of small harvest the price would be just high enough to compensate for the smallness of the crop, and in years of good harvest the price would be just low enough to compensate for the largeness of the crop. If the relative elasticity of demand for the crop of any year, therefore, were unity, there would be no need for any government interference in order to insure stable gross incomes for the producer.

If, however, the demand were relatively elastic, a small crop would bring in a smaller income than a large crop. Hence, in years of small crop the government—if it wished to stabilize the gross incomes of farmers—would have to take supplies off the market and thereby raise the price. But in years of large crop the income of farmers will be larger than normal, so that the government will have to put still further supplies on the market and so lower the price.

If the demand for the crop were relatively inelastic, a small crop would bring in a *larger* income than normal, as we have seen, and the government would have to put supplies on the market, and so lower the price, in order to bring the farmers' income back to normal. But with a large crop, the farmers' income would be smaller than usual, and the government would have to take supplies off the market in order to raise the price and consequently the farmers' income. This shows how important the distinction between a relatively elastic and a relatively inelastic demand can be. In the case of an elastic demand the government must increase both gluts and scarcities, and in the case of an inelastic demand it must diminish both gluts and scarcities, in order to achieve the same result—a stable farm income.

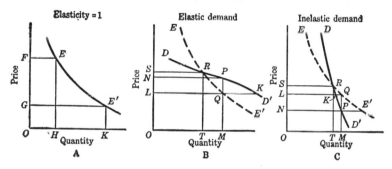

Fig. 45. The Stabilization of Gross Income

GRAPHIC ILLUSTRATION. This argument is shown graphically in Fig. 45. Figure 45A shows a demand curve of unit elasticity *EE'*. No matter what the size of the crop, be it small (*OH*) or large (*OK*), the total value of the crop is the same. In the first case, it is *OHEF;* in the second case, it is *OKE'G*—an exactly equal area.

Fig. 45B shows a relatively elastic demand curve for the crop, *DD'*. Suppose in this case that the average crop over a number of years is *OT,* and the average price *TR;* the average value of the crop, i.e., the average income from the crop, is therefore equal to *OTRS*.[1] Then

[1] To find the average price, *TR,* and the average crop, *OT,* we do not take the arithmetic mean of all the prices or of all the outputs in the period under review, for the product of these arithmetic means will not give the average gross value. Instead we must calculate the gross value of the crop in each year, and take the arithmetic mean of these figures. This is the *average gross value*. Then from the demand curve we must find the output and the price which yields this average gross value. *OT* is the output and *TR* the price so discovered.

through the point R draw a curve ERE', of unit elasticity. (This is a rectangular hyperbola.) If, then, the crop is abnormally large (say, equal to OM) the price which the farmer should receive in order to give him his average income will be MQ, where Q is on the curve EE'. The price which would obtain in the absence of government intervention would be MP, where P is on the demand curve DD'. In order that the price MQ may hold in the market, the government must sell out of its previously accumulated stocks an amount equal to QK, so that the total amount on the market in that year is LK. Thus the farmers' income will be equal to the crop (OM) multiplied by the new price (MQ), or the area $OMQL$, which is equal to $OTRS$ (the average income) by the construction of the curve EE'. If the government had not thrown the amount QK onto the market, the price would have been MP and the farmers' income $OMPN$, which is greater than normal. Similarly, in a year of short crop the government must in this case actually take some of the crop off the market and so raise the price even above what it would have been. The effect of government intervention in this way would be to increase price fluctuations but to do away with fluctuations in the total value of the crop.

Fig. 45C shows an inelastic demand for the crop, DD'. Again through the point R, where SR (or OT) is the crop and TR the price, which yields the average gross income, $OTRS$, we draw a curve of unit elasticity, EE'. Now, when there is a large crop, OM, the farmers' income, in the absence of regulation, will be $OMPN$, which is smaller than the average income, $OTRS$. Consequently, the government must take off the market an amount equal to QK, leaving an amount LK which will sell for a price OL, thus making the farmers' income equal to $OM \times OL$, or the area $OMQL$—which is equal to the average income $OTRS$. When there is a small crop, the government must throw some of its stores onto the market in order to bring down the price. In this case, therefore, the effect of government action will tend to make the prices as well as the gross incomes more equal in different years.

Ever-Normal Granary

Principles like these are clearly of vital importance in assessing any policy of an *ever-normal granary*. We cannot yet make any final judgment on such a policy. However, we can perhaps see that there is more justification for it in the case of commodities with a relatively inelastic demand than in the case of commodities with a relatively elastic demand. In the first case such a policy not only will equalize incomes but will diminish the fluctuation of prices. In the second case making incomes more equal actually necessitates an increased fluctuation of prices.

Does Private Speculation Stabilize Farm Income?

An interesting problem of a similar type concerns private speculation. How far would the activities of *private* speculators, apart from government intervention, serve to increase or diminish the fluctuation of farm income? It was explained in Chapter 8, page 138, that if time arbitrage is properly carried out and there is a reasonably accurate and widely known expectation of future events, speculation will tend to diminish the year-to-year fluctuation of the price of a storable commodity, such as wheat. Speculators will buy up part of

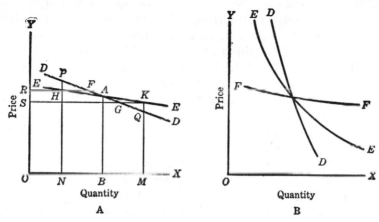

Fig. 46.   Speculation and Gross Income

the crop in years of big harvest in order to sell it in years of small harvest. This will diminish the fluctuation in price from year to year. Whether these operations will reduce the fluctuations in farm income from year to year will depend on how elastic is the demand curve of the market apart from the speculators, and on how much their operations in fact reduce the price fluctuations.

The demand curve of the market without speculators—*DD* in Fig. 46A—is the curve showing the relation between the size of the crop and the price at which it could be sold, if it all had to be sold for consumption within the year. Speculators take part of the crop off the market in years of good harvest when the price is low and put it back on the market in years of poor harvest when the price is high. They have the effect, therefore, of diminishing the fluctuations in price. The demand curve in the presence of speculators—*EE* in Fig.

46A—will be more elastic than in the absence of speculators. A small crop (*ON*) would command a price *NP* in the absence of speculation. Speculators, however, sell from their stocks an amount *HF*, making the total sales to nonspeculators equal to *RF,* and the price equal to *OR*, or *NH*. A large crop, *OM*, would command a price *MQ* in the absence of speculation. Speculators, however, buy up and store an amount *KG*, making the total sales to nonspeculators equal to *SG*, and the price *OS*, or *MK*.

WITH INELASTIC DEMAND. Now if the demand of the market without speculators were relatively inelastic, as *DD* in Fig. 46B, the action of speculators would make this demand more elastic. If the demand in the presence of speculators had unit elasticity, *EE,* the speculation would diminish not only the fluctuations of prices but also the fluctuation in the total value of the crop, for in this case the size of the crop would not affect its value. If, therefore, the speculators push the demand curve from the position *DD* to a position between *DD* and *EE,* they will have diminished the fluctuations in gross income. But if they push the demand curve into a still more elastic position—for example, *FF*—they may actually increase the fluctuations in the gross income. Such fluctuations will be in the opposite direction to those in the market without speculators. A small crop now brings a smaller gross income than a larger crop.

WITH ELASTIC DEMAND. With the demand curve in the absence of speculation relatively elastic, as it is drawn in Fig. 46A, the presence of speculation will make the demand still more elastic. In this case speculation as always will decrease the fluctuations of price. But it will of necessity increase the fluctuations of gross income.

Gross Income and Net Income

A large crop will probably involve the farmers in more expense than a small crop for, even though the acreage sown is the same, and the larger crop is due solely to the benevolence of the elements, there will be extra charges for reaping and handling. To insure that the *net* income of growers will be independent of the size of the crop, then, the total demand curve for the crop should not have unit elasticity, but should have an elasticity of slightly more than 1. Then a large crop will bring in a somewhat larger gross income to compensate for the increased expenses.

Fluctuations Due to Fluctuating Demands

Up to this point the problem of stabilizing income has been discussed on the assumption that demand is stable and that therefore fluctuations in prices or incomes from year to year are due to changes in output. For some periods (e.g., 1923–1929) this may have been approximately the case. In other periods, however (e.g., 1929–1948), price fluctuations have been due mainly to changes in demand itself arising from changes in income, and the fluctuations of output have been secondary. The problem of stabilizing gross income of producers when demand is fluctuating is illustrated in Fig. 47. *OR* represents the

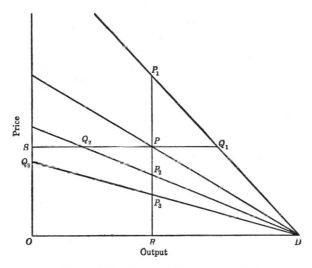

Fig. 47. Stabilization with Fluctuating Demand

annual output of the commodity, in this case assumed to be constant. *RP* is that price which will yield the *average* income which it is desired to stabilize, *ORPS*. If the demand curve passes through *P*, as *DP*, the income is average and no action is necessary. If the demand is greater than *DP*, say *DP₁*, in the absence of governmental action the price will rise to *RP₁* and income will be above average. To bring the price (and therefore the income, as output is assumed stable) down to the average price *RP* the stabilization authority must put an amount *PQ₁* on the market, increasing total sales to *SQ₁*. If the demand is below average, say *DQ₂*, the price in the absence of regulation will be *RP₂*. The authority will have to take an amount *PQ₂* off the market, reducing total sales to consumers to *SQ₂*. If the fall in demand is very great, say to *DQ₃*, stabilization of gross income will be impossible, as no amount of restriction of sales to consumers will raise the price sufficiently to bring income up to the average. In Fig. 47 the assumption has been made that the shifts in demand are due to cyclical changes in income, not to changes in tastes, hence, the shifts in demand do not affect the amount of the commodity that would be bought at zero price, *OD*, and all the demand curves pass through *D*. This is the most likely case, as a cyclical shift of tastes is difficult to imagine. However, it is evident that if any commodity were subject to regularly fluctuating tastes, the same type of analysis could be applied.

Criticism of Buffer Stocks Plan

It will be observed that the attempt to apply an ever-normal granary (sometimes called a *buffer stocks* plan) under circumstances of fluctuating demand would require the augmentation of consumption in years of good demand and its restriction in years of poor demand. As years of good demand are the boom years and years of poor demand are depression years, the result of the ever-normal granary plan would be to feed the boom by starving the depression—a most undesirable result. The stability of one element of the economy—the income of producers of the particular commodities stabilized—would be obtained only at the cost of unstabilizing what may be a much more important element in the economy, consumption. Particularly in the case of foodstuffs the buffer stocks method of stabilization might well prove disastrous if the cause of instability were unstable demand. If the economy is going to be unstable, it is much better for the instability to be reflected in farm income than in food consumption. Only if the basic cause of unstable farm incomes is fluctuating crop outputs is there much to be said for the buffer stocks plan, and only then if the demand is inelastic, so that the operation of the plan tends toward stabilizing prices and consumption as well as producer income.

CROP-RESTRICTION POLICIES

The United States Cotton Restriction

We have already examined some of the difficulties into which a restriction scheme may run, especially where there is no effective control of the volume of production. We may now examine an extension of this problem, of considerable practical importance: the case in which a government enforces the restriction of production within its own boundaries of a crop with a world market and with other centers of production. The cotton policy of the United States since 1933 is a case in point.

In Fig. 48, as usual, price is indicated along the axis *OY* and the quantities produced and consumed, or the rates of production and

consumption, along *OX*. Suppose the figure refers to cotton. Then
let $S_uS'_u$ be the normal supply curve for cotton, for producers within
the United States. Let $S_fS'_f$ be the normal supply curve for cotton for
foreign producers—i.e., all producers outside the United States. Then
the total supply curve for cotton, $S_fS_tS'_t$, is obtained by adding, for
each price, the quantity which will be produced by the United States
producers to the quantity which will be produced by foreign producers.
Thus, the meaning of these curves is that at any price, *OY*, American

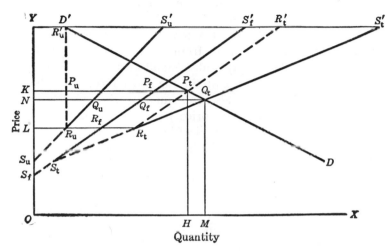

Fig. 48. Restriction of Part of a Crop

producers will produce at a rate equal to YS'_u, foreign producers will
be willing to produce at a rate YS'_f, and therefore the total rate of
production at that price will be $YS'_u + YS'_f = YS'_t$.

The normal price will be given at the point Q_t, where the total
supply curve cuts the total demand curve, *D'D*. *ON* ($= MQ_t$) is the
normal price: NQ_t ($= OM$) is the total quantity produced. NQ_u is the
quantity produced in America and NQ_f is the quantity produced
abroad.

Now suppose that the American government effectively prevents
American producers from producing any quantity greater than LR_u.
The American supply curve then becomes the dashed line $S_uR_uR'_u$.
Under the restriction scheme, if the price falls below *OL*, at which
the American producers will normally produce the allotted quantity
LR_u, they will automatically lower their production, following the
supply curve R_uS_u. If the price rises above this, they are prevented
from expanding their output by government authority, and therefore

their supply is perfectly inelastic. The foreign supply curve presumably remains the same. The *total* supply curve then becomes the dotted line $S_fS_tR_tR'_t$, where $R_tR'_t$ is parallel to the foreign supply curves $R_fS'_f$. The normal price rises to $HP_t (= OK)$, P_t being the point where this new total supply curve cuts the total demand curve. Then the American production has fallen from NQ_u to KP_u; foreign production has expanded from $NQ_f (= Q_uQ_t)$ to $KP_f (= P_uP_t)$. Whether the total gross income of the American producers has risen or fallen depends, of course, on the actual shape of the curves. In this case it is evident that the gross income of American producers has declined sharply from $(ON \times NQ_u)$ to $(OK \times KP_u)$, and the gross income of foreign producers has increased from $(ON \times NQ_f)$ to $(OK \times KP_f)$. Unless the shape of the supply and demand curves is very peculiar indeed, there must always be a gain in the gross income of the foreign producers, for the price and also the quantity they produce increase. For the American producers the price increases but the quantity produced diminishes. Unless the diminution in quantity is very small, therefore, they are unlikely to gain in gross income. A scheme like this is unlikely to increase the gross income of American producers unless (1) the foreign supply is very inelastic or (2) the legal maximum American crop is very little less than the normal crop.

If there is any elasticity of supply for foreign production, the result of an American crop restriction is that the foreign producers increase their production to make up in part the deficiency in the American crop. Consequently, the foreign producers get most of the benefit of the increased price.[2] This particular analysis has a good many applications. It applies not only to government restriction but to any attempt to gain monopoly prices by restriction of only a *part* of the total production, whether on the part of a government, a steel combine, or an agricultural cooperative. It explains why voluntary combinations of a monopolistic intent are so fragile. If all the producers of one commodity restricted their output, they might all benefit, but the bulk of the benefits of restriction go to the people who do not restrict their outputs, and not to the people who do. Consequently, in any scheme of this kind there is a constant temptation for the participants to break away from it—if they can. This tendency has been noticeable, for instance, in the organization of milk marketing cooperatives.

[2] The following dramatic figures illustrate the point:

	1928–1930	1959–1960
United States production of cotton (million bales)	14.4	14.4
Foreign production of cotton (million bales)	12.2	32.5
World production of synthetic fibers (million bales cotton equivalent)	0.9	22.0

THE COBWEB THEOREM

Another interesting application of supply and demand analysis is to the explanation of certain curious cyclical movements which are to be found in the prices and outputs of many agricultural commodities. In the case of commodities like fresh vegetables, potatoes, and pigs, a fairly regular cycle is noticeable. In one year the quantity supplied is small and the price is high. The high price encourages producers to plan for an increase in production which, however, matures in the next year or the year after. When this increased production comes on the market, the price is forced down. Consequently, many producers go out of production; and when their decisions are made effective—in another year or two—the quantity supplied is again small and prices are high, and so the cycle goes on.

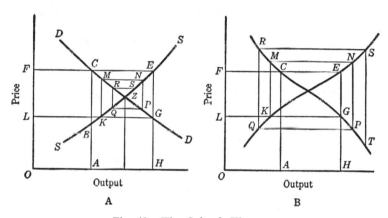

Fig. 49. The Cobweb Theorem

Fig. 49 illustrates this process. Here *DD* represents the relationship between the quantity supplied in any one year and the price which must be charged in order to sell that quantity. *SS* represents the relationship between the price in any one year and the quantity which will be produced in the year *following*—the *year* being the period of time between the decision to produce and the completion of production. These, it should be noticed, are not the usual supply and demand curves; they have a special meaning of their own, appropriate to the problem in question.

Suppose in one year there is a production equal to *OA*. The price will be *AC,* according to the meaning of the curve *DD*. If the price in that year, however, is *AC,* the production in the second year will be

FE, according to the meaning of the curve *SS.* Therefore, the price in the second year will be *HG.* The production in the third year will be *LK.* If *LK = OA,* the cycle will start all over again and will be repeated indefinitely, as long as the conditions which define the curves remain the same. But if the shape of the curves is such that, as in Fig. 49A, *LK* is greater than *OA,* the cycle will be repeated, following the path *KMNPQRS* . . . etc., with ever-diminishing range. In practice, of course, long before the cycle has a chance to be repeated the character of the curves themselves may change, but it is important to see what would happen if conditions did not change. Eventually, in this case we will reach the center, *Z,* and equilibrium will be established. If, however, after the end of the first cycle the production in the third year, *LK,* were less than that in the first, *OA,* the cycle would go on with ever increasing amplitude, following a course such as *CEGKMNPQRST,* as in Fig. 49B. Again, this cannot go on forever. Either it will come to a position of neutral equilibrium, following the same path in every cycle, or the whole position of the curves will change. This theorem is usually called the *cobweb theorem,* from the nature of the diagram which illustrates it.

INTERRELATIONSHIPS AMONG DEMANDS AND SUPPLIES

In all our previous analysis we have tacitly assumed that the demand curves and the supply curves for various commodities are independent. In fact this is not usually the case, and we must now extend our analysis to include some important cases where the demand or supply curves for various commodities are interdependent.

Complementary, Independent, and Competitive Relationships

Two commodities may be related in demand or supply in any of three ways. They may stand in a *complementary* relationship, they may be *independent,* or they may stand in a *competitive* relationship. They are complementary in demand, or in *joint demand,* when a rise in the consumption or purchases of one causes a rise in the demand for the other; that is, a rise in the quantity of the other which would be purchased at each hypothetical price. They are independent in demand when a rise in the purchases of one has no effect on the demand for the other. They are competitive in demand when a rise in the purchases of one brings about a fall in the demand for the other.

Knives and forks, razors and razor blades, pipes and tobacco, right shoes and left shoes, pens and ink, are all examples of joint (complementary) demand. These are commodities which must be consumed in certain more or less definite proportions. Each pair is consumed as a single commodity, for each is useless, or at least of much less use, without its counterpart. At the other extreme are pairs or groups of commodities which are good substitutes for each other—beef and lamb, cotton and silk, oranges and grapefruit, oatmeal and corn flakes. These are competitive in demand, for any one of a group can be used as a substitute for any other in the fulfillment of a want. The more easily two commodities can be substituted one for another, the more competitive will be their demands. Two commodities have independent demands if they cannot be substituted one for another in consumption—cheese and spark plugs, molasses and taffeta, pussy cats and powerhouses.[3] If two commodities are complementary in consumption then we may say that they are *negatively substitutable*.

Dependence in Supply

As in demand, so in supply we can distinguish three cases. Two commodities are complementary in supply, or in joint supply, if a rise in the output of one must necessarily be accompanied by a rise in the supply curve of the other. They are independent in supply if a rise in the output of one does not affect the supply curve of the other. They are competitive in supply if a rise in the output of one must necessarily be accompanied by a fall in the supply curve of the other. Complementarity in supply arises from the fact that many processes of production have multiple end products. Beef and hides are both obtained from cattle, wool and mutton from sheep, grain and straw from wheat, and steel and slag from blast furnaces. In these cases and in many others if we want one commodity, we must also produce the other; just as if we want a wife to come to a dinner party we must usually take the husband also.

Competitiveness in supply arises because many groups of products are produced with the same factors of production. Consequently, if the production of one commodity increases, resources which are neces-

---

[3] This statement is true only as a first approximation. The true test of independence in demand is that a rise in consumption of one commodity (A) will not affect the demand for the other comodity (B). If the demand for commodity A is relatively elastic, a fall in the price of A will raise its consumption and also the amount spent on it. Consequently, there will be less to spend on all other commodities, and for this reason demand for all of them—including B—will fall. In this case even if the commodities have zero substitutability, they will be slightly competitive. If the demand for A is relatively inelastic, commodities with zero substitutability will be slightly complementary in demand. Only if the elasticity of demand for both commodities is unity is the above statement wholly true. Nevertheless, for most commodities the inaccuracy is inconsiderable.

sary for the production of the competing commodity are withdrawn. Various agricultural crops, for instance, compete for land. If there is an increase in the production of wheat, there is likely to be a decrease in the supply of oats and barley, particularly if wheat, oats, and barley can all play the same part in the crop rotation.

EXAMPLE: A RISE IN DEMAND FOR BEEF MAY CAUSE A FALL IN THE PRICE OF HIDES. The problems created by dependent supplies or demands can best be illustrated by an example. Consider, for instance, two commodities produced under conditions of joint (complementary) supply. Beef and hides are both produced by the cattle industry. Suppose, then, that there is a rise in the demand for beef. The immediate result, as we have seen, will be a rise in the price of beef. The rise in the price of beef will make the cattle industry more prosperous than before,

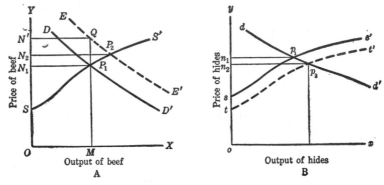

Fig. 50. Joint Supply

and it will expand. The rate of production of cattle will increase, and therefore the rate of production of *both* beef and hides will increase. The price of beef will then fall to some point a little above its old level, and the price of hides will fall *below* its old level. The net result of a rise in demand for beef, therefore, is a rise in the price of beef and a fall in the price of hides—assuming, of course, that the demand for hides does not change. This situation is illustrated graphically in Fig. 50. *DD'* is the old demand for beef, *SS'* the long-run supply curve for beef. In Fig. 50B, *dd'* is the demand curve for hides, *ss'* the original long-run supply curve for hides.[4] Now if there is a rise in the demand

[4] The nature of the supply curves drawn in this example requires some explanation. The profitability of cattle production depends on the price of *both* beef and hides. The total quantity of beef, therefore, which will be produced at each price of beef depends in part on the price of hides. The greater the price of hides, the more beef will be produced at each price of beef. That is to say, instead of having a single supply curve for

for beef to EE', the immediate result will be a rise in the price of beef to MQ, or ON'. This high price encourages production, which rises from N_1P_1 to N_2P_2 and the price falls finally to ON_2—still, however, higher than the original price, ON_1. Meanwhile, as the production of beef has expanded, the production of hides has also expanded, from an original n_1p_1 to n_2p_2. Correspondingly, the price of hides has fallen from on_1 to on_2.

Factors Determining Extent of These Changes

1. ELASTICITIES OF SUPPLY AND DEMAND. The extent of these changes depends on two things. First, as always, it depends on the elasticities of supply and demand in question. If the cattle industry as a whole is elastic in supply, i.e., if a small rise in its profitability causes a large influx of resources into it, then a rise in demand for beef will produce but little effect on the price of beef. It may, however, produce an appreciable effect on the price of hides. If the supply of cattle is inelastic, then a rise in demand for beef will produce a considerable effect on the price of beef, but it will not cause much expansion of the cattle industry and will therefore not affect greatly either the output or the price of hides. If the demand for hides is elastic, a greater output of hides will, of course, produce less effect on the price than if the demand were inelastic.

2. POSSIBILITY OF SUBSTITUTION. In the second place, the extent of these changes depends on the degree to which beef and hides can be substituted in the productive process. If the proportions of beef and hide produced are absolutely inflexible, any increase in the output of beef must also produce the same proportionate increase in the output of hides. If cattle always yielded beef and hides in the same proportion, an increase of 1 percent in the output of beef could only be brought about by an increase of 1 percent in the output of cattle, which would also bring about an increase of 1 percent in the output of hides. If, at the other extreme, it were possible to breed cattle without skins, then an increase in the output of beef might be obtained without any change in the output of hides. In practice the truth generally lies between these two extremes. There are some processes in which the proportions of the products are absolutely fixed—some

---

beef we have a series of supply curves, each corresponding to a certain price for hides. The greater the price of hides, the farther toward the right will the supply curve for beef lie. Similarly, for each price of beef there is a different supply curve for hides. Fig. 50, then, assumes that the supply curve SS' is that supply curve for beef which is consistent with a price of hides equal to on_2, and that the supply curve for hides, ss', is consistent with the price of beef ON_1, and the supply curve tt' is consistent with the price of beef ON_2.

chemical processes, for instance. But in most cases some variation is possible in the emphasis on the different products of the same process. Although we cannot breed cattle without skins, we can at least breed them specially for beef—we may be able to get more and better beef inside each hide. We could conceivably breed specially for hides, though this is not in fact the case in the cattle industry, the hide being a relatively small part of the total value of a beast. In the sheep industry, however, we find this specialization carried to considerable degree. Some sheep are bred specially for their wool, such as Merinos, and in this case the mutton or lamb is merely a *by-product*. Some sheep, on the other hand, are bred for their meat, and in this case it is the wool which is the by-product. A by-product may be defined as one of two or more joint products whose total value is small compared with that of its fellow products.

If we suppose that the proportion of beef to hide in a beast can be changed easily, then the result of our increase in demand for beef will be to shift the proportion in the favor of beef. That is, the fact that the price of beef has risen while the price of hides has fallen will make it profitable to breed cattle which contain more and better beef inside each hide. Consequently, there will not be so much of a rise in the output of hides as there might be if the proportion of beef to hide produced by a single beast were absolutely inflexible. If, therefore, beef and hides are substitutable in production, a change in the demand for beef will bring about a smaller change in the price of hides than it would if beef and hides could not be substituted one for another.

Competitive Supply

The analysis of competitive supply follows the same lines. Suppose, for instance, that cotton and tobacco are in competitive supply, for both are grown in the same region on the same kind of land. Then a fall in demand for tobacco will lower the price of tobacco, drive resources out of the tobacco industry, make the rent of the tobacco-cotton land cheaper, lower the costs of production of cotton, raise the supply of cotton, and therefore lower the price of cotton.

Complementary (Joint) Demand

Similar propositions can be derived from the study of complementary and competitive demands. Consider first the case of a rise in the supply curve of a commodity which is jointly demanded with another. For instance, if an improved pig is discovered which will produce bacon much more quickly and cheaply than previous pigs, there will be a rise in the supply of pigs for, at each price now, more will come on to the market than before. This will cause a fall in the price of pigs and of bacon, and a rise in the consumption of pigs and bacon. A rise in the consumption of bacon, however, may well cause a rise in the demand for eggs, for more people will now have bacon and eggs for breakfast or lunch than before. A rise in the demand for eggs will usually bring about a rise in the price of eggs. Thus an improvement in pigs may raise the price of eggs. This can be illustrated with supply and demand curves, just as in the last case. The extent of these movements again depends upon two things. The first is the elasticity of demand and of supply—especially the elasticity of demand for bacon and the elasticity of supply of eggs. Second, it depends on how much the proportions in which the two commodities are bought can be varied. If we imagine that there is a law which makes it obligatory for each housewife to drop one egg in the pan for every three rashers of bacon, and if eggs were used only for frying with bacon, then any increase in the consumption of bacon will be accompanied by an exactly proportionate increase in the consumption of eggs. If at the other extreme eggs and bacon were not used together at all, then of course an increase in the consumption of bacon would cause no appreciable change in the consumption of eggs.

Competitive Demand

The case of competitive demands can be analyzed in the same way. Suppose, for instance, that beef and pork are competitive in consumption. Then the improved pig, which we saw might result in a rise in the price of eggs, will cause a fall in the price of beef. The increased supply of pork will lower its price and increase its consumption. Consumers will turn away from the dearer commodity, beef, toward the cheaper pork. The demand for beef will decline, and the price and output of beef will also decline, except in the unlikely circumstance of a perfectly elastic supply of beef.

Measurement by Cross-Elasticities

The concept of competitiveness and complementarity is vague enough so that it can be sharpened in a number of different ways by giving different exact definitions. The definition used above is perhaps the simplest, but other definitions are also possible. We can define and measure these relationships, for instance, in terms of the *cross-elasticities* of demand or supply (see p. 200). We define the *cross-elasticity* e_{ab} as the change in the quantity of A produced by a unit change in the price of B. Then in the case of demand, if e_{ab} is positive, a rise in the price of B, which usually lowers the quantity of B demanded, raises the quantity of A demanded; the commodities are competitive in demand. Similarly if e_{ab} is negative the commodities are usually complementary in demand. In the case of supply the situation is usually reversed; if e_{ab} is positive, a rise in the price of B, which raises the quantity supplied of B, also raises the quantity supplied of A: the commodities are complementary in supply. Similarly if e_{ab} is negative the commodities are competitive in supply. These definitions do not diverge from the previous definitions as long as the regular elasticity of demand for each commodity is negative and the elasticity of supply, positive; if this is not true, however, the definitions may diverge.

GENERAL EQUILIBRIUM OF DEMAND AND SUPPLY: TWO COMMODITIES

In analyzing the equilibrium price of a single commodity by means of demand and supply functions it is always assumed that all other variables of the system are held constant. This *particular* equilibrium analysis, as it is called, must be used very carefully if it is not to involve logical fallacies, and it must always be regarded as a stepping-stone to a general equilibrium analysis in which the whole price structure is determined simultaneously, as on page 58. We can now proceed to the explicit analysis of the general equilibrium of supply and demand for two commodities, which will illustrate many of the problems involved in general equilibrium.

Extended Demand and Supply Functions

Consider first commodity A, the demand function for which we can write

$$d_a = F_{da}(p_a, \ p_b) \tag{1}$$

that is, the quantity demanded (d_a) depends on both the price of $A(p_a)$ and the price of B (p_b). Similarly the supply function is

$$s_a = F_{sa}(p_a, \ p_b) \tag{2}$$

that is, the quantity of A supplied depends on the price of both A and B. Various cases of this function are shown in Fig. 51. In each figure D_0 is the demand curve for commodity A when $p_b = 0$, D_1 is the demand curve when $p_b = 1$, D_2 is the demand curve when $p_b = 2$, and so on. Similarly S_0, S_1, and S_2 are the supply curves for A when $p_b = 0$, 1, and 2 respectively. P_0, where the demand curve D_0 and the supply curve S_0 intersect, shows the equilibrium price and quantity of A when $p_b = 0$. Similarly P_1, P_2, etc., show the equilibrium price and quantity

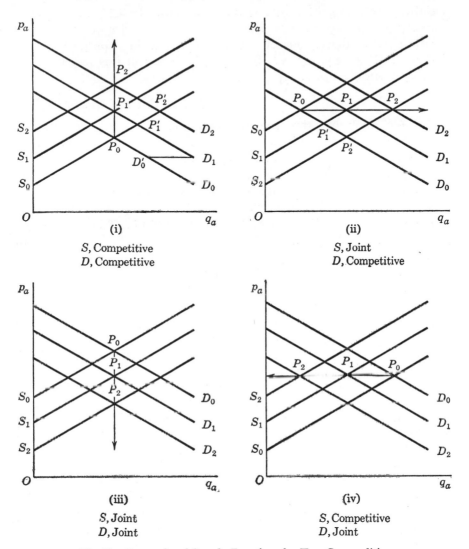

Fig. 51.   Demand and Supply Functions for Two Commodities

of A when $p_b = 1$, 2, etc. The horizontal distance between successive curves measures the absolute cross-elasticity in this range. Thus in Fig. 51(i), $D'_0 D_1$ is the increase in the quantity of A demanded which results from a unit increase in the price of B, when the price of A is given by the position D'_0. In Fig. 51(i) the cross elasticity of demand is positive; that is, a rise in the price of B, which usually lowers the quantity of B demanded, raises the quantity of A demanded; the two commodities

are therefore competitive in demand. The cross-elasticity of supply is
negative: the supply curve moves to the left as the price of B increases,
indicating that the commodities are competitive in supply. The line
$P_0P_1P_2$ ... is the equilibrium path as p_b increases: in this case it moves
roughly vertically upwards.

Various Cases of Cross-Elasticity

Suppose now that the competitiveness of supply diminishes: the
cross-elasticity of supply increases, that is, becomes a smaller negative
number; the successive curves S_0, S_1, S_2 squeeze together and the distance
between them diminishes; the equilibrium path bends more to the
right. When the cross-elasticity of supply is zero, the commodities are
independent in supply; the curves S_0, S_1, S_2 all collapse into the single
curve S_0' and the equilibrium path shifts to $P_0P'_1P'_2$. If now the cross-
elasticity of supply grows further and becomes positive we move to
Fig. 51(ii), with joint supply and competitive demand. The equilibrium
path $P_0P_1P_2$ rotates further and assumes a roughly horizontal position.
Now suppose the cross-elasticity of demand diminishes; D_0, D_1, D_2, etc.
squeeze closer together; when the cross-elasticity of demand is zero these
curves all collapse into D_0 and the equilibrium path is $P_0P'_1P'_2$. If the
cross-elasticity of demand further diminishes and becomes negative
we go to Fig. 51(iii), with both supply and demand joint; the equilibrium path again assumes a roughly vertical position, but this time
pointing downward; a rise in the price of B lowers the price of A
without much change in quantity. Finally, if supply now becomes more
competitive, the equilibrium path swings around further to the position
of Fig. 51 (iv), in which supply is competitive, demand is joint, and
a rise in the price of B lowers the quantity of A, but does not much
affect the price.

Equilibrium of the Whole System

The equilibrium of the whole system can now be shown in Fig. 52.
In this construction we measure the quantity of A horizontally and to
the right of the origin O; the price of A vertically and above O; the
price of B horizontally and to the left of O; the quantity of B vertically
and below O. The first quadrant is then identical with Fig. 51(i); the
points $_aP_0$, $_aP_1$, $_aP_2$, etc., are the same as the points P_0, P_1, P_2 in Fig. 51(i)
and show the equilibrium path. The demand and supply curves are
omitted from Fig. 52 for the sake of clarity. Then from the points $_aP_0$,
$_aP_1$, $_aP_2$, etc., we can construct points in the second, or p_a–p_b quadrant,
A_0, A_1, A_2, etc., as shown in the figure, by drawing a line horizontally
from a point $_aP_1$ to meet a line drawn vertically from a point $p_b = 1$.

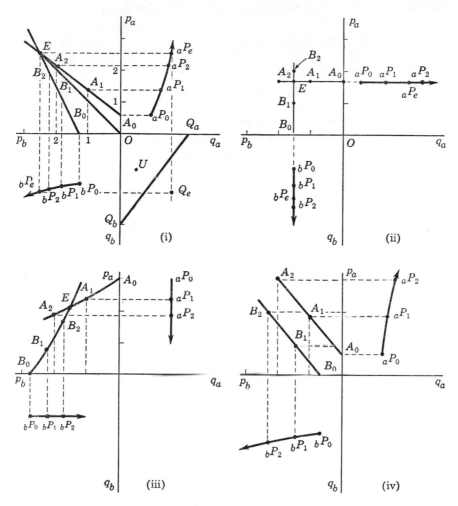

Fig. 52. General Equilibrium of Two Commodities

The line $A_0A_1A_2$, may be called the partial equilibrium-price path of A; it shows the equilibrium price of A for each price of B.

Similarly in the third, or p_b-q_b quadrant we can draw the points $_bP_0$, $_bP_1$, $_bP_2$, etc., which show the equilibrium position of B for $p_a = 0, 1, 2$, etc. This line is the equilibrium path for B, and is derived from a figure (not shown) similar to Fig. 51(i), but for commodity B instead of commodity A. These paths are likely to be somewhat similar, because of the reciprocal relations of the cross elasticities: if A for instance is in joint demand with B, so that e_{ab} is negative, B is almost certain to be in joint demand with B so that e_{ba} is also negative. Exceptions to this rule, however, are possible; A may be useless without B, for instance, while B is useful without A. From the points $_bP_0$, $_bP_1$, $_bP_2$, etc., we then derive the points B_0, B_1, B_2 exactly as A_0, A_1, A_2, etc., were derived from $_aP_0$, $_aP_1$, $_aP_2$, etc. $B_0B_1B_2$ is the partial equilibrium price path for B.

Where the two partial equilibrium price paths intersect at E is the general equilibrium of the whole system, for only at this point do we have a combination of the two prices such that the partial equilibrium value of each is consistent with the value of the other. At a point such as A_2, for instance, A is in equilibrium but B is not, at B_2, B is in equilibrium but A is not. Only at E are both in equilibrium together. The point $_aP_e$ then gives the equilibrium price and quantity of A, the point $_bP_e$ for B.

Fig. 52(ii) shows a similar diagram corresponding to case (ii) of Fig. 51, where supply is joint and demand is competitive; the equilibrium price of each commodity in this special case is independent of the price of the other, but E is still the equilibrium point. Fig. 52(iii) shows the case corresponding to Fig. 51(iii), with both commodities joint. Case (iv) of Fig. 51 is similar to Fig. 52(ii), and is not drawn.

Failure of Solution

It is interesting to inquire as to the circumstances under which the system yields no real or significant solutions. One case is shown in Fig. 52(iv). Here the two commodities are highly competitive, with cross-elasticities of demand and supply numerically very high. The partial equilibrium paths $A_0A_1A_2$ and $B_0B_1B_2$ are parallel, and now no longer intersect at finite prices. This case is highly unlikely, as cross-elasticities of the size needed to produce it are unlikely to occur. Nevertheless Fig. 52(i) suggests that when the two commodities are competitive both in demand and in supply, this operates to raise the price of both of them, and also makes the equilibrium more *shiftable*, that is, a given change in the parameters of the system will produce a large change in the position of equilibrium. Curious cases are also possible under conditions of joint demand and supply (case (iii)) if the cross-elasticities are large. Thus if in Fig. 52(iii) we increase numerically the cross-elasticities, so that the distances such as $_aP_{0a}P_1$ increase, the partial equilibrium path $A_0A_1A_2$ swings counterclockwise, pivoting on A_0, and $B_0B_1B_2$ swings clockwise, pivoting on B_0. A situation is possible in which these two partial equilibrium paths coincide, in which case *any* point in the segment where they coincide is an equilibrium position! This case, however, also requies cross-elasticities which are so high as to be quite unlikely. While we have not proved, therefore, that there must be an equilibrium position of the system with positive prices, we have proved that it is highly likely.

Negative Prices

Under some circumstances the equilibrium E may move out of the second quadrant into one of the others, where the price of one or both of the commodities is negative. A negative price means simply that the commodity has become a discommodity; we pay people to take it away. There are many cases of such discommodities, so that the solution is by no means absurd. If, for instance, we have a process of joint production which produces one commodity in large quantity for which there is little demand, this commodity can easily have a negative price. Mine dumps, calcium chloride in the Solvay process for making sulphuric acid, and garbage and sewage of all kinds are examples of such negative prices. *Both* commodities A and B, however, cannot have a negative price unless there is some third commodity with a positive price jointly produced with them; otherwise the process will simply not be carried out. In Fig. 52(iv), therefore, if the commodities become so competitive in both demand and supply that the partial equilibrium-price paths intersect in the fourth quadrant with both prices negative, this must be regarded as an inadmissable solution.

Failure of Solution in Inflation

We may note that in inflation a process similar to that of Fig. 52(iv) may go on; a rise in the price of one commodity may greatly increase the demand for another and diminish its supply, not so much because of the interrelatedness of the demand and supply themselves, but because the rise in price is a signal which produces an expectation that other prices will rise. In hyperinflation there is no equilibrium of the price system; all prices rise continuously, as they would do in Fig. 52(iv). We shall return to this problem later.

Constraints on Demand and Supply Functions in a Closed Economy

If the two-commodity system described above is part of a larger economy, there are no necessary constraints on the nature of the supply and demand functions; it is possible to have a rise in demand for one commodity without any fall in demand for the other; or it is even possible to have a rise in demand for both, which represents a shift away from the other commodities in the economy. In a closed economy, however, there are constraints imposed on the supply and demand functions—on demand through the limitation of income, and on supply through the limitation of production possibilities. These two sources of constraint are ultimately both derived from the existence of an alternative cost, or production possibility function, like the line BD in the deer and beaver case of Figs. 3 and 4, pp. 54–56. What this constraint means is that out of the set of all supply and demand functions which could be postulated, only a certain subset is consistent with the constraint conditions.

Thus suppose in Fig. 52(i) the line Q_aQ_b in the fourth quadrant represents the production opportunity boundary, when A and B are the only two commodities in a closed society. The line corresponds exactly to the line BD of Fig. 3, p. 54. As the figure is drawn, we see that the point Q_e, representing those quantities which are consistent with the equilibrium of demand and supply, lies beyond the line Q_aQ_b, and is hence beyond the capacity of the society. Under these circumstances, the demand and supply functions originally postulated are inadmissable. The supply and demand functions for commodity A of Fig. 51(i), or the corresponding functions for commodity B, must be moved to the left, thus moving the lines $_aP_{0a}P_2$ and $_bP_{0b}P_2$ toward their respective price axes until Q_e moves on to the line Q_aQ_b.

A still further constraint is imposed by the condition that the relative prices of the two commodities must equal their alternative cost. The relative price is the slope of the line OE in the second quadrant; assuming constant alternative cost, the alternative cost is the slope of Q_aQ_b in the fourth quadrant. The angle OQ_bQ_a must be equal to the angle p_aOE. Even with these constraints an indefinitely large number of supply and demand functions is possible, but a rise in demand for A implies a fall in demand for B. By contrast, a rise in supply for A, due to an improvement in its methods of production, will push the line Q_aQ_b to a new position with OQ_a larger than before, so there is not the same necessity for a fall in the supply of B.

General Equilibrium

It is not difficult to generalize this model to any number of commodities by means of algebra; every commodity that we add adds three equations (a demand function, a supply function, and the conditions of equilibrium) to the system, and likewise adds three unknowns—its price and the quantities demanded or supplied. With n commodities therefore we have $3n$ equations and $3n$ unknowns. The system may likewise fail to have real or relevant solutions under somewhat extreme conditions. There is likewise a constraint placed on the independence of the equations by the necessity for the set of outputs to conform to the production opportunity function, and for the set of relative prices to conform to the set of alternative costs. An interesting question arises if the equilibrium of demand and supply produces a set of outputs which lies *inside* the production opportunity boundary, say at a point such as *U* in Fig. 52(i). There is then unemployment of resources which are available for use, and it is a very interesting and important question whether this position is stable or not. This question, indeed, lies at the heart of the Keysnian economics, and we shall return to it later.

QUESTIONS AND EXERCISES

1. Suppose that the following schedule represents the total demand curve of all private individuals for wheat in any given year:

If the Total Output Is: (million bushels)	The Price Will Have to Be: (cents per bushel)
110	60
100	70
90	82
80	92
70	100
60	105
50	109
40	116
30	132
20	158

a. Plot this demand curve on squared paper.

b. Now suppose that over a period of ten successive years the annual *crop* amounted to outputs of 80, 60, 70, 40, 50, 80, 60, 50, 40, and 70 million bushels, respectively. Calculate and tabulate the gross value of the crop in each of these years, if the demand curve scheduled above was the demand curve of each of the ten years.

c. Calculate the *average* annual gross value of the crop over the ten years, and the output and price which would yield this value.

d. Construct a schedule showing what price would have to be received for each of the outputs in the schedule in order to make the gross value of the crop in each year equal to the average annual gross value. Plot this schedule on the same paper as the demand curve. It will be a curve of unit elasticity.

e. From the demand curve find the total amount which must be offered on the market in order to fetch the prices discovered in part (d). From these amounts make a schedule showing how much the government would have to buy or sell for each total output.

f. Draw up a schedule showing how much the government would have to buy or sell in each of the ten successive years of part (b). Notice that the government would have to sell a total greater than the amount which it would have to buy over the ten years. Does this mean that stabilization of the gross value of a crop is impossible?

2. Under what circumstances do you think that government interference with speculation in commodities is justified?

3. Prove that if the supply of foreign cotton is perfectly elastic, a restriction of the United States crop will not affect the price of cotton but will merely cause an increase in the foreign output exactly equal to the amount by which the United States crop has been restricted.

4. What conditions of supply and demand are likely to lead to fluctuations of price around an equilibrium level rather than to the establishment of a price at an equilibrium level?

5. Suppose that in Fig. 49 (A and B) the supply curve shows the relationship between the price in one year and the amount of production in the next year. Starting in both A and B with a production equal to OA, plot in each case two diagrams, one showing the fluctuation of price from year to year, the other showing the fluctuation of output. Measure the number of years along the horizontal axis, and the price or output along the vertical axis.

6. Discuss the problem of the stabilization of producer income when *both* output *and* demand fluctuate.

7. In the *cobweb theorem* diagram (Fig. 49) suppose that p_0 is the excess of the actual over the normal price at C, p_1 at G, p_2 at M, and so on. If the demand and supply functions are linear, with absolute elasticities of e_d and e_s, show that $p_1 = \dfrac{e_s p_0}{e_d}$, $p_2 = \dfrac{e_s^2 p_0}{e_d^2}$, and so on. From this show that the cobweb will be converging, neutral, or diverging according as $e_s \underset{>}{\overset{\leq}{=}} e_d$.

8. Consider a system with two commodities, A and B, with demand and supply functions as follows:

$$
\left.
\begin{aligned}
q_{ad} &= A_d + e_{ad}p_a + f_{ad}p_b &\quad \text{(i)} \\
q_{as} &= A_s + e_{as}p_a + f_{as}p_b &\quad \text{(ii)} \\
q_{bd} &= B_d + e_{bd}p_b + f_{bd}p_a &\quad \text{(iii)} \\
q_{bs} &= B_s + e_{bs}p_b + f_{bs}p_a &\quad \text{(iv)}
\end{aligned}
\right\} \text{(1)}
$$

p_a, p_b, are the prices of A and B; q_{ad}, q_{bd}, the quantities demanded; q_{as}, q_{bs} the quantities supplied; these are the six unknowns of the system. Of the parameters, the constants A_d, A_s, B_d, B_s measure the *size* of the demand or the supply; thus the greater A_d or B_d, the larger the demand. A_s and B_s are likely to be negative, but a rise in their algebraic value also raises the supply. The absolute elasticities of demand and supply are: e_{ad}, e_{as} for A, e_{bd}, e_{bs} for B. The absolute cross-elasticities are: f_{ad}, f_{as}, f_{bd}, f_{bs}.

Answer the following questions:

a. Assuming an open system, that is, that A and B are not the only commodities in the economy, what are the two equations of equilibrium necessary to determine the system?

b. Discuss the economic significance of the *sign* of each of the twelve parameters (that is, whether it is +, 0, or −). Discuss also the economic significance of a rise or fall in the magnitude of each of the parameters.

c. Derive equations for the equilibrium paths $_aP_0\,_aP_1\,_aP_2-$ and $_bP_0\,_bP_1\,_bP_2$ of Fig. 52(i), and also for the partial equilibrium paths $A_0A_1A_2$ and $B_0B_1B_2$.

d. Solve the latter two equations to get explicit equations for p_a and p_b in terms of the twelve parameters.

e. Substituting the values of p_a and p_b in the original demand equations (1) and (3), get explicit equations for q_{ad} and q_{bd}. Check by deriving similar equations from equations (2) and (4) for q_{as} and q_{bs}.

f. Discuss so far as you can the comparative statics of this system, by finding out what happens to the prices and quantities when each of the twelve parameters changes.

g. Now suppose that we are dealing with a closed, two-commodity economy, with constant alternative costs, so that there is a production opportunity boundary,

$$\frac{q_a}{A} + \frac{q_b}{B} = 1 \qquad (2)$$

$(q_a = q_{as} = q_{ad},\; q_b = q_{bs} = q_{bd})$. What is the economic significance of the parameters A and B?

Show that in equilibrium,

$$\frac{p_a}{p_b} = \frac{B}{A} \qquad (3)$$

Show now that only ten of the twelve parameters of equation (1) can be independently determined.

9. Give the twelve parameters of equation (1) in question 8 any plausible numerical values you wish, and plot the various equilibrium paths in a figure like Fig. 52(i) to find a graphical solution. Compare this with an algebraical solution of the same equations. Now assume numerical values for the parameters A and B in equation (2) of question 8. Change two of the parameters in equation (1) to make the solution conform to equations (2) and (3). Discuss the comparative statics of this system. Suppose we impose a further condition, $q_a = Kq_b$. What is the economic meaning of this condition, and what does this do to the system? (see p. 55).

10. Suppose each of the four cross-elasticities of equation (1) in question 8 can be either (+) or (−). List the 16 possible combinations, and try to find examples or pairs of commodities (such as beef and hides) for as many combinations as you can.

CHAPTER 13

THE PRICES OF FACTORS
OF PRODUCTION

We saw in Chapter 6 that an important part of what is called the theory of distribution consists of the study of the forces which determine the prices of factors of production, or the services of original suppliers. Analysis by supply and demand functions can throw a lot of light on this problem, for any problem involving prices can be analyzed by this means. We can use the tools of supply and demand in solving problems relating to wages or to rents just as we can in solving problems relating to the price of butter.

FACTORS OF PRODUCTION

The prices which form the subject matter of this chapter are the prices of the *services* of property, not of the property itself from which the services are derived. These services are the *factors of production,* although this term is sometimes carelessly used to mean the property from which the service is derived. Thus, labor is a factor of production derived from the human body. Land service is a factor of production derived from land. The services of houses, of machines, and of other material equipment are factors of production derived from the forms of property which yield them. There is, indeed, a relation between the prices of the services of any particular piece of property and of that property itself. The price of a house or a piece of land depends on the rent which it is expected to yield. We shall investigate this relationship in a later chapter. Meanwhile, it is important to notice that it is the price of the services of property, that is, of the factors of production, which concerns us here. To make the discussion more vivid we shall take labor as a typical factor of production and conduct most of the argument in terms of the problem of the determination of wages. The principles enunciated in this case, however, apply also to the prices of other services, like those of material property, subject of course to the peculiar circumstances of each case. They do not necessarily apply to the problem of the determination of the rate of interest. That is a special problem which we must leave until we have seen something of the theory of money.

A Wage as a Price

The nature of a wage as a price needs to be clarified. The economist usually regards labor as a commodity and a wage as a price of this commodity. The labor movement has protested this view and has even succeeded in writing into the Clayton Act of 1914 and the constitution of the International Labor Office a declaration that labor is not a commodity. The truth is that labor is *more* than a commodity; the industrial relationship in which a man is employed by an employer is a complex relationship involving many aspects of human life and surrounded by considerations which are outside the economist's abstraction. Nevertheless, in one of its aspects, and in the aspect with which the economist is most concerned, labor *is* a commodity; it is bought and sold, it participates in an exchange relationship, and one of the aspects of this exchange is its *price,* or ratio of exchange. In the labor bargain the worker gives up something—time or effort, however this may be measured—and receives something, which consists in part of a money wage including fringe benefits like pension rights or vacations with pay, in part of the various other benefits or costs which surround the fact of employment, such as status, companionship, conditions of work, and so on. The most general concept of the price of labor is the ratio, in this exchange, of what he gets to what he gives up. Where some of the items are incommensurable we simplify this concept and measure it, say, by money received per hour of work.

Measurement of Wages

There are many different methods of measuring both work and wages. The two commonest methods are: first, the simple hourly wage, which is the ratio of the amount of money received divided by the amount of time worked; and second, piece wages, which are measured by the ratio of the money paid to some measure of the actual work done, without specific regard to the time taken to do it. There are many variants on these methods, involving various forms of incentive payments, bonuses, disciplinary fines, fringe benefits, and so on. For most purposes of this analysis, however, we shall assume that all these methods can be reduced to an hourly wage equivalent, and that their effects can be measured by changes in the product of the hour of labor.

The Determination of Wages in a Competitive Market

The *equilibrium price* of the services of any form of property bought and sold in a competitive market is determined by the familiar principle of *clearing the market*. The equilibrium price is that at which the quantity of the service which its owners are willing to offer is equal to the quantity of the service which its employers are willing to take. Take, for example, the case of a particular form of labor, such as weaving. For a given place and a given period of time a demand schedule can be constructed showing the relation between the price of weaving (i.e., the hourly wage of weavers), and the number of hours of weaving that will be purchased at each hypothetical price by the employers. Similarly, a supply schedule can be constructed, showing the relation between the hourly wage of weavers and the number of hours of weaving which they will offer at each wage. Then, as we have seen before, unless the wage is at the point where the quantity of labor offered by the workers is equal to the quantity of labor which employers are willing to take, there will be forces coming into play to move the wage nearer the equilibrium level. If the wage is above the equilibrium level, there will be some workers who are willing to work at that wage but who cannot find employment. If the market is a competitive one, they will undercut the workers already in employment. The wage will fall. As it falls, employers will offer rather more employment, and some workers will be attracted away into other occupations, until finally a wage is reached at which all who wish to be employed at weaving will be employed.

Similarly, if the wage is too low, employers will want more labor than the workers are willing to offer, and there will be a *shortage of labor*. Consequently, if there is a competitive market, employers who cannot get the labor they require will raise wages in order to attract workers. This will force the other employers to raise their wages, and so wages generally will rise until more workers are attracted into weaving, fewer weavers are demanded, and the equilibrium wage is again reached.

Effect of Monopolies

If there are monopolies either on the side of labor or on the side of employers, it does not necessarily follow that the wage will tend to be where the quantity of labor which employers will take is equal to the quantity which workers will offer. Suppose, for instance, that there is a strong trade union of weavers, strong enough to prevent the employment of any nonunion men. Then the union may force the wage up to the point where there is a large number of workers who would like to obtain employment in weaving at the prevailing wage who cannot find employment at that wage, and yet who cannot gain employment by offering to work for less because the union will not allow individual bargaining. Similarly, there may be an employers' association, or an understanding among employers, which will keep the wage down to a point where some employers feel a shortage of labor. In their own private interest these employers may wish to bid up the wage they offer; but because of their agreement with other employers they prefer to suffer a shortage of labor rather than to overcome the shortage by raising wages.

Importance of Elasticities of Demand and Supply

Evidently in this case as in the case of any price, the elasticities of demand and supply play a great part in determining the flexibility of wages and the power of monopolistic combinations to raise or lower them above the equilibrium level. If the demand for any particular kind of labor is very elastic, the wage is likely to be much more flexible than if the demand is elastic, for the principles which were developed in Chapter 11 hold here also. If the demand for weaving is highly inelastic, a weavers' union will be able to raise the wage of weavers without materially affecting the volume of their employment. If, on the other hand, the demand for their labor is elastic, any attempt to raise wages above the equilibrium level will result in a large fall in employment. Likewise, if the supply of a particular kind of labor is inelastic, a combination of employers to force down wages is much more likely to be successful than if it is elastic. For with an inelastic supply of labor a low wage will create but little scarcity of labor. But if the supply of labor is elastic, an attempt by a combination of employers to force the wage below the equilibrium level is almost sure to fail. With an elastic supply, a low wage means a severe labor shortage, and some employer will be tempted to raise wages in the attempt to obtain the labor he needs.

THE COST CONCEPT

Interrelations of Factor Prices and Commodity Prices

The fuller study of the forces which underly the demand and supply of factors of production is taken up in Part II. The key to this relationship however is the concept of *cost*. Even though we cannot at this point explore all the implications of this concept, to go further with the theory of factor prices we must look a little more deeply into the relations of factor input to cost, cost to supply, and supply to output. We are already familiar with the concepts of alternative cost and of resources cost. In what follows *cost of production* usually refers to the *factor cost* of commodities, which is close to the concept of *resources cost,* and may be defined as the value of factors used up in the production of a given amount of commodity. Thus, suppose that in the production of 10,000 gallons of milk we had to use $1200 worth of labor, $200 worth of seed and fertilizer, $400 worth of depreciation of cows and equipment; suppose, too, that the capital employed in the enterprise in land, buildings, and equipment would not be forthcoming unless the owner were paid $200; the total cost of the milk would be $2000. The average cost is then the total cost divided by the output, which is $0.20 per gallon.

Why Cost Includes Normal Profit

It must be noted carefully that in economics we define cost in a way that differs from the cost concept of the accountant. The accountant is interested in measuring profit, so he defines cost in such a way as to exclude profit. The economist is interested in measuring supply price, that is, the price that will just be sufficient to persuade factors to cooperate in the production of a given amount of a commodity. The economist's concept of cost therefore includes a *normal profit,* that is, that sum which is just necessary to pay to the owner of the capital employed in order to persuade him to keep his capital in this particular occupation. Similarly it includes the wages which are necessary to persuade the workers to work in this occupation, and payments to other factors necessary to persuade their owners to supply them to this occupation. The concept of average cost as including normal profit has the great advantage that it is equal to the *supply price* of the producer's output, in the sense that if the price of the product falls below the average cost, its producer will go out of business. Only the output with average cost equal to or less than the actual price of the product will be produced, for it will not pay to produce if the average cost is greater than the price.

The Average Cost Distribution

We can now draw up a table showing the distribution of producers according to their average costs. Let us suppose that an investigation of a milk industry has revealed the results shown in Table 17. From this table the supply curve for milk can immediately be derived. If the price is below 20 cents, presumably no milk will be supplied, as there are no firms with costs low enough to make the production profitable. At a price of 20 cents, 3 firms will find it profitable to produce, and will produce 180,000 gallons. At a price of 21 cents these 3 firms will continue in production, of course, for if it pays them to produce at 20 cents, it will all the more pay them to produce at 21 cents. But at 21 cents 5 more producers find it profitable to produce; these add 300,000 gallons to the

TABLE 17. A COST DISTRIBUTION

Average Cost (cents per gallon)	Number of Firms	Total Output (thousand gallons)
20	3	180
21	5	300
22	10	600
23	11	630
24	20	1100
25	18	900
26	9	400
27	4	150
28	1	30

total output, which is therefore equal to 180,000 + 300,000 gallons, or 480,000 gallons. At 22 cents, 10 more producers come into the field, adding another 600,000 gallons, making 1,080,000 gallons in all. So we construct the whole supply schedule, as in Table 18A, by adding the successive increments of output produced at successively higher costs.

The relation between cost and supply is now clear. Suppose, for instance, that there was a general rise in the cost of production of milk, so that the costs of each producer rose by 1 cent per gallon. It would now take a price of 21 cents to persuade the 3 lowest-cost producers to produce their 180,000 gallons, 22 cents would be necessary to attract the next 300,000 gallons, 23 cents for the next 600,000, and so on, as in Table 18B. It is evident that the rise in costs has led to a fall in the quantity that would be supplied at each price—i.e., to a fall in supply. It follows that a rise in costs—unless demand is perfectly elastic—will lead to a rise in the price because of the fall in supply.

It is important to realize that the connection between *cost* and *price* is always of this indirect nature. There is no law which says that because

TABLE 18. COST AND SUPPLY

A		B	
Price (cents per gallon)	Output (000 gallons)	Price (cents per gallon)	Output (000 gallons)
19	0	20	0
20	180	21	180
21	480	22	480
22	1080	23	1080
23	1710	24	1710
24	2810	25	2810
25	3710	26	3710
26	4110	27	4110
27	4260	28	4260
28	4290	29	4290

a commodity has cost $40 per ton its price must be $40 per ton. If a man builds a house at the South Pole at a cost of a million dollars, the mere fact that it cost a million dollars would not enable him to receive that much for it. But there is, nevertheless, a close relationship between costs of production and price. The price of a commodity depends on its demand and supply curves, and the position of its supply curve depends on its costs of production.

Why Costs Rise or Fall

Average cost can rise or fall for two quite different reasons, which it is important not to confuse. It can rise or fall because there is a fall or a rise in productive efficiency, that is, in the amount of factors necessary to produce a unit of product. Or it can rise or fall because of a rise or fall in the price of the factors. The total cost of a factor is its price multiplied by the quantity employed. The total cost of a given amount of product is the sum of the *prices times quantities* of all the factors. Cost here is usually measured in money, but this is not merely a monetary phenomenon; a change in the relative prices of factors will change the alternative costs of commodities, for those which use more of a factor whose relative price has risen will become dearer relative to those commodities which use less.

DETERMINANTS OF THE DEMAND FOR A FACTOR

The Demand for a Factor as a Derived Demand

We are now in a position to investigate some of the forces which determine the demand for a factor of production, such as labor. The demand for a factor is usually a *derived* demand. Some people, it is true, are hired to perform direct personal services for others, but this is a small proportion of the labor force. Most labor is hired because with its aid the employer can produce or acquire some further commodity for which there is a demand, and which can therefore be sold. There is a demand for weavers because of the demand for cloth. There is a demand for automobile workers because of the demand for automobiles. Likewise there is a demand for the services of land because of a demand for the things which land will grow, and a demand for the services of machines because of a demand for the product of these machines.

The demand for a factor, like any other demand, is a function which tells us how much will be bought at each price. This function has two major parameters: the *magnitude* of the demand, that is, whether it is large or small; and the *elasticity* of the demand, that is, whether the quantity is responsive to a change in price.[1] Both these parameters are determined by three principal conditions. The first is the proportion which the total cost of the factor bears to the total cost of the product, which might be called the *importance* of the factor. Importance here does not mean being essential; all factors may be equally essential, in the sense that they cannot be dispensed with, but a factor which contributes only a small part of the total cost is *unimportant*. The second is the nature of the demand for the product of the factor. The character of the supply of the product is also relevant. The third is the degree to which the factor has good substitutes, or the substitutability of the factor for others. This is close to the concept of *essentiality*; if a factor is essential, no matter how unimportant in the above sense, it has no substitutes; if it has good substitutes, that is, high substitutability, it is not essential.

Three Propositions on the Magnitude of Derived Demand

We can now derive three propositions on what determines the magnitude of derived demand. To fix ideas, we will use the demand for a factor as an illustration, though the propositions hold for any derived demand.

Then proposition M1 is: *The demand for a factor will be larger, the more important the factor in the process of production,* that is, the larger the proportion of the total cost of the product accounted for by the factor. A corollary of this proposition is that a rise (or fall) in the importance of a factor will raise (or lower) the demand for it, other things of course being held constant. Thus if we move to a new process of production of cloth in which there is a decline in the proportion of the total cost of the cloth made up by the wage of weavers, the demand for weaving will fall.

Proposition M2 is: *An expected rise in the demand for a product will cause a rise in the demand for any type of factor which produces the product.* If it is expected, for instance, that at each price of cloth more will be demanded than before then, at each price of weaving, i.e., at each hourly wage of weavers, more hours of weaving can be sold than before. The full proof of this proposition must be left until later. It can be seen immediately, however, that the proposition is a reasonable one. For suppose the demand for cloth increases. Then, unless the supply of cloth is perfectly inelastic, its production will also increase. An increased production of cloth will necessitate an increased employment of weavers even at the old wage. That is to say, the demand for weaving will have increased.

---

[1] If the demand function is linear, of the form $q_d = K + ep$, then K, the amount that will be demanded at zero price, is a good measure of the magnitude of the demand, and e, as we saw on p. 189, is a measure of the absolute elasticity. It is usually negative.

UNCERTAINTY OF FUTURE DEMAND. It should be observed that it is the *expected* demand for a product that helps to determine the demand for the labor producing it. When labor is employed, the product which justifies that employment is not yet produced. It will not be finished and sold until some time in the future, a time which may be long or short. When labor is employed, then, it is not because of the present demand for its product, but because the employer expects that there will be a demand for the product at the time when it comes on the market. The expectation may be fulfilled or it may not. If a change takes place in the demand for weaving, it is because of a change in the opinion of employers regarding the demand for cloth in a few weeks or months. The employers may be right or wrong, but it is their opinion, and not the accuracy of that opinion, that determines the demand for weaving.

Proposition M3 is: *The magnitude of the demand for a factor will be larger, the less substitutable it is for others.* The corollary is that, if a factor becomes more substitutable for others, that is, less essential, the demand for it will decline. If substitutes for a factor appear on the market at an attractive price, employers of factors will begin to turn to the substitutes and diminish their purchases of the original factors. We should add therefore a further lemma, that if the price of substitutes declines, the demand for the factor will decline also. That is to say, substitutable factors are in competitive demand; a fall in the price of any one lowers the demand for the others. Factors may also be in joint demand, that is, be negatively substitutable; machines and their operators are a good example. In this case a fall in the price of one factor will raise the purchase of another with which it is in joint demand.

Three Propositions on the Elasticity of Demand for a Factor

Three corresponding propositions can also be stated regarding the determinants of the elasticity of demand for a factor. These attempt to answer the question, What determines whether a fall in the price of a factor will produce a large or a small change in the quantity purchased?

Proposition E1 may then be stated: *The more important, that is, the greater the proportion of the total cost of the product accounted for by the factor, the more elastic is the demand for it likely to be.* If a factor of production plays only a small part in the making of the final product, a fall in the price of the factor will cause little change in the price or output of the final commodity and therefore little change in the quantity of the factor bought. If there were only one kind of paint which could be used on automobiles, and if the price of this paint were halved, there would be very little effect either on the price or on the output of automobiles, or on the quantity of paint bought by the automobile manufacturers, for paint is a very small part of the total cost of a car. If, however, the wages of automobile workers were halved, there would be a very appreciable effect on the price and the output of cars, and on the employment of the workers, for labor plays an important part in the production of automobiles.

Proposition E2 is: *The more elastic the demand for a product and the less elastic the supply, the more elastic is likely to be the demand for the factors which go to make the product.* This proposition rests on the assumption that the lower the price of any type of factor, the greater will be the supply of any product which it goes to make. Suppose, for instance, that the wages of automobile workers are reduced. If all other things remain the same, this will have the effect of making the production of automobiles more profitable. Even if the price of automobiles remains the same, the output of the industry will expand. There will be an *increase in supply,* for what we mean by an increase in supply is an increase not merely in the quantity supplied but in the quantity supplied at each price. The same proposition can be illustrated with reference to the cost tables (Tables 17 and 18, p. 251). If the price of one of the factors of production of milk, for instance, rises and if all producers have to pay this higher price, the average cost to each producer rises. We move therefore from a position such as illustrated in Table 18A to a position shown in Table 18B where the rise in cost produces a fall in supply. A rise in the price of a factor then leads to a fall in supply of the product. Unless demand is perfectly elastic this will lead to a rise in the price of the product and a fall in output of the product. The fall in output of the product will lead to a fall in the employment of the factor. By this circuitous route therefore we pass from the rise in the price of the factor to a fall in its employment. This is what is meant by a *demand* for a factor.

The absolute elasticity of demand for a factor is the increase in its employment which results from a unit fall in its price. The demand for labor, for instance, is more elastic, the greater the increase in employment which follows from a given fall in the wage. If the demand for automobiles is elastic, the increase in supply which we noted will bring about a relatively large increase in the total output and therefore a large increase in the employment of labor. If, however, the demand for automobiles is inelastic, the increase in supply caused by the fall in wages will have little effect on the output and on the amount of employment. That is, the more elastic the demand for automobiles, the more elastic will be the demand for automobile workers. In contrast, the *less* elastic the overall supply of automobiles, the more will a given fall in supply affect the output, and therefore the more elastic will be the demand for automobile workers.

Finally, Proposition E3 is: *The better, and the cheaper, the substitutes*

for a factor of production, the more likely is it to have an elastic demand.
Suppose that machines can easily be substituted for labor, and labor for
machines. Then if the price of labor is raised, machines will tend to take
its place; if the price of labor is lowered, it will take the place of machines.
A lowering of the wage will result in a sharp increase in employment, for
an extra quantity of labor will be required to replace the discarded
machines. Similarly, a raising of the wage will result in a sharp decrease
of employment, for the high-priced labor will be replaced by machines.
In this case the demand for labor is elastic. If, on the other hand, a factor
has no substitutes in any particular process, i.e., if it is completely in-
dispensable, a rise or fall in the price of the factor will affect its employment only in so far as it affects the general output of the product. The
demand for labor will be more inelastic.

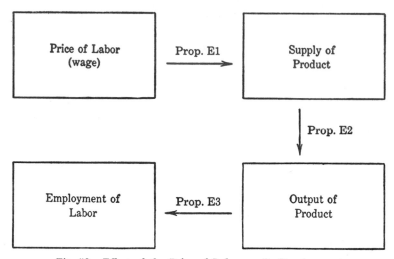

Fig. 53.   Effect of the Price of Labor on Its Employment

DIAGRAMMATIC REPRESENTATION OF THE PROPOSITIONS ON ELASTICITY.
The last three propositions relating to the elasticity of demand for labor
(or any other service) may be illustrative by Fig. 53. The elasticity shows
how much a change in the wage (the price of labor) affects the amount of
employment. There are three steps connecting these two quantities, each
corresponding to one of our three propositions. The wage affects the
supply curve of the product, the supply curve of the product affects the
output of the product, and the output of the product affects the amount
of employment. These influences are shown by the arrows in the figure.
The stronger each of the three influences represented by the arrows, the
greater will be the effect of a change in the wage on the quantity of

employment, i.e., the more elastic will be the demand for labor. The strength of the first influence, that of the price of labor on the supply of the product, depends on how important a part labor plays in the process; the more important the part, the greater the influence. This is proposition E1. The strength of the second influence, that of the supply of the product on the output of the product, depends on the elasticity of demand for the product. This illustrates proposition E2. Finally, the influence which the output of the product exerts on the employment of labor depends on the degree to which labor is substitutable for other factors. If labor cannot be substituted for other services, a change in output must produce a proportionate change in the employment of labor. If labor can be substituted easily for other services, then a rise in wages, leading to a decline in output, will produce a greater proportionate decline in employment, for not only will there be a smaller output but each unit of it will be produced with a smaller amount of labor than before. This illustrates proposition E3.

The Derived Demand Model

These relationships can be illustrated even more exactly by the model shown in Fig. 54. Here we measure the quantity of output demanded (q_d) or supplied (q_s) along OQ_u, the price of output (p) along OP_u, the price of input or factor (p_i) along OP_i, and the quantity of input or factor (q_i) along OQ_i. Then $D_1D'_1$ is the demand curve for the output or product, C_1P_1 the initial supply curve, P_1 the initial point of equilibrium with a price P_1Q_1 and quantity of output OQ_1. The curve $K_0K_1K_2$ shows how the minimum supply price varies with the price of the input, the minimum supply price being the price at which nothing will be supplied, measured by the intercept of the supply curve on the price axis. Thus OK_0 is the minimum supply price, when $p_i = 0$, and is equal to the average cost of the most efficient (least cost) producer when $p_i = 0$; this is the average cost per unit of output incurred through the purchase of all other inputs except the one in question. As p_i rises from zero to OM_1, the minimum supply price rises from OK_0 to OC_1; as p_i rises to OM_2 the minimum supply price rises to OC_2. As the minimum supply price rises, the whole supply curve rises with it roughly parallel to itself, as a rise in p_i raises the cost of all firms by about the same amount. We neglect here any possible change in the absolute elasticity of supply due to the change in p_i, which might happen if high-cost firms used the factor in a different proportion from that of the low-cost firms.

Thus when $p_i = OM_1$, the supply curve is C_1P_1, the quantity of output is OQ_1, and we need only one more relation, that between the quantity of output and the quantity of input, to determine the quantity of input. This relation is given by the line OS_2S_1: at output OQ_1, input is Q_1S_1 ($= OL_1$). The ratio of input per unit of output at S_1 and S_2 is the slope of the lines OS_1, OS_2, or $\tan Q_1OS_1$, $\tan Q_2OS_2$. The point H_1, then, in the $p_i - q_i$ field of the third quadrant, lies on the demand curve for input, showing how much will be bought (OL_1) at a price of input OM_1.

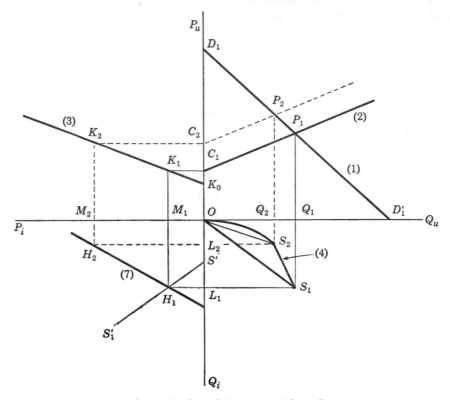

Fig. 54.   Derivation of the Demand for a Factor

Similarly, following the dashed line clockwise from M_2, if the price of input is OM_2, the supply curve will be C_2P_2, the price of output Q_2P_2, the quantity of output OQ_2 and the quantity of input Q_2S_2. The absolute elasticity of demand for input in that range will be L_2L_1/M_1M_2.

The six propositions on derived demand can all be deduced from this model. Thus if an input becomes more important, that is, a larger proportion of total cost, the total cost of all other inputs declines; the line $K_0K_1K_2$ shifts downward, the supply curve C_1P_1 shifts to the right, OQ_1 increases, OL_1 increases; that is there is a rise in the quantity of input bought at each price (proposition M1). The line K_0K_2 will also become steeper, a rise in price produces a larger fall in supply (C_1C_2 is larger), a larger fall in quantity of output (Q_1Q_2 is larger), a larger fall in quantity of input (L_1L_2 is larger); the demand for input is therefore more elastic (proposition E1). If the demand for output, $D_1D'_1$, rises, OQ_1 rises, OL_1 rises, that is, the demand for input rises (proposition M2). If the demand for output becomes more elastic, Q_1Q_2 increases, L_1L_2 increases; the demand for input also becomes more elastic (proposition E2). If the input suddenly has better, or cheaper substitutes, S_1 moves towards Q_1, the angle Q_1OS_1 will decline (less input per unit of output), and OL_1 will decline, that is, the demand for the input falls (proposition M3). With better substitutes also a rise in the price of the input will lower the ratio of input per unit of output; the angle Q_2OS_2 will be smaller, L_1L_2 will be larger, and the elasticity of demand for input will be larger (proposition E3).[2]

[2] Assuming linear functions, a simple formula can be derived for the demand for input. Thus suppose the demand for output is

$$q_d = K_d + e_d p \qquad (1)$$

and the supply of output is

$$q_s = -C_s e_s + e_s p \qquad (2)$$

e_d is the absolute elasticity of demand (a negative number in this case) e_s is the absolute elasticity of supply; C_s is the minimum supply price ($= OC_1$ for the supply curve C_1P_1 in Fig. 54). Then suppose the equation of the line $K_0K_1K_2$ is

$$C_s = F + w p_i \qquad (3)$$

The more important the factor, that is, the larger the proportion of total cost for which it accounts, the smaller will be F ($= OK_0$) and the larger will be w, for the smaller will be the average cost in the absence of any charge for the factor ($p_i = O$) and the faster total cost will rise as p_i increases. We have also a production function

$$q_i = S_0 + sq \qquad (4)$$

s also depends on the importance of the factor, but it also may change radically if the factor is substitutable for others (see Chapter 25). We also have the fundamental condition of equilibrium, represented by the point P_1,

$$q_d = q_s = q \qquad (5)$$

Substituting from (1), (2) and (3) in (5) we have

$$K_d + e_d p = -(F + w p_i) e_s + e_s p, \text{ or}$$

$$p = \frac{K_d + e_s F + e_s w p_i}{e_s - e_d} \qquad (6)$$

Substituting now in (1) or (2) and (6) in (4) we have

$$q_i = S_0 + \frac{s e_s (K_d + e_d F)}{e_s - e_d} + \left(\frac{s e_d e_s w}{e_s - e_d} \right) p_i \qquad (7)$$

This is the equation of the demand function of the factor. From it the six propositions outlined above can easily be derived. The lines corresponding to these equations in Fig. 54 are indicated by the equation number.

Complementarity and Competitiveness in Demand for Factors

The analysis of complementarity and competitiveness in demand for two or more commodities, outlined in the previous chapter, is also of great importance in interpreting the demand for factors of production. Where two factors of production are substitutable in production their demands will be competitive. A rise in the price of one without any change in the price of the other will cause a fall in the employment of the first but a rise in the employment of the second. Land and labor are frequently in this relationship. Where land is cheap and labor is dear, *extensive* farming is the rule, using much land and little labor. Where land is dear and labor is cheap, we have intensive farming, using little land and much labor.

Two factors of production may, however, stand in a relation of complementary demand. A good example is the demand for machines and for skilled machinists. In this case a scarcity of one factor will cause a fall in the demand for the other. If there are few machinists there will be little demand for machines. If there are few machines there will be little demand for machinists. A fall either in the wages of machinists or in the price of their machines will bring about a rise in the employment of *both* machinists *and* machines. A fall in the price of machines, therefore, may cause a decline in the demand for unskilled labor and a rise in the demand for skilled labor. This example should warn us against the fallacies which result from treating factors of production in too broad categories. From the point of view of economic analysis it is hardly too much to say that there is no such thing as labor as a whole, and the movement of such a whole must always be analyzed in terms of movements in its component parts.

THE SUPPLY OF FACTORS

The derived demand, or input-output system described above is still indeterminate; to determine the magnitude of the various variables we need a supply function for the factor. Suppose, for instance, in Fig. 54, $S_1 S'_1$ is the supply curve for the factor, H_1 where the supply and demand curves for the factor intersect gives the price of the factor, $L_1 H_1$, and all the other quantities of the system are now determined from this. The supply of each kind of factor presents peculiar problems of its own; we can begin by analyzing some of the forces which underly the nature of the supply of labor, by which we mean the relationship between the price of labor and the quantity of labor offered for sale at each hypothetical price. Usually this is a direct relationship, in which a greater quantity of labor of a particular kind is called forth at a high wage rather than at a low wage. Under certain circumstances, however, an inverse relationship is possible, in which a higher wage calls forth less labor than a lower wage.

Two Factors in the Supply of Labor

Labor is usually measured by *hours* of work. As we have seen, other methods of measurement have been devised which attempt to take into account the intensity as well as the duration of labor. These refinements will not concern us, important as they may be in practice, for no matter how labor is measured, the ensuing principles are valid. We shall therefore make the simplifying assumption that the quantity of labor of any given kind can be measured in hours. The total quantity of any given type of labor offered to employers then depends on two factors. One is the number of hours each worker is willing to work. The other is the number of workers. Thus the quantity of weaving offered for sale may increase because of a rise either in the number of hours worked by each weaver or in the number of weavers. To find out how the total number of hours of weaving offered will vary with the hourly wage of weavers, we must answer two further questions. The first is: How does the hourly wage affect the number of hours per week which an individual weaver is willing to work? The second is: How does the wage affect the number of individuals willing to work at weaving?

The Number of Workers and the Supply of Labor

If we can assume, as frequently we can, that the number of hours to be worked by each individual is fixed by custom or by contract, the problem of the supply of labor resolves itself into the second of the two questions above. In many industrial processes the hours of work are fixed either by law or by agreement with a trade union. The only way in which an employer can then obtain more labor is by taking on more men, and the only way in which the workers can offer more labor is through more men offering to work. In this case the relationship between the wage and the quantity of labor offered is a direct relationship. A rise in the wage offered to any particular occupation, other wages remaining the same, is bound to attract men into it out of other occupations, or perhaps even out of idleness. The higher the wage, therefore, the more labor will be offered, and the lower the wage, the less labor will be offered—labor, of course, of a particular kind. This is not to say that if wages are lowered in all occupations simultaneously there will be less labor offered. In this section we are discussing not the supply of labor as a whole but the supply of labor of a particular kind.

The Elasticity of the Supply of Labor

In the above circumstances the elasticity of the supply of labor will depend almost entirely on the *mobility* of labor into the occupation in question and out of other occupations. If the type of labor under consideration is mobile, and if the occupation is one which is easy to enter and which does not require much skill or unusual ability, then its supply will be elastic. A small rise in its wage will attract large numbers of workers away from other occupations, a small decline in wage will drive large numbers of workers away into other occupations. If, on the other hand, the occupation is difficult to enter or to leave, if it requires a great degree of skill which is not easily acquired or easily abandoned, or if it requires unusual ability, then the supply of labor will be inelastic. A high wage will not tempt may newcomers in; a low wage will not drive many old-timers out. Here is a phenomenon which is common to all supply curves. The longer the period which the curve represents, the more elastic it will be. A temporary rise in wages may attract few people into an occupation. The same rise in wages maintained over a number of years may attract large numbers into it. This is particularly true of occupations which require long training. In this case a rise or a fall in wages must be maintained perhaps for a generation or more before it produces its full effect on the quantity of labor supplied.

The Supply of Labor from the Individual Worker

It is not always true, of course, that the number of hours of work performed by an individual worker cannot be varied. In many cases considerable variation in individual effort is possible. Particularly is this so where the worker is himself employing his own labor. The labor of the artist, the writer, the independent craftsman, the farmer, and, above all, of the businessman himself falls into this category. Even the worker whose daily stint is fixed by agreement or custom has a certain ability to vary the number of days' work done in a year, as the wartime phenomenon of absenteeism clearly showed. Under these circumstances a peculiar phenomenon sometimes appears, as shown in Fig. 55. Here we plot the hourly wage vertically, and the number of hours worked or the quantity of labor supplied, horizontally. There will be some physiological upper limit on the number of hours worked per day, OH, and a lower limit on the wage, OW, at which a mere subsistence can be earned by working OH hours, equal to $OH \times OW$, or the area OWW_0H. Under no circumstances will any labor be supplied below the wage OW, and only at OW if there are no other employment opportunities. In that case however, WW_0 will be supplied at OW. As we raise the wage from OW the amount of labor supplied is likely to *decrease,* as people find they can earn their subsistence by working fewer hours, and the disutility of hours close to the maximum OH is very great. If the worker simply wishes to earn a conventional subsistence, the supply curve of labor, say between W_0 and W_1, will be a rectangular hyperbola, with total income constant. Beyond W_1 however we suppose that further increases in the wage result in a desire for more income; once the hours of work are easily tolerable, as at W_2, then a further rise in the wage may arouse still more the desire for income rather than leisure, and the supply curve may follow the usual upward-sloping

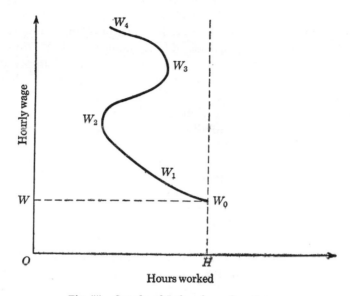

Fig. 55. Supply of Labor from One Person

path of supply curves as between W_2 and W_3, with an increased wage calling forth an increased effort. It is possible that this effect also reverses itself at very high wages, when all conventional material wants are satisfied, and leisure now emerges as a "rich man's good"; then a further rise in wage may once more reduce the quantity of labor offered, as between W_3 and W_4. Segments such as W_0W_2 and W_3W_4 are known as backward sloping or negatively elastic supply curves; we will study their origins more intensely in Chapter 27. We have suggested they are most likely to occur either at very low wages or at very high wages; in the intermediate range the supply of labor is more likely to be positively elastic.

THE IMPORTANCE OF BACKWARD-SLOPING SUPPLY CURVES. These backward-sloping supply curves for the labor of individuals can result in a backward-sloping supply curve for all labor of a particular kind only when the number of individuals in the occupation cannot easily change. If the number of workers in a particular occupation can change easily and quickly, a rise in wages will nearly always result in an increase in the total quantity of labor supplied, even if the quantity supplied by each individual declines. The decline in the quantity supplied by each individual will be outweighed by the rise in the number of workers supplying the labor. Where, however, the number of workers in an occupation is relatively fixed, the individual backward-sloping supply curve may be reflected in the general supply curve. As the number of individuals in an occupation frequently cannot be changed in short periods of time, a general backward-sloping supply curve is sometimes found in short periods, seldom, if ever, over long periods. The phenomenon is of considerable importance, therefore, in interpreting the short-period supply of some forms of labor. As we shall see in the next chapter, certain phenomena relating to the supply of agricultural produce can be interpreted only with the aid of this principle. Even more important, the supply of enterprise itself may be subject to this law. When times are good and the remuneration of the businessman is high, he may take time out, pay frequent visits to the club and the golf course, and neglect his business. When times are bad and his remuneration is low, he may stick close to the office, pay scrupulous attention to detail, and work two or three times as hard as he does in more prosperous times.

Supply of Other Factors

Some of the phenomena which occur in connection with the supply of labor also may be found in the case of other factors, though each factor has its own peculiarities. Thus land services in a particular place are often characterized by a highly inelastic supply; it is very hard, for instance, to increase the amount of land on Manhattan Island. Many of the peculiarities of land rent are accounted for by this inelasticity in supply. By contrast, there may be occasions in which a large landowner makes a decision as between the amount of land he will put into his own park and estate, which corresponds to the *leisure* use of human time, and the amount which he will rent out, which corresponds to the *work*, or income-producing use of human time. Backward-sloping supply curves for land are not inconceivable under these circumstances, where a higher price of land services (rent per acre) would actually diminish the amount of land rented, as the landlord might then feel that he was rich enough to withdraw some land from income-earning uses and put it into a park or garden. The supply of capital is too complex a problem to be considered fully at this time; even here, however, backward-sloping supply curves are possible. Thus a rise in the rate of interest may actually discourage saving, simply because making the capitalist richer in the present may lower his incentive to restrict consumption for future benefits.

ECONOMIC RENT

Economic Surplus

Part of the remuneration of any factor of production may be an economic surplus, the more traditional name for which is *economic rent*. Economic surplus may be defined as any payment to a factor of production which is in excess of its total supply price, that is, of the minimum amount which is necessary to keep the factor in its present occupation. There may be casual and accidental economic surpluses, positive or negative, as a result of chance or bargaining power. Usually however the term is restricted to the concept of an *equilibrium* surplus, for these surpluses may arise even in long-run equilibrium. Although first worked out in connection with the services of land (hence the name—economic rent), this concept applies to any factor of production which does not have a perfectly elastic supply. We may illustrate it first in the case of labor. Table 19 shows a small portion of a supply schedule for weaving.

TABLE 19.   SUPPLY SCHEDULE FOR WEAVING

Wage ($ per week)	50	51	52	53	54	55
Number of men offering labor	1000	1100	1200	1300	1400	1500

Here we have assumed that for every increase of a dollar in the weekly wage, 100 more men are willing to work at weaving. If the wage is $50 per week, 1000 men will offer their services. If the wage rises to $51 per week, the extra dollar will attract 100 new men to weaving. Therefore, $51 is the lowest wage which will make these 100 men offer their services. If the wage is $52 per week, another 100 men will offer their services. But the 100 who would work for $51 per week will now receive more than is necessary to keep them at the occupation of weaving. Each of these men would work for $51 per week, but in fact he receives $52 per week. Each therefore receives an economic rent of $1 per week, and the total economic rent received by the 100 men is $100. If the wage is $53 per week, the 100 men who would just be willing to work for $51 per week will get an economic rent of $2 each, or $200 in all, and the 100 men who would just be willing to work for $52 per week will receive an economic rent of $1 each, or $100 in all. The higher the wage, the greater will be the economic rent received by all those workers who would be willing to work at a lower wage, and the greater will be the economic rent received by all workers.

GRAPHIC ILLUSTRATION. This principle is illustrated graphically in Fig. 56. Here the wage is measured along OY, and the number of men who will offer their services at each wage along OX. The broken line $ABCDEFGHIJ$ is the supply curve. We have assumed a discontinuous supply curve for the sake of exposition, but as we can make the steps as small as we like our conclusions also hold for a continuous curve. Below a wage OA, then, there will be no labor offered. At the wage OA a number of men measured by AB offer their services. These are the men who are

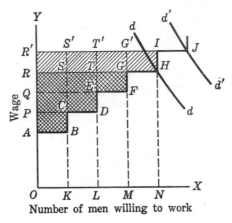

Fig. 56.   Economic Rent

most attracted by the occupation in question and who will therefore work in it at a low wage. At a higher wage, OP, an additional group of men, CD, will enter the occupation, bringing the total number to $AB + CD$, or PD. At a wage OQ a less eager group, EF, enters the occupation. At a wage OR a still less eager group, GH, and at a wage OR' an even less eager group, IJ, will be persuaded by the high wage to enter the occupation. If, now, the demand curve cuts this supply curve at H the wage will be OR. The first, most eager group, represented by AB, will receive this wage, OR. They would, however, have been willing to work for a wage OA. The total remuneration of the group at a wage OR is $OR \times OK$, or the area $ORSK$. At a wage OA the total remuneration would have been $OA \times OK$, or the area $OABK$. The economic rent of this first group, therefore, is the area of the rectangle $ARSB$. Similarly, at the wage OR the total economic rent received by the second group, CD, is the area $CSTD$; and that received by the third group, EF, is the area $ETGF$. No rent is received by the group *GH*, who are only just attracted into the occupation at the wage *OR*. The total economic rent received by all the workers at the wage *OR*, then, is the heavily shaded area *ARGFEDCB*.

Effect on Economic Rent of a Rise in Demand

Suppose, now, there is a rise in demand, the new demand curve passing through the point *J*. The wage will rise to *OR'*. The economic rent, therefore, received by the first group of men, *AB*, will increase, becoming the area *AR'S'B*. The economic rent received by all the workers together will also rise. It will now include the lightly shaded area *RR'IH* as well as the heavily shaded area, the total rent being represented by the area *AR'IHGFEDCB*.

Perfectly Elastic Supply Yields No Economic Rent

Thus we see that both economic rent and a less than perfectly elastic supply curve arise from the same cause—the *difference* in the eagerness with which the owners of various units of the factor in question will offer their services. If all the owners of a given factor are equally eager to sell all they own, there will be some price at which each will offer all the factor he possesses. A lower price than this will result in a complete absence of offers. Suppose that in the example in Table 19 a very large number of weavers are willing to offer eight hours of weaving per day at a wage of $50, and none below that wage. Then at any wage below $50 no weaving will be supplied. At a wage of $50 any amount of weaving may be obtained. The supply of weaving is perfectly elastic. No matter how great the demand for weavers, the equilibrium wage will be $50, which is the lowest wage that will persuade each weaver to offer his services. There is therefore no economic rent, no matter how great the demand for weaving.

To put the matter in another way. If the supply of any commodity is not perfectly elastic a higher price must be offered to induce a greater quantity of the commodity to come onto the market. The higher price is necessary to overcome the diffidence of those who are not eager to sell the commodity. At a high price, therefore, those who are more eager to sell will receive more than the least sum which will induce them to part with the commodity. This excess is economic rent. It should be noted that we have assumed in the above argument a fixed quantity supplied by each individual supplier. That is, in the case of weaving, we have assumed that an increased offer of weaving could come only through more men offering to weave, and not through the existing weavers offering to work for longer hours. If this assumption is relaxed the problem of economic rent becomes more complicated.

QUESTIONS AND EXERCISES

1. Suppose that the following schedules represent the demand and supply schedules for a certain form of labor—say, weaving. Assume that the number of hours worked per day is fixed by technical considerations, so that variation in the quantity of labor employed can come about only through a variation in the number of men employed.

At a wage of:	35	40	45	50	55	60	65	$ per week
Employers will employ:	50	45	40	35	30	25	20	thousand men
Employment will be wanted by:	20	30	40	50	60	70	80	thousand men

   a. If the market is perfectly competitive, what will be the equilibrium wage and the number employed at that wage?
   b. Suppose that there is a strong weavers' union with a membership of 25,000 men. Suppose, furthermore, that the industry has a closed shop policy so that only union men can obtain employment. What wage should the union try to get? How many men outside the union would like to get employment at that wage? Why are they unable to do so?
   c. Suppose the union had a membership of 40,000 men, and that it undertook to pay to its unemployed members an income equal to the weekly wage of its employed members. What wage would give the union members the highest weekly income, assuming that the employed members were taxed by the union to support the unemployed members, and that the expenses of administration were insignificant? How many members would be unemployed at that wage? (Note: Calculate the total payroll at each wage.)

2. Although the demand for houses is probably quite elastic, the demand for labor of various kinds and for raw materials in the building industry is probably very inelastic. How would you account for this? The supply of each kind of labor and raw material in the building industry is generally in the hands of a monopolistic organization. Because the demand for each of these things is inelastic, it is very difficult to reduce their prices. Why? If in a depression the prices of labor and materials in the building industry were reduced 25 percent, there would probably be a spectacular increase in building which would more than compensate all the elements in the industry for their reduced prices. Why, then, does not this happen?

3. Agricultural wages are generally higher in neighborhoods which are near industrial centers. Select the best explanation among the following:
   a. Farmers are more kindhearted when near the civilizing influence of a city.
   b. Workers who can get to a movie once a week are more efficient.
   c. City people come out and buy up all the cottages for summer homes.
   d. The attraction of high wages in the city naturally pulls up agricultural wages.
   e. Agricultural workers are relatively more scarce when they can easily get city jobs.

4. A trade union official in a textile town once advised his men to ask for a 10 percent cut in wages. Was he crazy? If not, why not?

5. Many people believe that there are "only so many jobs to go round" and that therefore if one man gets a job another must lose one. Do you agree? If not, how would you meet this argument?

6. Suppose a college suddenly decided to move to a small village in a rather remote part of the country. What do you think would be the effect of this move (a) immediately, (b) as time went by, on: (i) The wages of gardeners in the village; (ii) The rent of houses in the village; (iii) The price of building lots in the residential section; (iv) The rent of stores in the center of the village?

7. Illustrate with graphs the following propositions:

   a. If the supply of a particular kind of labor is perfectly inelastic, no change in demand for it will change the quantity of it which will be supplied.

   b. If the demand for a product rises, the price of those types of labor going to make it will also rise. The more inelastic the supply of any one of these types, the greater will be the rise in its price.

   c. If the demand for a product rises, the demand for the types of labor going to make it will rise. The greater the part played by the labor in the process, the greater will be the rise in demand for it, and the greater will be the rise in the price of the labor.

8. An oil company in Mexico found that in order to get more hours of labor it had to *reduce* the hourly wage which it offered. How would you account for this?

9. Prove that in the case of a factor of production whose supply is perfectly inelastic at all prices the whole remuneration of the factor is economic rent.

10. The concept of economic rent was first evolved in connection with the remuneration of land, hence the name rent. Why should economic rent be regarded as peculiarly characteristic of the remuneration of land?

11. If the cost distribution of Table 17 (p. 251) is a statistically normal distribution, what does this tell us about the general shape of the supply curve?

12. In Table 18A (p. 251) what would be the economic rent accruing to the various firms if each of the various prices listed were the equilibrium price. Repeat with the data of Table 18B. Discuss the possible impact on economic rent of a rise in wages in the above case. Who is likely to get the economic rent in the case of the milk industry? Why?

13. Calculate the parameters of the equations of footnote 1, page 259, which correspond to the lines of Fig. 54 by measuring the appropriate distances; thus, $OD'_1 = K_d$, $-OD'_1/OD_1 = e_d$, and so on. From these equations calculate parameters of the equation of the demand for input, and check by calculating and then measuring the intercepts on the axis of the line H_1H_2.

14. Show exactly how the six propositions on derived demand can be derived from equation (7) on page 259.

15. Let us define the *input price multiplier* M_i as the increase in the price of output which results from a unit increase in the price of input, other things being held constant. Show from equation (6), page 259, that M_i depends

only on e_d, e_s, and w, and discuss the effects of changes in these parameters on M_t.

16. Class exercise: to construct a supply schedule of books from a class. Let each person write down on a slip of paper the least price for which he would be willing to sell his copy of the text at the end of the course. (Some writers call this the "reservation price" of each person.) Let the instructor collect these slips and arrange them in order, the lowest price at the top of the pile. From these slips the supply curve can immediately be constructed. Suppose, for instance, that the first few slips showed figures of $0.25, $0.50, $0.75, $0.75, $1, $1, $1. Then if a buyer offered less than $0.25 for the books he would receive none. If he offered $0.25 he would receive one. At $0.50 per copy he would receive two; at $0.75, four; and at $1, seven; and so on. The supply schedule would be as follows:

Price ($)	0.25	0.50	0.75	1.00
Amount offered	1	2	4	7

If in this case the buyer wished to purchase seven books he would have to offer a price of $1.00 apiece. In that case the seller who cared so little for the book that he would sell it for $0.25 would receive an economic rent of $0.75. The one who would offer it for $0.50 would receive an economic rent of $0.50, and so on for the others.

The supply curve for the class should be plotted, and the total economic rent calculated for a series of possible prices.

CHAPTER **14**

THE DYNAMICS OF DEMAND
AND SUPPLY

The problem of the general dynamics of the price system is difficult and is hard to separate from the general problem of the dynamics of the social system, which in turn is the problem of what stable relationships exist between the values of social variables at different time intervals. Demand and supply analysis, furthermore, is essentially an equilibrium system, not initially designed for the discussion of dynamic problems. Nevertheless, with the tools now at hand we can develop substantial insights into the nature of the dynamic processes of a price system, mainly because of the possibility of interpreting this dynamic process as a succession of equilibrium states.

EFFECTS OF A SHIFT IN DEMAND

We shall illustrate these dynamic processes first by considering in detail the effects of a shift in demand from one commodity to another, starting from a position of equilibrium; the same analysis would apply to any movement from a disequilibrium to an equilibrium position. Suppose then, that all industries are just normally prosperous, no industry is more prosperous than another, and therefore there is no tendency for resources to move from one industry to another. Now suppose that there is a change in the tastes of consumers—for instance, that a change in fashion causes a marked shift in consumers' demand from silk goods to cotton goods. The results of this shift will depend on the period of time taken into account. We may consider three broad stages. First, there is the immediate, or *impact effect*. Second, there are the changes which will take place during the period of adjustment, or the *adjustment effects*. Third, there is the effect on the final position of equilibrium; this is the *final effect*.

271

In considering these effects we shall assume that the other factors affecting economic life remain unchanged. In fact this will never be the case. Nevertheless, this assumption is necessary in order to separate the effects of the particular change in tastes which we are considering from the effects of all other independent changes.

The Impact Effect

In considering the impact effect we shall assume that over a very short period of time the supply of both cotton and silk is perfectly inelastic. Let us also assume that there is no holding of supplies for future sale, so all that is produced in a given week must be sold in that week. These assumptions are rather unrealistic, but they can be relaxed at a later stage. We are considering the effects of a known shift in demand from silk to cotton, which takes place in a certain week, and which persists thereafter indefinitely. This situation is represented in Fig. 57.

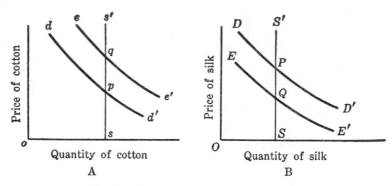

Fig. 57.   Impact Effect of a Shift in Demand

In Fig. 57A, *dd'* is the demand curve for cotton in the week before the change. That is, it shows the quantity of cotton which will be bought in that week at each hypothetical price. The total quantity of cotton coming on the market to be sold in that week is represented by *os*. It will have to be sold at a price *sp*. The perfectly inelastic supply curve for that week is *ss'*. Now suppose that in the next week the demand for cotton has risen to *ee'*. The quantity coming into the market is assumed to be unchanged. The price at which that quantity can be sold, however, has now risen to *sq*.

Similarly, in Fig. 57B the original demand for silk is *DD'*, the weekly quantity of silk coming into the market is *OS*, the inelastic supply curve for silk is *SS'*, and the new, decreased demand for silk is *EE'*. The result of the fall in demand is a fall in the price from *SP* to *SQ*.

The impact effect of a shift in demand from silk to cotton is therefore a fall in the price of silk and a rise in the price of cotton. These new prices will persist as long as the demands remain at their new levels, and as long as the quantities coming onto the market in each week do not change.

Intermediate Effects

However, the quantities coming onto the market *will* change. Under the stimulus of a high price of cotton new producers will enter the cotton industry, new workers will find employment in producing cotton, new land will be put down to cotton, and new cotton factories will be built. The output of cotton will increase. In each week after the initial change in demand an increase may be expected in the quantity of cotton placed on the market. This increase may be very slow at first, for it takes time before the effect of a higher price will show itself. Producers cannot enter an

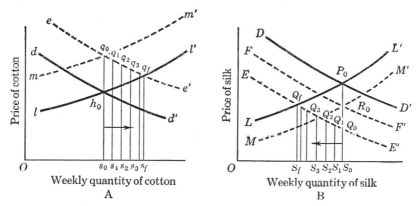

Fig. 58. Intermediate and Final Effects of Shifts in Demand

industry in the twinkling of an eye; plans have to be made, new fields must be plowed, new men must be trained, new warehouses and factories must be built, new machines must be constructed. All this takes time. Nevertheless, there will be a persistent tendency for the quantity of cotton placed on the market in each week to increase. But this increase will not go on indefinitely because if the demand remains unchanged at *ee'*, the price in successive weeks must fall. This is illustrated in Fig. 58A. Again, *dd'* is the old demand for cotton, and *ee'* is the new, increased demand. The quantity placed on the market in the week of the change is os_0. The price at which this quantity sells, after the rise in demand, is s_0q_0. Under the stimulus of this high price, however, in the next week a slightly larger quantity, os_1, will be placed on the market. This will sell at a rather lower price, s_1q_1. In the second week a still larger quantity will be placed on the market, os_2. This will fetch a still lower price, s_2q_2. So, as the weeks go by, the quantity placed on the market will increase under the stimulus of the high price, but the very increase in the quantity supplied will bring about a steady decline in the price.

Final Effects

This movement, however, will not go on forever. As the price falls, the force which makes for an increase in the weekly quantity supplied will also decline. Eventually there will come a week, f weeks from the initial change, when the force of expansion has worked itself out completely. The cotton industry will then be just normally profitable again, and the weekly quantity supplied, os_f, will show no tendency to increase in successive weeks thereafter. The price will be s_fq_f. This is the normal price under the new conditions. It is the price at which, when all necessary adjustments have been made, the industry will neither expand nor contract. The point q_f, therefore, must lie on the *normal* supply curve for cotton, ll', for any point on the normal supply curve shows what rate of production will be permanently maintained, without tendency to rise or fall, at the price indicated. Similarly, as the point h_0 represents the point of long-run equilibrium before the change in demand, this point also must lie on the normal supply curve. The output os_f and the price s_fq_f represent, therefore, the final effects of the original change in demand, the point q_f being the point of intersection of the new demand curve with the normal supply curve ll'.

EFFECTS IN A DECLINING INDUSTRY. In an exactly similar manner we can analyze the effects of the change in demand on the silk industry in Fig. 58B. In the week of the change there is a quantity OS_0 placed on the market and selling at a low price, S_0Q_0. This low price will cause a decline in the industry. The output of successive weeks will fall from OS_0 to OS_1, OS_2, etc. This decline, however, will not go on forever, for as the output declines the price will rise from S_0Q_0 to S_1Q_1, S_2Q_2, etc. As the price rises the industry will become relatively less unprosperous, and the force making for its decline will weaken. Finally, the output reaches OS_f, sold at a price S_fQ_f, at which the industry is once more normally profitable, and the decline will cease. The normal supply curve, LL' as before, must pass through points P_0 and Q_f.

FINAL RESULTS OF THE INITIAL CHANGE. The final results of a shift in demand from silk to cotton, then, are (1) a rise in the price of cotton, which will be greater, the more inelastic is the normal supply curve for cotton; (2) a fall in the price of silk, which will be greater, the more inelastic is the normal supply curve for silk; (3) a rise in the output of the cotton industry, due to an increase in the quantity of resources devoted to cotton production; (4) a decline in the output of the silk industry, due to a decrease in the quantity of resources devoted to silk production.

Effect on Remuneration of Factors of Production

Now, what will be the effect of these changes on the prices of the factors of production employed in these two industries? The rise in demand for cotton will, as we have seen, by making cotton production more profitable bring about a rise in demand for all the factors of production which go into the making of cotton. If the prices of all these factors of production were previously at their equilibrium level, this rise in demand may cause a reaction upon both the price of each factor and the quantity of it which will be employed. The extent of the reaction will depend, of course, on the elasticity of supply of the factor concerned. Suppose, for instance, that

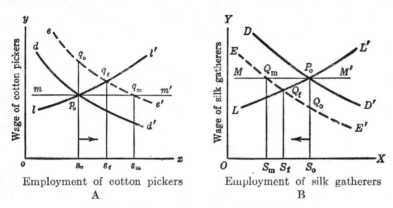

Fig. 59. Effect on Wages of a Shift in Demand

along the axis oy in Fig. 59A we measure the wage of the cotton pickers. Along ox we measure the amount of employment which they will be offered or will offer at each wage. Suppose that before the rise in demand for pickers a number equal to os_0 is employed at a wage s_0p_0. Now suppose the demand for pickers rises from dd' to ee'.

IMPACT EFFECT: FINAL EFFECT WITH ELASTIC SUPPLY. If the supply of pickers is perfectly inelastic, i.e., if there are only a given number of pickers whose force cannot be augmented, the wage of pickers will rise to s_0q_0. This might be the immediate effect. However, any rise in the wage of cotton pickers will be sure to attract workers into that occupation, and in consequence the number of people offering to work at cotton picking will increase, and the wage will decline. If ll' is the normal supply curve of cotton picking, the wage will decline (and probably fairly rapidly) to the level s_fq_f, where the amount of employment given is os_f. If, now, the

normal supply of pickers were perfectly elastic, represented by the line
mm', the final result of the rise in the demand for picking would be an
increase in the employment of pickers to os_m, without any increase in
their wage, for $s_m q_m = s_o p_o$.

The effects of this change on the wages of silk gatherers are illustrated
in Fig. 59B. If the supply curve of silk gathering, LL', is less than perfectly
elastic, the result of a fall in the demand for silk gatherers will be a fall in
their wage, from $S_o P_o$ to $S_f Q_f$. If, however, the supply of silk gathering is
perfectly elastic, as represented by the line MM', the final result will be
a decline in the number of silk gatherers employed from OS_o to OS_m,
but there will be no fall in the wage of the silk gatherers, as $S_m Q_m = S_o P_o$.

Elasticity of Supply a Result of Mobility of Factors

Now under what circumstances is the supply of cotton picking or of
silk gathering likely to be perfectly elastic? Suppose that the cotton fields
and the silk fields are adjacent, and that cotton picking and silk gathering
require just about the same amount of skill and training and are about
equally toilsome. That is to say, suppose that the nonmonetary advantages
of these occupations are identical and that there are no hindrances to
the free movement of workers between them. In that event it is clear that
there cannot be any permanent divergence between the money wage
of cotton pickers and of silk gatherers. Beginning with an equilibrium
situation with the money wages of cotton pickers and silk gatherers equal,
if the result of our shift in consumer's demand from silk to cotton is a rise
in the demand for cotton pickers which just equals the fall in the demand
for silk gatherers, we may suppose that the final result will be the transfer
of a number of workers from silk gathering to cotton picking. There will
be no change in the wage of either, for the supply of both kinds of workers
will be perfectly elastic. Any rise in the wage of cotton pickers, any fall
in the wage of silk gatherers, will bring about such a transfer of workers
from one field to another that wages will soon return to their original
levels.

Suppose now at the other extreme that we have a society in which silk
gatherers and cotton pickers each form a hereditary caste, into and
out of which nobody can move. Then the supply of both cotton picking
and silk gathering will be perfectly inelastic, at least over considerable
periods of time. A shift of demand from silk to cotton would result in a
fall in the wage of silk gatherers and a rise in the wage of cotton pickers
which will not be temporary but will persist. If we assume that the wage
in this case does not influence the number of surviving children raised by
the average family, this difference will persist indefinitely.

It is evident, then, that the elasticity of supply of a factor of production in any one use depends mainly on the ease with which similar factors of production can be *transferred,* either from other uses into the use in question or from the use in question into other uses. The more *mobile* is any factor of production between occupations, the more *elastic* will be its supply, and the more stable will be its price in any one occupation. It is because factors of production cannot be transferred easily from one occupation to another that their supply is less than perfectly elastic, and this fact also makes less than perfectly elastic the supply of the products which they produce, as we shall prove later.

EFFECTS OF A CHANGE IN TECHNIQUES

We have seen how a shift in demand affects the structure of prices and the distribution of resources, acting through the mechanism of price changes and their effect on advantage. Let us now see how a change in *techniques* will affect prices, advantage, and the distribution of resources. Suppose that the tastes of consumers in respect to cotton remain constant, but that an improved method of growing or manufacturing cotton and cotton goods is discovered, so that a given quantity of cotton or cotton goods can be produced with the expenditure of a smaller quantity of resources than before—i.e., with less labor, less land, and so on. This situation may be represented in Fig. 60.

As before, we measure the price of cotton along OY and the quantity which will be demanded or supplied in a week along OX. DD' is then the normal demand curve for cotton, representing the relation between the price and the quantity which will be bought in each week. This is assumed to be constant. LL' is the normal supply curve before the change, representing the relation between the price and the quantity which will continue to be supplied in each week at each price.

IMPACT, INTERMEDIATE, AND FINAL EFFECTS. Now suppose there is an improvement in techniques. The first result will be that cotton production will become abnormally advantageous, for the producers are still getting the same price for their cotton as previously, but they can produce it with greater ease and therefore with less expense than they previously could. Consequently, the industry will grow. New producers will be attracted into it. As the weeks go by the output will increase from OS_0 through OS_1, OS_2, etc., to OS_f. As the output increases, however, the price at which it can be sold will fall from S_0P_0, through S_1P_1, S_2P_2, etc., to S_fP_f. As the price falls the stimulus to expansion will decline until eventually the final output OS_f is reached, where in spite of the improvement in techniques the industry is once more normally profitable and the output ceases to expand. OS_f, then, is the new normal output; S_fP_f is the new normal price.

It follows that there must be a new normal supply curve, $L_f L'_f$ which cuts the demand curve at the point P_f. That is to say, the improvement in techniques has brought about a rise in normal supply. The quantity which producers will supply, or the rate of production which will finally be reached after all adjustments have been made, will be greater for each price than it was before. This is precisely what we should expect. The same conclusion can be reached by another way, by looking at the shift in

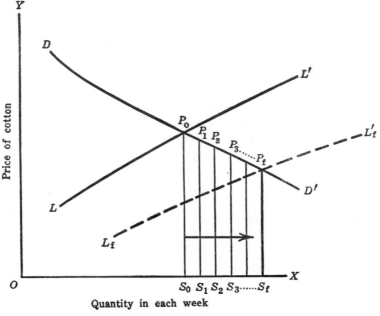

Fig. 60.   Effect of Change in Techniques

the supply curve from LL' to $L_t L'_t$ as due to a fall in the supply price of each output as a result of a decline in costs, following the technical improvement.

EFFECT ON DEMAND FOR OTHER COMMODITIES.   It is interesting to consider what will be the effect of this improvement in the techniques of cotton production on the demand situation of other commodities. We have seen that the improvement causes a fall in the price of cotton and a rise in the total consumption. If the elasticity of demand for cotton is unity, this fall in the price of cotton will not affect the total amount which consumers will spend upon cotton, for the fall in the price will be matched by a proportionate rise in the amount purchased. If, however, the demand for cotton is relatively elastic, the fall in price will result in a greater proportionate increase in the quantity bought, and therefore the amount spent by consumers on cotton will increase. This means that the consumers of cotton will have rather less to spend upon other things. Consequently, their demand for other things will decline. That is, if the prices of other things did not change, consumers would be willing to buy rather less of them in the mass.

Any decline in demand is most likely to fall on those things which are close substitutes for cotton.[1] Consumers will be buying an increased quantity of cotton and spending more money on cotton. We should therefore expect them to spend rather less money and buy rather smaller quantities of the substitute commodities—silk, wool, etc.—and possibly to reduce slightly their expenditures and purchases in the case of less related commodities. Thus an improvement in the techniques of cotton production might easily reduce the demand for silk and hence might reduce both the price and the output of silk. Nor is this the end of the adjustments. Consumers' expenditures on other things will decline, but if the demand for cotton is elastic, the producers of cotton as a class will have a larger gross income. This may result in an increased expenditure on the part of the cotton *producers* on other things, which may in part offset the decline in consumers' expenditures for them. It will be unlikely, however, to offset the decline completely in the case of each commodity concerned. For instance, if consumers of cotton as a whole are richer than the producers, we should not expect the increased demand of the producers to counterbalance the decreased demand of the consumers in the case of silk, but it might very well do so, and more, in the case of wool.

OTHER EFFECTS.   It is evident that here we are running into a series of ramifications of our analysis which we cannot pursue very far without a much greater body of factual information than we possess. Nevertheless, it is important to realize that these ramifications exist; that supplies react on demands and demands on supplies through an immense chain of related commodities, until the final consequences of a single change in the circumstances of production or consumption of even one commodity permeate the whole economic system, echoing and re-echoing ever more faintly from one effect to another until they finally die away.

THE PRICE STRUCTURE AND
ECONOMIC DEVELOPMENT

One important conclusion emerges from this analysis, that unless the technical improvements which constitute economic development take place uniformly for all commodities—and this is a most unlikely situation

[1] Even if there is unit elasticity of demand for cotton, a fall in the price of cotton is likely to bring about a *redistribution* of the demand for other things, even though the total amount spent on them remains the same. For this reason there may be a decline in demand in this case for cotton substitutes and a rise in demand for things which are complementary or even independent in demand.

—then economic development must produce a profound and irreversible change in the relative price and output structure. The prices of those commodities which have enjoyed a fall in costs will fall relative to those commodities the costs of which have not fallen. Furthermore, a technical improvement in the methods of producing those commodities which have inelastic demands will result not so much in the expansion of output and consumption of these commodities as in the expansion of output of other commodities which have an elastic demand, through the transfer of factors from the technically progressive industry into others. An important example of this principle is the effect of a technological improvement, especially a laborsaving improvement, in agriculture, for the demand for most of the products of agriculture, especially foodstuffs, is fairly inelastic. The result of such an improvement is not so much an increase in food output, as an increase in the output of other things; the society will produce about the same amount of food, or perhaps a little more, with less labor than before, and labor will be transferred from agriculture into other industries. In a later stage of development the same thing happens to many manufactured goods. An improvement in methods of their production results in low costs therefore, low prices, at which demand may be quite inelastic; and further reductions of cost result in transfer of resources out of manufacturing into service and professional occupations which have not experienced as much technological improvement. In practice therefore economic development always produces a profound transformation in the relative price structure, roughly expressed by saying that the price of goods, the cost of which has fallen, falls relative to the price of services, the production of which shows less improvement in productivity.

Effect of Prices on Future Supplies and Demands

In equilibrium price theory we assume that the relative price structure has one (or more) equilibrium positions, which are determined by the supply and demand functions, which in turn are determined, as we shall see more clearly later, by underlying preference and production functions. These underlying determinants are assumed to be independent of the price structure itself. This assumption is justified in equilibrium theory, and even in comparative statics. When however we are considering the dynamics of the price system, the possibility that the price structure of today may affect the *determinants* of the price structure tomorrow, or at other future dates, must be taken into consideration. In terms of supply and demand theory we need to ask the question: What is the impact of the present price structure on future supply and demand functions? There is an implicit assumption in equilibrium theory, for instance, that if the existing price structure is not in equilibrium, relative to existing demand and supply functions, then the only forces operating are those which change *prices* in directions that make them conform to the equilibrium set, with supply and demand functions remaining unchanged. We must now introduce the possibility that a disequilibrium price structure may also change the supply and demand functions themselves.

Effect of Surpluses

Thus suppose we have a disequilibrium set of prices in which some prices are "too high" (above the equilibrium level) and some prices are "too low" (below the equilibrium level). A commodity the price of which is too high will have a surplus (p. 175). This will undoubtedly create pressure for a fall in its price, but suppose the resistances are too great for these pressures to overcome, and the price does not fall? The existence of a persistent surplus will create strong incentives to increase the demand, to find new methods of utilization, new markets, and so on. Similarly there will be very little incentive to reduce costs or increase supply; the techniques of production are likely to be stagnant, and there will not be much resistance to cost-increasing changes. Demand therefore may rise, supply may stagnate or even fall, and the net result of these movements is to raise the equilibrium price itself. Here we see a disequilibrium, that is, a divergence between the actual and the equilibrium price, result in a reduction of the divergence, not by a change in the actual price, but by a change in the equilibrium price.

Effect of Shortages

Similarly, suppose we have a commodity the actual price of which is too low, that is, below the equilibrium price. There will be a shortage (p. 175) which means there will be no selling problem; anything produced is immediately snapped up by the market. In these circumstances there is no incentive to increase demand; little effort will be put into advertising or the search for new markets. On the other hand there are strong incentives to improve methods of production and to reduce costs, as any additional output is easily sold. Consequently supply will increase, demand will stagnate, and the equilibrium price will fall. Here again, the reduction of the divergence between the actual and the equilibrium price is achieved by lowering the equilibrium price towards the actual, not by raising the actual towards the equilibrium.

Output Adjustments

Similar processes may take place in the case of output adjustments. Suppose, for instance, that in Fig 58A (p. 275), with demand at ll' and supply at ee' and an excess of demand price over supply price equal to h_0q_0, that the cotton industry is prevented from expanding, because, say, of some kind of licensing or quota system. The existence of excessive profits removes incentives either to expand demand or to improve methods of production, and we may find costs creeping slowly upward, with the supply curve ll' moving upward and to the left. If this process goes on long enough it may move to the position mm', at which the point q_0 is a new equilibrium, with excess advantages eliminated and supply price equal to demand price once more at the original output, os_0, in spite of the rise in demand from dd to ee. Similarly in Fig. 58B, suppose demand is EE', and supply is LL', and output is OS_0, with an excess of supply price, P_0S_0 over demand or actual price Q_0S_0, indicating an abnormally unprofitable situation. If the industry is prevented by inertia or regulation from contraction, a great deal of energy may go into cost reduction and also into demand expansion through sales promotion. As a result of these activities, we might find the demand curve rising again, say, to FF' and because of the fall in costs, the supply curve moving downward and to the right to MM', with a new equilibrium at R_0, where advantages are again normal at the old output OS_0, in spite of the initial demand shift. In both these cases we again see the elimination of a divergence between actual and equilibrium values (output, this time) by a movement of the equilibrium value rather than by a movement of the actual value. In real cases, of course, both the actual and the equilibrium values may move toward each other; which moves the most depends on which is most easily movable!

External Economies and Negatively Elastic Supply

The dynamic approach to demand and supply illuminates, even if it may not completely resolve, a peculiar problem in demand and supply which arises because the size of the output of a whole industry may affect the costs of individual producers in it. In a small industry costs may be high simply because the industry is small; in a large industry costs may be lower simply because the industry is large. This is the phenomenon called by Marshall "external economies." It is an application of the general principle that the degree of specialization is determined by the extent of the market. In a large industry the specialization of processes and the specialization of firms themselves may be developed to a greater extent than in a small industry. Special machines, special tools, special processes may be possible in a large industry which a small industry is not big enough to support. An expansion of such an industry will thus *lower* its whole schedule of costs and will itself increase the quantity of product which the industry is willing to sell at each hypothetical price. In this case it is possible that a rise in demand, although it will at first cause an increase in the price of the product, will also cause an increase in output, a lowering of costs, and therefore a rise in supply and possibly a fall in price. Where a rise in demand can in this way cause a fall in price, the industry is said to be one of *decreasing cost*.

GRAPHIC ILLUSTRATION. These principles are illustrated in Fig. 61. In each diagram *DD* and *SS* represent the demand and supply curves of an industry in equilibrium. *SS* here may be called the *given-cost supply curve*. It shows how much will be produced by the industry at each price, on the assumption that the industry has a definite series of costs. Now suppose demand rises. The demand curve shifts to *D'D'*. If the costs of the industry do not change, the price will rise to *P'N'*, the output to *ON'*. This we may call the position of given-cost equilibrium.

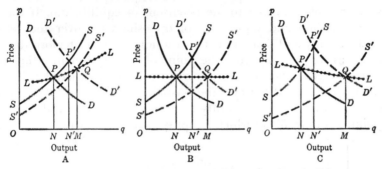

Fig. 61. Increasing, Constant, and Decreasing Supply Price

Greater output, however, will make possible a greater degree of specialization within the industry. Production will be more efficient and costs will fall. The given-cost supply curve, therefore, will shift to the right. As it shifts, the output will increase and the price will fall. As output increases, costs may fall still further, and the given-cost supply curve will shift farther to the right until finally it comes to rest at the position *S'S'*. In this position the price is *MQ*, the output is *OM*, and the supply curve *S'S'* is derived from that set of cost curves which is consistent with the output *OM*. This position is the *long-run equilibrium* of the industry. For every possible rise or fall in demand, whether great or small, there will be a series of points such as *Q*. These points lie along the beaded curve *LL*. This is Marshall's "long-period supply price curve." It tells us what, in the final adjustment, when the costs are consistent with the equilibrium output, will be the price and the output corresponding to each possible level of demand.

If now a rise in demand, and therefore in output, causes only a small movement in cost and short-period supply, as in Fig. 61A, the curve *LL* will slope upward, though with a greater elasticity than the short-period supply curves. If the rise in output causes a larger movement in cost curves and in short-run supply, as in Fig. 61B, the curve *LL* may be a straight line parallel to the output axis. That is, the long-period supply price curve will be perfectly elastic, and the industry will be one of "constant supply price" in the long run. If a rise in output causes a large fall in cost curves the result may be as pictured in Fig. 61C, where the long-period supply price curve slopes downward and has a negative elasticity. This would be an industry of *decreasing supply price* in the long run.

Multiple Equilibrium Positions

The possibility of decreasing supply price or negatively elastic supply curves introduces some curious complexities into the equilibrium and the dynamics of demand and supply. In the first place it opens up the possibility of multiple solutions to the equations of equilibrium. If the elasticities of demand and supply are of opposite signs over the relevant range, the supply and demand curves cannot intersect at more than one point, for as we go away from the point of intersection in either direction the divergence between, say, supply price and demand price must continually increase. If however the elasticity of supply and demand have the same sign, there is a possibility that they may intersect at more than one point, as in Fig. 62, in which a supply curve of negative elasticity, *SS'*,

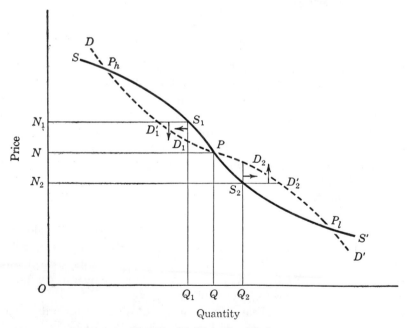

Fig. 62. Multiple Equilibria

intersects a demand curve (also of negative elasticity) at three points, one at a high price, P_h, one at a low price P_l, and one intermediate, P. This possibility gives rise to a famous case for government intervention in the price system, for from a social point of view it is clear that position P_l with low costs and price is much to be preferred to P_h with high cost and price. If, however, P_h is a stable equilibrium, market forces in themselves will not move it away from P_h. But if government can intervene, through a tariff or subsidy, to expand the industry until the output passes the presumably unstable equilibrium at P, the system will then move of its own accord to the new, and socially superior, equilibrium at P_l. This is the essence of the *infant industry* argument for a tariff, which is in turn merely a special case of the general argument for the protection and subsidy of infant industries. Without such assistance, it is argued, the infant will always remain such at P_h; and it needs assistance to push it from P_h beyond P so that it can become an *adult* at P_l.

THE GENERAL DYNAMICS OF DEMAND AND SUPPLY

"Walrasian" and "Marshallian" Dynamics

When we look at the actual dynamics of the system, however, a strange paradox emerges. We saw in Chapter 10, p. 175, that we could look at the dynamics of the equilibrium of demand and supply in two ways. Looking at Fig. 62 in the Walrasian quantity-dependent way, we see that point P is a stable position of equilibrium for, at a higher price than ON, say, ON_1, there is excess supply, $D'_1 S_1$, and price will fall, whereas at a lower price, ON_2, there is excess demand and price will rise. Similarly it can be shown that on this criteria positions P_h and P_l are unstable. If however we use the Marshallian criterion, with price dependent, we see that at a somewhat lower quantity than OQ, say OQ_1, the supply price $Q_1 S_1$ is above the demand price, $Q_1 D_1$, the industry is abnormally unprofitable and will contract toward P_h. Similarly at output OQ_2 there is an excess of the demand price $Q_2 D_2$ above the supply price $Q_2 S_2$, the industry is abnormally profitable and will expand toward P_l. P is now an unstable position, P_h and P_l are stable.

Reaction Curves and Dynamic Paths

This apparent paradox points up a very important proposition which we shall meet several times: that the stability of an equilibrium cannot be known until we have specified the dynamic machinery which surrounds it. It can be argued, for instance, that the "paradox of negatively elastic supply" is quite unreal and arises from an illegitimate application of dynamic assumptions. In actual fact the economy moves from day to day by a complex set of adjustments in which both price and quantity adjustments play a part. No model can hope to reproduce the complexity of this process. Nevertheless a simple model of price and quantity adjustments will throw light on the process. Thus in Fig. 63 we have a

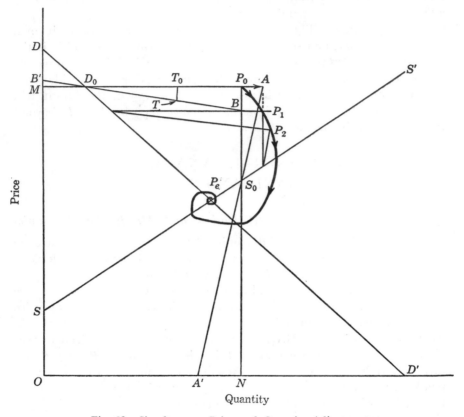

Fig. 63.   Simultaneous Price and Quantity Adjustments

conventional supply curve, SS', and demand curve, DD'. Consider now the possible meaning of a point such as P_0 which is not on either curve. It represents a combination of price paid (P_0N) and quantity produced (P_0M). Let us suppose that these have been set as a result of past decisions. Suppose now that the demand curve represents the quantity that will be bought at each price (a Walrasian demand curve) while the supply curve represents the price at which the production of each quantity will be normally profitable (the Marshallian supply curve). At the point P_0

there is an excess supply, D_0P_0, this being the excess of actual output, MP_0, over the amount bought, MD_0. An excess supply we suppose results in a lowering of price in the next time period. The amount of lowering can be represented by a *reaction curve* or function, $B'B$, the vertical distance of which from the line MP_0 at each price represents the lowering (or raising) of price. If we suppose that the amount by which the price is changed is proportional to the excess supply or demand, $B'B$ will be a straight line going through D_0. At D_0 there is no excess supply or demand, and price will remain constant. Thus at P_0 the price will fall in the next period by an amount P_0B.

Similarly we can suppose that the increase in quantity produced in the next period is a function of the excess of the actual price over the supply price, a function represented by the line $A'A$. This goes through S_0, indicating that when the occupation is normally profitable there is neither expansion nor contraction of output. If the change in output is proportional to the excess of actual over the supply price, $A'A$ is a straight line. Thus from P_0 in the next period output will expand to MA. The price-output combination at the end of the first and beginning of the second period is then represented by P_1, where $AP_1 = P_0B$ and $BP_1 = P_0A$. Repeating the construction from P_1 brings us to P_2 at the beginning of the third period, and so we can go on, tracing out a dynamic path which in this case will be a spiral, circling and continually approaching the ultimate point of equilibrium P_e. From any point in the figure a similar series of spiral paths can be drawn which express the whole of the dynamic properties of the system.

Dynamics of Negatively Elastic Supply

It is interesting to apply this model to the case of the negatively elastic supply curve of Fig. 62. This is done in Fig. 64. It will be seen by examining the dynamic paths (lines marked with arrows) that the apparent Walrasian equilibrium at P is in fact unstable, and the two Marshallian equilibria at P_h and P_l are in fact stable. No matter how close a dynamic path comes toward P, say, from below to the left, it must cut SS' vertically from below and must swing round to cut DD' horizontally from the left. There is some line on the figure such as HPK which is the *watershed:* from all points to the left of this line the dynamic path eventually takes us to P_h, or at least as close to it as we wish, and from all points to the right of it the dynamic paths all move toward P_l. At any point on HP or KP the dynamic path moves to P, but this is a path of unstable final equilibrium in the sense that any random movement off the path to the right eventually lands up at P_l and any movement to the left lands up at P_h.

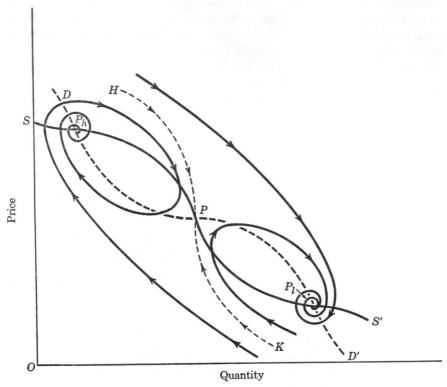

Fig. 64. Multiple Equilibria with Simultaneous Adjustments

Threshold Systems

The realism of dynamic models may be further improved if we introduce a *threshold factor*. By this I mean that when there is a force making for change it may have to reach a certain magnitude (threshold) before any change takes place at all. The function relating force to change then is a *step function*. Thus in terms of Fig. 63, instead of the function relating excess supply to price change being given by the line D_0B, it might be given by D_0T_0TB. Up to an excess supply D_0T_0 there is no change in price at all: at that point there is a sudden change in price represented by the *step* T_0T. Dynamic systems of this kind are very common in nature; thus if I push my typewriter with a horizontal pressure no movement takes place until the pressure reaches the threshold at which static friction is overcome, and the typewriter then moves across the desk. The neurons of the nervous system operate on this principle of requiring a certain minimum input before they 'fire" in output.

Cumulative Threshold Systems

We can distinguish between cumulative and noncumulative threshold systems. In a noncumulative system the force for change does not cumulate through successive time periods; in a cumulative system, in each successive time period, the force is cumulated until finally it is large enough to fire the system. Price systems may exhibit thresholds of both kinds. Thus

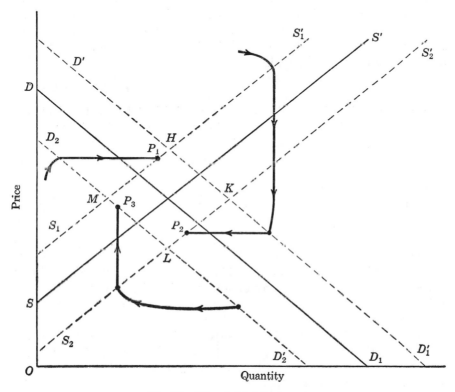

Fig. 65.   Threshold Adjustments

there is undoubtedly some *just noticeable difference* on either side of either a price or quantity equilibrium within which the force for change is not enough to overcome lack of perception or other noncumulative resistances. This may be illustrated in Fig. 65. DD', SS' are demand and supply curves. We suppose further that each curve is embedded in a *band,* bounded by $D_1D'_1$ and $D_2D'_2$ in the case of demand, and $S_1S'_1$ and $S_2S'_2$ in the case of supply, within which no dynamic effect occurs. That is, within the *demand band* any excess demand or supply is too small to produce any effect, and within the *supply band* any excess or deficit of actual over supply price is too small to cause any expansion or contraction of output. The price-quantity adjustment dynamic paths will be like the solid lines marked by arrows in the figure. It is clear that all dynamic paths originating outside the diamond-shaped *equilibrium area HKLM* will end at points such as P_1, P_2, or P_3 on the boundaries of this area. Any point within the equilibrium area will have no dynamic path from it, and will be an equilibrium point. Noncumulative thresholds thus give the system a certain amount of *slack* and give us a set of equilibrium positions rather than a single point. Which element of the equilibrium set is actually reached depends on the history of the system and the actual dynamic path followed.

Oscillatory Systems

In a cumulative threshold system the possibility of severe and almost perpetual oscillation is introduced. Thus suppose that in Fig. 65 again the system has reached the equilibrium area at P_1; at this point there is pressure to lower price and to raise output, but these pressures are not enough to produce action. Suppose however that these pressures cumulate, as indeed they are likely to do. The pressure to lower price comes from the existence of an excess supply; as period succeeds period this results in a cumulative rise in surplus stocks of the commodity, and eventually this will produce an explosive fall in price. Similarly the pressure to raise output comes because the price is above the supply price and production is abnormally profitable. The pressure may be resisted for a while, but eventually there may be an explosive rise in output. Suppose this shifts the system to P_2; now there is pressure to raise price and lower output. This will not result in an immediate change, but may cumulate until there is another convulsive shift, say back to P_1, and the system may then continue to oscillate between these two positions. More complex dynamic patterns can be assumed, but it is probably not worthwhile to pursue them at this point.

THE INCIDENCE OF TAXATION

As a final exercise in supply and demand analysis, let us return to the problem of the effects of taxation, for we now have an analytical apparatus which can throw light on another important problem—the *incidence* of taxation. By the problem of the incidence of taxation we mean, Who really pays taxes? That is to say, who is really worse off, and by how much, because of a given tax? We saw on pages 207–211 that a tax on a given commodity will generally raise the price to the consumer and lower the price to the producer. This, however, does not answer the question of who really pays the tax. Let us return to our previous illustration of a specific tax on cigarettes. Because of this tax the consumer pays a higher price and smokes a smaller quantity. If his demand is inelastic, he will spend more on cigarettes than he did before; if it is elastic he will spend less. Everyone who is a smoker, however, is a little worse off because of the tax, for the price of cigarettes is raised.[2]

Effect of a Tax on Industry, Falling on Immobile Factors

But that is not the whole story. What happens to the producers and to the factors of production employed in the making of cigarettes? The immediate result of the tax will be a decline in the output of the industry, and therefore a decline in the demand for all the factors of production involved in the industry. In the case of those factors which are mobile, i.e., which can get out of the industry, some will remove themselves, with more or less difficulty. The difficulties experienced by these factors in moving out of the industry must be charged to the tax. However, for any factor whose supply is perfectly elastic, enough of the factor will move out of the industry to bring the price of that factor back to where it was before. Consequently, in the final result the burden of the tax will *not* be borne by the owners of those factors of production—be they the services of men or of things—which can move easily out of the industry. Their remuneration will finally be pretty much what it was before, either inside the industry or in some industry into which they have moved. But the immobile factors in the industry which cannot easily get out of it, i.e., which are inelastic in supply, will have to bear the brunt of the tax. If there are any factors in the industry whose supply is perfectly inelastic, no units of the factor will be able to escape the tax, for none can escape the industry. The demand for such a factor will fall, but as the quantity supplied cannot change, its price will fall in proportion to the fall in demand.

Suppose, for instance, that there is land which can be used only for tobacco growing. Then a tax on tobacco will reduce the demand for that land, and will reduce the price of its services. But the owners of the land will not be able to do anything about this fall in rent. They will have to be content with the decreased rent and will continue to use their land for tobacco. However, if the reduced demand for tobacco pickers causes a reduction in their wage, they can do something about it—they can escape into other industries.

Effect of a Tax on Economic Rent

Wherever economic rent exists, the effect of a tax is always to reduce it. Even where the supply curve of a factor is not completely inelastic,

[2] Ignoring the medical factors.

a fall in the demand for the factor will lower its price, and will lower the economic rent on those units of the factor which would still be supplied at even lower prices. This is seen again in Fig. 56, page 266. If a fall in the demand from $d'd'$ to dd causes a fall in price from OR' to $OR,$ the total economic rent of all units of the factor will fall from the triangular area $AR'I$ to the area $ARG.$ The more inelastic the supply of the factor in the range between J and $H,$ the greater will be the fall in the economic rent. Where the supply curve is neither perfectly elastic nor perfectly inelastic, then, as in Fig. 56, some units of the factor will escape into another industry, i.e., those units which are least satisfied with their lot, represented in the figure by $IJ.$ The remaining units will suffer a loss in their remuneration. As, however, this is merely a loss in economic rent, they will not be able to escape the loss, for they will still receive more than the minimum sum required to keep them in the industry. If any factor is perfectly inelastic in supply over the whole range of the supply curve, i.e., if it will be supplied in a given quantity no matter what price it receives, the whole remuneration of the factor is economic rent, for even at a zero price it will still be supplied in the same quantity as at all other prices. In that case the reduction in demand for the factor consequent upon a tax will be reflected wholly in a reduction in the economic rent, for no units of the factor will be able to escape from the industry.

On Which Factors Does a Tax Fall?

Thus, the more inelastic the supply of a factor, the more does it bear the burden of a tax. It is because land is reputed to be a factor which is inelastic in supply that the burden of a tax is frequently supposed to rest on the landowner. This will be the case, however, only where the tax is a general one on all the commodities which may be grown in a given area. If the tax is laid upon one only of a number of commodities which may be produced in a given area, the landowner may escape the tax as easily as the worker by turning his land over to another employment. A tax on corn alone, for instance, would result in a considerable turnover of land as well as labor to wheat and other crops. A tax on all agricultural products would be more difficult for the landowner to escape. Frequently, however, it is some form of labor rather than land which is most inelastic in supply to a given industry, and which therefore would have to bear the chief burden of a tax. A tobacco auctioneer, for instance, may be fastened down to the tobacco industry more firmly than any acre of tobacco land in the country, and consequently may suffer more than any landlord by a decline in the tobacco industry. Similarly, the services of highly specialized equipment may be very inelastic in supply, especially in short periods. The owners of a tobacco-curing plant may suffer by a tax on tobacco more than a landowner.

Elasticity of Supply as Dependent on Period of Time Taken

One general rule which we have noticed applies in this case also. It is that the longer the period of time taken into consideration, the more elastic will be most supply curves. Over long periods the supply of special skills or of special equipment may be almost perfectly elastic, and the owners of labor services and of equipment will gradually be able to shift the burden of the tax. Over long periods also there is more justification for regarding land as peculiarly inelastic in supply, especially if it is specialized to the production of some commodity, for differences in the suitability of different acres of land for a particular employment may persist indefinitely. These differences are permanent, and lead to less than perfectly elastic supply curves for land even in long periods, whereas the differences which give rise to inelastic supply curves for labor and equipment may be only temporary.

Where All Factors Are Mobile, a Tax Falls on Consumers

If all the factors of production used in an industry are perfectly mobile, and if there are no difficulties of organization involved in using larger or smaller quantities of factors, then the supply of each of the factors and also the supply of the product will be perfectly elastic. In this case a tax will fall ultimately on consumers. It is true that the industry will decline and that some trouble will be given to factors thereby in getting out of the industry. However, once equilibrium is established again the price of each factor will be what it was before, and the price received by producers as a whole for the product will be the same as before— though of course the quantity of factors employed and the total output of the product will be smaller. But the price to the consumer will be higher by exactly the amount of the tax, as in Question 2, page 217.

We can therefore formulate the following proposition: The burden of any commodity tax will be shifted from the consumer to the factors of production engaged in making the commodity only in so far as the supply of these factors is less than perfectly elastic.

The Dynamics of Incidence

We still have not exhausted the subject of incidence, however, for we must go on to consider possible dynamic effects of the distortion of the price set which occurs as a result of different taxes (or subsidies) on different commodities. As we have seen, supply and demand functions themselves may adjust to strain imposed by a disequilibrium in demand and supply. In an industry with external economies, as in Fig. 61 (p. 283), a tax, by leading to a contraction of the industry, may raise its costs and eventually even raise the supply price, as in a movement from Q to P in Fig. 61C. Here the consumer's price is eventually raised by *more* than the tax—the consumer pays not only the whole tax but also bears the loss due to rising costs. Conversely, a subsidy will result in an expansion of such an industry, lower costs, and perhaps eventually in a price to the consumer lower than before by more than the subsidy, reflecting the fall in costs. This again is the classic case for the subsidization or protection of infant industries.

The distortion of the price system by taxes and subsidies may also have a substantial effect on the relative impact of technical change. We may suppose that at any one time the amount of resources available for technical change is fairly limited, and that it will be divided among various commodities and industries partly according to the expected payoffs of such expenditure; partly according to the visibility of different lines of development; partly according to habit or tradition; partly because of *slack*—funds which happen to become available, perhaps as a windfall, and are invested in research and development to make them less visible! A tax, suddenly imposed, may easily create a situation in which there are strong incentives to reduce costs, so that part of the effect of the tax may be a reduction in the supply price itself. The *burden* of the tax is thereby reduced or, if cost reduction at one point implies a failure to reduce costs somewhere else (which is not necessarily true, but is not impossible), then the burden falls on those commodities and factors which are deprived of cost-reducing activity.

Taxation and Development

These considerations suggest that the distortion of the price set through taxes and subsidies may be an important element in policies directed toward affecting the speed or course of economic development. This subject is too large to be discussed here; the possibility of this function of the price system, however, stands as an important challenge to economists of the next generation. We are familiar with two great functions of the price system in the allocation of resources and the distribution of income; this third function of directing the course of economic change and development has received shockingly little attention. It may well be, for instance, that the price system which is in some sense *optimal* for allocation or for distribution is not optimal for development. This is a genuine dilemma, for one of the problems of the price system is that it seems to have to bear too many responsibilities. The resolution of the dilemma may come by developing *substitutes* for the price system in terms of other forms of social organization in specific areas.

A broad principle which seems to emerge is that if the price set in the present is distorted in the direction which economic development is likely to take it in the future, there may be *parametric* change—for instance, in productivities—in the direction of speeding up the development itself. Thus suppose we have a society (like California) in which some commodity (water) is fairly plentiful now, but is likely to be scarce in the future. If the commodity is taxed and made more expensive *now,* this will direct development resources into improvements which economize its use; the society will then be better prepared to meet the future scarcities. If by contrast the commodity is subsidized and made cheap in the present, development resources will not go into improvements which economize its use, and the society will be ill-prepared for its future scarcity. A similar line of argument might produce the general conclusion that in a poor country capital should be made cheaper and labor dearer, to force development into economizing on labor by the use of capital. It is one thing to state these general principles, however, and quite another —and more difficult—thing to carry them out.

Questions Reserved

We have now reached the end of this part of our inquiry. We have asked ourselves why particular prices are what they are. We have given an answer to this question in terms of two powerful weapons of analysis— supply and demand. We have not as yet delved deeply into the question of *why* supply and demand are what they are, although we have gained some ground on that point. This question, however, is taken up in Part II. There we shall go into the theory of production and of the individual firm to seek for the underlying forces which determine the position of supply curves. We shall also go into the theory of consumption and of individual choice to seek for the underlying forces which determine the position of demand curves. Another topic, so far mentioned only in passing, is that of monopoly and the effects of monopolistic elements in the competitive system. This also is taken up in Part II. These deeper questions cannot be analyzed until we have studied economic behavior and organization.

QUESTIONS AND EXERCISES

1. Suppose that (a) lemons can be grown only on a certain very limited area of land in California; (b) imports of lemons into the United States have been prohibited for some time past. Suppose now that doctors discover

that a sure way to avoid colds is to eat two lemons a day. What do you think would be the effect of this discovery on the following?

a. The normal demand for lemons.

b. The normal supply of lemons.

c. The price of lemons (i) immediately and (ii) eventually.

d. The output of lemons (i) immediately and (ii) eventually.

e. The wages of lemon pickers (i) immediately and (ii) eventually.

f. The profits of lemon growers (i) immediately and (ii) eventually.

g. The rent of lemon-growing farms (i) immediately and (ii) eventually.

h. The orange industry (i) immediately and (ii) eventually.

2. Suppose in the above case that, coincident with the doctors' discovery, the prohibition on the import of lemons is removed. Compare the effects of the discovery in this case with the effects in the last case.

3. Discuss the probable effects of a tax on sugar refined in the United States.

4. The government of Northern Ireland placed a tax on *all* butter sold in Northern Ireland, whether produced at home or imported. The proceeds of this tax were given as a subsidy to the Northern Ireland butter producers. Discuss the probable effects of this policy.

5. Suppose in the case of the milk industry of Tables 17 and 18a, p. 251, the demand schedule was as follows:

Price (¢ per gallon)	20	21	22	23	24	25	26	27	28
Purchases (000 gallons)	5500	4900	4290	3710	2810	2200	1600	1200	1000

a. What would be the equilibrium price and output?

b. Suppose now that each producer with costs above 22 cents per gallon received a subsidy per gallon produced, equal to the excess of his cost per gallon over 22 cents. Thus a producer with costs of 25 cents per gallon would get a subsidy of 3 cents for every gallon produced. What now will be the equilibrium price and output, and the total subsidy paid?

c. Repeat part (ii), assuming the subsidy is equal to the excess of cost per gallon over 23 cents.

d. Repeat part (ii), assuming that a tax of 1 cent per gallon is levied on all milk sold. What will be the total yield of the tax?

e. Repeat part (ii), assuming a tax of 2 cents per gallon on all milk sold. What is now the total yield of the tax? If the subsidy is paid out of the proceeds of the tax, what is the *net* yield of the tax (gross yield − subsidy)?

Comment on the economic significance of these results.

6. What will be the effect of a tariff on the remuneration of factors of production employed in the protected industry? Who really benefits from a tariff? Who suffers?

7. (a) Suppose that the supply curve in Fig. 62, p. 284, *coincided* with the demand curve over a certain range of output. What would be the economic significance of such a demand and supply? (b) Discuss the case in which the demand curve lies wholly above or below the supply curve.

8. Under certain agricultural marketing schemes (e.g., hops in Britain, tobacco in the United States) each producer is allotted a marketing quota, and is

penalized if he sells more than his quota. Discuss the probable effects of such a scheme on the remuneration of the various factors of production involved and on the price of the product. Who gets most of the benefit from such a scheme?

9. It has been claimed that government assistance to agriculture is useless, as all subsidies eventually find their way into the pockets of the landowner in the form of higher rents. Discuss this criticism.

10. Show that by the construction of Fig. 61, p. 283, it is impossible to construct a long-run supply curve, *LL*, which will intersect the original demand curve, *DD*, at any point other than *P*, assuming the demand curves do not cross. What meaning remains, if any, for a supply curve such as *SS'* in Fig. 62, p. 284?

PART II

The Theory of
Economic Behavior

CHAPTER 15

THE ECONOMIC ORGANIZATION

THE NATURE OF ORGANIZATIONS

Persons and Roles

Persons, almost without exception, participate in organizations. That part of a person's life and behavior which is relevant to a particular organization is called a *role*. Thus sitting at the dinner table with the family discussing family problems a man has a role as a father in a family; working on an assembly line or at an executive's desk the same man may have a role as part of a firm; in a church or club he may have a role as a member; when he votes or works in a political campaign he has a role as a citizen of a state. In each of these cases he is part of an organization, and one person usually belongs to many organizations. The basic unit of the organization, however, is not the person but the *role*, even though the fact that many roles may be united in a single person is often of great importance. The person, indeed, may be thought of as a biological organization uniting and organizing his many roles.

Economic Aspects of Organizations

All organizations have economic aspects, in so far as they, or persons acting in their constituent roles, produce, consume, or exchange commodities. When the production, consumption, and exchange of commodities is the primary purpose of an organization, we may call it an *economic organization*. What economics is really dealing with, however, is the economic aspects of all organizations; churches, clubs, political parties, symphony orchestras, municipalities and national states are all part of the economic system in their roles as producer, consumer, and exchanger of commodities. Economic theory has traditionally laid great stress on two classes of organization; the *household*, which is at the same time an original supplier of factor services such as labor, and an original demander of consumer goods and services; and the *firm*, which is an economic intermediary, organizing a process of production by which inputs of factors and goods are turned into an output of goods and services.

Boundaries of Organizations

It is not always easy to draw a sharp boundary between what is inside an organization and what is outside it. Is a student, for instance, a member of a university, or is he just a customer? Is every person in the labor force of a corporation a member of the organization, or should we regard only management, or only the board of directors, or the shareholders as members? Is Congress, which votes the budget, a customer or a member of the Department of Defense? These are difficult questions, to which it is often impossible to give clear answers, for what we include inside the "skin" of an organization often depends on the particular problem we are considering. For purposes of theory we shall simply assume that some such line can be drawn for the particular purpose in mind, which will distinguish the organization from its environment.

The Position Statement

The next concept is that of a *state* or condition of an organization at a moment of time. These states are in fact very complex, and contain much that may not be relevant to a particular problem. An abstract description of such a state or condition, containing those elements which are relevant to a problem, may be called—borrowing and extending an expression from accounting—a *position statement*. A position statement is a "snapshot" of the organization as it exists at a moment of time. It may, of course, include much of the past history in the form of memory and records, and it will include images of the future in the shape of plans and ideas, but these exist as patterns or structures at a moment.

Events, Episodes

The history of an organization consists of a succession of consecutive position statements, like the frames on a movie reel. An *event* in its most elementary form consists in some specific difference between one position statement and the next. In common speech an event often refers to what is better perhaps termed an *episode*—a sequence of events forming a definite pattern.

The Decision as a Choice

The next important concept is that of a *decision*. At any one moment of time, the state or position statement of an organization will contain a certain number of images of possible future states. A decision is an act of choice among possible future states, as they are imagined or expected at the time of the decision. If there is only one possible future state no decision is involved; the organization simply proceeds from its present state to the next, which is the only one open to it. To have a decision there must be at least two possible futures; in practice there are frequently a large number. A commonplace decision situation is that faced by a person in a restaurant who looks over a menu. The menu is the list of possible immediate futures. Realizing any one of these excludes the others—if he orders steak he cannot usually also have stew. The decision is the order he gives the waiter; normally we expect the order to be followed in a few minutes by an expected dish, which will be followed shortly by a feeling of satisfaction at having eaten what we wanted.

Learning Through Disappointments

Decisions, however, can easily result in *disappointments,* and this is the key to much of the dynamic path of an organization. We can, for instance, order a dish from the menu, only to be told after the waiter has gone to the kitchen that the dish is no longer available. Disappointments, then, result when the "menu" is false, that is, when the present image of future possibilities is not realistic, and we choose a future which in fact turns out not to be available. Through a succession of disappointments or successes a learning process takes place by which the current "image of the menu" or set of images of possible futures is determined.

Behavior as a Rule of Decision

What we generally mean by *behavior* is a rule or principle by which decisions are governed. Behavior may be random, governed, for instance, by the throw of dice or an equivalent mental process. We could decide on a dish in a menu, for instance, simply by jabbing at it with a pin with our eyes shut. This, incidentally, is not necessarily always irrational; if we do not care very much what we choose, and if the act of choice is itself costly, random selection may be quite rational. Usually, however, we do care what we choose, and in this case a rule of behavior becomes necessary.

Maximizing Behavior

Economists have generally assumed a rule known as *maximizing behavior.* All that this means in its most general sense is that when a person has a choice and has to make a decision, he picks out of the set of possible futures that one which seems to him *best* or preferable to all the others.

In this general form the principle may seem so obvious as to be hardly worth stating, and if indeed the only test of what is best is what people actually choose, then the principle seems to say little more than "people do what they do." Nevertheless the principle turns out to be astonishingly powerful if it is stated carefully, and if something can be known about preferences apart from the simple observation of single decisions.

Satisficing Behavior

The only serious competitor to this rule is what Herbert Simon has called *satisficing behavior*. This arises where the acquisition of knowledge about possible alternatives is itself costly and where therefore the *search* for images of possible futures has to be cut off at some point. Thus to return to our illustration of the menu: if we are faced with a very long and elaborate menu it may take too long, especially if we are hungry, to read the whole menu. What we do then is read down the list until we find something we like well enough—that is, which reaches a certain stand-ard of satisfaction, and we choose this, without reading further down the menu to see if there is something we might like even better. Similarly a firm may be content with a policy which gives it a satisfactory target level of profits without making a further search which would reveal a still more profitable position. "Satisficing" however does not disturb the fundamental principle that we select the best out of the set of possible futures before us; it merely limits the set of possible futures.

The Order of Preference

Maximizing behavior implies the ability to arrange the set of possible futures in an *order of preference*. There are several ways of defining such an order; perhaps the simplest way is to say that for every element of the set S_i we can divide the remaining elements into two subsets, in one of which all the elements are better or preferred, and in the other of which all the elements are worse or not preferred to the element S_i. This is called a simple ordering; a good example would be a set of alternatives where we could attach a different ordinal number—first, second, third, and so on, to each member of the set. For maximizing behavior to be possible it is not necessary to put the whole set of alternatives into such an ordering; strictly, it is sufficient if we can divide the set into two subsets, one containing a single member which is first or best, and all the rest which are second or inferior to the first. For some problems, however, we need to know more than this, for we may want to know what a decision maker will do if his first choice is not available, or if his first and second choices are not available, and so on, in which case we need to know the order of at least the top members of the set of alternatives.

Maximands and Minimands

If there is some quantity or number associated with each member of the set of alternatives such that, the bigger the number, the more the alternative is preferred, the set of alternatives is said to have a *maximand,* and that set will be preferred in which this maximand is maximized, that is, is larger than the corresponding number associated with any other member of the set of alternatives. Thus suppose we have a set of objects and always prefer a heavier to a lighter object; all we have to do to find the best or most preferred object in the set is to weigh them all, and find which weighs the most; the heaviest is then the "best." Exactly the same principle applies if each element can be given a number such that the *smaller* number is always preferred; in this case we *minimize* a *minimand.* This however is the same as maximizing the reciprocal of the minimand, so the two principles are formally identical. For some purposes, for instance, we assume that cost is minimized—that is, that the alternative with the least cost is the best. Sometimes we assume that profit is maximized, that is, that the alternative with the greatest profit is the best. In most cases of actual choice there is no single maximand, but there may be maximands which give us at least a first approximation to the basic ordering. It is hardly an exaggeration to say that the whole of this volume consists in the working out in detail of these very simple principles.

THE BALANCE SHEET

Let us then, begin what is going to be a long argument by considering how to describe the position or state of an economic organization in some abstract way that will avoid unwanted detail. We can begin with the accountant's concept of the *balance sheet,* which is itself often called a position statement. In its primary form this is simply an aggregate or inventory of items of value (assets) pertaining to some specific organization or group of organizations. It is an aggregate of assets defined by their relevance to the organization for which the accounts are made. These assets may be both positive or negative: positive assets are items of value over which the organization has certain rights of use, control, and exchange; negative assets (liabilities) represent claims which others have against the organization, or which represent deductions of some kind from the positive assets.

Net Worth

If now a sum of the positive and negative items is to be calculated, in order to express the total net position of the organization, the various items must be capable of measurement in some common unit of value, such as the dollar. If all the items can be so valued the value of the positive and negative assets can be summed, and the algebraic sum is called the *net worth*. The net worth, that is to say, is the sum of the positive assets, less the sum of the negative assets or liabilities; it is the net value of all the assets which can be related to the organization. Ordinarily these aggregates are expressed in the form of a balance sheet, in which the positive assets are listed on one side (the left-hand side in American convention) and the liabilities and the net worth are listed on the other side. As the net worth (N) by definition is the sum of the positive assets (A) less the sum of the liabilities (L), or $N = A - L$, the sum of the positive assets must be equal to the sum of the liabilities plus the net worth, or $A = N + L$. The two sides of the table therefore have an equal sum—that is, the balance sheet *balances*.

Equities

In American practice the liabilities and net worth are called *equities*. They represent the distribution of claims on the total of positive assets between those claimants who are in some sense *outside* the organization, whose claims are liabilities, and those claimants who are *inside* the organization, whose claims are net worth. The distinction between liabilities and net worth is not always perfectly clear, as claimants which for some purposes might be regarded as outside the organization, such as bondholders, for other purposes (for example, in financial reorganization) might well be regarded as insiders. Lack of clarity in a distinction, however, in no way detracts from its importance.

The Personal Balance Sheet

We may illustrate these concepts first with reference to a personal or household balance sheet. Suppose, for instance, that John Doe or his family owns houses and land worth $10,000, a car worth $500, personal effects (furniture, clothes, etc.) worth $1,000, corporation bonds worth $5,000, a promissory note from Mr. Smith worth $500, an account receivable for $100 for services rendered to Mr. Robinson, and cash worth $400. These things are his *assets*. He may also, however, have certain claims against him called *liabilities*. Suppose he has debts consisting of a mortgage with $6,000 outstanding, accounts payable to various companies amounting to $300, a promissory note to Mr. Brown for $100, and a tax bill for $200. With this information we can calculate his *net worth* by the process of adding up the values of all his assets and subtracting from this total the sum of the liabilities or claims against him. In this case the total of his assets is $17,500. The total of his liabilities is $6,600. His net worth, therefore, is $17,500 − $6,600, or $10,900. The net worth may be visualized as the sum which would be left to his estate if it were liquidated—i.e., if all his assets were turned into cash and all the claims against him settled.

Claims

The balance sheet in Table 20 gives a classification of these assets and equities together into five groups. These are not necessarily the classifications usually made by the accountant, for we are here discussing economic principle rather than accounting practice. We divide assets into three groups: (a) things, (b) claims, and (c) cash. Things are those items

TABLE 20.   BALANCE SHEET, JOHN DOE

Assets		Equities	
(a) Things		(d) Liabilities (claims)	
Houses and land	$10,000	Mortgage	$ 6,000
Car	500	Accounts payable	300
Personal effects	1,000	Notes payable	100
		Taxes payable	200
(b) Claims			
Bonds	5,000	(c) Net worth	10,900
Promissory note	500		
Accounts receivable	100		
(c) Cash	400		
Total	17,500	Total	17,500

of property the value of which enters into no other balance sheet than the one in which they figure. Cash (from which we exclude bank notes and deposits) also enters into no other balance sheet than the one in which it figures. Claims, however, have the property of appearing on two balance sheets. They appear as an asset on the balance sheet of the person who makes the claim and as a liability on the balance sheet of the person against whom the claim is made. In the example, for instance, one of John Doe's assets is a $500 promissory note receivable from Mr. Smith. This promissory note, therefore, represents a $500 liability—a note payable to John Doe—on the balance sheet of Mr. Smith. Similarly, the account receivable from Mr. Robinson becomes an account payable to John Doe on the balance sheet of Mr. Robinson. All the items under (b) on the assets side of Table 20 will therefore be found on the liabilities side of other balance sheets, and all the items under (d) on the liabilities side will be found on the assets side of other balance sheets.

The Summation of Balance Sheets

Imagine a society in which all property is held by individuals, and all balance sheets are individual balance sheets. If *all* the balance sheets of this society were collected and all the asset items were listed on one side of an enormous sheet and all the equity items on the other side, the claims on the asset side and the claims (liabilities) on the equities side would exactly cancel out. Each claim would be represented in two places on this total balance sheet—once on the assets side and once on the liabilities side—for each claim is the asset of one person and the liability of another. The sum of the (a) and (c) items on the assets side would therefore be equal to the sum of the (e) items on the equities side. That is, the total value of the things and cash held by the society would be equal to the total of all individual capital—i.e., to the total net worth of the society.

Insolvency and Bankruptcy

When the value of the liabilities of an organization exceeds the value of its assets, its net worth is negative, and the organization is then said to be *insolvent*. Insolvency does not necessarily mean the immediate end or "death" of the organization, however, as it can sometimes meet its current bills and continue to operate even though it could not pay all its debts if it were called upon to do so. When a person or an organization is insolvent, however, its creditors usually have the legal right to *bankrupt* it—that is, to force it to suspend operations in its present form—and sell or otherwise reorganize its assets in such a way that they can be distributed among the creditors. In a complete bankruptcy the assets are usually liquidated—i.e., sold and converted into cash—and the creditors receive a portion of their claims according to some principle of proportionate distribution. Usually some claims—e.g., taxes—have to be paid in full. Then the remainder is distributed in proportion to the original claim of each creditor.

Suppose, in the case of John Doe, whose balance sheet appears in Table 20, that a fire destroys his uninsured property to the value of $11,700. He will then be insolvent, as his assets have declined in total value by a sum greater than his net worth ($10,900). His creditors may not, in that case, bankrupt him, for he still has an asset not reckoned in the account—his body—and they may hope that in time he will be able to recover his financial solvency once more. If, however, he is bankrupted, his assets will be liquidated—realizing, if their valuations on the balance sheet are correct, a sum of $5,800 ($17,500 − $11,700). Out of this we may suppose that $200 must be paid for taxes, which have a prior claim. The remaining $5,600 will then be divided among his creditors in proportion to their claims. The total of such claims is $6,400. Each creditor, therefore, will get $56/64$, or $7/8$, of his claim.

The fact that every private liability is an asset in some other balance sheet is one of the main sources of interrelations among economic decisions and events. Thus one bankruptcy can easily set off a whole chain of bankruptcies as the liabilities of the bankrupt organization become worthless or diminished in value. Those liabilities are the assets of other firms or households and, if their value shrinks sufficiently, these firms or households in turn may find themselves insolvent or bankrupt; their liabilities in turn diminish, which impairs the assets of still other organizations. The effect of course gradually loses force as it is dissipated among more and more organizations, and ceases when it meets an organization which can suffer a diminution in net worth without bankruptcy. This process is illustrated in Exercise 7, page 323.

The Difficulties of Valuation

It must not be thought that the valuation of the "things" possessed by a society is a simple, easy, or even certain process. There are many undoubtedly valuable things that are not ordinarily valued at all. The human body is the prime example. In a slave society it is evident that the human body is as much part of the inventory of stock as—shall we say—domestic cattle, and the value of human bodies is entered into the balance sheets of their owners. In a free society where each man possesses his own body it is not customary to put a valuation on it or to enter such a valuation on the balance sheet. In strict logic, however, our accounting will not be satisfactory without this, and indeed some of the ills of our present society can be attributed to the fact that our system of accounting makes no allowances for the changing value of our bodies. Perhaps the reason for our careless personal accounting is that the only time we are compelled to make an exact reckoning of a personal estate is immediately following its owner's demise, in which case his person is a liability to the estate rather than an asset. There is, however, a slowly growing recognition that a value should be placed on the human body in accounting. When a concern insures the lives of important members of its personnel, it is making a partial valuation of their bodies. There are also many other things which are valuable but on which we do not easily place dollar valuation. These things do not have to be material and tangible. A patent or a copyright, for instance, is an asset of its owner but is not a liability of any other person.

All Valuations a Matter of Estimate

The difficulties of valuation, however, extend far beyond the case of things which are not usually valued. Even those values which normally figure on balance sheets are calculated by a process of estimate according to certain rather arbitrary principles. We cannot at this point go into the theoretical and practical problems connected with valuation, for these would require a volume in themselves. Dollar values are derived from physical quantities of assets by multiplying the physical quantity by a price or valuation coefficient. Thus the value of 100 bushels of wheat at $2 per bushel is $100 \times \$2$, or $200. In balance sheet valuations the values are all strictly derived from valuation coefficients rather than from exchange ratios, though all valuation coefficients are ultimately derived from exchange ratios, past, present, or future.

It should be observed that in spite of the uncertainty which surrounds many estimations of the dollar value of assets, the principle of the cancellation of claims still holds. No matter how inaccurate the estimates of the value of assets, the total capital of a society will always be equal to the estimated value of the things and the cash which it possesses. Any error in valuing assets will be reflected in a like error in the net worth. If, for instance, in Table 20 the "true value" of John Doe's houses and land were $8,000 instead of $10,000, his net worth would have a true value of $8,900 instead of $10,900. Whatever change is made in any of the asset items is reflected in an equal change in the net worth.

TYPES OF EVENTS

A *simple event* is defined as a single change in the state or condition of an organization. In terms of the balance sheet a simple event is defined as a change in *two* items of the balance sheet, each of which offsets the other in such a way that the balance sheet continues to balance. It is impossible for a single item to change without such an offsetting change in at least one other, for if an item changes on one side of the balance sheet the total on that side will change, and either there must be an offsetting change which will restore the original total on the first side, or a change which will yield the new total on the other side. A simple event is thus seen as one *double entry* in double-entry bookkeeping. Eight basic types of simple event may be distinguished, as shown in Table 21. They are classified in two ways; first, according to their effect on net worth, second, according to their effect on the total of assets or of equities.

Thus events may be divided into: (A) *income events,* which increase net worth; (B) *exchange events,* which leave net worth unchanged; and (C) *outgo events,* which diminish net worth. They can also be divided into: (1) *expansion events,* which increase the total of assets and so increase the economic size of the organization; (2) *neutral events,* which leave the total of assets unchanged; and (3) *contraction events,* which decrease the total of assets. There are no events in the C1 or A3 boxes

TABLE 21. CLASSIFICATION OF SIMPLE EVENTS

Effect on Asset Total \ Effect on Net Worth	Income Events (Net Worth Increased) (A)	Exchange Events (Net Worth Unchanged) (B)	Outgo Events (Net Worth Decreased) (C)
Expansion Events (Asset Total Increased) (1)	A1 Assets + Net Worth +	B1 Assets + Liabilities +	C1
Neutral Events (Asset Total Unchanged) (2)	A2 Liabilities − Net Worth +	B2 Assets + Assets − B2′ Liabilities + Liabilities −	C2 Liabilities + Net Worth −
Contraction Events (Asset Total Decreased) (3)	A3	B3 Assets − Liabilities −	C3 Assets − Net Worth −

of Table 21, since it is impossible to expand assets and diminish net worth, or to diminish assets and increase net worth. There are two types of events, similar in essence, in the B2 category, for either the exchange of one asset for an equal value of another asset, (B2) or the exchange of a liability for an equal value of another liability (B2′) will leave both net worth and total assets unchanged.

THE EVENTS TABLE. All these various types of event are illustrated in an *events table* such as Table 22. Here we take the balance sheet of John Doe (Table 20, page 307 and follow it through a series of events. Each event is represented by the change in two items between two successive balance sheets, as shown by the two arrows. We are not at the moment concerned with the time interval between successive events, though for some purposes this is important.

Income Events

An income event of type A1 is recorded in columns I–II in Table 22. Here we suppose John Doe earns $200 in wages and in so doing creates a wage claim on his employer, recorded as an increase of $200 in John Doe's accounts receivable (line 6), and as an increase of $200 in net worth (line 13) Any kind of production is an income event: thus suppose Doe grows potatoes worth $50. This is reflected in an increase of $50 in his real assets (line 3) and an equal increase in his net worth, recorded in columns II–III. A very important class of income events is the upward

TABLE 22. AN EVENTS TABLE

Assets	I	II	III	IV	V	VI	VII	VIII	IX	X	XI	XII	XIII	XIV	XV
1. Houses and land	10,000	10,000	10,000	10,000→11,000	11,000	11,000	11,000	11,000	11,000	11,000	11,000	11,000	11,000	11,000→10,500	10,500→18,000
2. Car	500	500	500	500	500	500	500	500→0	0	0	0	0	0	0	0
3. Personal goods	1,000	1,000	1,000→1,050	1,050	1,050	1,050→1,300	1,300	1,300	1,300→1,700	1,700	1,700	1,700	1,700	1,700	1,700
4. Bonds	5,000	5,000	5,000	5,000	5,000	5,000	5,000	5,000	5,000	5,000	5,000	5,000	5,000	5,000	5,000→0
5. Notes	500	500	500	500	500	500	500	500	500	500	500	500	500	500	500→0
6. Accounts receivable	100	100→300	300	300	300	300	300	300	300	300	300	300	300	300	300
7. Cash	400	400	400	400	400	400	400→600	600→1,100	1,100→700	700	700→600	600→400	400	400	400
8. Total	17,500	17,700	17,750	18,750	18,750	19,000	19,200	19,200	19,200	19,200	19,100	18,900	18,900	18,400	20,400
Equities															
9. Mortgages	6,000	6,000	6,000	6,000	6,000	6,000	6,000	6,000	6,000	6,000	6,000→5,900	5,900→5,930	5,930	5,930	5,930
10. Accounts payable	300	300	300	300	300	300→550	550	550	550	550→350	350	350	350	350	350
11. Notes payable	100	100	100	100	100→0	0	0→200	200	200	200→400	400	400	400	400	400→2,400
12. Taxes payable	200	200	200	200	200	200	200	200	200	200	200	200→0	0	0	0
13. Net worth	10,900	10,900→11,100	11,100→11,150	11,150→12,150	12,150→12,250	12,250	12,250	12,250	12,250	12,250	12,250	12,250→12,220	12,220	12,220→11,720	11,720
14. Total	17,500	17,700	17,750	18,750	18,750	19,000	19,200	19,200	19,200	19,200	19,100	18,900	18,900	18,400	20,400
Type of event	A1	A1	A1	A2	B1	B1	B2	B2	B2′	B3	B3	C2	C3	Complex	Complex

(Columns XIV and XV are grouped under the heading "Complex.")

revaluation of assets. Thus suppose Doe finds that his house and land have increased in value as a result, say, of neighborhood developments, from $10,000 to $11,000. This is recorded in event III–IV; house and land (line 1) rises by $1,000, and so does net worth. The other type of income event (type A2) is rare; the best example would be the forgiveness of debt. Thus in event IV–V we suppose that the owner of Doe's $100 note payable (line 11) is an old friend who simply cancels the debt; Doe's net worth increases by $100, but the total of assets or equities is unchanged. Another possible example would be Doe carrying his own garbage to a dump, thus getting rid of a physical liability, or discommodity.

Exchange Events

Events of type B1 (exchange-expansion) are not uncommon. A purchase on credit is a good example. Thus suppose in event V–VI, Table 22, Doe buys a refrigerator for $250 on credit; personal goods, line 3, rises by $250, so does accounts payable (line 10). Net worth does not change, but the total of assets increases. Any kind of borrowing operation which increases claims is of this type, and is the main means by which expansion of Doe's assets beyond his net worth takes place. Thus suppose in event VI–VII he borrows $200 cash on a note: cash (line 7) rises by $200, so does notes payable (line 11).

Events of type B2 (neutral exchange) are of great importance. All purchases and sales for cash fall in this class. Thus suppose Doe sells his car for $500, as in event VII–VIII. Neither net worth nor the asset total change—there is merely a redistribution among assets. A cash purchase is similar: thus in event VIII–IX Doe buys furniture for $400. As we shall see more clearly later, production events also fall into this class, as when flour is ground into wheat. The purchases of stocks or bonds for cash, the receipt of cash by the payment of accounts receivable, the payment of wage claims, the bartering of goods for goods, or securities for securities, or securities for goods, all fall into this class.

Type B2' events—liability exchanges—have much the same kind of effect. The commonest B2' type effect is the refinancing of debt, that is, the exchange of one kind of debt for another. Thus in event IX–X of Table 22 we suppose that one of Doe's creditors to whom he owes $200 consents to accept a note instead of the account payable.

Type B3 events (contraction-exchanges) mainly involve the repayment of debt. Thus in X–XI we suppose Doe makes a cash payment of $100 on his mortgage; cash declines and mortgage (line 9) declines also by $100. Paying off account payable or notes payable by cash, and the payment of taxes is a similar operation. Thus in event XI–XII Doe pays $200 of tax liabilities with cash, and the total of assets declines by $200.

Type C2 neutral-outgo events mainly consist of accruals of interest on liabilities and accruals of tax liabilities. Thus in event XII–XIII, interest of $30 accrues on the mortgage, and there is a corresponding reduction in net worth.

Type C3, contraction outgo events, are of great importance and represent as it were the main counterpart of income events. Any kind of depreciation or consumption is an event of this kind. Thus in event XIV–XV we suppose that Doe registers $500 depreciation on his house: both total assets and net worth decline by $500. Similarly when he eats food, wears out clothes, burns gasoline in his car or gas to heat his house, and so on, there is a similar decline in net worth and in assets. When he buys services, which may be thought of as goods with a very short length of life, the good depreciates or is consumed immediately and the event is registered as a simple decline in cash. Losses of goods or other assets by fire or theft similarly involve a fall in both assets and net worth. Even where the physical goods are unchanged, a downward revaluation necessitates a similar decline in net worth. Thus the event recorded in XIII–XIV could also have been a revaluation of the house as a result say of deterioration of the neighborhood, or a general deflation of real estate prices.

Production and Transfer Events

Income and outgo events can further be divided into production (or consumption) events and transfer events. From the point of view of the individual these are very similar, but from the point of view of the total economic system they are quite different. A transfer event is one which raises the net worth of one party but lowers the net worth of another: it is an income event to the first, but an outgo event to the second. Thus a gift is an income event (type A1) to the recipient, an outgo event (type C3) to the giver. Similarly forgiveness of debt is a type A2 income event to the beneficiary, a type C3 outgo event to the benefactor. In a production event, by contrast, the assets and net worth of one party increase without any diminution of those of another. Thus when Doe earns wages (an A1 event), to his employer, as we shall see more clearly in the next chapter, this is an exchange event of type B2 or B1, exchanging money (or accounts payable) for the goods which are the product of the work. Similarly, a consumption event is one in which the assets of one person decline without any rise in the assets of another. When goods depreciate, are consumed in the enjoyment of them, or are destroyed by accident (C3 events), the net worth of the owner declines, but there is no compensating increase elsewhere. When goods are consumed in producing other goods, however, we have an exchange event, not an outgo event. Events of type C2 are more likely to be transfers: thus when interest or tax liability accrue, this may appear as a liability to the debtor but an asset to the creditor, and as a decline in net worth of the debtor. There are some tricky problems here relating to whether interest and taxes are *paid for* anything, which we must reserve till later.

Complex Events

Finally we must recognize a class of complex events involving changes in more than two items in the balance sheet. Suppose for instance that John Doe builds an addition to his house, costing $7500, and he finances this by giving the builder $5000 worth of bonds, cancelling the $500 note which the builder owes him, and giving the builder a personal note (that is, a promise to pay at some future date) for $2000; this is all reflected in the change from XIV to XV in Table 22. Any complex transaction can be analyzed into a series of simple events. Thus the above transactions would have exactly the same result as the following series of events, assumed to be simultaneous: (1) type B2, sale of $5000 (B1) bonds for cash; (2) type B2, repayment of note (B2) by $500 cash; (3) type B1, borrowing $2000 cash on a note; (4) type B2, paying $7500 cash for the house. Even though all complex events can be reduced analytically to a number of simple events, each involving only two changes in the balance sheet items, some complex events are not only simultaneous but are also logically connected, so that the simple events into which they are broken can occur only in the *package* of the complex event. Thus suppose John Doe hires a man for $30 to build a table worth $50 from John Doe's own wood worth $20. This would be reflected in a rise of $50 under an item, say, furniture, a fall of $20 in an item, wood, and a fall of $30 in cash, or perhaps immediately a rise of $30 in accounts payable as a wage claim. These three items are inseparably connected in fact, even though the complex event could be analyzed into three hypothetical simple events.

Recurrent and Continuous Events

An event which recurs after the passage of some fixed interval of time is a *recurrent* event. Thus interest may accrue every month, wages may be paid every week, and so on. If the interval between successive recurrent events is very small the events may be said to be *continuous;* thus depreciation takes place continuously, wage claims are built up continuously as work is done, and so on. For most accounting purposes however continuous events are treated as if they were recurrent and discontinuous.

Controlled and Uncontrolled Events

Events can be *controlled* or *uncontrolled*. An uncontrolled event is one that is a result of a decision on the part of some other party, or on the part of nature, over which our John Doe has no control. Thus John Doe may offer to sell his car for $500; whether this offer results in an event however such as the sale depends on whether somebody else decides to buy the car at that price. A controlled event—from the point of view of John Doe—is one which depends directly on John Doe's decision; if he decides to buy a car which someone else is offering for sale, and can either pay cash or arrange credit, this is a controlled event from his point of view, as he has in effect chosen between two or more events, or between an event and no event. Uncontrolled events may be predicted with varying degrees of certainty, ranging from absolutely certain to completely unpredictable.

DECISIONS AND THE EVENTS TABLE

Event and Opportunity Decisions

Decisions are of two kinds: The first kind may be called *event* decisions, which are decisions to bring about a controlled event. A decision to buy or sell in a competitive market or make any transformation in the position of the organization or organism which is open and part of the field of choice is an *event* decision. The second kind may be called *opportunity* decisions, which alter the expectations about uncontrolled events, by altering the field of choice of those *other* parties whose decisions determine the uncontrolled events. Thus a decision to change the price at which an organization is offering to buy or sell alters the opportunities of some other party, and hence may affect the decisions of this second party, and hence may affect the uncontrolled events relevant to the first party. John Doe, for instance, having offered to sell his car for $500 and getting no offers to buy at that price, may lower the price to $400 in the expectation that an uncontrolled event—the sale of the car—may take place. The balance sheet alone therefore is not a complete statement of the *position* of an economic organization; we must also include the results of opportunity decisions, which consist essentially of *offers* to accept uncontrolled events. Thus when a storekeeper puts price tags on his goods, he is in effect offering to sell them to anyone who makes a decision to buy at that price. Offers may, of course, be more complicated than a simple offer to buy or sell at a fixed price; there may be, for instance, an offer to buy and sell at some unspecified price, to be arrived at by bargaining.

Expectational Decisions

Opportunity decisions are profoundly affected by the whole system of expectations about the future on the part of the decision maker, and we may wish to treat expectations as produced by a third class of decisions, which we might call *expectational* decisions. Expectations change as a result of the passing of time, the accumulation of knowledge of past events, and the receipt of new information. Where there is ambiguity in the interpretation of information, as there frequently is, it might be argued that we make a choice among alternative expectations. Ideally, there should be a simple maximand in this case, which is the *truth* of the expectations; in the case of expectations, the truer the better, and we should always choose that expectation which seems to us to be truest. Where, however, there is no objective measure of the truth of an expectation we cannot deny the possibility that our expectations themselves are influenced by our general set of values, and that we frequently chose the pleasantest expectation rather than the truest. These considerations however get us into deep psychological waters from which the simple-minded economist is apt to retreat.

Negotiated Decisions

Many decisions take place as a result of agreement, following a period of negotiations; these might be called *negotiated* decisions. A negotiated decision is usually the result of a complex series of event and opportunity decisions which preceded it, and it can perhaps be analyzed into these simpler types of decision. Nevertheless it represents a case of such importance that it seems to deserve a special category. Any event that involves a second party requires agreement of some kind—explicit, tacit, or perhaps even imposed. In the simplest case an opportunity decision is taken by one party, a corresponding event decision by the other party, as when a person buys something in a store. In the negotiation process a succession of different opportunities is offered by the various parties, until one set is presented (perhaps even by a third party) to which the negotiating parties both agree.

The Events Table Analyzed

With these considerations in view let us return to the events table (Table 22) to see what additional information might be needed to classify the events and describe the decisions which led to them. Event I–II, the event between columns I and II, is the earning of a wage claim. This may be a recurrent event if John Doe has a regular job, and it is then a result of a decision made at the time the contract of employment was made—plus, one should add, decisions not to break the contract. It might also be the result of casual employment, in which case it usually represents an opportunity decision on the part of the employer (an offer to employ at a certain wage) and an event decision on the part of Doe (the decision to take the offer). Employment contracts are also frequently the result of negotiated decisions.

Another type of event which is frequently recurrent is the repayment of debt on contract and the accrual of interest on debt, as in X–XI and XII–XIII; these events are often combined in a single complex event, and are the automatic result of some previous decision to accept a contract. Tax accruals and payments (XI–XII) likewise may be thought of as the result of a previous "contract" with a government or other taxing body, even though the contract has special coercive features. Depreciation (XIII–XIV) may be regarded as a kind of contract with nature implicit in the very owning of depreciable property. It is in essence a continuous event, though it is always recorded as a series of recurrent events. Rates of depreciation, however, may vary as a result of decisions about types of use, or even accounting practice, which are subsequent to the basic contract decision to own the property.

Events such as domestic production (II–III) and purchases from stores (V–VI and VIII–IX) are likely to be simple controlled events, with the store (or nature!) providing the opportunity and Doe making the event decision. Events involving credit and refinance (VI–VII and IX–X) are more likely to be negotiated decisions, as the granting of credit involves a relation of trust between the parties which simple cash transactions do not. An event such as the sale of a car (VII–VIII) may be controlled, if there are dealers standing ready to buy at standard prices; or it may be the result of an opportunity decision, such as a want ad in the newspaper which then results in an event decision on the part of the buyer; it may also be a negotiated decision between buyer and seller. Events such as IV–V (the forgiveness of debt) present some peculiarities; they are uncontrolled, but may be anticipated. The receipt of a legacy would be a similar case. Where such an event is anticipated it may be legitimate to write it up as asset, expectations (an A1 type event), in which case when the expectations are actually realized there is simply an exchange event, of type B2 in the case of an expected legacy (expectations diminish, cash increases) or a type B3 event in the case of debt forgiveness (expectations assets diminish, liabilities also diminish).

Insurance

Some types of events not covered in Table 21 should be mentioned as presenting peculiar difficulties. Insurance presents some special problems. In the case of property insurance the chance of diminution of the value of property, for example, by fire or theft, should be valued as a contingent liability and either entered among the liabilities or (more logically) entered as a special deduction from the value of the assets to obtain a *net value* for these assets. A contingent liability is best regarded as a deduction from the value of the relevant assets, rather than as an ordinary liability, because it does not appear as an asset in the balance sheet of some other party, as does a true liability. Insurance diminishes these contingent liabilities: the payment of an insurance premium therefore should appear in the balance sheet as an event which diminishes cash and also diminishes the contingent liability by an equal amount.

Life Insurance

Life insurance presents yet another problem, as the value of John Doe's person, or mind and body, as we have seen, is not usually included in his balance sheet, as conceptually and logically it should be in a complete position statement. The chance of death is a contingent liability which represents a deduction from the value of the person; even where the value of the person is not listed, this liability should logically be listed as a deduction from the net worth. A pure life insurance payment therefore, as in what is called term insurance, can be thought of as either a type B2 asset transfer, with cash diminishing and the net value of the person increasing; or it can be thought of as a type B3 transfer with cash diminishing and the contingent death liability also diminishing, with net worth remaining unchanged. If, however, we have as part of the value of the person some item such as peace of mind, the act of insurance may increase the value of this item, and so increase net worth. It is this peace of mind or satisfactions derived from greater certainty that is the service we are really buying when we buy term insurance, just as what we are really buying when we buy a house is the prospective enjoyment of living in it.

Education Payments

Payments for education raise somewhat similar conceptual problems, and should often be regarded as an increase in the value of the person, hence as an asset transfer (type B2) with cash diminishing and the value of the person increasing. Our failure to include the value of a person in his accounts should not blind us to the conceptual necessity of including such a value in a complete position statement.

Income and Outgo

With these considerations in mind we can now go on to examine the concept of *income*—a concept which looks easy at first sight, but which actually hides surprising difficulties. We have already defined an income event for John Doe as one in which net worth increases. His total income in any period is then the sum of the increases in net worth in all income events. Similarly, an outgo event is one in which his net worth declines. His total outgo in a period is then the sum of the decreases in net worth in all the outgo events of the period. Saving is a word often loosely defined; the most logical definition, however, is that it is the net increase in net worth during a period; a decrease in net worth is called dissaving. It then follows that John Doe's total saving in a period is the excess of his total income over his total outgo, for the net increase in net worth must be equal to the sum of all the increases less the sum of all the decreases.

Receipts, Expenditure, and Hoarding

The concepts of income and outgo must be distinguished sharply from concepts involving the receipt and expenditure of money (cash). A *receipt event* may be defined as one in which cash increases; an *expenditure event* is one in which cash declines. The total receipts in a period is the sum of the increases in cash in all receipt events, and the total expenditure is the sum of the decreases of cash in all expenditure events. The excess of total receipts over total expenditure is sometimes known as *hoarding* (a rather poor term, but there seems to be no other). It is exactly equivalent to the increase in John Doe's stock of cash, for every receipt adds to the stock of cash and every expenditure subtracts from it.

For the individual, income, outgo, and therefore saving include transfer income or outgo. For society as a whole, however, as we shall see more clearly later, transfer incomes cancel out when we add up the total of all incomes, as each transfer event is an income event to one party and an outgo event to another. Whereas the saving of an individual includes the excess of his transfer income over transfer outgo, or transfer saving, for society as a whole, total saving excludes transfer saving, and is equal to the total value of production events less the value of consumption events.

These concepts are illustrated in Table 23, which summarizes the events of Table 22. We see that only income events produce income, only outgo events, outgo; in the above case only exchange events produce receipts or expenditures, though it is possible for income or outgo events to do this; for example, a gift of cash is both income and receipt to the recipient, outgo and expenditure, to the donor.

TABLE 23. JOHN DOE: EVENTS

Event	Type	Name	Income	Outgo (in dollars)	Receipts	Expenditure
I–II	A1	Earns wages	200			
II–III	A1	Grows potatoes	50			
III–IV	A1	Revalues house	1000			
IV–V	A2	Forgiveness of debt	100			
V–VI	B1	Buys refrigerator on credit				
VI–VII	B1	Borrows cash			200	
VII–VIII	B2	Sells car			500	
VIII–IX	B2	Buys furniture				400
IX–X	B2'	Refinances debt				
X–XI	B3	Pays on mortgage				100
XI–XII	B3	Pays taxes				200
XII–XIII	C2	Interest accrues on debt		30		
XIII–XIV	C3	Depreciation of house		500		
Totals			1350	530	700	700

Total savings = income − outgo = 1350−530 = 820.
Increase in net worth, I to XIV = 11,720−10,900 = 820.
Total hoarding = receipts minus expenditure = 700−700 = 0.
Increase in cash stock, I to XIV = 400−400 = 0.

QUESTIONS AND EXERCISES

1. Continue the events of Table 3 for John Doe starting from position XIV, registering the following events or episodes, and adding any items to the balance sheet which you deem necessary. (Note: Break up complex events into simple events.)

a. John Doe buys and eats a dinner for $3 in a restaurant.

b. He receives a $250 check in payment of interest on bonds owned and banks it. (Count bank deposits as cash.)

c. He gets a pay check for $200 and banks it.

d. He buys a TV set for $200, paying $50 cash and contracting to pay $10 a week plus 1 percent per week interest on the balance until the debt is paid off.

e. He pays $100 premium on a term life insurance contract.

f. He loses his wallet with $150 in it.

g. He pays $200 in taxes.

h. He receives a bill for $300 for taxes on his house.

i. He is repaid the $500 note, plus $30 interest.

j. He pays off $500 of his accounts receivable with cash.

k. He loses $100 in gambling.

What was his income, outgo, saving, receipts, expenditure, and hoarding during this period?

2. List one economic event if possible in each of the eight categories of Table 21 which might occur in the history of the following organizations:
   a. A local church
   b. A local school system
   c. An orphanage
   d. The United States Government
   e. A manufacturing corporation
   f. An insurance Company
   g. A commercial bank
   h. A beaver colony

3. What is the nature of the decision or decisions which might be associated with the following events, and what alternative futures might be envisaged, and what values might be involved?
   a. A family buys a new car.
   b. A student enters college as a freshman.
   c. A firm lowers the price of its product.
   d. A firm builds a new plant in Jonesville.
   e. A man joins a church.
   f. A man emigrates to another country.
   g. Two cars collide.
   h. One country declares war on another.

4. Can any of the above decisions be said to violate the rule of maximizing behavior? If so, how?

5. In the following situations involving a decision or set of decisions, what is the maximand or minimand by which the success of the decision is judged?
   a. A game of golf
   b. A footrace against opponents
   c. A footrace to break the world's record
   d. A game of chess
   e. A weight-reducing diet
   f. A gambler at a casino
   g. A speculator on the stock market
   h. A business corporation

6. In a straight-life insurance contract, a person pays the same premium to the insurance company each year until he dies, even though the actuarial value of the policy, as measured, say, by the premium on one-year renewable term insurance is less than the straight-life premium when he is young and greater when he is old. Break down into simple events the complex events involved in taking out and paying for a straight-life policy.

   Discuss similarly the events (simple or complex) involved in taking out fire or automobile insurance. Suppose taking out insurance makes people more careless. How do we put this in our accounts?

7. The following tables represent, in simplified form, the balance sheets of four firms.

FIRM A

Assets		Equities	
Goods and cash	$100,000	Due to other firms	$ 80,000
Due from firm B	20,000	Net worth	90,000
Due from firm C	40,000		
Due from firm D	10,000		
Total	$170,000		$170,000

FIRM B

Assets		Equities	
Goods and cash	$ 72,000	Due to other firms	$ 70,000
Due from firm C	20,000	Due to firm A	20,000
Due from firm D	18,000	Net worth	20,000
Total	$110,000		$110,000

FIRM C

Assets		Equities	
Goods and cash	$ 38,000	Due to firm B	$ 20,000
Due from firm D	32,000	Due to firm A	40,000
		Net worth	10,000
Total	$ 70,000		$ 70,000

FIRM D

Assets		Equities	
Goods and cash	$ 50,000	Due to firm C	$ 32,000
Due from others	20,000	Due to firm B	18,000
		Due to firm A	10,000
		Net worth	10,000
Total	$ 70,000		$ 70,000

Calculate the total value of goods and cash owned by these four firms. Show that this total is equal to the sum of the net worths of the four firms, plus the net amount due to other firms outside the four. Prove from this that in a closed society the total value of goods and cash must be equal to the total of net worths.

b. Suppose that a hurricane destroyed $40,000 worth of the goods belonging to firm D. Suppose further that in bankruptcy the assets of a firm are liquidated (turned into cash) and then divided among the creditors in proportion to each creditor's claim. What will be the effect of the hurricane on the balance sheets of the four firms? Which firms will be insolvent? (Assume that all insolvent firms are bankrupted.) Show that the total loss of net worth in the four firms is equal to the $40,000 of value destroyed by the hurricane.

CHAPTER 16

THE FIRM AS AN ECONOMIC ORGANIZATION

TYPES OF ORGANIZATION OF FIRMS

In the previous chapter a general theory of an economic organization was developed using a person, household, or single spending unit (John Doe) as examples. In the course of social development specialized economic organizations (firms) appear in many forms, and we need now to consider how far the theory of the previous chapter must be modified to fit the case of a firm. It is not easy to tell where households end and firms begin—there is a continuum of types of organization. At one end of the scale we have the primitive family of hunters, the peasant farmer, and the independent craftsman where there is virtually no distinction between the household and the "business." The division of labor between the sexes is perhaps the first sign of such a distinction—what the man does is business, what the woman does is household. With the growth of specialization in crafts and in the production of intermediate products the activities of production and exchange for the market become still more distinct from the activities of household production and consumption for domestic use. However, as long as the craftsman or peasant himself owns his shop, his farm, and his tools or animals, the household and the business are essentially part of a single organization. It is not until we get specialized ownership of physical capital, so that the worker no longer owns the physical things—whether land, cattle, or tools and equipment—with which he works, that the firm emerges as a distinct form of organization.

The Firm as Developing First in Trade and Agriculture

It is not easy to put one's finger on the exact date when the *firm* appears in history. In a sense the Egypt of the first Pharoahs was a firm—almost,

324

indeed, a one-firm state. Even before the first cities there seem to have been traders and merchants, whose business activities would be distinct from their household activities. In agriculture, the estate owned by a land-owner who also owns the livestock, equipment, and frequently the workers themselves (slaves) is clearly a type of firm and appears early in the development of civilization. Here we see clearly that the organization of the firm is built around the specialization of *enterprise* as an administration of a complex of productive capital brought together in a common ownership. The landed aristocracy did not derive their incomes from activity of their own; they derived them from the sheer fact of ownership, like a shareholder in a modern corporation. The landowner, both ancient and modern, was frequently an absentee from his estate; the work of detailed management was done by hired managers, just as absentee stockholders hire managers to manage the business which they own.

The Domestic System

In industry the specialization of enterprise and the organization of the firm begins with what is called the *domestic system*. This is a system in which the individual craftsman still works in his own home and with his own tools, but the activities of marketing are taken over by a specialized merchant or middleman. This is what we should expect, for of all the activities which a purely independent craftsman has to perform, marketing is least like his other activities. An independent weaver, for instance, has to buy his own yarn and sell the cloth which he makes from it. Both these activities may be troublesome to him, for his skill at weaving is totally different from the skill required in buying and selling. Consequently, those weavers who find that they are more skilled at buying and selling than at weaving may specialize in the trade of buying and selling—i.e., they may become merchants. A merchant clothier of the fifteenth century in England bought yarn, gave it out to weavers to weave, paid them for their work, and took the cloth they wove. Notice now the subtle and significant change which has taken place in the status of the weaver as he is transformed from an independent craftsman to a domestic worker. Although he works in his own home and with his own loom he is in effect an employee of the merchant, for he does not own the yarn on which he works or the cloth which he produces. It is *because* the merchant owns the yarn and the cloth that the weaver is an employee. The merchant does not buy cloth from the weaver, for the weaver does not own the cloth; he buys the *labor* of the weaver and the services of the weaver's looms and workrooms.

The Factory System

The next step is more spectacular but not, perhaps, really so significant as the change from the craft to the domestic system. This is the development of *factories*. The factory is a child of power; as long as the only power used in production was the power of human or even of animal muscles, there was little point in collecting workers and their implements together into factories. But once devices were discovered, first for using water power and later for using the power of coal and steam, the difficulties of transporting power led to the building of factories and the aggregation of workers into industrial towns. As power could not go to the worker, the worker had to go to the power. However, the power supplied by a single water wheel or a single steam engine was sufficient to drive a number of machines. For purely technical reasons an efficient source of power could not be devised which was small enough to drive a single machine. This fact in itself was probably enough to make factory production profitable. Another development which favored the growth of factories was the increasing specialization of processes, making it convenient to have a number of machines of different types located in the same building so that materials in process could be passed quickly and cheaply from one operation to the next.

The Private Entrepreneur

The growth in the size of the industrial unit, or "plant," led to an expansion of the form of enterprise run by a manager-capitalist, or *small businessman*. The small businessman generally owns the capital of his business; that is, he owns the raw materials and equipment used in the course of the process. He also directly supervises the management of the enterprise. He himself performs the operations of purchase and sale; he personally supervises the workers and is responsible for the efficient cooperation of the various inputs which he uses. In this form of enterprise the worker is a worker pure and simple, who sells nothing but the only thing he owns—his labor. The employer is also completely specialized, performing none of the common tasks of labor himself but confining himself to the operations of buying, selling, and supervising.

There is no necessary physical reason why this type of enterprise should have been the result of the growth of factory methods. It is conceivable that the factory system could have been introduced by workers' cooperatives in which the capital equipment and raw materials were owned by the workers themselves, acting as a group. Although the ownership of the capital of the productive processes was now outside the reach of a single worker, owing to the great size of the capital involved, it might not, perhaps, have been impossible for a group of workers to own their own factories, machines, and raw materials. In some fields, as we shall see, the cooperative form of enterprise has been successful. In the field of manufacturing industry, however, it has been a relative failure. For reasons connected with the natural differences and capacities of men, the form of enterprise which is owned and guided by those who are not employed by it has been the most successful.

The Partnership

As the size of the unit of enterprise increased, the organizational form of the enterprise developed. An early stage in this development was the *partnership*, in which two or more persons owned a business between them. Partnerships are of several kinds. In one kind each partner owns an equal share in the business and takes an equal responsibility for the conduct of the business. In another kind some partners own large shares, some, small shares of the business. In yet another kind some partners take an active responsibility for the conduct of the business and other partners merely contribute ownership, i.e., are "sleeping partners." The fundamental principle of the partnership, however, is the same in all cases. In so far as any one of the partners performs services (e.g., of management) for the business, he should be paid for those services just as any input has to be paid for. Then any excess of the value of outputs over the value of inputs, i.e., any *profit*, should be divided among the partners in proportion to their share in the capital of the business.[1]

DEFECTS OF THE PARTNERSHIP. There are two features of the partnership which frequently cause inconvenience. One is the fact that a partnership is merely an agreement between individuals and not an organization which exists apart from the individuals who compose it. Hence, important decisions can rarely be taken without the consent of all the partners. This limits severely the number of people who can participate in a partnership. Hence also, if one of the partners dies or wishes to withdraw from the partnership, the whole agreement must be redrawn.

The other inconvenient feature is that the partners are usually liable, each individually, for all the debts of the business. Thus, if a partnership fails, all the property of the partners, whether it pertains to the business or not, passes into the possession of the business when it is liquidated. Suppose, for instance, that Mr. A and Mr. B were equal partners in a business which failed with debts amounting to $50,000 and assets amounting to $20,000. Suppose that Mr. A's property outside the

---

[1] This rule is by no means universal. The forms of the partnership are legion, for there is a wide choice in the terms of the contract which is drawn up. The above-mentioned form is, however, the simplest and most logical.

business amounted to $10,000 and Mr. B's amounted to $20,000. Then Mr. A would have to hand over all his property to satisfy the claims of the business, and Mr. B also would have to hand over all his property, in spite of the fact that their original shares were equal. In this case the creditors would not lose, for they would be able to draw upon not only the property of the business itself but also the personal property of the partners. This feature is called *unlimited liability*.

Intermediate Forms

In order to remedy these defects many forms of business organization have been tried. For instance, there are limited partnerships, in which the liability of some of the partners is limited to the share of capital which they hold. In this case if the business fails, the limited partners do not lose their personal property outside the business. The difficulties which arise because the partnership is merely an agreement between individuals are avoided in the form of organization known as the joint-stock company, in which the organization is permanent, management may be delegated by the owners to one or more directors, and the shares of ownership are transferable. In this case the organization exists apart from its owners, who may change, and the owners do not have to take any active part in the management. However, the joint-stock company may still have unlimited liability. In that case the shares of ownership involve the owners in responsibility for the debts of the company even up to the extent of their whole personal capital.

The Corporation

The most highly developed form of organization, and one which is perhaps most characteristic of the present time, is the corporation. The corporation is a joint-stock company with limited liability. In England it is usually called a *limited liability company*. It is a *legal person*, which exists, can buy, sell, own, borrow, or lend as an entity apart from the stockholders who own it. The debtors of a corporation can lay claim only to the property which belongs to the corporation as such. They cannot lay claim to the private property of the shareholders, except in some special cases.[2]

Although the stockholders theoretically own the corporation, as a group they seldom play an active part in the management of the organization. They elect a board of directors, each stockholder having a number of votes in proportion to the number of shares which he owns. To these directors the stockholders delegate the responsibility for the success or

[2] Some states provided for the double liability of stockholders in the case of banks, where the stockholders may be called upon for twice the value of their stock if the bank is liquidated.

failure of the organization. The directors in their turn delegate the day-to-day management of the corporation to paid managers and reserve to themselves only the right of decision on fundamental matters of policy.

THE CORPORATION A LEGAL CONCEPT. It should be remembered that the corporation is a *legal* rather than a strictly economic concept, and is as much a part of the political organization as of the economic organization of society. The corporation is in fact, if not in theory, one of the brood of smaller leviathans which cluster around the great leviathan of the state. That is to say, it is an instrument of local economic government, much as the county or town authorities are instruments of local political government. It is not, perhaps, farfetched to draw an analogy between the relationships of corporations to the state today and the relationships of the feudal lords to the king in medieval times. The king granted certain rights and privileges to the barons because he could not otherwise administer his kingdom. The power of the barons in theory derived from the king, but in practice frequently the king was controlled by the barons. Similarly, the great corporations are the "barons" of modern life. Their privileges are in theory derived from the state. Again, however, in practice the "barons" may sometimes control the "king." Between the formal structure of political and legal relationships and the real structure of power and policy making there is usually little correspondence. Law is fiction; power is personal, though law is the framework within which power works.

ECONOMIC CONSEQUENCES OF THE CORPORATION. The corporation, therefore, is not necessarily to be identified with any particular form of economic organization, such as "big business." It is true that the corporate form of organization is particularly appropriate for large-scale enterprises. It may be equally appropriate, however, in small-scale enterprises. Whenever men unite in an enterprise which they wish to keep in some measure separate from their other concerns, and in which they wish to be able to delegate responsibility, the corporate form is usually the most satisfactory. Nevertheless, the legal institution of incorporation has had important economic consequences. It has in particular permitted an enormous extension of specialized financial relationships, providing for almost every degree of risk or of ownership in which an investor might wish to indulge. The variety of corporation securities is almost inexhaustible, ranging from mortgage bonds, ordinary bonds, cumulative preference shares, ordinary preference shares, ordinary shares, even down to nonvoting ordinary shares. This variety has in itself elaborated the possibilities of fraud, for the financial structure of a corporation can become so complex that no investor, unless he is a financial genius, can find out what assets really correspond to the equity that he possesses.

THE PYRAMIDING OF CONTROL. Another important consequence of
the corporate form is the development of the holding company and the
pyramiding of control. Because of the "dollar democracy" of the corporation (one share, one vote) any person or group who could control even
51 percent of the voting stock could control the corporation. Suppose,
for instance, that corporation A had $1,000,000 in voting stock. Anyone
who controlled $501,000 of this could control the corporation. Suppose
now that a corporation (B) was floated, with a capital of, say, $501,000,
for the purpose of holding stock in A. Anyone who held $251,000 of
stock in B could control both B and A. Similarly, if another corporation
(C) was formed to hold the stock of B, anyone who held $126,000 of
stock in C would control both B and A. The corporate form, therefore,
makes it relatively easy to build up vast industrial "empires" of control,
such as the Insull empire, on a relatively small amount of actual ownership, unless specific legislation hinders this process.

The Survival of Older Forms of Enterprise

It must not be thought that the older forms of enterprise have been
superseded altogether by the newer forms. Although one type of enterprise may be dominant at one period of history and another at another
period, examples of almost all previous forms can be found at any
one time. In our day the independent craftsman, selling the product
of his labor directly to the consumer and working with his own tools
and equipment, still survives in the person of the barber and the shoe-
shiner. The domestic system still survives in many industries—in the
clothing industry, for instance, where shirts are "put out" to be finished
as home, or in the cattle-feeding industry where the stock are frequently
owned by the dealer who buys and sells them. The small independent
employer is to be found in most industries. In agriculture the independent
farmer still predominates, and the small family "works" is still the main-
stay of many a town. Nevertheless, it would be true to say that the
dominant form of business organization in our day is the corporation.

The Cooperative Society

Through all these many forms of organization one principle holds:
profits, the difference between the value of outputs and the value of
inputs, belong to the owners of a business in proportion to the share
which they own. This principle applies even to another form of business organization—the cooperative society—which has risen into importance in the past hundred years. A cooperative society is a business
owned by the people who purchase from it, or who sell to it, in the proportion of the amount of their purchases or sales. In the case of a corpora-

tion the ultimate owners of the property of the corporation, and therefore of the profits which it makes, are stockholders—people who may not and usually do not buy from the corporation. A cooperative society may be defined as a corporation which is financed entirely by fixed-interest securities (bonds) and in which the ownership resides in the people who buy from it or sell to it. Its profits, consequently, also belong to the people who buy from it or sell to it, in proportion to the amount which they have bought or sold. That is, profits are distributed in the form of a rebate or dividend given to each member in a fixed proportion not of the capital stock which he owns but of the purchases or sales which he has made.

The Consumers Cooperative

A consumers cooperative is a retailing business, purchasing inputs in the form of wholesale goods, of the labor of storekeepers and managers, of the services of stores, and so on; selling outputs in the form of commodities to consumers across the counter. Its profits belong in the first instance to the business as such, just as in the case of the corporation—i.e., any addition to the net value of the property of the business is profit. These profits, however, must at some time be distributed among the members. Whereas in the case of the corporation the profits are distributed among the owners according to the proportion of the capital stock which each owns, in the case of the cooperative the profits are distributed among the members in proportion to the amount of purchases which they have made. There are also marketing cooperatives, especially in agriculture, which are distributing businesses buying products from the farmers, often processing them in some way, and selling them again to other merchants or to consumers.

FACTORS IN ITS SUCCESS. The consumers cooperative has been a very successful form of business organization in Europe, rather less so in the United States. There is nothing inherently superior about the cooperative as a form of organization. Under certain circumstances, and in certain fields, it seems to be superior to other forms; in other circumstances and other fields it is not. The success of the cooperative form of organization in the retail field in Europe is due to a number of causes, some of which were peculiar to the times, others of which are more fundamental. Thus the consumers cooperative movement in Europe came at a time when considerable economies were possible in the large-scale organization of retailing; the movement seized these economies and consequently made large profits. Part of the profits it used for paying dividends to its members; part were used to finance its expansion. The success of the cooperatives in Europe also seems to be due in part to the class structure of most European countries. The more rigid the class structure of society, the more difficult it is for a man with ability who originates in the working class to attain a managerial position. There may then be a large untapped reservoir of managerial ability among the working classes. The cooperative movement is frequently able to tap this ability, and consequently to obtain its managers at very low wages.

Cooperative Financial Institutions

In the United States the cooperative form of organization seems to have been most successful in the case of financial institutions. The credit union has had a modest success in the field of personal and household finance; this is an organization the members of which usually have some other membership in common, such as the employees of a factory. It lends money to its members and borrows money both from its members and from outside sources. The mutual savings banks and mutual life insurance companies, some of which are very large and successful, also have the cooperative form in the sense that they are owned not by outside stockholders but by their depositors or policyholders, though they are usually run by a self-perpetuating board of managers.

Separation of Ownership from Management

In any business the ultimate control of policy is supposed to lie with the owners, for it is their property which is being handled and their money which is being spent. Nevertheless, in those forms of business in which ownership is separated from management the danger always exists that the management will wrest the real control of the business from the owners. Even in such a simple form as the partnership it is possible for an active and unscrupulous partner to run the business for his own ends, while his sleeping partner sleeps on unaware. In the case of the great corporations the stockholders are almost inevitably sleeping partners. There is a form of election of directors by the stockholders, but the latter are frequently ignorant of the details of the business, and the real control of the corporation passes into the hands of a small clique. This is not to say that the management of corporations is necessarily corrupt or not in the stockholders' interests. It does mean, however, that once an owner relinquishes the management of what he owns, he also relinquishes his control and takes an unavoidable risk of bad or corrupt management. The unjust steward is a risk that anyone must take who yields his property to stewardship.

EXISTS EVEN IN COOPERATIVES.   The same difficulty arises also in connection with cooperative societies. In the case of consumers cooperatives the members, being the owners of the profit, elect the directors just as the stockholders elect the directors in a corporation. Where the number of members is large, the knowledge that each member can have about the affairs of the society is slight, and the control which the membership exercises over the management is inevitably weakened. The danger of corrupt management is probably less in a cooperative society than in a corporation, for the opportunities for personal profit are less. However, the danger of inefficient management is a real one, as many cooperative societies have found to their cost.

POSITIVE ASPECTS.   There are important positive aspects of the separation of ownership from management; indeed it can be said that one of the main functions of the financial system is to achieve precisely this separation. One of the main problems which faces any society is how to organize matters so that those persons who have unusual competence in the administration of property and the organization of production can gain control over more property than they personally own. If there were no financial system and no forms of economic organization beyond the household every owner of property would have to administer it himself—or herself as, simply because women live longer than men, a large proportion of the equity (that is, real ownership) of the property of most societies is in the hands of elderly ladies. The system of finance and economic organizations permits those who own capital, but do not have the capacity or the will to administer it, to relinquish its management and administration to those who have the capacity and the will but who do not have the ownership. In this sense the separation of ownership from management is an essential element of any complex society, and the fact that it is is open to abuse should not blind us to its necessity.

The Centrally Planned Economy

Yet another form of economic organization is the centrally planned economy, of which the countries of the socialist camp (as they call themselves) are examples. In the extreme case the whole of the economic life of a country is organized into a single firm, which is also the state. Thus if we imagine, say, General Motors growing until it absorbed the whole American economy, it would approximate in form, if not perhaps in spirit, to a centrally planned economy. In such a country everyone is an employee of the single firm-state, and all capital is owned by it. The people are theoretically the owners or stockholders; in practice, however, the separation of ownership from management is virtually complete, and the firm-state is run by a minority party. The economics of centrally planned economies, however, presents so many special problems that they will be treated separately.

Types of Firms: Manufacturing, Trading, Financial

Firms may be divided roughly into three main types according to the nature of the business which they carry on; manufacturing, trading, and financial firms. Manufacturing firms are engaged mainly in producing and selling goods or services; they tend to have a large proportion of their assets in physical goods (buildings, machines, raw materials, finished products) and their financial assets mainly consist of cash, bank deposits, and other fairly liquid assets needed in the conduct of their production processes. Trading firms are concerned mainly with the purchase, storage, handling and sale of commodities rather than with changing their physical form. The distinction between manufacturing and trading firms is not very great, as both are engaged in adding value to the goods which they purchase—one, by changing them to a more highly valued form, the other, by changing them to more highly valued times, places, or ownership. Financial firms are rather more distinct; their assets are mainly in the form of financial assets (liabilities of other individuals or firms) and they make profits mainly because the rate of return which they receive on their financial assets is greater than the rate of interest which they pay on their liabilities. Banks and insurance companies fall generally into this type, though insofar as they earn income by direct charges for services rendered they become more like manufacturing firms producing services. This classification is a rough one; firms of a pure type are very rare, and most firms participate in some degree in manufacturing, trading, and financial operations. Here we shall be dealing mainly with manufacturing and trading firms, as we are mainly concerned with the pricing of goods and services. The theory of the financial firm will be developed more fully in Volume II: *Macroeconomics*.

THE EVENTS TABLE APPLIED TO A FIRM

The Balance Sheet: Assets of Firms

We can now apply the concepts of the position statement and the events table to the firm, as in the previous chapter we applied it to the person or household. As in the case of the person, the first approximation to the position statement of a firm is its balance sheet. This does not differ in any essential concept from the balance sheet of a person, though additional subdivisions are needed. On the assets side we need to subdivide the "things" item into: (1) fixed assets which have a fairly long life and against which depreciation is charged at intervals; (2) raw materials and goods in process, representing items which are consumed (transformed) in the process of producing the final finished product; (3) finished goods ready to be sold (in the case of trading firms the item (2) may not be present). The claims items may include (4) stock of other corporations and (5) bonds of other corporations or of governments. (6) promissory notes (really a form of bond) of persons or other firms and (7) accounts receivable. The cash item may include (8) savings or time deposits, (9) checking deposits, (10) legal tender money. (8) and (9) are really claims on banks, and perhaps should be classified under claims. Even legal tender, as we shall see more clearly later, is best re-garded as a generalized claim on goods offered for sale. However, assets which are liquid enough to be immediately acceptable for any purchase are usually regarded as equivalent to cash.

Liabilities of Firms

On the liabilities side we find claims: (11) mortgages; (12) bonds (funded debts due to others); (13) notes payable to others (again a form of bond); (14) accounts payable—current bills for purchases on credit from the supplier including wage claims on the firm; (15) taxes payable, which ordinarily include only taxes owed for the current year and do not include any capitalized value of future taxes. As we shall see later, this is a fact of crucial importance for public finance. The total of items (11) to (15) are the total of *contractual* claims; they represent claims for definite sums. The amount by which the total value of the assets exceeds the total value of the contractual claims is the total of *residual claims* or net worth. In the case of a private business the residual claim is the value of the business to the owner. It will appear as an asset in the owner's personal balance sheet. In the case of a partnership the residual claim is divided among the partners according to some prearranged plan. If, for instance, a firm has two equal partners and a total residual claim of $100,000, each partner will count his property in the business as a $50,000 asset in his personal balance sheet.

CORPORATE NET WORTH. In the case of a corporation the residual claim represents the total book value of the stock of the corporation. Suppose a corporation has 1,000 shares of stock and a total residual claim (net worth) of $1,200,000. The book value of each share is one-thousandth part of the total residual claim, or $1,200. Corresponding to this claim against the corporation there is a sum of roughly $1,200,000 in assets in the personal balance sheets of all the stockholders. In each case it is seen, then, that *all* the items on the equities side of the balance sheet of a firm are represented as assets in the balance sheets of other firms or individuals. This is what we should expect, as a firm is only a vehicle of ownership. Ultimately, the real ownership of all the "things" possessed by a society must be found in individual persons. So the existence of firms does not invalidate our conclusion that the total value of the goods and cash held by a society should be equal to the total sum of the net worths of the individuals of that society.

In a corporation the residual claim is usually divided into three parts. One part is called the *capital stock* and represents the *nominal* value of the stock of the corporation. Another part is called the *surplus* and represents that part of the excess of the total residual claim over the nominal value of the stock which may be regarded as permanent. The third part is called *undivided profits* and represents that part of the excess of the total residual claim over the nominal value of the stock which is *not* regarded as permanent. Suppose that in the example above the total residual claim of $1,200,000 were divided as follows: (16) capital stock, $1,000,000; (17) surplus, $150,000; (18) undivided profits, $50,000. This would mean that the total equity of the shareholders was $1,200,000. The corporation would expect to reduce this by $50,000 in the near future by declaring a dividend—i.e., by taking $50,000 in cash from its assets and distributing it among the shareholders, thus reducing the assets by $50,000 and also therefore reducing the residual claim by $50,000. The *permanent* equity of the stockholders is then divided, in the accounts though not in any real sense, into two parts: one representing the nominal value of the capital stock; the other the increase or surplus of the permanent equity over this nominal value.

Insolvency and Bankruptcy

When the total of liabilties, or contractual claims against a firm, is greater than the total of assets of all kinds the firm is *insolvent*. The net worth in this case may be considered negative if it is defined as the difference between assets and liabilities. A firm may be insolvent for a considerable period, however, without going out of existence, as long as all its creditors do not demand payment at once. It is possible for a firm to meet its *current* obligations for a time, although it could not possibly meet *all* its obligations. When the insolvency of a firm is so manifest, however, that its creditors have given up hope of ever seeing it restored to solvency, the firm is *bankrupted*. Its existence as an entity ceases, although it is sometimes resurrected by a process known as corporate reorganization, in which, say, the previous shareholders are eliminated and the previous bondholders become shareholders in a new corporation which retains the physical assets of the old one. In any case the bankruptcy of one firm results in downward revaluations of the assets of its creditors, which may in severe cases, as in Exercise 7, p. 323, set off a chain of further bankruptcies.

Events in a Firm

The history of a firm can be written in the form of an events table such as Table 22 (p. 312). The eight classes of simple events noted in Table 21 (p. 311) apply to the firm just as to the household. There are, however, a number of peculiarities in the case of the firm, arising mainly from the character of a firm as an economic intermediary and a profit-making organization. Thus in the case of the firm we have to distinguish between the total income generated by the firm's operation (often called value added) and the profit of the firm itself. The value added in any period is the excess of the value of total sales of goods and services over the value of purchases of goods and services from other firms. It will be equal to the total wage bill, plus accruals of interest on debt (contractual claims), plus total profit, less income arising from assets (e.g., bonds) extraneous to the central productive process. There is therefore in the firm a distinction between *income events* which increase value added, and *profit events* which increase the net worth of the firm, profit being defined as the gross increase in net worth. It is profit in the firm, however, which is analogous to income in the household, and we shall therefore treat A-type events as profit events.

Profit Events

Let us consider first events of type A1 of Table 21 (p. 311) (profit-expansion events) which increase both the total value of assets and the net worth. There are two subclasses of these events, the most important of which is usually the revaluation of finished goods at the moment of sale. Thus suppose we have a weaving firm that sells 100 yards of cloth at $2 per yard for $200. Up to the moment of sale the cloth has been carried on the books "at cost," the meaning of which we will see later; suppose however the value at cost was $180. The sale then is a complex event, composed of two simple events: first, a revaluation of the cloth from $180 to $200, resulting in a rise of $20 in asset totals and a rise in net worth of $20, (a type A1 event) followed immediately by an exchange of $200 worth of cloth for $200 of cash or accounts receivable (a B2 type event, exchange-neutral). In the case of John Doe in the previous chapter we treated the sale of his car as a simple event of type B2; even in the case of the household if the car had been carried on the books at less than the value for which it was sold, the event should properly be regarded as a complex A1–B2 event like the above.

The second subclass of profit-expansion events is the revaluation of existing assets. This can happen if the book value of inventories of finished goods or goods in process increases. It can happen if an inflation forces the revaluation of fixed assets. An important subclass of this type is the accrual of interest or dividends on securities held by the firm. We should note that it is the accrual which constitutes the profit event, raising the value of the asset and of net worth; the *payment* of interest or dividends received is a type B2 event, with cash rising and the value of securities falling. Type A2 events (profit-neutral) are rare in the firm as they are in the household; corporate reorganization however falls conveniently in this category, when certain claims by old stockholders are compulsorily forgiven.

Exchange Events

Exchange events are central to the operation of a firm. Type B1 (for example, credit purchases, cash borrowings) and type B3 (repayment of debt, tax payments) are similar to the corresponding events in the household but are apt to be quantitatively more important in a firm, for expansion events are, of course, the principal means by which a firm expands, and for many firms the net worth is a fairly small proportion of total equities. Type B2' (refinance) operations are also similar in principle, though also much commoner, in the firm than in the household. It is Type B2 (exchange-neutral) events where the firm exhibits marked peculiarities, for the asset transformation involved in production mainly fall in this category. Thus when a firm produces 100 yards of cloth other assets are reduced or liabilities, increased: there is a diminution in stocks of yarn; a diminution through depreciation in the value of machines, buildings, and equipment involved; an increase in wage claims (accounts payable) of the labor employed which may soon be transformed into a diminution in cash when wages are paid, and possibly (depending on the method of accounting) an associated increase in liabilities as interest accrues on debt. The sum of all these diminutions in assets or increase in liabilities is the total cost of the finished goods; if this sum is $180 the process of production then involves a complex event of types B2 and B1, with finished goods increasing by $180, and various other assets decreasing, and liabilities increasing to total $180, so that net worth remains unchanged. This process by which asset and liability values are shifted into finished goods is known as *costing*.

Some events which are classified as outgo events (type C) in the case of the household may be costed in the case of the firm and so appear as exchange events of type B. Thus events such as accrual of interest and taxes, which we treated as type C2 (outgo-neutral) events, lowering net worth and increasing liabilities, may be costed in the firm and treated as B1 events, increasing the value of assets (finished goods) by as much as the increase in liabilities and so not changing net worth. Similarly depreciation and consumption, which in the household is a C3 event, diminishing both asset total and net worth, in the firm is costed as a B2 event, with finished goods increasing in value and goods in process and fixed capital diminishing. There are difficult problems (and a long controversy) in accounting practice as to which of these items should be costed, and how. It is often hard to allocate what are called overhead costs, such as depreciation, maintainance of plant and equipment, taxes, and interest accruals to particular products, and this allocation often has to be done by a farily arbitrary process known as cost accounting. There is also a view among accountants that interest accruals should not be costed, but treated as a deduction from net worth, that is as a C2 type event. Whatever the accounting practice, if we regard the firm as a pure intermediary, it is clear that it cannot have consumption or outgo of its own, and that therefore all type C events should in theory be costed. A possible exception may be made in the case of unpredictable losses, for instance destruction of assets by fire, storm, or theft; these should obviously not be costed to the particular goods produced in the period of their occurence, and may properly be treated as a C3 type event. Even here, strictly speaking, a contingencies reserve should be established as a deduction from the value of assets, and the cost of carrying this, or of paying insurance premiums, should certainly be costed and included in the cost value of finished goods. These noncosted events of types C2 and C3 may be called *loss events;* they are parallel in the case of the firm to outgo events in the case of the household.

Transactions within the net worth category present some problems which are special to the firm. An A1 type event resulting in an increase in assets and a corresponding increase in net worth is usually reflected in an increase in undistributed profits. Sometimes the firm may transfer a sum from undistributed profits to surplus or reserve: this is a purely nominal transaction, merely giving part of the net worth a different name; it is significant only as a declaration of intention. Similarly a stock dividend is a nominal transfer from undistributed profits to capital stock. Thus suppose the firm of p. 336, with capital stock, $1,000,000, surplus, $150,000, and undivided profits, $50,000, were to declare a stock dividend of $25,000. Each stockholder would get $25 of stock for each $1,000 he previously possessed, and the position statement would then read: capital stock, $1,025,000, surplus $150,000, undistributed profit, $25,000. There is no change in the total net worth, only in the names by which it is called.

A cash dividend is quite another matter: this is an event of type C3, analogous to consumption or outgo in the case of the person; it is a decline in cash assets, and an equal decline in net worth. We must distinguish very carefully between the *earning* of profit, which is the process by which net worth increases through revaluations of assets (or liabilities), either at the moment of sale or through windfalls, and the *distribution* of profit, which is a reduction of net worth. Business savings is the *net* increase in net worth in a period, which is equal to the total amount of profit earned (the gross increase in net worth) less profit distributions in dividends or other withdrawals.

It is not always easy to distinguish between profit withdrawals and purchases of management services. This is especially so in the case of small businessmen, partnerships, and even small corporations. Here what looks like a profit withdrawal is often in fact a purchase of management service, as when a small businessman transfers money from his business to his private account; or where what appears on the books as payment for management actually includes a share of profits, as when the director-managers of corporations vote themselves salaries beyond the current market price of their services. Indeed, what we count as a withdrawal and what as a cost of purchase of input depends on the purpose we have in mind. Thus when calculating the rate of return on the net worth of an enterprise, we include all payments for hired capital (debt) and all payments for management in *cost,* but allocate business savings, plus withdrawals to owners in their capacity as owners, as *profit.* The economist calculating the supply price of a product, however, as we saw on page 250, includes a *normal* profit on the net worth of the enterprise in his total cost, on the grounds that, without this, capital will not be supplied to that particular line of production. What is the level of normal profit depends on many things—the riskiness, the respectability, the illiquidity, even the fashionableness of the enterprise. The more risky, the less respectable, the less liquid, and the less fashionable the enterprise, the higher will have to be the rate of normal profit which will attract capital into it, and the higher therefore the supply price of the product.

It must be emphasized that it is the *rate* of profit which is significant in attracting or repelling capital, not the absolute amount. Two firms both earning $100,000 profits a year are not equally profitable if one has a net worth of $1,000,000 and the other of $2,000,000; the first earns 10 percent, the second, only 5 percent per annum. The rate of profit may then be defined as the rate of growth of net worth in the absence of withdrawals.

The profit-and-loss events (types A and B) which change net worth are usually summarized for an accounting period, such as a year, in an income statement, or profit-and-loss account, Thus our example of cloth weaving might be placed in tabular form as follows:

TABLE 24. PROFIT-AND-LOSS STATEMENT

Sales (revenues)	$200	Expenses (cost)	
		Labor	$ 60
		Materials	100
		Other	20
		Total expenses	180
		Net profit	20
Total	$200	Total	$200

Any Revaluation of Assets Produces Income

As we have seen, under usual accounting procedures any *revaluation* of assets will be reflected in income. A rise in the values of existing assets will be recorded as positive income; a fall, as negative income—that is, as a subtraction from income. Many difficult questions in accounting and in economic theory arise because of this identity between revaluation and income, for there are some items of revaluation which do not seem properly to fall in the same classification as others.

Inventory Valuation

A good example of this problem is the controversy between two systems of inventory valuation, known as the *last in, first out* method (LIFO) and the *first in, first out* method (FIFO). Inventory valuation is necessary for two purposes: for showing the value of goods in stock in the balance sheet; and for showing the change in the value of inventory between the opening and closing dates of the income period. Thus suppose that in the previous example $150 worth of the cloth produced was sold, and the remainder remained in stock, this being an addition to the total inventory of cloth. It would clearly be misleading to record in the income statement only sales, for against the expenses recorded there is not only the increase in cash of $150 but also an increase in cloth. The question is, How should this increase in cloth be valued? It might, of course, be valued at the current selling price of cloth, in which case the value of the sold cloth and of the unsold cloth would still be $200, and it would make no difference to the net income whether the cloth was sold or not. Current accounting practice does not favor this procedure. Generally inventories are valued at cost, or at "cost or market, whichever is the lower." If the price structure and the techniques of production do not change there is no ambiguity in cost. Thus in the above example the cost of the cloth was $180, so that the cost of a quarter of it would be $45, and the profit-and-loss statement would look like Table 25.

TABLE 25. PROFIT-AND-LOSS STATEMENT, WITH INVENTORY

Sales	$150	Expenses	$180
Increase in stock	45	Net profit	15
	$195		$195

FIFO. Suppose, however, that wages and the price of yarn have risen during the income period, so that the cost of cloth has been rising. The inventory consists of cloth of different ages, and therefore of different costs. The most obvious procedure is to take the cost of the most recently completed items of stock. This assumes in effect that those items which were sold were the oldest items in the existing stock. This is the FIFO method. This method has many advantages. It has one important disadvantage, however, that in times of rising prices the rise in the value of the stock of goods is reflected in an increased net income figure, and falling prices likewise lead to a decrease in the net income figure. These changes in recorded income are in some sense spurious, or at least are a different kind of income from that which is generated by production. Thus suppose that in the previous example the cost of cloth has risen so rapidly that at the end of the income period it was double the average value during the period. The value of the increase in stock would then be $90, and the statement would look like Table 26. The increase in the

TABLE 26. PROFIT-AND-LOSS STATEMENT IN A PERIOD OF RISING PRICES AND COSTS

Sales	$150	Expense	$180
Increase in stock	90	Net profit	60
	$240		$240

value of the existing stock has inflated the net profit figure considerably. On the other hand, suppose that the cost of cloth had fallen so sharply that at the end of the period it was only half what it had averaged during the period. The profit-and-loss statement would look like Table 27. In this case the net profit has been wiped out altogether and turned into a loss.

TABLE 27. PROFIT-AND-LOSS STATEMENT IN A PERIOD OF FALLING PRICES AND COSTS

Sales	$150.00	Expense	$180.00
Increase in stock	22.50	Net profit	−7.50
	$172.50		$172.50

LIFO. In all three cases (Tables 25, 26, and 27) the *physical* events are identical; the changes in the physical items in the balance sheet are identical. The difference in results arises from differences in methods of valuation. It is the feeling that accounting should in some sense give a single measure of the results of these complex changes in the *physical* balance sheet that has led to the introduction of the LIFO method of inventory valuation. By this method the stock is valued at the prices of the *earliest* items recorded. This means in effect that the inventory is valued at constant prices, and hence its value does not reflect the shifts in the price structure. Thus suppose in the above example the increase in stock was 25 yards, and that the cost of the first cloth made by the enterprise was $1.60 per yard. The change in inventory would be recorded as $40, no matter what the current cost or price. This method has the disadvantage in that the value of inventory as recorded in the balance sheet is unrelated to current values and, especially in times of inflation or deflation, becomes a quite misleading figure. It does, however, get rid of the distortions in the income statement which are the result of fluctuating price and cost levels.

Capital Gains from Inflation

Similar problems arise in the valuation of all assets. Thus suppose a man buys a house for $10,000 and sells it some years later for $15,000. Does the $5,000 difference represent income, neglecting maintenance and carrying cost? In terms of conventional accounting it does: if the house is carried on his books at $10,000 and he gets $15,000 for it, there is a rise in his net worth of $5,000 as a result of the transaction; as we have seen, it is this rise in net worth which constitutes income. If, however, he has to buy another house with the money he may find that the *income* is somewhat illusory; if all houses have risen in about the same proportion, he will have to spend the $15,000 in buying a house just about as good as the one he sold. Measured in terms of houses, then, his net worth has not increased at all. The increase in dollars is merely a reflection of the fact that the value of the dollar has declined, and that $15,000 at the later date represents the same quantity of house or real purchasing power as $10,000 at the earlier date. The apparent $5,000 income is not all illusion, however, as the man is clearly better off than he would have been had he *not* bought his first house, but had held on to his $10,000 in the form of cash or bonds. If he had done this his net worth in terms of houses would have been only two-thirds as great at the later date than it would have been had he bought the house.

Are Capital Gains Income?

The rise or fall in the value of existing stocks of assets because of changes in their price, or valuation ratio, may best be called capital gains and losses, following the terminology of the United States income tax.

From the point of view of society as a whole they should clearly not be included in income, as they do not represent any value of physical or real production. From the point of view of individuals, however, they represent *relative* shifts in the distribution of income: a rise in prices makes those who hold real goods better off at the expense of those who hold money and bonds, and a fall in prices does the opposite. In individual accounting, therefore, there is something to be said for retaining capital gains and losses, if not directly in the income category, at least as a kind of porch or appendix. The United States income tax recognizes the anomalous position of capital gains and losses by taxing them at a different rate from ordinary income.

QUESTIONS AND EXERCISES

1. The following are the items in the balance sheet of a cloth manufacturing firm: *Assets (in thousands of dollars):* (a) fixed assets, 760; (b) goods in process, 300; (c) finished goods, 200; (d) stock of other corporations, 10; (e) bonds of governments and other corporations, 120; (f) notes receivable, 10; (g) accounts receivable, 30; (h) savings deposits, 20; (i) checking deposits, 25; (j) legal tender, 5. *Equities:* (k) mortgage on property, 100; (l) bonds payable, 50; (m) notes payable, 100; (n) accounts payable, 20; (o) taxes payable, 10; (p) capital stock, 1000; (q) surplus, 150; (r) undistributed profits, 50.

   Arrange these data in the form of Table 20, p. 307, and calculate the total assets and total equities. Draw up an events table like Table 22, p. 312, showing the successive positions of the balance sheet for the following events: (a) sale on credit of 10,000 yards of cloth costing $18,000 at $2 per yard; (b) production of 5,000 yards of cloth involving costs of $4,000 for goods in process, $1,000 depreciation, $4,000 labor costs (wage claims); (c) payment of $4,000 in wages; (d) payment of $10,000 accounts receivable by bank deposit; (e) transfer of $5,000 to savings deposit; (f) accrual of $3,000 semi-annual interest on mortgage, costed as overhead to finished goods; (g) payment of $2,000 interest on mortgage by bank check; (h) uninsured loss by fire of empty warehouse, valued at $75,000; (i) transfer of $40,000 from surplus account to undivided profits; (j) stock in another corporation, carried on books at cost of $10,000, sold for $30,000, paid by bank check; (k) government bonds sold for $20,000, book value also $20,000, paid by check; (l) $10,000 transferred from savings deposit to checking deposit; (m) purchase of new warehouse for $80,000, paid by check; (n) sale of 5,000 yards of cloth, costing $9,000, for $8,000 bank deposit; (o) repayment of $10,000 bank loan. Classify each event by the eightfold classification, breaking up the complex events. Draw up a profit and loss account for this period of operations.

   Calculate the quantities for the following identities:

   Increase in net worth = Business savings = profits − dividends

   Increase in cash (checking deposits plus legal tender) =

   $$\text{receipts of cash − expenditures of cash}$$

2. Suppose the above firm was a partnership with three equal partners. What would the above operations have done to the net worth of each partner? How would you distinguish in this case between capital gain (or loss) and income?

3. A firm may be at the same time solvent but illiquid, or conversely, insolvent but liquid. Draw up two balance sheets, using as many of the categories of Exercise 1 as you need, to illustrate these two conditions. Show how the liquidity of a firm can depend on its credit position—that is, its ability to have expansion events.

4. How would a nonprofit institution such as a university be distinguished from a profit-making institution in the form of its accounts? Cooperatives have sometimes been defended (and attacked) on the ground that they are nonprofit institutions. How far is this description accurate?

5. From looking at its balance sheet, how would you decide whether a firm should be classified as a manufacturing, trading, or financial firm?

6. Classify the events of Question 1 as far as possible into controlled and uncontrolled events from the point of view of the firm. Discuss the type of decision or decisions which may have resulted in each event.

7. Consider a cloth manufacturer with the following (simplified) balance sheet (in thousands of dollars): *Assets:* (a) finished goods, under 1 week old, 100; (b) finished goods, 1-2 weeks old, 100; (c) finished goods, 2-3 weeks old, 100; (d) goods in process (yarn), 100; (e) cash, 100; (f) other assets, 500. *Equities:* (g) debts, 400; (h) net worth, 600.

   Suppose in every week the following events take place: (a) 50,000 yards of cloth are sold for cash; (b) 50,000 yards of cloth are produced, using up 100,000 pounds of yarn and employing 500 men; (c) unsold cloth in stock becomes 1 week older; (d) 100,000 pounds of yarn is bought and a week's wage for 500 men are paid in cash. The table below shows the prices and average wage in successive weeks.

| | | Week | | | | | | |
	1	2	3	4	5	6	7	8
Price at which cloth is sold (dollars per yard)	2.00	2.00	2.00	2.40	2.80	3.20	3.60	4.00
Price at which yarn is bought (dollars per pound)	.50	.50	.50	.60	.70	.80	.90	1.00
Average weekly wage (dollars)	100.00	100.00	100.00	120.00	140.00	160.00	180.00	200.00

Construct an events table showing the events of the 8 weeks as a succession of balance sheets, (a) under FIFO, (b) under LIFO inventory valuations. Construct the corresponding profit-and-loss statements for each week.

CHAPTER 17

THE THEORY OF THE TRADING FIRM

PROFIT MAKING IN THE EVENTS TABLE

If we are to analyze the processes and decisions which go to produce the events table of a firm we must simplify the model and break up the decision-making process into component parts. Let us begin by considering a simple trading firm, a simplified model of a firm trading on the wheat market. The only assets are wheat and money. The firm starts with a physical position statement at P_0 with 600 bushels of wheat and $400 of money, and then follows the events table, Table 28. P_0, P_1, etc., are successive positions; 1, 2, etc., are successive events; in this

TABLE 28. THE PROFIT-MAKING PROCESS

	Position						
	P_0	P_1	P_2	P_3	P_4	P_5	P_6
Event	1	2	3	4	5	6	
Price (dollars per bushel)	2.00	3.00	2.50	2.00	3.00	2.00	
Wheat bought (+) or sold (−)	+100	−600	+400	+400	−700	+400	
Money paid in (+) or out (−)	−200	+1800	−1000	−800	+2100	−800	
Wheat stock (bushels)	600	700	100	500	900	200	600
Money stock (dollars)	400	200	2000	1000	200	2300	1500

case there are only two types of event—a purchase of wheat for money, or a sale of wheat for money. Events 1, 3, 4, and 6 are purchases of wheat; 2 and 5 are sales. The price of wheat in each event is the ratio of money paid or received to wheat bought or sold. Given the purchases and sales, we can immediately calculate, as in the last two lines of the table, the successive *positions* of the physical balance sheet. These are represented in the points P_0, P_1, $\cdots$ P_6 in Fig. 66A. P_0 is the original position. On the first day the exchange opportunity line is P_0P_1, and we suppose the firm moves to P_1 by buying wheat. Then next day the price is higher; the opportunity line is P_1P_2, and the firm sells wheat, moving to P_2 The

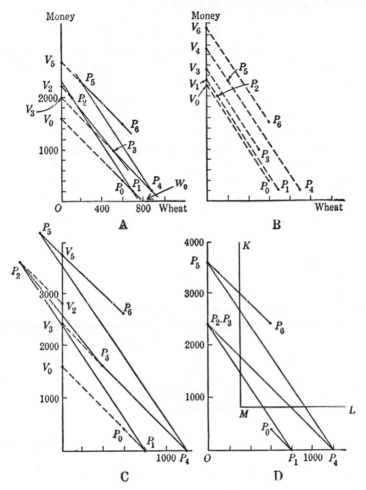

Fig. 66. The Profit-Making Process

third day the price is lower and the firm buys along the new opportunity line P_2P_3 to P_3. The fourth day the price is lower still, but the firm still buys along the new line P_3P_4 to P_4. So we go on. It is clear that these operations are profitable, for by the time we get to P_6 we have reached a position with the same amount of wheat as we started, and a good deal more money. The profitableness of the operations consists in moving through a succession of swings *outward* in the figure, so that on the whole we are increasing our assets. If the operations were unprofitable —as of course they may be—the firm would find itself moving *in* toward the origin. It might find itself, for instance, buying dear and selling cheap, following a path such as $P_6P_5P_4P_3 \cdot \cdot \cdot$ etc.

The Exchange Opportunity Line

The exchange opportunity lines are similar in principle to the production opportunity boundaries of Figs. 3 and 4 in Chapter 4. They show the field of choice which is open to the firm as it contemplates its opportunities of exchange in a market from a given position. If the price or ratio of exchange is independent of the amount exchanged we say that the market is *perfect;* the exchange opportunity line is then straight, with a constant slope equal to the price or ratio of exchange; if the price of wheat is $2 per bushel, for every $2 of money given up we get one bushel of wheat, for every bushel of wheat given up we get $2 of money, no matter how much we buy and sell. Thus from the point P_0 in Fig. 66A the firm can move to any point on the line V_0W_0, neglecting for the moment possibilities of borrowing or lending. Actually the firm could move to any point within the triangle OW_0V_0 by throwing away wheat or money, so that the exchange opportunity line is, properly speaking, a boundary between those points which are attainable (the *feasible set*) below and to the left of the line, and those which are unattainable, above and to the right of it. Ordinarily, however, the firm will always move to the boundary, and we can treat the line itself as the feasible set of positions. In this case we have supposed the firm moves along the opportunity line to P_1; at this point the price changes, so that we have a new opportunity line of which P_1P_2 is a segment; at P_2 the price changes again, and so we go on. The total process is seen as the result of a series of decisions as to which out of all feasible positions open is the *best;* the firm went from P_0 to P_1 presumably because it thought that P_1 was *better* than any other point on the opportunity line.

THE PROFIT-MAKING PROCESS

This process of moving *out* in an asset space (which in general will be of many dimensions) through a succession of transformations is the essence of the profit-making process. Profit making, that is, is the process of growth of the whole asset complex. If we are to measure this growth, however, we must reduce the n-dimensional asset complex to a single dimension of a unit of account, say, dollars. This can only be done by *valuing* all the physical assets, by multiplying their quantity by a coefficient of valuation. This is the same as the index-number problem which we shall meet in Volume II: *Macroeconomics* (p. 23) in the measurement of economic aggregates, though it is not generally recognized as such, even by accountants! Let us assume here a very simple method of valuation, which corresponds roughly to the accountants' FIFO method (see pp. 341–343). We will suppose that all wheat stocks are valued at the initial price of $2 per bushel. The total value of the wheat stock, and the net worth (value of wheat plus money), are shown in Table 29. The succes-

TABLE 29.   THE CALCULATION OF PROFIT: WHEAT AT $2 PER BUSHEL

Event	P_0 1	P_1 2	P_2 3	Position P_3 4	P_4 5	P_5 6	P_6
Wheat stock	600	700	100	500	900	200	600
Value of wheat stock	1200	1400	200	1000	1800	400	1200
Money stock	400	200	2000	1000	200	2300	1500
Net worth	1600	1600	2200	2000	2000	2700	2700
Total profit		0	600	400	400	1100	1100
Profit in each event	0	600	−200	0	700	0	

sive positions of net worth are shown in Fig. 66A by projecting valuation lines from the various positions to the money axis at a slope equal to the valuation coefficient of $2. Thus from P_0 we project the line P_0V_0 at a slope of $2 per bushel to meet the money axis at V_0; OV_0 is then the corresponding net worth. Thus the net worth at P_0 and P_1 is OV_0 ($1600), at P_2 it is OV_2 ($2200), at P_3 and P_4 it is OV_3 ($2000), and at P_5 and P_6 it is OV_5 ($2700).

Difficulties in Measuring Profit

The paradoxical nature of the measurement of net worth (and therefore of profit, which is simply the growth in net worth) is shown in the movement from P_2 to P_3, which apparently results in a loss of $200, because 400 bushels of wheat are bought at $2.50 and are valued at $2. Nevertheless it is clear from subsequent events that the movement from P_2 to P_3, and again to P_4 (which registers no gain or loss), actually lays the foundations for the subsequent gains at P_5 or P_6, and that if the firm had not moved down from P_2, at an apparent loss, it would not have made the subsequent gains. The dependence of the measure of profit on the system of valuations is brought out clearly in Table 30, which represents the physical data of Table 29 but values the wheat stocks at $3 instead of at $2. Comparing the course of net worth with that in Table 30, we see that at the higher valuation the loss from

TABLE 30. THE CALCULATION OF PROFIT: WHEAT AT $3 PER BUSHEL

				Position			
	P_0	P_1	P_2	P_3	P_4	P_5	P_6
Wheat stock	600	700	100	500	900	200	600
Value of wheat	1800	2100	300	1500	2700	600	1800
Money stock	400	200	2000	1000	200	2300	1500
Net worth	2200	2300	2300	2500	2900	2900	3300
Total profit		100	100	300	700	700	1100
Profit in each event		100	0	200	400	0	400

P_2 to P_3 is turned into a gain, and that the great gain from P_4 to P_5 is wiped out! The course of net worth is shown in Fig. 66B.

What Determines Profit?

It should now be easy to see that the larger the *swings* in a profitable succession of transformations, the greater the total profit. Suppose, for instance, that with the price history of Table 28, we double the purchases and sales. The result is shown in Table 31. Comparing the total profit figure (net worth minus initial net worth) of Tables 31 and 29,

TABLE 31. CALCULATION OF PROFIT: LARGER TRANSACTIONS

				Position			
	P_0	P_1	P_2	P_3	P_4	P_5	P_6
Wheat sales (−) or purchases (+)	+200	−1200	+800	+800	−1400	+800	
Money paid in (+) or out (−)	−400	+3600	−2000	−1600	+4200	−1600	
Wheat stock 600	800	−400	+400	+1200	−200	+600	
Money stock 400	0	3600	1600	0	4200	2600	
Value of wheat stock at $2 1200	1600	−800	800	2400	−400	1200	
Net worth 1600	1600	2800	2400	2400	3800	3800	
Total profit	0	1200	800	800	2200	2200	
Profit in each event	0	1200	−400	0	1400	0	

we observe that at any time the profit in Table 31 is double what it is in Table 29.

The negative stock of wheat in positions P_2 and P_5 can be achieved through the sale of *wheat futures*—promises to pay wheat in the future, which is the same as a wheat debt. Similarly we could go to the fourth quadrant with negative money stocks by borrowing money to buy wheat, and incurring a money debt. We assume here that these debts cost nothing to incur, and carry no interest, otherwise the opportunity line will bend at an angle at the axes.

In the present case it is clear that if there were no limits on the amounts bought and sold, and if markets remained perfect indefinitely, and if the future course of prices was certain, then profits could be made at an infinite rate by buying indefinitely large amounts when the price was going to rise, and selling indefinitely large amounts when the price was going to fall. That is, the larger the swings the larger the profit, and if there is no limit on the magnitude of the swings, there is no limit on the magnitude of the profit.

THE LIMITATION OF PROFIT BY MARKET IMPERFECTION

Boundary Conditions

We know in fact, of course, that the swings cannot be indefinitely large, and profits are always finite. We must ask ourselves, then, what *limits* the size of the swings, or successive transformations? There are two main answers. One is the development of imperfections in the market and the other is the presence of uncertainty. The simplest kind of imperfection we might call a *boundary imperfection*. This is a point at which the exchange opportunity suddenly disappears. Suppose, for instance, that in the previous example there was no possibility of borrowing, either money or wheat. The market opportunities would be bounded sharply by the two axes—i.e., all movements would have to be confined to the first quadrant. The maximum profit is then obtained if we adopt the following principle: move to the money axis (i.e., hold all assets in the form of money) whenever the *next* change in price is a fall, and move to the wheat axis (i.e., hold all assets in the form

TABLE 32. THE PROFIT-MAKING PROCESS: BOUNDARY LIMITS

	P_0	P_1	Position P_2	P_3	P_4	P_5	P_6
Wheat stock	600	800	0	0	1200	0	600
Money stock	400	0	2400	2400	0	3600	2400
Value of wheat at $2	1200	1600	0	0	2400	0	1200
Net worth	1600	1600	2400	2400	2400	3600	3600
Total profit		0	800	800	800	2000	2000
Profit in each event	0	800	0	0	1200	0	

of wheat) when the next change in price is a rise. This is illustrated in Table 32 and Fig. 66D. We observe that a mere fall in price is not sufficient to cause a move to the wheat axis. When price falls at position P_2 from \$3 to \$2.50, we do not move at all, because the price is going to fall further. If we refer back to Fig. 66A we can readily see that if the firm had not moved to position P_3 from P_2, but had stayed at P_2 on that "day" and then had moved toward the wheat axis to a new position 4, profits would have been higher. In P_6, I have brought the position to the original wheat stock in order to compare it with the other examples; in a continuing process it would, of course, go right on to the wheat axis, assuming that a rise in price is forthcoming. All that this principle amounts to, of course, is the familiar one of "getting in at the bottom and out at the top." The principle can be applied to any boundary condition—thus there may be a maximum amount of debt possible, in which case the boundaries may lie in the fourth or second quadrants. There may also be boundaries imposed by the unwillingness of the trading firm to allow either its money or its wheat stock to fall below a certain minimum, in which case the boundaries will be in the first quadrant, such as MK and ML in Fig. 66D.

Imperfect Markets: Discontinuous Imperfection

The boundary conditions above are an extreme case of a wide class of phenomena known as market imperfections. We have defined a perfect market for the individual buyer or seller as one in which the terms of trade, or the ratio of exchange, does not vary with the amount exchanged. In an imperfect market there are points at which the terms of trade *worsen* for the marketer as he contemplates increasing the quantity exchanged. For a buyer this means that the price rises against him, for a seller it means that the price falls against him. If there are a finite number of points (quantities exchanged) at which the price changes suddenly, we may say that the market exhibits *discontinuous imperfection*. It is not uncommon, for instance, for a trader to find that the price at which he can buy is higher than the price at which he can sell. This produces an *angle* or kink in the exchange opportunity line at the existing asset position. It is possible also that a trader finds that a particular market is perfect up to a point, but that only a certain quantity can be bought or sold (for instance, if there are quotas on purchases or sales). Beyond that point there may be a sharp rise in the buying price for further purchases, or a sharp fall in the selling price for further sales, as, for instance, the marketer expands into grey (semilegal) or black (illegal) markets. Such a condition is illustrated in Table 33. We suppose the marketer again starts with 600 bushels of wheat and \$400. The table

TABLE 33. EXCHANGE OPPORTUNITY SCHEDULE

	Sales							P₀	Purchases		
1. Position	S₆	S₅	S₄	S₃	S₂	S₁		P_0	B_1	B_2	B_3
2. Wheat stock (bushels)	0	100	200	300	400	500		600	700	767	867
3. Money stock (in dollars)	1280	1160	1040	920	760	600		400	160	0	−300
4. Total wheat bought (+) sold (−)	−600	−500	−400	−300	−200	−100		0	100	167	267
5. Total money bought (+) sold (−)	+880	+760	+640	+520	+360	+200		0	−240	−400	−700
6. Average price	1.47	1.52	1.60	1.73	1.80	2.00		2.40	2.40	2.40	2.62
7. Increment price		1.20	1.20	1.20	1.60	1.60	2.00		2.40	2.40	3.00
8. Change in wheat		−100	−100	−100	−100	−100	−100		−100	+67	+100
9. Change in money		+120	+120	+120	+160	+160	+200		−240	−160	−300

then shows his exchange opportunity for various hypothetical quantities bought or sold. This is not, like Tables 28 to 32, a record of actual transactions, but a schedule of hypothetical transactions or opportunities.

Positions S_1–S_6 show his positions after various sales, positions B_1–B_3, after various purchases of wheat. Line 7, the increment price is the crucial data which shows the price at which successive increments of quantities can be exchanged. Thus it is assumed that the first 100 bushels can be sold at $2 per bushel, the next 200, at $1.60 per bushel, and the next 300, at $1.20 per bushel. These figures are of course greatly exaggerated, beyond what is likely to occur in most actual markets, for the sake of graphical clarity. Similarly the first 167 bushels can be bought at $2.40; this brings the marketer down to a zero money stock, so that he must borrow to buy more wheat: the increment price, $3, here presumably includes interest and borrowing charges. Lines 8 and 9 show the amounts of wheat and money bought or sold between each position; the ratio of the change in money to the change in wheat is the increment price.

Lines 2 and 3 show the stocks of wheat and money after the various transactions: they are calculated from lines 8 and 9 by adding or subtracting the increments or decrements. Thus moving from P_0, the initial position, to S_1, we sell 100 bushels of wheat for $200 of money; the trader's wheat stock falls from 600 to 500 bushels, his money stock rises from $400 to $600. Lines 4 and 5 show the total amount of wheat and money acquired or given up in moving from P_0 to the position indicated.

Thus in moving from P_0 to S_6 the marketer gives up 600 bushels of wheat and acquires $880 of money. The ratio of the total money acquired (or given up) to the total wheat sold (or bought) in moving from the initial to a final position is the *average price* (line 6).

These exchange opportunities are described also in Fig. 67. In Fig. 67A we plot the various asset positions open to the marketer starting from P_0; the points S_1, S_2, to S_6 and B_1 to B_3 correspond to the positions of Table 33. These plot out the exchange opportunity line. The increment price between any two positions is the slope or gradient of this line. Thus between P_0 and S_1, P_0Q_1 of wheat is sold and Q_1S_1 money received: the increment price is Q_1S_1/P_0Q_1, or tan $S_1P_0Q_1$. The average price paid or received in reaching any position, such as S_6, is the slope of the line (S_6P_0) from the position (S_6) to the point of origin. Thus in getting to S_6 from P_0 the marketer sold a total of P_0Q_6 bushels of wheat and acquired Q_6S_6 dollars. The average price is Q_6S_6/P_0Q_6, which is the tangent of the angle $S_6P_0Q_6$. In Fig. 67B we plot the line $s_6s'_3s_3s'_1s_1pp'b_2b'_2b_3$ which shows the increment price for various amounts of sales or purchases. The line $a_6a_3s_1p$ shows the average price for various quantities of sales, and the

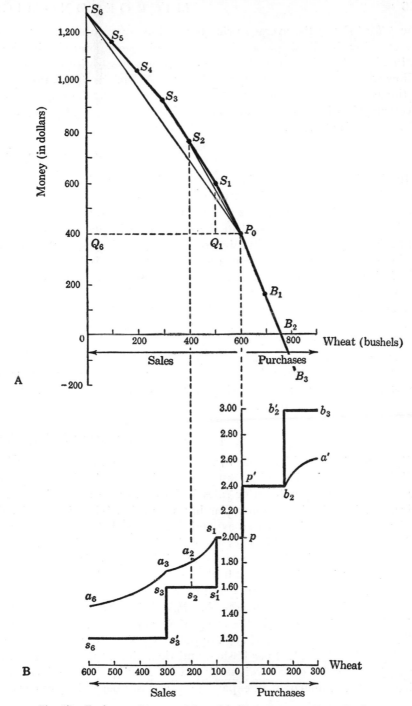

Fig. 67.   Exchange Opportunities with Heterogeneous Imperfection

line $p'b_2a'$ shows the average price for various quantities of purchases. We can visualize the shape of this curve if we image a point starting from P_0 in Fig. 67A and moving along the exchange opportunity line, and we follow what happens to the slope of the "chord" such as S_6P_0. From P_0 to S_1 the average and increment prices are the same; at S_2 the slope of S_2P_0 (average price) is greater than the slope of S_1S_2 (incremental price), so in Fig. 67B, a_2 is above s_2.

Price Discrimination

In the above example we have assumed that the various markets, for example between P_0 and S_1, between S_1 and S_3, or between S_3 and S_6, are separated, in the sense that a buyer buying from our trader at \$1.20 in the range S_3S_6 cannot resell to the buyer who is buying at \$2 in the range P_0S_1. The practice of selling or buying in different quantities to or from different buyers or sellers at different prices is known as *price discrimination*. It is clearly impossible to do this unless the markets are separated, for if the various buyers or sellers are in contact there will be resales or repurchases. Thus if the buyers between S_3 and S_6, buying at \$1.20, can resell to those between P_0 and S_1 at any price between \$1.20 and \$2, it will pay them to resell and pay the other buyers to buy from them rather than from the original trader. A market in which all marketers are in contact in this way is said to be homogeneous; it has the property that for a given commodity at one time all transactions will take place very close to one price.

Homogeneous Imperfection

For a particular trader, however, a market may be homogeneous but still discontinuously imperfect. Suppose, for instance, in the example of Table 33, that *all* purchases or sales had to be made at the increment price, not just the incremental purchases or sales. That is, in Fig. 68 similar to Fig. 67A, in order to expand sales beyond S_1, the trader must reduce the price of all his sales to \$1.60; immediately beyond S_1 the exchange opportunity line drops to S'_1, as, if he lowers his price to \$1.60, he must lower it on the first 100 bushels of sales as well as on subsequent sales. The exchange opportunity line now goes from S'_1 to S_3 at a slope equal to \$1.60 per bushel: we note that $P_0S'_1S_3$ is a straight line; average price therefore is constant in the range S'_1S_3, and equal to the increment price. Similarly at S_3 the exchange opportunity line drops to S'_3; where the slope of $P_0S'_3 = \$1.20$ per bushel, and then rises at the same slope to S_6; $S_6S'_3P_0$ also lie on a straight line, with average price = increment price = \$1.20. Similarly, if in expanding purchases beyond B_2 our trader must raise the price to \$3 on all bushels bought, the exchange opportunity line will be $P_0 B_2 B'_2 B_3$; here we neglect costs of borrowing.

Continuous Market Imperfection

A case which is too refined an ideal type to be found in practice, but which is very useful in analysis, is that of continuous imperfection, where

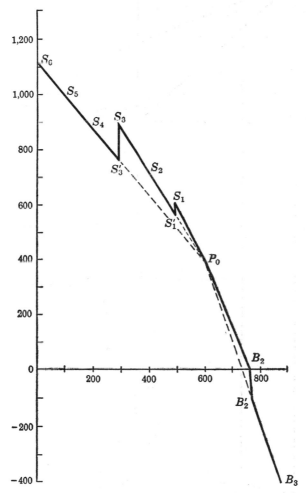

Fig. 68. Exchange Opportunities with Homogeneous Imperfection

the average price varies continuously with the amount bought or sold. This is shown in Fig. 69. In Fig. 69A we have a continuously curved exchange opportunity line in a field like Figs. 67A and 68. Again P_0 is the

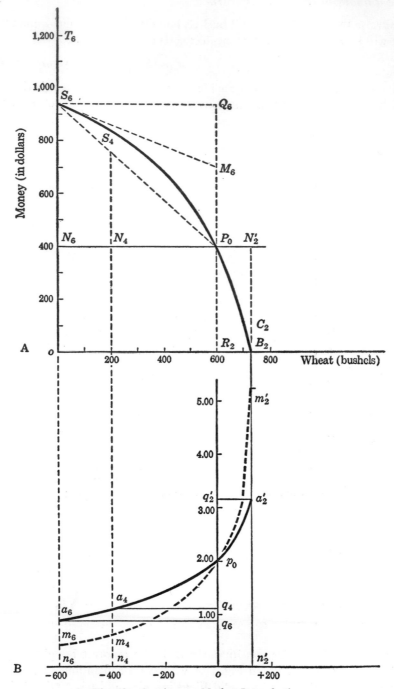

Fig. 69.   Continuous Market Imperfection

starting point: as the trader contemplates larger and larger sales the average price which he expects to receive declines continuously, following the curve p_0a_6 in Fig. 69B; as he contemplates larger and larger purchase the price which he expects to pay continuously rises, following the curve $p_0a'_2$. We must be particularly careful to notice here that these functions describe potential opportunities, not a succession of events. They must be read as a series of hypothetical propositions in the form "If he wants to sell x bushels he will receive y dollars, at an average price of y/x."

Marginal Terms of Trade

The slope of the exchange opportunity line is an important quantity, analogous to the previous concept of increment price; we may call it in general the *marginal terms of trade*. It is defined as the ratio of a small increment (plus or minus) in money stock to the corresponding small increment (minus or plus) in commodity or other asset stock, resulting from the exchange of a small quantity. In the case of sales this is the same thing as the *marginal receipts,* defined as the increase in total receipts from sales as a result of a unit increase in sales. Similarly in the case of purchases it is the same thing as the marginal expenditure, defined as the increase in total expenditure which results from a unit increase in purchases.

Use of the Term "Marginal"

This is the reader's first serious encounter with the word *marginal,* which is an important technical term in economics and will be frequently encountered in what follows. It came into economics as a loose translation of the German *Grenz* used as a prefix, which literally means border or edge. It is used in two rather different senses; when it refers to an object, as in the phrases marginal land or a marginal firm, it means an object which is literally a borderline case, for instance, land either just in use or just not in use, or a firm on the edge of going out of (or coming into) business. When it is used to modify a *variable,* as in the above expression, marginal receipts, it means the rate of change, at some point, of the marginal variable with respect to some other, that is, the change in the marginal variable which results from a unit change in some other, usually understood by convention. Thus if one variable, R, is a function of another, Q, then marginal R would be the change in R, dR, divided by the corresponding change in Q, dQ; in the limit, this becomes the differential coefficient, dR/dQ. Thus, if R is total receipts and Q is the quantity sold, and we have a total receipts function $R = F(Q)$, marginal receipts at any point is dR/dQ, which is the slope at a point of the total receipts curve. In a figure such as Fig. 69A the exchange opportunity line between P_0 and S_6 is *also* a total receipts curve, if we measure total receipts vertically upward from P_0 as origin, and measure quantity sold horizontally to the left of P_0. Similarly the portion P_0B_2 is a total expenses curve, measuring total expenses vertically downward from P_0 as origin and total quantity bought horizontally to the right of P_0. This is why the marginal terms of trade is identical with the marginal receipts or marginal expenses, depending on the portion of the curve we are in.

Construction of Average and Marginal Curves

In order to construct the average price curve $a_6a'_2$ and the marginal terms of trade curve $m_6m'_2$ from the exchange opportunity curve S_6B_2 proceed as follows. From any point on the exchange opportunity line such as S_6 draw the horizontal line S_6Q_6 and the tangent to the exchange opportunity line, S_6M_6, to meet the vertical line $P_0M_6Q_6$. Then the average price at which the quantity S_6Q_6 has been sold is P_0Q_6/Q_6S_6 ($= n_6a_6$ in Fig. 69B), that is, money received/wheat sold, and the marginal terms of trade at S_6 are M_6Q_6/S_6Q_6 ($= n_6m_6$ in Fig. 69B) which is the slope of the exchange opportunity line at S_6. We are assuming here that the market is homogeneous, so that n_6a_6 is the price received for all units sold when on_6 ($= Q_6S_6$) are sold. Conversely, to construct the exchange opportunity line from the average price curve, take any point on the average price curve such as a_6; draw the horizontal line a_6q_6 to meet the vertical line from o at q_6; the area of the rectangle $a_6q_6on_6$ is then the total receipts (price times quantity) of money from the sale of on_6 of wheat; this is equal to N_6S_6 in Fig. 69A.

Construction of Exchange Opportunity Line

To construct the exchange opportunity line from the marginal terms of trade curve is more difficult, but it can be done. Selling one bushel from the point P_0 brings in op_0; selling two bushels brings in an additional amount somewhat less than op_0, following the marginal terms of trade curve; selling the 600th bushel or, more accurately, expanding sales from 599 to 600 bushels, brings in an additional amount of money equal to n_6m_6. We can think of the area $n_6m_6p_0o$ as divided into 600 little vertical rectangles, each of which represents the increase in money resulting from an extra bushel of sales; the sum of all these little rectangles is the total increase in money as a result of selling 600 bushels, and is equal to N_6S_6. which is therefore equal to the *area* under the marginal terms of trade curve, $n_6m_6p_0o$. Similarly at any other point such as S_4 (sales of 400 bushels) we have N_4S_4 = area $n_4a_4q_4o$ = area $n_4m_4p_0o$ or, on the buying side, $B_2N'_2$ = area $oq'_2a'_2n'_2$ = area $op_0m'_2n'_2$.

Perfect Heterogeneity

A trading firm is unlikely to be faced with very heterogeneous markets, which are a mark of a high degree of monopoly; for the sake of completeness however we may note the extreme case of perfect heterogeneity, in which each bushel is sold at a different price. In this case the average price curve becomes a marginal terms of trade curve, for the trader can persuade each marginal customer to buy from him (or sell to him) by shading the price to that customer without lowering the price at which he sells, or raising the price at which he buys to any other. There is then a new exchange opportunity line lying above the old one (not shown in the figure) running from about T_6 to P_0 to C_2.

Pluperfect Markets

Another special case which may not be common but which is worth mention is where the terms of trade *improve* for a trader as he increases the quantities exchanged. This is sometimes called a *pluperfect* market. In this case the market opportunity boundary bounds a *concave set* curved the opposite way from Fig. 69, where it bounds a *convex set*. The marginal receipts and the average price *rise* with increased sales, and *fall* with increased purchases, so that the exchange opportunity curve becomes steeper as we move to the left of P_0 and less steep as we move to the right, while the average price and marginal receipts fall as we move from left to right instead of rising as in Fig. 69B. The reader may verify this for himself in Exercise 1 at the end of this chapter. A possible case of pluperfect markets is where there are discounts for quantity, so that one can buy a larger amount for a smaller average price. This factor would make the market unsymmetrical, with a pluperfect buying market to the right of P_0 and an imperfect selling market to the left of P_0.

DECISION MAKING IN THE TRADING FIRM

Maximizing Behavior

The problem of decision making in the trading firm arises because the exchange opportunity boundary defines a set of possible controlled events, each one of which is a *move* from the original position, say P_0 in Figs. 67–69 to some other asset position within the exchange opportunity boundary. The question then is which is the best move to make, and what criterion should be adopted to identify the *best* position. Suppose there is some way in which we can give any two points P_i and P_j in the field of Figs. 67A, 68A, or 69A numbers, N_i, and N_j, such that if N_i is bigger than

N_j, then P_i is a better position than P_j. Then we can reduce the problem to one of maximizing behavior. We simply find that P_m for which N_m is larger than any other N. Then P_m is the *optimum* position where N is *maximized*, and the behavior will consist in moving from P_0 to P_m.

Maximization of Subjective Net Worth

A simple case of maximizing behavior in the case of the trader would be where he had a subjective estimate of the capital value of each bushel of wheat stock, and maximized his subjective net worth which, in this simple model, is the total dollar value of his wheat stock plus his money stock. The coefficient by which bushels of wheat must be multiplied to turn them into dollars of value is the *valuation coefficient*. Thus if this is $3 per bushel the value of 600 bushels is $3 × 600 or $1800. If now we have a constant valuation coefficient, v, we can give each point in the field of the exchange opportunities such as M_i money and W_i bushels of wheat a number, $N_i = M_i + vW_i$, which is the corresponding net worth. Then the point representing that combination of M and W for which N_i is a maximum is the optimum, and the trader will move to it.

Linear Programming

Where the exchange opportunity boundary is linear (composed of straight lines) this problem can be solved by a procedure known as *linear programming*. Thus suppose in Fig. 70 in each diagram, P_0 is the initial

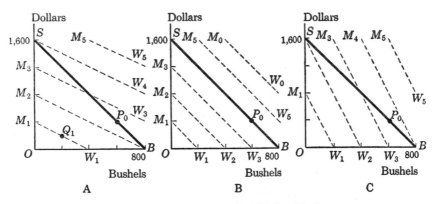

Fig. 70.　Linear Programming, Perfect Market

position ($400, 600 bushels) and SP_0B is the exchange opportunity boundary, with a perfect market at a constant selling or buying price of $2 per bushel. Let us suppose for the sake of simplicity that the other boundaries are set by the condition that neither the money stock nor the wheat stock should fall below zero. Then all the opportunities lie within the triangle *OSB,* each point of which is a member of what is called the *feasible set* of possible alternatives. Algebraically this can be represented by three inequalities: $M \gtrless O$ defines all points on or above the line *OB,* $W \gtrless O$ defines all points on or to the right of *OS,* and $M \lessgtr 1600 - 2W$ defines all points on or below *SB.* Each inequality defines what is called a *half space* on one side or the other of the line represented by the equation of the two sides of the inequality; the triangle *OSB* is the *intersection,* which contains the points common to the three half spaces.

The Line of Equal Net Worth as an Indifference Curve

Then in Fig. 70A we suppose a valuation coefficient of $1 per bushel. Then the line $M_1 W_1$ shows all those combinations of money and wheat for which the net worth is $400; for example, M_1 ($400 *M,* 0 *W*) W_1 (0 M_1 400 bushels *W*), or Q_1 (200 *M,* 200 bushels *W*) for which the total value of money and wheat stock together (net worth) is $400. Similarly $M_2 B$ shows all those combinations with a net worth of $800, $M_3 W_3$ those points with a net worth of $1200, and so on. Assuming that net worth as so computed is the measure of the goodness or preferability of each position, these lines of constant net worth are our first encounter with an important analytical device, the *indifference curve:* any point on, say, $M_1 W_1$ is just as good as any other, so the trader is presumably *indifferent* between them. On the other hand he will always *prefer* (choose) a move to a higher indifference curve, in this case a move to a point representing a higher net worth, such as from any point on $M_1 W_1$ to any point on $M_2 B$. The dotted lines of equal net worth may be visualized as the contours of a three-dimensional surface, with net worth measured vertically at right angles to the plane of the paper.

Positions of the Optimum

In Fig. 70A it is obvious by inspection that the point *S* is the optimum, being that point within the feasible set *OSB* which is on the highest indifference curve, SW_4; points on $M_5 W_5$ would be preferred, but are not accessible. The actual computation of the optimum point is a tedious mathematical process, necessary in complex cases which cannot be solved by inspection, but without much economic significance. In Fig. 70B we suppose that the valuation coefficient is $2 per bushel; in this case one of the indifference curves coincides with the exchange boundary, *SB.* The trader is therefore indifferent among all points on *SB.* Any one is as good as another, and if there is the slightest trouble involved in moving, he will presumably stay were he is at P_0. In Fig. 70C we suppose the valuation coefficient is $4; $M_1 W_1$ is now the line on which all points have a net worth of $800, and so on. In this case the point B is the optimum. We emerge then with a rule of behavior: If the valuation coefficient is less than the average price (Fig. 70A), sell wheat right up to the boundary below which wheat stocks cannot be allowed to fall. If the valuation coefficient is equal to the average price, it does not matter whether you buy or sell. If the valuation coefficient is greater than the price, buy all the wheat consistent with the minimum money stock. The valuation coefficient, it must be emphasized, is a subjective variable, which is related to the trader's expectations about the future course of prices. If the valuation coefficient is actually equal to the price on the next trading day, following this rule actually maximizes profits within the limits set by the minimum wheat and money holdings. In fact, of course, expectations may not be fulfilled, and losses or less than maximum profits may result.

Maximization in an Imperfect Market

These principles can easily be applied to an imperfect market, as in Fig. 71. Here we suppose that there is a kink in the exchange opportunity line

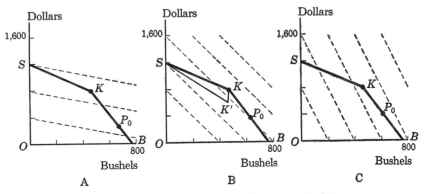

Fig. 71.   Linear Programming, Imperfect Market

K, representing a sudden lowering of the average price and worsening of the marginal terms of trade as the trader sells more than 200 bushels. The dashed lines again represent indifference curves of equal net worth. Suppose that p_1 is the marginal terms of trade (marginal receipts) between S and K (this is the slope of the line SK) and that p_2 is the marginal terms of trade between K and B (marginal receipts between P_0 and K: marginal expenses between P_0 and B), equal to the slope of KB. The slope of the equal-net-worth lines (dashed) is the valuation coefficient, v. If v is less than p_1, as in Fig. 71A, the optimum position is clearly S. As v rises the dashed equal-net-worth lines steepen; when $v = p_1$ an equal-net-worth line coincides with SK, and the trader is indifferent to any position on SK (not shown in figure). As v rises further, when it lies between p_1 and p_2 we have a situation such as Fig. 71B, where K is the optimum. When $v = p_2$ the trader is indifferent to any position on KB. When v is greater than p_2, as in Fig. 71C, B is the optimum position. We observe that the optimum point, where it is unique, is always at a kink or corner on the boundary; this is what is called an *extreme point*.

In Heterogeneous Markets

An interesting problem arises when the market is imperfect but homogeneous, so that the reduction of the price at K is a reduction of the average price on all sales. Then, as we saw in Fig. 68, the exchange opportunity boundary has a "sawtooth" because of the abrupt drop in receipts at K: it has the shape $BKK'S$. The exchange opportunity set (the *feasible set* in the language of linear programming) is no longer convex,[1] but has a cave in it, $SK'K$. As any position P' within the triangle SKK' not including the like SK, is inferior to some positions on the line SK, for if we take any such point P' a point P'' can be found on SK for which both M and W are larger, so that unless v is negative the net worth must be larger at P'' than at P'. The previous solution therefore holds, except that if $v = p_1$ the optimum position is at S, and not between S and K. The figure $OSKB$ in Fig. 71B is called the *convex hull* of the figure $OSK'KB$; the solution for a nonconvex set therefore is the same, roughly, as that for its convex hull. The convex hull may be visualized as the tightest bag that a nonconvex set can be put in!

Maximizing in Continuously Imperfect Markets

When the market is continuously imperfect the exchange opportunity boundary is a continuous curved line, as SP_0B in Fig. 72. The maximum net worth is then where one of the equal-net-worth indifference lines touches the exchange opportunity boundary, as at M in Fig. 72A and 72C, or P_0 in Fig. 72B. In Fig. 72B the valuation coefficient v (the slope of the dotted indifference lines) is just equal to the marginal terms of trade at the point of origin, P_0; then there is no incentive to trade at all, the existing position is best, and the trader will neither buy nor sell. If the valuation coefficient is lower, as in Fig. 72A, the point of tangency M is on the highest indifference curve possible within the area $OSMB$, the trader will sell P_0Q of wheat and acquire QM money. If O is the lower boundary of the wheat stock, the trader will go to this when v rises to the slope of the exchange opportunity curve (the marginal terms of trade)

---

[1] A convex set may be visualized as a set of points contained within a boundary such that a straight line joining any two points on the boundary will not go through any points not in the set.

at S. If v is less than in Fig. 72B, the trader will buy, as in Fig. 72C, where he moves again to the point of tangency at M. When the valuation

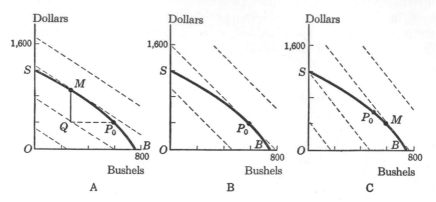

Fig. 72.   Maximizing Behavior in Continuously Imperfect Market

coefficient is at or above the marginal terms of trade (the slope of the exchange opportunity line) at B, the trader will buy up to his limit.

Behavior Under Uncertainty

The assumption of a constant subjective valuation coefficient and of maximizing subjective net worth implied in the analysis of Figs. 70, 71, and 72 must be regarded only as one possible first approximation to the very complex problem of describing the principles of behavior. The fuller treatment of this problem must wait until Chapter 27. Even at this stage, however, we must take some account of the vital problem of the impact of the uncertainty of the future on present decisions, for this is crucial to the decision-making process.

Up to this point we have assumed implicitly that the various opportunity functions were certain. In fact this is rarely, if ever, the case. To return first to the example of the pure marketer of Fig. 66. He moves in the direction he does along any of his market opportunity lines in anticipation of a change in price. Thus he moves down from P_0 to P_1, buying wheat because he thinks the price is going to rise. If he is absolutely sure the price is going to rise, and if there are no market imperfections, we have seen that it will pay him to go as far as he can in the direction of acquiring wheat and getting rid of money. However, he is never *quite* sure. Suppose that in fact he is disappointed, and the price falls. Then the further he has gone in the purchase of wheat, the worse off he will be; he should have gone the other way, selling wheat and acquiring money. As he moves down from P_0, then, his chance of gain increases if things turn out as he hopes—but also his chance of loss increases if things do not turn out as he hopes. He will stop, generally, at the point where the chance of loss, if things turn out badly, is greater than he can stand. That is, there is some point beyond which he feels the risk of being wiped out if things go badly outweighs any possible gain, no matter how great.

The problem is illustrated for the simple marketer in Fig. 73. P_0 is the

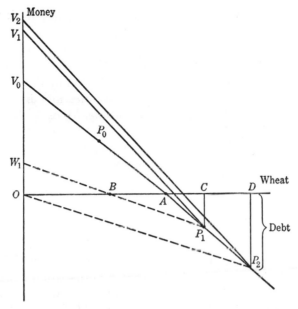

Fig. 73.   Uncertainty as a Limit

initial position in a wheat-money field. We suppose the exchange opportunity line is $P_0AP_1P_2$. The slight steepening of the line at A represents interest on the debt incurred to purchase wheat beyond his net worth. If now he anticipates that the price will rise to, say, the slope of P_1V_1, then if he goes to P_1 the first day, and then sells the next day, moving, say, all the way to V_1, his gain will be V_0V_1. If he goes to P_2 and then sells at the high price, he will move to V_2, with a greater gain (V_0V_2). Obviously, the further he goes downward along the opportunity line on the first day, the greater his profits on the second day—if things turn out as he *hopes*. Suppose, however, that things turn out badly, and the price falls, and that also he is forced to liquidate his debt. If he has moved to P_1, incurring a debt P_1C, he will have to sell at least CB of wheat to pay off the debt; and if the remainder of his wheat stock is valued "at market" (this now being below cost), his net worth will be OW_1—a severe loss of V_0W_1. If he goes to P_2 and the worst happens, he will be wiped out altogether, and his net worth falls to zero. It is clear that a reasonably cautious man would be extremely hesitant to go beyond the point P_2, no matter how attractive the gains hoped for, if the loss feared amounted to irretrievable disaster.

The Fear of the Worst as a Limit

This is not to say, of course, that disaster will never be risked. It does mean, however, that equal possible gains and losses are not of equal significance—that even if moving along an opportunity path increased equally the possibility of both gains and losses, the fear of loss would eventually outweigh the hope of gain. At this point the movement will cease, even though it is not checked by imperfections in the market or in cost curves. Exactly the same kind of considerations apply to movement in expectation of a fall in price. Suppose, for instance, that the marketer moves into the second quadrant, borrowing wheat (i.e., selling wheat futures) in order to increase his money stock. If his expectation is disappointed and the price of wheat rises, he may again suffer severe losses, and perhaps even be wiped out, when he has to purchase wheat to make good his undertaking to deliver. Uncertainty, therefore, results in what are apparently "boundary maxima," which may operate even when imperfections in the opportunity functions yield "true" maxima. That is, we may stop an operation, whether marketing or production, before the point of maximum profit under *favorable* anticipations, because of the fear of the losses which would result if things turn out badly.

We can interpret Fig. 73 also as if the slopes of the lines P_1V_1 (or P_2V_2) and P_1W_1 (or P_2O) represented subjective valuation coefficients, the first, under conditions of optimism, the second, under conditions of pessimism. The subjective valuation coefficient is an index, as it were, of the traders expectations about the future: the higher he thinks the future price will be, the higher will be his average valuation coefficient. He may envisage a number of possible future prices, with a probability figure attached to each. In Fig. 73 we suppose in effect that he focuses on two sets of possible futures: one with a higher probability (in the case of Fig. 73, that price will rise) which determines the *direction* of his movement from P_0, and another with lower but still not zero probability (that the price will fall), indicated by the slope of P_1W_1 or P_2O, which determines how far he will go. Whether this is in fact the way people think and behave can only be determined by a great deal more factual inquiry than has yet been done.

The Preferred Asset Ratio Theory of Behavior

Another approach to the description of trading behavior which is useful in developing some models of the market is through the concept of a preferred asset ratio. Thus in Fig. 74 we suppose a perfect market with an

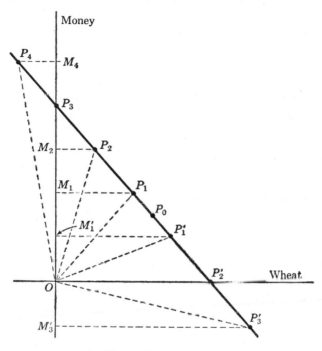

Fig. 74. Preferred Asset Ratios

initial position P_0, and an exchange opportunity line $P_4P_0P'_3$. As the trader sells, moving to positions such as P_1, P_2, and on, he diminishes the proportion of wheat in his total assets and increases the proportion of money. If he buys, moving to P'_1, P'_2, and on, he diminishes the proportion of money and increases the proportion of wheat. It is a reasonable interpretation of his behavior therefore to suppose that there is some proportion of, say, money to total assets—his *preferred liquidity ratio*—at which he feels most comfortable in the light of his expectations of future prices, and that he simply moves to the point on the exchange opportunity line at which this preferred asset ratio obtains. If in Fig. 74 we suppose that his valuation coefficient is the same as the market price, so that OP_3 is the total net worth, the line OP'_1 shows all those positions where the preferred money ratio is 25 percent, OP_1 shows all positions where it is 50 percent, OP_2 where it is 75 percent, OP_4 where it is 125 percent (through the sale of wheat futures), OP'_2 where it is zero, OP'_3 where it is -25 percent, and so on. If the trader confidently expects the price to rise he will move, say, to P'_3 where his preferred money ratio is -25 percent; if he thinks the price is slightly more likely to rise than to fall he may move to, say, P'_1 where the preferred money ratio is 25 percent, but he will not prefer a lower money ratio for fear of loss if price should fall, as shown previously. If he is very confident the price will fall he may go to P_4 with a preferred money ratio of 125 percent; if he is less confident he may go to P_2 with a preferred money ratio of 75 percent; if he thinks the price will remain where it is, or has about an equal chance of rising or falling, he may simply stay where he is at P_0, content with his present asset ratio.

Derivation of the Trader's Market Curve

From these various models of behavior we can derive some propositions about the nature of the trader's *market curve*, that is, the curve which shows how much he will buy or sell, with a perfect market, at different prices.[2]

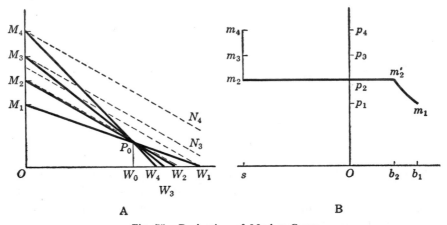

Fig. 75. Derivation of Market Curve

Let us take first the linear programming model of Fig. 70, where we assume a constant valuation coefficient and maximization of subjective net worth. In Fig. 75A we suppose a trader with initial position P_0, and a constant

---

[2] The market curve is important in determining equilibrium market price, as shown in Chapter 7. By summing the individual market curves along the quantity axis we get the total market curve, which shows the net amount all marketers will buy($+$) or sell($-$) at each price. Where this curve cuts the price axis is the equilibrium price, where the amounts offered for sale and for purchase are equal and their sum is zero. The market curves of Figs. 75 and 76 of the present chapter should be compared with those drawn in Chapter 7, Figs. 15, 16. and 19.

valuation coefficient equal to the slope of the parallel dotted lines M_4N_4, M_3N_3, and so forth. We have drawn four exchange opportunity lines corresponding to four different prices: M_1W_1, with price OM_1/OW_1 ($=op_1$ in Fig. 75B), M_2W_2, with price op_2, M_3W_3 with price op_3, and M_4P_4 with price op_4. We suppose the axes form the boundaries of the system, as in Fig. 70—any other boundaries can easily be drawn. Then at price op_4 and op_3 all the wheat is sold; sales are os ($= W_0O$). The price op_2 is just equal to the valuation coefficient, so that the exchange opportunity line M_2W_1 coincides with an indifference curve. At a price just above op_2 the trader will sell all his wheat; and at a price just below he will "sell" all his money, buying ob_2 ($= p_2m'_2, = W_0W_2$) of wheat. At prices below op_2 he will still sell all his money, but at lower prices he can buy more wheat, following the curve m'_2m_1; at price op_1 he buys ob_1 ($= W_0W_1$) of wheat for P_0W_0 of money. His market curve is then $m_4m_2m'_2m_1$. We see that it is perfectly elastic in the middle section where the price is equal to the valuation coefficient; the above assumptions produce an "all or none" type of behavior—he moves either to one boundary or to the other. We may note that individual market curves of the type in Fig. 75B may still be summed to produce a total market curve and market supply and demand curves, so that the analysis in Chapters 7 and 8 is not affected.

If now we suppose that the boundary of behavior is set not at a fixed stock of wheat or money but by a preferred asset ratio, we get the situation of Fig. 76. Here we suppose the same four prices and exchange opportunity

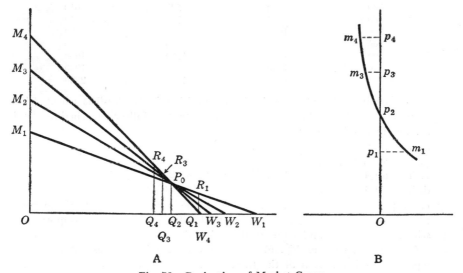

Fig. 76. Derivation of Market Curve

lines as in Fig. 75. We suppose, however, that the trader seeks to move to a position where the ratio of money to total assets, with wheat valued at the market price, is constant; R_4, R_3, P_0 and R_1 are the four positions corresponding to prices op_4, op_3, op_2, and op_1, and $M_4R_4/M_4W_4 = M_3R_3/M_3W_3 = M_2P_0/M_2W_2 = M_1R_1/M_1W_1$. The corresponding market curve is $m_4m_3p_2m_1$ in Fig. 76B, where $p_4m_4 = Q_2Q_4$, $p_3m_3 = Q_2Q_3$ (sales) and $p_1m_1 = Q_2Q_1$ (purchases). It will be seen that on this assumption the market curve is steep (inelastic), and a change in price produces much smaller shifts in sales or purchases than in Fig. 75. Many other models of behavior can be constructed. What is significant is not so much whether any particular model is "realistic," but whether there are models which would destroy the principle of equilibrium price (see Chapter 7). To do this, the model would have to produce the result that the trader will sell less or buy more at higher prices than at lower; it seems almost impossible to produce a behavior model with this property (see also pages 635–639).

QUESTIONS AND EXERCISES

1. The following table represents three different exchange opportunity lines: case A, columns 1 and 2; case B, columns 1 and 3; case C, columns 1 and 4.

(1) Wheat Stock	(2) Money Stock	(3) Money Stock	(4) Money Stock
900	−200	−290	−110
800	0	− 40	40
700	200	190	210
600	400	400	400
500	600	590	610
400	800	760	840
300	1000	910	1090
200	1200	1040	1360
100	1400	1150	1650
0	1600	1240	1960
−100	1800	1310	2290

Suppose in each case that the initial position is 600 bushels wheat, $400 money. In each of the three cases calculate the following schedules and arrange in tabular form:

a. The marginal terms of trade.

b. The average price.

c. The total amount of wheat bought (+) or sold (−).

d. The total amount of money paid (−) or received (+).

e. Suppose now that the market has perfect heterogeneity, so that the average price becomes the marginal terms of trade of a new exchange opportunity schedule. Calculate and tabulate this schedule.

On a graph such as Fig. 67 plot the various schedules as curves; use a separate graph for each of the three cases.

2. Suppose that a tax of $50 were imposed on all exchanges, no matter what the amount exchanged. Recalculate the exchange opportunity schedules and schedules a to d in the three cases of Question 1. Graph the results. Draw in each case the convex hull of the exchange opportunity line.

3. In each of the cases in Questions 1 and 2, suppose that the marketer has a subjective valuation coefficient of (a) $1.00, (b) $1.50, (c) $2, (d) $2.50, (e) $3; calculate and tabulate the amount of wheat which he will buy or sell at the different valuation coefficients. In case A, perfect markets, calculate and graph the market schedule of the marketer.

4. The following table shows the (constant) subjective valuation coefficient (v) and the initial position (stocks of wheat W_0, and money M_0, of eight marketers:

					Marketer			
	1	*2*	*3*	*4*	*5*	*6*	*7*	*8*
v	2.30	2.20	2.10	2.00	1.90	1.80	1.70	1.60
M_0 (dollars)	300	100	800	100	1000	500	100	1770
W_0 (bushels)	500	1000	900	600	5000	1000	500	2000

Suppose each maximizes subjective net worth, subject to the boundary constraint that neither M nor W should fall below zero. Calculate (a) the amount each will buy and sell at prices ranging by 10 cent intervals from $1.60 to $2.30 per bushel (the individual market schedules); (b) the market demand and supply schedule and the total market schedule (see Chapter 7). What will be the equilibrium price, and how much will each marketer buy or sell at that price?

5. Comparing Tables 29 and 30 (pp. 349–350), we see that the total profit is the same in both cases by position P_5, in spite of the great difference in the course of profit up to that position. Why is this? Does this mean that profit is not so arbitrary as it might seem from comparing Tables 29 and 30 up to P_5?

6. The concept of an *attainability function* defining the boundary between possible or attainable positions and impossible or unattainable positions is a perfectly general one. As an exercise in the method of plausible topology, discuss the probable shapes of the possibility boundaries in fields with the following axes:

a. The legal weight of the golf ball and the average score of golfers.

b. The average speed of automobiles and the number of fatal automobile accidents.

c. The area of a country and the proportion of national income derived from exports.

d. The ratio of Negroes to whites in a census tract and the number of mixed marriages per thousand population.

e. The national income of a country and the percentage of national income devoted to defense.

7. In Fig. 66, page 347, the profit-making process seems to be identical with the process of growth of assets—i.e., of accumulation. How could a firm make profits and still not accumulate assets over the years? How would this be represented in the diagrams?

8. A wheat marketer can buy or sell in unlimited quantities at $2 per bushel, can borrow money at 1 percent per month, and can sell next month's wheat futures at $1.98. He has no wheat but $40,000 of money. Draw his exchange opportunity line, from the second to the fourth quadrants. The following month the price rises to $3. Calculate his net profit for various quantities of wheat bought in the first month and sold in the second (say, 10, 20, 30, 40 thousand bushels) and also for various quantities of wheat futures sold (say, 10, 20, 30, 40 thousand bushels). Repeat with a price of $1 in the second month. Calculate the exact point in each case at which his net worth would be reduced to zero. Call this the *wipe-out point*. (Note that when he sells futures his cost is positive, being an addition to his money stock, and his revenue is negative, being the subtraction from his money stock when he buys the wheat to fulfill his contract to deliver—i.e., pay back his "wheat debt.") What will be the effect of a rise in the rate of interest on the wipe-out point? Is there an analogy to the rate of interest in the case of selling wheat futures? Does this example throw any light on the possible effects of a rise in the rate of interest on the behavior of a marketer?

CHAPTER 18

THE MANUFACTURING FIRM

The manufacturing firm differs from the trading firm in that it adds to the processes of purchase and sale a process of production that is, of transformation of some assets—cash, raw materials, goods in process, and some fixed assets through depreciation and maintenance—into finished product, which is then sold. In a simplified model we can regard production as the transformation of money stocks into stocks of finished product through the purchase of labor, raw materials, and so forth, and their transformation into finished product. The exact nature of the production transformation function will be examined in Chapter 20. Here we will simply assume a *cost function*, relating the amount added to the stock of product to the value of the diminutions in other assets which have been necessary to produce the product. Thus we can again take a very simple model, let us say of a wheat producer, in which we suppose that for every quantity of wheat produced—that is, added to the stock through production—there is a corresponding diminution in "money," which here essentially stands for the value of the other assets used up in production.

COST CURVES

Cost Schedules

CONSTANT AVERAGE TOTAL COST.   Suppose then that we start with a firm owning no wheat and $1000 of money, and that it then proceeds to use its money to produce wheat, following the *total cost curve*. The simplest case, case 1, is shown in Fig. 77A. Here in the upper part of the figure we measure the money stock vertically and the wheat stock horizontally. P_0 is the initial position. We suppose that the firm can produce wheat at a constant average cost of $2 per bushel. The line P_0W is the production

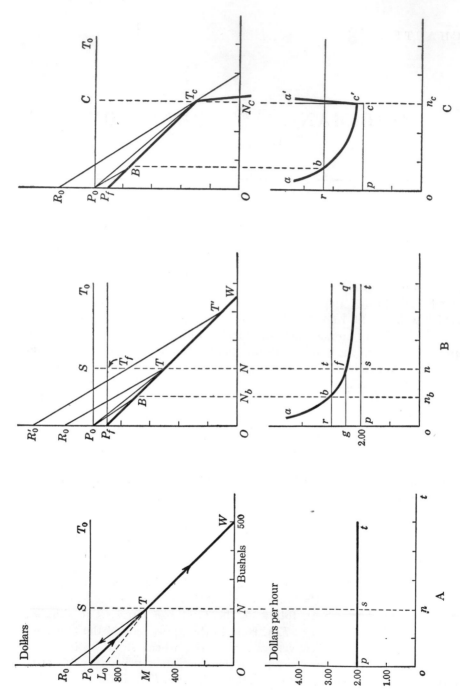

Fig. 77. Production Opportunity and Cost Curves

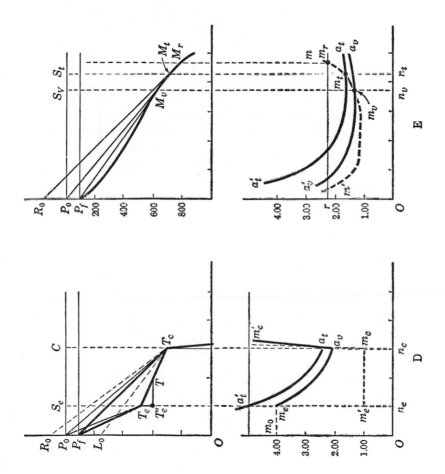

opportunity line, showing what stocks of wheat and money are open to the firm through production. It is also the total cost curve, with total cost measured downward from the line $P_0 T_0$, and output (production of wheat) measured horizontally from $P_0 O$. Thus at the point T the firm has produced $P_0 S$ bushels of wheat, at a total cost of ST; the money stock is reduced from the initial OP_0 to NT, and the wheat stock has increased to ON ($= P_0 S$, as we started with no wheat). The *average total cost* is the total cost divided by the output; at output $P_0 S$ this is $ST/P_0 S$ ($= op$ in the lower part of the figure), where pst is the average cost curve. No matter where T is on the line $P_0 W$ the average total cost is the same ($=$ tan $SP_0 T$). This case is illustrated in Table 34.

TABLE 34. COST SCHEDULES: CONSTANT AVERAGE TOTAL COST

Output (bushels)	Total Cost (dollars)	Average Total Cost (dollars per bushel)	Stock of Money (dollars)	Stock of Wheat (bushels)
0	0	0	1000	0
50	100	2.00	900	50
100	200	2.00	800	100
150	300	2.00	700	150
200	400	2.00	600	200
250	500	2.00	500	250
300	600	2.00	400	300
350	700	2.00	300	350
400	800	2.00	200	400
450	900	2.00	100	450
500	1000	2.00	0	500

Cost Schedules with Fixed Cost and Constant Average Variable Cost

The next case, case 2, is shown in Fig. 77B. Here we suppose a *fixed cost* of $P_0 P_f$ which will be incurred even if there is no production at all. Once a manufacturing firm is set up with buildings and machinery, this equipment will depreciate even in the absence of production. Furthermore there are certain maintainance functions which must be performed and paid for if a continuing capacity and organization is to be maintained— office staff, executives, janitors, and so on—which also involve deductions from total assets even if no production is carried on. The total fixed cost is then best defined as the total cost at zero output. In Fig. 77B we suppose that at output $P_f S$ the total cost is divided into the total fixed cost, ST_f, and the total variable cost, $T_f T$—the variable cost being that part of total cost which varies with output, such as direct wage bills, materials used up, and so on. The production opportunity boundary is now P_0P_fW, and the total cost curve is the same line, measured downward from P_0T_0. Here we assume that the average variable cost is constant, again equal to op ($2). This is T_fT/P_fT_f in the upper figure ($= \tan T_fP_fT$); this is constant for all points on the line P_fW. This case is further illustrated in Table 35.

TABLE 35. COST SCHEDULES: FIXED COST, CONSTANT AVERAGE VARIABLE COST

Output (bushels)	Total Cost (dollars)	Average Total Cost (dollars) per bushel)	Fixed Cost (dollars)	Average Fixed Cost (dollars per bushel)	Average Variable Cost	Money Stock	Wheat Stock
0	100	∞	100	∞	2.00	900	0
50	200	4.00	100	2.00	2.00	800	50
100	300	3.00	100	1.00	2.00	700	100
150	400	2.67	100	0.67	2.00	600	150
200	500	2.50	100	0.50	2.00	500	200
250	600	2.40	100	0.40	2.00	400	250
300	700	2.33	100	0.33	2.00	300	300
350	800	2.29	100	0.29	2.00	200	350
400	900	2.25	100	0.25	2.00	100	400
450	1000	2.22	100	0.22	2.00	0	450
500	1100	2.20	100	0.20	2.00	−100	500

We notice that the average total cost (nf) is equal to the average variable cost (ns) plus the average fixed cost (sf); this is always true. By moving T along the line P_fW we can visualize how the average total cost (ST/P_0T $= \tan SP_0T$) starts at infinity, falls very rapidly at first then more slowly, approaching the average variable cost as output increases.

Cost Schedules with Capacity Output and Nonconstant Marginal Cost

Case 3, Fig. 77C is a fairly common condition, where the firm has constant average variable cost up to some output P_0C at which the capacity of the existing plant is reached; any attempt to increase output beyond this point results in a very rapid rise in total or average cost. Here the various curves are identical with those of Fig. 77B up to the output P_0C, the capacity output.

Marginal Cost

Case 4, Fig. 77D, is a more general case, in which the average variable cost is not constant; we suppose that it is high at first, for when the plant is being operated at very low levels production will be inefficient and costs will be high. At a certain output S_e, however, we reach an efficient level of production, and costs fall. Here we need a new and very important concept, that of the *marginal cost*. This is defined as the increase in total cost which results from a unit increase in output. It is a concept parallel to that of the marginal receipts or marginal expenses of the previous chapter. In the geometry of Fig. 77 it is the slope, or gradient of the total cost curve. Thus consider the little triangle $T_e TT'_e$ in Fig. 77D; $T_e T'_e$ is the increase in total cost which results from an increase in output $T'_e T$; the marginal cost is therefore $T_e T'_e / T'_e T$ which is the slope of the line $T_e T$. If the marginal cost is constant the total cost curve will be a straight line. Thus in Fig. 77D the marginal cost is \$4 per bushel between P_0 and S_e, and \$1 per bushel between S_e and C. At C we suppose again that capacity is reached, total cost shoots off to infinity, and marginal cost likewise becomes infinite. In the lower portion of Fig. 77D the marginal cost curve is $m_0 m_e m'_e m_c m'_c$: it is \$4 per bushel between 0 and n_e, drops to \$1 per bushel at n_e, continues at \$1 till n_c and then shoots up indefinitely at capacity output. This corresponds exactly to the steep total cost curve between P_f and T_e, the flat one between T_e and T_c, and the vertical one after T_c.

The average variable cost is the same as the marginal cost from P_f to T_e (= \$4 per bushel), then falls to $n_c a_v$ at n_c; $m_0 m_e a_v m'_c$ is the average variable cost curve. The average total cost falls rapidly from infinity at P_0 to $n_e a'_t$ at S_e (equal to the slope of $P_0 T_e$), then falls somewhat less rapidly to $n_c a_t$ at C, equal to the slope of $P_0 T_c$; $a'_t a_t m'_c$ is the average total cost curve. The

TABLE 36. COST SCHEDULES: FIXED COST, VARIABLE MARGINAL COST

Output (bushels)	Total Cost (dollars)	Average Total Cost	Average Variable Cost	Marginal Cost	Money Stock (dollars)	Stock Wheat (bushels)
		(cost in dollars per bushel)				
0	100	∞	?		900	0
50	300	6.00	4.00	4.00	700	50
100	500	5.00	4.00	4.00	500	100
150	550	3.67	3.00	1.00	450	150
200	600	3.00	2.50	1.00	400	200
250	650	2.60	2.20	1.00	350	250
300	700	2.33	2.00	1.00	300	300
350	∞	∞	∞	1.00	−∞	?
				∞		

marginal cost over a range of output is the increase in total cost divided by the increase in output: thus between outputs of 50 and 100 total cost increases by 200, output, by 50, and the marginal cost in this range is 200/50, or \$4 per bushel. To indicate that this is the mean marginal cost over the range between the two outputs we put the marginal cost figure between the two outputs, and in plotting the marginal cost curve we plot the mean marginal cost also between the two outputs (Table 36).

Cost Schedules: Continuous Variation

Finally, case 5, Fig. 77E, is the most general case of all where we suppose that the marginal and average costs vary continuously with output. This is illustrated in Table 37.

TABLE 37. COST SCHEDULES, WITH CONTINUOUS FUNCTIONS

(1)	(2)	(3)	(4)	(5)	(6)	(7)	(8)	(9)
		Total	Total					
	Total	Fixed	Variable	Average	Average	Margi-	Wheat	Money
Output	Cost	Cost	Cost	Total	Variable	nal	Stock	Stock
(bushels)	(dollars)	(dollars)	(dollars)	Cost	Cost	Cost	(bushels)	(dollars)
					(dollars per bushel)			
0	100	100	0	∞	?		0	900
50	225	100	125	4.50	2.50	2.50	50	775
100	290	100	190	2.90	1.90	1.30	100	710
150	350	100	250	2.33	1.67	1.20	150	650
200	410	100	310	2.05	1.55	1.20	200	590
250	470	100	370	1.88	1.48	1.20	250	530
300	530	100	430	1.77	1.43	1.20	300	470
350	595	100	495	1.70	1.41	1.30	350	405
400	665	100	565	1.66	1.41	1.40	400	335
450	745	100	645	1.66	1.43	1.60	450	255
500	880	100	780	1.76	1.56	2.70	500	120

In Fig. 77E, the total cost curve is $P_0P_fM_vM_t$ (columns 1 and 2 of Table 37). The average total cost curve is a'_ta_t (columns 1 and 5), the average variable cost curve is a'_va_v (columns 1 and 6) and the marginal cost curve is $m'm$ (dotted), from columns 1 and 7.

The Average-Marginal Relationship

Some points about the geometry of these curves, which have some importance later, should be noted. The marginal cost curve rises through the minimum points of the average variable and average total cost curves. That is, marginal cost is equal to the average total cost when the average total cost is a minimum, and is equal to the average variable cost when the average variable cost is at a minimum. The proposition can easily be proved from the total cost curve. Thus as we move a point from P_f along the total cost curve, the average variable cost is the slope of the straight line joining the point on the cost curve to P_f. This slope falls until we reach M_v, at which P_fM_v is tangent to the total cost curve; as we increase output beyond this point the slope of the line to P_f rises again. M_v is therefore the point of minimum average variable cost; at M_v, however, the slope of the total cost curve (the marginal cost) is equal to the slope of the line $P_f M_v$ (the average variable cost), as this is the condition of tangency. Similarly we can show that M_t, where $P_0 M_t$ is a tangent to the total cost curve, is the point of minimum average total cost, and is also the point where the marginal cost (the slope of the total cost curve at M_t) is equal to the average total cost (the slope of the line $P_0 M_t$). At the corresponding minimum points m_v and m_t in the lower part of the figure, therefore, the marginal cost curve must intersect the average variable and average total cost curves.

Another proposition, sometimes useful in drawing the curves, follows from the above proof: where the average (variable or total) cost is falling with increase in output, as it is to the left of the minimum point, the marginal cost will lie below the average cost; where the average cost is rising, the marginal cost will lie above it, as it does to the right of the minimum point. The marginal cost must be rising where the marginal cost curve cuts the average cost curve; if it is falling, the average cost is a maximum, not a minimum, which is a very unlikely case. It follows that as the average variable cost is less than the average total cost, if there is any fixed cost, the minimum average variable cost comes at a lower output than the minimum average total cost. Where there is a discontinuity or "extreme point" on the total cost curve, the marginal cost will take a sudden jump, as in Fig. 77D. These propositions apply to any average-marginal relationship.[1]

EQUILIBRIUM POSITIONS OF THE FIRM

Sale of Product

The firm is not content with merely producing, of course, and the next step is the sale of the product. Suppose first that the firm sells in a perfect market at a given price for all sales. If, say in Fig. 77A the firm moves to point T on its production opportunity line, it will then have an exchange opportunity line TR_0 where the slope of TR_0 $(= MR_0/MT)$ is the selling price of the product. If the firm sells all it has produced in the period, it moves along the path $P_0 \rightarrow T \rightarrow R_0$. $P_0 R_0$ is the total increase

[1] The average-marginal relationship can easily be proved by algebra. Let a be the average total cost of x units, a_1 the average total cost of $x + 1$ units. Then the total cost of x units is ax, and of $x + 1$ units is $a_1(x + 1)$. The marginal cost of the $(x + 1)$st unit is $a_1(x + 1) - ax$, or $(a_1 - a)x + a_1$. If the average cost is constant as output changes, $a_1 = a$, and the marginal cost is equal to the average cost, a_1. If the average cost is increasing as output increases, $a_1 > a$, $(a_1 - a)x$ is positive, and the marginal cost is therefore greater than the average cost. If the average cost is decreasing as output increases, $a_1 < a$, $(a_1 - a)x$ is negative, and the marginal cost is less than the average cost.

in money stock as a result of the combined operation of production and sale; it measures also the total profit on the operation. If the firm distributes this profit in dividends, it moves from R_0 to P_0; this completes a simple production cycle, $P_0 \rightarrow T \rightarrow R_0 \rightarrow P_0$. The firm does not have to complete such a cycle in each period, of course; it could move to any point within the triangle $R_0 P_0 T$, and start the next cycle from there.

In the case of Fig. 77A and 77B, the more the firm produces, the greater the profit; thus if it goes from T to T' in Fig. 77B profit increases from $P_0 R_0$ to $P_0 R'_0$; this is assuming that the price of the product is greater than the minimum average total cost. If the price of the product is less than the minimum average cost, the production cycle would be, say $P_0 T L_0$ in Fig. 77A, and the owners of the firm would incur a loss equal to $P_0 L_0$; that is, they would have to put an amount of money equal to $L_0 P_0$ into the firm just to restore its asset position at the beginning of the cycle. In Fig. 77B, *or* in the lower part of the figure is the price corresponding to the slope of the lines $T R_0$ or $T' R'_0$. At an output $O N_b, = on_b$ the price is just equal to the average total cost, and profit is zero; the production cycle $P_0 P_f B P_0$ brings us back to P_0. At an output ON, the total profit is the rectangle *ftrg* in the lower figure; profit per unit is price minus average total cost, or *ft*.

Trading and Manufacturing Firms Contrasted

We should note here an important difference between the trading and the manufacturing firm. The trader must hold stocks of goods while he waits for the price to rise; purchase and sale cannot be simultaneous. The manufacturer however can be producing and selling his product at the same time, though he will need a certain stock of finished goods to allow for fluctuations in rates of production and sale. The production cycle is not therefore limited by the need for liquidity, for instance, in the same way that the trading operation may be limited. In the figures of Fig. 77, then, the boundary imposed by moving down the production opportunity line into the *negative money* quadrant beyond W in Fig. 77A and 77B is less restrictive than might be thought at first glance, for at the same time that production is diminishing the money stock, sales are replenishing it.

The Capacity Boundary

It would seem therefore as if Fig. 77A and B represent *firms without limit*, with neither a maximum profit nor any clear boundary; as firms do not in fact become indefinitely large, there must be some kind of limit or boundary not included in these first two cases. One of these, as in Fig. 77C and 77D, is the existence of a *capacity output* at which cost begins to rise sharply. Thus in Fig. 77C, if the price is below *op*, the minimum

loss is at no production at all; when the price is equal to $n_c c'$, the slope
of line $P_0 T_c$, profit is zero at the output ON_c, and there will be losses at
either greater or smaller outputs. At a price or (the slope of $T_c R_0$) ON_c
is again the point of maximum profit; B is the zero profit or break-even
point. This is a linear programming type of solution; the optimum position must be at one of the extreme points P_0 or T_c of the feasible set
bounded by $OP_0 P_f T_c N_c$; it will be at P_0 (no production) for all prices
below op, and at T_c (capacity output) for all prices above op.

Firms Operating with Price above Average Variable Cost

In the case of Fig. 77D we have a somewhat similar solution. If the price
is above the minimum average total cost, $n_c a_t$, the exchange opportunity
line $T_c R_0$ will have a slope greater than $P_0 T_c$, profits will be positive
($P_0 R_0$) and maximized at T_c. If the price is below the minimum average
total cost, $n_c a_t$, but above the minimum average *variable* cost, $n_c a_v$, the
exchange opportunity line from T_c will be between $T_c P_0$ and $T_c P_f$ (not
drawn): there will be losses, but the loss will be less than the loss $P_0 P_f$,
which would result from closing down the operation altogether and producing nothing. If the price falls below $n_c a_v$, however, the exchange opportunity line from T_c will have a slope less than $T_c P_f$ such as $T_c L_0$;
the loss by producing will be $P_0 L_0$, whereas the loss by not producing and
shutting down the plant will be only $P_0 P_f$; it will pay to shut down and
produce nothing at P_f.

The General Optimum; Price = Marginal Cost

In the general case, Fig. 77E, the most profitable output, when the price
is above the minimum average variable cost, is where the exchange
opportunity line *touches* the production opportunity line, as at M_r. It is
clear that the line $M_r R_0$ is as far "out" as any line of this slope can be
which has any point in common with the production opportunity curve.
That is, $P_0 R_0$ is the maximum profit obtainable at a price equal to the
slope of $M_r R_0$ (= or in the lower figure). At the point M_r the price
is equal to the marginal cost, for the slope of the exchange opportunity
line is equal to the slope of the production opportunity curve. In the lower
figure therefore the optimum output is at the point m_r where the price
line $m_r r$ cuts the marginal cost curve. If the price is below $n_v m_v$, the least
average variable cost, the minimum loss is greater than $P_0 P_f$, and it will
pay to shut down the plant.

Reasons for the Capacity Limit

The assumption of the existence of a *capacity output*, which is made
explicitly in cases 3 and 4 (Fig. 77C and D) above, and is implicit in the

rising marginal cost curve of Fig. 77E (case 5), needs further examination. In the short run, where we are producing something on a given farm, or in a given factory, the existing fixed capital facilities clearly impose a *capacity limit* of some type; this limit may be absolute, as assumed in Fig. 77C and D, or it may be flexible, reflected for instance in continuously

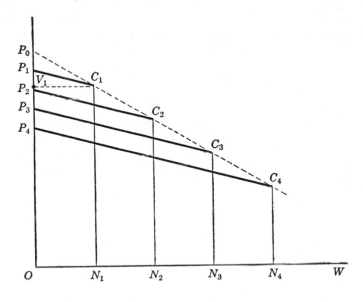

A

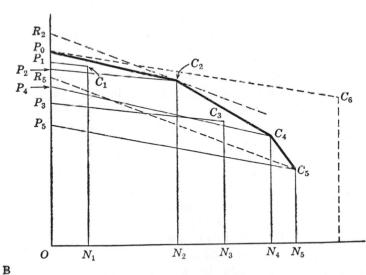

B

Fig. 78. Long-Run Production Opportunity Curves

rising marginal and average costs due to overtime payments, extra wear
and tear, costs of night shifts, and so on, as we try to squeeze more and
more production out of a single plant. Even in case 5, Fig. 77E, with a
given plant an absolute capacity will eventually be reached at which the
marginal cost becomes infinite.

Long-Run Cost Curves

Suppose, however, that we are considering the initial decision of how
large a plant to build in the first place; the larger the plant, the larger
the capacity, so it seems as if we can put the capacity point at any level
of output we wish by building a large enough plant. The larger the plant,
however, the larger the fixed cost. We may have, therefore, a situation like
that of Fig. 78. Here we suppose that with a small plant, with fixed costs
P_0P_1, we have a small capacity output at C_1; the production opportunity
curve we suppose is like Fig. 77C, $P_0P_1C_1N_1$. With larger plants we have
larger fixed cost, but we suppose no change in marginal cost, so we have a
succession of short-run production opportunity lines, $P_0P_2C_2N_2$, $P_0P_3C_3N_3$,
and so on, corresponding to larger and larger plants. The envelope of
these short-run production opportunity curves is the long-run production
opportunity line, $P_0C_1C_2$, etc. If each bushel increase capacity increases
fixed costs by a fixed amount c (equal to, say, P_0P_1/ON_1) and if the short-
run marginal cost is constant, $= m$, the long-run production opportunity
envelope will be a straight line, and long-run average total cost, a, will
be constant, corresponding to case 1, Fig. 77A. In Fig. 78A, $a = V_1P_0/V_1C_1$
$= (V_1P_1 + P_1P_0)/V_1C_1 = m + c$.

Long-Run Increasing Cost: Linear Optima

Suppose now that c is not constant, and suppose also that by increasing
fixed costs by investment in improved plant we can decrease m. The
situation is then much more complicated, as in Fig. 78B. Here we have
a number of short-run production opportunity curves, each corresponding to a particular kind of plant, but with different marginal costs and
capacities. These may intersect each other in various ways—thus going
from P_4C_4 to P_3C_3 we lower capacity, but also lower marginal cost—the
latter might be a smaller but more modern plant with more costly machinery. The problem of the optimum kind of plant and optimum output
then becomes a typical problem in linear programming. We draw (or
compute) the convex hull of the various short-run production opportunity curves—in Fig. 78B this is the dotted line $P_0C_2C_4C_5N_5$. For any
price less than the slope of P_0C_2 the optimum point is P_0, and there will
be no production, for production to *any* point on the convex hull and
subsequent sale of product brings us back to a point on the money axis

below P_0. At any price between the slope of P_0C_2 and the slope of C_2C_4, C_2 is the optimum point; thus if the exchange opportunity line has the slope of C_2R_2 the profit at C_2 $(= P_0R_2)$ is greater than at any other of the extreme points. Similarly if the price is between the slope of C_2C_4 and C_4C_5 the optimum point will be C_4. Points such as C_1 and C_3 which lie within the convex hull are simply irrelevant; they cannot be an optimum at any price, as there are always points on the convex hull which are superior to them.

Long-Run Cost Curve Cannot Show Decreasing Cost

We see that the long-run production opportunity boundary *must* be convex, treating Fig. 78A (constant long-run average cost) as a limiting case of convexity. Thus suppose in Fig. 78B a new process were discovered with capacity at C_6; this would immediately make all the previous extreme points irrelevant, as they would lie below the new convex hull P_0C_6. This means that the long-run average cost must either be constant in respect to output, or must rise eventually with increasing output; it cannot fall with increasing output. There are good reasons for supposing that the long-run average cost boundary will be convex in the sense of eventually increasing average or marginal cost. This discussion, however, must be postponed until we have examined further the production function in Chapter 25.

Imperfect Selling Markets

Now let us remove the limitation that the selling market is perfect, and allow imperfect markets for product. The exchange oportunity line is now no longer straight, but may have various "kinks" or curvatures, as in the previous chapter. Let us take two cases to illustrate; first, a simple case in which the firm can sell a certain amount at a fixed price, and no more. This would be the case, for instance, where a firm was allocated a certain quota of sales at a fixed price and forbidden to sell any more. Let us also suppose a total cost curve of the type of Fig. 77C. This is shown in Fig. 79A. $P_0P_fT_cN_c$ is the total cost curve.

A MARKET QUOTA. Now suppose the firm can sell an amount M_1T_1 (and no more) at a price equal to the slope of T_1R_1 (M_1R_1/M_1T_1); if it proceeds along the production oportunity line to T_1 it can then move along the market opportunity line to R_1. If however it moves to T_2 on the production opportunity line, it can only move to R_2 in the market opportunity line, where $M_2T_2 = M_1T_1$. Similarly from T_c it can only move to R_3. The envelope (or convex hull) of all the various opportunity lines is $R_1R_3T_cN_c$. R_1R_3 is a straight line parallel to P_fT_c. Where the optimum point will be at the end of a cycle of production and sale

depends on how the firm values stocks of product. Suppose the firm
maximizes its subjective net worth, as in the previous chapter; then if
the valuation coefficient of the product (wheat) is less than the slope of
R_1R_3, the indifference curves will be parallel to a line such as $R_1R'_1$,
and the optimum point will be at R_1, with the firm producing its sales

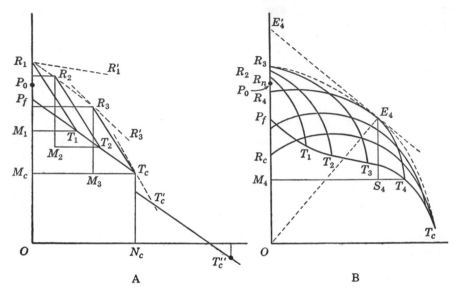

Fig. 79. Optimizing Production with Imperfect Markets

quota, M_1T_1, and selling it all to R_1, the production-sales-dividends cycle
being $P_0 \rightarrow P_f \rightarrow T_1 \rightarrow R_1 \rightarrow P_0$. If the firm values stocks of wheat
more highly, at a valuation coefficient greater than the (constant)
average variable cost but less than the selling price of the quota—that is,
between the slopes of R_1R_3 (which is equal to the slope of P_fT_c) and the
slope of T_cR_3—the optimum point will be R_3. The firm will produce to
capacity to T_c, sell its quota (T_cM_3), and retain the excess of production,
M_3M_c, as an increase in its stocks of wheat. It is only likely to do this,
of course, if it expects the quota system to end, or quotas to be increased,
and the price to rise in the fairly near future. If the firm is very optimistic
about future markets, its valuation coefficient may even exceed the present
sales price; its indifference curves would then be parallel to a line such
as $T_cT'_c$, and T_c will be the optimum point. The firm will produce to
capacity, but will sell nothing and hold all its production as an increase
in the stocks of wheat, M_cT_c.

A LIQUIDITY PROBLEM.   With imperfect markets we see immediately that the manufacturing firm acquires a possible liquidity problem, which it does not have under perfect markets. Under perfect markets there is really no liquidity problem in manufacturing, though there is in trading, as stocks of goods can be sold in unlimited quantities, and hence turned into money without any decline in value. With imperfect markets, however, if a manufacturer is accumulating unsold stocks and thereby diminishing his money stock, moving downwards and to the right in the money-commodity diagram such as Figs. 77 or 79, he may eventually reach a boundary at which he cannot continue manufacturing for want of money to pay money costs, such as wages and raw materials. As he moves downward and to the right, therefore, say, in Fig. 79A, he will value commodity less and money more. Thus from, say, a position such as T_c he is most unlikely to complete another such cycle, which would take him, say, to T''_c, where money stock is actually negative, unless he had most unusual expectations of the future of the market. There is a strong tendency therefore for the optimum to move to R_1 and for production to be limited to the quota.

CONTINUOUS VARIATION. In Fig. 79B the general case is presented, with continuously varying marginal cost and marginal revenue. $P_0P_fT_c$ is the production opportunity line, the mirror image of the total cost curve. From any point on this curve, such as T_4, the firm has an exchange opportunity curve, such as T_4R_4; these curves, T_1R_1, T_2R_2, etc., are identical in shape, the market being assumed invariant with the amount of production. These exchange opportunity curves will have an envelope, $R_3E_4T_c$; the optimum point obviously must lie on this envelope, which is the boundary of the feasible set. If we suppose that all that is produced is sold, the maximum profit is at R_3, where the envelope curve cuts the money axis. If the firm expects the market to improve, however, it may set a high value on stocks of product, in which case it may prefer some point such as E_4, with a cycle such as $P_0 \rightarrow T_4 \rightarrow E_4$, with M_4T_4 being produced, T_4S_4 sold, and M_4S_4 added to stocks. We can continue the exchange opportunity lines into the second quadrant, in which case sales would exceed production and stocks would decline.

TOTAL COST AND TOTAL REVENUE CURVES

The case in which all product is sold is of great importance, and is, of course, bound to be realized in the long run, as a firm cannot decumulate, and will not accumulate stocks of its product indefinitely. It can be treated more conveniently, with some loss of generality, by calculating the total revenue received from the sale of each volume of output, as in Table 38. Here we assume the same cost functions as in Table 37. Columns

1, 2, and 6 are the same as columns 1, 2, and 7 of Table 37. Column 3 shows the price at which each output can be sold; this is the sales curve. Column 4 shows the total revenue, obtained by multiplying each output in column 1 by the price at which it can be sold in column 3. Price is sometimes called average revenue, and the sales curve the *average revenue curve,* because it bears the same relation to total revenue that average cost does to total cost. We have, that is,

$$\text{Average cost} = \frac{\text{Total cost}}{\text{Output}}$$

and

$$\text{Price} = \frac{\text{Total revenue}}{\text{Output}} = \text{Average revenue}$$

Column 4 is the net revenue, obtained by subtracting each total cost figure from the corresponding total revenue figure. This is the realized profit, or the increase in money stock if all the output is sold. Column 7 is the marginal revenue, a concept exactly analogous to marginal cost. It is defined as the increase in total revenue per unit increase in output.

TABLE 38. PROFIT MAXIMIZATION

(1) Output (bushels)	(2) Total Cost (dollars)	(3) Price or Average Revenue (dollars per bushel)	(4) Total Revenue (dollars)	(5) Net Revenue (dollars)	(6) Marginal Cost (dollars per bushel)	(7) Marginal Revenue (dollars per bushel)
0	100	2.60	0	−100		
					2.50	2.50
50	225	2.50	125	−100		
					1.30	2.30
100	290	2.40	240	−50		
					1.20	2.10
150	350	2.30	345	−5		
					1.20	1.90
200	410	2.20	440	30		
					1.20	1.70
250	470	2.10	525	55		
					1.20	1.50
300	530	2.00	600	70		
					1.30	1.30
350	595	1.90	665	70		
					1.40	1.10
400	665	1.80	720	55		
					1.60	0.90
450	745	1.70	765	20		
					2.50	0.70
500	880	1.60	800	−80		

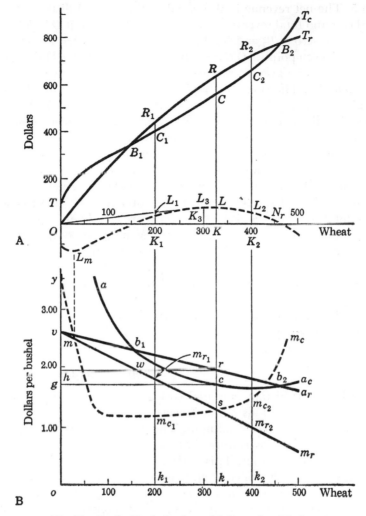

Fig. 80. Profit Maximization with Imperfect Markets

Thus over the range from 0 to 50 bushels the increase in total revenue is $125; marginal revenue is then $125 for 50 bushels, or $2.50 per bushel. We see now from the table that the net revenue is a maximum (about $70) when the marginal cost and the marginal revenue are equal, between 300 and 350 bushels. This again is no accident, but a necessary condition.

GRAPHIC ILLUSTRATION. The figures of the table are reproduced in Fig. 80. In Fig. 80A we plot the total cost curve, T_c, and the total revenue curve, T_r, from columns 2 and 4, and the net revenue curve, N_r, from column 5. The net revenue is also equal to the vertical distance between the total cost and total revenue curves. Thus at any output OK, $KL = CR$. Net revenue is zero at B_1 and B_2. These correspond to what are sometimes called "break-even points." OT is the total fixed cost. In Fig. 80B the curves va_r and vm_r are the average revenue and marginal revenue curves, from columns 3 and 7. The curves aa_c and mm_c are the average total cost and marginal cost curves from columns 5 and 7 of Table 37. It will be observed that the net revenue is a maximum, KL, at output OK ($= ok$) where the marginal cost and marginal revenue curves intersect at s; that is, where marginal cost equals marginal revenue. Marginal cost is the slope of the total cost curve, and marginal revenue is the slope of the total revenue curve. At an output such as ok_1, where marginal cost (k_1m_{c1}) is less than marginal revenue (k_1m_{r1}), the total revenue curve is steeper than the total cost curve and the two curves are clearly *diverging* with increase of output; i.e., net revenue is getting larger as output increases, and is therefore not at a maximum. Similarly, at an output such as ok_2, where marginal cost exceeds marginal revenue, the total cost curve is steeper than the total revenue curve and the curves are converging with increasing output—i.e., net revenue is increased by *diminishing* output, and again is not at a maximum. At output OK the total cost and total revenue curves are parallel, and net revenue therefore is neither increasing nor decreasing.

The Second-Order Conditions

It will be observed that marginal cost and marginal revenue are also equal at the point m. This point, however, represents a minimum value of net revenue, L_m, not a maximum. The equality of marginal cost and marginal revenue means simply that net revenue is neither increasing nor decreasing with output. This is true both at maximum and at minimum points, or anywhere net revenue is not changing with output. For a maximum not only must marginal cost equal marginal revenue, but the marginal cost curve must also cut the marginal revenue curve from below. That is, at slightly smaller outputs than the optimum, marginal revenue must be larger than marginal cost, and at slightly larger outputs it must be smaller. This is what is known as *second-order condition* for a maximum.[2]

---

[2] The student who is familiar with the differential calculus will recognize the marginal analysis as an example of the theory of maximization. Thus we have: net revenue (N) = total revenue (R) − total cost (C). The conditions for maximizing N with respect to output (q) are (1) the first-order condition, $\dfrac{dN}{dq} = \dfrac{dR}{dq} - \dfrac{dC}{dq} = 0$, or $\dfrac{dR}{dq}$ (marginal revenue) $= \dfrac{dC}{dq}$ (marginal cost), and (2) the second-order condition, $\dfrac{d^2N}{dq^2}$, negative—i.e., the excess of marginal revenue over marginal cost must be declining.

Under perfect markets marginal revenue and price are identical, as we have seen, so that the maximum condition reduces to the equality of *price* and marginal cost already noticed. With imperfect markets, however, price is greater than marginal revenue, and at the point of maximum net revenue price (*kr*) is greater than marginal cost (*ks*).

Further Geometric Properties

One or two further points of geometry should be noticed. The distance *cr* in Fig. 80B is the difference between the price and the average total cost, or the net revenue per unit of output. This is not generally at a maximum when the net revenue is a maximum. If we draw OL_3 to touch the net revenue curve in Fig. 80A, OK_3 is the output at which the net revenue per unit is a maximum. We see that this will always be at a smaller output than *OK* where the net revenue is a maximum, unless the maximum net revenue is itself zero—i.e., if the net revenue curve touches the horizontal axis from below. Then K_3 and *K* would coincide. Net revenue in Fig. 80B is measured by the area of the rectangle *crhg*—this being the net revenue per unit of output (*cr*) multiplied by the number of units of output (*gc*). Total revenue is the area of the rectangle *okrh* and total cost is area *okcg*.

Total revenue is also equal to the area under the marginal revenue curve, being the sum of all the individual marginal revenues. Thus suppose the marginal revenue of the first unit of output were $2.60 and of the second unit $2.59. The first unit would add $2.60 and the second $2.59 to total revenue, so that the total revenue at the end of the second unit would be $(2.60 + 2.59). That is, in Fig. 80B total revenue at output *ok* is also the area *ovsk*, = area *ohrk*. Subtracting the area *ohwsk* from both these areas, we have area *hvw* = area *wrs*. If the marginal revenue curve is a straight line, the triangles *hvw* and *wrs* are not only equal in area but congruent. In that case, *hw* = *wr*. This gives us a convenient method for constructing the marginal curve corresponding to an average curve. If the average curve is a straight line, the marginal curve will also be a straight line passing through the point at which the average curve cuts the vertical axis, *v*. If from a point on the average curve *r* we drop a perpendicular *rh* to the vertical axis and bisect *rh* in *w*, *vw* is the corresponding marginal curve. Even if the average curve is not a straight line the construction can be used to find the marginal quantity corresponding to each average quantity. Thus if *vr* were *tangent* to an average curve at *r*, *ks* would be the corresponding marginal quantity. The area under the marginal cost curve is similarly the total *variable* cost, if the marginal cost of the first unit of output excludes the fixed cost. If the marginal cost of the first unit includes the fixed cost, then the area under the marginal cost curve is the total cost. In this case the area *between* the marginal cost and marginal revenue curves is the net revenue. Thus in Fig. 80B, at an output ok_1 net revenue would be the area $mm_{c_1}s$— the area vmy, where y is the point at which the marginal cost curve cuts the vertical axis. The point m is clearly a maximum *negative* value of net revenue. As we move beyond m the positive area increases; at s it is a maximum; beyond s—e.g., at the output ok_2—the area $sm_{c_2}m_{r_2}$ represents a subtraction from the value at s. This constitutes another proof that s, the point where marginal cost and marginal revenue are equal, is the point of maximum net revenue.

Marginal Cost-Marginal Revenue Defines Envelope Boundary

The condition that marginal cost equals marginal revenue actually defines a wider set of optima than the above model does, where all product is sold in a single cycle. Thus if we refer back to Fig. 79B (p. 388), we see that for any amount of product, such as M_4T_4, the optimum volume of sales is S_4T_4. T_4E_4 is the exchange opportunity line from T_4, which is the same as the total revenue curve from T_4 as origin, with sales measured to the left of T_4 instead of to the right of the origin as in Fig. 80. E_4 is the point at which the exchange opportunity line touches the opportunity envelope, $R_3E_4T_c$; at any point short of this the firm can move to a position with more money and more product by a different combination of production and sales. At E_4, then, the slope of the total revenue curve, T_4E_4 is the same as the slope of the opportunity envelope at E_4. The slope of the opportunity envelope at E_4, however, is the same as the slope of the production opportunity line at T_4. To prove this, suppose the point T_4 is displaced, say downward along the production opportunity curve T_4T_c by a small amount: the line T_4E_4 may be supposed rigid for small displacements, so the point E_4 will be displaced in exactly the same amount and direction as the point T_4. The slope of the production opportunity line at T_4 is the marginal cost at output M_4T_4; the slope of the exchange opportunity line T_4E_4 at E_4 is the marginal revenue when sales are T_4S_4. When marginal cost of output equals marginal revenue of sales we have, then, a relative optimum *combination* of production and sales, and must be on the envelope boundary, $R_3E_4T_c$.

We can illustrate the above proposition arithmetically: Suppose marginal cost of output were $2 per bushel, and the marginal revenue of sales were $2.50 per bushel. Then by increasing output by one bushel and increasing sales by one bushel we would subtract $2 and add 1 bushel to our stocks through production, and add $2.50 and subtract 1 bushel from stocks through sale; the result of these two operations would be an increase of 50 cents in money holdings, and no change in wheat holding, which is clearly a move to a superior position no matter what our valuation of wheat is. Thus as long as marginal revenue from sales exceeds the marginal cost of output, the firm can improve its position by increasing output and sales equally. If the marginal cost of output exceeds the marginal revenue from sales it can similarly be shown that the firm can increase its money stock without change in its wheat stock by diminishing both sales and output equally. Only if the marginal cost of output equals the marginal revenue from sales is it impossible for the firm to improve its position by changing both output and sales equally.

In general, however, the condition that the marginal cost of output should equal the marginal revenue from sales is a necessary but not a sufficient condition for an optimum; it defines *any* point on the envelope boundary $R_3 E_4 T_c$. To define *which* point on the boundary is the optimum we must assume something further about asset preferences. Thus if we assume that sales equal output, as in the model above, this immediately assumes no change in wheat stock as a result of the production-sale cycle, which defines the optimum at R_3 in Fig. 79B. We can, however, generalize this second condition to include various levels of asset preference or valuation of product. Thus suppose the firm has a subjective variation of wheat equal to the slope of $E_4 E'_4$; then OE'_4 is the highest subjective net worth it can achieve, and E_4 is the optimum position at the end of the first cycle, where $E'_4 E_4$ touches the envelope boundary at E_4. Or we could define an asset preference by the slope of a line from the origin, such as OE_4; where such a line cuts the envelope boundary (E_4) would be the optimum position.

OTHER LIMITS ON THE FIRM

The Manufacturing Firm Without Limits

Up to this point we have assumed that the only factor limiting the operation of the manufacturing firm has been "imperfection" in some sense—either imperfection of the selling market, of the buying market, or of the production opportunity or total cost curve. If all markets were perfect and if the firm never ran into increasing cost, there would be no limit to the extent of its operations, either in marketing or in production—it would always pay to increase output. We see this clearly in Fig. 81A, which shows a firm with a perfect market for output and constant marginal cost. OR is the total revenue curve, TC the total cost

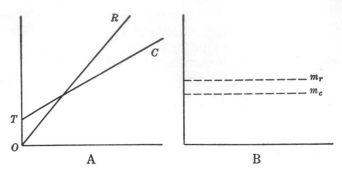

Fig. 81. The Firm Without Limits

curve—and it is clear that there is no maximum position of net revenue, which increases indefinitely with increase in output. The marginal cost curve, m_c, and the marginal revenue curve, m_r, are shown in Fig. 81B; these are parallel, and never meet. It is clear that if there is to be a maximum position of net revenue, then either the marginal revenue curve must turn down—i.e., there must be imperfection in the selling market—or the marginal cost curve must turn up—there must be "increasing cost."

Uncertainty as a Limit

As we saw in the case of the trading firm (page 366), even in the absence of market imperfection, the uncertainty of the future might limit the operations of a firm. The same principle clearly applies to the manufacturing firm. Even if its markets are perfect, the future market price is still uncertain. This uncertainty is particularly important in decisions regarding capacity. Thus in Fig. 78B, page 385, if expectations of price are high and certain, the firm may go to position C_5, with a high profit; if, however, things turn out not so well and the price is low, say, equal to the slope of C_2R_2, if the firm builds a high capacity plant at C_5 it will make a substantial loss (P_0R_5). If it goes to a high capacity by incurring large debts, such losses might make the original owners lose control to the bondholders, which would be most unacceptable. Uncertainty, therefore, by again bringing in the fear of the worst rather than the hope of the best as the main limiting factor, tends to restrict capacity and lower the scale of the firm; a reduction of price uncertainty may lead to larger capacity, even without a rise in the average realized price.

Asset Preferences as Limits

The existence of both uncertainty and imperfection leads to constraints on the position of a firm due to certain *asset preferences*—i.e., there will be certain proportions of various kinds of assets in its total position which the firm will not care to violate. These preferences may be boundaries—i.e., the firm will not mind certain proportions being in excess, say, of some boundary figure but will get seriously disturbed if the proportions fall below the boundary. A good example of such a preference boundary is the reserve ratio of a bank. As we shall see, banks are most unwilling to allow the ratio of reserves to deposits to fall below a certain minimum. Indeed, there is usually a legal limit to this ratio. All firms, however, keep an eye on various aspects of their asset *structure*, especially their liquidity position, in view of the uncertainties of the future. Some assets depend for their value on a narrow range of future circumstances; if things turn out only slightly worse than expected, they may lose all or the greater part of their value. These we will call *specific* assets. Other assets will retain their value even though the future turns out very differently from what is hoped—these are *flexible* assets. Generally speaking, fixed assets—buildings and machinery—tend to be more specific, and raw materials and money are flexible, though there may be exceptions to this rule. An increase in uncertainty itself will tend to shift asset preferences toward flexible and away from specific assets, simply because with flexible assets there is less chance of disaster if things go wrong and there is a better chance of being able to take advantage of presently unforeseen opportunities. In particular the demand for liquid assets (e.g., bank deposits and government bonds) is strongly influenced by the prevailing state of uncertainty—the less certain the future, the greater the demand for liquid assets, which are, as it were, a sort of insurance against the unforeseeable.

The flexibility or specificity of assets is strongly affected, as far as the individual firm is concerned, by the nature of the market for them. Generally speaking, assets which have perfect markets are more flexible than those which have imperfect markets. With perfect markets, even if price changes unfavorably, there is no difficulty in changing the proportions of the assets in the total structure, because they can be exchanged in indefinitely large amounts without difficulty or loss due to the mere amount exchanged. Assets that have sharply imperfect markets, however, are likely to be specific to the firm, for they cannot be transferred into other assets in large quantities without loss. Because of this a firm with imperfect markets may stop short of the point of profit maximization under favorable expectations, because of the danger of getting "stuck" with unsalable assets if markets take a turn for the worse. Even with perfect markets, of course, the fear of a fall in the price of existing assets may make firms keep their asset structure more liquid than profit maximization requires.

Learning in the Dynamics of the Firm

The behavior of a firm in the present depends largely on its image of the world, that is, the beliefs of its decision makers regarding the nature and environment of the organization—its markets, its opportunities, and the uncertainties associated with them. These images are *learned* as a result of past experience—partly through the memory of uncontrolled events, partly through a process of deliberate search for information and testing of images for reality. This is an aspect of economic behavior which is hard to bring into the analytical framework of economics; it is essential, however, to any dynamic theory, and we must be particularly wary of policy conclusions based on the assumption of accurate or costless information. The information problem, by which we mean how a firm's decision makers acquire "true" images of their opportunities and "wise" rules of choice, grows in importance as we move from perfect to imperfect markets or cost functions. A constant can be known by a single observation; thus a firm with a perfect market can find out the whole nature of its present market opportunity by simply observing the constant price at which transactions are being carried on in the market. A linear function can be known fully from two observations; given two points on a straight line we can immediately deduce all the others. This is one reason why the reduction of problems to linear functions, as in linear programming, open up possibilities of finding useful solutions. The higher the degree of a function the more information is needed to define it. Hence it is often difficult for firms to know the magnitudes of their marginal costs or revenues, and difficult for them to know whether their operations are in fact at an optimum point. It is not surprising therefore that in such cases we get a great many rules of thumb which represent satisficing—getting along with adequate if not maximum success because the cost of maximizing—or of getting the information necessary for maximization—is too high. These considerations, however, would soon carry us beyond the relatively elementary analysis of this volume.

QUESTIONS AND EXERCISES

1. A diagram such as Fig. 81A is often used in business under the name of a break-even chart; the point Q where total cost equals total revenue is called the break-even point. Explain carefully the assumptions which underlie such charts, and discuss critically their usefulness in the making of business decisions.

2. Suppose a firm has the choice of two processes: (a) with a fixed cost of $5000 and constant variable cost per unit of product thereafter of 50 cents per unit, and (b) with a fixed cost of $10,000 and a constant variable cost of 25 cents per unit. Draw the break-even curves for both processes on the same figure, with a perfect market for the product at prices of $1, 90 cents, 80 cents, down to 10 cents. What factors might affect the decision to select one process rather than the other?

3. A group of students wish to put out a newspaper. The data in front of them are as follows:

   a. There are three alternative methods of production:

      i. The university will duplicate any number of copies for 10 cents per copy.
      ii. A printing firm will charge them $50 for setting up type, and 5 cents per copy printed.
      iii. They can buy a duplicating machine for $120, and produce the paper themselves, with free labor, with materials costing 1 cent per copy.

   b. They reckon that if they charge 10 cents per copy they will sell 1800 copies, and that for every 1 cent addition to this price they will lose 200 copies in sales, and for every 1 cent subtraction from this price they will gain 200 copies in sales.

   c. Suppose, furthermore, that the university charges them a flat activities fee of $30 for permission to produce the paper. Then, using graph paper:

      i. Draw on one sheet the three total cost curves corresponding to the three methods of production listed in a, including the activities fee.
      ii. Indicate by letters the curve which shows the least total cost for each output.
      iii. Calculate and draw the total revenue curve.
      iv. Calculate, and draw on another graph, the average and marginal cost and revenue curves corresponding to curves ii and iii above.
      v. Label the points of intersection of the marginal cost and marginal revenue curves, and comment on the significance of each.
      vi. Then, for the three different assumptions listed below, calculate the following for the level of operations which fulfil the relevant assumption: (a) the total profit (net revenue); (b) the price charged per copy; (c) the quantity sold; (d) the average cost; (e) the profit per paper; (f) the production method used (i, ii, or iii in a).

      The three assumptions are as follows: (a) The students are in business for profit, and maximize net revenue. (b) The students are motivated by a desire to spread their ideas, and therefore wish to sell the maximum number of papers at which they will incur no losses. (c) The students have been pushed into getting out a paper, somewhat against their will, and want to do it with the least trouble to themselves, so want to operate at the smallest output consistent with breaking even (no gain or loss).

      vii. What is the largest activities fee which the university can charge and still allow the students to produce the paper without loss? What then will be (a) the price, (b) the quantity sold, (c) the method of production?

4. Suppose the following schedule represented the average variable cost schedule of an automobile, over a period of six months:

Miles Run	Average Variable Cost (cents per mile)
1,000	3.0
2,000	3.0
3,000	3.0
4,000	3.0
5,000	3.02
6,000	3.05
7,000	3.10
8,000	3.175
9,000	3.278
10,000	3.410
11,000	3.573
12,000	3.775
13,000	4.023

Suppose that the total fixed cost in this period amounted to $100.

Calculate, for each thousand miles from 0 to 13,000 (arranging the results in tabular form): (a) the total variable cost; (b) the total cost; (c) the average fixed cost; (d) the average total cost; (e) the marginal cost.

On one graph (A) draw the total cost curve and the total variable cost curve. On another graph (B) draw the average total cost curve, the average variable cost curve, the marginal cost curve, and the average fixed cost curve.

From the graph find the point of minimum average total cost and determine how many miles should be run in order to operate the car at the minimum average total cost. Show that at this point the average total cost and the marginal cost are equal.

5. In the above example, suppose that a benevolent uncle offered to pay the owner of the car 5 cents for every mile driven. Calculate the total revenue and the net revenue accruing to the owner of the car under these circumstances, for each thousand miles from 0 to 13,000. On graph A draw the total revenue curve and also the net revenue curve, showing the net revenue at each number of miles. How many miles will the owner of the car have to run in order to get the greatest net revenue? Show, on graph B, that at this number of miles the marginal cost is 5 cents per mile.

6. Using the cost figures in Table 37, page 381, calculate the most profitable (or least unprofitable) output when the price is $1.20, $1.40, $1.60, $1.80, $2.00. (Use graphs.) What do you deduce from these results about the effect of the price of a product on its output?

7. The following table shows five different total cost schedules.
In each case calculate the following schedules: (a) total variable cost; (b) average total cost; (c) average variable cost; (d) marginal cost. On separate figures for each case draw the curves corresponding to these schedules.

Output (tons)	(1)	Total Cost (dollars) (2)	(3)	(4)	(5)
0	1000	1000	1000	1000	1000
10	1100	1024	1221	1050	1050
20	1157	1061	1335	1100	1100
30	1180	1120	1410	1150	1150
40	1200	1190	1464	1200	1200
50	1226	1287	1509	1250	1250
60	1264	1388	1538	1300	1300
70	1315	1512	1555	1350	1350
80	1385	1670	1570	1400	Inf.
90	1480	1870	1583	1450	Inf.
100	1700	2160	1595	1500	Inf.

Show that in each case the average-marginal relationship is sustained. Show that in cases where there is a minimum value for either average total or average variable cost, the marginal cost is equal to the average cost at its minimum value. Is this true also in case 5? Suppose now that in cases 1, 2, and 3 the total cost went to infinity at an output of 80 tons. What does this do to the various curves? What would be the *meaning* of such an assumption and how realistic do you think it might be?

8. The following table shows six marginal revenue schedules:

Sales	(1)	(2)	Marginal Revenue (3)	(4)	(5)	(6)
0	100	100	100	100	100	100
1	100	90	80	90	99	90
2	100	80	60	81	97	82
3	100	70	40	73	94	76
4	100	60	20	66	90	72
5	100	50	0	60	85	70
6	100	40	−20	55	79	70
7	100	30	−40	51	72	72
8	100	20	−60	48	64	75
9	100	10	−80	46	55	76
10	100	0	−100	45	45	76

a. Calculate the corresponding total revenue schedules and the average revenue schedules in each case.

b. Plot on squared paper the total, average, and marginal revenue curves in each case.

CHAPTER 19

THE DERIVATION OF SUPPLY
CURVES FROM COST CURVES

Our first important application of the theory of the firm will be to show certain possible relationships between the cost curves of firms with perfect markets and the supply curves of competitive industries.[1]

In deriving a supply curve for a product we have to explain two things: First, how and why does the output of a single enterprise change in response to changes in the price of its product? Second, how does the *number* of enterprises change as the price of their product changes?

The Supply Curve of an Individual Enterprise

The analysis of marginal cost in the preceding chapter will almost immediately give the answer to the first question. It was there shown that the most profitable output of an enterprise with a perfect market for output is that at which the price of the product is equal to its marginal cost. Assuming, then, that an enterprise tends to produce the most profitable quantity of output, we know that high prices will permit the output to expand to a point where the marginal cost has risen to the high price, and that low prices will force the output to contract until the marginal cost has fallen to the low price, and if low enough will force the firm to suspend operations altogether. Thus the marginal cost schedule, or curve, itself shows immediately what will be the most profitable or least unprofitable output at which to produce, for a series of hypothetical prices.

Suppose we have in Fig. 82 a marginal cost curve, *MC*, and an average total cost curve, *ATC*, of an enterprise with a perfect market for its product. Suppose the price of the product is *OL*; the marginal revenue

---

[1] The supply curve is the relation between the price of a product and the amount that will be voluntarily produced at each price. See Chapters 10–12.

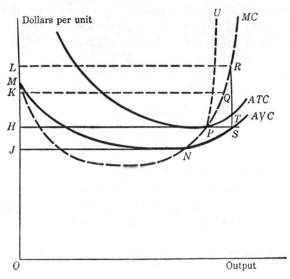

Fig. 82.   The Supply of Product from a Firm

curve and the average revenue curve will coincide, and will be *LR. R* is
the point of maximum net revenue (see page 392), where marginal cost
equals marginal revenue equals price. *LR* then is the optimum output.
At a lower price, *OK, KQ* is the optimum output—smaller than *LR,* if
the marginal cost curve is positively sloped. Similarly, at the price *OH,*
HP is the optimum output. At this price, however, where *HP* touches
the average total cost curve, the price is equal to average total cost at the
optimum output, and net revenue is zero. This means, as we have seen
earlier, that the firm is just normally profitable. At a price below *OH,*
say *OJ, JN* is the most profitable output, but even at the most profitable
output net revenue is negative and the enterprise is making less profits
than are necessary to keep it alive. Obviously, then, at prices less than
OH the enterprise, in the long run, will produce nothing. At the price
OH it will produce *HP,* and at higher prices it will produce more, following the marginal cost curve *PR.* The supply curve of product from the
enterprise, then—i.e., the relation between the price of the product and
the amount which the enterprise will produce—on the assumption of
maximization of net revenue, is *OHPR.* The price at which a certain
quantity will be supplied is called the *supply price* of that quantity. The
supply curve relates supply price to quantity supplied; it must not be
confused with the *sales curve* which relates price to the amount that
can be sold. The supply curve concept is strictly valid only on the assumption of perfect markets for output.

In the short run—by which we mean any period for which the firm has a fixed cost—the firm will continue operation even if the price is below the minimum average total cost, provided that the price is not below the minimum average variable cost. Thus if *AVC* is the average variable cost curve, with a minimum at *N*, then at prices between *OJ* and *OH*, even though the firm is not making enough to keep it in business indefinitely, it will lose less by operating than by shutting down. The short-run supply curve then is *OJNR*.

THE SUPPLY SCHEDULE FOR AN INDUSTRY

If the supply schedules of all the firms, actual or potential, associated with the production of a given commodity are known, the supply schedule for the commodity as a whole can be deduced by simple addition. Table 39 gives the supply schedules of four firms which comprise an industry.

TABLE 39. DERIVATION OF TOTAL SUPPLY SCHEDULE

Supply price (dollars per ton):	0	2	4	6	8	10	12	14	16	18
Output (tons)										
Firm A	0	0	25	43	55	63	70	75	80	85
Firm B	0	0	0	30	50	65	75	83	87	90
Firm C	0	0	0	0	0	40	60	75	85	90
Firm D	0	0	0	0	0	0	50	65	75	82
Total	0	0	25	73	105	168	255	298	327	347

Firm A is a low-cost firm. Its minimum average cost is $4 per unit of output, attained when it has an output of 25 units. Consequently it will produce nothing at a price lower than $4, but it will come into the industry as soon as the price rises to that level and will start producing 25 units of output. When the price rises to $6 per unit, firm B, which is the second most favorably situated in respect to its costs, will enter the industry. Firm B starts with an output of 30 units, at which its average cost is at a minimum of $6. At a price of $6, then, the schedule shows that firm A produces 43 units, this being the output at which its marginal cost is equal to $6, and firm B produces 30 units, 73 units in all. Similarly, at a price of $10 per unit, firm C enters the industry, making the total output 168 units; at a price of $12 per unit firm D enters the industry, making the total output 255 units, and so on. It is evident that as the supply price rises, the output of the industry increases for two reasons: (1) the output of each existing firm increases, and (2) new firms enter the industry.

What Determines the Elasticity of Supply?

The schedule showing the relationship between the price and the total output of an industry is what we have previously called the *supply schedule.* The question now arises, What determines the elasticity of this schedule? What determines the response of output to a change in price? The answer is that the supply will be more elastic if (1) a given increase in the output of the single firms produces only a small increase in the marginal cost of production in the firm, and (2) a given increase in the price makes it profitable for a large number of new firms to enter the industry. If it is easy for the individual firm to expand its output, as reflected in the fact that this can be accomplished without much increase in the marginal cost, and if it is easy for new firms to enter the industry, then the supply will be elastic, for a given increase in price will result in a large increase in output. If, on the other hand, it is difficult for the individual firm to expand its output, as reflected in the fact that it cannot expand without suffering a considerable increase in the marginal cost, and if it is difficult for new firms to enter the industry, then the supply will be more inelastic.

Perfectly Elastic and Perfectly Inelastic Supply

The supply will be perfectly elastic over a range of output if either the existing firms can expand output without any rise in the marginal cost or there are a number of firms whose minimum average cost is equal to the price of the product, so that a small rise in that price will bring these firms into the industry and a small fall will drive them out. The supply will be perfectly inelastic if the existing firms are producing at their absolute maximum capacity, so that an increase in output will result in an infinite increase in the marginal cost, and if no new firms can come into the industry.

The Equilibrium of an Industry

We can now formulate the general condition for the equilibrium of an industry. An industry is said to be in equilibrium when there is no tendency for it to expand or to contract. It will be in equilibrium, therefore, if the least profitable firm in it (commonly called the marginal firm) is normally profitable. If the profits of the least profitable firm are less than normal, this firm and others in like case will eventually leave the industry. Their departure will lessen the total output, which will raise the price of that output, making the remaining firms more profitable. Firms will continue to leave the industry until the least profitable firm is normally profitable. In this condition the least profitable firm would gain no advantage in moving out of the industry, and the industry therefore will cease to decline. If, on the other hand, the least profitable firm is making profits above normal, this probably means that a new firm coming into the industry would also be able to make profits above normal. Consequently, there will be a tendency for new firms to come in,

and the industry will expand. As it expands, its total output will rise
and the price of its product will fall, making the profits of existing
firms less, and lessening the temptation for new firms to come in. When
the profits of the least profitable firm are normal again, the industry will
cease to expand, for any new firm coming into it will probably make
less than normal profits.

Graphic Derivation of the Normal Supply Curve

Just as we have derived the normal supply schedule of an industry
from the cost schedules of its component firms, so we can derive the
normal supply curve from the cost curves of the component firms.

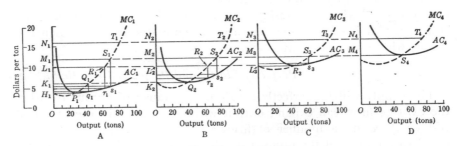

Fig. 83.　The Cost Ladder

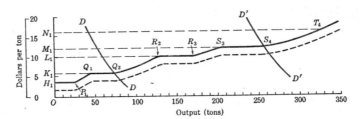

Fig. 84.　The Derived Supply Curve

Fig. 83 shows the average cost curves (AC) and the marginal cost
curves (MC) for four single-product firms comprising an industry. Firm
A has the lowest minimum average cost, firm D, the greatest. The exposition is confined to four firms for the sake of convenience; in fact, of
course, a perfectly competitive industry would have a large number.
From the cost curves we can derive the normal supply curve for the
product of the industry, as follows: When the price of the product is
less than OH_1, nothing will be produced. At a price equal to OH_1,
firm A will find it profitable to enter the industry, and will produce at
an output measured by H_1P_1 (Fig. 83A). As the price rises from OH_1 to
OK_1, the output of firm A rises from H_1P_1 to K_1Q_1, following its marginal cost curve. Transcribing this movement to Fig. 84 (the supply

curve) we see that the quantity supplied rises from nothing to K_1Q_1 as the price rises from O to OK_1, following the curve $OH_1P_1Q_1$. At the price OK_1, firm B will enter the industry, for OK_1 is equal to its minimum average cost. It produces at this price an amount K_2Q_2. The total quantity supplied by the industry at this price is therefore $K_1Q_1 + K_2Q_2$, or K_1Q_2 in Fig. 84. As the price rises from OK_1 to OL_1, the output of both firms increases, following their marginal cost curves, till at the price OL_1 their combined output is $L_1R_1 + L_2R_2 (= L_1R_2$ in Fig. 84). At this price, firm C comes into the industry, and the total output increases by an amount L_3R_3 to L_1R_3 in Fig. 84. At a price OM_1 the fourth firm enters the industry. The supply curve for the industry, therefore, is the curve $OH_1P_1Q_1Q_2R_2R_3S_3S_4T_4$, etc., of Fig. 84.

The Elasticity of Supply

It will readily be seen from the figures that the elasticity of the supply curve depends on the two aforementioned factors. The first is the slope of the marginal cost curves, for the steeper the marginal cost curves are, the steeper the supply curve will be. The second is the difference between the minimum average cost of successive firms on the cost scale. Thus, a rise in price of $4 per ton is necessary, after firm B has been brought in, to bring in firm C. The supply in this range is more inelastic than in the next price range, where a rise of only $2 per ton in price is sufficient to bring in firm D. If we think of the succession of firms from A to D as a ladder of costs, then the steeper the ladder, the more inelastic the supply.

These conclusions tally well with the concept of elasticity of supply as it was used in Part I. We see now clearly that the elasticity of supply is a measure of the *ease* with which an industry may be expanded. A steeply rising marginal cost curve is a sign that an enterprise is running into increasing difficulties as it tries to expand its output. A steeply rising *cost ladder* means that it is difficult for new firms to enter the industry. If, therefore, it is difficult for an industry to expand its output, the supply will be inelastic; if it is easy, the supply will be elastic. If the cost ladder is horizontal, or nearly so—i.e., if the cost curves of all the firms lie at about the same level—there will be perfect elasticity of supply.

LONG-RUN AND SHORT-RUN SUPPLY

The Period of Adjustment

We have already noticed that our definition of cost, and therefore of supply, must always have reference to a specific length of time. This is necessary because adjustments take time; consequently, the shorter the period of time under consideration the less adjustment can be made. In any situation there is a period so short that no adjustments can be made to changing circumstances; this we may call the *instantaneous* period, though it may cover a finite period of clock time. At the opposite extreme there is what is called the *long period;* this again is no very definite number of days or years, but is a period long enough to permit all adjustments to be completed. In between these two periods are an indefinite number of *short periods* representing various temporary adjustments which are not in themselves complete. Suppose, for example, that a man is proceeding along a road at a steady pace when suddenly the road is blocked by a landslide ahead. For a brief moment the change in circumstances produces no change in the man's behavior; he continues walking along the road at the old pace; this is the instantaneous period. Following that come various short-run adjustments to the new situation. He may stop altogether and take stock of the situation, he may scramble over the obstacle at a reduced pace, he may turn back to find another road, and so on. If the road is a well-traveled one, however, there will be an ultimate, long-run adjustment to the landslide: the obstacle will be cleared away, or the road will be rebuilt over it with perhaps a heavier gradient than before.

Instantaneous and Long-Run Adjustments

Similarly, in the problem of supply we can distinguish three broad periods of adjustment, with three different types of cost and supply curves. At one extreme there is the instantaneous period, so short that no adjustments can be made. Cost curves in this period are vertical, and supply curves perfectly inelastic. A change in demand or a change in price produce no change in output; the wheels of production grind on from force of habit in exactly the old fashion. At the other extreme there is the long run, the period long enough to allow all adjustments to be made; long enough, for instance, to allow for the liquidation of plant and equipment and their replacement by other forms. The long-run supply curve is likely to be the most elastic of all the supply curves, for it represents the maximum possible adjustment of output to price or demand. The long-run supply curve also has the property of being *reversible*. That is to say, if the conditions of long-run cost are unaltered, the same supply curve shows the reactions of output either to a rise or to a fall in price. Thus, if H_1T_4 in Fig. 84 is a long-run supply curve, it will show with equal accuracy the effect either of a rise in demand from DD to $D'D'$, or of a fall in demand from $D'D'$ to DD. If cost curves are unchanged and an industry is in equilibrium, a rise in demand followed by a fall in demand to its original position will eventually return the industry to its initial equilibrium.

The Short Run and the Concept of Capacity

Between the instantaneous no adjustment and the long-run full adjustment there lies the indefinite morass of the *short period*. Short-period supply curves present many difficulties, mainly because the analytical apparatus so far constructed is not fitted to deal with the kind of dynamic problems that characterize temporary adjustments. Much of the analysis up to this point has been essentially static in character, and hence is best suited to the solution of those problems of long-run equilibrium where the adjustment is not a function of time but is complete, and therefore independent of particular time periods. Care must be taken, therefore, not to load too much on an inadequate analytical apparatus in the interpretation of short-run adjustments.

When economists talk about *the* short run they usually mean a period of time too short to make changes in the quantity of plant and equipment —i.e., in the *capacity* of an industry—but long enough to make changes in the degree of utilization of that capacity. In point of fact, of course, adjustments in capacity and in the utilization of existing capacity are likely to proceed simultaneously, so that it is impossible to take any definite period—say, a year—and call it the short period. The actual adjustments made in a short period of time—e.g., to changes in demand— depend very much on the expectations of the future. Thus the adjustment which may be made to a change in demand or in price expected to be temporary might be very different from that made to a supposedly permanent change.

Fixed Cost in the Short Run. The best practical definition of the short run is that period in which decisions are made in the light of the existence of some fixed cost, and in which, therefore, average variable cost is the lower limit of price below which the plant will be shut down. The longer the period of time we take into account, the less fixed costs become, and in the long run fixed costs are zero and total and variable costs are equal. In the instantaneous period *all* costs are fixed and marginal cost is zero. What is institutionally defined as fixed cost therefore has an important bearing on the chronological length of these various economic reaction periods. Thus in Japan the labor force is regarded as more a semipermanent part of the firm that it is in the United States, so that the wages bill is a fixed cost for a longer period of clock time than it is in the United States. In the United States wages may be regarded as a fixed cost only for a week; hence when demand slacks off American businesses lay off their workers, treating wages as a variable cost. In Japan there is much more reluctance to dismiss workers, hence firms are likely to keep operating (wages being treated for a considerable period as a fixed cost which must be paid whether output is produced or not) for a considerable period in the face of adverse market conditions or low prices. This may account in part for the remarkable mildness of depressions in Japan.

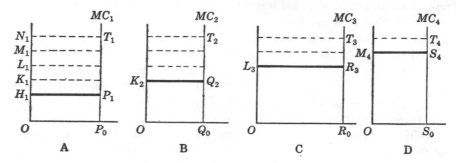

Fig. 85.   The Instantaneous and Short-Run Cost Ladder

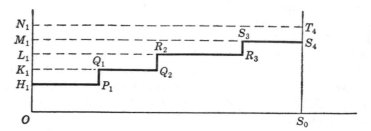

Fig. 86.   Derivation of Instantaneous and Short-Run Supply

Short-run supply curves are illustrated in Figs. 85 and 86. The instantaneous period (which may be, as we have seen, an appreciable period of clock time in cases where long-term obligations for the purchase of input are the rule) is shown by the marginal cost curves OP_0T_1, OQ_0T_2 OR_0T_3, OS_0S_4 of Fig. 85, constructed like Fig. 83. The supply curve which is derived from these cost curves, where marginal cost is zero up to capacity output and then springs upwards indefinitely, is the perfectly inelastic supply curve S_0T_4, constructed as in Fig. 84, where OS_0 in Fig. 86 = $OP_0 + OQ_0 + OR_0 + OS_0$ in Fig. 85. In the short period, as we have seen in the previous chapter, cost curves are likely to approximate to $H_1P_1T_1$, $K_2Q_2T_2$, $L_3R_3T_3$, and $M_4S_4T_4$ for successive higher cost firms, with marginal cost positive but constant up to capacity; in this case marginal and average variable cost curves are identical. The derived supply curve is $H_1P_1Q_1Q_2R_2R_3S_3S_4T_4$ in Fig. 86. If there are a larger number of firms, the section from H_1 to S_4 may be fairly smooth, and with positive elasticity. At S_4 where the capacity of all existing firms is reached the supply curve becomes perfectly inelastic.

Supply curves for different reaction periods are brought together in Fig. 87. ST is the instantaneous supply curve, where OS is the output

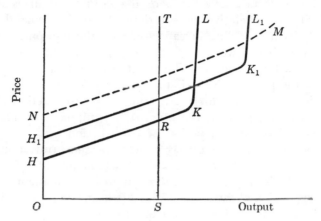

Fig. 87. **Supply Curves of Different Periods**

of firms actually operating. HKL is the short-run supply, where some variable costs are taken into consideration; if price falls below SR some firms drop out as price falls below their minimum variable cost; all firms have dropped out by the price OH. On the other hand at prices above SR there may be firms which have temporarily gone out of production but which have some capacity and come into operation, so that the short-run supply curve runs from R to K. At K, however, we suppose the capacity of all existing plant is reached, and supply becomes very inelastic. There may be some slight elasticity in practice due to overtime work, and so on, but there will be a distinct kink in the supply curve at K. If we take a longer period of adjustment the variable and marginal costs are higher, but the capacity of the industry is greater; a longer short-period supply curve will be something like $H_1K_1L_1$. In the true long run the kink disappears altogether, capacity becomes infinite, and the long-run supply curve will be like NM. We get, therefore, a gradual transition from ST to NM as we increase the period of adjustment.

Asymmetry of Response to Rise or Fall in Demand

As we have seen, firms will continue producing once they have a certain capacity established, even if the price of their product falls below the minimum average total cost, provided that the price exceeds the minimum average *variable* cost. They will not *expand* their capacity, however, unless the expected price is at least equal to the average *total* cost of the product of the expanded capacity. Because of this there is a certain asymmetry between the response to a rise or to a fall in demand in a given time period. A rise in demand which is thought to be permanent may attract new firms, or may cause old firms to expand their capacity, in a relatively short time. A fall in demand, however, will not result in a decline in capacity until the equipment on which the capacity is based wears out; the equipment will continue to be employed for a long time even though its full costs are not covered by the price of the product. That is to say, the short run may be a much longer period of time when the adjustment is a contraction than when it is an expansion, particularly where the equipment or fixed capital is long-lived relative to its period of construction.

One important result of the asymmetry of short-run supply is that industries with highly fluctuating demands tend to suffer from chronic overcapacity. A rise in demand is thought to be permanent, and results in a rapid expansion of capacity; a subsequent unexpected fall in demand does not lead to a rapid reduction of capacity, but results rather in a long period of unprofitable production, if the firms in the industry have perfect markets, or perhaps in much idle capacity if the industry is monopolistic.

The chronic overcapacity of the construction industries (e.g., steel, housing, etc.) is responsible for a good many of the woes of capitalist society and may, at least in part, be attributed to the above phenomenon. Such an industry is like a beetle trap—easier to get into than out of. There is little wonder that it tends to become overcrowded.

ECONOMIC RENT

Economic rent is defined as any payment to a supplier in excess of the minimum sum necessary to keep him supplying. It comes into being whenever a supply curve is less than perfectly elastic, and markets are homogeneous and competitive, for then the price which is just sufficient to call forth the "last" unit of a product from the least willing supplier of a given quantity is more than sufficient to compensate the more willing suppliers, who would still be willing to supply at lower prices. See Part I, Chapter 13, pages 265–267.

Net Revenue as Economic Rent

Now, when an industry has a number of firms some of which have high costs and others low costs, it is evident that if the price is high enough to keep the high-cost firms in the industry, it will be greater than is necessary to keep the low-cost firms in the industry. The low-cost firms, then, are apparently receiving more than is strictly necessary to keep them operating; they are the recipients of economic rent. The net revenue of such a favored firm is the measure of this economic rent or surplus, for when the net revenue is zero a firm is just normally profitable, and if the net revenue is positive the firm is receiving more than is necessary to keep it alive. Fig. 83, page 406, will serve also to illustrate this concept. When the price of the product is as low as OH_1, even the first firm has a zero net revenue. If the price rises to OK_1, the net revenue, or economic rent, in firm A rises to the area $K_1Q_1 \times Q_1q_1$. If the price rises to OL_1, the economic rent in firm A is the area of the rectangle $L_1R_1 \times R_1r_1$, the economic rent in firm B is the rectangle $L_2R_2 \times R_2r_2$, and there is no economic rent in firm C. If the price rises to OM_1 the economic rent in firm A is $M_1S_1 \times S_1s_1$, in firm B is $M_2S_2 \times S_2s_2$, in firm C is $M_3S_3 \times S_3s_3$, and in firm D is nothing. An increase in demand, therefore, where the supply is not perfectly elastic, will increase the economic rents in all the firms. If, for instance, the demand in Fig. 84 were the curve DD, only two firms would be in the industry, the price would be OK_1, and only the first firm would enjoy an economic rent. If the demand rose to the position $D'D'$, the price would have to rise to OM_1 to overcome the barrier of increasing cost, four firms would be in the industry, and the first three firms would be receiving economic rent. In a perfectly competitive industry there will of necessity be a large number of firms—we merely use four firms as a convenient expository device.

No Economic Rent with a Perfectly Elastic Supply

If all the cost curves of all firms in an industry are identical, the supply curve will be perfectly elastic. Such an industry would be described as an industry of *constant cost*. It should be noticed that to have an *industry* of constant cost it is not necessary for the individual enterprise to have constant costs. It is possible for the average cost and the marginal cost of each enterprise to vary with its output, and still the industry as a whole may have constant cost and a perfectly elastic supply curve. If in Fig. 83 the minimum average cost of all the firms were on the same level, the industry would be a constant-cost industry even though for each firm a rise in price would lead to a rise in cost. In this case an increase in demand would result in the addition of new enterprises to the industry, but not in any increase in price, and not, therefore, in any increase in cost. In such an industry there are clearly no economic rents. The price of the product will be determined

by the minimum average total cost of each firm. Each firm will then
be normally profitable when the industry is in equilibrium, no matter
how great the demand or how great the output of the industry. There
will be no *net revenues* except in periods of transition when the industry
is moving from one point of equilibrium to another.

Who Gets Economic Rent?

In the discussion of the present chapter we have assumed implicitly
that the net revenue accrues to the owner of the business. In fact,
one or more of the factors of production employed by the business may
receive part or all of the economic rent resulting from the favorable
position of a business. We shall return to this topic in the next chapter,
when we have discussed more fully the nature of the production function.

THE EFFECT OF A CHANGE IN COST CURVES

With the analytical tools now at our disposal we can go to work on the
proposition that a fall in the average cost of production of individual
enterprises *at each output* will result in an increase in supply, i.e., in a
movement of the supply curve of the industry to the right.

Change in Cost and in the Cost Curve

In the case of demand there is a vital distinction between a *change
in demand* and a *change in the quantity demanded*. A change in demand
means a shift of the whole demand curve, a change in the quantity
demanded at each hypothetical price. A change in the quantity
demanded means a change in the quantity demanded *as a result of* a
change in price, the demand curve itself remaining unchanged. Similarly
in the case of cost curves, a shift in the whole cost curve of an enterprise
must be distinguished from a change in cost which is due to a change in
output. In the first case there is a new cost of production at each
hypothetical output. In the second case the cost curve is unchanged,
but the cost changes because of a movement along the curve. The first
we shall call a *change in the cost curve* to distinguish it from a mere
change in cost.

Fall in Cost Curves Equivalent to an Increase in Supply

We shall show in the next chapter that an improvement in the
techniques of production will lower the average total cost at each
hypothetical output, i.e., will lower the average total cost curve. An
improvement in techniques will also probably lower the marginal
cost at each output, although this result is not absolutely necessary.

In any case, however, a study of Figs. 83 and 84 (p. 406), will show that an improvement in techniques, a fall in the price of inputs or anything resulting in a lowering of the cost curves will cause a movement of the supply curve to the right, and therefore, probably, a fall in price and a rise in the industry's output. Suppose that for some reason every cost figure in Fig. 83 fell by $2 per ton. That is, every cost curve, both marginal and average, moved $2 per ton downward toward the output axis. Then the supply curve, Fig. 84, would also move downward by $2 per ton to the position marked by the dotted line. A fall in the cost curves, therefore, results in a fall in the *supply price* of each quantity of output. If cost curves fall, that is to say, the industry will be prepared to supply any *given* quantity of output at a smaller price than before. This means also that at any *given* price the industry will be prepared to supply a *larger* quantity than before. A fall in the supply price at each output is equivalent to what we have called an *increase in supply,* i.e., a rise in the quantity which will be supplied at each price. In terms of geometry, a movement of the supply curve downward toward the output axis is the same thing as a movement to the right away from the price axis. It is this movement to the right which we call a rise in supply.

The Paradox of Decreasing Supply Price

With the apparatus of this chapter we can see more clearly the nature of the problem of apparently decreasing supply price (see Part I, Chapter 14). In Chapter 18 we saw that with *given* conditions of technological opportunity, as in Fig. 78, the total cost curve of a firm even in the long run could not possibly exhibit significant *concavity*— that is, the marginal cost must either be constant or increase with increasing output. This means, as we have seen in the present chapter, that the supply curve from an individual firm cannot exhibit negative elasticity; it may be perfectly elastic, but after a point it is almost certain to exhibit positive elasticity and slope upwards. Similarly the whole *cost ladder* approach of Figs. 83 and 84 rules out any possibility of a negatively elastic (downward sloping) supply curve for a competitive industry. At higher prices there must be either the same number of firms, or more firms in an industry than before, with the same or larger total output. Under no circumstances can a higher price go along with a smaller number of firms or lower output. Nevertheless we do seem to have circumstances in which a rise in demand leads to a fall in price, which would seem to imply a supply curve of negative elasticity. The resolution of this dilemma has already been indicated in Chapter 14, Fig. 61 (p. 283), where we suppose that an expansion of the industry, by allowing for increasing specialization, causes the cost curves of each firm, or of most firms, to fall, thus lowering the *given-cost* supply curves. What we have here is a related rise in both demand and given-cost supply. If the rise in supply or fall in cost curves is large enough this may even lead to a rise in demand producing a fall in price, and of course a large rise in output. Thus in Fig. 61 we suppose an original equilibrium at *P* with supply and demand curves *SS* and *DD;* demand then rises to *D'D';* as a result the industry expands and cost curves fall, with a new given-cost supply curve at *S'S',* and a new equilibrium at *Q.* Whether the supply curve which is the locus of these equilibrium points, such as *LL,* can be regarded as a true long-run supply curve is a matter of some debate. It can be argued that it is impossible to separate out in practice the changes in cost curves which are due to an expansion of a particular industry, and those which are due to the expansion of the economy as a whole. It might be better, therefore, to stick to the given-cost supply curves for a description of temporary equilibrium, and to discuss the whole impact of development on cost curves as a dynamic problem when it comes to analyzing the impact of development on the price structure.

The Effects of Uncertainty

Up to this point in the chapter we have assumed that the various cost and revenue functions are certain and known, and that therefore the maximization of net revenue is a reasonable rule of economic behavior. We may now wish to inquire what modifications the presence of uncertainty introduces into the analysis. Suppose, for instance, returning to Fig. 82, page 403, that the entrepreneur hopes for a price of *OL,* but fears that the price might be only *OH.* If he follows only his most hopeful expectation he will of course produce *LR* (= *HS*). Suppose now, however, that he produces *LR* but the price in fact turns out to be *OH.* He will then incur a loss (negative net revenue) of *HS* × *ST,* whereas had he been more cautious and only produced *HP* he would at least have made normal profits. Uncertainty, then, is likely to make producers commit themselves rather less than they would at each expected price if they were quite certain of realizing the price. That is, the supply curve from the firm will be more inelastic than the marginal cost curve above the point *P*—say, *PU* rather than *PR.* From the point of view of the entry of new firms also the presence of uncertainty will make prospective new firms hestitant to commit themselves. This makes for steepness in the cost ladder, and hence also for more inelastic supply curves, especially in the short run. Thus we see that the presence of uncertainty modifies the above analysis, but does not affect its basic principle. It is noticeable that a reduction of uncertainty—e.g., by government guarantees of price in agricultural production—has a marked effect in increasing the elasticity of supply. A guaranteed low price may be more effective in calling forth output than the uncertain prospect of a high price.

SOME APPLICATIONS OF THE FOREGOING ANALYSIS

Fixing Price According to Cost of Production

We frequently hear the complaint that the price of a certain commodity is "below the cost of production" and that the government should step in and fix a *"fair"* price which will be *"equal* to the cost of production." The milk industry, and agricultural production in general, seem to be particularly subject to this complaint. Our analysis of cost will show the fallacy in most of these arguments. We have seen that there is no such thing as *the* cost of production of a commodity. There are as many costs of production as there are firms, and as many costs of production within a firm as there are different quantities of output. When, therefore, an industry demands that the price of its product be fixed so as to cover *the* cost of production of the commodity, the question at once arises, *"Whose* cost of production?" We have seen that in equilibrium the price of the product of a competitive industry is of necessity equal to the marginal cost of production in all firms and to the average total cost of production in the marginal firms. How, then, does the complaint arise that the price is "below cost"?

Low Prices a Symptom, Not a Cause

The answer seems to be that a cry for fixing prices generally arises from an industry which is larger than its equilibrium size. In such an industry there are a number of *submarginal* producers who are making less than normal profits and who therefore should leave the industry and employ their resources elsewhere. The "cost of production" which is not "covered by the price" is the average cost of these submarginal producers. If the price could be fixed to cover the cost of production of these producers, the industry would be permanently too large, would be prevented from finding its position of equilibrium, and there would be a permanent maldistribution of resources. Low prices and unprofitability in any industry are a *symptom* of a deep-seated economic complaint. To treat the complaint of maldistribution of resources by fixing prices is like treating jaundice by painting the patient pink.

In any case the fixing of prices at a level high enough to keep the submarginal producers in the industry cannot be achieved unless there is restriction of production by all, or most, producers below the level which would be most profitable to each individually. If prices are fixed above the level at which the quantity demanded and the quantity supplied are naturally equal, then unless there is control of production, the output of the industry will increase to a point where the whole output cannot be sold at the fixed price (see Chapter 11 in Part I). Then either the price-fixing scheme collapses or rigid control of production must be introduced.

The Case for Intervention

The above argument is not, however, necessarily a proof that government should keep its hands off the affairs of a competitive industry. If the submarginal producers find it very difficult to transfer themselves to another industry, or if all producers have about the same cost curves, the "automatic" mechanism may not work at all well. The automatic adjustment of an industry by the forcing out or the attraction of submarginal or supermarginal producers is something that works best when there is a moderately inelastic supply, a steep "cost ladder" between different firms, and consequently a relatively small number of firms which are actually on or around the margin of profitability at any one time. In such an industry any overexpansion is easily remedied by the dropping of a few firms, and the automatic adjustment takes place without a great deal of personal suffering. If, however, the cost ladder is almost horizontal and the supply very elastic, but firms find it difficut to leave the industry, then the adjustment to a new equilibrium may take a long time and cause a good deal of suffering. Indeed, in such a case there may be no movement toward equilibrium at all, but a perpetual cyclical movement, the industry swinging continually between overexpansion and overcontraction. If the cost ladder is steep and there is a fall in the price of the product, most firms will still be able to continue in operation with some reduction in economic rent, and only a few firms will find their position in the industry untenable. But if the cost ladder is horizontal, a fall in price will make almost *all* the firms in the industry unprofitable. This sad condition will remain until some firms are forced out.

Now, however, it is not clear *which* firms should be forced out. Suppose that with 10,000 milk farmers almost all milk production is unprofitable, while with 9,000 milk farmers the price of milk would be great enough so that almost all milk production would be profitable. If there are 10,000 milk producers, evidently the only final answer to the problem of the industry, apart from the monopolistic exploitation of the consumer, is to get rid of a thousand milk producers. But who is to be driven out, if all 10,000 of them are about equally profitable? It may be that they will all hang on to the industry at an unprofitable level of prices for some time, and then quite suddenly 2,000 or more may get disgusted and quit the business. This may make production highly profitable for those who remain, until the high profits once more attract large numbers of new producers.

Efficiency and Profitability

A further problem arises where the least "desirable" producers are the most tenacious. An unprofitable situation in the milk industry may result in forcing out the clever producers who are able to seek opportunities elsewhere, leaving the slothful and insanitary back-country muck dairymen in possession of the industry. According to our definitions, in this case the technically efficient dairymen, with their spotless sheds and tested cows, might well be "high-cost" producers, while the technically inefficient producers might be "low-cost." That is to say, technical inefficiency may be balanced, and more than balanced, by the low alternative cost of the skill and enterprise involved. During the depression of the 1930s, for instance, it was a curious sight to see coal mines fitted with the very latest in technical equipment lying idle because they could not meet the competition of the hill scratchers who dug coal out of the mountains with pickax and bucket. It is evident that there may be a conflict between economic efficiency, as measured by low alternative cost, and engineering efficiency, as measured by some physical standards. Where such a conflict exists there is often a tendency to overemphasize the engineering aspect of the problem at the expense of the economic. A good example of such overemphasis is found in the breeding of farm animals. Too often animals are bred for arbitrary "points" rather than for economic efficiency, and the ritualistic ideals of the dog show predominate to the exclusion of the more humdrum calculations of the accountant. In this kind of conflict we should constantly be on the watch for the specious allurement of purely technical ideals. Nevertheless, there may be a case for government intervention where the commodity produced by the technically inferior methods is itself inferior and where the public does not have an adequate opportunity for judging its inferiority. It might, for instance, be undesirable to let economic efficiency triumph over technical efficiency in the milk industry, if the technically inefficient plants produced unsafe milk and the public were not capable of judging its quality. The case for regulation here, however, rests on grounds other than the instability of the industry.

The Infant Industry Argument for Tariffs

An important application of our analysis of long-period supply and of industries of possibly decreasing supply price is found in one of the few theoretically sound nationalistic arguments for a protective tariff. If an industry of decreasing supply price inside a country is small, its cost curves will be high and it may be at a comparative disadvantage in international trade. If there is complete free trade, then, the industry will never grow in the country concerned, because its larger foreign rivals will always have a cost advantage over it. If, however, the industry is protected from foreign competition by a tariff when it is young, it will grow; and as it grows the cost curves of the firms in it will fall, until it stands in a position of comparative advantage in respect to foreign industries. Then the tariff can be withdrawn and the industry can stand on its own feet. The price of the product may then be lower than it would have been without the tariff, and consumers will benefit from the economies of specialization.

The infant industry argument applies equally well to the case of a subsidy given to a small, struggling industry in the hope that it will eventually grow to a size where it can stand on its own feet. Indeed, there are many reasons for preferring a subsidy to a tariff as a means of protecting infant industries. Subsidies are more direct in their effects, and their costs are more obvious. For this reason industries themselves are likely to prefer tariffs, the cost of which is obscured by the complexity of its expression, appearing as it does in higher prices and depressed export markets which may not seem to be very clearly related to the tariff which produces them. Both subsidies and tariffs, however, are difficult to get rid of once they have been established, for vested interests with political influence grow up behind them. Even, therefore, when the "infants" have grown to lusty maturity, it is difficult to wean them from the government pap which has nourished them. For this reason, if for no other, there is something to be said for J. S. Mill's dictum that even though there may be occasional sound arguments for a protective tariff, politicians could never be trusted to know when these occasions might arise!

Economic Development and the Terms of Trade

The infant industry argument is part of a much larger problem which is receiving increasing attention, that of the relation of economic development to the terms of trade. By the terms of trade of a country we mean the quantity of imports of goods and services which it gets per unit of goods and services exported. The more imports a country can get per unit of exports, the better off it will be. The terms of trade, however, are a function of the world price set; the higher the prices of a country's exports and the lower the prices of its imports, the more favorable its terms of trade. In the course of world economic development, those countries and regions which lag behind a general technological advance may find that the terms of trade turn against them. This will happen if what they are exporting suffers a decline in relative demand, either because advanced processes economize its use if it is a raw material, or because substitutes are developed, or because the developed countries find superior ways of producing the same thing. This worsening of the terms of the trade not only makes the poor countries poorer but also makes their development all the more difficult, and it is argued that successful world development requires substantial subsidies from the rich to the poor countries to counteract the worsening of their terms of trade.

The facts of the case are still somewhat ambiguous and vary from country to country. Price theory certainly suggests that the problem may be real. It suggests also, however, that the solution lies not in the artificial support of low prices, but in either a transfer of resources out of the low-price industries into occupations with better terms of trade, or in the directing of aid and investment effort toward the lowering of cost curves and the increases in productivity in the export industries.

QUESTIONS AND EXERCISES

1. What would you expect to be the effects of a tax on pigs on (a) the price of pigs, (b) the number of producers in the pig industry, (c) the cost of production of pigs? Assume that it is easy to get into and out of the pig industry.

2. "It is possible for the supply curve of a single enterprise to be inelastic, and yet for the supply curve of the industry of which the enterprise forms a part to be perfectly elastic. Similarly, it is possible for the supply curve of an industry to be inelastic in the short run, and yet perfectly elastic in the long run." Discuss and illustrate.

3. In the course of the expansion of the automobile industry there was a tremendous expansion of output and an equally remarkable reduction in the price. How do you account for this fact, when we usually assume that an increased output will result only from a *higher* price?

4. "It is seldom, if ever, true to say that the price of a product is determined by its cost of production. It is much truer, though not the whole truth,

to say that the cost of production is determined by the price." If this is so, what is the "whole truth"?

5. Discuss the correctness or completeness of the following statements:

a. An industry is in equilibrium when no firms are leaving it and no firms joining it.

b. A firm is in equilibrium when it is producing at its lowest cost.

c. No extraordinary profits can be made in a perfectly competitive industry.

d. A firm must be making profits if the price of its product is equal to or greater than the marginal cost of production.

e. In an industry which is in equilibrium the least profitable firm will be making normal profits.

f. The price of a product will tend to be equal to (i) the marginal cost of *all* firms in the industry, (ii) the average total cost of the marginal firm in the industry.

6. If new firms join an industry, they will compete for factors of production employed by the other firms and will therefore raise the prices of these factors of production. What effect will this have on the cost curves of firms already in the industry? What effect on the supply curve? How far does this element (which we have hitherto neglected) affect the validity of our analysis?

7. The proposal is often made for a "scientific" tariff which will "equalize the cost of production at home and abroad." How would you criticize such a proposal in the light of our analysis of cost and of comparative advantage?

8. "The farmer demands a living price for milk." Discuss.

9. "It is not an exaggeration to say that, at the present day, one of the main dangers to civilization arises from the inability of minds trained in the natural sciences to perceive the difference between the economic and the technical." (Lionel Robbins, *The Nature and Significance of Economic Science,* 2nd ed., p. 34.)

Discuss this statement with particular reference to (a) the problem of war, (b) government agricultural policy, (c) architecture.

10. Illustrate graphically the proposition that fluctuating demands may lead to chronic overcapacity in an industry that has large fixed capital.

CHAPTER 20

PRODUCTION FUNCTIONS WITH ONE VARIABLE INPUT

We have seen how the structure of cost functions underlies the decisions in the firm and the structure of supply functions. We must now carry the analysis back a stage further to show how cost functions in turn are derived from production functions. A production function is a *feasible set* of quantities of inputs and outputs which shows what quantities of inputs (factors) can be transformed into what quantities of output (product). The total cost of any quantity of output is simply the *value* of the inputs given up in its production. Clearly, then, production functions and cost functions must be closely related—indeed, the properties of the cost functions are for the most part derived from properties of the production functions. The main purpose of this chapter is to discuss the properties of production functions, and to show how the properties of cost functions are derived from them.

PRODUCTION RELATIONSHIPS

In the first place inputs and outputs are related in a qualitative way. If we put turnip seed into the sea we will not get potatoes as a result; but if we put seed potatoes into land we probably will get potatoes. The production of any commodity involves certain techniques, i.e., certain *kinds* of inputs which must be used in order to get the *kind* of output wanted. Any process of production, then, is much like a recipe in a cookbook. Indeed, cooking is a very good example of a process of production, for it clearly involves taking certain inputs—raw materials in the form of ingredients, the time of the cook, the heat of the oven, and so on—mixing them all together, and producing a product (output).

Quantitative Relations

A cookbook, however, would not be much use if it were merely
qualitative, if it merely said, "Take sugar and butter and flour, mix
them together, and bake." Besides telling the cook what *kinds* of things
to put into a recipe, it also tells her what *quantities*. The process of
production has a quantitative as well as a qualitative aspect, for inputs
and outputs are closely related in *quantity*. Small quantities of input
will yield only small quantities of output. If the *proportions* of inputs
are varied, the quantity or quality of outputs will also be varied. Generally, these quantitative relationships are fairly definite. If we put 4 eggs,
2 cups of milk, 3 cups of flour, ½ cup of melted butter, 4 teaspoons of
baking powder, and 1 teaspoon of salt into a waffle mixture and obey the
instructions, we should expect to get ten waffles out of it, no more and
and no less. If we got twenty waffles or five waffles we should be not
merely surprised, but indignant. Similarly, when an iron manufacturer
goes to his cookbook, or whatever the equivalent is in the iron industry,
and mixes so much ore, so much lime, so much coke, and so much heat
for so many hours, he knows almost exactly how much iron he will get
as a result. In some processes, like agriculture, the result is less certain.
The farmer may plant so much seed potato on so many acres and give
it so many hours of attention; but he may raise either a fine crop of
potatoes or a fine crop of blight. From year to year the results of the
application of agricultural recipes varies. Nevertheless, this variation is
due merely to changes in inputs over which the farmer has no control,
such as the weather. The farmer is merely a cook working with a remarkably unreliable oven. Even here, however, over a number of years,
the farmer knows pretty well what size of crops he will get in response
to various quantities of seed, land, and labor used. We shall not go far
wrong in assuming that in any process the quantity of output is determined by the quantities of input of all kinds which go into it.

The Physical Production Schedule

For any process of production, then, we can draw up a schedule showing the relations which may exist between input and output quantities.
This may be called the *physical production schedule*. Just as we should
read a demand schedule: "If the price were *p* then the amount purchased would be *q*," so we read the physical production schedule: "If
we put *a* units of this input with *b* units of that input with *c* units of
the other input, we shall get *x* units of output." There will be a large
number of kinds of inputs and outputs in most processes. This makes
the study of these relationships more difficult, as we now have a large

number of *dimensions,* or kinds of quantities, instead of only two as in the demand schedule. However, let us take the simplest possible case first, with one variable input. The general case is postponed to Chapter 25.

A Simple Case: One Variable Input

Suppose a process of production uses two inputs, which we shall call *labor* and *land,* and produces a single output, which we shall call *potatoes.* Let us assume at first that the quantity of land to be used by the process cannot be varied, and is equal to 8 acres, or land units. A land unit will be an area of land for a given time—say, an acre for a month. In this case the quantity of labor applied to the 8 acres of land can be varied, and the quantity of output depends on the quantity of labor applied. The unit of labor will be the work of one man for a given period of time— say, a man-hour, or a man-month. For shortness we shall call the labor unit a *man.* In these examples we are not considering the *time* at which these inputs are applied. That part of the analysis will come later; here our concern is merely with the relationships between the *quantities* of inputs and outputs.

A Total Product Schedule

Just as we can construct a schedule to show the relation between, say, output and cost, so we can construct a schedule to show the relation between the quantity of labor applied to our 8 acres of land and the quantity of product which will result in each case. This is shown in columns 1 and 2 in Table 40, and is called the total product schedule. This schedule should be read as follows: If no labor is applied to the 8 acres, there is no product; if one unit of labor is applied, there will be a product of 8 tons; if two units of labor are applied, there will be a product

TABLE 40.   PRODUCTIVITY SCHEDULES

(1) Quantity of Labor Applied to 8 Acres of Land (men)	(2) Total Product (tons)	(3) Average Physical Productivity (tons per man)	(4) Marginal Physical Productivity (tons per man)
0	0	?	
1	8	8.0	8
2	24	12.0	16
3	34	11.3	10
4	40	10.0	6
5	42	8.4	2
6	44	7.3	2
7	46	6.6	2
8	48	6.0	2
9	49	5.4	1

of 24 tons, and so on. The successive figures on the schedule denote alternative ways of using the 8 acres.

Average and Marginal Productivity

We saw how from the total cost schedule two other important schedules could be derived—the average total cost and the marginal cost schedules. Similarly, from the total product schedule two important schedules can be derived—an average physical productivity schedule (columns 1 and 3) and a marginal physical productivity schedule (columns 1 and 4). The average physical productivity of an input is defined as the ratio of the total product of a process to the quantity of the input necessary to produce that total product. Thus if 2 men produce 24 tons of potatoes, the average physical productivity is 12 tons per man. The marginal physical productivity of an input may be defined most simply as the increase in the total product resulting from the addition of one unit to the quantity of the input employed, under the condition that the quantities of all other inputs do not change. Thus the addition of the first man in Table 40 increases output from 0 to 8 tons; if the quantity of labor used is increased from 1 to 2 men, the product increases from 8 to 24 tons, i.e., by 16 tons; a further increase of one man, from 2 to 3, increases the product by 10 tons; and so on. If the quantity of input increases by a and the quantity of output responds by increasing x units, the marginal physical productivity over the range in question is x/a.

The Law of Diminishing Returns

There are several important things to notice about Table 40. The first is that both the average physical productivity and the marginal physical productivity rise at first, reach a maximum, and then fall as the quantity of labor applied to a fixed quantity of land is increased. This is, of course, a property of the figures for the total product assumed in our illustration, but it represents a principle of great importance, usually described as the *law of diminishing returns*. As the expression "diminishing returns" is a loose one, capable of several meanings, we shall avoid it as far as possible, and refer to this principle as the *law of eventually diminishing marginal physical productivity*. It could also be stated as a law of eventually diminishing *average* physical productivity, for if one eventually diminishes, so does the other.[1] The expression is clumsy, but it is better to be clumsy than vague.

[1] This statement is not absolutely true. It is possible for the marginal physical productivity to be increasing as the quantity of input increases, even when the average physical productivity is decreasing, if the latter is decreasing slowly at a decreasing rate. But this case is so improbable that it can be ruled out with safety.

Its Exact Statement. Note that it is a law of *eventually* diminishing marginal physical productivity. It may be stated thus: As we increase the quantity of any one input which is combined with a fixed quantity of the other inputs, the marginal physical productivity of the variable input must eventually decline. It must be clearly understood that when we say "increase the quantity of one input" we mean in different experiments. To find the effect of a fourth man working with 8 acres we must not start working with 3 men and then add a fourth when the process is halfway through. We must take first 8 acres and 3 men and see how many potatoes we get. Then in a separate experiment we must take 8 acres and 4 men and see how many potatoes we get. The difference in the output is the marginal physical product of the fourth man. In this sense, then, the first man put to the 8 acres gives us 8 tons of potatoes, the second man gives us an additional 16 tons, the third an additional 10 tons, the fourth an additional 6 tons, the fifth an additional 2 tons, and so on. The more labor added to our 8 acres, the more potatoes we have.

But the output of potatoes does not increase in proportion to the quantity of labor used. That is, the output rises at a decreasing rate. If we increase the number of men on our acres to a large enough number, we shall find that eventually the addition of more labor does not enable us to get any more potatoes. The land has reached the physical limits of its productive capacity, and the marginal physical productivity of labor is then zero. If we add still more men they may get in each other's way and trample down the plants, and an extra man may actually reduce the yield of potatoes. If a thousand men had to work on 8 acres the crop would probably not be large! The marginal physical productivity may then be negative. In practice, negative marginal productivities may be avoided by simply not using surplus factors, but even this is not always socially possible.

The Law Applies to Any Factor of Production

The law of eventually diminishing marginal physical productivity is a general law applying to any factor of production or input whatsoever. It is perhaps easier to visualize a varying number of men being applied to a fixed quantity of land. The law applies, however, if a fixed number of men are spread out over varying quantities of land. Suppose that we have only 5 labor units (men) to work with, but that we can spread them over as much or as little land as we like. By conducting a series of experiments we might then be able to construct a table such as Table 41, which would show how much product could be produced by 5 "men" on varying quantities of land.

TABLE 41. LAND PRODUCTIVITY

(1) Number of Acres to Which 5 Men Are Applied	(2) Total Product (tons)	(3) Average Physical Productivity of Land (tons per acre)	(4) Marginal Physical Productivity of Land (tons per acre)
0	0	?	
			7.0
1	7	7.0	
			8.0
2	15	7.5	
			5.0
3	20	6.67	
			5.0
4	25	6.25	
			5.0
5	30	6.00	
			5.0
6	35	5.83	
			4.0
7	39	5.57	
			3.0
8	42	5.25	
			3.0
9	45	5.00	

Table 41 is similar to Table 40, with land in the place of labor. The average physical productivity of land and the marginal physical productivity of land are calculated as are the corresponding concepts for labor. It will be observed in this case also that the average and marginal physical productivities at first rise and then decline as the quantity of land is increased. Just as the physical productivity of labor must decline because of the physical limitations on the product from a given area of land, so in this case the fact that there is a definite physical limit to the amount that a fixed quantity of labor can produce, no matter how much land it has to work on, means that the physical productivity of land will eventually decline as labor is spread over a larger and larger area.

Productivity Schedules and Cost Schedules

The next task is to show how cost schedules can be derived from the productivity schedules in the simple case where only a single input can be varied in quantity. If we know the prices of the inputs used and the quantities of input necessary to produce a given quantity of product, we can calculate immediately the total outlay required to produce such a quantity. Table 40, page 425, for instance, shows that a product of 8 tons can be obtained with 8 acres of land and one unit of labor. If, then, the price of land were $20 per unit and the price of labor $20 per unit, the total outlay on 8 tons would be $160 for land plus $20 for labor, or $180. So we could calculate the total outlay for each quantity of output; and if we knew the normal profit at each output, we should have the whole total cost schedule. In this example we assume that normal profits are zero —the problem of allocating normal profit is difficult and must be left to a later stage of our analysis. The inclusion of normal profit in total cost, however, makes no great difference to the argument of the present chapter, and the exposition will be simplified by assuming that total outlay and total cost are identical.

The total cost schedule derived from the product schedules in Table 40, on the assumption that land costs $20 per unit and labor costs $20 per unit, is shown in Table 42. A close examination of the schedule will show that *because* increasing quantities of labor produce a less than pro-

TABLE 42. DERVIATION OF COST SCHEDULES

(Assumptions: Land = $20 per unit, labor = $20 per unit. Variable quantities of labor working with 8 acres of land.)

(1)	(2)	(3)	(4)	(5)	(6)	(7)	(8)
		Outlay on Labor	Outlay on Land		Average Total		Marginal
Total Prod- uct (tons)	Quan- tity of Labor	(Total Variable Cost) (dollars)	(Total Fixed Cost) (dollars)	Total Outlay (Cost) (dollars)	Cost (dollars per ton)	Average Variable Cost dollars	Cost (dollars per ton)
0	0	0	160	160	∞	?	
8	1	20	160	180	22.5	2.50	2.50
24	2	40	160	200	8.33	1.67	1.25
34	3	60	160	220	6.47	1.76	2.00
40	4	80	160	240	6.00	2.00	3.33
42	5	100	160	260	6.19	2.38	10.00
44	6	120	160	280	6.36	2.73	10.00
46	7	140	160	300	6.52	3.04	10.00
48	8	160	160	320	6.67	3.33	10.00
49	9	180	160	340	6.94	3.67	20.00

portionate increase in the total product, after a certain point an increase in the total product can be obtained only under the penalty of increasing average cost. The average total cost in the table reaches a minimum of $6 at an output of 40 tons.

Cost and Product Curves

The graphic treatment of these various relationships is shown in Fig. 88. At the top left of the whole figure we plot the total product curve, *OMNPR*, with labor measured on the horizontal and product on the vertical axes. This is columns 1 and 2 of Table 41. From this, in the lower left of the figure we derive the average physical product curve, $a_p nr$, and the marginal physical product curve, $m_p mnpcd$, from columns 1 and 3 and 1 and 4 of Table 41. At any quantity of input *OH* the marginal physical product is the slope of the total product curve at the corresponding point *P*, and the average physical product is the slope of the line *OP* (not drawn in figure) or *HP/OH*. We now relabel the horizontal axis *OX* so that the scale now reads "total outlay on labor." We suppose here the price of labor is \$20 per unit, so that 1 unit represents an outlay of \$20, 2 units of \$40, and so on. Perfect markets are of course assumed throughout. The curve *OMNPR* now represents the *total variable cost curve*, with total variable cost measured along *OX* and output along *OY*. If the figure

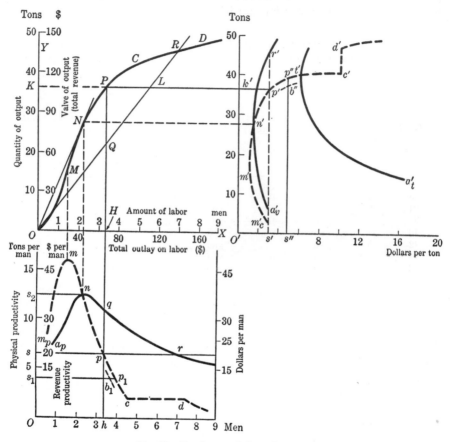

Fig. 88.   Product and Cost Curves

is looked at from the right, the reader will see that the curve has much the same shape as the total cost curve of Fig. 77E, page 377. If the origin were moved to the left a distance equal to the total fixed cost (160), the curve would then represent the total cost curve. From this total variable cost curve the marginal cost curve, *m′_cm′n′p′c′d′*, is derived in the top right figure. This is from columns 1 and 8 of Table 42. The average variable cost curve, *a′_vn′r′*, and the average total cost curve, *a′_tt′*, are similarly derived from the total cost curve, or from columns 1 and 7 and 1 and 6 of Table 42.

We can now notice several things about the relationships of these curves. (1) The point of inflection of the total cost or total product curve, *M,* is the point of maximum marginal physical product, *m,* and also the point of minimum marginal cost, *m'.* (2) The point where the tangent from the origin, *ON,* touches the total product or total cost curve at *N* is the point of maximum average physical product, *n,* and also the point of minimum average variable cost, *n'.* This assumes of course that only one factor varies. (3) It will be observed that the *average-marginal relationship* holds for the relations of average and marginal physical product, as well as for average and marginal cost. That is, the marginal physical product curve cuts the average physical product curve at its highest point, just as the marginal cost curve cuts the average cost curve at its lowest point. (4) In the range of input quantities where marginal physical product is rising $(m_p m)$, there is a corresponding range of output quantities where the marginal cost is falling $(m'_c m')$. Similarly, where marginal physical product is falling, in the range *mc,* marginal cost is rising in the range *m'c'.* In a range where marginal physical product is constant with respect to input *(cd),* marginal cost is constant with respect to output *(c'd')* and the total product, or total cost curve, is a straight line *(CD).* We thus see the intimate connection between the principle of eventually diminishing returns and the principle of eventually rising cost. Exactly similar propositions hold for the relation of average physical product and average variable cost.

Revenue Curves

Now let us suppose that there is a perfect market for the product at a price of $3 per ton. Assume no fixed cost. Measuring dollars along *OX,* the straight line *OR* is the total revenue curve. The net revenue is at a maximum, *PL,* at the output *OK.* Here the price *k'p'* is equal to the marginal cost, *s'p'* being the marginal (and average) revenue curve. The curves *OR* and *ONPCR,* however, can be given another significance. Suppose now we relabel the vertical axis *OY,* multiplying each quantity of output by its price, so that 10 tons becomes $30, 20 tons $60, and so on. Then with the *OX* axis measuring the quantity of labor (men) and the *OY* axis measuring dollars, the line *OMNPR* is now a total revenue curve, showing what *value* of product is produced with each quantity of input. The line *OR* now is a total cost curve, showing the total cost of each quantity of input. That is, at any input *OH* the total cost of the input is *HQ.* When both axes register dollars *OL* is a 45 degree line—i.e. ,in dollars $HQ = OH$. At the input *OH,* then, *HP* is the total revenue, *HQ* is the total cost, and QP is the net revenue. We also have, however, as OL is a 45 degree line, $QP = PL$; i.e., QP is also the maximum net revenue. Moving down now to the bottom left-hand figure, we again relabel the vertical axis, multiplying each ton by its price—in this case $3. Thus 15 tons per man becomes $45 per man, and so on. The curves of the figure now represent the average (a_pnr) and the marginal (m_pmcd) *revenue* product. At any input oh, hq is the average revenue product—i.e., the total revenue divided by the quantity of input—and hp is the marginal revenue product, i.e., the increase in total revenue which results from a unit increase in input. If now os is the price of the input, assuming a perfect market, we see that the quantity of input at which net revenue is a maximum is oh ($= sp = OH$) where the price of the input is equal to its marginal revenue product.

The Marginal Conditions for Input

This is another application of the general marginal principle. In the general case where the market for input is not perfect the principle may be expressed as follows: Net revenue can be increased by increasing input if the marginal revenue productivity of the input is greater than its marginal cost, and can be increased by decreasing input if the marginal revenue productivity is less than the marginal cost. This method of statement implicitly takes care of the "second-order conditions" (see page 392) and ensures that the condition defines a maximum, not a minimum. The marginal cost of input is of course the increase in the total cost which results from a unit increase in input. A simple arithmetical example will illustrate the point. Suppose at a certain level of employment of input (say, labor) the marginal revenue product of labor were $50 per man-week, and the marginal cost of labor were $40 per man-week. That is to say, the addition of a man-week to the total amount of labor employed would increase the total revenue by $50 and would increase the total cost by $40. Clearly the increase in labor employed would increase net revenue by (50 − 40) or $10, and it will pay to increase the quantity of labor employed. As this quantity is increased, however, the marginal revenue productivity will decline, and if the market is imperfect the marginal cost will rise. When, say, the marginal revenue productivity has declined to $45 per man-week and the marginal cost of labor has risen to $45 per man-week, it will no longer pay to increase employment, for an increase in employment adds just as much to revenue as it does to cost and there is no increase in net revenue. If now the firm goes beyond this point, to where, say, the marginal revenue productivity is $40 and the marginal cost is $50, it will clearly pay to reduce employment back to the point of equality of marginal revenue productivity and marginal cost of input.

Where the market for input is perfect the marginal cost of input and its price are identical, so that the marginal condition becomes the one formulated above—price equals marginal revenue productivity.

Imperfect Input Markets

An imperfect market for input is a situation in which the price and the marginal cost of input are not independent of the amount bought, but at some point rise as the amount bought increases, or fall as the amount decreases. This situation is sometimes called *monopsony* (monopsony is from the Greek for *one buyer*, just as monopoly is *one seller*), as it is often found where a number of sellers face a single buyer. A mine in an isolated region may find itself in this situation where it can, for instance, lower the wage of miners without driving many away, but where it might have to raise the wage substantially to attract more miners into the area. Under these circumstances the marginal cost curve will rise

TABLE 43. MARGINAL COSTS OF LABOR AND OUTPUT

		Perfect Markets		
(1)	*(2)*	*(3)*	*(4)*	*(5)*
		Marginal	*Marginal*	*Marginal*
	Quantity	*Physical*	*Cost of*	*Cost of*
Output	*of Labor*	*Cost*	*Labor*	*Output*
0	0			
8	1	0.125	20	2.5
24	2	0.0625	20	1.25
34	3	0.1	20	2.0
40	4	0.166	20	3.33
42	5	0.5	20	10.0
44	6	0.5	20	10.0
46	7	0.5	20	10.0
48	8	0.5	20	10.0
49	9	1.0	20	20.0

	Imperfect Markets		
(6)	*(7)*	*(8)*	*(9)*
	Total	*Marginal*	*Marginal*
Price of	*Cost of*	*Cost of*	*Cost of*
Labor	*Labor*	*Labor*	*Output*
20	0		
21	21	21	2.62
22	44	23	1.44
23	69	25	2.50
24	96	27	4.48
25	125	29	14.50
26	156	31	15.50
27	189	33	16.50
28	224	35	17.50
29	261	37	37.00

more steeply, with given production functions, than if the markets for input are perfect. Let us define the marginal physical cost of output as the increase in physical input which must accompany a unit increase in physical output. This is the reciprocal of the marginal physical productivity. Then the marginal (money) cost of output is the marginal physical cost multiplied by the marginal cost of input, the marginal cost of input being the increase in its total money value which accompanies a unit increase in its employment. Thus suppose that at a given output of potatoes the marginal physical cost is 0.1 men per ton; that is to say, the addition of 1 ton to output involves the addition of 0.1 men to input. If the marginal cost of labor is $25 per man, this means that the addition of 1 man adds $25 to the total cost of labor. The marginal cost of output then is $2.50 per ton; adding 1 ton to output adds 0.1 men to input, which adds $(0.1 × 25) to total cost. The point is illustrated in Table 43. Columns 1 and 2 show the production function of Table 42. Column 3 is the marginal physical cost in each range of output. Column 4 shows the marginal cost of labor on the assumption that the price of labor is constant at $20 per man; in this case the marginal cost of labor is constant also and equal to its price (wage). Column 5 shows the marginal cost of output, obtained by multiplying columns 2 and 4. It is identical with column 8 of Table 42. Then in columns 6 to 9 we recalculate the marginal cost on the assumption of an imperfect market for labor—i.e., we suppose in column 6 that the price of labor rises with increase in the quantity bought. Coumn 7 then shows the total cost (price times quantity) of labor, and column 8, the marginal cost of labor, the first differences of column 7. Column 9 then shows the new marginal cost of output, by multiplying column 3 by column 8. Comparing column 9 with column 5, we see that the introduction of imperfection in the input market steepens the marginal cost curve, because the marginal cost of labor rises as the quantity employed rises.

Effect of Imperfect Markets for Output

Similarly imperfect markets for output will make the marginal revenue productivity curves steeper, and hence make the demand for input less elastic. This is shown in Table 44, which continues Table 40.

Columns 1 and 2 are the same as columns 1 and 4 of Table 40.

Column 3 shows the marginal revenue of product on the assumption of a perfect market at a price of $3. Column 4 is the corresponding marginal revenue productivity (column 2 multiplied by column 3), corresponding to the curve $m_p mcd$ in Fig. 88, with the dollars-per-man vertical axis. Column 5 shows a hypothetical marginal revenue schedule with an imperfect market, with marginal revenue falling with increase in output and sales. Column 6 is the corresponding marginal revenue productivity (column 2 multiplied by column 5). It will be seen that

TABLE 44. MARGINAL REVENUE PRODUCTIVITY

(1)	(2)	(3)	(4)	(5)	(6)
		Marginal		Marginal	
	Marginal	Revenue	Marginal	Revenue	Marginal
Quantity	Physical	of	Revenue	of	Revenue
of Labor	Productivity	Product	Productivity	Product	Productivity
0					
1	8	3	24	3.0	24
2	16	3	48	2.5	40
3	10	3	30	2.0	20
4	6	3	18	1.5	9
5	2	3	6	1.0	2
6	2	3	6	0.5	1
7	2	3	6	0	0
8	2	3	6	−.5	−1
9	1	3	3	−1.0	−1

the marginal revenue product falls more steeply when there is an imperfect market; the decline in marginal revenue augments the decline in marginal physical product.[2]

SOME APPLICATIONS

Rent in the Individual Enterprise

In the preceding chapter we noticed that in any industry with a less than perfectly elastic supply curve those firms with lower costs apparently received a positive net revenue, described as *economic rent*. We must now examine this phenomenon further, for it seems as if the existence of economic rent would conflict with the principle of equal advantage as applied to profits. We shall prove that any economic rent in an enter-

---

[2] If Q is the quantity of output, L, the quantity of input, R, the total revenue, C, the total cost, then the marginal physical product is $\dfrac{dQ}{dL}$, the marginal revenue of output is $\dfrac{dR}{dQ}$, and the marginal revenue productivity is $\dfrac{dR}{dL} = \dfrac{dQ}{dL} \cdot \dfrac{dR}{dQ}$, or the marginal physical product multiplied by the marginal revenue of output. Similarly the marginal physical cost is $\dfrac{dL}{dQ}$, the marginal cost of input is $\dfrac{dC}{dL}$, and the marginal cost of output is $\dfrac{dC}{dQ} = \dfrac{dL}{dQ} \dfrac{dC}{dL}$, or the marginal physical cost multiplied by the marginal cost of input.

prise tends to be appropriated by the owners of *specific* inputs. A specific input is defined as one which is perfectly inelastic in supply to the enterprise concerned, for which the entrepreneur can find no substitutes, and which is absolutely necessary for carrying on his business.

SPECIFIC INPUTS ABSORB ECONOMIC RENT.   Suppose that, in the example in this chapter, a potato producer is working with 8 acres of land, and that the position and quality of this particular plot of land are such that the potato producer is earning extraordinary profits—i.e., he receives an economic rent. In that case the owner of the land would be able to raise the price of land services until he had appropriated all the extraordinary profits of the potato grower, leaving him with normal profits. The potato grower will not be forced off the land unless the landlord tries to exact a rent which will leave less than ordinary profits, i.e., which will result in a negative net revenue for the grower. If, for instance, in the example in Table 42 the price of potatoes were $6, the farmer would evidently be "breaking even," or earning normal profits, at the minimum average cost output of 40 bushels. At this point his net revenue is zero, as the total fixed cost ($160) is just equal to the excess of total revenue ($240) over total variable cost ($80). If, however, the price were less than $6 per bushel the farmer would be making less than normal profits if the rent were $20 per acre, and the landlord would have to reduce the rent if he is to hold the farmer on his land. Similarly, if the price were above $6 per bushel the landlord would be able to raise the rent above $20 per acre without driving the farmer away.

CALCULATION OF ECONOMIC RENT.   Thus the economic rent at any given price is equal to the difference between the total revenue and the total variable cost at the most profitable output, as this is the total fixed cost which would make the net revenue zero. The principle is illustrated in Fig. 89, drawn from Table 42. Output is measured along OX (or ox), total cost along OY, average or marginal cost along oy. OTD is the total variable cost curve, $m'_c t'$ is the marginal cost curve, $a'_v A_0$ is the average variable cost curve, and $a'_t A_{20}$ is the average total cost when land rent is $20 per acre. These curves are identical with the corresponding curves in Fig. 88, except that the axes are reversed to make them look more familiar. Suppose now that the price of the product is os ($6.) To calculate the economic rent we draw st' to cut the marginal cost curve in t'; st' ($= ok$) is then the most profitable output. The total revenue is then $ok \times os$, or the area of the rectangle $okt's$. The total variable cost is $okuw$. The economic rent then is the area of the rectangle $wut's$. Economic rent can also be calculated from the lower part of the figure. Project $t'k$ down to cut the total variable cost curve in T. Draw the tangent to the curve at T, TO_t, to meet the vertical axis at O_t. OO_t is then the economic rent.

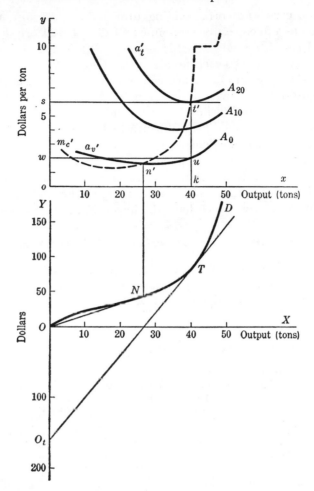

Fig. 89. Economic Rent

If the origin is shifted to O_t, then OTD becomes the total cost curve, O_tT the total revenue curve, and it is evident that net revenue is a maximum of zero at the point T.

It will be observed that the average total cost curve, a'_tA_{20}, is tangent to the horizontal line st' at t'; that is, the average total cost is a minimum at t'. This is a general property; at each price there will be an average total cost curve (including rent), and the minimum value of the average total cost will be equal to the price. The minimum point of each of these average total cost curves also lies on the marginal cost curve. That is, for each marginal cost curve there is a whole family of average total cost curves, each one corresponding to a given fixed cost. Curves corresponding to a fixed cost or economic rent of 0, 10, 20, are shown in Fig. 89 at A_0, A_{10}, A_{20}.

If now we include the economic rents in our average total cost, we can show that the minimum average total cost of *all* firms, not merely of the marginal firm, will be equal to the price of the product when an industry is in equilibrium. It is the differences in the average *variable* cost curves between different firms which constitute the "cost ladder" in Figs. 83 and 84. If the demand for the product rises, and therefore the price rises, the price of those fixed inputs which receive economic rent will also rise, until the minimum average total cost of each firm is equal to the price of the product. Then the rents of the fixed factors will be greatest in those firms which have the lowest average *variable* cost curve.

Changes in the Price of Variable Inputs: the Demand for Input

In the simple case of an enterprise with one fixed and one variable input we can now consider the effects of a change in the price of the variable input, both on the amount of the product and on the quantity of the variable input purchased.

EFFECT OF DOUBLING PRICE OF LABOR. Let us recalculate the schedules of Table 44 on the assumption that the price of labor is not $20 but $40.

TABLE 45.   CALCULATION OF COST SCHEDULES WHEN LAND = $20 PER UNIT, LABOR = $40 PER UNIT

(1) Total Product	*(2)* Quantity of Labor	*(3)* Outlay on Labor (dollars)	*(4)* Outlay on Land (dollars)	*(5)* Total Cost (dollars)	*(6)* Average Total Cost (dollars)	*(7)* Marginal Cost (dollars)
0	0	0	160	160	∞	
8	1	40	160	200	25.0	5.00
24	2	80	160	240	10.0	2.50
34	3	120	160	280	8.2	4.00
40	4	160	160	320	8.0	6.66
42	5	200	160	360	8.6	20.00
44	6	240	160	400	9.1	20.00
46	7	280	160	440	9.6	20.00
48	8	320	160	480	10.0	20.00
49	9	360	160	520	10.6	40.00

This calculation is performed in Table 45. It will be observed that the result of doubling the price of the variable input is to double the marginal cost at each level of output (Table 45, column 7, being compared with Table 42, column 8). The average total cost at each output is increased but not doubled. The average variable cost at each output is doubled, as the student may verify by making the calculations for himself.

The result of a rise in the price of a variable input, therefore, is a general rise in the cost curves of all the firms comprising an industry. However, a rise in the cost curves of all firms will lower (shift to the left) the supply curve of the product (page 414). If there is no change in demand for the product, there will then be a rise in the price of the product and a fall in its total output, partly because of a decline in the output of each firm after the rise in the marginal cost curve, partly because of a reduction in the number of firms. The rise in costs will push a number of firms which previously had been profitable below the line of normal profits and drive them from the industry. The rise in the variable cost curve will tend to lower the rents of the fixed input, and the rise in the price of the product will tend to raise the rents. The decline in the output of the industry will also go hand in hand with a decline in the purchases of the variable input. Therefore, the demand curve for the variable input can also be derived from the production schedules of the firms in the industry and from the demand for the product of that industry.

GRAPHIC ILLUSTRATION. The solid lines in Fig. 90—A_1V_1, A_2V_2, etc.— represent the average variable cost curves of four firms. The solid lines A_1M_1, A_2M_2, etc., represent the marginal cost curves of the same firms.

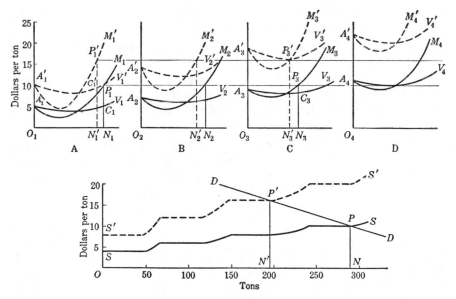

Figs. 90 and 91. Effect of Rise in Wages

The line SS in Fig. 91 is the supply curve of the industry, constructed from the cost curves after the principles of Fig. 84 (p. 406). DD is the demand curve for the product, PN the equilibrium price, ON the equilibrium output of the industry. Firm D is the marginal firm. If the price of labor now doubles, labor being the only variable input, in each firm both the marginal cost and the average variable cost will be doubled at each output. The new average variable cost and marginal cost curves are shown by the dotted lines, $A'_1V'_1$, $A'_1M'_1$, etc. The new supply curve is $S'S'$ (Fig. 91), where the supply price of each quantity of output is twice as great as before. The new equilibrium price is $P'N'$ and the new equilibrium output is ON', P' being the point where the demand curve cuts the new supply curve. Under these conditions firm D has to drop out of the industry, and firm C becomes the marginal firm.

EFFECT ON RENTS.   What happens to the rents in the individual firms depends on the circumstances of the case. In our example it is evident that the rent of firm C has declined from $P_3C_3 \times O_3N_3$ to zero, as firm C is now the marginal firm. In firm A, however, the rent originally was $P_1C_1 \times O_1N_1$. With the price and output scales the same as those in Fig. 83 this amounts to 5×81, or \$405. After the rise in the price of labor the rent is $P'_1C'_1 \times O'_1N'_1$, which on the same scale amounts to 6.7×78, or \$522. There is no rule, therefore, which will tell us a priori whether the rent in a firm will rise or fall when the price of the variable input rises. It depends on whether the tendency exerted in the direction of a rise in rents by the rise in the price of the product is outweighed by the tendency exerted in the direction of a fall in rent by the rise in variable costs. Probably rents will tend to rise in low-cost firms and fall in high-cost firms.

Fig. 90 shows the effect of the rise in the price of labor on the output of each firm. In firm A output falls from ON_1 to ON'_1 in firm B it falls from O_2N_2 to $O_2N'_2$ and in firm C it falls from O_3N_3 to $O_3N'_3$. If, however, we know the production schedule of each firm, we can immediately find how much labor is needed to produce any given quantity of product and can therefore find how great a diminution in the quantity of labor employed results from the rise in the wage. That is, we could calculate the elasticity of demand for labor. The quantity of labor bought by each individual firm does not decline very greatly, even when the price of labor doubles, for the decline in output in each case is relatively small (e.g., $N_1N'_1$). But the fact that one firm goes out of the industry means a considerable decline in the quantity of labor employed. Indeed, it is probable that the magnitude of the effect of a rise in wages on an industry depends more on its effect on the number of firms engaged in the industry than on its effect on any individual firm. The effect on the number of firms we may call the *industry effect* and the effect on the individual firm, the *firm effect*.

Importance of Elasticity of Demand

We can see immediately from Figs. 90 and 91 that the elasticity of demand for the product is of prime importance in determining the effect of a change in the price of an input (e.g., wages). If the demand for the product is inelastic, a rise in wages will result in a large rise in the price of the product and in little change in the number of firms and in the output of the industry. In that case there will be little change also in the quantity of labor employed. That is, an inelastic demand for a product is likely to result in an inelastic demand for any input which goes to produce it (see page 255). Conversely, if the demand for the product is elastic, a rise in wages will produce a relatively small change in the price of the product, and a large reduction in the number of firms, in total output, and in the volume of employment of labor.

The Demand for Input and Marginal Productivity

The demand for input can also be analyzed by means of the marginal revenue productivity curve. We saw on page 432 that net revenue is not a maximum if the marginal revenue productivity of any input is not equal to its marginal cost. When the market for the input is perfect its marginal cost is equal to its price, and the condition for maximum net revenue is that the *price* of each input should equal its marginal revenue productivity. This means that if the marginal revenue curve does not change as the price of input changes, the marginal revenue productivity curve is itself the demand curve for the input, at least below the point of maximum average revenue. Thus in Fig. 88, in the lower part of the figure we have the marginal revenue productivity curve $mnpcd$. If the price of the input (in this case the wage) is os (on the dollars-per-man scale), the total amount of input employed (assuming maximization of net revenue) is sp. At a lower price (wage), os_1, more will be employed, s_1p_1. When the wage is equal to os_2, the maximum average revenue product, the net revenue is zero; for wages above this level net revenue is negative and the firm will eventually go out of business, so that the long-run demand curve for the input is s_2npcd.

The total demand for the input can be derived by adding up the individual demand curves from each firm. This analysis is essentially similar to the derivation of supply curves from the marginal cost curves of individual firms. It suffers also from a similar defect. A change in the price of an input, as we have seen on page 414, is likely to have an effect on the price of the *product* unless the demand for the product is perfectly elastic. If the price of the product changes, however, this changes the marginal revenue productivity curve, for it (assuming perfect markets for the firm's product) is derived by multiplying the marginal physical productivity (assumed invariant) by the price of the product. Thus a fall in the wage will lower the equilibrium price of the product, and so will lower the marginal productivity curve. Thus suppose in Fig. 88 again the wage falls from os to os_1. As a result of this the marginal revenue product curve itself may fall, and the amount of employment will not be s_1p_1 but s_1b_1. The firm's demand for labor, that is, will be less elastic than the marginal revenue productivity curve. A similar difficulty is found in the derivation of the supply curve. Thus suppose there is a rise in the price of the product from $o's'$ to $o's''$ (Fig. 88, right-hand side). Output rises from $s'p'$ to $s''p''$, following the marginal cost curve. As a result of the rise in output, however, there may be a rise in the price of input, which will raise the marginal cost curve. In this case the output at price $o's''$ will be not $s''p''$ but $s''b''$. Here again the supply curve of product from the firm will be less elastic than the marginal cost curve.

Just as the total elasticity of supply for a product may depend much on the steepness of the cost ladder and the industry effect, so the total demand for an input may depend more on the steepness of the productivity ladder—i.e., the intervals between the maximum average productivity of successively less productive firms—than on the steepness of the marginal productivity curve for any one firm. If a large proportion of the output is produced by marginal firms or firms close to the margin, a rise in the price of input (e.g., in wages) will drive a lot of firms out of business and the demand for the input (e.g., labor) will be elastic.

QUESTIONS AND EXERCISES

1. Suppose that the following represented a production schedule for wheat, applying different quantities of labor to 10 acres of land:

Quantity of labor man-months)	0	1	2	3	4	5	6	7	8	9
Product (bushels)	0	100	220	340	450	540	605	645	665	675

Assuming that labor and land are the only factors of production, and neglecting normal profits, calculate and draw, as in Fig. 88, page 430.
a. The total product curve.
b. The average physical productivity curve.
c. The marginal physical productivity curve.
d. The total variable cost curve.
e. The total revenue curve.
f. The net revenue curve (fixed cost = 0).
g. The average and marginal revenue productivity curves.

h. The average variable and the marginal cost curves.

Assume that the price of labor is $80 per unit and that the price of wheat is $1 per bushel. Under these circumstances what is the most profitable output? What is the total economic rent of the land? The rent per acre? With the fixed cost equal to the total economic rent, draw the average total cost curve and show that it reaches a minimum point at the most profitable output.

2. Repeat Question 1 with the following production schedule:

Quantity of labor	0	1	2	3	4	5	6	7	8	9
Product	0	100	200	300	400	500	600	600	600	600

Comment on the properties of this production function, and on the realism of the assumptions involved. What kinds of production function, in this type of analysis, must be assumed to obtain the types of cost curves represented in Fig. 77A, B, C, D, and E? What character would the demand for input take on these various assumptions? Is there a "linear programming" type of solution in this case for the demand for input?

3. The following tabulation gives a relationship between the quantity of concentrates fed to a cow and the amount of milk obtained:

Concentrates fed (pounds)	0	4	8	12	16	20	24
Milk obtained (gallons)	1	2	2.8	3.5	3.9	4.0	3.9

Assume that all other inputs are held constant, and that their total cost is 20 cents. Suppose the cost of concentrates is 3 cents per pound, and the price of milk is 30 cents per gallon.

a. Plot the marginal physical and marginal revenue productivity curves for concentrates.

b. Calculate, using graphs if necessary:

   i. The most profitable amount of concentrates to feed.

   ii. The most profitable amount of milk to produce.

   iii. The output of milk at which its average total cost is the least.

c. The output at which the average total cost of milk is least is smaller than the most profitable output, which in turn is less than the maximum possible output. Are these relationships generally true? Under what circumstances might they not be true?

d. Are there any circumstances under which a cow with a high maximum yield might be *less* profitable than one with a low maximum yield? Illustrate graphically.

4. "If it were not for the law of diminishing marginal physical productivity we could grow all the world's food in a flowerpot." Discuss.

5. a. Prove that when the marginal physical productivity of a single variable input is zero, the total product is as great as it can possibly be.

b. Prove that if the law of diminishing marginal physical productivity holds, in every process of production in which there is a necessary fixed factor there must be some absolute maximum to the amount of product obtainable.

c. What would be the significance of a negative marginal physical productivity? Would such a case ever occur in practice?

6. Construct an arithmetical example to show that when the average physical productivity of an input does not vary with the quantity, the marginal physical productivity is equal to the average physical productivity and is also constant.

7. "The principle that the marginal cost eventually rises as output increases (the law of increasing cost) is essentially the same as the principle that marginal productivity declines as we increase the employment of an input (the law of diminishing returns)." Discuss.

8. "It is no more true to say that wages are determined by the marginal productivity of labor than it is to say that prices are determined by cost of production." Discuss.

9. When we draw up a production schedule we assume that the *methods* (techniques) of production are given. Any change in techniques operates through changing the whole production schedule. Consider, therefore, the effect of an improvement in the techniques of production of potatoes on:

a. The production schedule.

b. The cost curves of potato firms and the potato industry.

c. The supply curve for potatoes.

d. The demand curve for potato labor.

e. The rents of potato land.

f. The price of potatoes.

g. The price of potato labor.

CHAPTER 21

FURTHER PROBLEMS IN THE
THEORY OF MONOPOLY

We have by no means exhausted the discussion of the production function in Chapter 20, and the reader who wishes to pursue this study further may now wish to turn to Chapters 25 and 26, where the more general theory of the firm with many inputs and outputs is considered. Nevertheless there are still some important aspects of the theory of behavior of the firm which can be handled with the simple apparatus already developed, and which will be treated in the next three chapters.

What usually goes by the name of the *theory of monopoly* in economics is little more than the theory of the firm itself, under the assumption of imperfect markets and stable transformation functions. The latter assumption means that the market environment of the firm, as described in its sales or purchase functions, is not affected by any behavior of the firm itself. This invariance of the market environment is assumed also for the firm in perfect competition, simply because the firm is too small a part of the total system to have any noticeable effect on its own environment. A firm will not have imperfect markets, however, unless it is a fairly large part of its own market system, the *market system* being defined as the firm plus its market environment. Under these circumstances the firm will find that its own behavior affects the behavior of others, and therefore its market environment. Pure monopoly, then, is better regarded as a level of analysis rather than as a description of any specific institutions in the real world, for there probably never has been a pure monopoly. All actual firms will find that their transformation functions will be affected in some degree by the value of their various variables, such as profits. If, for instance, they are making very high profits, this will encourage other firms to produce products which are in some degree substitutes for the product of the first firm, which will lower its sales curve, or perhaps its labor force will demand and obtain higher wages, which will raise its purchase curve. It is useful, nevertheless as a step in the analysis to develop some special cases at the simple monopoly level.

The "standard case" has already been discussed on pages 389–392. Here we saw that net revenue would not be at a maximum if marginal cost were not equal to marginal revenue. We shall now proceed to some special applications of this general principle.

PRICE DISCRIMINATION

A problem of great interest in the theory of monopoly, which can be handled very conveniently by the marginal analysis, is that of price discrimination.

In the preceding chapter we assumed that the firm sold each units of its output at the same price. It is not always necessary to do so; indeed, it will be necessary only if its customers can easily resell to one another the commodity which it has sold to them. If resale is possible without trouble, the firm which sells some of its output at a low price and some at a high price will find that the output sold at a low price will be resold in the high-priced market. Suppose, for instance, that a monopolist sold his product to Mr. A for $10 per ton and to Mr. B for $5 per ton. If resale were possible it would clearly pay Mr. B to buy all he could at $5 per ton and resell it to Mr. A at some price between $5 and $10 per ton. In that case the monopolist would find that he could not sell to Mr. A at the high price, for Mr. A would buy the resold product from Mr. B. The monopolist therefore would be forced to charge the same price to both Mr. A and Mr. B. This is an application of the "principle of arbitrage" noted in Chapter 8, Part I.

If Mr. A and Mr. B do not know each other, cannot meet each other, and cannot trade with each other, resale is impossible and there is nothing to prevent the monopolist from charging each a different price. This practice is known as *price discrimination*. It is possible only when a monopolist is faced with two or more separated markets. The problem arises, then, what are the most profitable prices to charge in two or more separated markets? A common example of two separated markets for a commodity is the home market and the foreign market. A monopolist may sell at one price in his own country and at another price abroad, for the people who buy from him in the one market cannot very well sell in the other.

Marginal Revenue Equal in Each Separated Market

This problem is essentially a part of the *sales* problem; i.e., how to get the greatest total revenue from any given total volume of sales.

Where there are two or more separated markets, the solution is that the greatest total revenue from a given volume of total sales is obtained when the marginal revenue in each of the separated markets is the same. For, clearly, if the marginal revenue in one market is greater than that in the other, it will pay to shift sales (by raising price or lowering selling costs) out of the market in which the marginal revenue is low into the market in which it is high.

Suppose, for instance, that in the "home" market the marginal revenue is $10 per ton and in the "foreign" market the marginal revenue is $15 per ton. Under these circumstances, if a ton of sales is withdrawn from the home market (say, by raising the price at home) and transferred to the foreign market (say, by lowering the price abroad), the result is a loss of $10 of revenue in the home market but a gain of $15 of revenue in the foreign market, representing a net gain of $5 of revenue from the same *total* volume of sales as before. As such transference proceeds, however, the marginal revenue in the home market will rise as sales are lowered, say, to $12 per ton, and the marginal revenue in the foreign market will fall as sales are increased, say, also to $12 per ton. At this point it will no longer be possible to increase total revenue by transferring sales from one market to the other; the maximum total revenue from a *given* volume of sales has been reached. If the total volume of sales is increased the marginal revenue in each market will decline, but it still remains true that unless the marginal revenue in each market is the same gains can be made by shifting sales from one market to the other.

Marginal Revenue in Each Market Equal to the Marginal Cost

We still need, however, to solve the problem of the optimum size of *total* sales. This also can be done with the marginal analysis.

Let us define the *total marginal revenue* as the increase in the total revenue which results from a unit increase in total sales, divided equally over all the various separated markets. The total marginal revenue is then equal to the arithmetical average of the marginal revenues in the various markets. Suppose that in one market the marginal revenue is $10 per ton and in another it is $8 per ton. Then, by selling half a ton in each market the amount added to the total revenue will be $5 + $4, or $9; $9 per ton is therefore the total marginal revenue. When the marginal revenue in each market is the same, then, each is equal to the total marginal revenue. But the most profitable total output of the monopolist is that at which the total marginal revenue is equal to the marginal cost. Hence at the most profitable output, the marginal revenue in each separated market will also be equal to the marginal cost.

GRAPHIC ILLUSTRATION.   The graphic solution of the problem of price discrimination between two separated markets is shown in Fig. 92. In 92A we have the sales (demand) curve, R_1A_1, and the marginal revenue curve, R_1M_1, in one market—let us say, the home market. In 92B we have the demand curve, R_2A_2, and the marginal revenue curve, R_2M_2, in another market, separated from the first—let us say, a foreign market. These curves are drawn as straight lines for convenience, but it is not necessary to assume straight-line curves for this particular

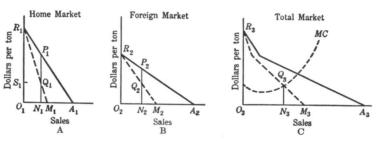

Fig. 92.   Price Discrimination

analysis. In C we have the aggregate demand curve in both markets, R_3A_3. This shows how much would be sold in both markets at various prices if the same price were to be charged in each market. It is formed by adding the horizontal ordinates of figures A and B. Thus $O_3A_3 = O_1A_1 + O_2A_2$. The curve R_3M_3 is similarly the aggregate marginal revenue curve in both markets. It shows how much can be sold in the two markets at various levels of marginal revenue, if the marginal revenues are the same in both markets. This curve is constructed by adding together the quantities sold in the two markets at each level of marginal revenue. Thus when the marginal revenue in both markets is O_1S_1, O_1N_1 is sold in Market A and O_2N_2 in Market B and O_3N_3 $(= O_1N_1 + O_2N_2)$ in both markets together. The curve R_3M_3 is *not* the "marginal" curve corresponding to the average curve R_3A_3.

The dashed curve MC in Fig. 92C is the marginal cost curve of the monopolist. His most profitable output is O_3N_3, where his marginal cost is equal to his aggregate marginal revenue. He will sell O_1N_1 in Market A, for at this volume of sales the marginal revenue in Market A is equal to his marginal cost. He will also sell O_2N_2 in Market B. In order to sell O_1N_1 in Market A he must charge a price N_1P_1 there, for P_1 is on his sales curve. Similarly, in Market B he must charge a price N_2P_2 in order to sell O_2N_2. It will be observed that the price in Market A is higher than the price in Market B. This is because the demand in Market A is more inelastic, at the equilibrium output, than the demand in Market B.

Higher Price in Less Elastic Market

It can be shown in general that if the elasticities of demand in the two markets are the same, the prices which it will pay best to charge in the two markets will be the same; but if the relative elasticities of demand in the two markets differ, the higher price will be charged in the less elastic market. It is difficult to prove this without the use of mathematics; a mathematical proof is appended below.[1]

We have seen that the more elastic is the demand schedule, the less is the divergence between the marginal revenue and the price. When the marginal revenues in the two markets are equal, the price will be higher in the less elastic market, for in that market there will be a

[1] Let p_1 be the price in the first market; p_2 be the price in the second market; q_1 be the quantity in the first market; q_2 be the quantity in the second market; r_1 be the total revenue in the first market; r_2 be the total revenue in the second market; m_1 be the marginal revenue in the first market; m_2 be the marginal revenue in the second market; e_1 be the elasticity of demand in the first market; e_2 be the elasticity of demand in the second market.

Then

$$m_1 = \frac{dr_1}{dq_1} = \frac{d(p_1 q_1)}{dq_1} = p_1 + q_1 \frac{dp_1}{dq_1} = p_1\left(1 + \frac{1}{e_1}\right) \tag{1A}$$

$$\text{for} \qquad e_1 = \frac{dq_1}{dp_1} \cdot \frac{p_1}{q_1}$$

Similarly,

$$m_2 = p_2\left(1 + \frac{1}{e_2}\right) \tag{1B}$$

The expression $(1 + 1/e)$ is important. We may call it the "coefficient of imperfection," for when the market is perfect, e is infinite and this coefficient is unity; when the elasticity is zero this coefficient is infinite. It is equal, as we see in equations (1A) and (1B), to the ratio, $\dfrac{\text{marginal revenue}}{\text{average revenue}}$.

When the ratio, marginal revenues in both markets are equal,

$$p_1\left(1 + \frac{1}{e_1}\right) = p_2\left(1 + \frac{1}{e_2}\right) \tag{2}$$

This is the condition which must be fulfilled if the total revenue from both markets is to be maximized. It is evident immediately from equation (2) that when $e_1 = e_2$, then $p_1 = p_2$.

Now we know that a monopolist will never sell at outputs where the demand is relatively inelastic (e between 0 and -1), for then, it is clear from equations (1A) and (1B), the marginal revenue will be negative. As marginal revenue is equal to marginal cost at the most profitable output, and as marginal cost is always positive, the marginal revenue at the most profitable output must also be positive; i.e., the demand must be relatively elastic (e between -1 and $-\infty$). When the demand is relatively elastic in both markets, equation (2) shows that the price will be higher in the less elastic market. For instance, if $e_1 = -2$ and $e_2 = -10$, e_1 being the less elastic market, then from equation (2) $p_1 = \frac{9}{5}(p_2)$; p_1, the price in the less elastic market, is greater than p_2.

This proposition does *not* hold for the absolute elasticities.

greater divergence between the price and the marginal revenue than there will be in the more elastic market.

Price Discrimination Between Different Quantities

Besides charging different prices to different buyers or in different markets, a monopolist may also charge different prices for various quantities of the same commodity sold to a single buyer. He may, for instance, charge a high price if the buyer buys small quantities, and a lower price if the buyer buys large quantities. This device is used sometimes in retail stores as a special price policy ("five cents each, three for a dime"). It is also used by electricity companies and other public utilities, as a regular price policy.

Marginal Outlay Determines Purchases

The effectiveness of this device rests on the fact that the quantity which determines whether a buyer will expand his purchases is not the *price* he has to pay (the average outlay) but the amount which an additional unit purchased will add to his total bill—the *marginal outlay*. If, for instance, I am considering whether or not to install an electric cooker, I shall calculate the cost of electricity used in running it according to the amount which each extra unit adds to my electricity bill. What I pay for electricity used for lighting and other purposes should not influence my decision. If the electricity company charges me, let us say, 6 cents per unit for lighting and 3 cents per unit for cooking, I may find it worth while to buy as much electricity as if the price were 3 cents for all units, and the company will be able to extract from me a greater sum than if it had charged a flat rate for all units. This principle is illustrated in Table 46.

TABLE 46. PRICE DISCRIMINATION BETWEEN DIFFERENT QUANTITIES

1. Price of electricity (cents per unit)	9	8	7	6	5	4	3
2. Consumption (units)	0	20	40	80	200	400	600
3. Increase in consumption (units)		20	20	40	120	200	200
4. Differential revenue (cents)		160	140	240	600	800	600
5. Total differential revenue (cents)		160	300	540	1140	1940	2540
6. Total flat-rate revenue (cents)		160	280	480	1000	1600	1800

The first two rows of this table show a demand schedule of a consumer for electricity. They show that if the price is 8 cents per unit, he will buy only 20 units; if the price is 7 cents, he will be a little more extravagant and buy 40 units; if the price is 6 cents, he will buy 80 units, and so on. The third row shows how much he will increase his consumption for each unit change in price. Suppose the electricity company charges 8 cents for the first 20 units used and 7 cents for the next 20 units used. The consumer will buy his first 20 units at 8 cents, for he thinks that it is worth paying 8 cents per unit, let us say, to light two of his rooms. If the price came down to 7 cents per unit he would light two more of his rooms and consume 40 units. But if the company charges 7 cents for this additional 20 units, he will still find it worth while to light his two other rooms. Therefore, if the company charges 8 cents for the first 20 units and 7 cents for the next 20 units, the consumer will buy 40 units in all; he will pay 160 cents for the first 20 and 140 cents for the second 20 (shown in the fourth row of the table) and will therefore pay 300 cents for the 40 units. If, however, the electricity company had charged a flat rate of 7 cents for all units bought, the consumer would still have bought 40 units, but he would have paid only 280 cents for them, as shown in the sixth row of the table. Similarly, if the company charged a flat rate of 6 cents per unit, it could induce the consumer to buy 80 units, and would receive 480 cents; but if the company charges 8 cents for the first 20 units, 7 cents for the next 20 units, and 6 cents for the next 40 units, the same consumer will still be persuaded to buy 80 units, but will pay the company a total of 540 cents for these 80 units. So we can go on all through the table.

This Is Possible Only If Buyers Cannot Resell

If a monopolist could shade his price according to quantity to follow the consumer's demand curve exactly, his marginal revenue would be equal to the price that he charged for the last unit bought, for he could increase his sales by offering to sell an extra unit at a lower price without lowering the price of the other units he sells. In practice, of course, it is not possible for a monopolist to adjust his price scale accurately to the demand for each buyer. Nevertheless, the practice of charging lower prices for larger quantities is very common. It may, of course, be combined with the practice of charging different prices to different buyers; thus an electricity company may have one scale of prices for commercial buyers and another scale of prices for domestic buyers. It should be noticed that this type of discrimination also is possible only if the buyers are unable to resell what they have bought. If resale is possible, then, as we have seen, any buyer who buys at a low price will undercut the monopolist himself by reselling to those buyers who have to pay a high price to the monopolist. This principle applies as much to the practice of charging different prices for different quantities as it does to the practice of charging different prices to different people.

If buyers can resell, it will pay some of them to buy large quantities —thus getting the product at a low price—and to resell some of their purchases to those who buy only small quantities and who therefore would have to pay a high price to the monopolist. If a householder could retail electricity to his neighbor, it would obviously not pay the electricity company to charge smaller prices for larger quantities, for such a policy would merely encourage people to buy large quantities of electricity for resale.

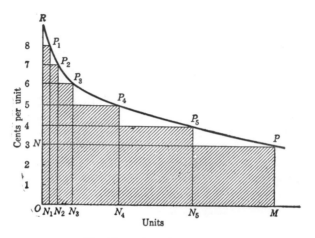

Fig. 93. Price Discrimination

GRAPHIC ILLUSTRATION. Fig. 93 illustrates the process of discriminating according to quantity. RP is the demand curve of a single buyer of electricity. If the seller wishes to sell an amount equal to OM, he can achieve this end by charging a flat rate of ON, in which case the total revenue will be $OM \times ON$, or the area $OMPN$. But if he charges N_1P_1 for the first ON_1 units, N_2P_2 for the next N_1N_2 units, N_3P_3 for the next N_2N_3 units, and so on, and MP for the last N_5M units, he will still be able to sell an amount OM, but his total receipts from this consumer will be the shaded area of the figure. Evidently, if the gradations could be made in infinitely fine steps, the "stairs" of the shaded area could be made smaller and smaller until the total receipts amounted to the whole area under the demand curve, $RPMO$. The maximum possible gain from quantity discrimination, then, is the area NRP. This is sometimes called the consumer's surplus. It represents the difference between what a consumer pays when there is a flat rate for all quantities and the maximum amount which can be extracted from him by skillful pricing. The seller must be careful, however, not to schedule a reduction in price at a quantity which is greater than that which would be bought by the consumer at the preceding price on the schedule. Suppose, for instance, that the electricity company scheduled a price of 8 cents for the first 20 units, 7 cents for the next 50 units, 6 cents for the next 100 units, and so on. A consumer with the demand curve in Fig. 93 would stop short at 20 units and would never extend his purchases into the low-price quantities, because at 7 cents a unit he would only purchase 40 units altogether. Not unless his total purchases at 7 cents amounted to at least 70 units would he be tempted to purchase more by reason of the 6-cent price for quantities greater than 70 units.

DISCONTINUOUS FUNCTIONS

Some interesting problems arise in the theory of the firm when the various cost and revenue functions are discontinuous—that is, exhibit sharp jumps, corners, or changes. There are several cases where discontinuous functions are plausible. Thus in Fig. 77C and D (p. 376) we have already considered the possibility of discontinuous cost curves. In Fig. 77C, for instance, we suppose a constant marginal cost up to some capacity output, after which marginal cost rises sharply and indefinitely. In Fig. 77D marginal cost is high but constant at first, then drops suddenly to a lower level, and then again rises indefinitely when capacity is reached. These types of cost curve are particularly likely to occur when there are alternative methods of production in each of which marginal cost is constant over a wide range, as in Exercise 3, page 399. Another possibility, which has been advocated[2] is that when a plant is engineered for a certain capacity output, marginal and average costs are likely to fall over the whole range of output up to capacity and then to rise very sharply.

These cases are illustrated in Fig. 94. In Fig. 94A we have a case similar to Fig. 77C: OCC' in the upper part of the figure is the total cost curve, $m_0 m_c m'_c$ is the marginal cost curve. Here we notice an immediate difference from the case of perfect markets for output. With perfect markets the firm will either produce at capacity, or not at all: the horizontal marginal revenue curve can only cut the marginal cost curve in its vertical section. With imperfect markets for output, under-capacity operation may be the most profitable, if the marginal revenue curve such as $r_0 r_m$ cuts the marginal cost curve in its horizontal section, as at x. The corresponding average revenue curve is $r_0 r_v$, and the corresponding total revenue curve is $OR_m R$; the maximum net revenue is $R_m C_m$, at

[2] W. J. Eiteman and G. E. Guthrie, "The Shape of the Average Cost Curve," *American Economic Review*, December, 1952, pp. 832–838.

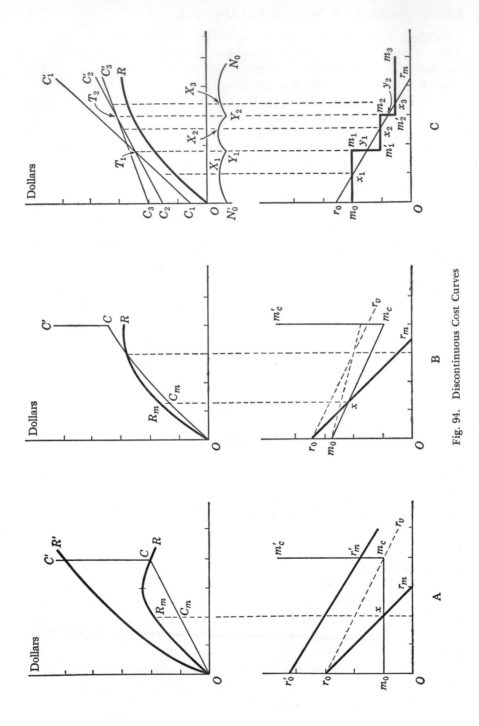

Fig. 94. Discontinuous Cost Curves

an output equal to $m_o x$. If the marginal revenue curve cuts the marginal cost curve in its vertical sector, like the curve $r'_o r'_m$, corresponding to the total revenue curve OR', the firm will have its most profitable output at capacity, and its maximum net revenue will be CR'. This clear association of undercapacity operation with an imperfect market is a proposition of great practical importance.

Fig. 94B shows a slightly more extreme case where the marginal cost actually falls up to capacity, as the marginal cost curve $m_o m_c m'_c$ shows. Here again undercapacity operation may be most profitable if the marginal revenue curve, such as $r_o r_m$, cuts the marginal cost curve in its declining section, as at n. Again, $R_m C_m$ is the maximum net revenue. The importance of this case lies in the fact of the great shiftability of the point of maximum profit. If the slopes of the marginal cost and marginal revenue curves are nearly equal, a small rise in the demand for the product may shift the most profitable point to the capacity output, and a small fall may eliminate production altogether, which would happen if r_o fell below m_o, assuming no fixed costs.

Fig. 94C shows the case with three alternative methods of production, I, II, and III, with total cost curves $C_1 C'_1$, $C_2 C'_2$, and $C_3 C'_3$. The least total cost curve, which is the significant one, is $C_1 T_1 T_2 C'_3$. Method I has the least total cost between C_1 and T_1, method II between T_1 and T_2, method III between T_2 and C'_3. The corresponding marginal cost curve is $m_0 m_1 m'_1 m_2 m'_2 m_3$. Here we may actually have a marginal revenue curve such as $r_o r_m$ cutting the marginal cost curve in five places! OR is the corresponding total revenue curve. It will be seen that the outputs at x_1, x_2, and x_3 represent *relative* maxima; that is, at these outputs the net revenue is larger than at any other point in the immediate neighborhood. The points y_1 and y_2 represent relative *minima*; the net revenue is smaller at these points than at any other in the immediate neighborhood, because of the discontinuities at T_1 and T_2. This is shown clearly in the net revenue curve $N_0 X_1 Y_1 X_2 Y_2 X_3 N'$, showing the vertical difference between OR and $C_1 T_1 T_2 C'_3$; the net revenue in this case happens to be negative, but this does not invalidate the general principle; the points X_1, X_2, and X_3 are points of minimum loss.

Discontinuous Sales Functions

Another interesting possibility of discontinuity is in the firm's demand or sales functions. Suppose, for instance, that the firm produces a multiple-use commodity, in which the demand is very elastic in each use up to a point of saturation after which demand becomes very inelastic. In the extreme case the demand curve will be a step function, as in Fig. 95. Above the price OA we suppose nothing will be sold; at OA the first

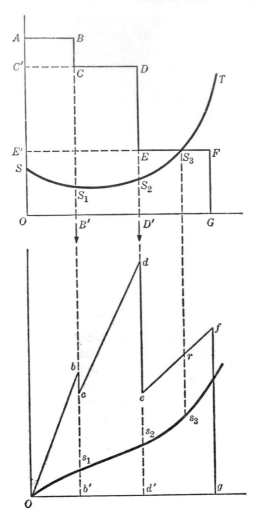

Fig. 95. Discontinuous Sales Curves

use comes into play, and *AB* will be sold. Lowering the price below *OA* does not expand sales beyond *AB* until the price *OC'* is reached, when sales expand suddenly into the second use, to *C'D*. A third use comes in at price *OE'*, expanding sales to *E'F*, and so on. The total revenue curve corresponding to this sales (average revenue) curve is shown in the lower part of the figure, *obcdefg*, assuming no price discrimination. Thus at sales equal to *ob'* total revenue suddenly drops from *b'b* (= area *OABB'*) to *b'c* (=*OC'CB'*) as sales are pushed into the second use.

The Discontinuous Marginal Revenue Curve

The marginal revenue curve in this case is very curious. It may be visualized best perhaps if we imagine ourselves driving a little car over the saw teeth of the total revenue curve and observing its changes in angle; from o to b marginal and average revenue are the same, equal to OA. At b the slope suddenly changes from OA to minus infinity, and the marginal revenue curve rushes off from B through B' to minus infinity. At c the slope is again reversed to a positive number ($B'C$) and marginal revenue rushes back from minus infinity at $B'C$. From c to d marginal revenue is again constant at $B'C$; at d it again goes off to minus infinity, and returns to $D'E$ at e.

Relative and Absolute Maxima

Suppose now that we have a marginal cost curve ST. This strictly cuts the marginal revenue curve at three points S_1, S_2, and S_3. Indeed, it cuts the marginal revenue curve *twice* at each of the points S_1 and S_2, once on its way down to minus infinity and once on its way back! This curious phenomenon has, however, a very simple interpretation, as we see from the total revenue and total cost curves in the lower part of the figure. At the output ob' there is both a relative maximum net revenue at b and a relative minimum at c. Similarly, there is a relative maximum at d and a relative minimum at e. There is also a relative maximum of the conventional type at r, corresponding to the point S_3 in the upper figure. There is no way of telling which of the three relative maxima, b, d, and r, represents the highest absolute value of the net revenue except by inspection. In the figure d is clearly the absolute maximum; this, however, is a mere accident of the functions selected.

Boundary Maxima

In the two previous cases the *formal* conditions of the marginal analysis have survived the discontinuities of the functions; that is, the maximum position is still formally at a point where marginal gain is equal to marginal loss, even though the formal condition loses much of its significance when the functions are discontinuous. In the case of the *boundary maximum,* however, not even the formal condition is retained. A boundary occurs when there are limits imposed, say, by law or custom, beyond which some variable is not allowed to go. Minimum wage laws, usury laws, price controls, output quotas, are examples of such boundaries. If the greatest value of the maximand (say net revenue) is found at the boundary, it is said to be a boundary maximum. At the boundary, however, the marginal conditions may not be satisfied

at all. The case is illustrated in Fig. 96. The maximand is measured along
OY, some related variable along OX. We suppose this has a boundary at
OH. In the figure there is a regular relative maximum at M, where all
the marginal conditions will be fulfilled. There is likewise a relative minimum at N. The boundary maximum at B, however, is clearly the highest
possible value of the maximand. If the boundary did not exist there might

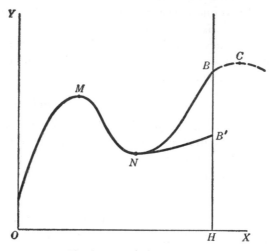

Fig. 96.   Boundary Maxima

be another relative maximum at C. Because of the boundary, however, B
is the best position, in spite of the fact that the marginal conditions are
not fulfilled there. It should be observed, however, that the mere presence
of boundaries does *not* mean that the boundary itself is the maximum.
Thus in Fig. 96, if the maximand went from N to B' instead of to B, M
would be the absolute maximum and the organization would not proceed
to the boundary but would stop at M.

EFFECT OF A CHANGE IN DEMAND

The marginal analysis throws some light upon the effects of a change
in demand for the product of a monopolist. We will discuss the effects
of a fall in demand; an exactly similar analysis, of course, holds for a
rise. As the general demand curve of the public for the product of a
monopolist is the same as his sales curve, a fall in demand means a shift
in the sales curve to the left. The marginal revenue curve will therefore also move to the left and will intersect the marginal cost curve at
a point representing a smaller output. A fall in demand for the product

of a monopolist will thus cause a reduction in the output of the product. In general there will also be a reduction in the price of the product, although circumstances are conceivable in which a fall in demand may lead to a rise in the price of the product. In Fig. 97A, *RA* and *RM* are the sales curve and the marginal revenue curve before the fall in demand, *ON* is the equilibrium output, and *NP* is the price, at which the marginal

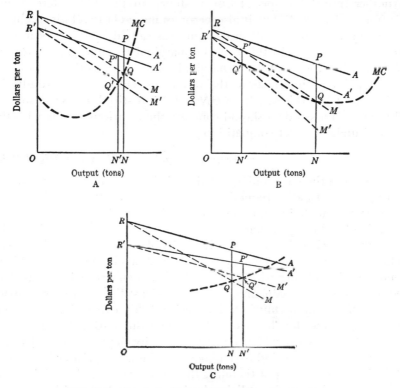

Fig. 97.   Effect of a Fall in Demand on Monopolist

revenue is equal to the marginal cost, *NQ*. *MC* is the marginal cost curve. After the fall in demand, *R'A'* is the new sales curve, *R'M'* the new marginal revenue curve. The marginal revenue is now equal to the marginal cost, *N'Q'*, at the output *ON'* sold at a price *N'P'*. There is evidently a fall in output from *ON* to *ON'* and a fall in price from *NP* to *N'P'*. The extent of the fall in output depends on the slope of the marginal cost curve. If the marginal cost curve is steep there will be a small fall in output. If the marginal cost does not change much as output changes, however, the output will have to fall a good deal before the marginal cost is again equal to the marginal revenue.

Fig. 97B shows a case in which a fall in demand causes a rise in the price of a monopolist's product. In this case the symbols have the meaning assigned to them in Fig. 97A. But the marginal cost falls with increasing output in the significant range, and therefore a very large decline in output, from ON to ON', results from the fall in demand. The decline in output is so great that it permits an actual rise in price—from NP to $N'P'$.

Another interesting special case is shown in Fig. 97C. Here demand falls from RA to $R'A'$, but it also becomes more elastic. This might happen, for instance, if the fall in demand was caused by the appearance of a substitute product. In this case the marginal revenue curves, RM and $R'M'$, actually cross; and if the marginal cost curve cuts them to the right of their point of intersection, the fall in demand actually results in a *rise* in output—in this case from ON to ON'. It still, however, results in a fall in price. The student should compare these various results with those obtained under perfect competition.

Why Does a Monopoly Have Rigid Prices?

We see from these examples that there is likely to be a larger reduction in price and a smaller reduction in output when the marginal cost is rising sharply with increased output. This condition, however, is characteristic of a firm working at full capacity. Where a firm is working at an output well below the capacity of its plant, the marginal cost curve will be flat or may even slope downward as in Fig. 97B. When a monopolist is working with *excess capacity*, then a fall in demand may lead to a still further reduction in output and a still greater excess capacity, and will not lead to much fall in price. This conclusion has a good deal of importance for the theory of economic fluctuations. One important feature of our society which tends to intensify depressions is that when the money demand for industrial goods declines, the prices of these goods fall little and their output therefore declines greatly. This may in part be due to conventional price policies; businessmen may not wish to go to the trouble of adjusting their prices to meet new conditions. We now see, however, that the policy of rigid prices may have a foundation also in self-interest. If most plants are working under capacity their marginal cost curves will be flat or even negatively sloped, and a fall in demand will result in a large fall in output and little or no fall, or even a rise, in price, as can be seen from Fig. 97B, assuming profit-maximizing behavior.

TAXATION

The effect of taxes on a profit-maximizing monopolist, as on any firm, depends principally on whether the tax is a fixed sum or whether its total amount varies with output.

The effect of a fixed tax is shown in Fig. 98A. OQC is the total variable cost curve. OPR is the total revenue curve. In the absence of fixed costs, ON is the output at which the net revenue, QP, is a maximum. If the fixed input is not owned by the monopolist himself, a rent may be charged equal to QP, or OK. The total cost curve is then KP; the most profitable output is still ON, at which the monopolist's net revenue is

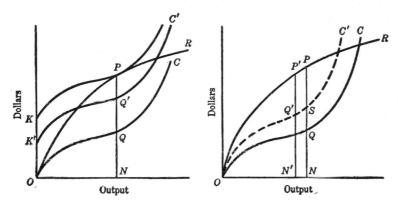

Fig. 98. Taxation of Monopoly

zero. If, now, a fixed tax equal to OK' is laid on the monopolist, there is no change in the most profitable output, ON, for there is no change in the *marginal* cost curve and none in the revenue curves, so that the marginal cost will still be equal to the marginal revenue at the output ON. But the economic rent will be reduced from QP ($= OK$) to $Q'P$ ($= K'K$). The total fixed charge cannot exceed the sum QP. Therefore, if there is a tax equal to QQ', the total cost curve including the tax but excluding rent will be $K'Q'C'$, and the rent will be that sum which will make the total fixed charge equal to QP, or $Q'P$. A lump-sum tax on a monopoly, then, is equivalent to a tax on economic rent. Unless it exceeds the economic rent, it will not affect the output of the monopolist, unless, of course, the parties concerned are not following their own interest. Even a lump-sum tax may affect the output of a monopolist if it forces him to devote greater attention to *finding* his most profitable output. If the tax exceeds the economic rent, it will force the monopolist out of business and reduce the output to zero.

The effect of a tax which varies in total amount with output is shown in Fig. 98B. Suppose there is a specific tax on each unit of the commodity produced. The total cost, including the tax, is now greater than before at each output; but instead of increasing by a fixed amount, it increases by an amount which is proportionate to the output. That is, at large outputs the tax is greater than at small outputs. If in Fig. 98B the original total cost curve is OC, the total cost curve after the tax will be OC'. The effect of a specific tax is similar to the effect of a rise in the price of input. The marginal cost curve rises, for the marginal cost at each output is increased because of tax. The output will therefore tend to decline, and the price of the product will rise. The rent of the monopoly will also decline. In Fig. 98B the original output will be ON, where the net revenue or rent is a maximum at QP. After the imposition of the tax the slope of the new cost curve, OC', at the output ON' is greater than that of the old cost curve; i.e., the slope of OC' at S is greater than that of OC at Q. In other words, at the old output, after the tax, the marginal cost has risen. But previously the marginal cost was equal to the marginal revenue at this output. Now, however, as the marginal revenue has not changed, the new marginal cost must be greater than the marginal revenue. The net revenue can therefore be increased by reducing the output to ON', where $Q'P'$ is the new maximum net revenue, ON' the most profitable output. The amount by which a given specific tax will reduce the output and raise the price will depend on the character of the demand for the monopolist's product. If the demand is very elastic, there will be a large reduction in output and a small rise in price. If it is not very elastic, the reduction in output will be smaller and the rise in price larger.

Conclusions Modified

The presence of discontinuities and boundaries may, of course, modify these conclusions in regard to changes in demand and taxation. Generally speaking, positions of maximum profits at boundaries or at discontinuities tend to be rather insensitive to changes in the environment, and may survive considerable changes, for instance, in levels of demand or of taxation, without shifting. Thus suppose in Fig. 97A the marginal cost curve were vertical (at capacity output, as in Fig. 94A or B); it is evident that a fall in demand would not affect output at all, as long as the firm was producing. No matter what the demand, within wide limits the firm would produce at capacity. Taxes, even variable taxes, would have a similar effect, for a tax can always be treated as a fall in the demand curve.

The conclusions of the elementary marginal analysis in regard to the effect of changes in environment may be modified also if account is taken of the asset preferences of the firm. The assumption underlying simple profit maximization is that the firm is concerned only with the gross increase in total value of its assets and is indifferent to the structure and composition of these assets. If, however, the firm is concerned for the composition of its assets—for example, if it wishes to preserve some proportion of liquid to nonliquid assets—it may well prefer a position with less than maximum total profit but in which the composition of assets resulting from the operation is superior to that which would emerge at the profit maximum position.

In a case of this kind even a fixed tax is likely to affect the output and sales positions of a firm, at least in the short run, because of the effect of the tax on the composition of assets. If the tax is collected in money, this has the immediate effect of making the firm less liquid, and hence it may attempt to recover its liquidity by cutting down production and selling off inventory, even under a fixed tax.[3]

SATISFICING AND SEARCH. A further question is how far conclusions derived from the assumption of profit maximization have to be modified in the light of more realistic *behavioral* theories of the firm. It is the *image* of the world in the mind of the decision maker which determines his decisions, not the *realities*. This image is the result of his past experiences. Those experiences however may be organized in a process of search for better information, a process which is itself costly and subject to marginal controls, in the sense that it will be carried only to the point where the marginal rewards of better information cease to justify the marginal costs. If the search tends to stop when some satisfactory level of profits is reached—satisficing behavior (see page 304)—then a reduction of profits below this level by a tax may force further search. The results of search and of stimuli to search are often unpredictable; in justification of the profit-maximization assumption, however, we may suppose that if the maximum position is what the search is "looking for," then the more search activity, the better the chance of finding the maximum position or of getting closer to it. Hence the profit-maximization analysis is not irrelevant to behavioral theory, even though its results have to be interpreted in terms of the probable direction of change rather than as absolute predictions.

One final question may be raised regarding the aim of profit maximization itself, as in practice firms have other goals besides profits, such as security, stability, reputation, the quiet life, and so on. Here again, however, if the departure from maximum profits, even under conditions of costless search, or "perfect knowledge," tends constantly in the same direction, the conclusions derived from profit maximization analysis can still be interpreted in terms of the probable direction of change.

[3] For a detailed discussion of this problem, see K. E. Boulding, *A Reconstruction of Economics*, New York, Wiley, 1962, pp. 104–107.

QUESTIONS AND EXERCISES

1. "A perfect monopoly is almost as inconceivable as perfect competition." Discuss.
2. "A monopoly price is one which is raised above the competitive level." What do you understand by the "competitive level"? Is the price charged by an unrestricted monopolist necessarily above the competitive level? If not, how could you tell whether the price of a monopolist was or was not above the competitive level?
3. "A monopoly is most likely to be successful in the case of commodities whose demand is relatively inelastic." Discuss.
4. Prove that a monopolist will never wish to produce at an output where the elasticity of demand for his product is numerically less than one. (Note: Prove first that when the marginal revenue is positive, the elasticity of demand is numerically greater than 1.)
5. "In making any decision the businessman merely has to ask himself whether his proposal will add more to the total revenue than to the total cost. If it does, he will proceed with the proposal in question. Otherwise he will not." Discuss, in the light of the marginal analysis.
6. Analyze the effect of an increase in demand for the product of a monopolist on (a) his price, (b) his output, (c) his demand for inputs.
7. Who is injured by the existence of a monopoly?
8. Compare and contrast the effects of various kinds of taxes on commodities produced under conditions of monopoly and of perfect competition.
9. Milk cooperatives usually charge a higher price for milk in the "liquid" market (for direct consumption) than for milk in the manufacturing market (for butter and cheese). Why? What assumption does it imply about the demand in these two markets?
10. Discuss in detail the effects of a subsidy given to a monopolist (a) when the subsidy is a fixed amount irrespective of output; (b) when the subsidy is a fixed sum on each unit of output produced; (c) when the subsidy is a fixed percentage of the price of each unit produced; (d) when the subsidy is progressive, i.e., increases per unit as the output increases.
11. Prove that the maximum tax which can be extracted from a monopolist without driving him out of business is greater in total when the tax is a fixed sum than when it is a specific tax on each unit of output.
12. Suppose a monopolist is selling a product at its most profitable price at $20 per ton. Suppose that (a) a specific tax of $10 per ton is laid on the commodity, and (b) an ad valorem tax of 50 per cent of the price of each unit of the commodity is imposed. Compare and contrast the results of these two taxes. (Note: Treat the ad valorem tax as a deduction from revenue, as on page 209.)
13. The following table shows the marginal revenue and marginal cost schedules for a monopolist producing a patented refrigerator.

Output of Refrigerators (units)	Marginal Revenue (dollars per unit)	Marginal Cost (dollars per unit)
0	200	100
100	185	95
200	171	91
300	158	93
400	146	96
500	135	100
600	125	105
700	116	112
800	108	122
900	101	137
1000	95	157
1100		

a. Calculate, for each output, the total revenue, the price of the product, the total variable cost, the average variable cost, and the net revenue.

b. Draw on one graph (A) the marginal cost curve, the marginal revenue curve, the sales curve, and the average variable cost curve. What is the most profitable output?

c. What is the maximum amount which the owner of the patent could exact from the monopolist without driving him out of business? Is this economic rent? Explain.

d. Calculate the average total cost, at each output, on the assumption that the total fixed cost is equal to the maximum amount receivable by the owner of the patent. Draw on graph A the average total cost curve. Show that it touches the sales curve.

e. On another graph (B) plot the total variable cost curve, the total revenue curve, and the total cost curve, calculated according to the assumptions in d. Compare graphs A and B, and note any significant conclusions.

f. What will be the effect of (a) a flat tax of $40,000, (b) a flat tax of $50,000, (c) a tax of $30 on each refrigerator, on the refrigerator company?

g. In the case of the above refrigerator company, what subsidy (per refrigerator) would expand the output to 950 refrigerators? Assuming that the net revenue is all economic rent, what fixed tax would now leave the concern normally profitable?

14. The following table shows two straight-line demand curves facing a monopolist in two separated markets, A and B.

Price	0	10	20	30	40	50	60	70	80	90
Sales in A	90	80	70	60	50	40	30	20	10	0
Sales in B	150	120	90	60	30	0	0	0	0	0

a. Plot the sales curve and the marginal revenue curve for each of these markets, and the aggregate sales curve and the aggregate marginal revenue curve, as in Fig. 92.

b. For *each level* of marginal revenue, 0, 10, 20, . . . , 80 use the above graphs to calculate:

    i. Sales in market A.

   ii. Sales in market B.

  iii. Aggregate sales in both markets.

  iv. The price in market A.

   v. The price in market B.

  vi. The total revenue from market A.

 vii. The total revenue from market B.

viii. The aggregate total revenue from both markets.

  ix. The aggregate average revenue from both markets per unit of sales.
Assume that price discrimination is practiced so as to maximize the total
revenue from any given volume of sales. Arrange the results in tabular form.
c. Suppose that the average variable cost in this firm is constant with
respect to output. For various levels of this constant average variable
cost (10, 20, 30, etc.) calculate (i) the total variable cost and (ii) the total
economic rent (net revenue), at various levels of output 0, 10, 20, . . . 120,
assuming that there are no fixed costs. Arrange results in tabular form.
d. Plot on a single sheet, with sales (output) along the horizontal and
revenue along the vertical axis, the family of net revenue curves corresponding to various levels of average variable cost.
e. Show that the maximum net revenue is always at that level of output
where marginal cost is equal to the aggregate marginal revenue.

15. A monopolist with the demand curves of Exercise 14 is now prohibited
by law from charging different prices in different markets; he must now
charge a uniform price for all sales.

  a. Calculate, for levels of output 0, 10, 20, . . . , 120:

    i. The uniform price at which each quantity can be sold, using both
       markets.

   ii. The total revenue from each level of output.

  iii. The marginal revenue at each level of output.

  iv. The total variable cost and the net revenue (assuming no fixed
      costs) on the assumption of various constant average variable cost
      levels, e.g., 20, 25, 30, 35, 40, 45.

Arrange results in tabular form.
b. Plot on the same figure the family of net revenue curves at various
levels of average variable cost derived from the figures in a (iv). Comment
on any peculiar features of this family of curves, comparing them with
the family of curves derived in Exercise 14, part (d).
c. Plot the aggregate demand curve of the monopolist from the figure
in a (i). On the same figure plot the marginal revenue curve which corresponds to this aggregate demand curve. How does this curve differ
from the aggregate marginal revenue curve of Exercise 14? Interpret
the peculiarities of the family of net revenue curves derived in part b by
reference to the marginal revenue curve. Show, in particular, that where
a marginal cost curve cuts the marginal revenue curve in three places,
the net revenue curve will exhibit two maxima.
d. Plot on one figure:

    i. The total revenue curve under price discrimination from Exercise 14, b (viii).

    ii. The total revenue curve under uniform pricing from Exercise 15, a, ii. Comment on the relationship of these two curves.

e. Assume again that average variable (= marginal) cost is independent of the volume of output. Plot on another figure curves showing the equilibrium output at various levels of average variable cost, (i) under price discrimination, and (ii) under uniform pricing.

f. On another figure, plot (i) the price in A, (ii) the price in B, and (iii) the average price, from Exercise 14, b (viii), all under price discrimination, and (iv) the price under uniform pricing, for various levels of constant average variable cost.

16. In the light of the above two exercises, write an essay on the effect of compulsory uniform pricing on a monopolist who has previously been practicing price discrimination, with special reference to the effect on prices and sales.

17. In Fig. 95, what would be the total revenue curve and the marginal revenue curve under conditions of perfect price discrimination? How would price discrimination affect output in this case? Can the results of this case be generalized?

18. Price discrimination can also be practiced by a monopolist in the purchase of input as well as in the sale of output. Construct a diagrammatic analysis of this phenomonen, on the assumption of profit maximization, drawing out the parallels with the analysis of the sale of output. How do phenomena like overtime payment, secrecy in regard to salaries, quantity discounts fit into this analysis?

CHAPTER 22

IMPERFECT COMPETITION

We have now treated in some detail two extreme cases—perfect competition on the one hand and pure monopoly on the other. Both are important in actual economic life, for some industries, notably those producing the standard raw materials of commerce, operate under conditions close to perfect competition, and others, like the public utilities, operate under conditions close to pure monopoly. Probably, however, the bulk of economic activity is carried on in industries whose condition lies somewhere between these two extremes, in which neither the conditions of perfect competition nor the conditions of pure monopoly are completely observed. This state of industry is known as *imperfect competition*.

Forms of Competition

Within the general field of imperfect competition three important cases can be distinguished whose results differ significantly; we shall call the first *monopolistic competition,* the second, *perfect oligopoly,* and the third, *imperfect oligopoly*. In all cases of competition, whether perfect or imperfect, we assume freedom of entry of firms or of other resources into the industry. The four cases of competition are then defined by ringing the changes on two fundamental conditions: the homogeneity of the product and the number of firms. When many firms are producing a homogeneous product the result is perfect competition. When many firms are producing heterogeneous products, and the product of each firm is similar to but not identical with the product of other firms in the same industry, the condition is known as monopolistic competition. When a *few* firms are selling a homogeneous product there is a condition which may be called *perfect oligopoly*. When a few firms are selling heterogeneous products there is a condition which may be called *imperfect oligopoly*. Where there are only two sellers the condition is known as *duopoly*.

Definition of an Industry or Sector

It must be confessed that the various states of the market distinguished above are not sharply divided one from the other, and that what we have in fact is a complex continuum of market conditions. The simple model of the economy which we find in the theory of perfect competition, with economic activity divided into a number of *industries* each producing a single clearly identified *commodity* is far from the truth. Most firms produce many commodities, and most commodities are surrounded by a group of more or less good substitutes. Hence it is impossible to divide up the total of economic activity neatly into industries, each characterized by a particular market form and each producing a particular commodity, nor can we define an industry sharply as that economic activity which produces a particular commodity or group of commodities. What, for instance, is the steel industry? Does it include those firms which make frames for automobiles? If so, how far does one have to go down the process of production before the steel industry passes into the automobile industry? Worse still, does the steel industry include firms producing close substitutes for steel, such as aluminum? The labor movement evidently thinks so, for the aluminum workers are now included in the United Steelworkers of America!

Attempts have been made to describe the situation of the market in terms of the interaction of the totality of firms and segments of firms, without reference to any classification by industry[1]. Such analysis, however, easily slips into a rather sterile formalism, and we find that if we are to emerge from our analysis with any conclusions we have to think in terms of sectors or subsystems of the total economy, and so reintroduce the concept of the *industry*, in spite of the difficulties of exact definition. Thus we shall define an industry as a group of firms or segments of firms, closely related in the competitive process by reason of the great substitutability of their respective products, and distinguished from other firms by a gap in the range of substitute products.

Levels of Abstraction in Competition Models

These various *models* of different forms of competition can be regarded not only as corresponding roughly to different states of actual markets but also as different levels of abstraction. We have seen that the analysis of the firm under monopoly is really the analysis under the condition that the market functions relating sales or purchases to price structure are not only given for the firm but are independent of any other variables related to the firm itself. Thus no matter how high the profits of a pure monopoly,

---

[1] See Robert Triffin, *Monopolistic Competition and General Equilibrium Theory*, Cambridge, Mass., Harvard University Press, 1940.

the market functions will not be affected. At the next stage of analysis we may suppose that the market functions of the firm depend on some other variables—say profits—and that if profits are above normal new firms will be attracted into the industry and the market functions of old firms will move to the left (less can be sold or purchased at each price). This is the analysis of *monopolistic competition*. Perfect competition is simply a special case of this model where the number of firms is large and the commodity produced homogeneous, so that the market functions are perfectly elastic. Further stages of analysis introduce assumptions regarding the reaction processes by which firms react to the behavior of others, or anticipate the reactions of others to their own behavior. This gets us into problems of oligopoly.

THE SPATIAL MODEL

Perhaps the simplest approach to these complex problems is to start with the relationships of firms in an "ideal" geographical space, for the essence of the market relationship is "distance," and the analysis of the effects of spatial distance can easily be generalized to the analysis of difference among commodities on some scale of quality or preferability. *Likeness* and *closeness* are almost identical concepts! We begin then with a single firm (monopoly) in a space which consists of a straight line, XX' in Fig. 99. We suppose that potential customers (buyers) are distributed evenly along this line, and the firm is located at point *A.* Suppose first that it adopts what is known as the *mill base* system of pricing, with a price at its own location (or mill) equal to *AP,* and price rising to the buyers along *PT* and *PT'* as we move away from *A,* the slope of the lines *PT* and *PT'* being the cost of transport per ton-mile, or unit-mile. Then if we measure the amount sold in each point or small segment "mile" of the XX'

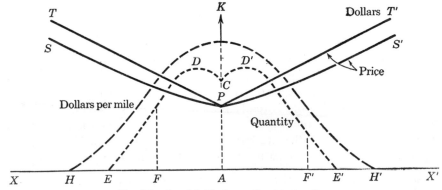

Fig. 99. Spatial Markets of a Monopolist

on another vertical scale, a curve such as *HKH'* will show the amount sold at each point: at points *H* and *H'* the price to the buyer is so high that he buys nothing: maximum sales are at point *A* where the price is lowest. The total sales equals the area under the curve *HKH'* above the line *HH'*. The relation between the price as given by *TPT'* and sales as given by *HKH'* is the particular sales or demand curve for the buyers for each "mile" of the line.

The Marginal Net Revenue Curve

The marginal revenue from including another mile of buyers, less the marginal cost involved, is the *marginal net revenue* from including another mile full of buyers. The marginal net revenue curve, showing at each point the marginal net revenue from expanding to include another mile of buyers, is likely to be shaped like *EDCD'E'* in Fig. 99. At very low volumes of sales and output, where sales are confined to a small area near the mill, marginal costs are apt to be high and marginal net revenue lower than at somewhat higher volumes. It is likely, therefore, that marginal net revenue will rise at first, from *C* to *D* or *D'* as the firm expands sales. Beyond a certain point, however, declining marginal revenues, and possibly increasing marginal cost, will lower the marginal net revenue till it falls to zero at some distance *AE* or *AE'* from the mill. The total net revenue is the area under the marginal net revenue curve in the relevant range: thus if the firm sells only to buyers between *F* and *F'*, the total net revenue will be the area *FDCD'F'*. The maximum net revenue is obtained when the firm expands to the points where marginal net revenue is zero; this is equal to the area *EDCD'E'*.

Optimum Price Policy

The position of the marginal net revenue curve is itself a function of the geographical structure of prices charged, which does not have to be the same as the mill price plus cost of transport. There will be some such structure represented, say, by the line *S'PS'*, at which the total net revenue is a maximum; this is achieved when the price at each mile is such that the marginal net revenue for that mile is maximized.[2] A divergence from

---

[2] If the demand function at each mile is the same, and is linear, for mile (x_i) suppose it is $s_i = k - ep_i$, s_i being the sales, p_i the price to the buyer, e the absolute elasticity. Then if t is the cost of transport per unit mile, the net price returned to the mill from sales at mile x_i is $p_i - tx_i$. The marginal net revenue from mile x_i is then $m = (k - ep_i)(p_i - tx_i) - C$, where C is the marginal production cost. This is a maximum when

$$\frac{dm}{dp_i} = 0 \quad \text{or} \quad p_i = \frac{tx_i}{2} + \frac{k}{2e}$$

That is, the buyer's price should fall only half as fast as the cost of transport. This however is a very special case.

the principle of charging the mill price plus cost of transport can only be profitable, of course, if the buyers are not in communication and cannot resell. Otherwise, if a buyer at the xth mile pays a price which differs from that paid by a buyer at the $(x + 1)$th mile by more or less than the cost of transport per unit mile, it will pay one buyer to resell to the other. The case is strictly parallel to the problem of price discrimination discussed in the previous chapter.

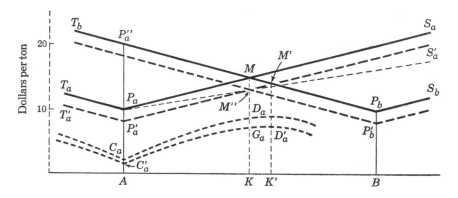

Fig. 100. Imperfect Competition: The Two-Firm Model

The Two-Firm Model: The Boundary of Indifference

Now let us suppose that we have two firms in the field, one ("Able") at A and one ("Baker") at B, as in Fig. 100. Suppose AB is 100 miles, and the cost of transport is 10 cents per unit mile. If the vertical axis now represents price, AP_a and BP_b are the mill prices, both assumed to be $10 per unit; then the line $T_aP_aS_a$ again shows the buyer's price charged by firm Able at any point on the base line; it rises as we move away from A at a slope equal to the cost of transport, assuming no price discrimination. $T_bP_bS_b$ is the corresponding buyer's price line for Baker. Where these lines intersect, at M, the price charged by both firms to a buyer at the corresponding location, K, is equal. To the right of K Baker's price to the buyer is lower than Able's, and if the commodities are similar in all other respects, all buyers will buy from Baker. Similarly to the left of K all buyers will buy from Able. K therefore may be called a *boundary of indifference*, for only at K is the buyer indifferent as to which firm he buys from. This boundary then divides the field into two market regions, one where Able is dominant to the left of K and one where Baker is dominant to the right of K.

The Price War

Suppose now that Able reduces its mill price to $8, while Baker retains its price at $10. Able now has a new buyer's price line, $T'_aP'_aS'_a$, and the boundary of indifference moves from K to K'. Able therefore gains, and Baker loses, all the customers between K and K'. Suppose now Baker is not content with this loss, and cuts its mill price to P'_b. The boundary of indifference is pushed back to M'' (K); Baker regains its lost customers, but both firms are now selling to their old customers at a lower price, and the net revenue of each will have fallen. This a phenomenon known as a *price war*, and it has many similarities to the corresponding phenomenon in the international system known as the *arms race*. Whether it will in fact take place or not depends on two main sets of circumstances: first, whether a price cut on the part of one firm will in fact increase its net revenue, if the other firm does not retaliate; and second, what is the first firm's estimate of the chances of retaliation. The larger initial gains, and the less the chance of retaliation, of course, the better the chance of a price cut.

Gains from a Price Cut

If the marginal net revenue per mile is high at the boundary of indifference, the gains from a one-sided price cut are likely to be greater—especially likely where the firm is operating under capacity. Thus suppose the marginal net revenue curve for firm Able in Fig. 100 were C_aD_a; the total net revenue, with both mill prices at AP_a, BP_b, would be the area AC_aD_aK, plus the corresponding area to the left of A. A price cut to AP'_a, with Baker's price still at BP_b, would lower the net marginal revenue curve to $C'_aD'_a$, with a loss of net revenue equal to the area $C'_aC_aD_aG_a$ (plus the corresponding area to the left of A), and a gain of net revenue equal to the area $KG_aD'_aK'$. If a small price cut produces a large shift from K to K' it is likely to be profitable—if there is no retaliation. On the other hand, if the situation of the two firms is symmetrical, if it is profitable for Able to cut price in the absence of Baker's response, it is also likely to be profitable for Baker to cut its price in response. The dynamics of the system then depends a great deal on the shortsightedness or long-sightedness of the parties—that is, whether each neglects or considers the response of the other party. Price wars are much less likely to occur where the parties are longsighted.

The Point of Market Extinction

Suppose now in Fig. 100 that the mill price of Able at A were AP''_a, where P''_a is on the line P_bT_b, and the mill price of Baker at B were still

BP_b. Baker could then undersell Able at all points to the right of A; if Able's mill price were even very slightly greater than BP''_a, Baker could undersell Able at all points, and Able would have no customers left. That is, as the excess of Able's mill price over Baker's increases, the boundary of indifference K moves towards A until at some point it is right at A; beyond this, Able's market completely disappears. This may be called the point of market extinction. There is a similar point for Baker as the excess of Baker's mill price over Able's increases.

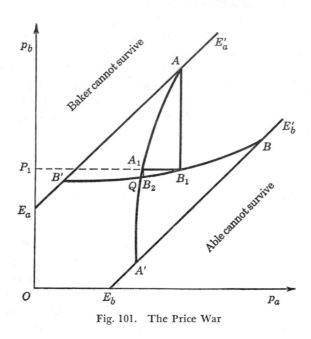

Fig. 101.   The Price War

The Strategy Field: Market Extinction Lines

The properties of the two-firm system can further be illustrated in Fig. 101, where we measure the mill price of A, p_a, horizontally and the mill price of B, p_b, vertically. Such a diagram can be called a *strategy field*, p_a symbolizing Able's strategy—a variable over which it has power—and p_b symbolizing Baker's strategy. The *results* depend on both strategies—that is, on the values of both p_a and p_b. This is known in game theory as an infinite game matrix, and the processes which relate to such strategy fields are often called—perhaps unfortunately—*games*. Within a field of this nature two different kinds of processes or games can be distinguished: first, the *game of coexistence* in which each party seeks to maximize its own long-run advantage on the assumption that the other party or parties continue to survive[3] and participate in the process; and the second, the *game of survival* in which one or more parties seek to eliminate one or more of the others. These concepts are elaborated further in Chapter 26. In Fig. 101 there are two 45 degree market extinction lines, $E_aE'_a$ for A and $E_bE'_b$ for B, the equations of which are $p_b - p_a = cs$, and $p_a - p_b = cs$, respectively, where c is the unit cost of transport and s the distance (AB in Fig. 100) between the two firms. We have then $cs = OE_a = OE_b$. At all points (combinations of p_a and p_b) to the left of and below $E_aE'_a$, p_a exceeds p_b by more than the cost of transporting the commodity from B to A, so that Baker can outsell Able anywhere and Able has no market. Similarly for all points above and to the left of $E_bE'_b$ Baker has no market. Only points between the parallel lines represent feasible combinations of the two prices.

In the dynamics of the system, we suppose that each firm can change its own price but not the other, so that Able can move only horizontally and Baker only vertically. Suppose now within the field of possible co-existence between the two parallel market extinction lines we have two *reaction curves:* AA' shows Able's reaction to a price set by Baker, and BB', Baker's reaction to a price set by Able. That is to say, if Baker set a price equal to OP_1, Able will set a price equal to P_1A_1, where A_1 is on Able's reaction curve AA'. Similarly if Able were to set a price P_1B_1, Baker would react by setting a price OP_1. If then we start from a point such as A, Baker will cut its price and move vertically to B_1, Able will retaliate by cutting its price to A_1, Baker will then cut its price to B_2, and so we go on, approaching the equilibrium point Q at the intersection of the two reaction curves. With the curves as drawn the equilibrium is stable. If we started, for instance, from A', Baker would raise its price, Able would counter with another raise, and we would find ourselves once more at Q. We must leave the question of what determines the position of these reaction curves, and also the question as to the circumstances under which competitors will coexist, or, alternatively, one will seek to eliminate the other to Chapter 26. We may note here, however, that the reaction curves themselves may not be stable; if, for instance, at Q both firms are unprofitable, either one may eliminate or absorb the other, or there may be collusion and a new set of reaction curves to raise the prices to higher levels.

PERFECT OLIGOPOLY

Suppose now that either the cost of transport c diminishes, or the firms move closer together ($s = AB$, in Fig. 100, diminishes) so that cs ($= OE_a = OE_b$) declines. The two market extinction lines move closer

[3] See M. Shubik, *Strategy and Market Structures*, New York, Wiley, 1959.

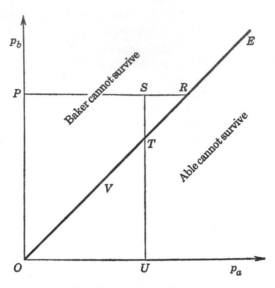

Fig. 102. Perfect Oligopoly

together, squeezing the area of possible coexistence between them until, when either the cost of transport c is zero, or the firms are in a single location, $s = 0$, $cs = 0$, we have perfect oligopoly, as in Fig. 102. Here the area of possible coexistence collapses into the 45 degree line, OE: $p_a = p_b$. Able cannot survive below OE, where $p_a > p_b$, and Baker cannot survive above OE, where $p_a > p_b$. If, e.g., firm Able lowers its price from PR to PS, Baker will immediately retaliate by lowering its price to the point T, (TU) or it cannot survive. If the firms are symmetrical, there is likely to be a *survival point*, V on OE, above which both firms, and below which neither firm can survive. In this case price cutting aimed at eliminating the competitor will simply push the position down OE towards O; any price cut even below the survival point V on the part of one firm will immediately be met by the other. If both firms are alike, the chance that the aggressor in the elimination competition will *not* survive is nearly 50 percent, as each firm has an even chance; hence the attempt to eliminate the competitor is unlikely, and coexistence will be the policy. Then each firm will seek that position on OE which maximizes its own net revenue. If the firms are symmetrical this will be the same for both. If they are unsymmetrical, the firm with the maximum net revenue at the *lowest* price sets the price to suit it, and the other firm must just follow, as the two prices cannot diverge. This is a phenomenon known as *price leadership,* frequently observed in industries approximating to perfect oligopoly, with a few firms producing a standardized product.

The marginal analysis throws up some interesting suggestions as to *which* firm is likely to be the price leader. In perfect oligopoly there is no *boundary of indifference*; each firm can sell over the whole market field. We must suppose therefore that there is some division of the market between the two firms. If the products are identical and the prices identical this distribution is random. The simplest assumption under these circumstances is that, as each firm has a 50 percent chance of selling to any particular buyer, the market will be divided equally. If now the two firms are symmetrical and have identical cost curves, we have the situation

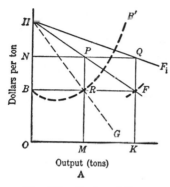

Fig. 103. Perfect Oligopoly,
Equal Costs

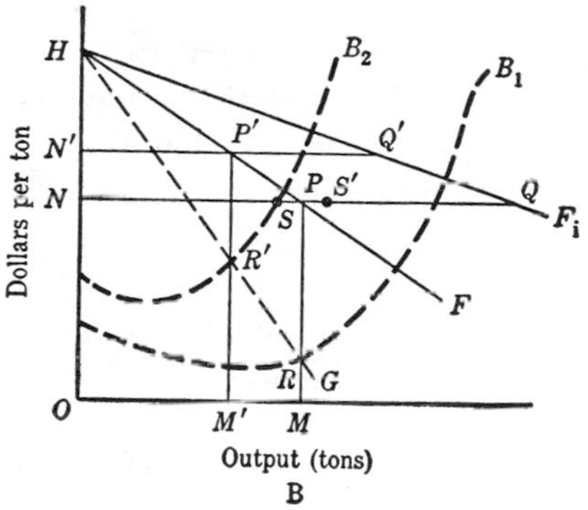

Fig. 104. Perfect Oligopoly,
Unequal Costs

of Fig. 103. The total demand curve for the product of the industry is HF_i. As the total sales of the industry at each price are assumed to be equally divided between the two firms, the individual demand curve (sales curve) of each firm will be *HPF*, where at any price, *ON*, charged by both firms the amount sold by each firm, *NP*, will be half the amount sold by the industry. This sales curve is drawn for each firm with the premise that the same price is charged by both firms, not, as is usual, with the premise that one firm alone changes its price. In perfect oligopoly, as we have seen, it is impossible for one firm to change its price alone. Then suppose *BRB'* is the marginal cost curve of either firm, both firms having identical cost curves. The marginal revenue curve for each firm is *HG*, this being the curve which is marginal to the average curve *HF*. Then each firm will set its price at the level *ON* (= MP), where it will sell an output *OM* and where its marginal cost is equal to its marginal revenue, *MR*. The total sales of the industry will then be *OK* (= *NQ*). For the sake of convenience the demand curves are drawn as straight lines, but the analysis does not, of course, depend on this assumption.

Where the demand curve is a straight line, however, we can show in this special case that the price and the output of the industry are the same as would result from pure monopoly. If our two firms are united into one, assuming that no economies or diseconomies result from the union, then the united firm will be able to produce twice as much output for a given marginal cost as either of the old firms. Thus at a marginal cost of OB each of the old firms could produce BR, and therefore at this marginal cost the united firm could produce BF ($= 2BR$). The marginal cost curve of the united firm will therefore pass through the point F. But the point F is also on the marginal revenue curve of the new firm, HF[4]. HF is the marginal curve to the average curve HQ. The output OK, therefore, is the most profitable output for the new firm, where its marginal revenue and marginal cost are both equal to KF; and the price it charges will be KQ, or MP. In all this analysis we have supposed that at the most profitable output the price is not less than the average total cost. Otherwise, of course, the industry will not exist at all.

Two Firms with Different Cost Curves

Now consider the case of two firms with different cost curves, as in Fig. 104. Suppose Able is a low-cost, or high-capacity, firm, with a marginal cost curve, B_1. Baker is a high-cost, or low-capacity, firm, with a marginal cost curve, B_2. The *capacity* of a firm is measured by the distance of its marginal cost curve from the vertical axis, for the farther the marginal cost curve lies to the right, the greater the output which can be attained at any given marginal cost. We again assume equal shares of the market, so that the revenue curves HQF_i, HPF, and HRG have the same significance as in Fig. 103. On these assumptions Able will be best satisfied at the output OM, where the price is MP, and its marginal cost and marginal revenue are both equal to MR. Baker, on the other hand, would prefer to produce at an output OM', with a price of $M'P'$, where its marginal cost and marginal revenue are both equal to $M'R'$. Here, then, is a conflict of policy between the two firms. The high-capacity firm, however, has a certain advantage, as the price it prefers, MP, is lower than the price $M'P'$, preferred by the low-capacity firm. The high-capacity firm (Able), therefore, will set the price to suit its own convenience, and the low-capacity firm (Baker) will be forced to follow suit, as the prices charged by the two firms cannot differ. If Baker set its price at $M'P'$, Able would be under no obligation to follow it, for Able prefers a lower price. If Able sets the price at MP, however, the other firm *must* follow it, or lose all its sales. If at the price MP Baker is unprofitable, it will go out of business and leave Able with a monopoly. It is quite possible, however, for Baker still to be making at least normal profits when the price is MP, even though

[4] See page 393 for the proof of this proposition.

it is not as profitable as it would be if it could set the price to suit itself. In this case the industry will be stable, and will attract enough firms to make the least profitable firm at least normally profitable.

A Special Problem

An interesting problem arises in connection with the interpretation of Fig. 104. *NP* shows how much each firm *can* sell at the price *ON*. There is no reason to suppose, however, that each firm has to sell as much as it can; if it wishes, it can sell less than the market will take simply by not having the product available when the last buyers come for it. Consequently, the demand curve for Baker, when Able fixes the price at *ON*, is not *HF* but *NPF*. That is to say, Baker can sell any amount not greater than *NP* at the price *ON*; and if it lowers its price, the other firm will be forced to follow and both firms will expand sales following the path *PF*. The marginal revenue curve of Baker, therefore, is *NPRG*. If now the marginal cost curve of this firm cuts this marginal revenue curve between *P* and *R*, no problem arises, and the above analysis stands. If however, as in the figure, the marginal cost curve B_2 cuts Baker's marginal revenue curve between *N* and *P*, at *S*, Baker will not wish to sell all that the market will take but will only sell an amount *NS*. That is, Baker has virtually perfect markets in this range, at the price set by Able, and will not wish to produce or sell beyond the output where price is equal to the marginal cost. This means, however, that Able now can sell an amount

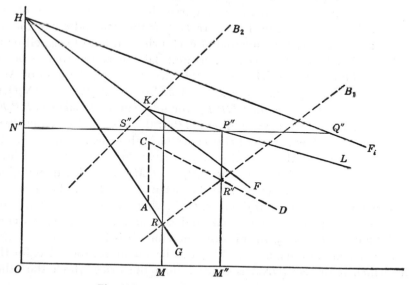

Fig. 105. Perfect Oligopoly, a Special Case

equal to $NP + SP$, or NS', where $SP = PS'$. Able's demand curve therefore is no longer HF, but is something like HKL in Fig. 105, K being the intersection of HF with the marginal cost curve B_2, and KL being drawn so that KF bisects any horizontal line such as $S''P''$ between the curve B_2 and KL. The marginal revenue curve corresponding to this demand curve is $HACD$, where CD is the curve marginal to KL. The optimum output of Able, OM'', is given by the point R'' where Able's marginal cost curve cuts its marginal revenue curve. The price will be $M''P''$; at this price Baker will only wish to sell an amount $N''S''$, leaving $S''Q''$, which by construction is equal to $N''P''$, to Able. A similar difficulty can also arise in the analysis of Fig. 106.

Price Leadership

We have obtained from our geometry a result which corresponds closely to reality. Many industries are characterized by the very phenomenon of *price leadership* by the high-capacity firm which we have seen emerging from our theoretical discussion. As we should expect also, the industries characterized by price leadership are those in which a simple, homogeneous commodity is produced by a small number of firms. The steel industry and the cement industry are excellent examples. In the steel industry, for instance, the United States Steel Corporation, having the greatest capacity, has been the price leader, and the other firms have followed the prices it set.

TWO FIRMS WITH DIFFERENT SHARES OF THE MARKET. A third situation, where two firms have identical cost curves but different shares of the market, is illustrated in Fig. 106. Here HQ_2 *is* the demand curve for the product as a whole. We assume that at each price set, both firms selling at the same price, Able gets three-quarters and Baker gets one-quarter of the total sales. Thus at a price ON_1 the total sales are N_1Q_1, the sales of Able are N_1P_1 [$= \frac{3}{4}(N_1Q_1)$] and the sales of Baker are N_1S_1 [$= \frac{1}{4}(N_1Q_1)$]. The sales curve of Able is then HP_1F_1; the sales curve of Baker is HP_2F_2. The marginal revenue curve of Able is HG_1; the marginal revenue curve of Baker is HG_2. The marginal cost curve of both firms is assumed to be the same, BB. Then Able would prefer to have the price set at the level ON_1, where it could sell an amount N_1P_1 ($= OM_1$), at which its marginal cost and its marginal revenue were both equal to M_1R_1. Baker would prefer to have the price set at the level ON_2, where it could sell an amount N_2P_2 ($= OM_2$), and where its marginal cost and its marginal revenue were both equal to M_2R_2. In this case, therefore, it is Baker, the firm with the smaller share of the market, which will be able to set the price, for the price which it prefers (ON_2) is smaller than the price which the other

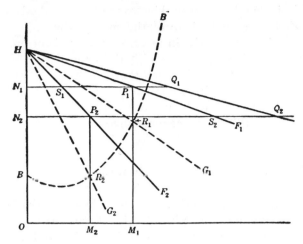

Fig. 106. Perfect Oligopoly, Unequal Shares of Market

firm prefers (ON_1). If the price charged by both firms were ON_1, then Able would sell an amount OM_1 (N_1P_1) at which its marginal cost and marginal revenue were equal. But Baker would then be selling only N_1S_1, an output at which its marginal revenue was greater than its marginal cost. Baker would therefore cut its price to ON_2 and force Able to do likewise. At this price Baker would sell N_2P_2 and Able, N_2S_2. If at this price both firms were at least normally profitable, the situation would be stable.

Price Leadership by a Firm with a Small Share of the Market

This result may seem surprising, for we should perhaps at first sight expect that the firm with the larger share of the market would act as the *leader*. We must remember, however, the peculiar assumptions which we have made, in particular the assumption that the marginal cost curves of the two firms are the same. This implies that all the firms have about the same capacity. In that case it is the *least* fortunate firm which is most active in setting the price. In the retail gasoline industry, for instance, when it is passing through one of its intermittent periods of stability, the situation outlined above frequently holds. The price is set by those firms which are not getting a very large share of the market. In the first instance they may have cut their price below that of the more fortunate firms in order to try to attract new customers. The other firms also cut prices to follow suit. At this lower price, the firms with the larger share of the market may still be making profits, though not maximum profits— i.e., they would prefer to have everybody charge a higher price. But the firms with the small share would be worse off if everybody raised prices, for having already a small share of the market the reduction in total sales, which would follow a rise in price, would hit them proportionately harder than it would hit the firms with the larger share of the market. Consequently, the firms with the small share of the market refuse to raise their price, and the firms with the larger share cannot compel them to do so. The relative permanence of cut-rate gasoline in many centers is probably an example of this phenomenon. The stations with the small share of the market, however, can set the price only as long as the capacity of all stations is approximately equal.

In our discussion of perfect oligopoly we have assumed that the share of the market possessed by each seller is not under his control but is determined by chance or by situation. It may be, however, that a firm cannot charge a price different from that of other firms but can make certain efforts to gain larger or smaller shares of the market by increasing selling costs. In such a case the problem becomes one of great complexity, and it is doubtful whether any general propositions can be deduced.

MONOPOLISTIC COMPETITION

Unlimited Market Space

Up to this point, we have simply assumed that we had two firms each located at a definite place. We must now extend the model and ask what will determine the location of the firms. If we have an unlimited market, which we can symbolize in Fig. 107 by an infinite line with buyers scattered uniformly along it, a single firm or monopolist is indifferent to where he locates. If he locates at A we may postulate a marginal net revenue curve, $M_a N_a M'_a$; he will sell within the range $M_a M'_a$, and not outside it. If now another firm comes in, he will maximize his total net revenue by locating at any point outside the range CB, where the marginal net revenue curves just touch at M_a or M'_a. If the second firm locates within the range CB, say at B', it will not only reduce the total net revenue

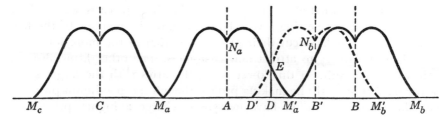

Fig. 107. Monopolistic Competition in Unlimited Space

of Able, as there will now be a boundary of indifference between the two firms at *D,* but its own net revenue (the area *DEN′_bM′_b*) will be less by the amount of the triangle *D′ED* than it would be if it located at *B.* In an unlimited linear market space then we will have a *line* of monopolists, each of which expands to the limit of its own market, and none of which are in competition with any other.

Limited Market Space: The Island

The situation is quite different if the market space is limited. Suppose we have an *island,* with coasts at *T* and *T′* in Fig. 108. It is easy to show that a single monopolist (Able) will locate at *A* in Fig. 108A at the center of the island, assuming that buyers are spread evenly along the line *TT′,* for the marginal net revenue curve *SN_aS* is then symmetrical about *N_a,* and the marginal net revenues at the points *T* and *T′* are equal (*TS = T′S′*). If the firm is located to one side of the center, say closer to *T* as in Fig. 108B the marginal net revenue on one coast *TS* is larger than on the other *T′S′,* and total net revenue will be increased if *A* shifted towards the center. Thus a shift from *T* to *V* and *T′* to *V′* would result in a gain of the area *SUVT* and a loss of *S′U′V′T′.*

Now suppose a new firm (Baker) decides to come into the island: where should it locate? Suppose in Fig. 108C it locates at *B.* If both firms charge

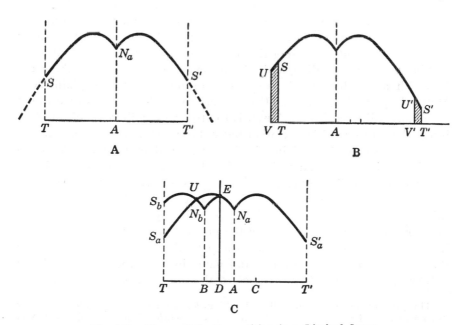

Fig. 108. Monopolistic Competition in a Limited Space

the same price, there is a boundary of indifference between them at D, halfway between A and B. Baker's net revenue is the area TS_bN_bED; Able's is reduced to $DEN_aS'_aT'$. Now as Baker moves toward A, D likewise moves toward A, and Baker's maximum net revenue is likely to be either when B is very close to, or at A. The mathematical problem here is tricky, as when B approaches A, Baker gains the area DEN_aA and N_bUE but loses the area S_aS_bU. It may, therefore, depending on the exact shape of the marginal net revenue curve, be possible that Baker has a maximum net revenue short of moving all the way to A. Another factor also will check Baker's motivations to settle close to A: the closer B gets to A the more the situation moves towards perfect oligopoly, and as Baker may have some intrinsic weaknesses through being a newcomer, if a game of survival follows it may not be Baker who survives! We can state a proposition thus, however—that Baker will move as close to Able as it *dares*.

The Principle of Minimum Differentiation

This is a principle of the utmost generality. It explains why all the dime stores are usually clustered together, often next door to each other; why certain towns attract large numbers of firms of one kind; why an industry, such as the garment industry, will concentrate in one quarter of a city. It is a principle which can be carried over into other differences than spatial differences. The general rule for any new manufacturer coming into an industry is: "Make your product as like the existing products as you can without destroying the differences." It explains why all automobiles are so much alike, and why no manufacturer dares make a car in which a tall hat can be worn comfortably. It even explains why Methodists, Baptists, and even Quakers are so much alike and tend to get even more alike, for if one church is to attract the adherents of another, it must become more like the other but not so much alike that no one can tell the difference. It explains the importance of brand names in commercial, social, and even religious life, for the best way of making a product as much like other products as possible without destroying the differences is to make it physically similar to the others but to *call* it something different, and to try to build up by advertising a preference in the mind of the buyer for the *name* of the product. Thus it also explains the importance of advertising, for a great part of advertising is little more than an attempt to establish a brand name in the minds of the public.[5]

Now suppose a third firm comes to the island; where will it locate?

[5] This principle deserves to be called *Hotellings law*, as it was first formulated clearly in an article by Harold Hotelling, "Stability in Competition," *Economic Journal*, Vol. 39, 1929, pp. 41-57).

The three-firm model, like the three-body problem in mechanics, is extremely difficult to solve explicitly. If a third firm (Charley) locates at *C* in Fig. 108C, this puts Able in a special position of being "in between" the other two, as long as we confine ourselves to a one-dimensional island. There may be a set of positions of the three firms in which all three can coexist, or there may not, depending on the shape of the marginal net revenue functions and the survival level of the net revenue. Competition for survival with three firms is greatly complicated by the possibilities of coalitions; thus a coalition of the two "outside" firms may be able to eliminate the "in-between" firm fairly easily; we may note the same problem in international relations, where in-between countries like Germany tend to be at a disadvantage.

Competition in a Plane Space

Once we go to the more realistic model of firms locating in a plane rather than on a line the problem of *in-betweenness* becomes less important. Thus in Fig. 109A we suppose a circular island with uniform distribution of buyers, in which it is easy to show that the best location

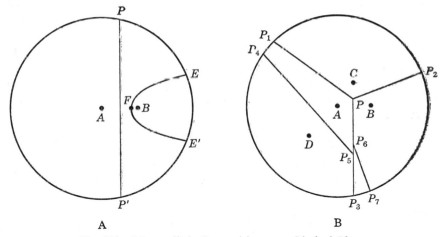

A   B

Fig. 109. Monopolistic Competition on a Limited Plane

for a single firm is at the center, *A*. A new firm coming in will locate at *B*, following the principle of minimum (advisable) differentiation and, if the mill prices are equal, the boundary of indifference will be *PP'*.[6] If a third firm comes in it is likely to locate at a point such as *C* in Fig. 109B where the firms form a rough triangle, and the market areas are P_1PP_3 for Able,

---

[6] If Able cuts its price the boundary of indifference becomes a hyperbola such as *EFE'* in Fig. 109A: this suggests that, in a plane, price differences have a more drastic effect than in the linear model and price cutting is more likely.

P_3PP_2 for Baker, P_2PP_1 for Charley. We may note that the firstcomer, if he locates in the middle, retains a certain market advantage even after the appearance of competitors. The question as to where a fourth firm would locate may be a matter of some doubt; he may squeeze in between two of the others, creating a new slice of pie-shaped market area, or he may go to a point such as D, which gives him a market area such as $P_4P_5P_6P_7$. Obviously, endless complications are possible. With a large number of firms all concentrated at a single spot and with free entry or exit of firms, we have perfect competition; when firms are scattered as in Fig. 109B we have monopolistic competition.

Equilibrium of an Industry

What we mean by *free entry* in such a case is not always easy to say. If the entry of another firm still permits the coexistence of all firms, and if the profits of the firms are then normal or above, and if there are no obstacles to the entry of such a firm, then we might suppose that there is free entry. What we mean by the equilibrium of the industry in these circumstances, however, may be ambiguous; we may mean that number and disposition of firms in which the addition of another firm would reduce profits below normal, or we may mean that number and disposition of firms in which an additional firm would trigger a game of survival in which one firm (not necessarily the newcomer) would be eliminated. In the case of perfect competition, these two concepts amount to the same thing; this is not necessarily so in monopolistic competition, where profits *may* be held above normal by fear of a game of survival if another firm intrudes.

Equilibrium of an Industry in Monopolistic Competition

We cannot construct a supply curve for an industry in imperfect competition as we can for one in perfect competition, for there is no *single* price at which all the product is sold; even in equilibrium each firm may charge a different price. But a construction similar to that in Fig. 83, page 406, can be applied to the case of monopolistic competition. Although there is now no single supply or demand curve, we can still interpret a general rise in demand, say, for breakfast foods as a whole, as meaning a rise in the sales curves of all the firms connected wth the industry. Figs. 110 and 111 show the cost and revenue curves (average and marginal) for a series of firms in an industry in monopolistic competition. In each case the dashed curve marked C is the marginal cost curve, the dashed curve marked R is the marginal revenue curve, the solid curve marked V is the average variable cost curve, and the solid curve marked S is the sales curve, or average revenue curve. In Fig. 110 the position of the curves is

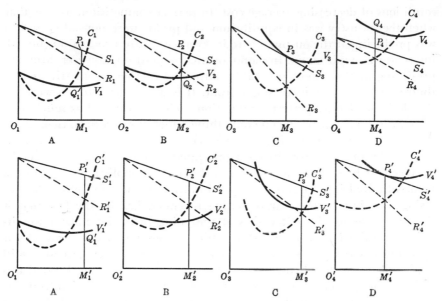

Figs. 110 and 111. Rise in Demand in Monopolistic Competition

such that firm C is the marginal firm, or the "no-rent firm." This firm's most profitable price is equal to its average variable cost, and therefore its fixed factors receive no rent. Firms A and B bear rent. Fig. 111 gives the effects of a "rise in demand" for the commodity. The rise in demand means a rise in all the individual demand curves (sales curves) of the various firms. It will be seen that firm D is now brought into the industry, whereas in Fig. 110 firm D would not be in the industry in equilibrium because even at its most profitable output (O_4M_4) the price (M_4P_4) is less than the average cost (M_4Q_4). The rise in demand clearly raises the output of each firm—e.g., of firm A from OM_1 to $O'_1M'_1$. It will probably raise the price charged by each firm—e.g., from M_1P_1 to $M'_1P'_1$. As we saw earlier in Fig. 97B, the rise in price, though probable, is not an absolutely necessary result. The rise in demand will increase the rents in the industry, as may be seen by comparing the rectangle $P_1Q_1 \times O_1M_1$ with $P'_1Q'_1 \times Q'_1M'_1$.

Monopolistic Competition Results in Production with Decreasing Average Cost

An important proposition is suggested by this analysis, that when an industry in monopolistic competition has reached an equilibrium without excess profits the size of each firm is smaller than the size at which the average cost is at a minimum, so that each firm will be producing under conditions of decreasing average cost. In perfect competition, we saw that when the industry was in equilibrium and profits were normal each firm was producing at the output where its average cost of production (including rent) was a minimum. In monopolistic competition, however, firms are producing at their most profitable output when they could still reduce their average cost by increasing output. It is not difficult to see why this should be so. Under perfect competition each firm can sell as much as it wants at the market price. The only thing which limits a firm, then, in its desire to expand output, is the fear of rising costs, so that a firm cannot possibly be producing at its most profitable output if it could lower its average cost by expanding its output. But in monopolistic competition a firm is limited in its desire to expand output not merely by the fear of rising costs but by the fear of falling revenues, i.e., by the fact that it cannot sell as much as it wishes at the going price but must lower its price (or raise its selling costs) in order to sell more. Consequently, it will stop expanding its output at a point where its average cost is still falling, if its marginal cost is equal to its marginal revenue. Beyond this point, although its average cost falls, the fall in cost is more than counterbalanced by the fact that in order to sell the increased output the price must be lowered or the selling cost raised.

EXAMPLE: THE RETAILING INDUSTRY. The industry which provides the services of retailing is a good example of monopolistic competition. Almost every store has a certain clientele which would buy from it even if its prices are somewhat higher than those of surrounding stores. Thus, physically identical commodities may sell for different prices even in neighboring stores. This would be impossible under perfect competition, and is a proof that an element of monopoly is present. The profits in the retail business are not unusually large, however, for it is usually an easy business to enter. If profits were above normal in any line of retail trade or in any locality, new stores would quickly open up and reduce profits to normal. Indeed, it may be that profits are actually below normal in the retail trade on account of the unshakable and unwarranted optimism of the small capitalist with a few thousand dollars.

The result of monopolistic competition, therefore, is not that profits are large but that the number of stores is greater than would be the case if perfect competition prevailed. Almost every retail store could lower the average cost of its services if it had a larger volume of sales. In most cases, however, it does not attempt to get this increased volume of sales, in spite of the lower cost, because of the loss in revenue involved in obtaining the increased volume. The loss in revenue may be due to lower prices or to increased selling cost, but it should be noticed that in either case this loss would not be present under perfect competition. If the industry were perfectly competitive, some of the weaker stores which are protected under monopolistic competition by their faithful clientele would be driven out. The remaining stores would expand their outputs to the point where the average total cost (including rent) of their services was a minimum. Monopolistic competition, however, enables the relatively inefficient firms to make normal profits, and so keeps these firms in the industry. It also enables all firms to maximize their profits at a level of output which is inefficient in terms of costs. These are wastes of monopolistic competition for which the consumer must pay in the form of higher prices.

Selling Costs in Imperfect Competition

An important aspect of the behavior of firms in various forms of imperfect competition, which arises directly out of the imperfection of competition itself, is that they devote a proportion of their activity to selling, the costs of which are known as selling cost. These may include advertising, the employment of salesmen, the use of attractive packaging, and so on.

The full treatment of selling costs must wait until more advanced techniques of analysis have been presented in Chapter 26. Nevertheless, some important conclusions can be drawn from the simple propositions (1) that the purpose of sales expenditures is to move the sales curve of the firm to the right, and (2) that the more effective is sales promotion as a method of increasing sales and the less effective is price reduction, the more likely are selling costs to be high. It is clear that a firm with perfect markets will not have any selling costs; there is no point in trying to increase the amount that can be sold at the market price when any amount within the limits of the firm's capacity is salable.

In general, the more homogeneous the product, the less important will selling cost be for the individual firm. Even in the case of perfect competition, of course, selling costs may be expended by an association of the industry as a whole, in an attempt to increase the total demand for the product—the "Drink More Milk" and "Eat More Fruit" campaigns are typical. Such *industry* advertising is also characteristic of perfect oligopoly. Individual selling costs incurred for its own benefit by the individual firm, however, grow in importance as the products become more heterogeneous. In perfect oligopoly, advertising by the individual firm may exist, in an attempt to give the firm a larger share of the market; but if the product is completely homogeneous the market will be divided at random and no amount of advertising will persuade a buyer that the product of one firm is better than that of another. The more imperfect oligopoly becomes, the more important becomes individual selling cost.

In monopolistic competition selling costs are extremely important, for the more inelastic the sales curve, i.e., the more differentiated the product, the less effective is a reduction in price as an instrument for increasing sales, and the more effective selling cost is likely to be. In terms of the spatial model of Fig. 100, a reduction in price is equivalent to a reduction in the mill price such as AP_a, but an increase in selling cost is equivalent to devoting expenditures to reducing the cost of transport, or rather, the slope of the line P_aT_a. Thus Able can push the boundary of indifference from K to K' either by reducing its mill price from AP_a to AP'_a, cost of transport being unchanged, or by reducing the cost of transport or price gradient line from P_aM to P_aM'. A distinction may be made, between a *real* decrease in cost of transport due to investment in better actual transport facilities and a manipulated change in the price gradient line through subsidy expenditures and "absorption of freight." The first corresponds in nonspatial differentiation to invading a competitor's market by improving the quality (desirableness) of the product, or improving the information available to buyers. The second corresponds to pure selling cost, for example, in the form of psychological advertising which does nothing to improve the product, as such, but inveigles people into buying it. It is not always easy to make a sharp distinction between these two cases, but the principle is fairly clear.

Because an increase in selling cost may be a substitute for a fall in price, many of the results of this chapter may need reinterpretation in terms of competitive increases in selling cost rather than in terms of competitive price cutting. Thus a fall in demand may lead to an increase in selling cost rather than to a decline in price, according to the relative effectiveness of these two methods of increasing sales. Similarly, in the case of imperfect oligopoly there may be advertising wars rather than price wars. The cigarette industry is probably a case in point, where, like the Red Queen in *Alice Through the Looking-Glass*, each firm has to run as fast as it can in the direction of selling costs in order to stay where it is. If, however, a fall in price is relatively more effective than an increase in selling cost as a means of expanding output, imperfect oligopoly will lead to price wars rather than to competitive advertising.

Weaknesses of the Models

The reader should not be deluded by the apparent neatness of some of the solutions of this chapter into thinking that the problems of oligopoly and imperfect competition are easy. In fact this represents still one of the least satisfactory fields of economics, in spite of much useful work in recent years. There is, for instance, no adequate theory of the *macroeconomic* impact of various states of the market, nor of the dynamics of these various situations; and until this gap in theory is filled, any overall appraisal of the effects of these different market forms must be made with great reserve. The most we can say for economic analysis in this regard is that the pursuit of various degrees of abstraction in the analysis seems to lead to cases that bear a striking resemblance to conditions which are observed in the real world. Nevertheless the real world is a mosaic of immense intricacy and complexity, and our models do little more than outline some rough abstract patterns which may be perceived in it.

QUESTIONS AND EXERCISES

1. It has been proposed to measure the degree of monopoly power possessed by any firm by the reciprocal of the elasticity of its sales curve. Criticize this proposal from both the theoretical and the practical standpoint.

2. Under what circumstances is price cutting likely to arise? How may it be prevented?

3. "One of the greatest evils of modern society is price cutting." "The benefits of economic progress must be passed on to the consumer in the form of lower prices. This can only be done by price cutting." Discuss these two statements.

4. Discuss briefly the truth, falsehood, or completeness of the following statements:
   a. Rent cannot exist except in an industry which is operating under conditions of monopolistic competition.
   b. Firms in an industry in monopolistic competition will be smaller than those in an industry in perfect competition.
   c. The profits of monopolistic competition are not permanent.
   d. No stable position of equilibrium is possible under oligopoly.
   e. In monopolistic competition, when the industry is in equilibrium, the marginal cost will be less than the average total cost (including rent) in all firms.

5. Make a tabular statement comparing and contrasting the conditions and results of (a) perfect competition, (b) monopolistic competition, (c) pure monopoly, (d) perfect oligopoly, (e) imperfect oligopoly.

6. What are the competitive and what are the monopolistic elements in monopolistic competition?

7. Analyze, as far as you can, the effect of taxation upon industries in monopolistic competition, in perfect oligopoly, and in imperfect oligopoly.

8. Analyze the situation when two firms in perfect oligopoly have different cost curves *and* different shares of the market.

9. Prove that in a model like that of Fig. 100, the further the distance between the firms (A, B) the more likely is competition to take the form of reducing or subsidizing cost of transport (or selling cost) rather than reducing the mill price (price cutting).

CHAPTER 23

APPLICATIONS OF THE MARGINAL ANALYSIS: THE REGULATION OF COMPETITION AND MONOPOLY

The previous chapters have formed a long, connected argument in which it has not been possible to follow the general plan of this work in regard to applications of the theoretical models. Now, however, that we have gained a broad view of the theory of economic behavior and the marginal analysis, it is possible to consider some applications of the theory, especially to problems of the regulation of competition and monopoly.

For a complete analysis of this problem we need first to understand what causes the emergence of different forms of market structure—monopoly, oligopoly, monopolistic competition—and second we need to have some analysis of the *social optimum* according to which these various forms can be judged. The first is the easier problem, and the marginal analysis throws a good deal of light on it. The question is, If the economic system is left to itself, without government intervention, what will be the result? Will there be universal perfect competition, universal monopoly, or a mixed system? The answer seems to be that an unregulated system would soon find itself in a "mixed" condition in which some industries were monopolies, some perfectly competitive, some in monopolistic competition, some perhaps in almost pure oligopoly. The question arises, therefore: What determines the character of an industry in the absence of state intervention?

Perfectly Competitive Industries

Two principal factors determine the nature of an industry. One is the character of the commodity which it produces. The other is the character of the process by which its commodity is produced. For an industry to be perfectly competitive, two things must be true. The commodity which it produces must be a relatively simple, homogeneous substance, easily graded into a small number of grades, and sold in bulk. Unless this is the case, the product of one firm will not be perfectly substitutable, in the minds of the buyers, for the product of any other firm in the industry, and therefore the market for the output of each firm will not be perfect. Also, the most profitable output of the individual firm must be small relative to the total output coming to the market. This latter condition will be fulfilled only if the average cost of production in each individual firm reaches its minimum at a relatively small output. It will also be fulfilled only if the commodity is readily transportable and if the buyers and sellers of the commodity are in close physical proximity. The average cost of production will reach a minimum in the case of any firm, as we have seen, because of the existence of inputs whose quantity cannot indefinitely be increased. In short periods capital equipment is typical of these fixed inputs. In long periods it is the quality of management which is fixed. In any process in which management is a detailed and complex function the point of minimum average cost will come at a relatively small output.

Agriculture as a Typical Competitive Industry

Agriculture and, to a lesser extent, mining provide the best examples of perfectly competitive industries. Most agricultural products are homogeneous substances, easily graded and defined. There is therefore little opportunity for product differentiation, especially by the individual producers of the standard raw materials—wheat, sugar, coffee, etc. The size of the firm is small, for the average cost apparently begins to rise at a relatively small output. This is due mainly to the fact that in agricultural processes management is a detailed and difficult process which cannot be reduced to a simple routine or delegated to employees. The farmer must catch the weather when he can; he cannot work to an eight-hour day or a set of book rules. Consequently, large-scale production has been much less successful in agriculture than in industry.

Natural Monopolies

At the other end of the scale are those industries which are *natural monopolies,* in which the size of the firm is so large in relation to the market that there is room for only one firm. As always, the exact definition of what is natural and what is artificial is no easy matter. No economic life can be carried on without some laws, and laws imply intervention by the state. There are doubtful cases in which firms have obtained monopolies by gaining control of the whole supply of some input necessary for the production of their commodity. The exclusive possession of patents is another possible case. Apart from these examples there are industries in which the productive process exhibits decreasing cost over a long range of output and in which, therefore, large firms will prosper at the expense of small firms until only a single firm is left. Whether this will occur or not depends largely on the physical character of the productive process.

A change in techniques may easily break up a natural monopoly through the introduction of new ways of providing the old commodity. The introduction of the automobile is an interesting example of a technical change leading to a reduction in the size of the unit of enterprise. The rail-road was an excellent example of a natural monopoly in many cases. It was a form of organization of transport in which the unit of enterprise had to be large or it could not exist. The automobile, on the other hand, is a form of organization of transport which lends itself admirably to small enterprise, whether the business enterprise of the independent trucker or taxi driver or the personal enterprise of the car owner.

Imperfect Competition

Wherever the cost curves of firms are such that the size of the in-dividual firm is large in relation to the size of the market, but where there is room for a few firms, imperfect competition in one or another of its forms is likely. Which form it will take depends mainly on the character of the commodity. With a chemically simple, definable com-modity product differentiation will not exist, so there will be pure oligopoly and price leadership. Steel is a good example. With a moderately homogeneous commodity in which small differences may exist from firm to firm, imperfect oligopoly with its attendant recurrent price cutting will be the rule. The gasoline industry and some other retail industries tend to fall into this class. With a complex and highly manufactured commodity the product of each firm is likely to be appreciably different from that of other firms in the same industry, and monopolistic competition will result.

The Social Optimum

The analysis of the nature of the *social optimum* is difficult and presents problems which may be impossible to solve in an exact form. Nevertheless the marginal analysis throws some light on the nature of *serious* diver-gences from the social optimum, and legal regulation is most clearly justified where these serious divergences can be detected. It is very difficult to say exactly what is the ideal state of society. It is much less difficult to detect situations which are clearly *not* ideal, and it is usually possible to say something about the direction of change which will improve matters. Therefore it is fortunately not necessary to have a clear or exact theory of the social optimum or ideal in order to be able to say something about desirable directions of change away from situations which are clearly not ideal.

THE REGULATION OF MONOPOLY

The first situation which can clearly be recognized as a divergence from the economic ideal is monopoly. In considering the problem of the regulation of monopoly, then, we must first answer the question: What is wrong with monopoly? Why do we have to bother about its regulation? There are many answers to this question. They can, however, be reduced to two principal propositions: (1) that monopoly distorts the distribution of resources among various occupations away from that which is socially most desirable, and (2) that monopoly allows the exploitation of one group by another. If an industry which formerly was operating under perfect competition were suddenly to be organized as a monopoly, its owners would find it profitable to restrict its output and to raise the price of its product. By eliminating those plants which were operating under the highest variable costs and so restricting the output, the owners could obtain a higher price for the product and thus a higher net revenue in the remaining plants. As the net revenue in the eliminated plants would be small in any case, there would clearly be a gain in total net revenue through their elimination. Those resources which were employed in the high-cost plants would be forced out of the industry and either would be unemployed or would have to find employment elsewhere. The fact that they did not seek employment elsewhere before the advent of the monopoly, however, implies that when the industry was perfectly competitive they were in their most advantageous occupation.

The formation of a monopoly, therefore, will drive some resources from the monopolized industry into an occupation which is *less* advantageous to them. Consequently, the principle of equal advantage is violated. A monopolist can maintain his own advantages at a level higher than the prevailing level only because he can prevent the movement of those resources which would like to move into his occupation. He can be said to *exploit* these resources. He can also be said to exploit consumers, who now have to pay a higher price than before. A monopoly, then, results in a general distortion of the distribution of resources, a smaller amount than is desirable going into the monopolist's occupation and a larger amount than is desirable going to other uses, with the results that, first, there is a general social loss, and second, the monopolist appropriates an unduly large proportion of what is left. A monopolist is like a greedy boy at a table, who not only seizes more than his fair share of the cake but also in the scramble causes some cake to be spoiled.

There are two broad policies possible in an attempt to deal with the monopoly problem. One is the policy of *dissolution*—that is, the attempt to split up the monopoly into a number of competing firms. This policy was tried in the early days of the antitrust laws but has not had much success in recent decades. It is doubtful whether it does much to solve the monopoly problem, as it is rarely possible to split a big firm into more than a few parts, which may leave us with a situation of oligopoly, some-times even worse than the monopoly which preceded it. A case can be made that splitting is good for the firms themselves; successful firms may grow until they are too big for their own best efficiency, and the shock of a split may put new life into the components, as it seems to have done with the Du Pont company in 1911. Nevertheless the alternative policy of *regulation* is much more popular. This involves the acceptance of monopolies as necessary evils in some cases and the regulation of their practices and policies by law. Regulation is practiced principally in those industries where there is a strong natural tendency for monopoly; i.e., where the optimum size of the firm is so large that the industry if left to itself would all come under the control of a single firm. The so-called public utilities—water, gas and electricity, telephones, railroads, and so forth—are for the most part natural monopolies, and there is therefore a reasonable fear that left unregulated in private hands they would prove instruments for the exploitation of the people.

Objects of Monopoly Regulation

It is one thing, however, to say that monopolies ought to be regulated and another thing to say *how* they ought to be regulated. From the point of view of the distribution of income it is fairly clear that they should not ideally be allowed to retain more than *normal* profits, though exactly how normal is to be defined in practice, and how above-normal profits are to be extracted from them without changing their policies in other directions, possibly adverse, is also not always clear. When we come to the question of what constitutes the *ideal output* of a monopolist, we find controversy not only in the matter of how to achieve the ideal output, but even in regard to the definition of the ideal.

The problem is illustrated in Fig. 112. Fig. 112A shows the curves of average revenue (AR), marginal revenue (MR), average cost (AC), and marginal cost (MC) of a monopolist. We suppose that average cost is rising with output. For convenience in drawing, all the curves are assumed to be straight lines, but this is not necessary to the argument. Then the output at which profit (net revenue) is a maximum is OA_1, at which

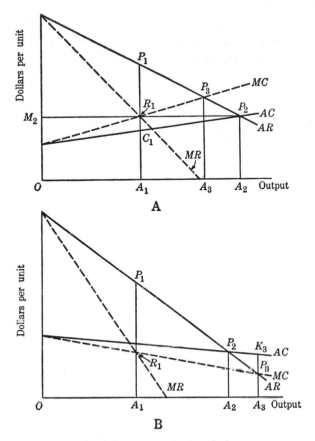

Fig. 112. Monopoly Regulation

marginal cost equals marginal revenue at R_1 (see page 391). The largest output at which profits are normal is OA_2, where the average revenue (price) is equal to the average cost, and the net revenue therefore is zero. If therefore the regulatory commission sets the price at A_2P_2, under the condition that all the output that can be sold at that price must be produced, profits will be normal. The condition is necessary because otherwise it might still pay the monopolist to restrict output and sales below the maximum amount which could be sold at the set price. Thus suppose the price were set at A_2P_2 ($= OM_2$), but that the firm were left free to produce and sell as much or as little as it pleased. The marginal revenue curve to the firm would then be M_2P_2, which intersects the marginal cost curve at R_1, and the firm would still restrict its output to OA_1, even though it now makes smaller profits than formerly ($R_1C_1 \times OA_1$ as against

$P_1C_1 \times OA_1$). In the present figure M_2P_2 goes through R_1, the inter-section of MR and MC, only because all the curves are straight lines; but even if the curves are not linear, M_2P_2 will cut MC well to the left of P_2, and there would be restriction of output.

Marginal Cost Pricing

Yet another criterion for determining the socially best output has been suggested, by Hotelling, Lerner, and others:[1] that the price should equal the marginal cost. In the figure this would mean an output of OA_3, where the MC curve cuts the AR curve at P_3. The price would then be A_3P_3. The reasons for this proposal are subtle, and cannot be explained in full here. Suppose, however, that the marginal cost is a measure of the value of resources used up in producing an additional unit of the product, and the price is a measure of the value of the product to the consumer. Then if the marginal cost is less than the price, there is evidence that an ex-pansion of the output in question will create more social value (as measured by the price) than the value of the resources used up, and there-fore it will be socially desirable to expand output. If the marginal cost is greater than the price, a contraction of output will release a greater value of resources than the value of the product, and there is a presump-tion that resources should be transferred to other commodities.

There are many objections to this proposal, both theoretical and practi-cal. We may notice, for instance, that the criterion is formally satisfied at R_1 (Fig. 112A) if the price is fixed at OM_2 but the monopolist is allowed to produce any quantity he wants. A condition must be added, therefore, that sales must not be less than the maximum possible at the fixed price. A more serious objection is illustrated in Fig. 112B. Here the meaning of the figure is identical with Fig. 112A except that we have supposed decreasing instead of increasing cost. Under these circumstances it will be observed that P_3, the point where price equals marginal cost, is at a larger output than P_2, the point where profits are normal. This means that if output is pushed to the point where price equals marginal cost, there will be losses (profits below normal) equal to $P_3K_3 \times OA_3$. If the enterprise is to continue, therefore, a subsidy at least equal to this amount must be paid, and the question arises how this subsidy is to be raised without creating further distortions in the system. The question will be discussed later (pages 646–648).

---

[1] For an excellent summary of this proposal and the controversy connected with it, the reader is referred to two articles by Nancy Ruggles, "Recent Developments in the Theory of Marginal Cost Pricing," *Review of Economic Studies*, Vol. 17, 1949–1950, pp. 107–126, and "The Welfare Basis of Marginal Cost Pricing," *ibid.*, pp. 29–46.

Difficulties of Marginal Cost Pricing

The practical difficulties are perhaps the most serious: long-run marginal cost is not really in the information system at all, and even if short-run marginal costs can be discovered, serious errors might be introduced by pricing according to short-run marginal costs. It should also be pointed out that under constant cost the *MC* and *AC* curves coincide in a horizontal line and that therefore P_3 and P_2 are the same point—that is, the "normal profits" criterion and the "price equals marginal cost" criterion are the same. The longer the period of time considered, the more likely are we to find approximately constant cost conditions, as in the long run most adjustments of capacity can be made. Under these circumstances it is not surprising that the less sophisticated criterion of normal profits has proved a more effective guide for regulation than the sophisticated criterion of equating price with marginal cost.

Difficulties of Normal Profits Pricing

Even if the *normal profits* criterion is accepted, the practical difficulties in the way of carrying out such a policy of regulation are enormous, though perhaps not insuperable. One difficulty is the *definition* of normal profit. Presumably, normal profit in this connection means a certain *rate of return* on capital, measured as a percentage per annum, which the investor could reasonably have expected to earn had he invested in some other unregulated enterprise of comparable risk. But the definition and calculation of the rate of profit is by no means an easy matter; for in order to calculate the rate of profit over any period of time less than the whole life of the enterprise, *valuations* of the property of the enterprise must be made at the beginning and at the end of the period. It is the making of these valuations which provides most of the difficulties of effective public regulation, for there is no agreement as to the principles according to which they shall be made. We must leave the detailed consideration of these difficulties until we have examined the theory of valuation.

Another practical difficulty is that of identifying the normal rate of profit itself. Any figure, such as 6 percent per annum, fixed by the courts, is bound to be arbitrary. It is not only difficult to discover what are the actual profits in the regulated business; it is even more difficult to discover what are the rates of profit in unregulated businesses, and still more difficult to estimate and allow for the differences in risk between various enterprises. But if the figure set by the courts is too high, part of the purpose of regulation is evaded, and if it is too low, there will be little new investment in the regulated industries, and even the old investment will in part be liquidated.

Public Operation of Monopolies

In view of these difficulties public ownership and operation of natural monopolies has been advocated, and in many cases it has been carried out. The Post Office is an excellent example of a business which seems universally to be best administered by the state. In many countries railroads are run by the state; and the municipally owned and operated water, gas, electricity, or transport company is a common occurrence. If the political system is efficient, the operation of monopolies by the state may be the most satisfactory solution of the problem. Where political life is corrupt, however, or even where it is honest but unintelligent, state or municipal operation is no guarantee of maximum social welfare. Even under state ownership, it should be noticed, the principles of profit making are not absent. When *all* the services and costs are valued properly, a government agency should usually be operated at the maximum output at which normal profits can be made. If less than normal profits are made there is evidence either of inefficient production methods or of a misuse of resources.

The misuse of resources involved in unprofitable public undertakings need not, of course, be due to any particular corruption or incompetence of public officials, but may simply be due to errors of forecasts. All investment is made in anticipation of future returns, and these anticipations are by their very nature subject to error. It should be pointed out, therefore, that public ownership involves public acceptance of the risk of loss as well as of the chance of profit. If a privately owned coal mine or railroad turns out to be unprofitable, the owners bear the bulk of the loss. If a publicly owned coal mine or railroad turns out to be unprofitable, the loss is distributed over the whole people in some degree. For this reason public ownership is not quite the unqualified blessing that it might appear to be at first sight: a town, for instance, which has incurred a mass of bonded indebtedness to acquire a transport system which turns out to be a financial burden may well envy its sister community which allowed its defunct trolleys to remain in private hands.

Another difficulty which is sometimes encountered by public enterprises is that they may be denied access to the private capital market, and hence their expansion or even modernization may wait upon the somewhat capricious decisions of legislative budget makers. This means that they may face a kind of monopsony in the capital market which may handicap them.

One possible method of regulation emerges from our analysis which has probably never been tried but is of some theoretical interest. The purposes of regulation are (1) to prevent the monopolist from making abnormal profits, (2) to expand the output of the monopolist beyond the point of greatest private profit. Both these ends might be achieved by the combination of a fixed tax with a variable rebate or subsidy. The effect of a variable subsidy is of course opposite to that of the variable tax studied on page 461. The marginal cost curve will be lowered (if the subsidy is regarded as a deduction from cost) and consequently the monopolist will expand his output under the influence of the subsidy. Any monopoly profits that accrue to him, however, can theoretically be absorbed by the state in the form of a fixed tax, for a fixed tax, as we have seen, should not affect the monopolist's output.

DUMPING AND PRICE DISCRIMINATION

Another important aspect of the monopoly problem we have already noticed (pages 446–453) under the heading of price discrimination, and many problems in the regulation of monopoly arise out of this practice. In international trade the policy of price discrimination between two markets is known as *dumping*. A steel combine, for instance, which has a monopoly within its own country may find that the demand for its product at home is less elastic than the demand abroad, for in foreign markets the fact that buyers have alternative sources of supply makes the demand for the product of the monopolist highly elastic. A high price will not restrict sales at home as much as it would abroad, for buyers at home cannot turn to other sellers. Consequently, the monopolist will find it most profitable to charge a high price at home where the demand is less elastic, and a low price abroad where the demand is more elastic. This policy often arouses the anger of competitors abroad, who accuse the company of selling below cost; the layman may well wonder how it could possibly pay anyone to sell below cost. The ambiguity of the word *cost* is well illustrated in this problem. If the monopolist wishes to maximize his profits he will, as we have seen, try to sell that quantity and charge that price in each market at which the marginal revenue is equal to the marginal cost. This means that the price in each market cannot be below the *marginal* cost, for except when the demand is perfectly elastic the price at any volume of sales is greater than the marginal revenue. However, it is quite possible for the marginal cost to be well below the average cost, as it will be if the plant is working at a smaller than optimum capacity. Consequently, it may profit a monopolist to sell at a price below his *average* total cost in some market, provided that the additional revenue received from the sale of an additional unit at least covers the additional cost of producing that unit.

Price Discrimination in Domestic Trade

Dumping is found in internal trade as well as in international trade. The milk cooperative, for instance, which sells milk at a high price to domestic consumers and at a low price to butter and cheese manufacturers is dumping. A celebrated example in the industrial sphere was that of the Goodyear Tire Company, which sold tires under its own name at a high price through the regular channels, and sold the identical tires through a mail-order house, under another brand name, at a lower price! The grocer who used to divide his tea into three parts—one selling at 20 cents, another at 30 cents, and another at 40 cents a pound—was following exactly the same principle. So is the doctor who charges a high fee to a rich patient and a small fee to a poor patient.

In all these cases it should be observed that the price discrimination is possible only because the markets are separated. It is possible on an international scale because of the difficulty of reselling, in its country of origin, material sold abroad. Frequently a tariff on imports of the commodity is necessary or at least helpful to the monopolist in maintaining the separation of markets. Discrimination in the milk market is possible only because domestic consumers cannot conveniently purchase from the manufacturers, or because an agreement or contract forbids the resale of milk sold for manufacture. Discrimination is possible in the retailing business because consumers do not generally buy and sell from each other. A drugstore which follows a policy of "25 cents for one, 26 cents for two!" would soon be run out of business if all its customers hunted in couples, and the above-mentioned tea merchant would soon find his little tricks unprofitable if the Colonel's lady who insisted on "the best" tea at 40 cents ever began to compare notes with Judy O'Grady who bought the same tea for 20 cents. Similarly, doctors can discriminate only because a poor person cannot retail his appendicitis operation to the rich.

Railway Rates

Another interesting, though complex, example of price discrimination is found in the theory of railway rates. Railroads usually charge a low rate per ton on bulky commodities of low value-density, such as wheat and coal, and a high rate on commodities whose value is great in proportion to their bulk or weight. Railroads also charge low rates over long hauls and higher rates over short hauls; they may charge one rate from west to east, and another rate from east to west; they may charge a low rate between two points where there are competing forms of transport and high rates between intermediate points on the same route where there are no competing forms of transport. All this complex structure of rates is an application of the principles of price discrimination which we have outlined. The principle of discrimination in this case goes by the name of "charging what the traffic will bear." If the demand for a particular form of transportation is highly elastic, the rate is likely to be lower than if the demand is more inelastic. Thus in the case of bulky commodities a high freight rate may prevent their transportation altogether; the demand for their transport is therefore elastic, and the rate will be relatively low. In the case of precious commodities transport charges may be only a small proportion of the total cost of getting them to the consumer. Consequently—with transport services regarded as an *input* in the whole process of production—the demand for this input will be inelastic (see Chapter 13 for proof of this proposition). The price will be considerably greater than the marginal revenue and will be relatively high. Similarly, when a railroad runs between two points which have water communication, the demand for the transport of those types of freight which can easily travel by water will be very elastic. The cost of transport by rail cannot greatly exceed the cost by water or the freight will travel by water exclusively. The railroad rate will therefore be low compared to the rate on shorter hauls where there is no competition and the demand for transport is inelastic.

The problem of railway rates is complicated by the fact that each class of transport may have a different marginal cost. In each line of traffic, then, the most profitable price is that which will make the marginal revenue equal to the marginal cost of the operations involved. As the marginal costs of different forms of transport differ, it is not true in this case that the marginal revenues in all lines of traffic will be equal. If, however, in any one line the rate is such that an alteration in the rate will increase the total revenue more than it increases the total cost, it will pay to make that alteration.

Discrimination as a Weapon to Achieve Monopoly

In all our discussion so far we have assumed that the monopoly is established, and we have seen that under those circumstances it frequently pays to charge different prices for different units of output. There is another field in which discrimination may be important: this is in the original *establishment* of a monopoly position by a *game of survival* (p. 475). A would-be monopolist may discriminate even more than considerations of immediate profit would demand in order to drive a competitor out of business. An oil company, for instance, may drive a competitor out of a certain district by cutting its price far below the point even where the marginal revenue in that market is equal to the marginal cost. By so doing it will reduce its profits temporarily, but this may be an *investment* in the hope of regaining still larger profits later when it has established a monopoly. The problems involved in this type of operation are complex and involve a consideration of the theory of capital. They cannot, therefore, be discussed fully at the present point. An analogous operation is found in the purchases of input as well as in the sale of output. A monopolist, by having, or pretending to have, a highly elastic demand for an input which is sold by another monopolist, may force the seller to sell the input at a price lower than that charged to competitors. The Standard Oil Company, for instance, in its early days frequently obtained special concessions in railroad rates for the transport of oil.

The Movement Against Price Discrimination

In the history of the United States there has been a strong movement to outlaw the practice of price discrimination. The feeling against it arises partly from the fact that it has been used as a method of obtaining monopoly, and also from the fact that in itself it is rightly regarded as a *symptom* of monopoly power. The practice is also associated in the popular mind with "unfair competition," whatever that may mean. Two acts of Congress are specifically directed against it—the Clayton Act of 1914 and the Robinson-Patman amendment to the Clayton Act of 1936. Both, of course, apply only to interstate commerce. Like many legislative enactments they are vague in the definition of what they forbid, and the definition of their prohibitions is still in some dispute. In principle they forbid charging different prices to different buyers except where the price differences are "justified" by cost differences. The idea that price differences must be justified by cost differences is common in the lay discussion of this topic. It overlooks the problem of the ambiguity of the word cost, however, and is not necessarily a safe guide to social policy. Does it mean that the price of any service should equal its *average cost?* In that case the problem is virtually insoluble, for wherever there is joint cost it is almost impossible to allocate the overhead costs over various products or services. Does it mean that the price of any good or service should equal its marginal cost? Carried to its extreme this policy might deprive the poor of medical services, for a doctor forced to charge the same price to all for his services might have to charge so much as to exclude all below the middle class.

Thus it is not easy to discover all the implications of price discrimination for social policy. Price discrimination may be a method for redistributing real income. The demands of the rich are generally more inelastic than those of the poor, so that a monopolist will usually tend to charge higher prices to the rich than to the poor. This will have the effect of lessening the apparent inequalities of income. But it can also be argued that this method of equalizing incomes is undesirable, and that direct, conscious taxation and subsidy are to be preferred to the *indirect taxation* involved in price discrimination. These problems involve political and social considerations which go far beyond the range of our present study.

SPECIAL CASES OF MONOPOLISTIC ORGANIZATION

Our analysis will enable us to interpret several important types of monopolistic organization. A monopolistic organization is a combination of firms in an industry that is not a natural monopoly. Its object is to establish a price and sales policy giving greater profits than would result from the uncoordinated action of individual firms. As we have seen, the least stable form of competition is imperfect oligopoly, or "cut-throat competition." In industries which have a tendency toward this sort of competition, where the product is fairly homogeneous and the number of firms is relatively small, monopolistic organizations are common. Such industries have a constant tendency to try to escape from imperfect oligopoly either into monopolistic competition through product differentiation, or into perfect oligopoly through price leadership, or into a form of monopoly.

The Basing Point System

An interesting example of an industry escaping from imperfect oligopoly into perfect oligopoly is the steel industry. Before about 1900 the American steel industry was a good example of imperfect oligopoly. Prices were generally quoted on the "mill base" system—i.e., the price was quoted at the foundry and the buyer paid this price plus the freight from the foundry. As we saw on pages 472–475, such a system will lead to an imperfect market for the output of each seller. The elasticity of demand for the product of the individual seller will be great, but not infinite; the product will be differentiated, but not sufficiently so to produce monopolistic competition. Such was the case in the steel industry. Price cutting was frequently profitable and frequently practiced. A price cut, say, in Pittsburgh, pushed back the boundary of indifference between

Pittsburgh and, say, Chicago by an appreciable amount and gave to Pittsburgh a number of customers who previously had been in Chicago's market area. In order to escape from this situation the basing point system known as "Pittsburgh plus" was established. On this system all steel firms, wherever located, charged the same price for steel delivered at any given location. This price was the Pittsburgh mill price plus the freight charge from Pittsburgh to the buyer. The result of this was to do away with the market areas, for all firms charged the same price at any given point. This is evidently an example of *price leadership,* the leader in this case being United States Steel. In the early days the system was established by a so-called gentlemen's agreement. Mr. Elbert Gary gave one of his celebrated dinners, and the price of steel quoted by all companies mysteriously adjusted itself to the Pittsburgh plus system. Thereby price competition was avoided, and steel firms confined themselves to the apparently less noxious form of competition in services, such as speed in delivery.

Discrimination Under Pittsburgh Plus

Under the Pittsburgh plus system the firms in Pittsburgh received the same price at the mill for their steel no matter where they sold it. Firms, elsewhere, however, received a lower price at the mill when they sold to buyers between their mill and Pittsburgh than when they sold to buyers on the other side. Suppose, for instance, that the Pittsburgh mill price is $40 per ton and the freight from Pittsburgh to Chicago is $5 per ton. At a point midway between Pittsburgh and Chicago the price will be $42.50 per ton. Chicago will receive a mill price of $40. At a point the same distance on the other side of Chicago the price will be $47.50 per ton, for $7.50 is the freight from Pittsburgh. Chicago will get this price, but will pay only $2.50 in freight, giving Chicago a mill price of $45. For all points west of Chicago (assuming, what is not quite true, that transport costs per mile are uniform) the Chicago mill price will be $45. This meant in effect a division of the market, but in a way which would not allow any firm to increase its market by a small amount by price cutting. Chicago was now not anxious to push sales in the eastern area, for such sales brought a lower mill price to her than western sales. Chicago therefore concentrated on the West, Pittsburgh on the East, without there being any movable boundary of indifference for buyers between them; for at any point, east or west, both quoted the same price to the buyer.

Cartels

Another interesting form of monopolistic organization is the cartel, or selling agency. A cartel is an organization of a number of producers for the common selling of their product. It differs from the gentlemen's agreement or from price leadership in that the title to the commodity passes from the hands of the individual producer into those of the cartel itself. The individual producer, however, retains his individuality as a unit of production and enterprise. Cartels are common in both industry and agriculture, though in agriculture they are usually dignified by the name cooperatives and frequently are organized according to the cooperative form of business enterprise. The principal problem of the cartel, if it wishes to make monopoly profits, is that of restricting the production of its members without interfering too vitally with their independence of management. If cartels are successful in this, they are usually faced with the possibility of a breakaway by some of their members.

EXAMPLE: THE ENGLISH MILK MARKETING BOARD. An interesting example of a compulsory cartel is found in the English Milk Marketing Board. Every milk farmer in England must sell his milk by a contract registered with the Milk Marketing Board. His buyer pays the money not to the farmer directly but to the Marketing Board. The board then pools all moneys received from the sale of milk, deducts its expenses, and pays out the rest to the farmer as a "pool price." Previous to the establishment of the board (in 1933) a peculiar variety of imperfect competition prevailed in the milk market. There was a contract agreement between farmers and distributors, without legal standing but very generally observed, at least until 1931. This fixed the price of liquid milk at a level which was probably higher than would have prevailed without the collective bargain. It was appreciably higher than the price which the farmer got for milk sold to be manufactured (i.e., for

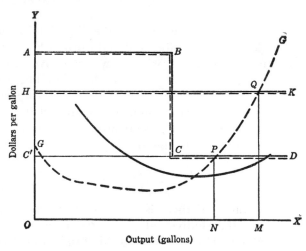

Fig. 113. Result of Forming a Cartel

butter, cheese, etc.). Consequently, the individual farmer found himself with a sales curve something like *ABCD* in Fig. 113. He could sell any amount up to a quantity *AB* in the liquid market at the price *OA*. If, however, he produced a surplus he had to sell it in the manufacturing market at a price *OC'*. If under these circumstances *GG* were his marginal cost curve he would produce an amount *ON*, where the marginal revenue was equal to his marginal cost, *PN*. The marginal revenue curve is also *ABCD*.

Now, after the cartel has gone into operation, he receives a uniform pool price, *OH*, which is somewhat less than the old liquid price but greater than the old manufacturing price. But he receives this price no matter how much he sells. The cartel, therefore, has given the producer a perfect market. If there are no restrictions on entering the industry, no license fees, etc., the effect of the cartel—a monopolistic organization—has been, paradoxically enough, to produce *perfect competition*.

Cartels May Increase Transport Costs

Unless the pool prices are adjusted properly for cost of transport, however, the result may be a distortion of the geographic distribution of the industry. This in fact happened. Normally it is liquid milk which is produced near the consuming centers, butter and cheese which are produced in the remoter districts. The result of the milk marketing scheme was to shift liquid milk production to the extremities of the island, thus increasing the total expenses of transportation of milk. The dealers paid their own costs of transport and were allowed a deduction from what they had to pay to the board according to the distance the milk traveled. This deduction at first proved to be greater than the actual cost of transport, so that the dealers made a profit on every mile a gallon of milk was carried. The result was naturally to send the liquid milk dealers out into the distant regions—e.g., Cumberland and Cornwall—for the farther they carried the milk, the more profit they made. Any monopolistic scheme is in danger of running into difficulties like this. The basing point system, for instance, results in a good deal of cross-transportation. Instead of each mill serving the area immediately around it, all the mills can sell over the whole country. Consequently, steel may travel farther, on the whole, between the mill and the buyer than it would under a mill base system.

Results of the Cartel

The result of the cartel, if there is no control or "rationing" of individual producers, is that individual producers increase their production. The farmer of Fig. 113 will increase his production from *ON* to

OM. If there are no restrictions of entry and no rationing of production, the cartel cannot give the members a profit which is above normal in the long run; for if the cartel succeeds in raising prices to the point where the industry is abnormally profitable, new producers will flock in. The total output of the industry will then increase until it becomes impossible for the cartel to maintain the price any longer. The cartel, therefore, cannot obtain a monopoly price for its product unless it can both ration the production of its members by *quotas* and restrict entry into the industry. Even here, of course, the profits may not remain with the members, but may be absorbed by the rent owners in the industry. The British hops marketing scheme (established in 1931) is a good example. Under this scheme no one may produce hops unless he possesses a quota. Hence the expansion of the industry is rigidly controlled. Those who were already in the industry in 1931 were allotted quotas of production, i.e., permits to produce a given amount. The result has been that the monopoly profits of the industry have been given to the owners of these quotas, which have become valuable items of property. Newcomers to the industry can enter only by buying a quota from an established producer. The price of the quota presumably is such that newcomers will make only normal profits. A similar situation has arisen in the American tobacco industry, where farms which happen to possess a quota allotment, simply because they were producing tobacco in 1943, now sell for several times the price of a similar farm without a quota, and all the monopoly gains seem to have been capitalized into the value of the farms.

Cartels Not Necessarily Monopolies

It will be seen from these examples that cartels are not necessarily monopolies, and do not necessarily have the power to exact monopoly prices or to give their members monopoly profits. Two conditions are necessary before a cartel can have monopoly power. First, it must be able to prevent any appreciable sales of its commodity through independent channels; otherwise, if the cartel attempts to raise prices above competitive levels, it will rapidly lose business to its independent competitors. Second, it must be able to control the admission of new members. Even if a cartel controls all sellers of its product, so that there is no problem of competition from independents, it will still be unable to obtain monopoly profits unless it can restrict admission. Otherwise, the existence of monopoly profits will attract members in until profits have been eaten away to normal levels. From the social point of view, therefore, it is very important that cartels—if we must have them—should be open, i.e., open to anyone who wishes to join.

It is important to note also that the diminution of profits as new sellers join the cartel may be accomplished in two ways, one of which is much more desirable, socially, than the other. If the output of the members is unrestricted the inflow of new members raises the total amount which the cartel has to sell, and hence the cartel must lower the price in order to sell the extra amount. If, however, the cartel has the power to restrict the output of each member, the adjustment to an inflow of new members may take the form of restricting the output of each individual member to the point where profits are not high enough to attract new entrants, not because of low prices but because of high costs. Under this system the cartel invariably results in a waste of resources and in the building up of idle capacity. The German potash cartel was a case in point.

The Trust and the Merger

The purely voluntary cartel is an unstable institution, for if it obtains a monopoly price by rationing the production of its members, there is a strong incentive for an individual to break away and obtain the benfits of the monopoly price without having to restrict his own production. In the absence of compulsory cartels, therefore, producers in search of monopoly organization have been forced into combinations of a much more drastic kind. The *trust* is an arrangement whereby the ownership, or at least the controlling share in the ownership, of the combining firms is vested in a single corporation, or trust. The legal form of the trust was made illegal in the United States by the Sherman Act of 1890. Nevertheless, the economic form survives in the *holding company*. This is a form of economic organization made possible by the institution of the corporation. The holding company is a corporation formed for the purpose of holding a controlling share of the stock in other corporations. By this means the policy of the subsidiary corporations may be brought directly under the control of the holding company, even though the subsidiary corporations maintain a degree of independent existence. In the *merger* the constituent corporations lose their identity altogether and are merged into a new corporation. Control over the constituent plants thus becomes absolute.

The Trust Movement

It is not the place of this volume to go into the elaborate details of what is known as the trust movement. We should, however, notice one or two points. The first is that there are two broad types of industrial combination. The first is the *vertical* combination of firms, one of which uses the product of the other. The combination of an ore mine and a steel mill would be an example. The second is the *horizontal* combination of a number of firms producing the same product. The second generally has more of a monopolistic motive than the first. Vertical combination may result in genuine economics and reductions of cost. Horizontal combination is likely to result in economies only if a better proportion of management to other expenses can be obtained. The problem of motives in the promotion of combinations is interesting. Frequently combinations have proved less profitable than their constituent parts, and the motive of power or prestige has played an important part in their creation. They are the battlegrounds of the captains of finance, and have often been promoted more for the promoters' than for the owners' benefit. Frequently, also, promoters have capitalized on the expected gains of combination, and then the investors have found that these gains were illusory. Nevertheless, there seems to have been a movement toward larger units of enterprise in many industries inspired by the economies of large-scale production and the elimination of the wastes of monopolistic competition as well as by the desire for monopoly profit.

The Labor Union as a Cartel

Many of the principles outlined above in connection with organizations of business also apply to interpreting organizations of labor. A labor union is a *labor cartel*. A cartel in the usual sense is defined as an organization of sellers for the joint sale of their product. A labor union is an organization of the sellers of labor (workers) for the joint sale of their product (labor). This is not to say, of course, that the cartel aspect of labor unions is their only one; they have many purposes, sociological and psychological as well as economic. But in their economic aspects unions must be understood principally as a subspecies of the cartel. Thus collective bargaining is always a sign of cartelization, for a collective bargain is one in which the terms of sale of the product of many buyers or sellers is arranged jointly by their representatives.

This is not to say, of course, that unions are necessarily monopolies; if they have nonunion labor competing with them (i.e., independent sellers of labor outside the cartel), or even when there is no nonunion labor in the field, if the union is *open* and does not restrict the labor of its members beyond the normal requirements of health and custom, then there is no monopoly. Unions differ from most business cartels in that the proceeds of the collectively arranged sale are not channeled through the organization but are paid to the members directly. Perhaps as a consequence of this, one is less apt to find the more objectionable aspects of cartelization in the labor movement, although parallels to almost all the cartel practices can be found. Thus, there is a certain amount of subsidization of idle capacity in the form of unemployment benefits or the *stand-in* arrangements of the musicians. One also finds unions which restrict entry by means of high entrance fees, onerous apprenticeship requirements, racial discrimination, or even by simple limitation of numbers. When such a *closed union* enjoys a *closed shop* it is very likely to have monopoly powers. Fortunately, these monopolistic situations are confined for the most part to craft unions; where they exist, however, they are a danger not only to the public interest but to the labor movement itself, for it is the labor monopoly that is the breeding ground of the labor racketeer.

THE WASTES OF COMPETITION

We have now said a good deal about the evils of monopoly. It must not be inferred, however, that competition is an unmixed blessing. Competition, like Janus, is a two-faced deity. On the one hand, it is lauded by economists as the mainspring of the economic system, the beneficent—if somewhat stimulating—source of efficiency, through whose operations the resources of society are pushed gently but firmly into those places in which they will do the most good. On the other hand, there is a good deal of talk about the wastes of competition, about its evil effects on society and upon humankind. On one side, it is the hero of the warfare of man against the Wicked Dragon, Monopoly; on the other it seems to be the enemy of the Beautiful Princess, Cooperation. This paradox is soon resolved when we realize that competition is a word with a number of different meanings. It may be perfect, oligopolistic, or monopolistic. It may refer simply to that ability of superior processes to displace inferior processes which is the necessary condition of any progress. It may refer to a particular condition of a market. It may refer to an interpersonal situation in which the gain of one is a loss to another. It may refer to the biological competition of populations in which a rise in one population causes a fall in the other. With so many meanings it is little wonder that there is confusion.

On the whole it seems fair to say that the major evils of competition are associated with the monopolistic aspects of competition rather than with perfect competition. These evils may be classified under two main heads: first, the evils which result from the fact that competition means the conflict of interest of one person against another; second, the evils which result from certain *wastes* of competition, such as competitive advertising. Both these evils are peculiarly characteristic of monopolistic competition. Under perfect competition, for instance, there are so many sellers and buyers that the action of any one of them cannot affect appreciably the fortunes of any other. Whenever people speak of competition being keen or intense they always refer to a state of imperfect competition, in which there are relatively few firms and in which, therefore, the action of one firm, say, in pushing sales or reducing prices, will affect the fortunes of the others.

Competitive Advertising

The wastes of competition are also characteristic mainly of imperfect competition. Perhaps the most important of these wastes from a social point of view is that involved in competitive advertising. There is a case for a certain amount of advertising, such as the purely informative advertising which is descriptive of the qualities and prices of commodities. This is a form of consumer education which is necessary if consumers are to make intelligent choices; in fact, it makes competition more nearly perfect. This virtuous advertising, however, does not bulk very large in the total. Most advertising, unfortunately, is devoted to an attempt to build up in the minds of the consumer irrational preferences for certain brands of goods. All the arts of psychology—particularly the art of association—are used to persuade consumers that they should buy Bumpo rather than Bango. Look through the pages of any magazine or newspaper, or listen to any program on radio and TV, and see how much space or time is devoted to an accurate description of the properties and prices of goods; the amount is surprisingly little. Instead, advertisements seek to associate the commodity in question with something else which the consumer likes or with the avoidance of something which the consumer seeks to avoid. Drinks are portrayed with beautiful flowers, cigarettes with beautiful girls, soaps are associated with love and marriage, and so on. There is very little place in the technique of advertising for the sober, truthful presentation of the qualities and prices of commodities.

Social Waste

There is a strong presumption that much competitive advertising is social waste. There seem to be only two arguments in its defense. From the economic side it might be argued that selling expenses increase the velocity of circulation of money and so increase employment. There are, however, cheaper and more dignified ways of increasing employment, and this argument breaks down completely in a time of full employment, and still more in a time of inflation. On the sociological side it might be argued that advertising has itself an entertainment and cultural value, and that it promotes mass communication in the form of cheaper magazines, newspapers, radio, and television. I am happy to leave this argument to the sociologists. With these possible exceptions competitive advertising does not result in the creation of wealth, for the consumer would spend his money in any case, advertising or no advertising, and he would probably spend it more wisely if there were no competitive—only informative—advertising.

No Competitive Advertising Under Perfect Competition

However, the wastes of competitive advertising are characteristic of monopolistic, not of perfect, competition. In perfect competition, as we have seen, there is no advertising of a competitive nature, for when each firm has a perfectly elastic sales curve it can sell all it wants at the market price and advertising will do it no good. It is useless for a single farmer to advertise "Buy Wheat," for even if his advertising has the effect of increasing the total demand for wheat, his share of that increase will be infinitesimal. It is useless for a single farmer even to advertise "Buy Giles's Wheat," for everyone knows that Giles's wheat is just the same as everybody else's wheat for miles around.

Monopolistic Competition Leading to Faulty Distribution of Resources

Another of the wastes of monopolistic competition is that it leads to a faulty distribution of resources and to excess capacity in those industries which operate under it. We proved in Chapter 22 that although perfect competition led to a state of affairs in which each enterprise produced at the output where its average cost (including rent) was least, this is not the case under monopolistic competition. The overabundant multiplication of small shops, of gas stations, of merchants of all kinds—in fact, all those things which are usually called wastes of distribution—is attributable to this property of monopolistic competition. Two railroad tracks where one would carry all the traffic; ten milk deliverers in every street where one could do the work much more easily; the litter of gas stations at the exit from every city where a few would sell gas more cheaply; even perhaps the extreme multiplicity of sects, both religious and political—are all evidences of monopolistic competition. If perfect competition could exist in these industries, these evils would disappear. Inefficient distributors would be driven out by the efficient ones, the number of distributors would fall, costs of distribution would be lower, and present wastes would be avoided. As it is, the inefficient distributors now shelter behind their little walls of monopoly and cannot be driven out into occupations where they would be of more benefit to society.

The Evils of Perfect Competition

It may be asked, however, with some justice: Are there not wastes of perfect competition just as destructive to human happiness as the wastes of imperfect competition? If perfect competition is a remedy for our economic ills, how does it happen that the agricultural industry, which perhaps approaches most closely to this idea, is constantly in difficulty? Is not the growth of product differentiation, of advertising, of trusts and combinations evidence of a desire to escape from the evils of unrestricted competition? These questions deserve examination. Even if monopoly were eliminated and all industries operated under conditions of perfect competition, there would still be economic dislocations. Any change in the structure of consumers' demands, for instance, will tend to bring about a shift of resources from one industry to another. (See Chapter 14 in Part I.) If, now, resources are difficult to shift from one occupation to another, the result of a change in demand may be that one industry is abnormally prosperous for a long period of time and another is abnormally unprosperous. Perfect competition works out to the general good only if resources are easily transferable from one industry to another. Where resources are highly specific to a single industry, there may be serious maladjustments of the system for long periods even in a perfectly competitive industry.

At the other extreme, an industry may be too sensitive to temporary shifts in its profitability. An industry in this condition is subject to cycles, such as the hog cycle, which are mainly the result of too easy, and too thoughtless, entry and exit. An industry may also run into difficulties of adjustment if all its firms are very similar, so that the cost ladder (page 407) is very flat. If under these circumstances the industry is unprofitable, some firms should get out of it; but as all the firms are so much alike, it is not clear *which* firms should get out. All firms may therefore hang on for a long time in an unprofitable condition in the hope that some other firms will abandon the struggle; then when things are very bad a large number of firms will leave suddenly, and the industry will become highly profitable, which may set off a new cycle.

Maldistribution of resources is not, of course, a *result* of perfect competition; it is likely to occur in all situations, and, indeed, monopoly or monopolistic organization will intensify the evil rather than cure it. But in some cases it can be argued that monopolistic organization will prevent the symptoms of the disease from becoming too unpleasant. It might similarly be argued that a doctor is justified in giving drugs to ease pain even if the drugs retard the final cure of the disease. So, if an industry is overexpanded, the result will be less painful to the individuals concerned if the effects of overexpansion are mitigated, or rather dispersed, by monopolistic organization than if the overexpansion is allowed to produce its entire effect in perfect competition. Even here, however, we must beware of lingering illnesses; it may be better to kill off an industry quickly by perfect competition than allow it to drag out a painful and burdensome existence to a long-delayed end under monopolistic regulation or government subsidy.

Evils of a Mixed System

In a system in which some industries are monopolistic and some approach perfect competition certain difficulties arise which might not arise under a system of universal monopoly or of universal competition. In a mixed system, such as in fact we have, serious dislocations of the price structure and unemployment of resources over long periods of time are all too likely to occur. In monopolistic industries prices are likely to be relatively stable, while output and employment fluctuate. In competitive industries output and employment are likely to be stable, while prices fluctuate. Suppose in a competitive industry the supply curve is inelastic. This will almost certainly be the case in short periods, and it may be so even over relatively long periods if there are unusual difficulties in the way of the movement of resources into and out of the industry. Then a fall in demand will bring about a sharp fall in the price of the commodity. The output of the industry will not be much affected. In the case of a monopoly, however, a fall in demand may be met in ways other than a fall in price. Selling costs may be increased and output may be reduced. Consequently, a fall in the demand for the product of a monopolist is likely to result in a small fall in price, or there may be no effect on the price (cf. pages 458–460). But where there is no effect on the price there will be a sharp fall in output and in employment.

These facts are of great importance in interpreting the phenomena of the business cycle. Suppose, for instance, that there is a general fall in the velocity of circulation of money, in bank loans, and bank deposits, leading to a fall in money incomes. This is characteristic of the period of recession. Then there will be a decline in the money demands for almost all commodities. This fall in demand, however, will not have a uniform effect on prices. The price of goods produced by competitive industries will decline sharply, but the output will not decline, and may even rise. The price of goods produced by a monopolistic industry will fall but little, if at all. The output of these goods, and the employment in these industries, will decline sharply.

How a Mixed System Intensifies Depressions

This is a regularly observed phenomenon of depression. In agriculture, for instance, prices fall, often catastrophically, while output and employment may even increase. In the construction and manufacturing industries prices stay up, but output and employment suffer a disastrous slump. The disparity between the two halves of the system produces evil secondary effects, intensifying the depression. Because of the reduced incomes of farmers and the high prices of industrial products, the purchases of industrial products fall still further, causing more industrial unemployment. Because of the industrial unemployment the demand for farm products falls still further, causing a greater fall in agricultural prices. If, now, industrial prices had been flexible and had fallen with the fall in demand, prices all round would have declined, but output and employment would have been maintained. Prices would reach a new stable level at that point at which the demand for money was satisfied.

The Flight from the Free Market

It is impossible to study the history of industrial combinations, of the labor movement, of the protectionist movement, of the agricultural organization movement, and of the socialist movement without realizing that all these historical movements of the past hundred years or more are in one sense aspects of a larger movement which can be described as the "flight from the free market." While the leaders of Western capitalism have been giving lip service to the principle of competition, they have been busily engaged in building up associations of all kinds for the purpose of limiting competition. A movement as universal as this cannot merely arise from what Adam Smith calls the "wretched spirit of monopoly"; there must be more fundamental causes. One of these causes, we have already seen, lies in the fact that an unregulated and unorganized economic order may produce not perfect, but imperfect, competition over large areas of economic relationships. There may, however, be even deeper causes. The completely unregulated market is subject to erratic and meaningless fluctuations in prices arising from *self-justified anticipations.* (See Chapter 9.) The deflationary phase of these fluctuations is extremely destructive to enterprise and employment. In some part the flight from the free market in all its forms can be interpreted as an attempt—perhaps in large part unconscious—to *protect* smaller groups from a general deflationary movement. Thus, the protectionist movement in commercial policy is in part an attempt to protect an individual nation from world deflation, and the failure of free traders to convince the world of practical men by arguments which would seem to be academically unimpeachable may be in great measure due to their failure to recognize the short-run deflationary effects of tariff removal and the inflationary effects of tariff imposition. Similarly, the labor movement in its economic aspects is an attempt to protect the organized worker from general deflationary movements, and the same may be said of agricultural and industrial combinations. In even broader terms it is an interesting question how far the strength of socialism is derived from experiences with the instability of the free market, and especially from the recurrent failure of capitalism to provide full employment. There are questions here which it is easier to raise than to answer: nevertheless it is clear that the monopoly problem is not going to be solved by preaching against or even by legislating against monopoly, unless at the same time something is done to counteract by other methods the deflations which have undermined confidence in the ability of the free market to do its proper job.[2] On the other hand, it may also be true that a genuine solution of the instability problem is impossible in a monopolistic economy. As we shall see in Volume II, the nightmare of the monetary stabilizer is a situation in which attempts to raise employment by monetary expansion result in a rise in money prices and wages rather than in a rise in output and employment. Hence, it may well be that in a monopolistic economy the only way to get full employment is to have a continuous inflation—a highly unsatisfactory state of affairs. The attack of the economists on monopoly has been ineffective mainly because economists have not seen that there was a real social question which monopolistic organization was trying to answer. The tragedy of our present situation is that monopoly is not only the wrong answer; it is an answer which may prevent the right answer being found.

QUESTIONS AND EXERCISES

1. "Under a system of perfect competition there would be waste of resources, for we cannot prevent people from making bad investments. Monopoly does nothing to prevent these wastes, though it may prevent the consequences of bad investment from falling on those who ought to bear them. In addition, monopoly produces many wastes of its own." Discuss.

2. Pure monopoly may be preferable to imperfect competition. Why, and under what circumstances?

3. Which is the greater evil, the fluctuation of prices or the fluctuation of outputs? Does your answer support the institution of monopoly?

4. What is conveyed to your mind by the phrase, "unfair competition"? Give examples. Try to define "fair competition."

5. "The tariff is the father of the trust." Do you agree?

6. "The monopolistic organization of industry is an expedient necessitated by the wastes of competition." Discuss.

7. "The troubles of the milk industry stem from the fact that the market is too competitive at the producer's end, and too monopolistic at the distributor's end." Discuss.

[2] How to do this is a principal subject of *Economic Analysis, Fourth Edition—* Volume II: *Macroeconomics*, New York, Harper & Row, 1966.

8. Suppose every industry were a pure monopoly. Would all industries then be able to make monopoly profits?

9. "A system cannot remain half slave and half free. Likewise, a system cannot remain half competitive and half monopolistic." Discuss.

10. What similarities and differences are there between the practices of:
    a. Industrial cartels?
    b. Labor unions?
    c. Agricultural cooperatives?

11. The following causes have been suggested for the growth of organization in labor, in business, and in agriculture:
    a. The need to protect groups against deflation
    b. The desire for monopoly profits
    c. The growth of skills of organization and the development of a class of professional organizers
    d. Growth of a moral feeling that cooperation is ethically superior to competition

    Can you suggest any other causes? How would you rate these various causes according to their importance? If you feel that your information is not sufficient to justify rating the causes, what sort of information would you need?

12. Suppose the mill price of steel at Pittsburgh is $40 per ton, and the freight rate is 1 cent per ton-mile. Assume that Chicago is 500 miles from Pittsburgh. On the Pittsburgh plus system draw up a schedule showing (a) the price of steel, (b) the price received by Pittsburgh mills at the mill, (c) the price received by Chicago mills at the mill, for points at hundred-mile intervals on a line drawn from Pittsburgh through Chicago to a point 500 miles west of Chicago. Illustrate the schedule with a diagram, plotting distance along the horizontal axis and price along the vertical axis.

    On a similar diagram draw the price structure under a mill-base plus cost-of-transport price system, and compare the two figures.

CHAPTER 24

THE ELEMENTARY THEORY OF
HOUSEHOLD DECISIONS

The household is one of the basic organizations of economic life. It is at the same time an original supplier of labor and other productive services, and it is an ultimate demander of final goods and services. An essential part of price theory is the development of models of household behavior which can help explain what determines the household's demand curves for its purchases, and its supply curves for its sales of productive services or of goods of household production.

As suggested in Chapter 1, the household is not very different in its essential problems and behavior from the firm. In that chapter we used the more familiar patterns of the household in the person of John Doe to illustrate some of the essential characteristics of all economic organizations. We shall now repay this small debt by extending to the household some of the concepts which we have now developed in the marginal analysis of the behavior of the firm. The *events table* of even a relatively simple household is a very complex mass of information, even though we must always remember that this is the basic reality which we are studying. We can gain insights into the forces which underlie the decisions and behavior of households, as described in the events table, by using simpler models which break down the problem into its parts.

The Utility Model

A model which has been of great importance historically, and which is still useful in organizing our thinking even though it has some limitations, is the *utility model* in which the household is assumed to guide its behavior by maximizing an ultimate psychological product called utility. In this model the household is regarded as a little firm at the final stage of the process of production. It buys consumer's goods as a firm buys inputs, and like the firm it transforms them into a final product whose worth may in some manner be estimated. The final product of the household, however, is not a physical product to be seen, tasted, and handled. It is a psychological product, utility. Just as a firm buys labor, land services, and raw materials and transforms them into a physical product, so a householder buys food, clothing, and amusements and out of them builds the edifice of his satisfactions. Utility, therefore, is the ultimate product of all economic activity—indeed, in its broadest sense, of all human activity whatever. Just as labor is bought in order to produce coal, and coal in order to produce steel, and steel in order to produce automobiles, and automobiles in order to ride down to the drug store and buy ice cream, so the ice cream is bought in order to produce those inner delights and satisfactions which its passage engenders. All physical goods are valuable only because they serve to produce utility. All physical goods, even final consumption goods, are really intermediate products. At the head of every process of production stands the satisfaction of a want. It is this want satisfaction that gives the process meaning. The *process of consumption* in the household, therefore, is not something separate and distinct from production; it is the final act in the economic drama, the culmination of a long series of processes held together by intermediate products.

THE UTILITY SCHEDULE

The Household as a Firm

If, then, the household is a little firm, buying inputs in the form of consumer's goods and producing utility, or want satisfaction, as a product, how much of the theory of the firm can be applied to it? We shall neglect here the problems which arise because the household consists usually of a number of persons, and assume that one person (the consumer) makes the economic decisions on behalf of the whole group. For the present we shall assume also, for purposes of exposition, that utility is a quantitatively measurable substance. In fact this is not so, and we shall see later how to escape from this unrealistic assumption. But for the moment suppose that we can strap a galvanometer to the seat of the emotions and record quantitatively the amount of enjoyment or utility which is produced under the stimulus of the consumption of various quantities of a commodity. Let us suppose that we can define a unit of utility called a *util*. Then just as we construct a series of experiments to show how the quantity of product varied with the quantity of labor

TABLE 47. UTILITY SCHEDULES
(per month)

(1) Quantity of Cheese (pounds)	(2) Total Utility (utils)	(3) Marginal Utility (utils per pound)	(4) Marginal Rate of Substitution (dollars per pound)
0	0		
1	10	10	0.50
2	30	20	1.00
3	48	18	0.90
4	63	15	0.75
5	74	11	0.55
6	81	7	0.35
7	84	3	0.15
8	84	0	0.00
9	80	−4	−0.20
			(Marginal utility of money = 20 utils per dollar)

applied, listing the results in a physical production schedule (Table 40, page 425, so we could conduct a series of experiments to find how great a total utility a consumer would register under the stimulus of various quantities of consumer's goods. Table 47, columns 1 and 2, represents such a schedule. Here it is assumed that the consumption of all other goods does not change, and a series of experiments with different quantities bought or consumed of a variable commodity (cheese) shows what in each case will be the total utility registered. We have assumed in the table that as the quantity of cheese rises, the total utility derived from its consumption rises also, but not proportionately. Total utility rises at a decreasing rate, and as the quantity of cheese increases to the point of satiety, between 7 and 8 pounds, the total utility reaches a maximum. Beyond that point any increase in our consumption of cheese makes us sick, or at least gives us a smaller total satisfaction than before.

Marginal Utility

The *marginal utility* of any quantity of commodity is the increase in total utility which results from a unit increase in consumption. Comparing Table 47 with Table 40, page 425, we see that the total utility corresponds to the total product and the marginal utility, to the marginal physical productivity. The *form* of the schedules is also assumed to be similar. Just as the marginal physical productivity at first rises, reaches a maximum, and then falls off, so in Table 47 the marginal utility rises, reaches a maximum, and then falls continuously as the quantity of commodity increases. Corresponding, therefore, to the law of diminishing returns or the law of eventually diminishing marginal physical productivity is an exactly analogous law, the *law of eventually diminishing marginal utility.*

The more exact statement of the law of diminishing marginal utility must be left to Chapter 27. But even at this stage we can show that it is a reasonable assumption. It may be stated as follows: As a consumer increases the consumption of any one commodity, keeping constant the consumption of all other commodities, the marginal utility of the variable commodity must eventually decline. If I go to one movie a month I shall probably get a good deal of satisfaction from it. One movie may whet my appetite so that two movies might give me more than twice as much satisfaction. But probably the third movie will not increase my satisfaction as much as the second, the fourth not as much as the third, the fifth not as much as the fourth, and so on.

Reasons for Diminishing Marginal Utility

1. COMMODITIES ARE IMPERFECT SUBSTITUTES. There are several good reasons for supposing that the marginal utility of a commodity falls eventually as the quantity consumed increases. The first is that commodities are not perfectly substitutable one for the other. That is to say, there are certain appropriate proportions in which commodities tend to be consumed. We would be worse off with an ounce of butter and no bread, or a loaf of bread and no butter, than with half an ounce of butter plus half a loaf of bread. In a series of experiments successively increasing the consumption of butter while keeping the consumption of bread and other things constant, we should find that when the *best proportions* of butter to bread had been passed, successive ounces of butter would add less and less to our enjoyment. As our consumption of butter increases with a constant amount of bread, pretty soon we do not have enough bread to spread our butter on.

2. SATIABILITY OF PARTICULAR WANTS. Another fundamental reason for assuming a diminishing marginal utility is that no *particular* want is insatiable. No matter how great a quantity of other things we might consume, our consumption of salt, for instance, will never rise above a certain quantity. Even if we could consume as much of a commodity as we wished without any sacrifices, we should still not consume an infinite amount. The point of satiety in consumption is the point where the total utility cannot be increased by further consumption, and therefore the marginal utility is zero. But at smaller quantities of consumption the marginal utility is positive, and total utility is rising. Between a level of consumption where the marginal utility is positive and a higher level where it is zero, then, the marginal utility must have been declining.

THE DERIVATION OF DEMAND CURVES

In Chapter 20, pages 432–433, the demand curve of an individual firm for input was shown to be derived from its productivity curves. An exactly similar analysis can be applied to the derivation of the demand of an individual consumer for consumption goods. At this stage of our analysis we shall derive the demand curve for one commodity—cheese—on the premise that the consumption of other commodities remains unchanged. We shall remove this unrealistic assumption in later chapters.

The Marginal Utility of Money and the Marginal Revenue of Utility

The first problem, then, is to find an equivalent for the concept of the marginal revenue productivity of page 432, in terms of utility, for we have seen that *marginal utility* is analogous to marginal physical productivity. This problem is solved if we can assume a relationship between a sum of utility and a sum of dollars. In order to turn the marginal physical productivity into a marginal revenue productivity we multiply by the marginal revenue of output; thus if the marginal physical product is 8 tons per man and the marginal revenue of output is $4 per ton, adding a man will increase output by 8 tons and revenue by $32, and the marginal revenue product is $32 per man. The problem therefore is to find a concept in the theory of consumption analogous to the concept of marginal revenue in the theory of production. Such a concept is found in the idea of the *marginal utility of money*. This is the increase in total utility which results from the addition of one "dollar" to the total expenditure of a consumer. Suppose the marginal utility of money is 20 utils per dollar. Then adding one util to the total utility is equivalent to adding one-twentieth of a dollar to the total expenditure. The reciprocal of the marginal utility of money, then—in this case $\$\frac{1}{20}$ per util—may be called the *marginal revenue of utility*, as it measures the equivalent, in monetary terms, of the addition of one util to the total utility product. It is the marginal revenue of utility which is analogous to the marginal revenue (of product) in the theory of production.

Marginal Rate of Substitution

If, then, the marginal utility of a commodity is multiplied by the marginal revenue of utility, or, what is the same thing, if the marginal utility of a commodity is divided by the marginal utility of money, a quantity analogous to *marginal revenue productivity* is obtained.

To take an arithmetical example. In Table 46 the marginal utility of the third unit of cheese is 18 utils per pound. Suppose that the marginal utility of money is constant, and equal to 20 utils per dollar. Then the increase in the consumption of cheese from 2 to 3 pounds is equivalent in utility to an increase in money expenditure of $18/_{20}$, or $0.90. (One pound = 18 utils: 20 utils = $1; therefore one pound = 18 utils = $0.90.) This quantity has been called the *marginal rate of substitution*;[1] it is related to the marginal utility just as the marginal revenue productivity is related to the marginal physical productivity. The marginal rate of substitution, then, is that sum of money which will afford the same satisfaction as one unit of the commodity in question. The marginal rate of substitution also varies with the quantity of consumption; its schedule is shown in column 4 of Table 47 on the assumption that the marginal utility of money is constant, and equal to 20 utils per dollar. If the marginal utility of money is not constant, as will in fact be the case unless the commodity in question is only a small part of the consumer's total expenditure, we can still construct a relative marginal utility schedule if we know the schedule giving the marginal utility of money for each quantity of cheese consumed.

Demand Schedule Identical with Marginal Rate of Substitution Schedule

If now we assume that the behavior of the household is governed by the principle that the consumer maximizes total utility, at each price of a commodity the consumer will buy that amount at which the marginal cost to him of a unit of the commodity (equal to the price of the commodity if the market is perfect) is equal to the marginal rate of substitution, so that the marginal rate of substitution schedule is identical with the *demand schedule*, at least in the segment where the marginal rate of substitution is falling. This is exactly similar to the proposition that if the firm maximizes net revenue, its demand schedule for an input with a perfect market is identical with the corresponding marginal revenue productivity schedule. Thus, if the consumer is buying an amount at which the price is less than the marginal rate of substitution, he can increase his total utility by consuming an extra unit. Suppose in Table 47 that the price were $0.35 per pound, and the consumer consumed only 3 pounds, the marginal rate of substitution being $0.90 per pound. Under these circumstances, by consuming an extra pound the con-

---

[1] This quantity is sometimes called the relative marginal utility. The term marginal rate of substitution is used because the quantity measures the amount of money which could be *substituted* for one unit of commodity without causing any gain or loss in utility.

sumer will give up $0.35 in money, but will gain in utility an amount which he thinks would be worth a sacrifice at $0.90. Obviously, then, he will gain in utility by buying and consuming an extra pound; and as long as the price is less than the marginal rate of substitution, he will be able to increase his total utility by increasing his consumption, for the gain from the increased consumption is more than the loss from the sacrifice of money. To put the matter in another way: again referring to the conditions in Table 47, if the price were $0.35 per pound and the marginal utility of money were 20 utils per dollar, we see that a sacrifice of $0.35 would be equivalent to a loss of 20 × 0.35, or 7 utils. If, therefore, the marginal utility is greater than 7 utils per pound, there will be a gain in total utility from expanding consumption. If the marginal utility were 18 utils per pound, for instance, the increase of a pound in consumption would cause a gain of 18 utils and a loss of 7 utils for the $0.35 given up. The consumer would therefore expand his consumption to include the sixth pound, whose marginal utility is 7 utils per pound. In Table 47, columns 1 and 4 give the demand schedule of the consumer for cheese on the assumption that he does not change his consumption of other things.

No Assumption of Measurable Utility

Although for purposes of exposition we assumed a quantitatively measurable utility, in fact this assumption is not necessary to the argument. The marginal rate of substitution is a magnitude measured in dollars per pound which does not contain the imaginary util. We can therefore postulate a marginal rate of substitution schedule without making any assumption regarding the cardinal measurement of utility. The only assumption necessary is that the utilities of a quantity of money and a quantity of commodity can be *compared*. We must be able to say that this quantity of money has a utility greater than, equal to, or less than the utility of a certain quantity of commodity. But we do not have to assume that we can measure by *how much* the utility of one thing is greater than that of another.

Utility an Intensive (Ordinal) Magnitude

A magnitude such as utility is termed an *ordinal* magnitude as distinct from a *cardinal* magnitude. A cardinal magnitude, such as length, weight, or time, is one in which the ratio of two quantities is subject to exact numerical calculation. It makes sense to say that A is 2.756 times as long, or as heavy, or as voluminous as B. Length, weight, and volume are therefore cardinal magnitudes. It makes sense to say that A is brighter, or redder, or wetter, or rougher than B. But unless we adopt an arbitrary standard of measurement from some cardinal quantity, it does not make sense to say that A is 2.756 times as bright, or as red, or as wet, or as rough as B. Brightness, redness, wetness, roughness are all ordinal magnitudes as far as their ordinary meaning is concerned. Such magnitudes can only be measured quantitatively by selecting, more or less arbitrarily, some cardinal magnitude which is connected with the ordinal magnitude. Brightness can be measured in terms of foot candles, redness in terms of the proportion of light waves of a certain wave length, and so on. But all these measurements are to some extent arbitrary. Utility, therefore, does not stand alone as an ordinal magnitude; there are many such, even in the physical sciences, and the difficulties of measuring utility are not fundamentally greater than the difficulties involved in measuring any other ordinal magnitude.

THE DIVISION OF EXPENDITURE

The principle that the quantity bought is that at which the price equals the marginal rate of substitution is necessary but not *sufficient* to determine the demand for a single commodity. The reason is that the marginal utility of money, on which the marginal rate of substitution depends, is itself dependent on the household's income, which in turn depends on the disutilities of earning it. Furthermore the marginal utility of purchase of one commodity depends on how much we are buying of others.

We cannot in the present chapter develop fully the theory of the consumer who is faced with the problem of consuming many commodities. We shall, however, indicate the main lines along which the solution of this problem is found. Suppose, first, that a consumer is faced with the problem of spending a given amount of money in a given time —say, $5000 in a year. He must divide this total expenditure among a large number of competing uses. He must spend some on bread, some on butter, some on shoes, some on coats, some on travel, and so on through the thousand and one varieties of expenditure. The problem is to formulate a principle which will indicate the *best* distribution of a given expenditure among a number of alternative uses.

The Weighted Marginal Utility

Let us again assume for purposes of exposition that total utility can be measured in terms of utils. Then the *weighted marginal utility* of a commodity may be defined as the increase in the total utility of the consumer which results from a unit increase in *expenditure* on the commodity in question. The weighted marginal utility is equal to the marginal utility divided by the price of the good concerned. Suppose the marginal utility of cheese at a certain level of consumption was 18 utils per pound and the price of cheese was $0.35 per pound. Then the weighted marginal utility would be 18/0.35, or 51.4, utils per dollar. That is to say, an increase of $1 in the expenditure on cheese would increase purchases by 1/0.35, or 2.86 pounds; and as an increase in consumption of 1 pound increases the total utility by 18 utils, an increase in consumption of 1/0.35 pounds will increase the total utility by 18/0.35 or 51.4 utils.

The best division of expenditures is that at which the weighted marginal utilities in all lines of expenditure are equal. In other words, the expenditure of an extra dollar in all lines of expenditure must have the same result in increasing utility. Otherwise it would pay to transfer expenditure from commodities where the weighted marginal utility is low to commodities where it is high. Suppose for instance that the weighted marginal utility of food is 50 utils per dollar, when the weighted marginal utility of cloth is 30 utils per dollar. In that case, if the consumer spends a dollar less on cloth he will lose 30 utils, and if he spends a dollar more on food he will gain 50 utils. The transfer of a dollar from cloth to food will result in a net gain of 20 utils, and therefore the transfer will be made.

As the transfer proceeds, however, the marginal utility of food falls, for the amount purchased is increasing, and the marginal utility of cloth rises as the amount purchased diminishes. The weighted marginal utility of food will likewise fall, say, to 40 utils per dollar, and the weighted marginal utility of cloth will rise, say, to 40 utils per dollar. At that point nothing is gained by transferring expenditure from cloth to food, and the total utility is therefore maximized.

The Equimarginal Principle: General Applications

1. To Expenditure of Time. This is a general principle of great importance; we may call it the *equimarginal principle*. Stated in general terms it runs as follows: In dividing a fixed quantity of anything among a number of different uses, just so much will be apportioned to each use to cause the gain involved by transferring a unit of dividend into one use to be just equal to the loss involved in the uses from which the unit of dividend is withdrawn. It obviously applies no matter how many the number of uses to which the dividend can be put. It applies no matter what the dividend is. It applies to the expenditure of twenty-four hours a day of time as well as to the expenditure of money. In considering whether or not to go to the movies we must balance the advantage (utility) to be derived from the two hours spent

in the movies against the advantage to be received from two hours spent in some other way (reading, studying, gardening, or in bed). The principle of diminishing marginal utility applies here as much as to the consumption of commodities; if we had been to the movies six times during the past week, the marginal utility of time spent at the movies will be low, and if we have been neglecting our studies and have an examination coming up soon, the marginal utility of time spent in study will be high. Consequently we are likely to choose study rather than the movies; what is gained by devoting two hours to study will be greater than what is lost by not going to the movies. If, on the other hand, we have been burning a lot of midnight oil and have not been to the movies for a month, the marginal utility of movies may be high, and that of study may be low, and we shall choose the movies.

2. To the Distribution of Assets. The equimarginal principle applies not only to the distribution of income, whether of money or of time, but also to the distribution of assets among various forms, liquid or illiquid. Thus an individual who possesses, say, $10,000 worth of assets of one kind or another—bank notes, bank deposits, savings deposits, bonds, stocks, real estate, furniture, clothes, utensils, household goods, stocks of food, and so on—is faced with the problem of the way in which the total value of his assets is to be divided among the many asset forms. The redistribution of assets is of course accomplished by exchange: if a man feels that he has too much in the form of cash and not enough in the form of shirts, he has the recourse, usually of going out to buy shirts—a process which increases his stock of shirts at the expense of his stock of cash. Or, anticipating an inflation, one may exchange cash and bonds for stocks; or anticipating a deflation, exchange stocks and real estate for cash and bonds. As long as an individual feels that the psychological gain from expanding his holdings of one form of asset by one dollar's worth is greater than the psychological loss from contracting his holdings of another asset by a dollar's worth, it will be worth his while to shift his distribution of assets by exchanging the more- for the less-valued form. The individual will only be in equilibrium, as an asset holder, therefore, when his psychological valuation of an extra dollar's worth of any form of asset is the same. This is the equimarginal principle.

3. To Resources in General. The apportionment of the general resources of a society among various alternative uses is the most fundamental of all economic problems, and its formal solution is again an example of the equimarginal principle. The ideal apportionment is clearly that in which there is nothing to be gained by transferring marginal units of resources from one use or occupation to another.

This involves us, however, in some notion of *social utility* which is not possible to define very exactly, though the concept clearly has meaning. The *principle of equal advantage* (see Chapter 6) is a special case of the equimarginal principle. If we adopt it as a social optimum it means that we rely on the judgment of individual persons as to whether there is net gain in shifting from one occupation to another. Some people would question this solution on the ground that the judgment of the elite, or some self-conscious party is superior to the judgment of the individuals who actually make the changes. Whatever the definition of social utility, however, the formal equimarginal principle still applies. The best distribution of resources is that in which the marginal social utility in each use is the same.

Limitations of Equimarginal Principle

1. INDIVISIBILITY OF GOODS.   There are some qualifications and limitations of the equimarginal principle which must be noticed. The first is that it can only be fully satisfied if the resources (money, time, etc.) can be divided and the commodities bought with these resources are divisible into very small parts. Where a commodity is indivisible—like a house or a car—only certain quantities of it can be bought; consequently, expenditure on these things and our holdings of them can increase only in large jumps. In a given period of time a man can buy one car or two cars; he cannot buy 1½ cars. He can spend, say, $2000 or $4000 on cars (if cars all cost $2000 each); he cannot spend $3000. Perhaps, however, the weighted marginal utility of money spent on cars would be equal to the weighted marginal utility of money spent on other things only when $3000 is spent on cars. If, therefore, the man buys only one car for $2000, he will feel that he is spending a little too much on other things in comparison with automobiles. If he spends $4000 he will feel that rather too much is going toward cars and not enough toward other things. It is like trying to build a number of towers of equal height with building blocks of different sizes; the towers built with big blocks are sure to be either a bit too tall or a bit too short. Wicksteed[2] suggests that this is responsible for the fact that we all feel that we would be a lot better off if we had just a *little* more money, no matter how much we have. On those items of expenditure in which the units are large we tend to spend a little too much, and we therefore feel that this expenditure, although not justified at our present income, would be quite justified at a rather higher income

[2] P. H. Wicksteed, *The Common Sense of Political Economy*, 4th ed., London, Macmillan, 1910, chapter 3.

level. But of course even if we get a larger income we still find it impossible to adjust our expenditures exactly according to the equimarginal principle, and so still feel that we could do with just a little more!

3. INDEFINITE BUDGET PERIOD. Another thing which limits the application of the equimarginal principle is the fact that our budget period is not definite. The equimarginal principle assumes that we have a definite quantity of resources (say, time or money) to spend. But of course we have only a definite quantity within a definite period of time. That period of time which we usually reckon in calculating how much income, for instance, we have to divide may be called the *budget period*; it is usually a year, though it may be any period. Many things which are bought within one budget period, however, are used in another budget period—e.g., cars and furniture. When buying an armchair I do not merely compare the benefits received from this chair in the current year with the loss involved in giving up the things on which I otherwise would have spent the money, for I must take into account the benefits to be enjoyed in many years to come. Consequently, some capital accounting must enter into household budgets and household behavior. Many of the economic *events* of the household, as we saw in Chapter 15, imply a horizon of budgeting which extends over long periods, even to the whole life of the person; thus buying a house, taking out a mortgage, buying life insurance, and indeed any form of saving implies a long-term budget of some kind.

The flexibility of the budget period, we should notice, to some extent modifies the difficulty introduced into economic adjustments by the indivisibility of commodities. In one year it may be true that either $2000 or $4000 must be spent on a car, but over two years it is quite possible to spend $3000 by buying three new cars over the two years. The longer the budget period, therefore, the less troublesome becomes the fact of indivisibility. But no matter how long the budget period, some indivisibility will occur.

THE EQUILIBRIUM OF THE CONSUMER

In view of the essentially dynamic and whole-life character of the household's events table, it may be questioned whether the concept of a short-run equilibrium of household behavior is useful. Nevertheless, as long as we constantly bear in mind that short-run equilibrium models are merely intellectual tools to help us grapple with the larger problem, they have a distinct, if limited, value.

The Homeostasis Model

The simplest short-run equilibrium model is that of pure *homeostasis*. By this we mean that the household adjusts all its behavior to simply maintaining a given state, condition, or position statement. Income is earned and exchanges are made simply because there is a constant process of consumption, depreciation, and erosion of the state going on. We eat to maintain our bodies; we buy food to replace the food eaten up; we earn money to replace the money spent; we buy a haircut because our hair grows, and we go to the movie because the psychological state of "just having been to a movie" gradually erodes and has to be replaced. We buy clothes because they wear out, gas because it burns up, and so on. The more elaborate and costly the state that we maintain, the larger will be the annual depreciation and consumption, and the larger income we will have to earn in order to maintain it. Big houses, rich furniture, fine clothes, elegant states of mind depreciate rapidly, and need a correspondingly large income to maintain them.

The Whole-Life Model

We can now extend the model to include a succession of such homeostatic states over the whole life of the person or household. The fact that both persons and households go through a fairly regular life cycle gives this concept a degree of regularity and predictability, through the "seven ages of man." The anticipation of a life cycle—birth, childhood, adolescence, college, a job, marriage, children, promotion, children's marriage, retirement, old age, death—means that we do not merely maintain homeostatic states, but we behave in such a way as to change them in a fairly regular sequence. The engaged couple scrimps and saves and likewise hoards, building up not only assets but liquid assets; upon marriage they buy furniture, perhaps go into debt, and dishoard. Children bring new patterns of consumption and saving; retirement and old age bring still another pattern. In all this variegated pattern of earnings, consumings, savings, receipts, expenditures, hoardings, and so on, the equimarginal principle holds good as the formal statement of rational behavior, for all it really says is that we do only what we think is worth the cost, the problem of cost arising because scarce resources of some kind have to be allocated.

What Determines Earnings?

The most fundamental problem is perhaps that of determining the allocation of an individual's time between work and leisure. This distribution determines that part of income which may be called *earnings*, and like any other distribution of a resource it falls under a general equimarginal principle. Thus, work means the sale of the services of resources which a man owns, such as the sale of the services of his body as labor. Leisure means the use of his resources for his own enjoyment. Everyone has twenty-four hours a day to spend according to the equimarginal principle, as we have seen. Part of this may be devoted to earning a money income, part to producing goods for our own use, and part to occupations which do not add to our assets but may even diminish them—that is, leisure. With freedom to choose how much time to spend on each, a person will so divide his time between "work" and "leisure" that the gain in utility resulting from a small unit increase in one exactly balances the loss in utility resulting from a small unit decrease in the other. If, for instance, to use a numerical example, we spent 6 hours on work and 18 hours on leisure and if, with this distribution of time, the marginal utility of time spent on leisure was 10 utils per minute and the marginal utility of time spent on work was 12 utils per minute, it would pay us to transfer a minute from leisure (thereby losing 10 utils) and to add that minute to work (thereby gaining 12 utils), a net gain of 2 utils. It would pay to transfer time from leisure to work until the rising marginal utility of time spent on leisure met the falling marginal utility of time spent on work. Similar considerations apply to the distribution of other resources—e.g., land—to earning or nonearning uses.

The Distribution of Earnings Between Saving and Consumption

The problem of what determines the individual's total income will be studied further in later chapters. Even if income is given, however, there is still a problem of the allocation of income between consumption and saving (i.e., accumulation). Formally, we can again invoke the equimarginal principle; we can regard accumulation as one method of disposal of income, and say that the equilibrium distribution of income between consumption or between the various lines of consumption, and saving is that at which the marginal gain from an increase in consumption is just equal to the marginal loss from the resultant decline in accumulation. It is not satisfactory, however, to leave the matter there; we need to know something of the *nature* of the gain or loss (utility) functions involved, for only then can we know whether people will think it worth while to save much or little. Our consumption depends on the elaborateness of the state we are trying to maintain; saving will depend on whether or not we are trying to move toward a more or less elaborate state in the future.

Factors Affecting Saving

1. SIZE OF INCOME. The most obvious factor affecting saving, whether as an absolute quantity or as a proportion of income, is the size of

income itself. Saving is a luxury. At very small incomes the imperious demands of subsistence press upon the scanty means and saving is impossible; indeed at very low levels of income saving is negative, the minimum consumption being larger than income. At larger incomes we would expect saving to be larger, both in absolute amount and as a proportion of income.

2. RAINY DAY SAVING. The amount saved by a consumer is likely to depend also on the expected future-time shape of his income, that is, on his expected life pattern. If he thinks his future incomes are going to be larger than his present incomes, the incentive to save will be small. If he expects his incomes to be smaller in the future, the incentive to save will be great. Such saving may be called *rainy day* saving. Saving for old age is its most typical form. If this were the only type of saving, in a stationary population there would be no *net* saving, for the old would spend what the young saved. In this type of saving we save to redistribute our consumption over the span of our life, and not primarily to accumulate a capital fund. It usually results in the accumulation of a capital fund by an individual only if he anticipates that his present income is larger than his future income will be. If we knew that our future income was going to be larger than our present income, it would be rational to "dis-save" in the present—that is, to decumulate or borrow in the present in order to increase our consumption and to accumulate or pay back loans in the future when our income is large. The young heir who borrows in anticipation of coming into his fortune later is therefore following exactly the same principle as the thrifty peasant who saves for his old age. Rainy day saving derives its justification from the principle of the diminishing marginal utility of outgo. If this principle holds, then we will gain on balance by taking a dollar from a year of large income and adding it to a year of small income. That is, we shall gain by making our outgo more equal in all the years of our life. If the schedule relating outgo and total utility were the same in all the years of our life, and if the rate of interest at which we could borrow or lend were zero, we should adjust our saving so as to make our outgo in each year equal. If our outgo in one year were greater than in another, in the above case, what we should lose in utility by withdrawing a dollar of outgo from the high outgo year would be less than what we should gain in utility by adding a dollar of outgo to the low-outgo year.

3. CERTAINTY OF FUTURE INCOMES; "INSURANCE SAVING." In the third place, the amount an individual will save depends upon the certainty with which his future income can be anticipated. This type of saving necessarily involves building up an individual fund of capital. It derives its justification from the fact that an individual whose income suddenly

disappears through, for instance, the loss of his job is in a much worse position if he has no capital fund to draw from. A man who possesses, say $100,000 worth of property has much less need of life insurance than a man who possesses no property. Other things being equal, we should expect a man with a safe job to save less than a man with an uncertain job. This may be called *insurance saving*. It must not be confused with the insurance premium itself in its pure form, which is a form of ex-penditure—the purchase of a consumption good known as *protection*. Pure insurance does not result in the building up of an individual capital fund; insurance saving does.

4 SHIFTLESSNESS. In the fourth place, the amount of saving depends on the carefulness with which the future is anticipated, i.e., on the degree to which present income is preferred merely because it is present, because we have not the imagination to visualize future needs. This is a nonrational element of time preference which we may call shiftless-ness. The more shiftless we are, the more we live only in the present, the less likely are we to save even in times of relatively high income, although if we had the imagination to do so we would be better off over our whole life. The element of shiftlessness often goes along with an uncertain or casual income, but it should not be confused with the effects of uncertainty itself. Uncertain incomes in themselves should promote saving. In so far, however, as they go hand in hand with a careless attitude about the future, the element of shiftlessness involved may serve to make people with uncertain incomes actually save less than people with equivalent safe incomes.

5. INTEREST RATES. Finally, the amount saved depends on the *result* of saving, i.e., on the real rate of interest which saving will bear, and on the certainty with which that rate of interest may be anticipated. If the real rate of interest on invested funds is high and safe, a con-sumer may generally be expected, on purely rational grounds, to save more than when the rate of interest is low or uncertain. That is, a high safe rate of interest will encourage saving. However, in this problem it is risky to make a priori judgments of this nature, based on the doubtful assumption that saving is postponed consumption.

Nonrational Saving

Saving is perhaps the least rational—i.e., the least planned—of all the forms of disposal of income. For one thing, the phenomenon of saving and of capital accumulation is surrounded by all manner of social taboos—e.g., the taboo against the squandering of capital, and the feeling that saving is done, not to spend again, but to provide a fund from which a perpetual income may be drawn for one's descendants. Again, saving is frequently not a planned part of the budget but a buffer which adjusts changes in outgo to changes in income. That is to say, the standard of life of the consumer has a certain inertia of its own; once a certain standard is established it takes some time to make the consumer adjust himself to a different one.[3] When the money income of the consumer is rising or when prices are falling, his standard of life will frequently lag behind the rise in the purchasing power of his income; he will find himself saving. Conversely, if the consumer finds that his money income is falling or that prices are rising, he will for a time maintain his old standard of life, even though it means that he may consume more than he gets. The amount which a consumer will save in a given time may consequently depend as much upon the rise or fall of his income or the prices of the things he buys as upon the rational calculations which he makes in planning his budget. It has been suggested by Duesenberry,[4] for instance, that the highest previously attained income may be an important variable in the savings or consumption function. The studies of consumer behavior by the Survey Research Center[5] confirm the hypothesis that income is an important determinant; they also bring out the wide variations in individual behavior in this regard and the many variables which may be involved. Age, family status, occupational status (farmers and small businessmen save more than others of comparable income), asset totals and distributions, all are significant variables.

Liquidity and Hoarding

In the above discussion we have used the word saving to mean the increase in the consumer's net worth, income to mean gross additions to, and outgo to mean gross subtractions from his net worth, income being the value of his production, outgo, the value of his consumption, saving, the value of his total accumulation. In the complete picture of the consumer's behavior we also need to consider the *forms* in which he holds his assets—e.g., whether liquid or nonliquid—and also his expenditures and receipts. An expenditure is a transfer of an asset from a liquid to a nonliquid form; a receipt is a transfer from a nonliquid to a liquid form. Thus, when a consumer makes a purchase, he diminishes his stock of money and increases his stock of the thing purchased.

[3] Milton Friedman has elaborated this idea, and even presented some evidence in its favor, in his "permanent income hypothesis" in *A Theory of the Consumption Function*, New York, National Bureau of Economic Research, 1957.

[4] James S. Duesenberry, *Income, Saving, and the Theory of Consumer Behavior*, Cambridge, Mass., Harvard University Press, 1949.

[5] See the annual "Survey of Consumer Finances" in the *Federal Reserve Bulletin*, Washington, D.C., U.S. Government Printing Office.

Purchase and expenditure are thus not the same things as consumption, though they may be followed by it. Similarly, when the consumer makes a sale, he increases his stock of money and decreases his holdings of the thing sold; receipts are not the same thing as income, though they are closely related to it.

Besides the problem of income, outgo, and saving, then, there is an additional problem of receipts, expenditure, and hoarding—hoarding being the change in the consumer's stock of money. Consumers make expenditure mainly in order to replace what they have consumed; hence, for some purposes the assumption that consumption and consumer's expenditure are identical is not wholly unrealistic. Nevertheless, we cannot afford to neglect the possibility that consumers make expenditures not merely to replace what they have consumed, but in order to change the form of their asset holdings. For instance, a consumer feels that he is holding too much money; he will increase his expenditures beyond his consumption and so expand his holdings of nonliquid and diminish his holdings of liquid assets. Conversely, a consumer who wishes to increase his liquid assets will diminish his expenditures even though his consumption may not be diminished; the result will be to increase his liquid assets at the expense of his nonliquid assets. The formal solution of the problem of expenditures and asset forms again lies in the equimarginal principle: the equilibrium distribution of assets between different types—e.g., liquid and nonliquid—is that at which the marginal gain of adding to one type is just equal to the marginal loss of the thereby necessitated subtraction from another. This equilibrium is perpetually disturbed by consumption and production, which add to and subtract from assets of different kinds, and it must continually be restored by expenditures (purchases) and receipts (sales).

DEMAND AND HOUSEHOLD BEHAVIOR

The crucial question which the price theorist wants to ask of the theory of household behavior is what light it throws on *ultimate demand,* that is, on the relation between the set of prices or exchange opportunities open to the householder and the set of quantities of consumption or purchases of the corresponding commodities. *Original supply*—the relation between prices of factors and the amounts supplied by households—is in a sense part of the same problem. With the simple apparatus of this chapter we can only consider single price-quantity relations; the study of more elaborate relationships must be postponed to Chapter 27.

Change in Demand: Tastes

Demand has two major parameters, magnitude and elasticity. The magnitude of a particular demand can best be studied by considering how a demand rises or falls. Thus a consumer's demand curve will shift if his tastes change. A change in taste toward an increased desire for a commodity will be reflected in a shift in the total utility curve upward, as in Fig. 114A. At each quantity of the commodity the total utility will be greater than before. At a quantity *ON*, for instance, the original total utility was *NP*. After an increase in desire for the commodity the total

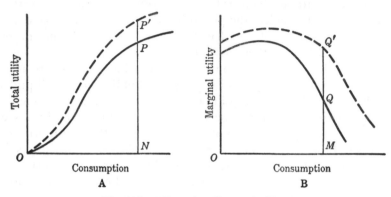

Fig. 114.   Effect of a Change in Taste

utility will be *NP′*. If *OP* is the original total utility curve, *OP′* is the curve after the increase in desire. This new total utility curve will probably be steeper than the old, at each level of consumption. As the steepness of the total utility curve is the marginal utility, the marginal utility will also be increased at each level of consumption—say, from *MQ* to *MQ′* in Fig. 114B—when *OM* units are consumed. The marginal utility curve, therefore, will move upward and to the right. The marginal rate of substitution curve will do likewise, as the marginal rate of substitution is equal to the marginal utility multiplied by an almost constant figure —the marginal revenue of utility. But the marginal rate of substitution curve is the same as the demand curve of the consumer for the commodity in question. An increase in desire for a commodity will therefore shift the demand curve of an individual consumer upward and to the right, i.e., will cause an increase in his demand.

Change in Income

From our utility curves we can also prove that a rise in a consumer's money income will raise all or most of his demand curves. A rise in money income will operate principally by lowering the marginal utility of money. It may have a significant effect on the marginal utility curves themselves, but that problem is reserved for Chapter 27. Here we can show that even if a change in money income does not affect the total and marginal utility curves for a commodity, the change in the marginal utility of money is sufficient to affect the demand. It is generally assumed that the marginal utility of money declines with an increase in money income; i.e., that a dollar means less to a rich man than to a poor man. A rise in money income will therefore increase the marginal rate of substitution of a given level of consumption of most commodities, for if the marginal utility does not change, it is now divided by a smaller sum in order to calculate the marginal rate of substitution.

Suppose, for instance, that at a certain level of consumption of cheese the marginal utility was 20 utils per pound. If the marginal utility of money were 40 utils per dollar the marginal rate of substitution would be $0.50 per pound. If a rise in money income lowered the marginal utility of money to 30 utils per dollar, the marginal rate of substitution of the same quantity of cheese would be $0.67 per pound. A rise in money income therefore raises the whole marginal rate of substitution curve upward and to the right and causes a rise in the consumer's demand for commodities. A possible exception to this rule occurs in the case of inferior goods which are consumed at low but not at high incomes, like coarse foods. Here the rise in income lowers the marginal utility curve itself, and if this effect outweighs the fall in the marginal utility of money, the marginal rate of substitution curve may fall with rise in income.

Changes in Saving

Changes in the consumer's propensity to save also have an effect on demand curves similar to that produced by a change in money income. With an increased desire to save, the relative marginal utility curves and the demand curves will fall, mainly because of the rise in the marginal utility of money. Changes in the propensity to save frequently offset changes in money income or in prices, especially in the short run where savings act as a buffer. For instance, a rise in money income or a general fall in prices will often increase saving rather than expenditure. The rise in the propensity to save will offset the tendency for demand curves to rise as a result of increased money income.

Changes in Asset Preferences

Changes in demand for commodities (or securities) may also come about as a result of changes in the *asset preferences* of individuals. If, for instance, there is a rise in liquidity preference, so that people now wish to hold a greater proportion of their assets in liquid form, the result will be a decrease in the demand for commodities, i.e., in the willingness to purchase at a given price, even though consumption might remain unchanged; people will allow their stocks of commodities to run down, and will try to build up their money stocks. Changes due to asset preferences will not generally be of long duration, and for purposes of long-run analysis they may perhaps be neglected. Over short periods, however, changes in asset preferences may be very important in explaining changes in demand.

The Elasticity of Demand

We can now proceed to a further understanding of the forces which determine the elasticity of consumer's demand for a commodity. The elasticity of demand for a single consumer depends mainly on the *steepness* of the marginal utility curve. The steeper this curve, i.e., the faster marginal utility declines with increase in consumption, the faster will the marginal rate of substitution decline and the less elastic will be the demand of the consumer for the commodity in question. In this problem also there is a close analogy between the forces which determine the elasticity of the demand of a single consumer for a product and the forces which determine the elasticity of a single producer's demand for input. The demand for input is more elastic, the greater are the possibilities of substitution. Likewise, the demand for a consumption good will be more elastic, the better its substitutes. If a commodity has good substitutes in consumption, a rise in its price will cause the consumer to turn to the substitutes, and so will diminish greatly his consumption of the dearer commodity. We saw that the demand for input was more elastic, the greater the part played by the input in the process of production. Similarly, the demand for a consumption good will also be more elastic if it absorbs a large proportion of total expenditure. Thus a commodity like salt, on which we spend a very small part of our total income, is likely to have an inelastic demand.

The Industry Effect

Corresponding to the *industry effect* in the case of supply is a similar effect in the case of demand. We saw that the elasticity of supply depended in great part not only on the effect which a rise in price had on the output of an individual firm but also on the effect of a rise in price on the *number* of firms. Similarly, the elasticity of the *total* demand curve of all consumers for a product depends not merely on how a change in price will affect the purchases of an individual consumer, but on how a change in price will affect the *number* of consumers. Many commodities have an almost completely inelastic demand as far as the demand of a single consumer is concerned and yet have an elastic total demand because a change in price causes a large change in the *number* of purchasers. The demand for a magazine is a good illustration. Largely because of the indivisibility of the unit, and because the expenditure on any one magazine forms a small part of total expenditure, the demand of a single individual for a given magazine is probably almost perfectly inelastic within the range in which he is willing to purchase it. If I am willing to buy one copy for 15 cents, probably I should not be induced to buy two copies even for a price of 1 cent, or even for no price at all. Nevertheless, the total demand for a magazine may be highly elastic, because although a reduction in price will not cause any one individual to buy two copies where previously he bought one, it may cause a large number of individuals to buy one copy who previously had not purchased the magazine.

QUESTIONS AND EXERCISES

1. Utility does not connote mere pleasure or physical satisfaction. It refers to the satisfaction of *any* want, physical or spiritual. The theory of utility does not merely apply to mundane matters; it applies to such things as friendship, love, forgiveness, honesty, and peace of mind as much as to the things more usually regarded as economic. Discuss and illustrate.

2. "High Heaven rejects the lore of nicely calculated less or more" (Wordsworth). Why?

3. "Saving is the least rational thing we do." Discuss the meaning of the word "rational" in respect to consumption.

4. Which of the following sentences best expresses the law of diminishing marginal utility?
    The more you have of anything, the less you want it.
    The less you have of anything, the more you want a good deal of it.
    The more you have of anything, the less you want more of it.
    The second drink is never as good as the first.
    The more you have of anything, the more fun you get out of it.
    Desire grows by what it feeds on.

5. Make a tabular statement, comparing and contrasting, as far as you can, the theory of production with the theory of consumption.

6. In discussing the demand for input we stated that the marginal revenue productivity curve of an individual firm *below the point of maximum average revenue productivity* was the demand curve. Is there any similar condition in the derivation of the demand for a consumer's good?

7. a. Using the figures of Table 47, page 522, calculate the sacrifice of total utility resulting from the money given up in the purchase of 1, 2, . . ., 9 pounds of cheese, assuming that the price of cheese is $0.35 per pound. Tabulate, and

calculate the *net gain* in utility for each amount purchased. Show that the net gain is greatest at the point where the price is equal to the marginal rate of substitution.

b. Repeat for a number of different prices of cheese, and show that for any price above $0.80 it does not pay to buy cheese at all.

c. What must be assumed about the nature of the utility function if the commodity is a necessity, so that there is *no* price above which it will not be bought? Construct a schedule with this property.

d. Suppose that with a marginal rate of substitution table as in Table 47, columns 1 and 4, the marginal utility of money is constant at 10 utils per dollar. Repeat parts a and b, calculating the new total utility schedule. Show that the results are not affected by the level of marginal utility of money assumed, and discuss their significance.

e. Illustrate all the above exercises by means of graphs.

8. Draw a set of curves showing how an individual's saving might be expected to vary with (a) income, (b) future income, (c) certainty of future income, (d) the age of the consumer, (e) the number of children in the family, (f) the rate of interest, (g) the cost of living. Draw a corresponding series of curves to show how his consumption might be expected to vary. Can the consumption curves always be deduced from the savings curves? If so, how? What is the relation between the savings or consumption functions of individuals and the overall consumption function of a society? How is a change in the distribution of income likely to affect the overall consumption function?

CHAPTER 25

THREE-VARIABLE ANALYSIS OF
THE FIRM

INTRODUCTION

The greater part of the techniques of price theory has now been covered in outline. The principal method used has been the graphical method. There is a good reason why the graphic method has proved so useful in economics. Economics deals with certain functional relationships between various economic quantities, such as demand functions, cost functions, and so on. The exact algebraic form of these functions is usually not known. That is to say, we may know that the quantity demanded, (q), depends on—that is, is a function of—the price, (p), but we are not justified usually in assuming any explicit relationship between these two quantities, such as, for instance, $q = 10 - 6p - p^2$. To write almost any significant economic relationship as an explicit equation would be to assume too much. On the other hand, we know *something* about the shape and nature of these functions; to write them as a purely general function, $q = F(p)$ would be to assume too little. Graphic analysis enables us to discuss the relationships of functions of which we know the general character but no more; it is, therefore, extremely well suited to the tasks of economic analysis. It has, however, this severe limitation. A curve in two dimensions can describe the relationships of only two variables. If, therefore, we wish to describe graphically the relationship of three variables, e.g., the quantity of A demanded, the price of A, and the income of the demander, we must use a surface in three dimensions.

Three-dimensional figures are not, of course, so easy to draw or to visualize as two-dimensional ones. Fortunately, in most cases there is a simple method for expressing the shape of a three-dimensional surface in a two-dimensional figure. This is the method of contour lines or *isomers* used in mapping. A contour line or isomer is a line on a plane surface joining all those points on the surface which have some other quantity in common. Thus in a geographical contour map the 100-foot contour is the line which runs through all points on the map which are 100 feet above sea level; it represents the coast line which would exist if the sea rose 100 feet. On a weather map the *isobars* are lines running through all places having the same barometric pressure, an *isotherm* is a line running through all places having the same temperature, and so on. By drawing a system of contours the shape of any non-re-entrant surface can be described on a plane diagram, and some of the difficulties involved in the construction of three-dimensional diagrams, themselves, obviated.

We can also represent relationships of three variables in schedule form by drawing a chessboard diagram in which each square represents a certain combination of two quantities, say X and Y, and the third quantity, Z, is written in the square.

When we go to problems involving four or more dimensions the graphic method becomes impossible and we must rely on analytical mathematics. Fortunately there seems to be a principle of diminishing returns to increasing the number of dimensions, at least in regard to the illustration of fundamental principles. Even though economic systems are by their very nature multidimensional, having in reality millions or even billions of variables, a large proportion of their most essential properties can be explained in models of two dimensions, and almost all the remainder in models of three dimensions. It is hard to think of any proposition in economics which requires a model of four or more dimensions to explain it. Although, therefore, our two- and three-dimensional models will constantly point toward the generalization to many dimensions of the propositions illustrated in them, we shall find that by thoroughly exploring the properties of the simpler models we shall be much better prepared to understand the properties of the more general models.

THE THREE-VARIABLE PRODUCTION SCHEDULE

We may conveniently begin our three-variable analysis by considering the relationships between *two* inputs and one output. A simple production schedule of the type illustrated in Table 40, page 425, is not now sufficient to show all the various relationships between the quantities of input and output. If the two inputs are labor and land, it is not sufficient to show how various quantities of labor will affect the product when a fixed quantity of land is used. We need a schedule to show not only how much product is produced with various quantities of labor applied to 8 acres, but how much product results from the application of various quantities of labor to 7, 6, 5, or any other number of acres. Such a schedule is illustrated in Table 48. The horizontal rows of this schedule show

TABLE 48. THE PHYSICAL PRODUCTION TABLE

Number of acres of land	0	7	23	36	41	45	48	50	52	54
9	0	7	23	36	41	45	48	50	52	54
8	0	8	24	34	40	42	44	46	48	49
7	0	9	24	32	36	39	41	42	43	44
6	0	10	24	30	32	35	36	37	38	39
5	0	11	22	26	28	30	31	32	33	34
4	0	12	20	22	24	25	26	27	28	29
3	0	12	16	18	19	20	21	22	23	24
2	0	10	12	13	14	15	16	16½	16	15½
1	0	6	7	8	8	7	6½	6	5½	5
0	0	0	0	0	0	0	0	0	0	0
	0	1	2	3	4	5	6	7	8	9

Number of man-months applied

how much product (tons of potatoes) will be produced when the various quantities of labor (shown on the bottom row) are applied to a fixed quantity of land (shown at the left of the row). Thus with 8 acres of land, 1 unit of labor produces 8 tons, 2 units 24 tons, 3 units 34 tons, and so on. This row corresponds to the production schedule in Table 40. Similarly, with 7 acres of land, 1 unit of labor produces 9 tons, 2 units 24 tons, 3 units 32 tons, and so on. The columns of the table show how much product results from the application of various quantities of land to a fixed quantity of labor. Thus 4 units of labor on 1 acre produce 8 tons, on 2 acres 14 tons, on 3 acres 19 tons, and so on, reading up the column. From the complete schedule we can find, therefore, how many tons of potatoes will be produced by any combination of quantities of labor and land. Each of the heavy figures represents the number of tons of potatoes produced by the quantity of land shown at the head of the row and the quantity of labor shown at the foot of the column in which the figure lies. Thus we see that 7 acres of land and 5 units of labor produce 39 tons of potatoes. This table represents, not successive results, but the results of alternative combinations of the two inputs. It should be read: "*If* 7 acres of land are used with 5 units of labor, *then* 39 tons of potatoes will result." In this part of our analysis we neglect the uncertainty of the results, and assume that the result of combining definite quantities of inputs can always be predicted by reference to the production schedule.

Returns to Scale

We have already examined the law of *eventually diminishing marginal productivity* in Chapter 20. We can see by examining Table 48 that this law applies to each column and to each row of the table. Now, however, a new property of the physical production schedule emerges when there are two variable inputs. We have seen what will happen to the product when one input is increased and the quantity of the other is kept constant. What will happen when *both* the inputs are increased in the same proportion? Instead of running our eye along one of the columns or rows of the table, let us run our eye diagonally from the bottom left-hand corner, i.e., from the zero point. In this way we can see what will happen when both inputs are increased in the same proportion. For instance, following the diagonal marked *B,* we see that with 1 unit of labor and 1 of land, 6 tons are produced; with 2 units of labor and 2 of land, 12 tons are produced; with 3 units of labor and 3 of land, 18 tons are produced; and so on. That is to say, as *both* inputs are increased in a given proportion, the output also increases in that proportion. Doubling both inputs doubles the output, trebling both inputs trebles the output, and so on. Similarly, diagonal *A* shows that 1 unit of land and 2 of labor produce 7 tons; 2 of land and 4 of labor, 14 tons; 3 of land and 6 of labor, 21 tons; and so on. Along diagonal *C,* 1 unit of labor and 3 of land produce 12 tons; 2 of labor and 6 of land produce 24 tons; 3 of labor and 9 of land produce 36 tons, and so on. The student may entertain himself by following out other diagonals to see whether this rule is universal in the figure.

The Laws of Returns to Scale: Homogeneity

This property of a table is called, mathematically, *homogeneity of the first degree.* We shall call it the property of *constant returns to scale.* It means that if we take any combination of inputs and outputs and increase all but one in a given proportion, that one must also increase in the same proportion. Increasing all inputs in the same proportion is increasing the *scale* of the process. One thing is a *scale model* of another if all the linear measurements of the one are the same proportion of the corresponding measurements of the other. If we wished to build a scale model of the Capitol we would make all our lengths a given proportion —say 1/1,000 of the lengths of the actual building. Similarly, in a process of production, if, when all inputs are changed by a given proportion, the output also changes in that proportion, then one process is a pure scale model of the other, and there are constant returns to scale. If, with all inputs changed in a given proportion, the output changed in a greater proportion, we should have *increasing* returns to scale. If, with all inputs changed in a given proportion, the output changed in a smaller proportion, we should have *decreasing* returns to scale. For instance, if, when the quantities of all inputs doubled, the quantity of output more than doubled, we should say that the process showed increasing returns to scale. And if under the same circumstances the output less than doubled, the process would show decreasing returns to scale.[1]

The Confusion of the Two Laws of Returns

A great deal of confusion has been caused in economics by the failure to separate these two quite different laws—the *law of change of marginal or average productivity*, and the *law of change of scale*. All too frequently economists have meant by *diminishing returns* the principle of eventually diminishing physical productivity of one factor as it is increased and the others held constant; and by *increasing returns* the postulate of increasing returns to scale when *all* factors are increased proportionately.

Diminishing Marginal Productivity and Substitution: Two Cases

Now *why* are we justified in assuming a law of eventually diminishing physical productivity? The answer is that the law of diminishing physical productivity is merely a way of expressing the fact that the inputs in a process are *not perfectly substitutable* one for the other. Unfortunately there seems to be no substitute for the deplorable word substitutable. Nevertheless, the concept of substitutability is one of the most important in the whole of economic analysis. We can see the truth of this relationship by examining two extreme cases.

FIXED PROPORTIONS. Table 49 is a physical production table in which the inputs can be used only in absolutely fixed proportions. A possible case of this might be the production of certain alloys where, if the ingredients are used in the right proportions, the desired product is obtained, and if

---

[1] This property can easily be generalized to n dimensions. If x is output, a, b, c, etc. are inputs, and the production function, i.e., $x = F(a, b, c \ldots)$, then suppose $kx = F(ha, hb, hc, \ldots)$. Then there are constant, increasing, or decreasing returns to scale according as $k = h$, $k > h$, or $k < h$.

they are used in any other proportions, it is not. Table 49 assumes that two inputs, A and B, in equal proportions will produce an output, but in any other proportions they will produce nothing.

TABLE 49. FIXED PROPORTIONS						
Units of A	Units of B					
	0	1	2	3	4	5
5	0	0	0	0	0	30
4	0	0	0	0	24	0
3	0	0	0	18	0	0
2	0	0	12	0	0	0
1	0	6	0	0	0	0
0	0	0	0	0	0	0

TABLE 50. PERFECT SUBSTITUTABILITY						
Units of A	Units of B					
	0	1	2	3	4	5
5	15	18	21	24	27	30
4	12	15	18	21	24	27
3	9	12	15	18	21	24
2	6	9	12	15	18	21
1	3	6	9	12	15	18
0	0	3	6	9	12	15

PERFECT SUBSTITUTABILITY. Table 50, on the other hand, is the physical production table for two inputs which are perfectly substitutable, i.e., which can be substituted one for the other at a given rate without the product being affected. Thus in Table 50, 1 of A and 3 of B, or 2 of A and 2 of B, or 3 of A and 1 of B, or even 4 of A and 0 of B all give the same product: 12. That is to say, we can use any combination of A and B, take away one unit of A and add one unit of B, and go on doing this without changing the quantity of product. Clearly, this could never be the case over the whole range, unless A and B were identically similar, or it would lead us to the preposterous conclusion that we could make a product without any quantity of an essential ingredient! Nevertheless, inputs may be perfectly substitutable over short ranges, though even this is unlikely.

Diminishing Productivity in These Two Cases

What has happened in Tables 49 and 50 to our law of eventually diminishing physical productivity? In Table 50 we see that along any row of the table the marginal physical productivity of input B is constant and equal to 3. That is to say, if we add 1 unit of B to a fixed quantity of A, the result is always an increase of 3 units of product. There is no diminishing marginal physical productivity at all, for the inputs are perfectly substitutable. Looking up the columns, we see that the marginal physical productivity of input A is likewise constant, and does not decline as we increase the quantity of A which we combine with a fixed quantity of B.

Table 49, on the other hand, shows that along any row the product remains at zero as the quantity of input B is increased, until the *correct* proportions are reached. Then the product immediately rises, and immediately falls to zero again as the quantity of B is increased beyond the correct proportions. That is, the marginal physical productivity, at the point of correct proportions, diminishes very rapidly indeed. For instance, with 2 units of A and 1 of B there is no product; adding one unit of B increases the product by 12 units; the marginal physical productivity over that range is 12. Adding another unit of B reduces the product again to zero; the marginal physical product is − 12. With infinitesimally small units of inputs which could not be substituted one for the other, the rate of diminution of marginal physical productivity would be infinite.

The Best Proportions

In the more usual case represented by our original Table 48, page 545, the inputs are substitutable to some extent; i.e., the proportions in which they are used can be varied in some degree. Nevertheless, they are not perfectly substitutable. There will be, as we shall see, some proportion which is the *best,* and too great a proportion of either input will yield worse results than the best proportions. It is the fact that some *proportions* of input are better than others which gives rise to the law of eventually diminishing marginal physical productivity. As we start adding a variable input to a *fixed* quantity of the other inputs, we shall first find that we *approach* the best proportions. The additional units of the variable factor therefore produce more than proportionable returns in product; the marginal physical productivity of that factor is increasing. Soon, however, we reach, and then pass, the best proportions. As our variable factor is increased from this point the proportions get worse and worse all the time. Consequently, the marginal physical productivity declines, and eventually the addition of more of the variable factor actually lessens the product—i.e., the marginal physical productivity becomes negative.

Increasing Returns to Scale Frequently Only Apparent

Thus the problem of diminishing returns, in the sense of diminishing marginal physical productivity, essentially relates to the problem of the *proportions* of the inputs used. The problem of increasing, decreasing, or constant returns to *scale* has nothing to do with the change in the proportions of the input quantities. Frequently, however, what appears to be variable returns to scale turns out to be nothing but a subtle example of variable marginal physical productivity. For instance, it is often the case that doubling the size of a factory, the number of machines in it, the number of men, and the quantities of materials employed more than doubles the output. We may be tempted to regard this immediately as an example of increasing returns to scale, or, as it is often called, the economies of large-scale production. However, we have overlooked one kind of input—management. What we have really been doing is to hold constant the quantity of one input, management, and to vary the quantities of all the others. It is possible that the proportion of management to the other inputs was better in the larger factory and that management was being underworked in the smaller factory, just as land might be underworked when it had only a small quantity of labor employed on it.

Possibility of Genuine Variability of Returns to Scale

This is not to say, however, that a genuine variability of returns to scale is not possible in economic life, though its presence is difficult to prove. It is perhaps difficult to see at first why, if we could double *all* inputs, including the quantity of management, we should not also double the output. Nevertheless, there are examples from nature which show that genuine variable returns to scale exist. For instance, a flea can jump over a scale model of the Capitol, scaled down to the size of the flea. If a flea were as big as a man, however, it could not jump over the Capitol in Washington. Indeed, it could not jump at all. Its legs would break. This is due to the fact that the strength of muscles and bones is proportional to their *cross section,* which is an area. The weight of an object is proportional to its *volume.* Now, as the size of any object is increased according to scale, its volume increases as the cube of the proportionate increase in length, but its areas increase only as the square. Multiply the length, breadth, and height of a flea by 1,000 and you will have increased all its areas by 1,000,000, and all its volumes by 1,000,000,000. You will have increased its weight by a thousand times more than the increase in its strength of bone and muscle. No wonder it would break in pieces! Sizes, therefore, and not merely the proportion of the parts, are important in nature and account for the different structures of things of different sizes—for the slender legs of the insect, the tiny legs of the mouse, the sturdy legs of man, the gigantic legs of the elephant, and the flippers of the whale.

The same may be true of enterprises. A moderately large enterprise may be more efficient than a small one simply because it is bigger. Quite apart from the possibility of varying the proportions of the factors, the very size of an enterprise may permit a better or worse use of the factors employed in it. Very large enterprises, however, may be unwieldy, and may even break under their own weight. Very large combinations, for instance, have occasionally broken down because of the sheer weight of bureaucracy necessary to maintain them. The possibility of genuine departures from homogeneity in the production schedule must therefore be taken into consideration. It is quite possible that at small scales there may be increasing returns to scale, but at large scales decreasing returns to scale may be the rule.

GRAPHIC REPRESENTATION. The graphic representation of Table 48 introduces some difficulties, as here we are dealing with three quantities —labor, land, and product—and consequently have to use three dimensions—length, breadth, and height—in order to represent their relations. Consider the little boxes in Table 48 containing the product quantities. The position of any one of these, relative to the axes OX and OY, shows from what *combination* of quantities of land and labor the product figure within it is derived. Thus the box at the top right-hand corner containing the figure 54, shows that nine units of labor combined with nine units of land yield 54 units of potatoes. Now suppose that on each of these boxes we build a little tower, equal in height to the figure in the box. We should then have a solid figure which would give all the relationships between the three quantities, labor, land, and product, just as a figure on flat paper will show the relationships between any *two* quantities. Part of this figure is shown in perspective in Fig 115.

If the units of land, labor, and product are extremely small, the steps in Fig. 115 will be smoothed out and will form a *surface* shaped like Fig. 116. This is the *physical production surface*. Any point on the surface, such as Q, represents a certain combination of labor, land, and product quantities. If we drop a perpendicular, QN, to the base, and drop perpendiculars NO_y to OY and NO_x to OX, then NQ represents the quantity of product produced by an amount OO_x of labor and an amount OO_y of land.

The Total Product Curve

A perpendicular slice of this figure parallel to OX, such as $O_yP_yX_y$, gives us a curve O_yQP_y, which is a total product curve like that in Fig. 89, showing the relation between the total product and the quantity of labor when the quantity of land is kept constant and equal to OO_y. Similarly, a perpendicular section such as $O_xP_xY_x$ cut parallel to OY gives us a total product curve O_xQP_x, showing the relation between the total product and the quantity of land, under the condition that the quantity of labor, OO_x, is constant. The symmetry of the principle of diminishing marginal physical productivity is evident from the figure; the curves O_yQP_y and O_xQP_x have the same general shape.

The Isoproduct Curve

Suppose now that we take a slice parallel to the base plane, such as RTR'; what is the significance of the curve RQR'? This is a line which

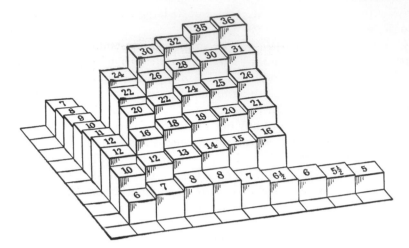

Fig. 115.   Physical Production Surface

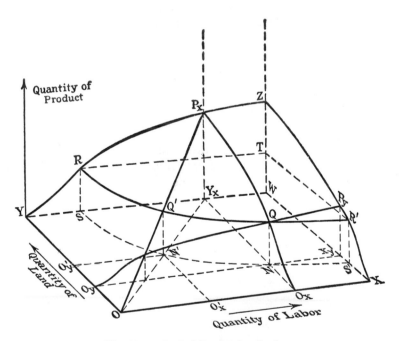

Fig. 116.   Physical Production Surface

connects all those points on the surface at which the product is equal to
SR; that is to say, it is a *contour line* of the surface. Its projection onto
the base, *SNS'*, we shall call an *isoproduct* curve or a product contour.[2]
Any point on it represents a combination of input quantities which will
produce the same output, *SR*. Thus, to return to Table 49, all those combinations in the product boxes which yield 24 tons of potatoes—for example, 6 of land and 2 of labor, 4 of land and 4 of labor, and 3 of land
and 9 of labor—will lie on an isoproduct curve. Just as isotherms are lines
which connect on a map all points having the same temperature, so isoproduct curves are lines connecting all points which yield the same
product.

The System of Product Contours

It is clear that just as we can represent a mountain on a flat map by
drawing its contours, so we can represent a physical production surface on
a flat diagram by drawing its contours, i.e., its isoproduct curves. Thus
in Fig. 117 the curve P_6 represents all those combinations of land and
labor quantities which produce 6 tons of potatoes; the curve P_{12} represents
all those combinations of land and labor quantities which produce 12 tons
of potatoes; and so on. Those who are accustomed to reading contour maps
will readily visualize this figure as a surface—a mountain rising up from
the origin. Fig. 117, then, is another way of describing the facts described
in Table 48.

Returns to Scale on the Physical Production Surface

Let us now see how returns to scale can be expressed in our figures. With
constant returns to scale we saw that increasing *both* labor and land in
the same proportion also increases the total product in that proportion.
This property of the physical production table is expressed in the
physical production surface, Fig. 116, by the fact that any line drawn from
the origin, *O*, to touch the surface will touch it at all points of its length.
That is to say, a slice of the surface through the origin perpendicular to
the base plane, such as OP_xY_x, will cut the surface in a straight line, OP_x.
To put it in another way, if the surface shows constant returns to scale,
it must be made by moving a straight line with one end fixed at *O* and
the other end moving over a path such as *YRZR'X*.

This follows from a well-known property of similar triangles. If from
any point, *Q'*, on the line OP_x a perpendicular *Q'N'* is dropped to the
base plane, the triangles *OQ'N'* and OP_xY_x are similar. Therefore,

---

[2] This curve is often called the *isoquant,* being a curve of equal quantities. As, however, there are many kinds of isoquants, I have thought it better to retain the name
given above.

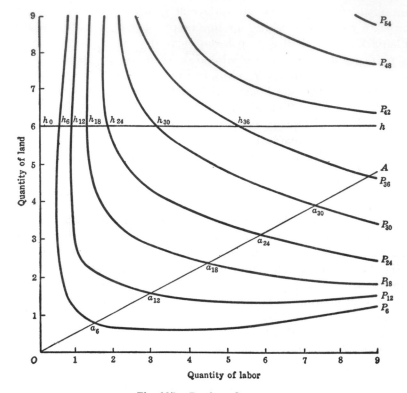

Fig. 117.   Product Contours

$ON'/OY_x = N'Q'/Y_xP_x$. Also, dropping the perpendiculars $N'O'_x$ to OX and $N'O'_y$ to OY we see that triangles $ON'O'_x$ and OY_xO_x are similar, and triangles $ON'O'_y$ and OY_xY are similar. Therefore

$$\frac{ON'}{OY_x} = \frac{OO'_x}{OO_x} = \frac{OO'_y}{OY} = \frac{N'Q'}{Y_xP_x}$$

That is, a given proportionate increase in both land and labor quantities will cause the product quantity to increase in the same proportion. If the line $OQ'P_x$ were curving upward there would be increasing returns to scale; if it were curving downward there would be decreasing returns to scale.

Properties of the Product Contour Map

Most of the properties of the physical production surface can be represented by means of a product contour map like Fig. 117. The use of such a map is therefore a great convenience, as it enables us to represent a relationship between three variables on a plane figure, and avoids the use of awkward three-dimensional diagrams.

If the production surface is homogeneous (with constant returns to scale), then *any* diagonal from the origin, such as *OA,* will be divided into equal segments by successive product contours. If the contours in Fig. 117 represent a homogeneous production surface and the product contours P_6, P_{12}, etc., cut the line *OA* at a_6, a_{12}, etc., then $Oa_6 = a_6a_{12} = a_{12}a_{18} = a_{18}a_{24}$, etc. This rule follows from the definition of a homogeneous production surface as one in which equal proportionate increases in both inputs produce equal proportionate increases in output. If there are decreasing returns to scale, successive intercepts on a diagonal will become larger and larger. Then $Oa_6 < a_6a_{12} < a_{12}a_{18} < a_{18}a_{24}$, etc. Similarly, if there are increasing returns to scale the successive intercepts will become smaller. In the case of decreasing returns to scale the mountain of the production surface becomes flatter as we climb, and the contours therefore become farther and farther apart. In the case of increasing returns to scale the mountain becomes steeper as we climb, and the contours get closer together.

The law of diminishing marginal productivity is illustrated by the intercepts made by successive contours on a line parallel with either axis. Consider the line h_0h. As the quantity of labor increases, with the quantity of land constant at Oh_0, the intercepts h_0h_6, h_6h_{12}, $h_{12}h_{18}$, etc., eventually increase, indicating the fact that to produce successive equal increments of product increasing increments of labor must be used.

Drawing the product contours corresponding to Table 50, we shall find that they are straight lines running diagonally across the figure. If, therefore, the product contours have no curvature, the inputs are perfectly substitutable. The product contours corresponding to Table 49, where no substitution is possible between the inputs, have an infinite curvature, for they have contracted to a point. The curvature of a product contour, then, is a possible measure of the degree of substitution of the two inputs. Where the product contours have a small curvature, the substitution of one input for another (represented by moving along the contour) does not greatly affect the *rate* of substitution. But if a product contour is curved sharply, as one input is substituted for another it takes more and more of the expanding input to replace one unit of the contracting input. This is a sign that the inputs are not easily substitutable.

THE "BEST COMBINATION" PROBLEM

When there are two variable inputs a problem arises because there are many ways of producing a *given* output. This was not true in the case in

which only one input could be varied; Table 40, for instance, shows that
to produce 24 tons of potatoes 2 units of labor must be used on 8 acres.
This is the only way to produce 24 tons with 8 acres, and it must therefore be the best way to produce 24 tons! Table 48, however, shows that
24 tons of potatoes can be produced either with 8, 7, or 6 acres and
2 units of labor, or with 4 acres and 4 units of labor or with 3 acres and 9
units of labor, as well as with an indefinite number of intermediate
combinations not shown in the schedule. Now, if the producer decides to
grow 24 tons of potatoes, which is the best of all these alternative ways of
doing it? We shall not yet inquire why he wants to produce 24 tons and
not any other quantity, for that part of the solution comes later. Before
the final solution can be given we must know the best combination of
inputs which will produce any given quantity of output.

Example. Table 51, section A, shows a number of these possible com-

TABLE 51. THE LEAST OUTLAY COMBINATION[a]

A. Quantity of labor (men)	2	3.0	4.0	5.0	6.0	7.0	8.0	9.0
Quantity of land (acres)	6	4.5	4.0	3.7	3.5	3.3	3.1	3.0
B. Labor @ $20 unit	$ 40	$ 60	$ 80	$100	$120	$140	$160	$180
Land @ $20 unit	120	90	80	74	70	66	62	60
Total outlay	160	(150)	160	174	190	206	222	240
C. Labor @ $10 unit	20	30	40	50	60	70	80	90
Land @ $10 unit	60	45	40	37	35	33	31	30
Total outlay	80	(75)	80	87	95	103	111	120
D. Labor @ $10 unit	20	30	40	50	60	70	80	90
Land @ $30 unit	180	135	120	111	105	99	93	90
Total outlay	200	165	(160)	161	165	169	173	180
E. Labor @ $10 unit	20	30	40	50	60	70	80	90
Land @ $40 unit	240	180	160	148	140	132	124	120
Total outlay	260	210	200	(198)	200	202	204	210

[a] Circled numbers equal least outlay combination.

binations. Which is the best? Will it pay to produce 24 tons with a lot of
labor and a little land or with a little labor and a lot of land or with
some combination in between? Obviously, from the point of view of the
producer the best combination of inputs is that which he can purchase for
the least amount of money. In order to find out how much money must
be expended (the total outlay) in the purchase of any combination of
quantities of input, however, we must first know the *prices* of these
inputs. In Table 51, section B, then, is calculated the total outlay required to purchase the various combinations shown in section A, on the

assumption that the price of labor is $20 per man-month and the price of land is $20 per acre for the appropriate period. The total outlay on labor in each case is the quantity bought multiplied by the price; the total outlay on land is also the quantity bought multiplied by the price, and the sum of these quantities is the total outlay expended on the purchase of the combination. In the case represented by section B of this table it is evident that the least outlay combination of inputs is 3 units of labor and 4.5 units of land, where the total outlay is $150.

The Least Outlay Combination Depends on the Relative Prices of Input

Now let us see whether the least outlay combination changes when we change the prices of the inputs concerned. Section C of Table 51 gives the case in which the price of *both* inputs is $10 per unit instead of $20 as in section B. It is evident that the least outlay combination is still 3 units of labor with 4.5 units of land, where the total outlay is $75. A proportionate change in the prices of *both* inputs therefore does not change the quantities of input which form the least outlay combination; it merely changes the total expense involved in purchasing the least outlay combination. In section D, however, the price of land has risen relative to the price of labor, land now being $30 per unit and labor $10 per unit. It will be seen from the table that the least outlay combination is now 4 units of labor and 4 units of land, where the total outlay is $160. Similarly, in section E, where the price of land is $40 per unit as against $10 per unit for labor, the least outlay combination is 5 units of labor and 3.7 units of land. Evidently, as land increases in price relative to labor, the cheaper input (labor) will oust the dearer input (land), and the proportion of labor used will increase relative to the amount of land used. That is to say, when one input increases in price relative to another, the cheaper input is substituted, up to a point, for the dearer input. This, of course, is what we should expect.

Geometric Solution: Outlay Contours

In the two-input case a geometric solution of the problem of finding the least outlay combination of inputs is possible. We begin in Fig. 118 by constructing lines of equal outlay, or outlay contours on a two-input field. Thus suppose the quantity of labor is measured along OX, the total outlay on labor along OY'. Then the line OR is the *total outlay curve* for labor; it shows how the total amount spent on labor varies with the amount of labor bought. If the price of labor is constant this curve will be a straight line through the origin. In Fig. 118, however a more general case is shown with three possible market situations. As the quantity of labor increases from O to Ot_5, the price gradually falls, indicating a condition in which the enterprise is getting a "reduction for quantity." The price of labor at any point on the outlay curve—e.g., at r_4—is the slope of the line Or_4, or t_4r_4/Ot_4. From the quantity Ot_5 to Ot_7 we assume that the price is constant. The outlay curve, r_5r_7, in this range is a straight line whose projection passes through the origin, O. Above the quantity Ot_7 we assume that the market is imperfect, i.e., that as the firm tries

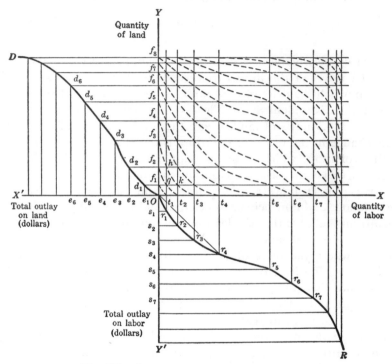

Fig. 118. Construction of Outlay Contours

to buy more and more labor the price rises against it. This is reflected in the increasing steepness of the outlay curve after r_7. The outlay curve for land, OD, is treated similarly. The slope of a total outlay curve at any point is the marginal cost of the input.

The Construction of Outlay Contours

Mark off on OX' distances Oe_1 representing 1 unit of outlay (one dollar), Oe_2 representing two dollars, and so on. Draw the perpendiculars from e_1 meeting the outlay curve OD in d_1, and from d_1 to OY meeting OY in f_1. Then Of_1 represents the quantity of land which can be bought with \$1.

Similarly, Of_2 represents the quantity of land which can be bought with \$2, Of_3 the quantity which can be bought with \$3, and so on. The range of points on OX, t_1, t_2, t_3, etc., are similar; Ot_1 represents the quantity of labor which can be bought with \$1, Ot_2 the quantity which can be bought with \$2, and so on. Perpendiculars drawn from their axes at the points f_1, f_2, f_3, etc., and from t_1, t_2, t_3, etc., form a rectangular framework as in the figure. Now consider the meaning of a line drawn diagonally across the corners of this framework, as f_3t_3. The point f_3 represents an amount of land equal to Of_3, combined with no labor; total outlay on land and labor is \$3. The point h represents a combination of Of_2 of land, costing \$2, and Ot_1 of labor, costing \$1; a total cost of land and labor of \$3. The point k represents a combination of Of_1 of land, costing \$1, plus Ot_2 of labor, costing \$2; total outlay, \$3. Similarly, the point t_3 represents a combination of Ot_3 of labor, costing \$3, with no land; total outlay, \$3. Evidently all the points on the line f_3t_3 represent combinations of input quantities which can be bought for a total sum of \$3. Likewise, all the points on the line f_4t_4 represent all those combinations of input quantities which can be bought for \$4; and so for the whole system of dashed lines in the figure.

Just as we called the line joining all those points representing combinations of input quantities which produced the same product an iso-product curve or a product contour, so we can call the dashed lines of Fig. 118 iso-outlay curves or outlay contours. They represent the contours of a total outlay surface in which the total amount spent on purchasing any combination of input quantities is measured vertically.

It will be observed that when both markets are imperfect the outlay contours are concave to the origin, as in the top right-hand corner of the figure. When in both markets the price is smaller for larger quantities— a state which we have called a pluperfect market (p. 361)—the outlay contours are convex to the origin, as in the bottom left-hand corner of the figure. When both markets are perfect the outlay contours are straight lines. The outlay contours are the contours of a three-dimensional outlay surface, in which the total outlay of any combination is measured vertically above the plane of Fig. 118. The surface is generated by erecting the outlay curves OR and OD in a vertical plane above OX and OY respectively, and by moving one curve at right angles to its plane with its origin moving along the other curve.

Least Outlay Combination Where Outlay and Product Contours Touch

In Fig. 119 a product contour (PP_1P_2) is superimposed on a system of outlay contours. For the sake of simplicity we suppose that the markets for input are perfect throughout, so that the outlay contours are straight lines. Let the product contour represent all those combinations of input quantities which will produce 24 tons of potatoes. Then the *cheapest* combination of inputs which will produce this amount is given by the point *P,* where the product contour is *touched* by an outlay contour. The outlay contours are marked with the total outlay which they represent; thus the point P_2 represents a combination which can be bought with

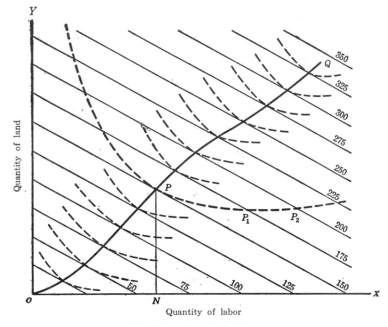

Fig. 119.   The Scale Line

$200; P_1 a combination which can be bought with $175; *P* a combination which can be bought with $150. Evidently, as long as we stick to the dashed product contour we cannot find any combination of input which will give us 24 tons of potatoes and which can be bought for less than $150. To take a quantity of labor represented by *ON* and a quantity of land represented by *NP,* therefore, is the cheapest way of producing 24 tons of potatoes. For any other quantity of potatoes also, we can draw a product contour and find the point where it is touched by an outlay contour.

The Scale Line

A line *OPQ* drawn through all these points shows all the combinations of quantities of labor and land that are cheapest for producing the amount of potatoes which they do in fact produce. This line may be called the *scale line,*[3] for it shows how the quantities of labor and land will rise as the scale of enterprise rises, i.e., as more and more output is produced. A combination of labor and land represented by a point which does not lie on the scale line cannot possibly be the most profitable combination to take, for from any point—say P_1—which does not lie on the scale line it will be possible, simply by moving toward the scale line along a product contour, to find another combination of input quantities which will give the same quantity of product at a lower total outlay. The most profitable combination of quantities, therefore, must lie somewhere on the scale line.

The Optimum Point

To find exactly *where* on the scale line is the most profitable output, or optimum point, of the whole field of input quantities, we must calculate for each point the total value of the product (its quantity multiplied by its price) and also the total cost (quantity times price of each input used). The difference between these quantities is the net revenue, which we assume to be the measure of profitability. Then in a figure like Fig. 80A (p. 391) we stretch the scale line along the horizontal axis and plot the net revenue on the vertical axis; the point of maximum net revenue, K in Fig. 80A will give us the optimum product. We now go back to Fig. 119 and find the product contour corresponding to this optimum product. If this is PP_2 then P is the optimum position in the field, ON is the amount of labor, and NP the amount of land that will yield the maximum net revenue. We can visualize the significance of this point if we suppose that above the plane of Fig. 119 we erect a total revenue surface, showing the total revenue or value of product corresponding to each combination of labor and land. Similarly, we can erect a total cost surface, showing the total cost corresponding to each combination of labor and land. The point where the vertical distance of the revenue surface above the cost surface is greatest is the absolutely most profitable combination of the two factors. The contours of the revenue surface will be identical in shape with the product contours, as each product contour, representing as it does all combinations of land and labor which produce a given output, must also represent those combinations which produce the value of that output. Thus if the price of 24 tons of product is $10 per ton, the 24-ton product contour is also the $240 revenue contour. Provided that all other

---

[3] The scale line is frequently called the *expansion path*. The term expansion path, however, is somewhat misleading, as it suggests that as a matter of historic fact a firm will expand along this line. This is not necessarily true; the scale line is merely a *construction* line by which the most profitable point in the field of the diagram can be discovered.

costs are held constant, the outlay contours will be identical in shape with the cost contours.

On the Scale Line, the Rates of Substitution for Product and Outlay Are Equal

Let us consider now the economic significance of the condition that defines the scale line—that is, that the outlay contours and product contours should be tangent. At such a point the slopes of the two contours are equal. The slope of a product contour at a point is the *rate of product substitution* of land for labor at that point. That is, it is the amount of land that can be substituted for one unit of labor and still leave the product unchanged. Similarly, the slope of an outlay contour is the *rate of outlay substitution* of land for labor, that is, the amount of land that can be substituted for one unit of labor and still leave total outlay unchanged. The condition that defines the scale line, therefore, is that

$$\text{Marginal rate of product substitution} =$$
$$\text{Marginal rate of outlay substitution} \qquad (1)$$

If this condition is not fulfilled we can get a larger product for the same outlay, or the same product for a smaller outlay, by substituting one input for another.

Rates of Substitution Equal to Ratios of Marginal Effect

If any three variables are related, X, Y, and Z, the rate of substitution of two of them, say of X for Y, which will keep Z constant is equal to the ratio

$$\frac{\text{Marginal effect of } X \text{ on } Z}{\text{Marginal effect of } Y \text{ on } Z}$$

Thus if increasing X by 1 unit increases Z by 6 units, and if increasing Y by 1 unit increases Z by 3 units, then if we increase X by 1 unit (increasing Z by 6) we shall have to decrease Y by 2 (decreasing Z by 6) units to keep Z unchanged.[4] Thus we have, as the marginal physical productivity is the marginal effect of input on output, and the marginal outlay is the marginal effect of input on total outlay,

[4] If $\dfrac{dz}{dx}$ is the marginal effect of X on Z, and $\dfrac{dz}{dy}$ is the marginal effect of Y on Z, then the marginal rate of substitution of X per unit of Y is

$$\frac{dx}{dy} = \frac{\dfrac{dx}{dz}}{\dfrac{dy}{dz}}$$

Marginal rate of product substitution of land per unit of labor =

$$\frac{\text{Marginal physical productivity of land}}{\text{Marginal physical productivity of labor}} \qquad (2)$$

and

Marginal rate of outlay substitution of land per unit of labor =

$$\frac{\text{Marginal outlay on land}}{\text{Marginal outlay on labor}} \qquad (3)$$

Now combining equations (1), (2), and (3) we have, on the scale line,

$$\frac{\text{Marginal physical productivity of land}}{\text{Marginal physical productivity of labor}} = \frac{\text{Marginal outlay on land}}{\text{Marginal outlay on labor}} \qquad (4)$$

This may be called the least outlay condition. It can also be put in the form:

$$\frac{\text{Marginal outlay on labor}}{\text{Marginal physical productivity of labor}} =$$

$$\frac{\text{Marginal outlay on land}}{\text{Marginal physical productivity of land}} \qquad (5)$$

The Scale Line Enables Us to Separate Problem of Proportions from Problem of Scale

One great advantage of the scale line as a weapon of analysis is that it enables us to divide the problem of production into two rough parts, the problem of the *proportions of input quantities,* on the one hand, and the problem of the *scale of operations,* on the other. If the scale line is a straight line through the origin, then any point on it represents a definite *proportion* of input quantities—a proportion represented by the slope of the line itself. In Fig. 119 the steeper the scale line, the greater the proportion of land used and the less the proportion of labor. If the scale line is not straight we cannot make any simple separation of the problem of proportions from the problem of scale. We can still distinguish, however, between swings of the scale line itself, which correspond roughly to changes in proportions, and movements along the scale line, which indicate changes in scale.

APPLICATIONS TO THE CASE OF PERFECT MARKETS FOR INPUT

We can now apply this analysis to some problems involving perfect markets for input. In a perfect market, as we have seen (p. 433), the price of input is the same as its marginal outlay, for if price does not change with change in the quantity bought, every unit increase in purchases increases total outlay by an amount equal to the price.

Equal Proportionate Change in Prices of All Inputs Causes Change in Scale Only

If the prices of the inputs change *in the same ratio,* there will be no change in the position of the scale line and hence, roughly, no change in the proportions of the inputs used. If, for instance, the prices of labor and land both double, there will be no change in the rate of outlay substitutions; $3\%_{10}$ is just the same as $6\%_{20}$. The slopes of the outlay contours will not therefore be changed, although there will be a change in the total outlay which each contour represents, i.e., in the *height* of the contour. The scale of the process is likely to decline, but there will be no change in the proportions of the inputs used.

Change in Relative Prices of Inputs Also Changes Proportions Used

If, on the other hand, the price of labor changes in a different ratio from the price of land, there will be a change in the rate of outlay substitution, and the proportions of input—the slope of the scale line—will change. Suppose the price of land increases from \$10 to \$15 per acre while the price of labor increases from \$30 to \$60 per man-month. The rate of outlay substitution of land for labor will rise from 3 acres per man-month to 4 acres per man-month. That is to say, the outlay contours will all become *steeper.* Consequently, they will touch the product contours at a point above the old point, where the product contour is also steeper. That is, the scale line will also become steeper; the result of an increase in the price of labor relative to that of land is to increase the proportion of land taken and to decrease the proportion of labor. This is what we should expect; the input which has become relatively cheaper is substituted in place of the input which has become relatively dearer.

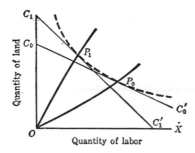

Fig. 120.   Effect of a Relative Rise in the Price of Labor

GRAPHIC ILLUSTRATION. This is illustrated in Fig. 120. P_1P_0 (dotted) represents a product contour, $C_0C'_0$ an outlay contour touching the product contour at P_0. OP_0 is then the scale line. Suppose the price of labor rises relative to the price of land. The outlay contours become steeper; $C_1C'_1$ is one of the new outlay contours, which touches the product contour at P_1. OP_1 is the new scale line. Obviously, the result has been to increase the proportion of land used at the expense of labor; the relatively cheaper land is substituted for the relatively dearer labor.

Change in Proportions Depends on Product Substitutability of Inputs

It is clear from Fig. 120 that the extent of the change in the proportions of inputs with the change in relative prices depends on the curvature of the isoproduct curves. If these are very slightly curved there must be a long swing from P_0 to P_1 before the rate of product substitution is equal to the new rate of outlay substitution. If the curvature is sharp the swing will be correspondingly small. The curvature of the isoproduct curve is, however, a measure of the degree of substitutability of the inputs (page 555). The more substitutable the inputs, therefore, the more the proportions of inputs will shift in response to a given change in relative prices, and the less stable will be the position of the scale line.

Scale Line Shiftable in Pluperfect Markets

To return for a moment to the general case of Fig. 118, it is easy to see that the position of the scale line, and therefore the proportions of inputs used, will be much more shiftable when the markets for input are pluperfect than when they are perfect or imperfect. In the bottom left-hand corner of the outlay map in Fig. 118 it will be seen that the outlay contours are convex to the origin. But the product contours also are convex to the origin because of the law of diminishing marginal productivity. It would be possible, then, when for both inputs large reductions in price could be obtained with increased purchases, that the outlay and product contours might almost coincide. If they coincided over some range, the position of the scale line would be indeterminate within that range, and a very small shift in the conditions of the problem would cause a large shift in the scale line and in the proportions of the inputs used. Imperfection in the input markets, however, makes large shifts in the proportions of input quantities unlikely.

Conditions of Constant Average Cost

With the analytical equipment now at hand it is not difficult to show that if the production function is homogeneous, markets are perfect, and

all inputs are variable, the average outlay, or average cost, will be constant.
In Fig. 121 a system of product contours (dashed) and cost contours (solid)
is reproduced as in Fig. 119. The product contours in this case, however,
represent a production schedule with constant returns to scale. Here it
can be proved that the scale line, *OS*, is a straight line from the origin.
It is a well-known property of any homogeneous system of curves, such
as the product contours in Fig. 121, that any straight line from the origin

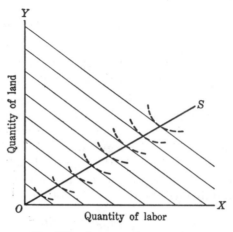

Fig. 121.　Constant Average Cost

will intercept them at points where their *slopes* are equal, and that, conversely, any line connecting the points on the various curves which have
a given slope is a straight line through the origin. But by definition we
know that on the scale line the slope of each product contour is equal to
the slope of the outlay contour at that point. And we know also that when
the markets for input are perfect the slope of all outlay contours is constant. The slope of any product contour, therefore, at the point of intersection with the scale line is equal to the given slope of the outlay contours, i.e., to the ratio of the price of the two inputs. So the scale line must
be a straight line through the origin. It follows that a given proportionate
rise in output is best attained by increasing both inputs in the same
proportion. If the prices of input are constant, the total outlay will increase in this same proportion also. For instance, a doubling of the
quantity of product will be obtained by doubling the total outlay or
the total cost. The total cost curve, instead of being curved as in Fig.
80, page 391, will be a straight line from the origin, such as *OQR* in
Fig. 81A. In that case the average cost and the marginal cost are the same
at all outputs and are equal to the constant gradient of the total cost curve.

Why Do Costs Rise with Increasing Output?

The above conclusion is of great importance, for in all our analysis of supply we have assumed that the average total cost was *not* constant, but had a minimum value. If the average total cost were the same at all outputs, no matter how great, and if the market for output were perfect at all outputs, there would be nothing to prevent an enterprise from increasing its scale indefinitely. There would be no output at which the net revenue is a maximum, for the net revenue, provided the price of the product is greater than its constant average cost, will always increase with increase in output. The marginal cost will be constant and equal to the average cost, and will always be below the price of the product. If the market for output is perfect, then, an enterprise is prevented from expanding indefinitely only by the fact of rising marginal cost as output expands. But how can marginal cost rise? Only if (1) the prices of inputs rise as more are purchased, (2) one or more inputs are fixed in quantity so that the law of diminishing marginal productivity comes into play, or (3) there are decreasing returns to scale at higher outputs. In short periods both (1) and (2) are likely to be true. Over long periods it is a little more difficult to explain why marginal cost should rise with increasing output, for the usual fixed costs—e.g., plant and equipment—can now be varied as plans are made for many years ahead. Even here, however, there may be one element of input which cannot be increased indefinitely—the input of management. Two managers are not twice as much management as one! Beyond a certain point further reorganization of management fails to increase its quantity. This alone would explain why firms seem to have an optimum size. Failing this, we have to fall back on an assumption of genuine diminishing returns to scale at high outputs to explain what limits the growth of firms.

DISCONTINUOUS FUNCTIONS

The previous analysis of this chapter has assumed continuous production or market functions. Frequently these functions are discontinuous, which creates both problems and opportunities. Thus, suppose we had a situation in which only certain specific combinations of factors were feasible, so that the production function shrank to a number of separated points. This is illustrated in Fig. 122. Here we suppose that the product contour shrinks to two points, P_1 and P_2, representing the only two possible combinations of inputs which can produce a given output: P_1, with a little labor and a lot of land; P_2 with a lot of labor and a little land. These represent two entirely different methods of production. The choice

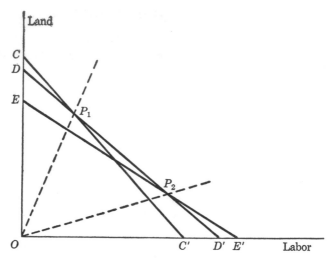

Fig. 122.   A Discontinuous Production Function

between the methods rests on the marginal outlays of the two inputs. Suppose the input market is perfect, so that the outlay contours are straight lines. Then if CC' is an outlay contour, P_1 is clearly on a lower contour than P_2, for the line parallel to CC' through P_2 (not drawn) represents a *higher* outlay. If the outlay contours are parallel to DD', both P_1 and P_2 have equal outlays; if the outlay contours are parallel to EE', P_2 is the preferred point with the least outlay. This is essentially a linear programming solution; it can easily be extended to cases where there are three or more alternative methods. In the above case if the ratio of the price of land to the price of labor is above that given by the slope of DD', the method of P_1 will be chosen; as this ratio falls there will be a sudden shift to the method of P_2 when labor has cheapened, relatively, to the ratio just beyond the slope of DD'. If the proportions of factors employed in each method are constant, the line OP_1 shows all combinations of input which would be used at different scales of output under the first method, and OP_2 the similar set of combinations under the second. What we have then is two possible scale lines, with the possibility of a sudden shift from one to the other when the relative prices of the inputs pass a critical point.

There can also be discontinuities in the outlay curves, when, for instance, a quota creates a two-price system. Thus suppose in Fig. 123 that the firm has a perfect market for land in all quantities, and for labor up to the amount OV, but that beyond the quantity OV the price of labor rises sharply. Overtime payment has something of this character.

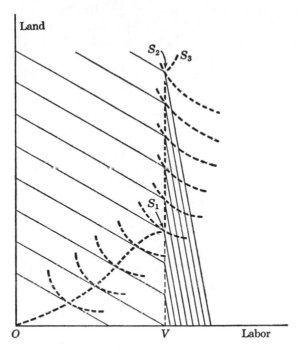

Fig. 123. A Discontinuous Outlay Function

The outlay contours all have a kink on the line VS_2. The scale line rises normally to the point S_1 at which the labor quota is reached, and then turns vertically upward to S_2 where the marginal rate of product substitution equals the higher price of labor. Then it will continue steeply, but not vertically, beyond S_2. If the optimum point is at a low scale between O and S_1 the quota is simply ineffective; if it is between S_1 and S_2, the amount of labor bought is equal to the quota; only at high scales beyond S_2 does the purchase of labor go beyond the quota to the higher price.

Extension to Case of More Than Two Inputs

One advantage of the scale-line method of analysis is that it enables us to extend our discussion easily to cases where there are more than two inputs. For three inputs we can construct a three-dimensional diagram with product contour surfaces and outlay contour surfaces. A product contour surface on such a figure will show all combinations of quantities of three inputs which cooperate to produce a given quantity of product. There will be a system of these surfaces, something like the skins on a quadrant of onion. Similarly, the outlay contour surfaces with perfect markets will form a system of planes lying diagonally athwart the three axes, like the pages of a tilted book. The outlay contours will touch the product contours along a line in 3-space, each point of which represents the cheapest combination of inputs to use in producing a given output. Thus there will be a scale line in our three-dimensional figure. We can also extend the analysis to four or more inputs, though visual geometry fails us here. The scale line is always a *line,* even in *n space,* and each point on it represents a definite combination of input quantities, no matter how many inputs there are.[5] The general conclusions developed for two inputs hold also in the case of many inputs. If the production function is homogeneous and the markets for input are perfect, the scale line will always be straight, and the average total cost will be the same at all outputs. A relative rise in the price of any input will swing the scale line away from the axis along which the input is measured and will therefore tend to alter the proportions of the inputs in favor of those whose prices have not risen. Similarly, an equal proportionate rise in the prices of all inputs will not change the position of the scale line, though it will in general change the scale itself.

QUESTIONS AND EXERCISES

1. Prove geometrically, from Fig. 118, that the slope of the outlay contour is equal to the ratio of the slopes of the total outlay curves from which it is derived, and discuss the economic significance of this proposition.

    Construct outlay contours by the method of Fig. 118 for the case in which *each* input can be purchased at a constant price up to a fixed quota, after which it cannot be obtained at any price.

2. Assume that Table 48 (p. 545) exhibited constant returns to scale.

    a. Draw as many diagonals as you can, like *A, B,* and *C,* passing through figures representing proportional increases in all inputs and outputs.

    b. What would be the output of potatoes when (i) $2\frac{1}{2}$ units of labor are applied to 3 acres, (ii) $1\frac{1}{2}$ units of labor are applied to $3\frac{1}{2}$ acres?

3. Construct a table similar in form to Table 48 and derived from the data given therein, to show the marginal physical productivity of labor for each quantity of land and of labor. Construct a similar table showing the marginal physical productivity of land for each quantity of land and labor. Show that in each case the law of eventually diminishing marginal physical productivity holds.

    Can we formulate a law to describe the change in the marginal physical productivity of one input as the quantity of the other is increased?

[5] The equation of the scale line in the n space with axes measuring quantity of inputs $a_1, a_2, a_n,$ *is given by the* $n - 1$ independent equations $\dfrac{r_1}{C_1} = \dfrac{r_2}{C_2} = \dfrac{r_n}{C_n} =$ where r_1 is the marginal physical productivity, and $C_2,$ the marginal outlay on the C_1 input.

4. The yield of agricultural crops per acre is considerably higher in Europe than in America, although the soil is intrinsically no more fertile. How could you connect this fact with the fact of Europe's dense population? How would you expect yields per man-hour to differ in the two continents? Yields per acre and per man in American agriculture have been rising sharply since the middle 1930s, while agricultural employment has been falling and arable acreage has remained roughly constant. How might these changes be interpreted in terms of a production function?

5. Show graphically the effect of an equal proportionate rise in the price of all the inputs of an individual firm on the following: (a) the total outlay curves, (b) the outlay contours, (c) the least cost combination of inputs, (d) the scale line, (e) the marginal cost curve, (f) the average cost curve, (g) the equilibrium output. Show also the effect on (h) the normal supply curve, (i) the price, (j) the output of the product, (k) rents of fixed inputs, and (m) the number of firms in the industry.

6. In the physical production schedule of Table 48, assume that the price of labor is $60 per unit, the price of land is $20 per acre, and the price of potatoes is $20 per ton. Assume that normal profit is zero. Then calculate for each one of the 81 combinations of input quantities shown in Table 48, the net revenue resulting from the employment of the combination. Tabulate the results in a similar table. Notice that the net revenue increases indefinitely as the quantities of land and labor increase; there is no maximum value. Why?

7. Discuss how the concept of a production function and the laws of returns might apply to the following processes: (a) cooking an omelet; (b) painting a picture; (c) writing a sonnet.

CHAPTER **26**

THREE-VARIABLE ANALYSIS
(Continued)

THE MARGINAL PRODUCTIVITY METHOD

The analysis of the optimum position of an enterprise with two or more inputs can be attacked by another method, involving the concept of marginal productivity. We have already seen (page 432) that if there is only one variable input the enterprise will not be at its most profitable point if the marginal revenue productivity of the variable input is not equal to the marginal cost of the input. This condition also holds in the case in which more than one input is variable, for each of the variable inputs. If the quantities of all the inputs are such that for any variable input the marginal revenue productivity is, say, greater than the marginal cost of the input, the net revenue can be increased by increasing the employment of the input. In those circumstances a unit increase in the quantity of the input employed will increase the total revenue more than it will increase the total cost. If, therefore, the marginal revenue productivity of any variable input is *not* equal to its marginal cost, the enterprise is not producing with the most profitable quantities of input and output, i.e., is not in equilibrium. It must be understood, however, that a change in the quantity of one input will change the marginal productivity *curves* of the other inputs, for the marginal productivity of one input depends on the quantities of the other inputs used with it.

GEOMETRIC ILLUSTRATION. These principles are illustrated geometrically in Figs. 124 and 125. In Fig. 124 it is assumed that the quantity of land is held constant, at an amount equal to OH in Fig. 125. In Fig. 124 the quantity of labor is measured along OX, dollars along OY. The curve OPQ is a total revenue curve. A quantity of labor ON, with the fixed quantity of land, yields a product which sells for an amount NP. (This is essentially the same as the *ONPCR* of Fig. 88, page 430.) We suppose for simplicity that the inputs have perfect markets; the total cost of labor curve will then be *ORS*. The slope of *ORS* is the marginal cost, in this case equal to the price of labor. As all other inputs are assumed fixed, the

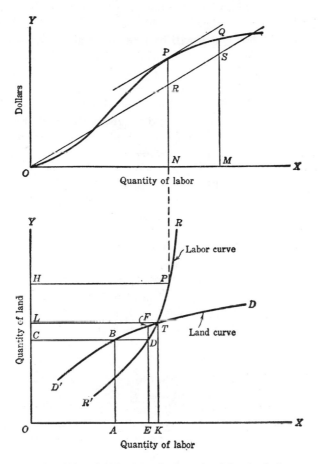

Figs. 124 and 125. Marginal Productivity Analysis

total net revenue will be a maximum when the difference between the total revenue and the total cost of labor is a maximum. This is at the quantity of labor *ON*, where the marginal productivity of labor, equal to the slope of the curve *OPQ* at *P*, is equal to the marginal cost of labor, equal to the slope of *ORS* at *R*. The excess of revenue over labor cost, *RP*, is a maximum at this point and as all other costs are supposed constant the total net revenue will likewise be at a maximum.

The Labor Curve and the Land Curve

In Fig. 125 the quantity of labor is plotted along *OX*, the quantity of land along *OY*. If *OH* represents the quantity of land to which labor was applied in Fig. 125, *HP* (= *ON* in Fig. 124) will represent the most profitable quantity of labor to use with the quantity of land *OH*. Similarly, for any other quantity of land—e.g., *OC*—there will be some quantity of labor which will be most profitable—say, *CD*. *D, P,* and other such points lie on a curve, *RR'*, which may be called the *labor curve.* Any point on it represents a quantity of labor which it is most profitable to employ with a given quantity of land. In an exactly similar fashion, again applying the principle that with a given quantity of labor the most profitable quantity of land to use will be that at which the marginal cost of land is equal to its marginal revenue productivity, we can obtain a curve *DD'*, the *land curve.* Any point on the land curve indicates a combination of input quantities such that, with the quantity of labor given, the quantity of land is the most profitable to use.

GRAPHIC SOLUTION. MOST PROFITABLE COMBINATION IS WHERE LAND AND LABOR CURVES INTERSECT. The point where these two curves intersect, *T*, shows the most profitable combination of land *and* labor, assuming that the quantities of both these inputs are variable. Suppose we start with a certain quantity of labor, *OA*. The most profitable quantity of land to use with this quantity of labor is *AB* (= *OC*), where *B* lies on the land curve. But with a quantity of land equal to *AB*, or *OC*, the most profitable quantity of labor to use is *CD*, where *D* is on the labor curve; it will pay to increase the purchase of labor. But with a quantity of labor equal to *CD* (or *OE*) the most profitable quantity of land to use is *EF*, where *F* is on the land curve. So we go on, continually approaching the point *T*. Then *TL* is the most profitable quantity of labor to use with an amount of land equal to *TK;* and *TK* is the most profitable amount of land to use with the amount of labor equal to *TL*. The net revenue cannot be raised by increasing *any* of the input quantities. The point *T*, therefore, is absolutely the most profitable combination possible, and the output corresponding to the product contour which passes through *T* is the most profitable output. It must be emphasized that both the scale line method and the marginal productivity method are *constructions* for finding the point *T*, and should give exactly the same result; sometimes one and sometimes the other will be found the most convenient.

THE DEMAND FOR INPUT

Both the scale line method and the marginal productivity method can be employed to analyze the problem of the demand for input for a two-input firm. We suppose, of course, perfect markets for input, otherwise the concept of a demand for input—that is, a function relating the price of input to the quantity purchased—loses its clarity. We cannot now assume that the demand for an input is identical with its marginal value productivity curve (page 441), because the position of this curve itself, for any given input, depends on the amount of other inputs employed. We must therefore analyze the effects of a change in the price of one input on *all* the variables of the enterprise.

Analysis by the Scale Line

The effect of a change in the price of one input in an enterprise using more than one variable input can be analyzed into two parts. There will be a *substitution effect;* i.e., a rise, say, in the price of one input will cause a substitution of a cheaper for the dearer input. The proportions of inputs will change to the disadvantage of the one which has suffered the rise in price. Such a change is reflected geometrically by a shift in the scale line away from the axis of the dearer input, as shown in Fig. 120, page 564. The second effect we may call the *scale effect*. If the price of even one variable input rises, the marginal cost of the product at each output will rise. The marginal cost will therefore meet the price at a smaller output than formerly. The rise in the price of input, by increasing costs, will act to reduce the scale of the enterprise. Both substitution effect and scale effect are illustrated in Fig. 126.

Here the quantity of labor is measured along OX, the quantity of land

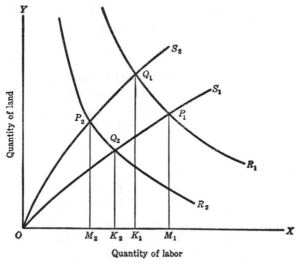

Fig. 126. Derivation of Demand Curves for Input

along OY. OS_1 is the original scale line; OS_2 is the scale line after the price of labor has risen, as in Fig. 120, page 564. R_1 is the product contour representing those combinations which produce the most profitable output before the price change; the point where OS_1 cuts this product contour, P_1, gives the best quantities of labor and land to employ—M_1P_1 of land and OM_1 of labor. R_2 is the product contour representing those combinations which produce the most profitable output after the rise in the price of labor; it is nearer the origin than R_1, indicating that the most profitable output is now smaller than before. Where this cuts OS_2, P_2 shows the most profitable quantities of labor and land to employ —M_2P_2 of land and OM_2 of labor. If there were no scale effect the new point of greatest profit would be Q_1, where the quantity of labor employed was OK_1 and the quantity of land K_1Q_1. Evidently with this condition an increase in the price of labor would cause a decrease in the purchase of labor and an increase in the purchase of land. If there were no substitution effect the new point of greatest profit would be Q_2, where the quantity of labor employed was OK_2 and the quantity of land was K_2Q_2. In this event the scale effect alone would bring about a reduction in the quantities of *both* land and labor when the price of labor rose. If the price of labor rises, then, both the substitution effect and the scale effect combine to cause a decline in the quantity of labor bought. The substitution effect will make for a rise, the scale effect, for a fall in the quantity of land bought. If, therefore, the scale effect is small compared to the substitution effect, a rise in the price of labor may cause a rise in the quantity of land bought. If the scale effect is large compared to the substitution effect, a rise in the price of labor may bring about a fall in the quantity of land bought as well as a fall in the quantity of labor.

Substitutability and Importance of Inputs

We have seen (page 555), that the substitution effect—the rotation of the scale line—will be small if the product contour is sharply curved, great if the product contour is but little curved. The magnitude of the substitution effect, therefore, depends, as we should expect, on the degree to which the inputs can be substituted. If they must be used in inflexible proportions, there will be no substitution effect at all.

The magnitude of the scale effect depends mainly on the degree of *importance* of the input in question. If the input plays a large part in the process, the scale effect will be large; if it plays a small part, the scale effect will be small. The more substitutable the inputs and the more important the inputs in question, the greater will be the decline in employment which follows from a given increase in the price of an input—i.e., the more elastic will be the demand for the input of an individual firm. (See Chapter 13.)

The Industry Effect

In considering the demand for input by a whole industry, we must take into account a further effect, the effect on the profitability of the industry, and on the entry or exit of firms, of changes in the price of an input. Referring to Fig. 90, page 439, we see that a rise in the price of one input would raise all the cost curves of each firm. The rise in costs would drive firm D out of the industry, thus reducing the total demand for all the factors used. Besides the scale effect on the output of each firm, a rise in the price of an input will have an *industry effect* on the number of firms in the industry. This industry effect will be large if the input is an important one, thus confirming the proposition that the demand for an input will be more elastic, the more important the input. This effect will also be large if there are a large number of firms on the margin, i.e., if the industry approaches the condition of *constant cost*. It will also be large if the demand for the product of the industry is elastic, small if the demand for the product is inelastic. As firms drop out, the total output of the industry falls and therefore the price of the product rises. If the demand for the product is inelastic, a small fall in output will cause a large rise in the price of the product, which will offset the rise in costs and so prevent more firms from dropping out. If the demand for the product is elastic, there will not be so much of this offsetting effect of a rise in price, and more firms will have to drop out following a rise in costs before the industry is normally profitable again.

It should be noticed that if the prices of all inputs rise in the same proportion there is no substitution effect. There is, however, a scale effect and an industry effect, so that the employment of all inputs will fall. This proposition is true only if the industry is small so that the effect of its factor payments on the demand for its product can be neglected.

Analysis of Demand for Input by Marginal Productivity Analysis

There is another method by which the demand for input from an individual firm may be analyzed, the method involving marginal productivity analysis as used on pages 432–434. Figs. 127A and 127B show the effect of a change in the price of one input on the quantity which will be bought, on the assumption that the quantity of other inputs used remains unchanged. Fig. 127A is similar to Fig. 124, page 573; the quantity of input (labor) is measured along the horizontal axis, and the total revenue derived from the sale of the output produced by each quantity of labor along the vertical axis, assuming that the quantity of other inputs (land) is constant. OPP' is the total revenue curve. When the price of labor is equal to the slope of the line ORS, the best quantity of labor to employ will be ON, where the marginal revenue productivity of labor is equal to

its price. When the price of labor falls to an amount equal to the slope of
the line $OR'S'$, the quantity which it will pay best to employ will rise from
ON to ON'. This is shown also in Fig. 127B, where the quantity of labor
is plotted along the horizontal axis as before, and the marginal revenue
productivity of labor on the vertical axis. At a price of labor equal to OR

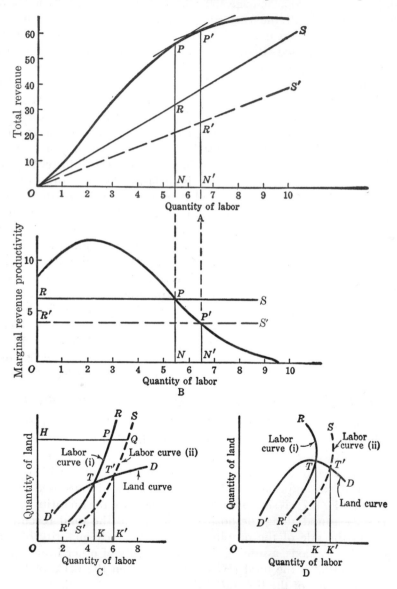

Fig. 127.   Derivation of Demand for Input from Marginal Productivity Analysis

the quantity of labor at which the marginal revenue productivity is equal to this price is ON, or RP. At the price of labor equal to OR' the quantity employed will be ON', or $R'P'$. It is evident from Fig. 127B that the *steeper* the marginal revenue productivity curve in the region PP', the smaller will be the effect of a given change in the price of labor on the quantity which will be brought. That is, if the marginal revenue productivity falls rapidly as the quantity of labor employed increases, only a small increase in employment is necessary to bring the marginal revenue productivity down to the new level. We saw, however, on page 548, that the marginal physical productivity of an input declines rapidly when the input is not highly substitutable for others. A change in the price of a nonsubstitutable input, therefore, will cause little change in its employment. That is, the demand for an input will be less elastic, the less suitable it is for others.

Fig. 127C shows the effect of a change in the price of labor on the land curve and the labor curve of Fig. 125, page 573. A change in the price of labor will not affect the land curve,[1] for it will not change the marginal revenue productivity curves for land. With a fixed quantity of labor the *fixed cost* will have changed, but this fixed cost plays no part in determining how much land shall be employed with the fixed quantity of labor. A fall in the price of labor, however, will move the labor curve to the right, from RR' to SS', for, as we have seen, with each given quantity of land (e.g., OH) the best quantity of labor to employ has increased (e.g., from HP to HQ). The final optimum point, then, with both land and labor variable, has moved from T to T'. The effect of a fall in the price of labor has been to raise the quantity of labor used from OK to OK' and to raise the quantity of land used from KT to $K'T'$. If the land curve bends back on itself, as it well may do, so that it has a negative slope in the range TT', the effect will be to lower the quantity of land used. This is illustrated in Fig. 127D. These two cases correspond to the two cases on page 576.

JOINT PRODUCTS

By means of the methods of the present chapter it is also possible to analyze the problem of joint products. A firm is said to produce joint products when as a result of a *single* process two or more products are made. In such a case the concept of the average total cost of a single product has virtually no significance. Suppose, for instance, that a farmer produces 15 tons of wheat and 10 tons of straw from his wheat field, at a total cost of $500. The average total cost cannot now be

---

[1] A possible exception to this proposition is where the inputs are themselves products of joint (complementary) or competitive supply; here a change in the price of one may change the marginal cost of the other.

calculated by dividing the total cost by the output unless the total cost can be *allocated* in some way to the two products. Usually, however, it is impossible to allocate the total cost. It is impossible, for instance, in the above example, to say that $400 went for producing the wheat and $100 for producing the straw. The marginal cost of each product still is significant. The marginal cost of wheat is the increase in the total cost of producing both wheat and straw when the production of wheat is increased by one unit without increasing the production of straw. The marginal cost of straw is the increase in the total cost of producting both commodities when the production of straw alone is increased by one unit.

If the commodities can be produced only in a fixed proportion, the problem of the most profitable output differs in no essential from the like problem in the single-product firm. Output can be measured in composite units, such as 1 ton of wheat plus 1 ton of straw, in the fixed proportions in which they must be produced. Then the most profitable output is that at which the marginal cost of a composite unit is equal to its combined price.

If, however, the commodities may be produced in variable proportions, the problem is more complicated. The most profitable situation now is that combination of outputs of the two commodities at which the marginal cost of each is equal to its price. In all this argument, of course, perfect markets are assumed. If the marginal cost of one product is less than its price, it will be possible to increase profits by increasing the output of that product.

The graphic solution of the problem is essentially similar to that of finding the most profitable combination of input quantities. It can be approached either by the scale line technique or by the marginal cost technique. Thus in Fig. 119, let OX and OY measure the quantities of the two products, A and B. Then the dashed lines represent cost contours, or isocost curves, for these products, showing what combinations would be produced at a given cost.[2] The slope of such a cost contour is the rate of cost substitution of the two products—the amount of product B which can be substituted for one unit of product A without changing the total cost. This is equal to the ratio of the marginal cost of A to the marginal cost of B. The solid lines in the figure now represent revenue contours, and show what combinations of product quantities yield given total revenues. In perfect competition they will be straight lines whose slope is equal to the ratio of the price of A to the price of B. Then a scale line can be drawn, showing the best way to increase the output of both

---

[2] The cost contours in the present case will be concave to the origin, as normally the marginal cost of each product increases with its output.

commodities. It is the locus of the points of tangency of the cost and revenue contours, as in Fig. 119. For all combinations on the scale line the ratio of the marginal costs of the two products is equal to the ratio of their prices.

The problem may also be solved by figures such as Fig. 125, page 573. If in these figures we again measure the quantity of product A along OX, and the quantity of product B along OY, then a curve such as $R'R$ can be drawn (the "A-curve") showing what is the most profitable quantity of A to produce for each given amount of B. With a production of B equal to OH, for instance, HP is the quantity of A at which A's marginal cost is equal to its price. Similarly a "B-curve," $D'D$, can be drawn showing the most profitable quantity of B to produce for each given amount of A. The point T where the two curves intersect is the most profitable combination of the two products, for only at this point is the marginal cost of each one equal to its price.

Most of the conclusions of the study of two inputs apply to the case of two outputs. Thus it can be shown that a rise in the price of only one output has a *substitution effect*—moving the most profitable combination to a point where a greater proportion of the higher-priced product is produced—and has also a scale effect, raising the whole scale of the enterprise. Thus a rise in the price of one joint product will always tend to raise its output. The output of the other product will be increased or decreased according as the scale effect or the substitution effect predominates—the scale effect raises and the substitution effect lowers its output. If the price of both products rise in the same proportion, there is no substitution effect, but the scale effect operates to raise both outputs.

Joint Products Under Monopoly

Some interesting modifications of the above analysis follow when the markets for the two products are imperfect. The cost contours as before will be concave to the origin. The revenue contours, however, will no longer be straight lines, as the prices of the products now depend on the outputs, and will generally fall as the corresponding output rises. The revenue contours can be constructed as in Fig. 128 by a method exactly like that of Fig. 118. Quantities of product X and Y are measured along OX and OY, total revenues, along OY' and OX'. OM_xX is the total revenue curve for X, OM_yY for Y. We draw construction lines, which are lines of equal revenue from *one* product, as in Fig. 118, and draw the dashed total revenue contours through the appropriate points. The total revenue surface is a *dome* with a maximum at M at the top of the dome. The revenue contours will make rough circles around this point. Only that part of the field between the origin and the top

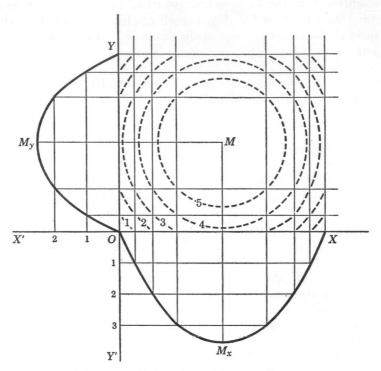

Fig. 128.　Derivation of Total Revenue Contours

of the dome is relevant, for an enterprise will never expand to outputs where marginal revenue is negative. The slope of a revenue contour at any point is now equal to the ratio of the marginal revenues of the two products, not to the ratio of their prices. A point is on the scale line if the ratio of the marginal costs of the two products is equal to the ratio of their marginal revenues. The most profitable combination of outputs is that at which the marginal cost of *each* product is equal to its marginal revenue. This is again the point where the *A* curve and the *B* curve (not shown, but like the labor and land curves of Fig. 127C) intersect; but each curve is now defined by the condition that for a given production of one product, the most profitable output of the other is that at which its marginal cost and marginal revenue are equal.

Some interesting problems arise when the demand for the two products is not independent. In such cases it can be proved that the total revenue surface, showing the total revenue receivable from any combination of output quantities, is more like a ridge than a dome. The lines of equal revenue can again be constructed by a method similar to Fig. 118 or 128; now, however, the construction lines which represent lines of equal revenue from a single product are not straight, but themselves are the contours of a surface. Thus in Fig. 129 the heavy solid lines are contours of a surface showing the total revenue from the sale of X, assuming X is competitive in demand with Y, so that for higher amounts of Y, the total revenue curve for X falls and shifts towards the OY axis. The heavy dashed lines are the similar curves of equal revenue from the sale of Y. The light dashed lines are constructed, as in Fig. 128, through points of

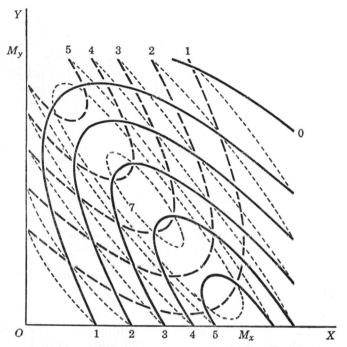

Fig. 129.   Total Revenue Contours with Complementary Goods

equal total revenue; the line marked 7, for instance, through the points of intersection of the 4-contour for X and the 3-contour for Y, and of the 3-contour for X and the 4-contour for Y. It will be seen that the total revenue surface is now rather like a ridge running at a roughly 45 degree angle between the points M_x and M_y on the axes, which represent the sales of each commodity which gives the maximum revenue when the sales of the other are zero. In the extreme case of X and Y being identical commodities the total revenue surface shrinks to a razor edge at a 45 degree angle across the axes. The more competitive and similiar the commodities are, the more a slight shift in the cost functions will shift output from one to the other.

It can be shown similarly that if the two commodities are complementary the total revenue surface becomes a ridge from the origin at a roughly 45 degree angle; in the case of perfect complementarity with two products which can be consumed only in given proportions (e.g., right and left shoes) the ridge contracts to a razor edge and becomes a simple total revenue curve for the joint commodity.

SELLING COST

Up to now the problem of selling cost has been virtually neglected; this is the problem of how much to spend on advertising, salesmen, free samples, door-to-door canvasses, and so on. Under perfect markets the selling problem does not arise. When a firm has a perfect market, it can sell all it wants at the market price, and there is no point in advertising. When a firm has an imperfect market, however, it is limited in the quantity it can sell; the market does not take with open arms everything which the firm has to offer but quickly becomes gorged, so that in order to increase sales at least one of two things must be done. Either the price must be lowered in order to tempt buyers into buying more or the buyer must be persuaded to buy more at each price. The process of persuading the buyers to buy more at each price is called *sales promotion*. The total of expenses plus normal profit involved in sales promotion is called *selling cost*. Those expenses (plus normal profits) which are not specifically connected with sales promotion are called *production cost*.

Distinction Between Selling Cost and Production Cost

The total cost of producing a given output may therefore be divided into two parts—total selling cost and total production cost. The exact point of division is not always easy to determine. Nevertheless, we may roughly define the selling costs as those which are incurred specifically in order to make the buyers buy more of the product at any given price; production costs are the residue. There will always be some costs which are difficult to apportion: should the cost of a cellophane wrapper, for instance, be included among production costs or selling costs? However, the distinction is made in practice, and, like most distinctions, the fact that it is not perfectly clear does not impair its usefulness.

The Total Selling Cost

As the main purpose of selling costs is to affect the revenue (through affecting the volume of sales), it is convenient to treat selling costs not as an addition to cost but as a deduction from revenue. The selling problem, like that of production, can be divided into two parts. There is first the problem of how to use a *given* expenditure on selling costs most effectively. This is analogous to the problem of how to produce a *given* quantity of product with the least cost. We cannot here go into the various techniques of selling. We shall simply assume that there are several ways of spending money on sales promotion in order to obtain a desired result, the desired result being that a certain quantity should be sold at a certain price. The least expensive method of producing this desired result will naturally be chosen; its cost will be called the *total selling cost* of selling a given quantity at a given price. In the second place, even if we knew the least total selling cost which would sell each possible output quantity at each possible price, we should still have to determine the most profitable combination of price, selling cost, and quantity of output.

The Selling Cost Table

In order to do this we first construct a table such as Table 52. Each of the boxes in this table represents a certain combination of price and total selling cost, the price being found at the bottom of the column in which the box stands and the selling cost at the head of its row. The box in the top right-hand corner of the figure represents a combination of a price of $6 per unit with a total selling cost of $140. The first (uppermost) of the figures in each one of the boxes represents the quantity of product (tons) which can be sold if a price is charged equal to the price at the foot of the column and a selling cost is incurred equal to the figure at the head of the row in which the box lies. Thus with a price of $6 per ton and a total selling cost of $140, a quantity amounting to 37 tons could be sold; with a price of $5 and a total selling cost of $120, 39 tons could be sold, and so on for each box of the table.

Total Gross Revenue

The center figure in each box is obtained by multiplying the first figure, representing the quantity of output sold, by the price at which it is sold, found at the bottom of the column. This gives what may be called the *total gross revenue*—the total revenue which is received, in the first instance, from the sale of the quantity of output shown in the box. Thus with a selling cost of $140 and a price of $6, 37 tons can be sold; 37 tons at $6 per ton is $222, and so for all the other boxes of the table.

Total Production Revenue

The bottom figure in each box represents what may be called the *total production revenue*. It is found by subtracting the selling cost at the head of the row from the second figure in the box, representing the total gross revenue. That is, the total production revenue is equal to the total

TABLE 52. RELATIONSHIP BETWEEN PRICE, TOTAL SELLING COST, AND (1) OUTPUT, (2) TOTAL GROSS REVENUE, (3) TOTAL PRODUCTION REVENUE

Total selling cost (dollars)	0	1	2	3	4	5	6
140	92 0 -140	90 90 -50	78 156 16	70 210 70	50 200 60	40 200 60	37 222 82
120	90 0 -120	88 88 -32	75 150 30	65 195 75	49 196 76	39 195 75	35 210 90
100	88 0 -100	85 85 -15	·70 140 40	60 180 80	48 192 92	37 185 85	30 180 80
80	85 0 -80	80 80 0	65 130 50	50 150 70	45 180 100	35 175 95	25 150 70
60	80 0 -60	70 70 10	60 120 60	45 135 75	40 160 100	30 150 90	20 120 60
40	70 0 -40	60 60 20	50 100 60	40 120 80	35 140 100	28 140 100	15 90 50
20	60 0 -20	50 50 30	40 80 60	35 105 85	30 120 100	25 125 105	10 60 40
0	50 0 0	40 40 40	30 60 60	25 75 75	15 60 60	·5 25 25	0 0 0

Price of output (dollars per ton)

gross revenue less the selling cost. This is the revenue which is passed back, as it were, from the selling department to the production department. It is the revenue figure in which the production department is primarily interested. Thus with a selling cost of $140 and a price of $6, a gross revenue of $222 is obtained; but as $140 of this has been spent in selling costs, only $82 remains to be passed on to the production department.

Diminishing Returns of Selling Costs

It will be noticed that the first figure (sales) in each box is an assumed figure, i.e., it is part of the data of the problem. The other two figures are derived from the first. In constructing the system of "first figures" (i.e., the relationship between price, selling cost, and the quantity which can be sold), we have made two important assumptions which are illustrated in the figures chosen. The first is that the greater the price with a *given* total selling cost, the less will be the quantity which can be sold. This is what is meant by an imperfect market. If the market were perfect, so that an indefinitely large quantity could be sold at the market price, the selling cost problem would not arise at all. The second is that the quantity which can be sold at *any given price* increases as the total selling cost rises, but that it increases at a *decreasing rate*. Obviously, as the aim of selling costs is to enlarge the quantity which would be sold at any given price, it is reasonable to assume that the greater the selling costs, the more will be sold. But for every commodity there must be some point of saturation beyond which higher selling costs will produce no increase in the total quantity sold. Although at first, then, successive increases in the total selling cost may produce greater and greater increments in the quantity sold, after a certain point, unit increases in the selling cost will result in smaller and smaller increases in sales until the point of saturation is reached. This principle is somewhat analogous to the law of diminishing returns. If the increase in sales which results from a unit increase in the total selling cost is called the *marginal productivity of selling costs*, then the principle may be stated as one of *"eventually diminishing marginal productivity of selling costs."*

Various Ways of Selling a Given Output

Now, consider the boxes which have been marked by a ring in Table 52. These boxes represent different combinations of price and selling cost, all of which have one thing in common: they all enable the seller to sell 50 tons of output, as evidenced by the first figure in each box. Evidently, in this case if nothing is spent on selling costs, the seller will have to give the product away in order to get rid of 50 tons. If $20 is spent on selling costs, $1 per ton can be charged and 50 tons can still be sold. If $40 is spent on selling costs, the price can be $2 a ton and 50 tons can still be sold. If $140 is spent on selling costs, the price can be as much as $4 per ton and 50 tons can still be sold. As the price rises, the total selling cost must also be increased if the same amount as before is to be sold.

The Best Way of Selling a Given Output

Again considering the ringed boxes, only this time looking at the bottom figures, we see that the box with diagonal shading shows the greatest total production revenue of any of the ringed boxes. If 50 tons are sold with a selling cost of $80 and a price of $3, the total production revenue received will be $70. If 50 tons are sold at a lower price—say, $2—and at a lower selling cost—$40—only $60 will be received in total production revenue. If 50 tons are sold at a high price—$4—and with a high selling cost—$140—again only $60 will be received in production revenue; the great selling cost more than outweighs the advantage of the high price which it makes possible. Evidently, the best way to sell 50 tons is at a price of $3 and with a selling cost of $80.

Similarly, the best way of selling 40 tons is with a price of $4 and a selling cost of $60, the best way of selling 25 tons is with a price of $5 and a selling cost of $20, and so on for any quantity of output. A small figure like Table 52 will not enable us to find very accurately the best way of selling intermediate quantities of output—say, 42 tons—but this could easily be remedied by making a larger and more detailed table. Those boxes which represent the best combinations of price and selling cost for producing a *given* output are shaded.

GRAPHIC ILLUSTRATION. Just as a three-dimensional physical production surface was constructed from the physical production data in Table 48, page 545, so three-dimensional figures can be constructed from the data in Table 52. We need not bother to try to draw these figures, for they can be represented perfectly well by contour lines.

THE SALES CONTOUR. The ringed boxes in Table 52 represent all

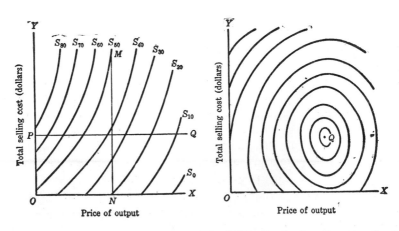

Fig. 130A. Sales Contours   Fig. 130B. Production Revenue Contours

combinations of price and selling cost which will enable the seller to sell 50 tons. In Fig. 130A this is represented by a "sales contour," S_{50}. The coordinates of all points on this line represent combinations of price and selling cost which will allow 50 tons to be sold; similarly, the coordinates of all points on S_{40} represent those combinations of price and selling cost which will allow 40 tons to be sold; and so on for the whole system of "sales contours," which are the contours of a "sales surface."

Production Revenue Contours

From the data given by these sales contours we can calculate, in the way shown in Table 52, the total production revenue obtained from each combination of price and selling cost. These figures are represented in the bottom figure in each box of Table 52. They can be shown by a system of "production revenue contours," as in Fig. 130B; the coordinates of any point on one of these contours represent a combination of price and selling cost which will yield a given production revenue. There will be some point, Q, representing a combination of price and selling cost at which the total production revenue is a maximum. In Table 52 this maximum value is $105, at a selling cost of $20 and a price of $5. To get a production revenue of rather less than this—say, $100—it is possible with the same price to have either a greater or a smaller selling cost, or with the same selling cost a greater or a smaller price. The contour which gives the combinations yielding $100 production revenue will therefore circle around the point Q; similarly, for all the other production revenue contours. These "circles" will not necessarily be smooth; they will probably be quite crooked. However, for simplicity in the diagram they are drawn smoothly.

The Sale Line

Fig. 130C combines the system of sales contours (solid lines) with a system of production revenue contours (dotted lines). For any sales contour, S_{50}, the point where it is touched by a production revenue contour, P, is the point whose coordinates show the best way of selling the quantity of output represented by the sales contour—in this case, 50 tons. That is to say, the best way of selling 50 tons of output in this case is with a price equal to PN and a selling cost equal to ON, for no other way gives a greater production revenue. Similarly, we can find the best combination of price and selling cost for selling any other output. All these points lie on a line $HPQK$, which we may call the *sale line*. It is somewhat analogous to the *scale line* in Fig. 119, page 560, in that it shows the best way of expanding or contracting sales. The best way to expand

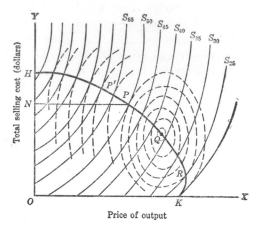

Fig. 130C. The Theory of Selling Cost

sales from, say, 50 to 55 tons is to move from a combination of price and selling cost represented by the point P to a combination represented by the point P'. Evidently, if the sale line is steep, the best way to increase sales is to raise selling cost a lot and reduce price a little. If the sale line is flat, the best way to increase sales is to raise selling cost a little and reduce price a lot. If the sale line is vertical, as at R, the best way to increase sales is to raise selling cost without lowering price. If the sale line is horizontal, the best way of increasing sales is to reduce price without raising selling cost. It is just conceivable that the sale line might bend backward, as in the figure between K and R. In such a region the best way to expand output is to increase both price and selling cost. This might be the case if an increase in selling cost is extremely effective in expanding sales while a change in price makes little difference to sales.

Why Sales Promotion Is Often Preferred to Price Cutting

We can now see why businessmen who are not in perfect competition and who therefore have a selling problem frequently prefer to increase their selling cost rather than to cut prices. That combination of price and selling cost which is absolutely the most profitable must lie somewhere on the sale line between K and Q, for only in this range is the total production revenue increasing as sales increase. If sales are pushed beyond the figure whose sales contour passes through Q, then as sales go up the total production revenue actually decreases. Obviously it could not pay to push sales to this point. In the range between K and Q, however, the sale line is likely to be relatively steep, as we see from the figure and as we have seen from our arithmetical example. Consequently, in the range of output in which the most profitable position is likely to lie it will probably pay better to concentrate on sales promotion rather than price cutting as a means of expanding output. This is not, of course, necessarily so—it is quite possible for the sales curve to be flat in this range if price cutting is effective in expanding sales and sales promotion is not. This seems to be the case in some businesses. Nevertheless, there will be a certain dominant tendency for sales promotion to be more effective in this range than price cutting.

One further conclusion of interest arises from this analysis. It is that probably the best way of expanding sales is not by increasing selling costs alone, or by cutting price alone, but by a combination of the two. This need not be so if the sale line is vertical. A vertical sale line, however, is a special case and is probably not common.

The Final Solution for the Profit Maximum

We can now bring together all the various elements of the *maximum-profit* problem into one final solution. First is the problem of *production*, solved by means of the scale-line analysis. From this we obtain a total cost curve, each point of which represents the total cost of the best way of *producing* a given output. Next is the problem of *selling*. This manifests itself as the best way of *selling* a given output—the best combination of prices to different people or for different quantities, or the best combination of price and selling cost, as found by the sale-line analysis. Then for each output we can postulate a *total production revenue,* this being the total revenue which is passed on to the production side of the business after all selling expenses have been met. And just as each total cost is the *least* total cost with which a given output can be produced, so each total production revenue is the *greatest* production revenue which can be obtained by selling a given quantity of output. We can then draw total cost and total production revenue curves, and find where the difference between them is greatest, or we can derive from them marginal cost and marginal production revenue curves, and find where they intersect. Either of these methods gives the most profitable output. Then we can go back to our scale-line figures and find out what is the best way to produce this output, and we can go back to our demand and sales figures and find out what is the best way to sell this output. Then the problem is mathematically solved! We may notice that all the analysis in Chapter 18 is valid if we interpret the marginal revenue to mean the marginal production revenue, and the price to mean the average production revenue. Our more detailed analysis, as usual, extends but does not destroy the simpler constructions.

SOME APPLICATIONS OF THE THEORY OF
SELLING COST

Taxation

The application of the theory of selling cost to problems of taxation is interesting. The analysis of Chapter 21 with regard to the effect of taxation applies perfectly if we replace price by *average production revenue,* and marginal revenue by *marginal production revenue.* Thus, Fig. 98 (p. 461) shows that a lump-sum tax will not lead to a change in output or to a change in average production revenue. There will therefore be no change in price or selling cost if the monopolist is already selling his output in the most economical way. A variable tax will reduce the output and raise the average production revenue. In this case there will be an effect on both price and selling cost, illustrated in Fig. 131. Here selling cost is measured vertically and price horizontally, as in Fig. 130C. *HK* is the sale line. Suppose S_n to be the *sales contour* showing all those combinations of price and selling cost which will sell an amount equal to the originally most profitable output. Then *OF* is the total selling cost, *FP* is the price. Let S'_n be the sales contour for the

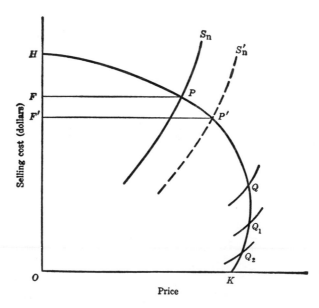

Fig. 131. Taxation and Selling Cost

smaller output which is most profitable after the tax is imposed. The new price will be $F'P'$, and the new selling cost OF'. The effect of the tax in this case is evidently to raise the price from FP to $F'P'$ and to lower the selling cost from OF to OF'. It is possible, however, that a tax may take out all its effect on the selling cost. If, for instance, the tax shifted the most profitable output from the one represented by the sales contour Q to the one represented by Q_1, there would be no change in price but a considerable reduction in selling cost. A case is even conceivable in which a tax causes a monopolist to reduce his price. A tax which reduced the most profitable output from the one represented by Q_1 to the one represented by Q_2 would have this effect, the sale line being re-entrant in this range.

Effect of a Change in Demand

Our theory of selling cost leads us to broaden our concept of the *demand* for the product of a monopolist. We must now think of the demand not as a simple relationship between the price and the quantity bought, but as a threefold relationship between price, selling cost, and quantity bought. That is, the demand for the product of a monopolist really consists of the whole system of *sales contours,* as in Fig. 130A, page 588. A change in demand means a shift in this whole system. In the simple case a fall in demand means that a smaller quantity than before can be sold at each price. For a monopolist, however, a fall in demand means that a smaller quantity than before can be sold at each combination of price and selling cost. A fall in demand therefore means that the whole surface, which the sales contours represent, has fallen toward the base plane. The whole system of sales contours in Fig. 130A will move upward and to the left; thus S_{60} might occupy the place now held by S_{80}, and so on. After the fall in demand more must be expended in selling cost in order to sell a given output at the original price, or a lower price must be charged in order to sell a given output with the original selling cost.

That is to say, in order to sell any given output either a lower price must be charged or a greater sum must be expended in selling cost, or both, than before the fall in demand. In any of these cases the result will be a decline in the total production revenue. At each output, therefore, the total production revenue, the average production revenue, and the marginal production revenue will be less than before; the average and marginal production revenue curves will have shifted downward and to the left. We have already analyzed the results of this in Fig. 97, page 459. There will usually be a decline in output and usually (though not always) a decline in the average production revenue. In the case of

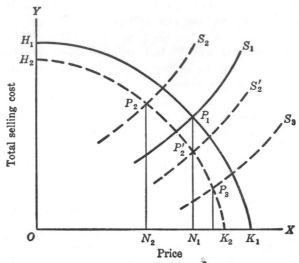

Fig. 132.   Selling Cost After a Fall in Demand

Fig. 97 itself, of course, the average production revenue and the price are identical.

Where selling cost is taken into account, the problem is more complicated. It is illustrated in Fig. 132. Price is measured along OX; total selling cost along OY, as in Fig. 130C; H_1K_1 is the original sale line before the fall in demand; S_1 is the sales contour corresponding to the original output. The effect of the fall in demand will probably be to shift the sale line downward and to the left, to the position H_2K_2, for the sales contours in Fig. 130A, page 588, and the production revenue contours in Fig. 130B, have all shifted to the left. Conditions are possible in which a fall in demand will not change the sale line, or will change it in the opposite sense, but they are not the most probable. The fall in demand will also have shifted the sales contours to the left. Let S_2 be the new sales contour corresponding to the original output. Then if the output did not change, the point which describes the best way of selling that output would shift from P_1 to P_2. In this case, evidently, there will be a considerable fall in price, from ON_1 to ON_2, and only a slight change in the selling cost, from P_1N_1 to P_2N_2. In fact, unless the marginal cost curve in Fig. 97 rises very steeply, the output will decline. If it declines only a little, it remains true that the principal result of a fall in demand is a fall in the price, and not in the selling cost. If it declines sharply, say, to the figure whose sales contour is S'_2, then P'_2 shows the best price and selling cost. The price may be unchanged at ON_1, but the selling cost will fall sharply to $N_1P'_2$. In exceptional cases where the fall in demand brings about a very large fall in output it is conceivable that the sales contour might shift to S_3, in which case the fall in demand would lead to a great fall in selling cost and an actual rise in price! Further complications of this topic arise out of the question whether the fall in demand affects principally the price or the selling cost at which a given output can be sold. It is conceivable, for instance, that the public might become less susceptible to the charms of advertising and more susceptible to the charms of low prices. However, we have probably pursued these abstract ramifications as far as our clumsy techniques will allow.

OLIGOPOLY AND VIABILITY

With a three-variable analysis we can pursue our studies of the interaction of two firms (duopoly) further than in Chapter 22. Let us suppose a strategy field as in Fig. 133, similar to Fig. 101 (p. 474) with two firms, Able and Baker, the mill price of Able's product, p_a, measured horizontally and the mill price of Baker's product, p_b, measured vertically. For each firm we can now postulate lines of equal net revenue in this field; these will be the contours of a net revenue surface, where the net revenue is measured vertically above the plane of the paper. For Able we suppose the curves (dashed lines) $A_0A'_0$, $A_1A'_1$, $A_2A'_2$, $A_3A'_3$, are such contours of a net revenue hill rising towards A_m; $B_0B'_0$, $B_1B'_1$, $B_2B'_2$, $B_3B'_3$, are similar curves for Baker, rising towards B_m. The assumption here is that if the price charged by the other firm is constant, a rise in the price of one firm will first raise, and then lower net revenue, as demand is choked off. If a firm's own price is held constant, a rise in the price of the other firm's product will drive demand toward the first firm and raise its net revenues. In Fig. 133 we neglect the market extinction curves of Fig. 101 (p. 474) supposing that market extinction occurs at prices higher than those in the figure. The line M_0A_m goes through the minimum points of all the A contours where p_b is a minimum, and the line N_0B_m goes through the points on the B contours where p_a is a minimum.

Reaction Curves on the Pareto Line

If now we suppose shortsighted behavior, so that each firm assumes that the price charged by the other firm will remain constant and selects its own price at the level that maximizes its net revenue, then the lines M_0A_m and N_0B_m are the *reaction curves* corresponding to $A'A$ and $B'B$ of Fig. 101 (p. 474). If, for instance, Able thinks Baker will maintain its price at OH, Able will charge a price HM_3 to maximize its net revenue.

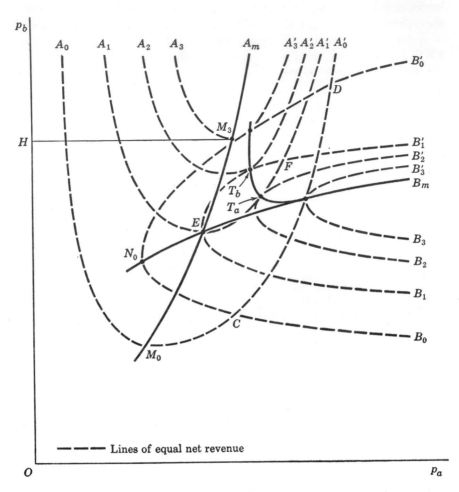

Fig. 133. Oligopoly

The point where the two reaction curves intersect is E, corresponding to Q in Fig. 101. Mutual shortsighted behavior will bring the system to this point. Both firms, however, can do better than at E anywhere within the lens-shaped area bounded by Able's net revenue contour at E, ET_aF, and Baker's net revenue contour at E, ET_bF. By bargaining, then, or even by a succession of "longsighted" unilateral moves, the parties can move to some point on the line T_aT_b, which is the locus of all points where one of Able's net revenue contours is touched by one of Baker's net revenue contours. This line may be called the *Pareto line* after the distinguished Italian economist Vilfredo Pareto, who developed the concept now usually called the *Paretian optimum*. A Paretian optimum is a point in a strategy field from which no movement can be made which benefits both parties. From any point *not* a Paretian optimum a movement *can* be made which benefits both parties. Thus from the point E a move to any point within the area ET_aFT_b will benefit both firms. From any point on the Pareto line T_aT_b, however, any move will make at least one party worse off, that is, move him to a lower net revenue. Exactly *where* on the Pareto line two longsighted firms will settle depends on the dynamics of the process which gets them there, a process which has strong random elements and cannot therefore be predicted.

Conditions of Coexistence

In all this we have assumed *coexistence*—that is, that each firm postulates the continued survival of the other. We now need to look at the circumstances under which one firm will try to eliminate the other in a *game of survival.* Suppose that the contour $A_0M_0A'_0$ is Able's net revenue contour representing the least net revenue at which Able can survive. If net revenue is defined to mean abnormal profits, this will be the contour of zero net revenue. Suppose $B_0N_0B'_0$ is the corresponding survival contour for Baker. If these intersect at C and D, then the area bounded by CN_0D is the *area of coexistence,* or *mutual survival,* for at any combination of prices within this area both firms can survive indefinitely. If, however, the survival contours were $A_3A'_3$ and $B_3B'_3$, which do not intersect, there would be no area of coexistence, and a game of survival would necessarily follow. We can distinguish, then, a number of conditions of coexistence, in Fig. 134. Here the area of Able's unconditional survival is shaded horizontally, to signify that Able can only move unilaterally in that direction, and Baker's area of unconditional survival is shaded vertically, as Baker can only move in that direction. Fig. 134A shows *no* coexistence. Fig. 134B shows conditional coexistence. There is a cross-hatched area of coexistence, but this is precarious, because Able, for instance, can move out of the area of coexistence to a point such as R where Able can survive and Baker cannot, and Baker can do likewise. There are strong temptations for a game of survival, therefore, and coexistence will only persist as long as this temptation is resisted. Fig. 134C shows a state of conditional viability for Baker, unconditional viability for Able. We can suppose some level of net revenue which is intolerably low even in the short run, corresponding, say, to price equal to average variable cost, below which the firm will simply shut down. Suppose the contours corresponding to this level are represented by the dashed lines in Fig. 134C. Then Able can move to a point R at which he is within his viability boundary, but Baker has to shut down. While coexistence is possible in the cross-hatched area, Able will constantly be

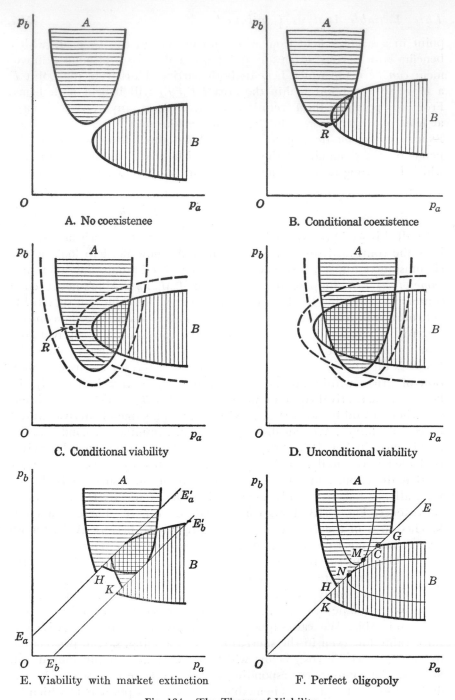

A. No coexistence

B. Conditional coexistence

C. Conditional viability

D. Unconditional viability

E. Viability with market extinction

F. Perfect oligopoly

Fig. 134. The Theory of Viability

tempted to eliminate Baker and enjoy monopoly profits. Figure 134D by contrast, shows a situation of unconditional viability for both parties. There is no position which is tolerable to one party, from which the other cannot move into the area of mutual coexistence; coexistence is secure, and there is no temptation to begin a game of survival.

So far we have neglected the problem raised by the existence of market extinction lines; their influence is shown in Fig. 134E. Here $E_a E'_a$ and $E_b E'_b$ are the market extinction lines, as in Fig. 101 (p. 474). These create, as it were, geological faults or cliffs in the net revenue surfaces.[3] Thus suppose we move vertically downward from point A, lowering p_b but keeping p_a constant. Above the line $E_a E'_a$, Able is the only firm in the field. As we cross this line, Baker enters the field and Able's net revenue is suddenly reduced. As we continue downwards, when we cross the line $E_b E'_b$, Able suddenly becomes no longer viable and its net revenue disappears. Able's survival area then, shaded horizontally, exhibits "kinks" at the line $E_a E'_a$ and is cut off sharply by the line $E_b E'_b$. Baker's survival area exhibits like properties. In Fig. 134E the introduction of market extinction has produced conditional coexistence again: Able could force a game of survival on Baker by going to the p_a at H; Baker could force a game of survival on Able by going to the p_b at K. As the firms get closer together or as cost of transport diminishes, then, unconditional viability for both becomes less likely. When the two market extinction lines coincide as in Fig. 134F we have perfect oligopoly, as in Fig. 102 (p. 476). The area of coexistence shrinks to the line HC. In Fig. 134F Baker will be the price leader under coexistence, and will move to N, where the line OE touches one of its net revenue contours (dashed). Able will not be able to achieve its preferred position at M, but may still be viable at N. If the two firms are exactly similar, so that H coincides with K and C with G, the system is rather stable, as neither side is tempted to start a price war or game of survival. In the asymmetrical case of Fig. 134F, Baker can move to K, at which point Able is not viable and Baker is; Baker therefore has a temptation to begin a price war. However, as the dynamics of a game of survival are so different from those of coexistence, it is hard to derive any very solid conclusions. For the sake of simplicity we have neglected the short run survival condition of Fig. 134C and D, but this can easily be introduced into E and F.

THE REALISM OF MAXIMIZING ANALYSIS

In the analysis of this part we are continually deriving conclusions from the basic assumption of *maximizing behavior*. In view of our earlier

---

[3] Strictly the cliff comes at the viability boundary of the other firm.

discussion of the possible lack of realism of this assumption in Chapter 15 (pp. 302–305) we should at least ask the question, How far a more realistic psychology of economic behavior would modify the conclusions we have drawn? The maximizing behavior assumption implies, in effect that the *search* for wider knowledge of alternatives is costless. In fact this is not so; hence the cost of finding out what policy would produce, for instance, maximum profits, may not be worth the gain in profits which would result. This leads to the conclusion that a search for new policies will only take place if profits, or whatever is the appropriate index of success, falls below a certain satisfactory point. If maximum profits are above the minimum survival value this means that instead of a single value of each variable—such as quantity of input bought, or amount spent on selling cost, or the price of the product—being selected at which profits are a maximum, a whole range of values are possible at which profits are above the satisfactory or *no-search* level. This is illustrated in Fig. 135; here we measure profits vertically, and any variable x which the firm has to make a decision about, horizontally. The curve PMP' shows how profits vary with x. On the assumption of maximizing behavior the value of X selected will be OV_m, where profits are at a maximum, V_mM. If, however, the firm satisfices, and VS is the satisfactory level of profits, the variable may fall anywhere between OV and OV' and there will be no search and no pressure for change. It is only when the variable falls below OV or above OV' that change occurs. What this means is that such an organization will have a good deal of slack: its situation will have to change a positive amount before anything is done about

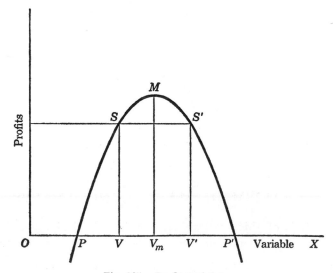

Fig. 135. Profit Satisficing

it. Still, the point V_m will be somewhere in the mid-range between V and V'; the conclusions which we have drawn from the maximizing assumption still serve to define the approximate middle of the range beyond which change will occur.

In the case of duopoly or oligopoly, the *satisficing* principle suggests that coexistence once established may be much more stable than a strict maximizing-behavior analysis would suggest, simply because the game of survival usually represents a very high cost of search. Hence firms develop "live and let live," "don't rock the boat" types of policy which have a lot of slack, in the sense that a very severe worsening of the situation is necessary before any change takes place. In the case of price wars and games of survival it may well be that psychological and sociological elements are more important than the strictly economic factors. The price cutter, like the international aggressor, is likely to be the man (or nation) that is excluded from the country club for strictly noneconomic reasons!

QUESTIONS AND EXERCISES

1. As an exercise in the use of contour lines, draw the contours of the following objects:
   a. A cone with its apex above the center of its base
   b. A cone with its apex above a point on the circumference of its base
   c. A half-cone, cut through the apex and center, and lying on the flat triangular side
   d. A similar half-cone, standing on its semicircular base
   e. A half-sphere, standing on its base
   f. A football at rest on the ground
   g. A baseball bat lying on its side
   h. A saddle-back mountain pass
   i. A square pyramid
   j. A corkscrew
2. Compare and contrast the theoretical problems presented by (a) the production of a given quantity of physical product, (b) the obtaining of a revenue from the sale of a given quantity of physical product.
3. Draw in perspective the three-dimensional figures represented in contour form in Figs. 130A and 130B. Draw representative sections of these figures showing (a) the relation between the sales and the total selling cost, price being constant; (b) the relation between price and sales, selling cost being constant; (c) the relation between production revenue and selling cost, price being constant; (d) the relation between production revenue and price, selling cost being constant.
4. Show that as the market for a firm's output became more nearly perfect, the sales contours in Fig. 130A would become steeper and farther apart. What would the sales contours be like for a firm with a perfect market for output?

What would its production revenue contours be like? Why must we assume that selling costs would be ineffective in a perfect market?

5. Continue Exercise 6, page 571, by drawing a ring around the maximum value of the net revenue in each row of the table. Join these rings by a line. This line is the *labor curve* in Fig. 125. It shows the best quantity of labor to use with each quantity of land. Similarly, ring the maximum values of the net revenue in each column of the table. The line joining these rings is the *land curve* of Fig. 125. Why do these curves not intersect?

6. The following table is a physical production function, showing the number of bushels of potatoes obtained with various amounts of land and labor

Units of Land	Bushels of Potatoes						
7	460	574	660	725	775	820	860
6	442	557	636	707	760	800	838
5	411	536	615	683	747	779	812
4	370	498	577	638	694	736	770
3	322	436	520	576	613	643	668
2	265	360	418	470	519	554	574
1	156	245	307	345	371	391	402
0	1	2	3	4	5	6	7
			Units of Labor				

a. On squared paper, with labor on the horizontal axis and product on the vertical axis, draw the family of seven physical production curves corresponding to the seven units of land. Label this Figure 1.

b. On another sheet of squared paper draw the product contours, with labor on the horizontal axis and land on the vertical axis, corresponding to quantities of product 100, 200, . . . 800. Label this Figure 2. Use the curves of Figure 1 to get the exact amount of labor corresponding to various amounts of land and product.

c. Suppose the price of potatoes at all outputs is $1 per bushel, labor is $100 per unit, land is $50 per unit. Then: (i) Draw the outlay contours in Figure 2, touching the product contours, and draw the scale line through the point of tangency. (ii) For levels of output 100, 200, . . . 800 calculate the least total input cost, the net revenue, and the marginal cost. (iii) At what level of output and inputs is net revenue a maximum?

d. Find the point on each of the curves in Figure 1 at which the slope of the curve is equal to the price of labor. From these points plot the labor curve on Figure 2. In a similar way draw the land curve. Show that these curves intersect at the point of maximum net revenue found in part c above.

e. For each of the cells in the physical production table calculate the net revenue, and pick out the largest net revenue figure. Does this correspond with the results of parts c and d?

f. Repeat parts c, d, and e on the assumption that the price of labor is $100 per unit and the price of land is $100 per unit.

g. Repeat parts c, d, and e on the assumption that the price of labor is $50 per unit and the price of land is $50 per unit.

h. Comment on these results.

7. a. In a figure like Fig. 118, page 558, plot the output of one joint product (*A*) along *OX*, the total revenue derived from its sales along *OY'*, the output of the other joint product (*B*) along *OY*, and the total revenue derived from its sales along *OX'*. Draw total revenue curves for each product, on the assumption of perfect markets for output. Construct the corresponding revenue contours, and draw a perspective drawing of the revenue surface which they represent.

b. Repeat the exercise on the assumption that the market for one product is perfect and for the other product is imperfect.

c. Repeat the exercise on the assumption that the market for both products is imperfect. Show that a dome-shaped revenue surface results.

d. Repeat the exercise on the assumption that the two products are (i) competitive in demand, (ii) complementary in demand. (Note that in this case the construction lines forming the network from which we draw the contours are not straight lines, but curved (see Fig. 129, p. 583). They are themselves the contours of surfaces showing the revenue derived from a *single* product for each combination of quantities of *both* products.)

8. The following schedule shows the total cost, in thousands of dollars, of producing various quantities of two products, A and B, in a single process.

Quantity of B	Total Cost ($000)								
800	540	600	670	750	840	940	1050	1170	1300
700	455	520	595	680	775	880	995	1120	1255
600	375	445	525	615	715	825	945	1075	1215
500	300	375	460	555	660	775	900	1035	1180
400	230	310	400	500	610	730	860	1000	1150
300	165	250	345	450	565	690	825	970	1125
200	105	195	295	405	525	655	795	945	1105
100	50	145	250	365	490	625	770	925	1090
0	0	100	210	330	460	600	750	910	1080
	0	100	200	300	400	500	600	700	800
					Quantity of A				

Suppose the price of product A is $1200 per unit, and of B is $500 per unit. Find the most profitable output of *both* products by the following methods:

a. Calculate from the table the net revenue at each combination.

b. For each quantity of B draw the marginal cost curves of A, and find at which output of A the marginal cost is equal to the price. From these results draw the *A*-curve. In a similar manner draw the *B*-curve. Find the most profitable output combination from these two curves.

c. Draw, by interpolation, the cost contours corresponding to the above table. Draw on the same figure the revenue contours. Draw the scale line. Calculate the net revenue for each combination on the scale line, and find where it is a maximum.

Repeat the exercises with different prices for A and B, and study the effects of these price changes. Can you construct a supply curve of either of these two products? Discuss the problem of supply when there are joint products.

CHAPTER 27

INDIFFERENCE CURVES AND THE THEORY OF OPTIMUM CHOICE

With all its defects, the assumption that rational behavior consists in maximizing something, that is, in finding the *best* alternative, at least gives us an important norm or first approximation which can then be modified in the light of more realistic models. What is maximized, however, is not always an objective maximand such as profits or efficiency, and the theory must be generalized to take account of the subjective maximand (*utility*), a quantity which simply describes the fact that one situation may be preferred to another. What we are looking for here is a general theory of optimum choice—that is, of the conditions which underlie the best position of any organization whether firm, household, government, church, school, or society.

The Preference Scale

A theory of optimum choice involves putting together two sets of relationships, one which describes what there is to choose among and the other which enables us to select out of the possible choices that which stands highest on some scale of value or preference. We have already seen how production functions, cost functions, and market functions impose limitations on possible choices. In essence they divide the universe into combinations of quantities that are available and that are not. We have called them *availability* or *possibility* functions. We now want to find ways of describing the preference, value, or welfare functions which indicate the *ordering* of the various conceivable combinations of quantities according to some scale of "better or worse," "up or down." Such an ordering is all that is necessary in order to pick out the *optimum*— that combination of quantities which stands higher on the "up-down" scale than any other. This "up-down" scale is a quite general notion. It

604

may refer to personal preference, to moral values, to group or social preferences, to anything where it makes sense to say that one set of things is "better" or "worse" than some other set.

The analysis of the previous two chapters indicates a convenient way of representing the preference function for combinations of two quantities, A and B. In Fig. 136 we measure A along the horizontal, B along the vertical axis. A and B can be anything we like, so long as they are

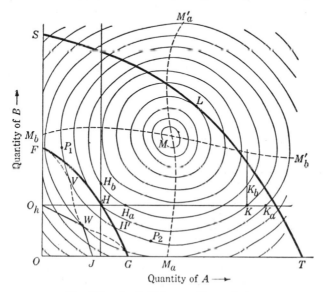

Fig. 136. An Indifference Curve System

quantities which are objects of preference or valuation. They may be quantities of commodities consumed, or assets held, or prices, or profits, or characteristics of any kind—even virtues and vices, if they are reasonably measurable. The solid circular lines in the figure then represent contours of a three-dimensional figure in which the third dimension measures the position of the various combinations on the scale of preference. This measure is what in Chapter 24 we have called *utility,* for historic reasons, though *preferability* would be a much better name.

INDIFFERENCE CURVES

These contours or lines of equal preference are called *indifference curves* because they represent combinations of quantities which are neither better nor worse than each other but are indifferent. If two points P_1 and P_2 are on an indifference curve it means that the combinations represented have equal values on the scale of preference which the set of indifference curves describes: we "don't care" whether we have a lot of B and little A, as at P_1, or a lot of A and little B, as at P_2. As drawn in the figure the indifference curves are roughly circular around the point M. This means that M is the absolute maximum of utility, the absolutely most preferred point, the top of the "utility mountain," or the point of satiety. This point may, of course, be a long way off or even at infinity, but the most general case is the one drawn. The line $M_bMM'_b$ is drawn through those points where the indifference curves are vertical. It shows the maximum preferability quantity of B for each quantity of A. Similarly, the line $M_aMM'_a$ is drawn through those points where the indifference curves are horizontal. It shows the most preferable quantity of A for each quantity of B. These two lines divide the field into four quadrants. In that bounded by M_bMM_a, both quantities are *commodities* in the sense that as we increase the quantity of either, the quantity of the other being held constant, we move to preferred positions. Thus moving from H to H_a we increase A, keeping B constant, and we move to a higher indifference curve, that is, to a preferred position. If we visualize the three-dimensional mountain, then as we move from H to H_a we are moving "uphill." Similarly, moving from H to H_b also means moving to a preferred position. In the quadrant bounded by $M_aMM'_b$ A is a *discommodity* though B is still a commodity. That is to say, moving from K to K_a increases A but is a move "downhill" on the utility mountain to a lower indifference curve or a less preferred position. Moving from K to K_b is still moving to a preferred position. In similar ways we can verify that in quadrant $M_bMM'_a$ A is a commodity but B a discommodity, and in quadrant $M'_aMM'_b$, both A and B are discommodities.

The Possibility Boundary

Now suppose we impose on this figure a *possibility boundary*, FHG, which divides the field into possible or attainable combinations which lie within the area OFHG, and impossible or unattainable combinations which lie outside that area. The problem now is which is the preferred or optimum position among all those which are possible, as clearly the unattainable is not particularly interesting. The answer is the point H, where the possibility curve is touched by an indifference curve. Again visualizing the utility mountain, it is clear that H is the highest point on the mountain which can be reached as long as we have to stay within the "possibility fence" FHG. At any point such as H' where the possibility curve cuts an indifference curve, it is possible to move to a higher indifference curve while keeping to the line FHG.

The Marginal Conditions for an Optimum

At this point of mutual tangency *H*, the slopes of the two curves are equal. The slope of the indifference curve may be called the *rate of indifferent substitution*. It is the amount of B which could be substituted for one unit of A without moving to a more or less preferred position. That is to say, it is the amount of B which is equivalent, in preferability, to one unit of A. This quantity is frequently called simply the *marginal rate of substitution*, but it seems wise to qualify the term to distinguish it from other rates of substitution. The slope of the possibility curve may be called the rate of alternative substitution, or the (marginal) alternative cost of B for A. It is the maximum amount of B which can be substituted for one unit of A. That is, it is the maximum addition to B which can be obtained by the sacrifice of one unit of A. The condition for an optimum is then that the marginal rate of indifferent substitution should be equal to the marginal alternative cost. This is not, however, a sufficient condition for an optimum. Suppose, for instance, the possibility line were *SLT*. The point *L* where the marginal conditions are fulfilled is only an optimum if we have to stay on the boundary *SLT*; if, however, we can move inside the boundary, we will move to the absolute maximum *M*, simply by discarding some of A and B. Suppose again that the possibility line were *FVWG*. The marginal conditions are satisfied at both *V* and *W* where the possibility line touched an indifference curve. *V* is a relative maximum, but *W* is a relative minimum. It is not an absolute minimum, as both *G* and *F* are on lower indifference curves than *W*. If the possibility boundary is discontinuous the marginal conditions may be formally satisfied, but are not very instructive. Thus suppose the possibility boundary was $O_h WJ$ in Fig. 136, where there is a discontinuity or kink at *W*. The marginal alternative cost shifts abruptly at *W*, which is in this case the optimum point. In all these problems, therefore, it is never wise to rely on the marginal condition alone; the whole field should be examined as far as possible to see where the optimum lies. Basically the problem is one of *selection* of some highest point within the possibility area. The marginal conditions are merely aids in this process.

Analogy with Production Functions

In the quadrant bounded by $M_b MM_a$ the similarity to the production function figures of Chapter 25 (e.g., Fig. 117, page 554) is striking. We can think of utility as the *product* of the other two quantities. If for a moment we suppose that utility is cardinally measurable, marginal utility is seen to be a concept analogous to marginal productivity. A vertical section of the three-dimensional figure plotted in Fig. 136 along the line O_nK gives a total utility curve, as in Fig. 114A. The slope of this curve at any point is the marginal utility of A. The marginal rate of indifferent substitution is then equal to the ratio of the marginal utilities of A and B, just as the rate of product substitution is the ratio of the marginal productivities.

Utility as an Ordinal Magnitude

One of the virtues of the indifference curve analysis, however, is that it applies to many problems where cardinal measurement of utility is not necessary. If we are given a field of indifference curves and a possibility area, all we need to know to find the optimum point is the *ordering* of the indifference curves. That is to say, we need to know of any two indifference curves which is the higher—i.e., which represents a superior position—but we do not need to know *by how much* one is higher than the other. This is what is meant by saying that utility is an ordinal rather than a cardinal magnitude—we must be able to rank or order the various utilities represented by the indifference curves in order from low to high, but we do not have to specify the magnitude of the intervals between them. In geometric terms, we can suppose that the indifference curves are contours of a utility mountain whose general shape we know but whose height we do not know. We can transform the mountain by compressing it or stretching it as much as we like, provided that all points which were previously on the same level remain on the same level, and any point which was previously above another remains so. Maximum properties in general survive transformations of this kind—the top of the mountain is still the top no matter how much we stretch or compress it according to the above rules. This is why confining utility to an ordinal magnitude seems to make so little difference to the analysis.

APPLICATION TO THE THEORY OF THE FIRM

Indifference curve analysis can be applied to the theory of the firm to release it from the previous assumption of profit maximization. Thus in Fig. 137 we suppose three possible cases. Profits are measured on the vertical axis, and some other variable of significance to the firm, A, on the horizontal axis. It does not matter for the present purpose what this variable is. It may be size of enterprise, it may be uncertainty, liquidity, security of control, public reputation, or quality of labor relations. We suppose in each case a profits curve which is a possibility function relating profits to A. This we suppose has a maximum value for

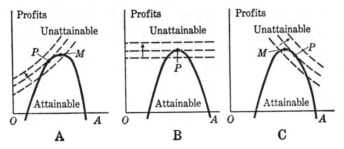

Fig. 137. Utility Maximization in the Firm

profits at *M*. All combinations of amounts of profit with amounts of A within the curve are attainable; outside it they are unattainable. In each case three indifference curves of a field are drawn.

In Fig. 137A these indifference curves slope upward, indicating that A is a discommodity, as in quadrant $M_aMM'_b$ of Fig. 136. Profits must increase in order to compensate for an increase in the disagreeable A. The optimum position is at *P* where an indifference curve touches the possibility boundary. This point is below the maximum profits point *M*, and at a smaller value of A. It is not worth going on to *M* because the gain in profits is accounted of less worth than the increase in the discommodity A which would accompany it.

In Fig. 137B the indifference curves are horizontal, indicating that A is neutral—that is, we do not care at all whether we have more or less of it. In that case the optimum point *P* coincides with the point of maximum profit.

In Fig. 137C, A is a commodity, and the indifference curves slope downward—we are willing to sacrifice profits in order to get more of A. In this case the optimum point *P* is below but to the right of *M*, indicating that we are willing to go beyond the point of maximum profits for the delights of getting more A. The principle of maximizing profits is thus seen as a special case in which the firm is indifferent to all those variables which are related to profits in a possibility function.

APPLICATION TO THE THEORY OF THE HOUSEHOLD

The theory of the household is a peculiarly important field for the application of indifference curve techniques, as there is clearly no objective maximand such as profits which can be maximized, and we must fall back on a more general theory of the optimum.

The Budget Problem: The Standard-of-Life Line

Let us take first what might be called the *budget problem*—that of dividing a fixed income or sum of money in the best possible way between competing lines of expenditure. Let us suppose first that there are only two commodities bought—say, food and clothing. The solid lines in Fig. 138 show the indifference curves of a consumer for combinations of these goods. Now let us suppose that the household has a fixed amount of money to spend on the two goods. If the whole sum is spent on cloth-

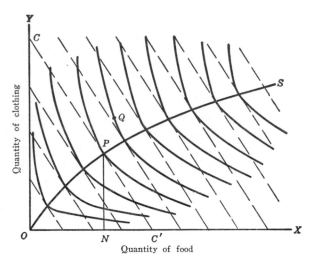

Fig. 138.   The Standard-of-Life Line

ing an amount, say, *OC* can be bought; if the whole sum is spent on food an amount *OC′* can be bought. All other combinations of quantities of food and clothing which can be bought with the given sum lie on the line *CC′*, which will be a straight line if the markets are perfect. This is an outlay contour as in Fig. 118 (p. 558); it is also a possibility boundary as the household cannot reach points beyond it as long as it is confined to the given total outlay. The optimum point is where it is touched by an indifference curve at *P*. There will be a family of such outlay contours corresponding to different total outlays. The locus of their points of tangency with the indifference curves is the line *OPS*. This is analogous to the scale line of Fig. 119. We may call it the *scale of living* or *standard-of-life* line, for it shows the best way of increasing purchases as the total outlay of the household increases. Given the total outlay of the household and its standard-of-life line, the optimum consumption pattern is found at the point of intersection of the standard-of-life line and the appropriate outlay contour.

The Standard-of-Life Line with More Than Two Commodities

The analysis can be extended, like the scale-line analysis, to cover the case of three commodities if the quantity of the third commodity is measured on the vertical axis. Then instead of indifference curves we have indifference surfaces, looking rather like the skins of an onion; instead of outlay lines we have outlay planes, rather like the pages of a book. The point where an outlay plane is touched by an indifference surface represents that combination of *three* commodities which gives the greatest satisfaction, and which we can buy with the total outlay represented by the outlay plane. The locus of all such points is again a standard-of-life line, but in three dimensions instead of two. Any point on the line now represents a combination of quantities of three inputs which is the best combination for a given total outlay. Similarly, with any number of commodities, *n*, we can construct analytically, if not geometrically, a standard-of-life line in *n-space*, each point of which shows the best combination of commodities which can be purchased with a given total outlay.

Proof of the Equimarginal Principle

If we suppose for the moment a cardinally measurable utility, it can easily be shown that the principle of equality of marginal rates of substitution is identical with the *equimarginal principle* developed in Chapter 24, page 528. We have seen that the marginal condition for an optimum is that the marginal rate of indifferent substitution should equal the marginal rate of alternative cost. For two commodities A and B, however, the marginal rate of indifferent substitution is the ratio of their marginal utilities, and in perfect markets the marginal rate of alternative cost is the ratio of their prices. If for instance the price of A is \$1 per unit and of B is \$4 per unit, giving up one unit of B releases money which can be applied to purchase 4 units of A, total outlay being constant. We can write the marginal condition for the optimum, then

$$\frac{\text{Marginal utility of B}}{\text{Marginal utility of A}} = \frac{\text{Price of B}}{\text{Price of A}}$$

Rearranging this equation we have

$$\frac{\text{Marginal utility of A}}{\text{Price of A}} = \frac{\text{Marginal utility of B}}{\text{Price of B}}$$

This is the equimarginal principle of page 528. Although in this form it apparently requires the assumption of a cardinally measurable utility, this is merely a matter of form, not of substance; and as we see, the principle can be stated in the form of equality of marginal rates of substitution in a manner that does not imply more than ordinal measurement of utility.

Release of the Budget Limitation

The picture of household behavior which is implied in Fig. 138 is of course drastically oversimplified. As we saw in Chapter 15 there are eight main categories, and at least twenty-five or thirty different types of economic events in any economic organization, even in the household. The theory of the household does not end with the problem of dividing a fixed money expenditure, or budget, among different commodities purchased; many different kinds of decision have to be made, all of which affect the total picture. These decisions, however, are all made within a framework of limitations, that is possibility boundaries. These are imposed partly by certain fundamental identities, some of which have been noted in Chapter 15 (p. 320). Thus we have

$$\text{Saving } (S) = \text{Income } (I) - \text{outgo } (O) \tag{1}$$
$$\text{Hoarding } (H) = \text{Receipts } (R) - \text{expenditure } (E) \tag{2}$$

To these we might add one more:

$$\text{Saving (increase in net worth) } S = \text{Hoarding } (H) + \text{increase in}$$
$$\text{nonliquid assets } (A') - \text{increase in liabilities } (O) \tag{3}$$

We can, therefore, distinguish a number of different types of decisions which the householder has to make: (1) how much income to earn; (2) how to divide it, according to the identity in equation (1), between saving and outgo; (3) how to divide saving into hoarding, increase in nonliquid assets, and increase in liabilities, as in the identity in equation (3); (4) how much to exchange for cash (R); if H is already decided upon, this automatically determines the volume of expenditure; that is, the budget outlay of Fig. 139, by the identity in equation (2).

Receipts and income are by no means the same concept. In farm households, for instance, receipts may be appreciably less than income, as part of the product of the household is consumed on the spot and does not go to market. This is true even of urban households where much time is spent on home repair and maintenance. On the other hand there are some households which indulge in a good deal of buying and selling; a household, for instance, which buys and sells a house in the course of a year will have receipts and expenditures far in excess of its income or outgo. There is a problem here of when does a household become a business. If a household, for instance, makes a regular practice of buying and selling houses, we should probably want to classify this activity as business.

Income: Earnings and Hours of Work

Income is derived from three sources: (1) work, that is, the use or sale of the activity of the person himself; (2) earning assets which yield profit, interest, or rent; and (3) gifts.

Let us consider first the problem of the determination of income or earnings from work. Suppose first that a man has the opportunity to work for as many hours as he pleases at a fixed hourly wage. In Fig. 139A the number of hours worked in a day is measured along the horizontal direction, the total income derived from such work along the vertical direction. We can then postulate a system of indifference curves, such as I_1, I_2, I_3, etc., which describe the system of preferences of the individual as between work and income. Any one of these curves—say, I_1—joins all those points which represent equally advantageous combinations of hours of work and income.

This system of indifference curves can also be regarded as the contours of a three-dimensional utility surface, in which utility is measured in the direction vertical to the plane of the paper. Any one familiar with contour maps will have no difficulty in visualizing the surface as something like a half-dome mountain, rising toward the top left-hand corner of the figure.

We have given this set of indifference curves certain properties. In the first place we have supposed that there is some income OS below which no work will be done at any wage; this is the *subsistence income*. If there are no other alternatives it will be determined by physical subsistence; otherwise, it will be the wage which can be earned in the next best alternative occupation. We have also assumed that there is some number of hours of work, OT_0, which represents the absolute maximum that is physically or psychologically possible. The right-angled line SW_0W_8 then represents the "zero" indifference curve, that is, a degree of utility of preference below which the occupation will not be entered at all.

The other indifference curves then have the following properties: (1) They all eventually slope upward and to the right, indicating that labor is a discommodity and we are operating mostly in the quadrant $M_aMM'_b$ of Fig. 136 (p. 605). There may be exceptions to this for low hours of labor, where work is a commodity and, like curve I_{11} we would be willing to sacrifice income for the privilege of working up to a point. At the maximum hours T_0 all the indifference curves become vertical, indicating that no amount of income would be regarded as compensating for an additional

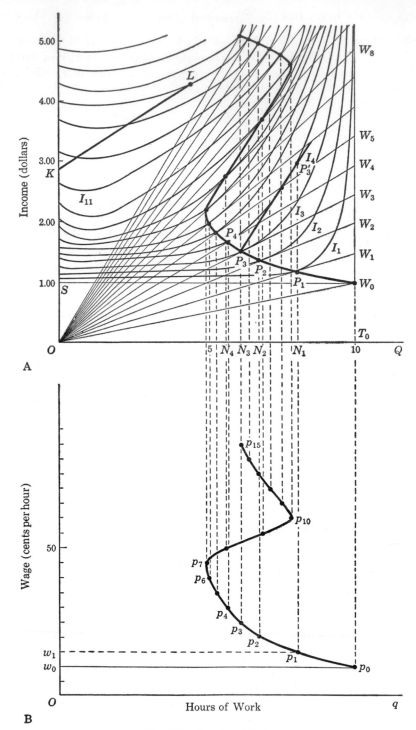

Fig. 139. Supply of Labor

amount of work. (2) This means that the slope of each curve (the marginal rate of substitution of work for income) will become greater at higher amounts of work: the tenth hour of work is likely to be much more distasteful than, say, the fourth, and would require a larger amount of income to compensate for it. (3) It is also assumed that the marginal utility of income declines with increasing income. If we follow any vertical line upwards we notice that the indifference curves are close together at low incomes, indicating that it takes only a little increase of income to get us to the next highest level of utility, but that at high incomes they are far apart, meaning that a larger increase of income is necessary to produce the same increase in utility.

The lines OW_0, OW_1, OW_2, etc. represent the possibility boundaries at successively higher wage rates, assuming each hour of work is paid the same. The slope of each line is the hourly wage. Thus if the hourly wage is $T_0W_1/OT_0 (= OW_1)$, OW_1 shows all combinations of income and hours worked attainable at that wage rate.

To find the *best* combination of hours and income for any given wage, we find where the income-hours line, e.g., OW_1, is touched by an indifference curve. The coordinates of this point (e.g., P_1) represent that combination of hours and income which gives the individual the greatest total utility consistent with a given hourly wage. This point is on the highest indifference curve which the individual can reach under the limitation that he receives only a fixed hourly wage.

The Supply Curve for Labor

It is only a little step now to derive from our system of indifference curves the supply curve for labor. The higher the hourly wage, the greater the slope of the income-hours line. As the wage rises from N_1P_1/ON_1 to N_2P_2/ON_2, the income-hours line steepens from OP_1 to OP_2, the point of equilibrium shifts from P_1 to P_2, and the number of hours worked changes from ON_1 to ON_2. As the wage rises further to levels indicated by the slopes of OP_3, OP_4, etc., the point of equilibrium changes to P_3, P_4, etc. So we can plot a complete supply curve for labor from the individual, as in Fig. 139B. Here the number of hours is measured horizontally on the same scale as in Fig. 139A. The hourly wage is measured vertically. Then the curve $p_0p_1p_2 \ldots p_{15}$ is the supply curve for labor from the individual in question. When the wage is $OW_0 (= W_0T_0/OT_0$ in Fig. 139A) the number of hours which the person is willing to work is w_0p_0 $(= OT_0)$; when the wage is $ow_1 (= T_0W_1/OT_0)$ the hours worked is w_1p_1 $(= ON_1)$, and so on. It will be observed that, as we have drawn the indifference curves, the supply curve for labor first has a negative slope at low wages, where a rise in wages enables the worker to earn a slightly better than subsistence income with less work. Then there may be a turning point as at p_7, after which a rise in wages raises the amount of labor offered; there may be another turning point, p_{10} at higher wages, where the worker now is able to afford more leisure as a rich man's good. The curve of Fig. 139B should be compared with that of Fig. 55 (p. 263).

Overtime Wages

Just as a seller can extract a greater amount of money from a buyer if he charges different prices for different quantities, as we saw in Chapter 23 (page 452), so a buyer of labor can extract a greater amount of labor for a given sum if he offers to pay different sums for different hours. Suppose, for instance, in Fig. 139A that the employer offers to pay an hourly wage equal to P_3N_3/ON_3 for the first ON_3 hours worked, and a higher wage, equal to the slope of the line $P_3P'_3$, for each hour worked thereafter. The income-hours line is now $OP_3P'_3$, and the highest indifference curve reached on this line is not I_3 but I_4, if we assume that the line $P_3P'_3$ touches the indifference curve I_4 at P_4. Such a practice is known as paying overtime rates. The figure shows that it may result in extracting from the worker a larger number of hours (ON_1) than he would be willing to work at any higher wage if the hourly wage were constant

Fig. 139A also tells how many hours a man will want to work at a given hourly wage if he has income from other sources. Suppose he has an income equal to OK from sources other than labor and that he can earn an hourly wage measured by the slope of the line OW_5. Then a line KL, drawn from K parallel to OW_5, represents the income-hours curve. If this curve touches an indifference curve at L, the coordinates of the point L give the number of hours he will work and the total income he will earn. We can see immediately from the figure that the larger the income from other sources, i.e., the greater is OK, the fewer hours will probably be worked.

Earnings from Property

A very similar analysis illustrates the decision in regard to the division of total assets into earning assets and liquid assets, which we suppose do not earn any income, but give a certain *"comfort."* In the distribution of assets, earning assets play the role of *work* and liquid assets of *leisure* in the distribution of time. In Fig. 139A, then, suppose we measure the amount of earning assets along OT_0, income as before on the vertical axis. If OQ represents total assets, and if, say, ON_1 is earning assets, N_1Q is liquid assets. If the rate of earnings is independent of the quantity of assets held, a straight line from the origin such as OW_0 will be an assets-income possibility boundary showing how much income we can get from each quantity of earning assets. Here the indifference curves may be thought of as measuring the utility of liquidity; there will again be some boundary at T_0W_8 representing the absolute minimum of liquidity, T_0Q, below which the person cannot permit himself to fall. In this case there is less likely to be a subsistence boundary; SW_0 is likely to coincide with OT_0. There may, however, be a fairly similar pattern of the supply curve, Fig. 139B, which now measures how total assets will be divided between earning and liquid assets for different rates of interest or profit (measured vertically). There may well be a section like p_0p_7 where a rise in the rate of return (interest or profit) actually results in a rise in the proportion of liquid assets as incomes rise beyond subsistence. There is also likely to be a section such as p_7p_{10} where a rise in rates of return will tempt the person into less liquidity as the high alternative cost of liquidity in terms of income foregone now becomes apparent. It is not even impossible that a section such as $p_{10}p_{15}$ might exist, where the person gets so rich as to be able to afford to carry large quantities of money with him, and not have to worry about earning more!

The Outgo-Saving Decision

With the indifference curve technique we can give at least a formal solution to the problem of the determinants of individual saving and hoarding. Thus in Fig. 140A we show the field of indifference curves for combinations of outgo and saving. The hypothesis suggested is that for a given amount of outgo an increase in saving will first increase utility, but utility will reach a maximum and will then decline. This can be seen by following a line such as NN_mN_1, and visualizing the utility surface above it; utility rises from N to a maximum at N_m and then declines as saving is increased further. We suppose, however, that increase in outgo always increases utility, as may be seen by following a vertical line in the figure. The curves as drawn also indicate the hypothesis that the volume of saving at which utility is a maximum is larger at larger levels of outgo. The line $N_mN'_m$, through the minimum points of the indifference curves bears to the right. For each level of income the possibility curve is a straight line making equal intercepts with the axes, such as ET_1S. If all the income were saved saving would be O_1S; if all were consumed outgo would be O_1E. The line ETS then represents the identity $I = O + S$ (page 612). The optimum point is the point of tangency with an indifference curve, T_1, where saving is O_1L_1 and outgo is L_1T_1. The locus of such points is a "scale line," $T_1T'_1$, showing the best way to change outgo and saving as income changes.

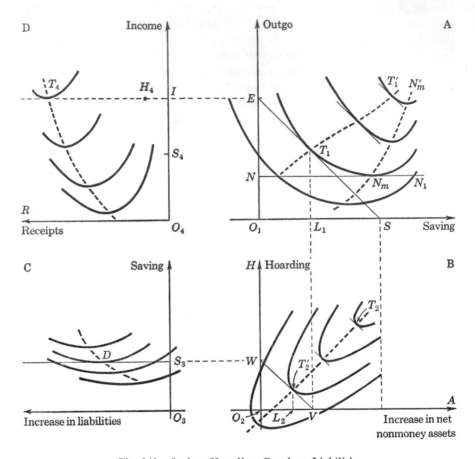

Fig. 140.   Saving, Hoarding, Receipts, Liabilities

The Hoarding Decision

We then project O_1L_1 down to O_2V in Fig. 140B, in which increase in
money stock (H) is measured vertically and increase in net nonmoney assets
(A) horizontally. If A′ is the gross increase in nonmoney assets and D
is the increase in liabilities (debt), $A = A' - D$ and $S = H + A' - D =
H + A$. The line WV then represents the combinations of H and A which
are possible with a total volume of saving equal to O_1L_1 ($= OV = OW$).
This line touches an indifference curve at T_2, so that O_2L_2 is the optimum
value of A and L_2T_2 of H. The indifference curves in Fig. 140B are drawn
so that both H and A show a utility maximum as one is increased while
the other is held constant.

The Expansion Decision

A household or any economic organization can expand the total of its assets and liabilities together by incurring debt (exchange expansion events, type B1 (p. 313)). This can be shown in several ways; one is in Fig. 140C, where saving (increase in net worth) is plotted against increase in liabilities. Saving is O_3S_3 ($= O_1L_1$); the optimum amount of increase in liabilities is S_3D where the line S_3D is the opportunity boundary, showing that, consistent with a given amount of saving, we can have any amount of increase of liabilities. S_3D touches an indifference curve at D. A rise in saving may lead to a greater willingness to expand, as in the figure, or it may not, depending on the psychology of the person and also on the rates of interest on liabilities and rates of return on assets. Fig. 140C is no more than a purely formal solution to this problem; we will, however, return to this problem in the next chapter.

The Receipts-Income Turnover Decision

Finally, in Fig. 140D we show the optimum amount of receipts corresponding to each level of income. We suppose a set of indifference curves in the receipts-income field. From the level of income O_4I ($= O_1E$) we draw the horizontal line to touch an indifference curve at T_4. IT_4 is then the optimum amount of receipts with the income O_4I. If now we draw IH_4 $= L_2T_2$ (hoarding), H_4T_4 is the optimum amount of expenditure. Similarly drawing $IS_4 = O_1L_1$ (saving), we have O_4S_4 as the optimum outgo. The optimum income, O_4I, we derive from Fig. 139, given the wage rate and rates of return on assets. It is not suggested, of course, that these decisions are made in the order named. The analysis is made more difficult also by the possibility that the various sets of indifference curves are not independent—thus a change in the rate of substitution of income for work may well go along with changes in the rates of substitution of saving for outgo and of money for other assets. Nevertheless we must suppose that the whole set of optimum positions is consistent with a set of preferences as above described, provided that each set of indifference curves is consistent with the others.

DERIVATION OF DEMAND CURVES

With the above apparatus we can proceed to a more detailed analysis of the derivation of demand curves from preference (utility) functions. We will first assume the budget limitation—i.e., constancy in total expenditure—and consider the effect of a rise in the price of one commodity or input. The treatment is strictly analogous to that of the demand for input of a firm. Just as a rise in the price of an input has two effects on the equilibrium position of a firm—a *scale* effect and a *substitution* effect—so in the case of a householder a rise in the price of one of his consumption goods will have two effects—a scale effect, which is called the *income* effect[1], and a substitution effect. That is to say, in most cases a rise in the price of a commodity will make a householder buy less of it for two reasons: first, the rise in price makes him poorer and so reduces his real income, and second, the rise in price makes him shift his purchases toward

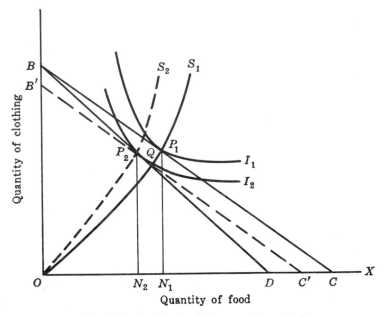

Fig. 141. Derivation of Consumer's Demand

the substitutes for the dearer commodity. We shall suppose first that the total expenditure is given and is not changed by the rise in price. We shall again assume that only two commodities are purchased, food and clothing, and shall study the effects of a rise in the price of food. In Fig. 141, then, as in Fig. 138, the quantity of food is measured along OX, the quantity of clothing along OY. Let BC represent the outlay curve for a given total expenditure, t dollars when p_c is the price of clothing and p_f the price of food. Then $OB = t/p_c$, and $OC = t/p_f$. Suppose that the price of food rises to p'_f. The quantity of food which can be purchased with a sum t dollars falls from OC to OD ($= t/p'_f$). The outlay line there-

---

[1] A better term would be the outlay effect for, as we have seen, income and outlay are not the same thing.

fore moves from *BC* to *BD,* as an outlay of $\$t$ will still buy a quantity *OB* of clothing. Suppose at the old price the outlay line *BC* is touched by an indifference curve, I_1, at P_1. P_1 will then lie on the standard-of-life line, OS_1, and the consumer will buy a quantity ON_1 of food and N_1P_1 of clothing. When the price of food rises, there is a new outlay line, *BD*; this is touched by another indifference curve, I_2, at P_2, which lies on the new standard-of-life line, OS_2. The result of the rise in the price of food, therefore, is a reduction in the quantity bought from ON_1 to ON_2. Thus the *law of demand* can be derived from the assumption of a scale of preference as embodied in the indifference curves.

Substitution Effect and Scale Effect

The fall in the consumption of a commodity which results from a rise in its price is due to a substitution effect—the movement of the scale line from OS_1 to OS_2—and a scale effect—the reduction in utility as observed in the passing from the indifference curve I_1 to the lower indifference curve I_2. That is, the rise in price causes a shift to other commodities and also a reduction in real welfare.

Industry Effect

In considering the forces underlying the total demand of all consumers for a commodity we must also note an effect analogous to the industry effect; when the price rises, some consumers may cease to consume the commodity altogether, and when the price falls, some consumers who had not previously consumed the commodity will begin to consume it.

Rise in Price Equivalent to Fall in Money Outlay

Another interesting property of this analysis is that it enables us to define the scale effect of a change in prices in terms of a change in money outlay. Consider the significance of point Q, Fig. 141, where the standard-of-life line OS_1 cuts the indifference curve I_2. This represents that combination of food and clothing which would give the same enjoyment as the combination represented by point P_2 (as it is on the same indifference curve); but as it is on the standard-of-life line OS_1, it also represents the best possible combination to buy at the *old* prices and at an income represented by the outlay line $B'C'$ drawn through Q parallel to *BC*. The money outlay which, at the old prices, would give the same satisfaction as does the present money income at the new prices, is then $OB' \cdot p_c$, or $OC' \cdot p_f$. This is smaller than the actual money outlay, showing that a rise in the price of even one commodity is equivalent to a loss of money outlay if prices remained the same. This construction gives us a theoretical solution to the problem of a cost-of-living index number, the change in the cost of living being measured by the reciprocal of the *income equivalent* of a price change. If after a rise in prices the income equivalent of $100 at the original price structure is $90—i.e., $90 at the old price structure is equivalent to $100 at the new—then we may say that the cost-of-living index has risen from 100 to 111.1.

Poor Man's Goods: A Backward-Sloping Standard-of-Life Line

There is one special case of the above analysis which is interesting. If there are two commodities, one of which is a rich man's good and the other a poor man's good (often called an inferior good), the character of the indifference curves will be as in Fig. 142. It will be observed that after

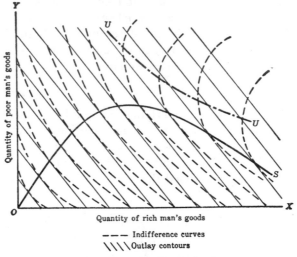

Fig. 142.   Poor Man's Goods

a while the indifference curves bend backward and become positively sloped, indicating that the poor man's good has become a positive nuisance. It will also be noticed that the point where this happens gets nearer to the X axis as the quantity of rich man's goods increases—the line *UU,* drawn through the points in the indifference curves where the poor man's good first becomes a nuisance, slopes downward. With such a system of indifference curves the standard-of-life line, *OS,* will actually bend backward as in the figure, indicating that as the standard of life increases beyond a certain point, a smaller quantity of the poor man's goods is actually bought. This is true to experience; the rich eat much less margarine and corn pone than the poor do.

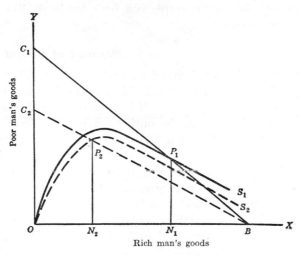

Fig. 143. Inverse Demand Curve

The Inverse Demand Curve

In this case it is possible for a rise in the price of the poor man's good to have a scale effect in the opposite direction to the usual one, so that this rise may actually bring about an *increase* in the quantity bought, because of the decline in the standard of life. This is shown in Fig. 143. Here OP_1S_1 is the original standard-of-life line. A rise in the price of poor man's goods pushes this line toward the X axis—the substitution effect operating to substitute rich man's goods—and the standard-of-life line moves to OP_2S_2. The rise in the price of poor man's goods shifts the outlay line from BC_1 to BC_2, for fewer poor man's goods can now be bought for the same money expenditure. At the original prices, N_1P_1 of poor man's goods will be bought, ON_1 of rich man's goods, where P_1 is the point of intersection of BC_1 and OS_1. After the rise in the price of poor man's goods, N_2P_2 of poor man's goods will be bought, and ON_2 of rich man's goods, where P_2 is the point of intersection of BC_2 and OS_2. It will be observed that N_2P_2 is greater than N_1P_1—i.e., the rise in the price of the poor man's goods has resulted in an increase in the consumption of them, as it has made people poorer. Thus even an apparent exception to the law of demand can be understood by means of the indifference curve analysis. It will be readily appreciated that this exception is likely to be very rare, for the commodity not only must be a poor man's good but it must also play a relatively large part in consumption; otherwise, the reverse income effect will not be large enough to offset the substitution effect which still, of course, makes for a decrease in the quantity taken when there is a rise in price. Probably the only example is a basic foodstuff, like bread, at a very low level of income.

Removal of Budget Limitation

The above derivation of demand curves must be modified somewhat if the budget limitation is removed. Thus a rise in the price of food is equivalent to a fall in real wages. If income remains the same and the same proportion of it is spent, the outlay curve, as we have seen, moves from BC to BD in Fig. 141. The fall in real wages, however, may result in a change in the number of hours worked; if the householder is operating in the segments p_0p_7 or $p_{10}p_{15}$ in the supply curve of Fig. 139B, the fall in income due to the fall in real wages is partly offset by the rise in the number of hours worked, so the outlay curve BD in Fig. 141 will rise, partly offsetting the fall in purchases of food. If this supplementary income effect is large enough, it may lead to an inverse demand curve, with a rise in the price of food actually leading to an increase in the quantity taken—not, this time, because food is an inferior good but because the householder works harder, work as opposed to leisure being the inferior good.

It is possible also that a rise in the price of food might lead to changes in saving and in hoarding which would change the total of expenditures relative to income and so shift the position of the budget line BD (Fig. 141). If, for instance, the rise in price led to dis-hoarding, expenditures would be increased and the scale effect would lessen the decline in purchases. These changes might also lead to inverse demands, at least in the very short run. These effects, however, are limited to short periods and are of the nature of once-over changes; they cannot be the source of permanent changes in demand.

The impact of price changes on the willingness to go into debt is a problem of considerable importance, but also great difficulty where simple conclusions may not be available. Thus a fall in the price of consumer durables, or of houses, may easily have a large effect on the willingness to go into debt, and hence may produce spectacular increases in total outlay and may, indeed, affect the whole pattern of life and consumption. The possibility of sharp discontinuities in the overall demand functions, then, cannot be ruled out.

THE DYNAMICS OF THE HOUSEHOLD

The problem of the dynamics of the household, that is, what determines the whole course of a household's events table, like the very similar problem in the case of the firm, is again too complex to permit of any simple solutions. An equilibrium analysis nevertheless suggests certain guidelines. We can suppose, for instance, that a *controlled event,* that is, one which results from a decision, will raise the expected *utility* of the household; otherwise the decision will not be made. We can also suppose that out of a range of possible controlled events, one will tend to be selected which raises utility the most. On the other hand we run into the problem of the *costs of search* in the household, just as in the firm. Existing patterns tend to have a certain stability, even if there may be, objectively, other patterns available which would make the household better off, simply because the search for these other patterns is too costly and difficult. A small change, therefore, which pushes a household over some "threshold of search" may have very large consequences. Insofar as selling cost represents a specialization of the search process, it may, especially when it is genuinely informative, lessen the costs of search for the household and so have some social benefits as well as social costs.

Another dynamic problem of great importance is the way in which a decision at one point of time may effect the *uncontrolled* events of the future. Thus a decision to buy a house on a mortgage will profoundly affect the uncontrolled events for years to come, and will also deeply affect the whole pattern of future consumption and expenditure. Thus instead of there being one best events table with small marginal variations from it leading to progressively worse situations, we may find a number of *gestalts,* to use a psychological term—life patterns which cluster sharply around a group of possible events—patterns of roughly equal value, separated from other such clusters by sharp cliffs in the utility function. This again suggests the possible importance of discontinuities in the utility function, leading to occasional drastic changes in life pattern.

QUESTIONS AND EXERCISES

1. The concept of marginal utility is subject to the objection that it implies a numerical measurement of total utility. How can we get over this difficulty? Translate into terms which do not involve the extensive measurement of utility:

   a. The law of diminishing marginal utility

   b. The equimarginal principle

   c. The proposition that a commodity is a discommodity if its marginal utility is negative

   d. The proposition that the marginal utility of "poor man's goods" falls to zero at a smaller consumption when we rise to a higher standard of life

   e. The law of the diminishing marginal utility of money

2. With this chapter in view, compare and contrast the analytical tools involved in the theories of production and consumption.

3. Diamonds are often cited as a possible exception to the rule that a higher price makes for a smaller volume of purchases, for a rise in the price of diamonds may increase their value as articles of display. How would you explain this phenomenon according to the indifference curve analysis?

4. "Economics is ultimately the theory of human choices. As such it covers not merely a part of life, but the whole. And the indifference curve is the map of human choice." Discuss.

5. Prove that by a sufficiently refined system of wage discrimination (e.g., overtime) any person, no matter what his income from other sources, could be persuaded to work any number of hours short of the physical or psychological maximum.

6. Draw a set of indifference curves for a trader on a field such as in Figs. 66, p. 347, 67, p. 355, 68, p. 357 and 69, p. 358, describing the preferences as between money and wheat stocks. Show how these may be used to describe the position of equilibrium of a trader. Show that if a trader has no costs, no asset limits, and a *constant* set of indifference curves (preferences), then he will make a positive rate of profit no matter what the sequence of price changes with perfect markets, or what the sequence of market function changes with imperfect markets, provided there is *some* sequence of changes.

7. Draw indifference curves in the fields of Fig. 79, p. 388 and derive a formal solution of the problem of how a firm will divide a given volume of production between sales and increase in inventory.

8. In Fig. 137, p. 609, suppose that the variable A represents a measure of the overall size of the enterprise. What types of business character would correspond to the three cases shown? Repeat this question on the assumption that variable A measures (a) liquidity, (b) man-days lost in strikes, (c) amplitude of fluctuations in profits, (d) amount paid in taxes, (e) percentage of income given to charity.

9. Apply the indifference curve analysis to the problem of joint demand. How will the indifference curves differ in the case of two commodities in (a) competitive demand, (b) independent demand, and (c) complementary demand? What kind of demand curves or surfaces (contours) can be derived from these indifference curves?

   (Note: The methods in Exercise 7, p. 603, can be applied to this problem. Derive the indifference curves from total utility curves, in a construction like Figs. 118, p. 558, 128 and 129, pp. 582, 583.)

10. In Figs. 139 and 140 what might be the effect on the indifference curves and on the optimum positions of the various variable of the following changes? (a) a general rise in the cost of living; (b) a rise in the rate of interest; (c) an increase in income tax rates; (d) a tax on food; (e) a decline in frugality; (f) expectations of inflation. Illustrate by diagrams.

11. Are there any kinds of input in a process of production which correspond to the "poor man's good" (inferior good)? If so, what peculiarities might be encountered in their demand?

CHAPTER 28

APPLICATIONS OF INDIFFERENCE CURVE ANALYSIS: WELFARE ECONOMICS

THE THEORY OF EXCHANGE AND THE PARETIAN OPTIMUM

With indifference curve equipment we can now return to an earlier problem—the theory of exchange between two individuals.

In the box diagram, Fig. 144, O_aX is the total quantity of commodity H in the possession of two exchangers, A and B, and O_aY is the total quantity of commodity K in their possession. The *distribution* of the two commodities between the two exchangers is shown by a point inside the rectangle O_aXO_bY. Thus at the point P_0, exchanger A has O_aH_a of H and O_aK_a of K; exchanger B has O_bH_b of H and O_bK_b of K. A's quantities are measured by the coordinates of the point relative to origin O_a, and B's quantities relative to origin O_b.

Suppose now that we start from a position such as P_0, and suppose that some price is set at which exchanges can be made. The exchange opportunity line for both parties is a straight line such as $P_0E_bE_a$, the slope of which is equal to the price. Thus suppose we move from P_0 to E_b. This means that A has acquired and B has relinquished LE_b of H, and A has relinquished and B has acquired P_0L of K. The price, or ratio of exchange, is therefore P_0L/LE_b units of K per unit of H, which is the slope of the line P_0E_b. We now impose two sets of indifference curves on the figure. The solid curves such as P_0A_0, E_bA_1 show A's preference function and the dashed curves such as P_0B_0, E_bB_1 show B's preference function. As drawn, A moves to preferred positions as he moves out from O_a, toward O_b, with more goods in his possession; B moves to preferred positions as

627

he moves out from O_b toward O_a. If the figure is turned through 180 degrees, it will be seen that B's indifference curves are of the conventional two-commodity pattern relative to B's origin at O_b. We may note in passing that the preference here is for a *distribution* of the commodities,

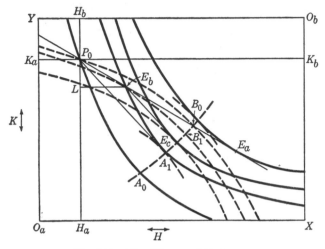

Fig. 144.   The Theory of Exchange

not for possession alone. If the parties are highly altruistic, so that each worries about the poverty of the other, the indifference curves may exhibit a maximum point within the box, as in Fig. 136.

Dynamics of Exchange

With indifference curves as in Fig. 144 and an exchange opportunity line P_0E_b, exchange will proceed to the point E_b with both parties moving to higher indifference curves and being better off; A's (solid) indifference curve at E_b is higher than the one at P_0, and B's (dashed) indifference curve at E_b is likewise higher than the one at P_0. At E_b, however, B will not wish to exchange any more, and beyond E_b, where the line P_0E_b touches a B-indifference curve, B is moving to worse positions. A would like to go on exchanging at this price up to E_a, where the exchange opportunity line touches one of his indifference curves, but he cannot do this because B is not willing to go beyond E_b. If no further price change is possible, E_b is the point of equilibrium. If, however, the price can be changed (in this case raised) to any level up to the slope of A's indifference curve at E_b, further exchange is possible. Thus suppose the price is raised and the exchange opportunity line shifts to E_bE_c. As we move from E_b to E_c both parties are again moving to higher indifference curves, until again one or the other reaches a point where the exchange opportunity line touches one of his indifference curves and exchange ceases. In the figure E_bE_c has been drawn so that E_c is on a point of tangency both of A's and B's indifference curves. At such a point no further movement can be made which will benefit both parties, no matter what the price.

The Contract Curve

The locus of such points of mutual tangency, $A_0E_cB_0$ is called the *contract curve*. From any point not on the contract curve an exchange opportunity can be found which will benefit both parties and move them toward the contract curve. No such opportunity can be found for a point on the contract curve. As long as price changes are possible, therefore, the equilibrium point must be on the contract curve, as for any point not on the contract curve a price can be found at which exchange is mutually profitable.

Bargaining Paths

From the point P_0, movement to any point on the contract curve between A_0 and B_0 will benefit both parties. At A_0, A is only just as well off as he was at P_0; B is making his maximum gain from exchange. At B_0, B is only just as well off as at P_0, and A is making his maximum gain. The exact point to which the system will move depends on the actual dynamics of the case—that is, on the succession of prices offered. By perfect price discrimination A can move B down B's indifference curve to B_0, or B can move A down A's indifference curve to A_0. There is one price at which both parties move straight to the contract curve, as on the path P_0A_1, where P_0A_1 is tangent to both indifference curves at A_1. There is nothing in the system to suppose, however, that this price is an *equilibrium price,* for any other exchange path within the area $P_0A_0B_0$ is equally plausible, depending on the bargaining ability of the two parties. The *final* price at which the two parties reach the contract curve must of course be equal to the marginal rates of indifferent substitution (the slopes of the indifferent curves) of both parties. Even this, however, is not determinate, as it varies from point to point on the contract curve.

Application to Collective Bargaining

This analysis is of general applicability to any bargaining situation, wherever two parties and two goods are involved. Thus Fig. 144 might apply to a collective bargain situation in which, say, O_aX, measures the wage and O_aY some other benefit, say, shortness of vacation. The dashed indifference curves now represent the employer's preference function (he likes lower wages, shorter holidays) and the solid lines the union preference function. The origin O_b is not significant here. As before, there will be a contract curve at the locus of the points of tangency of the two sets of indifference curves. From all points *not* on the contract curve adjustments can be made (trades) which benefit both parties, and much bargaining in practice consists on finding what these adjustments are. Once on the contract curve, however, movement can only be made which benefits one party and injures another. This involves conflict, whereas trades do not.

This analysis illustrates well an earlier proposition (page 33): that exchange involves both a community and a conflict of interest—community of interest in *reaching* the contract curve, conflict of interest in moving one way or the other along the contract curve.

The Paretian Optimum

The contract curve describes what is known as the *Paretian optimum* in exchange. This should be compared with the "Pareto line" in Fig. 133 (p. 596). A Paretian optimum is a condition in which any adjustment or change that is possible makes at least one party, in his own estimation, worse off than before. The conditions for such an optimum are best described in a negative form: the optimum has not been reached if any reorganization is possible which will make some people better off without making anyone worse off. Then the marginal conditions can be stated by saying that if the appropriate marginal rates of transformation between commodities or factors of two parties are *not* equal, keeping either utility or product constant, reorganizations can be made which will improve one party's position without worsening the other.

Seven Marginal Conditions

Seven such *marginal conditions* have been distinguished. (1) In exchange, as we see above, marginal rates of indifferent substitution of two owners should be equal. If owner A can give up $2K$ for $1H$ without feeling loss, and owner B can give up $3K$ for $1H$ without feeling loss, then if A gives B $1H$ and gets from B $2K$, A is no worse off and B is better off, as he would have been willing to give up $3K$ for $1H$. (2) In the reallocation of production: if two producers each produce two commodities the marginal rates of alternative cost should be equal. If giving up the production of $2K$ enables A to produce $1H$, and giving up $1H$ enables B to produce $3K$, then if A produces $1H$ more and B $1H$ less, $2K$ is lost from A but $3K$ is gained from B; no H is lost and $1K$ is gained on balance. (3) In the reallocation of factors: marginal physical productivities of a factor f for all producers should be equal. If $1f$ makes $2K$ with producer A and $3K$ with producer B, shifting $1f$ from A to B will result in a net gain of $1K$ for the same amount of factor employed. (4) In the substitution of factors: two factors f and g should have the same rate of equal product substitution in all occupations. If producer A can substitute $1f$ for $2g$ without loss of product, and producer B can likewise substitute $1f$ for $3g$, then if producer B lets $3g$ go and takes on $1f$, and producer A takes on $2g$ and releases $1f$, there is no change in product and $1g$ is released to make other things. (5) In the substitution of products: for two products H and K the rate of indifferent substitution for any household should equal the rate of equal product substitution for any firm. If household A can give up $2K$ for $1H$ without feeling loss, and producer B can produce $3K$ by giving up $1H$, then shifting production from $1H$ to $3K$ will enable the producer to give the householder $2K$ for $1H$; the household is as well off as before and the producer is $1K$ to the good. (6) In the substitution of leisure for product: the rate of indifferent substitution of factor use for product should equal the marginal rate of reward paid. If it would take an additional $2H$ to induce the owner of a factor to add $1t$ to its use, and if the owner can earn $3H$ by adding $1t$ to its use, then by adding $1t$ to its use the owner is better off. (7) In lending and borrowing (without uncertainty), the marginal rate of time preference should be the same for all individuals. Thus suppose H_1 and H_2 represent "this year's" and "next year's" income. If a lender feels that giving up $1H_1$ is just worth it if he gets $2H_2$, and a borrower feels that getting $1H_1$ is worth it even if he has to give up $3H_2$, then lending $1H_1$ and paying back $2H_2$ will leave the lender as well off as before but will make the borrower better off.

Trading Leads to the Optimum

These conditions are not, of course, sufficient to describe a social optimum. If, however, they are violated it means that trading of some sort is possible—that is, it is possible to reach bargains which will not make anybody worse off and will make somebody better off. Once they are all fulfilled together, however, all movement implies conflict—i.e., it is only possible to gain at the expense of someone else.[1]

CONFLICT AND THE SOCIAL OPTIMUM

Interpersonal Comparisons of Utility

Economists have frequently maintained that it is impossible to make interpersonal comparisons of utility; that is, that the welfare of one person cannot be compared with that of another. Whatever may be the case in

[1] For a more detailed exposition of these marginal conditions, see M. W. Reder, *Studies in the Theory of Welfare Economics*, New York, Columbia University Press, 1948; or K. E. Boulding, *Survey of Contemporary Economics*, edited by Bernard Haley, Homewood, Ill., Irwin, 1952, vol. II, chapter 1.

the Elysian Fields of pure economics, the social fact is that we make such interpersonal comparisons all the time, and that hardly any social policy is possible without them, for almost every social policy makes some people worse off and some, better off. The Paretian optimum itself is a special case of a social welfare function, for if we assume this to be a social ideal it implies that nobody should ever be made worse off, whereas most societies have defined certain groups (e.g., criminals or foreigners) who *should* be made worse off! It is true of course that, strictly, such interpersonal comparisons can be made only in a single mind; A, B, or even C may have notions about how a sacrifice of A's welfare for B's should be rated, and these estimations are likely to differ. The political process however is precisely the machinery by which these different estimations of social welfare themselves are weighed in terms of power to carry out a policy; the social welfare functions of those who have power obviously are superior to those of people who do not have power. The political process also involves the mutual *change* of social welfare functions under discussion and criticism. It is not absurd to suppose that this process might reach some kind of equilibrium, and if it did, no matter who was in power, the social welfare functions would be very similar.

The Conflict Field or Utility Space

We can represent the welfare (utility) of two persons or parties in a field such as Fig. 145. Here we measure A's welfare horizontally, and B's welfare vertically. These can very well be ordinal measurements; that is, for some purposes all we need to know is whether the welfare of one or the other party has gone up or down. Suppose for the moment, however, we assume cardinal measurement. In such a field we can distinguish four major types of movement. From a point such as P_0 a move to B is a *benign* move, in which both parties are better off: any movement "northeast" in the quadrant bounded by P_0N and P_0E is benign. The opposite move, southwest to M, is *malign*, in which both parties get worse off. A movement "northwest" to C_b is a conflict move, with B getting better off and A worse off. The opposite move "southeast" to C_a is a conflict move with A getting better off and B worse off.

Suppose now we have a series of conflict moves, in which, say, A does something which makes him better off but B worse off, moving, say, from P_0 to P_1, B retaliates by doing something which moves the situation to P_2, A moves it to P_3, B to P_4, and so on. In this case a succession of conflict moves results in an overall malign process—P_4 is clearly southwest of P_0 and both parties are worse off. On the other hand, it is also possible for conflict to be generally benign, as it would be if the moves went from P_4 to P_3 to P_2 to P_1 to P_0. An arms race or a price war is a good example of a generally malign conflict process; the succession of different political parties in office in a successful democracy is perhaps an example of a benign conflict process. If we define the *rate of conflict* as the ratio, the loss of the loser, per unit gain of the gainer, then two successive conflict moves in opposite directions with rates of conflict c_1 and c_2 will have a

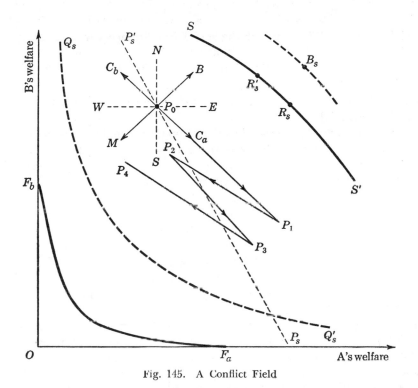

Fig. 145. A Conflict Field

generally benign, neutral, or malign direction, as the product c_1c_2 is less than, equal to, or greater than 1. Whether conflict moves return to the benign or malign quadrant depends on the length or extent of the move as well as on the rate of conflict. Generally speaking, a succession of conflict moves is more likely to be benign if rates of conflict are low, and if moves with high rates of conflict have a small extent.

The Social Welfare Function

When we make interpersonal comparisons between A's and B's welfare we can express these by drawing social indifference curves in the field of Fig. 145. All points on such an indifference curve represent combinations of A's welfare and B's welfare that are regarded as having equal social desirability. A social indifference curve through the point P_0, such as

$P_sP_0P_s$, divides the field into two (or perhaps one should say three) parts. A movement from P_0 upward and to the right of the indifference curve represents a social improvement, even though this includes conflict moves in the region P'_sP_0N or P_sP_0E, for in conflict moves in these regions the losses to one party are judged to be outweighed, socially, by the gains to the other. Similarly a move from P_0 to any point below and to the left of $P'_sP_0P_s$ represents a social loss, and a move to any point on $P'_sP_0P_s$ is socially neutral. The slope of the social indifference curve at any point is the rate of "social importance" of A relative to B. If B is entirely without value in the social estimation, the social indifference curves will be vertical straight lines; if A is entirely without value they will be horizontal straight lines. Even in these cases we may notice that all benign moves are socially beneficial.

MALEVOLENCE. If the social welfare function is malevolent toward one party, so that a decline in his welfare is regarded as a social advantage, the social indifference curves will have a positive slope; then even some malign moves will be regarded as socially beneficial. Thus suppose BM is a social indifference curve, with malevolence toward B; any move from P_0 below and to the right of BM will be regarded as socially beneficial, even in the malign segment MP_0S. A nation frequently damages itself in order to damage an enemy more; the Nazis damaged themselves in order to damage the Jews, Communists damage themselves in order to damage the bourgeoisie. The phenomenon, irrational as it may seem, is distressingly common. Social indifference curves are not necessarily—or usually—straight lines with a constant rate of social importance. When there is a sense of community between the two parties the social importance of each may increase as his welfare declines: when B's welfare is low and A's is high, a small increase in B's welfare compensates for a large decrease in A's welfare. The social indifference curve may even be asymptotic to both axes, like $Q_sQ'_s$, indicating that a situation where the welfare of either A or B is reduced to zero is worse than any position where the welfare of both is positive.

The Social Possibility Boundary

A utility field like Fig. 145 is likely to have a possibility boundary such as SS' beyond which the welfare combinations are unattainable, because of the ultimate scarcity of resources. If this boundary has a negative slope, as in the figure, then once the boundary is reached only conflict or malign moves are possible; benign moves are ruled out. Even then, however, there remains the possibility of diverting resources from conflict itself to *development*—that is, to pushing out the possibility boundary itself. Thus in Fig 145, conflict between the two parties might keep them shuttling back and forth between, say, R_s and R'_s, whereas if they were able to resolve the conflict and devote the resources tied up in it to development they might be able to push the possibility boundary out to B_s, where both would be better off.

A dangerous situation arises where the possibility boundary is perceived to be a highly concave set, like the line F_bF_a in Fig. 145. Here the welfare of each is greatly increased if the other is eliminated or reduced to a low state. There is strong temptation here to start a *game of survival*.

THE THEORY OF A COMPETITIVE MARKET

From the indifference curves of all individuals in a competitive market it is possible to obtain their demand-supply, or market curves, and hence the equilibrium price and quantity exchanged. In Fig. 146 we draw the indifference curves M_0I_0, M_1I_1 of a single marketer showing those combinations of stocks of money and of the commodity concerned to which he is indifferent. His stock of money is measured along the vertical axis, his stock of commodity along the horizontal axis. Any one indifference curve, such as I_0, shows all those combinations of holdings of money and commodity to which the marketer is indifferent. Over most of the range it will be observed that the indifference curve has a negative slope, indicating that if money is given up, commodity must be increased to compensate. We have drawn the curves, however, with the slope (i.e., the marginal rate of substitution) diminishing with increase in commodity, indicating that the more commodity a marketer has in his possession the less he values a marginal increase in terms of money. We have drawn the indifference curves sloping positively at high quantities of commodity, indicating that in this range the commodity has become a discommodity— i.e., the marketer would have to be offered money in order to persuade him to increase his holdings of commodity. Another property of the indifference curves as we have drawn them should also be noticed; the curves are parallel in a vertical direction—i.e., at a given quantity of commodity the slopes of the curves, or the marginal rate of substitution, is the same no matter how great the quantity of money. This assumption leads to an important simplification of the analysis, though it will be relaxed shortly. It corresponds to an assumption which is important in Marshall's analysis, that the marginal utility of money is constant. If we could assume a measurable utility, the marginal rate of substitution, in dollars per unit of commodity, as we have seen, would be equal to the ratio

$$\frac{\text{Marginal utility of commodity}}{\text{Marginal utility of money}}$$

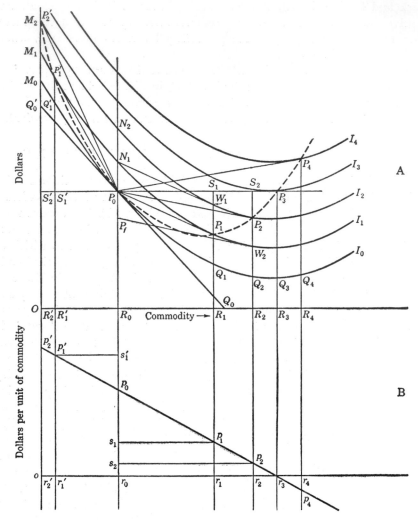

Fig. 146.   Derivation of Market Curve

If the marginal utility of money is constant, then the marginal rate of substitution depends only on the quantity of commodity, not on the quantity of money. The implication is that the total quantity of money held by the marketer is so large that changes in his stock of money do not affect his willingness to part with it; hence, his demand for or offer of commodity depends only on his willingness to part with or acquire commodity, not on his willingness to acquire or part with money. It should be observed that the condition that the marginal rate of substitution should be independent of the quantity of money is somewhat broader than the Marshallian assumption; the marginal rate of substitution could be independent of the quantity of money even if the marginal utility of money changed (presumably fell) with increase in the quantity of money, provided that the marginal utility of the commodity changed in the same proportion. Fortunately, however, the indifference curve technique enables us to escape from this grave restriction in a way that the older marginal utility analysis did not permit.

Derivation of Market Curves

From the indifference curves it is not difficult to derive the demand-supply or market curve of the marketer, showing what quantities of commodity he will offer to buy or sell if he is faced with a situation in which he can buy or sell unlimited quantities at fixed prices. Suppose P_0 represents the combination of money and commodity in his possession at the beginning of trading. The straight lines $P_0P'_2$, $P_0P'_1$, Q'_0Q_0, P_0P_1, P_0P_2, etc., are *opportunity lines* showing what combinations of money and commodity are open to the marketer by exchange at various prices, the slope of the line being the price at which exchange takes place. Thus the line P_0P_1 (and its projections, not drawn on the figure) shows those combinations which are open to the marketer when he starts exchanging from the point P_0 at a price P_1S_1/P_0S_1. Movements to the right from P_0 represent purchases of commodity—the stock of money declines as the stock of commodity increases. Movements to the left of P_0 indicate sales of commodity—stocks of money increase as stocks of commodity decline. It must be emphasized again that all we are considering here is simple exchange; there is no production or consumption, but simply a transformation of the form of assets by buying or selling; the price is the *transformation coefficient* showing how much money can be transferred into or out of one unit of commodity.

The equilibrium position at any price is the point where the opportunity line touches an indifference curve, this being on the highest indifference curve which can be reached as long as the marketer must stay on his opportunity line. Thus, P_1 is the equilibrium point when the price is equal to the slope of P_0P_1. P_0S_1 is the amount of commodity bought; S_1P_1 is the amount of money given up. The locus of all such points, the dotted line $P'_2P'_1$, . . . P_4, is an outlay-receipts curve with its origin at P_0, showing how much money will be paid out or received for different quantities of commodity bought or sold.

From Fig. 146A the marketer's demand-supply or market curve can immediately be derived, as in Fig. 146B. Commodity is measured on the horizontal axis as before, dollars per unit of commodity on the vertical axis. The line $p'_2, \ldots p_4$ is the marginal rate of substitution curve; its vertical ordinate at each quantity of commodity is equal to the slope of the indifference curves of Fig. 146A at the corresponding point. As we have assumed that the marginal rate of substitution is independent of the quantity of money, the whole system of indifference curves reduces to a single marginal rate of substitution curve, for at a given quantity of commodity all the indifference curves have the same slope. Thus at a quantity or_2 ($= OR_2$), the slopes of the indifference curves at Q_2, W_2, P_2, etc., are all equal to r_2p_2. Then the marginal rate of substitution curve $p'_2, \ldots p_4$ is the same as the demand-supply curve of the marketer, because the marginal rate of substitution must be equal to the price when the marketer is satisfied. Thus at a price r_1p_1 the marketer will buy r_0r_1 of the commodity, because when he has an amount or_1, the marginal rate of substitution (the slope of the indifference curve) is equal to the price (the slope of the opportunity line); in other words, the opportunity line is tangent to the indifference curve, as it is at P_1. The total market curve and the market price and quantity exchanged can be derived by summing the market (demand-supply) curves of all the individual marketers, so that from the indifference curves of all the marketers the market price and quantity could be obtained (see pages 128, 370).

A Limiting Assumption Removed

In Fig. 147 we remove the assumption that the marginal rate of substitution is independent of the quantity of money. The figure is essentially similar to Fig. 146, except that the indifference curves are drawn so that the marginal rate of substitution rises with increase in the quantity of money; thus, the slope of the curve at N_2 is greater than that of the curve at N_1. Instead of the whole system of indifference curves now reducing to a single marginal rate of substitution curve we have a whole series of marginal rate of substitution curves in Fig. 147B, m_0i_0, m_1i_1, m_2i_2, etc., each corresponding to an indifference curve in Fig. 147A. In this case higher indifference curves yield higher marginal rate of substitution curves. The demand-supply curve does not now correspond to any single marginal rate of substitution curve. The outlay-receipts curve— the dashed line $P'_1, \ldots P_2$ in Fig. 147A—is, as before, the locus of the points of tangency of successive opportunity lines $P_0P'_1$, P_0P_1, etc., with the indifference curves. At each point of tangency the price is equal to the marginal rate of substitution. In Fig. 147B, therefore, from each point on the quantity axes, say, r_1, we erect a perpendicular till it cuts the marginal rate of substitution curve m_1i_1 derived from the indifference curve at P_1 at p_1; r_1p_1 is then the price at which the market will be willing to buy the quantity r_0r_1. The dashed line $p'_1, \ldots p_2$ is the mar-

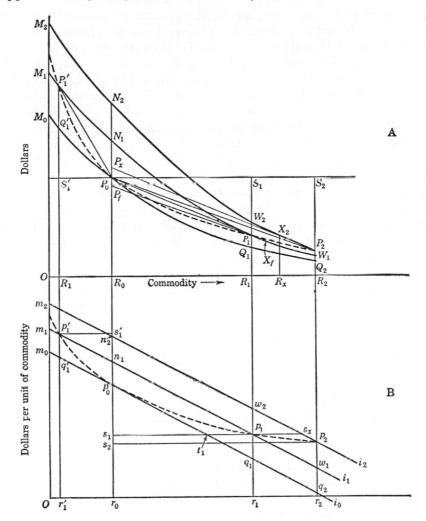

Fig. 147. General Derivation of Market Curve

keter's demand-supply curve. It will be observed that the demand section of the curve (p_0p_2) has a flatter slope than the marginal rate of substitution curves, and the supply section ($p_0p'_1$) has a steeper slope. If the marginal rate of substitution fell with increasing quantities of money, the above relationship would be reversed. The latter case, however, involving as it does an *increasing* marginal utility of money, is extremely unlikely.

The above analysis enables us to clear up some confusions relating to the concept of economic surplus. In the Marshallian economics the triangular area bounded by the demand curve, the vertical (price) axis, and the horizontal line at the market price is called the *consumer's surplus*. As the concept is related to purchases rather than to consumption, it is perhaps better to call it the *buyer's surplus*; the corresponding concept for sellers may be called the *seller's surplus*. The existence of a demand curve implies that the buyer would be willing to buy smaller quantities than he actually buys at a higher price than he actually pays. If, therefore, he is faced not with a perfect market at which he can buy as much as he likes at a given price, but a market in which he is subjected to price discrimination—a high price for the first unit bought, and successively lower prices for successive units purchased—he will be willing to buy the same quantity that he buys in the perfect market but will be forced to pay more money for it. We have already examined this phenomenon in Chapter 21. The buyers' surplus may then be defined as the difference between the total sum which could be extracted from him in the purchase of a given quantity of commodity by perfect price discrimination, and the sum which he would pay for the same amount in a perfect (one-price) market. Similarly, the seller's surplus is the difference between the sum which will extract a given quantity of commodity from the seller under perfect price discrimination, and the sum which will persuade him to supply the same quantity in a perfect market.

Perfect Price Discrimination

Under conditions of perfect price discrimination the outlay-revenue curve of the marketer is the same as his indifference curve through the point P_0, for perfect price discrimination must be defined as a situation in which the opportunity line is the same as the indifference curve at P_0. If he expands purchases, the price is continually lowered as his marginal rate of substitution falls, continually tempting him on; if he expands sales, the price is continuously raised as his marginal rate of substitution rises, again continually tempting him to increase sales. For complete mathematical accuracy we should have to assume that the opportunity line under perfect price discrimination lies infinitesimally above the indifference curve—otherwise, of course, the equilibrium is indeterminate.

Buyer's and Seller's Surplus

Suppose now in Fig. 147 that the marketer expands purchases under perfect price discrimination until he reaches the point Q_1; he will have bought R_0R_1, and will have paid a total amount S_1Q_1. In order to make him buy this amount under a uniform price, the opportunity line would have to be P_0P_1, which is tangent to the indifference curve at P_1. The amount paid under uniform pricing would then be S_1P_1. The difference between the amount paid for R_0R_1 under perfect discrimination and under uniform pricing is P_1Q_1 ($S_1Q_1 - S_1P_1$), that is, the buyer's surplus. Similarly, $Q'_1P'_1$ is the seller's surplus when the amount sold is $P_0S'_1$.

The Compensating Payment

Another important concept related to that of economic surplus is that of a *compensating payment*. This is the sum of money which would just compensate a marketer for a given change in price or in the conditions of the market. Thus, suppose in Fig. 147 that there is a rise in price from r_2p_2 to r_1p_1: the opportunity line shifts from P_0P_2 to P_0P_1. As a result of the rise in price, the marketer is worse off; his position of equilibrium moves from P_2 on indifference curve M_2 to P_1 on the lower indifference curve M_1. The compensating payment is that addition to his initial stock of money which will enable him to reach the indifference curve M_2 when the price is equal to r_1p_1. This sum is P_0P_x, where P_xX_2 is drawn parallel to P_0P_1, so that it represents an opportunity line, at a price r_1p_1, to touch the indifference curve M_2 at X_2. Similarly, the compensating *tax* for a fall in price from r_1p_1 to r_2p_2, which would make the marketer just as well off as he was before the fall in price, is P_0P_f, where P_fX_f is drawn parallel to P_0P_2 to touch the indifference curve M_1 at X_f. In the general case P_0P_f is not equal to P_0P_x. The concept of a compensating payment is of considerable importance in welfare economics.

If we take the more special case of Fig. 146, in which the indifference curves are parallel, the buyer's (or seller's) surplus becomes equal to the compensating payment which would compensate for the loss of the market, and the change in buyer's (or seller's) surplus due to a change in price is equal to the compensating payment for that change in price. Thus, in Fig. 146, the buyer's surplus when the price is r_2p_2 is P_2Q_2. The payment which would have to be made to a buyer to compensate him for the loss of the market (i.e., for the withdrawal of the privilege of exchanging at the price r_2p_2) is P_0N_2; this is the sum of money which added to his initial stock will bring him to the same indifference curve, I_2, that he can reach by exchanging at a price r_2p_2. If the indifference curves are parallel, P_2Q_2 is equal to P_0N_2. Consider now a change in price from r_1p_1 to r_2p_2. The compensating payment (in this case a tax) is equal to P_0P_f, where W_2P_f is drawn parallel to P_0P_2 to touch indifference curve I_1 at W_2. The compensating payment P_0P_f is clearly equal to P_2W_2, which in turn is equal to the rise in buyer's surplus from P_1Q_1 to P_2Q_2, as $P_1Q_1 = W_2Q_2$. Similarly, the compensating payment for a rise in price from r_2p_2 to r_1p_1 is P_0N_1, where N_1W_1 is drawn parallel to P_0P_1

to touch the indifference curve I_2 in W_1. We then have P_0N_1 equal to P_1W_1, which is in turn equal to the fall in buyer's surplus, $Q_2P_2 - Q_1P_1$.

The Demand Triangle

These various concepts may be expressed also in terms of Figs. 147B and 146B. Thus, in Fig. 147A the line S_1Q_1 is the sum (integral) of all the marginal rates of substitution on the curve P_0Q_1; this is equal to the area $r_0p_0q_1r_1$ in Fig. 147B. The line S_1P_1 in Fig. 147A is the total payment made in purchasing r_0r_1 at a price r_1p_1, and is therefore equal to the rectangle $r_0s_1p_1r_1$. The buyer's surplus, therefore, at the quantity r_0r_1 is equal to the area $r_0p_0q_1r_1$ less the area $r_0s_1p_1r_1$, which is the area of the complex quadrilateral $s_1p_0q_1p_1$, or $s_1p_0t_1 - t_1p_1q_1$. In the case of Fig. 146 the buyer's surplus reduces to the *demand triangle*, $s_1p_0p_1$, as the condition of parallel indifference curves makes q_1 and p_1 identical points. In the more general case of Fig. 147 the demand triangle $s_1p_0p_1$ has no significance whatever. Similarly, in Fig. 147 the total compensating payment at the price r_1p_1 is P_0N_1. $P_0N_1 + S_1P_1$ is the sum of all the marginal rates of substitution between N_1 and P_1, which is the area $r_0n_1p_1r_1$. S_1P_1, as we have seen, is equal to the rectangle $r_0s_1p_1r_1$. It follows that the total compensating payment for the loss of the market at the price r_1p_1 is the area $s_1n_1p_1$, which in this case is greater than the demand triangle. In the case of Fig. 146, however, the lines n_1p_1 and p_0p_1 coincide and the compensating payment is equal to the demand triangle $s_1p_0p_1$.

The Gain from Trade

The concept of a compensating payment can be used to measure the *gain from trade* in a whole market. In Fig. 148, B_1N_1, B_2N_2, . . . M_1S_1, M_2S_2, etc., are the individual demand-supply curves of all the people in a given market. Summing the positive segments of these curves gives us the market demand curve, $B_3H_2H_3N$. Summing all the negative segments gives the market supply curve, $S_3K_2K_1M$. The market price OP is of course that at which the quantity demanded PN is equal to the quantity supplied, PM. If a mirror image of the supply curve is drawn, S_3N, it will cut the demand curve at the market price at N, and we have the familiar Marshallian diagram. If now the marginal rates of substitution of all marketers are independent of their money holdings, the compensating payment for the marketer whose demand-supply curve is B_1N_1 is the area PB_1N_1; similarly, for all the other marketers. The sum of the areas PB_1N_1, PB_2N_2, etc., is therefore the total amount of money which would compensate the buyers for the loss of the market; it is equal to the area $PB_3H_2H_3N$. Similarly, the area $PS_3K_2K_1M$ is the total amount of money which would compensate the sellers for the loss of the market.

The total amount of money which would have to be paid to all the marketers to compensate for the loss of the market is the triangular area S_3B_3N; this is a measure of the gain from trade.

If now we relax the assumption of parallel indifference curves, a simple modification is introduced into the figure; instead of the compensating payment to marketer 1, being represented by the area B_1N_1P, it is now

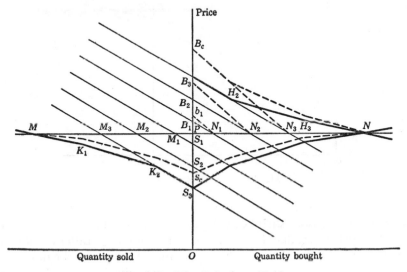

Fig. 148. The Gain from Trade

represented by the area b_1N_1P, enclosed by the dotted line b_1N_1—the marginal rate of substitution curve for marketer 1 at N_1. Similar marginal rate of substitution curves are drawn for the other marketers, and these are summed in the market marginal rates of substitution curves B_cN and S_cM. The triangular figure S_cB_cN now represents the total compensating payment. The assumption of a marginal rate of substitution increasing with increase in the quantity of money leads to a higher compensating payment for buyers but a lower compensating payment for sellers, as buyers are parting with money which is becoming more valuable to them as they part with it, while sellers are acquiring money which is becoming less valuable to them as they acquire it. The compensating payment triangle S_cB_cN is not likely to differ in area very much from the demand-supply triangle B_3NS_3.

Loss from Taxation

The above analysis leads to an interesting proposition in the field of taxation. In Fig. 149 we suppose a tax equal to P_bP_s per unit laid on a

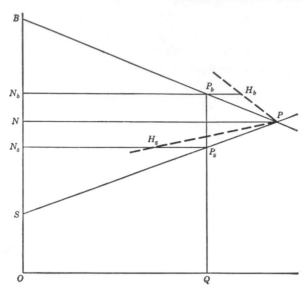

Fig. 149. Loss from Taxation

commodity whose market demand and supply curves are BP and SP. The volume of transactions shrinks to OQ as a result; the buyer's price is QP_b, the seller's price QP_s. Starting with the assumption of parallel indifference curves, the payment which would compensate the buyers for the imposition of the tax is equal to the rectangle NN_bP_bP; similarly, the sellers would have to be compensated by a payment of N_sNPP_s to make them as well off as they were before the tax. The total payment which would compensate the marketers for the imposition of the tax is therefore the area $N_sN_bP_bPP_s$. The total receipts from the tax amount to $N_sN_bP_bP_s$. The total receipts from the tax would therefore be insufficient to cover the compensating payment by an amount equal to the triangle P_bPP_s. This is one possible measure of the social *loss* due to the imposition of the tax. If the condition of parallel indifference curves is removed, and if PH_b and PH_s represent the market marginal rate of substitution curves, the total compensating payment would be $N_sN_bH_bPH_s$, and the loss due to the tax would be measured by the area of the complex polygon $P_sH_sPH_bP_b$.

TAXATION AND INCOME

The indifference curve analysis can also be used to study relationship of various forms of taxation to the willingness to earn income. In Fig. 150 the dashed lines are indifference curves on a money–hours of work diagram, like that of Fig. 139A, page 614. Suppose the initial amount of

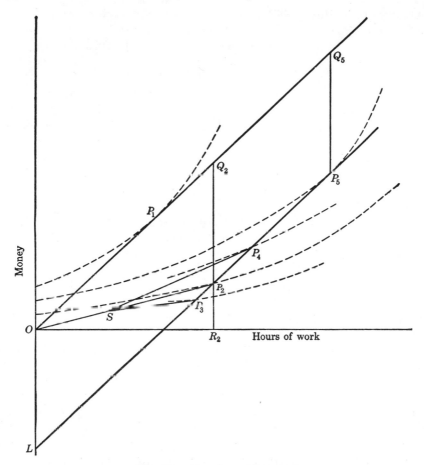

Fig. 150. Taxation of Income

money is zero, and that the individual can earn money at a constant wage equal to the slope of the opportunity line OQ_5. Suppose now that we wish to levy a tax on the individual equal to LO. If now we draw LP_5 parallel to OQ_5, all points of equilibrium after the tax equal to LO is paid must lie on this line. The various possible schemes of taxation may be represented by different opportunity lines which touch indifference curves at their intersection with LP_5. Thus, OP_2 is the opportunity line of income after tax when the tax is a proportional income tax, equal to a proportion P_2Q_2/R_2Q_2 of income earned. The line OP_2 touches an indifference curve at P_2. The line OSP_3 represents a progressive income tax; the line OSP_4 a regressive income tax; successive increases or decreases in the rate of tax may be represented by shifts in the slope of the net opportunity line. It will be seen in the figure that a progressive income tax reduces income and effort below the resultant of a proportional income tax yielding the same amount of tax, and also leaves the individual worse off—P_3 is on a lower indifference curve than P_2. A regressive income tax, on the other hand, spurs the individual to greater effort and income, and leaves him better off than a proportional tax; P_4 is at a higher level of effort and income, and is on a higher indifference curve than P_2. The theoretically best tax is a fixed tax independent of the amount earned. If this is levied at the start, the opportunity line net of tax is LP_5. This reaches a higher indifference curve at P_5 than any of the other net opportunity lines. It can easily be seen that P_5 is on the highest indifference curve which can be reached by any scheme of taxation, as it is on the highest indifference curve which can be reached on the line LP_5; and as long as the rate of wages and the total tax collected is unchanged, all points of equilibrium after tax must lie on LP_5. The conclusion therefore emerges that the best tax on purely economic grounds is not an income tax at all but a property tax assessed on income-earning power rather than on income actually earned. The administrative difficulties of such a tax make it impossible in practice; nevertheless, the theoretical conclusion at least raises the question whether the administrative advantages of a progressive income tax on individual incomes are worth the very real economic disadvantages of such a tax. It should be observed that the adoption of a fixed tax or even a regressive tax on individual incomes does not necessarily mean the abandonment of the progressive principle as *between* individuals. It would be theoretically possible, for instance, to assess fixed taxes on those individuals with large earning power which are proportionately heavier than those levied on individuals with small earning power. We should notice also that with any scheme of taxation, if there is no tax on any income earned *after* the point at which the person would otherwise stop earning more income, the net effect is the same as a lump-sum tax. Thus suppose we had a proportional income tax, with a net income line OP_2 up to an income R_2Q_2, and no tax on any income earned thereafter. The net income line would be OP_2P_5, and the person would proceed right to P_5.

THE SIGNIFICANCE OF WELFARE ECONOMICS

Many of the propositions of this chapter, especially those which use indifference curves or welfare functions to analyze the questions involved when we try to say whether one set of opportunities is better or worse than another, form part of a body of theory known as *welfare economics*. This represents a serious attempt on the part of economists to answer the question: What exactly do we mean when we say that one position of the economic system is better or worse than another in a strictly economic sense? It has now become clear that it is impossible to answer this question in the absence of an ethical value system, for as we have seen, even the Paretian optimum implies the ethical value of the absence of malevolence. When it comes to interpersonal comparisons and the evaluation of redistributions of income, we can postulate, as in Fig. 145, a social welfare function. Kenneth Arrow[2] has shown, however, that this cannot be derived from individual welfare functions, by addition or any other mathematical operation, except under very restricted and unlikely conditions. Samuelson[3] has pointed out further that we cannot be sure even that a *larger* real income is superior in welfare, unless all the commodities which compose it are identical and all increase; even then we cannot be sure that some might not be discommodities. With all these hesitations and qualifications it certainly looks as if welfare economics is in ruins—or at least comes up with practically nothing in the way of secure propositions.

Nevertheless, the effort has not been in vain, and it has been an exercise which the other social sciences might well emulate. What welfare economics really says is that there is a certain norm of exchange opportunities, divergences from which have to be specially justified. This norm essentially is that everyone should be able to exchange anything for anything else in any quantity at ratios equal to the alternative costs or, more generally, the rates of *real* transformation of the exchangeables. This principle itself provides plenty of opportunity for intervention in markets, either in the interest of correcting for unrecognized or unappropriable costs and gains—as when we subsidize education or tax cigarettes—or in the interest of controlling monopoly pricing, which would violate the principle. There are also many occasions on which a society may wish to violate the principle itself, in the interest of development or of more equitable distributions. The principle furthermore sheds little light on the best disposition of the *grants economy,* that is, of those unilateral transfers which are getting more important all the time. Nevertheless, when one sees around the world the enormous social losses which result from gross and unconscious violations of the principle, when one sees countries which have strangled their whole development because they have made the price system unworkable, one realizes that the message of welfare economics is not insignificant, and that it is often of great importance to point out that distortions of the price system

[2] Kenneth Arrow, *Social Choice and Individual Value,* New York, Wiley, 1951.

[3] Paul A. Samuelson, *The Evaluation of Real National Income,* Oxford Economic Papers N.S.2, Jan. 1950, 1–29.

have a social cost. Under some circumstances we may think the gains are worth the cost, but the assumption that such distortions have *no* cost will almost inevitably lead to disastrously costly policies.

QUESTIONS AND EXERCISES

1. Illustrate all seven of the marginal conditions for a Paretian optimum by means of graphs, using indifference curves and equiproduct curves, and draw the contract curve in each case.
2. From a system of indifference curves, such as in Fig. 144, how can we find the *range of prices* within which exchange is possible? Construct a system of indifference curves under which no such range of prices exists, and under which, therefore, exchange is impossible.
3. Draw a system of indifference curves, as in Fig. 144, for the case in which both parties are altruistic—that is, each values the welfare of the other. What now might happen to exchange? Illustrate how in such a system there might be gifts (unilateral transfers). Will there be a contract curve? What about the Paretian optimum under these circumstances?
4. Suppose that *both* the welfare dimensions of Fig. 145 are ordinal rather than cardinal quantities. What kind of transformations does this permit in the figure? What properties of the figure survive these transformations? What parts of the argument based on this figure depend on the assumption of cardinal measurement of A's and B's welfare. Is there any assumption of cardinal measurement of the *social* utility?
5. Generalize the discussion of Fig. 145 to three parties, A, B, and C, and draw the corresponding three-dimensional figure. Generalize, as far as possible, to *n* parties. Note that the concept of a conflict move now becomes more complex. Does any of the basic argument drawn from Fig. 145 have to be modified?
6. In a diagram such as Fig. 150, p. 645, or Fig. 139, p. 614, draw a part B as in Figs. 146 or 147, with *marginal rates of substitution* curves, and derive the supply curve for labor from these, as the market curve is derived in Figs. 146B and 147B.
7. The results of Fig. 150 have been obtained in part because of certain assumptions which were made in drawing the system of indifference curves. What are these assumptions? Discuss the effect of different assumptions regarding the shape of the indifference curve system on the results obtained. Prove that if the indifference curves are parallel, no tax system can be devised which will increase income and effort. Discuss, in Fig. 150, the relation of the *compensating payment* to the tax.
8. Apply the compensating payment analysis to the theory of the tariff. Show that the compensating payment is always greater than the receipts from the tariff.
9. Would the compensating payment concept have any significance in the case of *long-run* demand and supply curves?

10. An electricity company charges 8 cents per unit for the first 100 units, 4 cents per unit for the next 300 units, and 3 cents per unit for all subsequent units purchased. Draw the opportunity line facing a consumer under these circumstances. Draw on three separate diagrams systems of indifference curves together with this opportunity line (a) which will make the consumer buy 80 units only, (b) which will make him buy 350 units, (c) which will make him buy 500 units.

   Prove that under any circumstances if the consumer pays different prices for different quantities, he would be better off if the company charged a flat rate equal to the average price which he pays under differential pricing, though he would buy less electricity. Discuss the concept of the compensating payment under these circumstances.

CHAPTER 29

CAPITAL, TIME, AND VALUATION

Many of the problems relating to capital, time, and valuation revolve around the fact that the events of the events table (p. 312) take place not merely in succession but at specific dates with definite time intervals between them. Suppose, for instance, we take the very simple events table involved in the making and repayment of a loan. Here we find a number of *payments,* positive (receipts) or negative (expenditures), which are organized in a definite time structure, each at a particular date. A complete sequence of such payments, with dates attached, complete in the sense that all payments before the initial date or after the final date are zero, is sometimes called a *single investment,* though in view of the many other meanings of the word investment it might be better to call it simply a *payments record.* Thus in Table 53 we show the payments record of an investment which consists of making a loan for $1000, receiving $50 on every anniversary of the loan for five years, and then receiving $1050 on the sixth anniversary.

TABLE 53. A PAYMENTS RECORD

Year	0	1	2	3	4	5	6
Payment	−1000	50	50	50	50	50	1050

Here we notice that the payments record shows an excess of positive over negative payments, in the above case of $300. This will appear in the accounts as *income,* as it represents an increase in net worth. The crucial question however is *when* should it appear as income. The basic problems of valuation and income accounting all revolve around this apparently simple question. In the above case the answer seems obvious: we should allocate $50 to income in each year up to the sixth.

650

TABLE 54. INCOME ALLOCATION (DOLLARS)

	Year						
	0	*1*	*2*	*3*	*4*	*5*	*6*
Capital	0 1000	1050 1000	1050 1000	1050 1000	1050 1000	1050 1000	1050 0
Money Stock	1000	0 0	50 50	100 100	150 150	200 200	250 250	1300

In terms of the events table (54) what this allocation means is that the capital of the investment has *grown by* or accrued by $50 each year; thus at date zero we have an exchange event, $1000 cash is exchanged for $1000 of investment or capital, which represents the value of the loan. By year 1 this has grown to $1050; if we measure growth discontinuously, this represents an income-expansion event at year 1. Then immediately there is an exchange event; the payment of $50 exchanges $50 worth of investment for $50 money. This process is repeated each year, until in the sixth year the $1050 of capital is exchanged for $1050 cash, and we are left with $1300 cash, the increase in cash, $300, being the total income over the period.

Suppose now, however, that we had a payments record like Table 55, line 1, where we simply have a negative payment at the beginning and one positive payment at the end. The form of contract is not common for periods longer than a year but is by no means unknown. How now should we allocate the total income? If we follow the first rule and only allocate income at the time of actual payment (line 2), we allocate all the income to the last year. Capital then stays the same until the last year when it suddenly rises and falls. This, however is rather unsatisfactory for, in fact, the income is earned over the whole period. An obvious solution is to allocate it evenly, $50 to each year, as in Table 55, lines 4 and 5. Now, however, we notice something curious; suppose we define the *annual rate of return* as the ratio of income allocated in one year to the capital value at the beginning of that year. That is, the rate of return in year 1 is the income allocated to the end of that year, $50, divided by the capital at the beginning, year 0, $1000, or 5 percent per annum. Similarly the rate of return in the second year is 50/1050, or 4.76 percent per annum, and so on (line 6). We now notice that the rate of return apparently falls as time goes on, simply because a constant income is being divided by a constantly increasing capital sum. If now we wish to have a constant rate of return in each year, we must first calculate the constant rate of return which will just allocate all the income ($300) to the various years. This turns out to be 4.4697 percent per annum, and when income is calculated each year by multiplying the previous year's capital by this quantity

TABLE 55. ALLOCATION OF INCOME OVER TIME

				Year			
	0	1	2	3	4	5	6
1. Payment	−1000	0	0	0	0	0	+1300
2. Income	0	0	0	0	0	0	300
3. Capital	1000	1000	1000	1000	1000	1000	1300/0
4. Income	0	50	50	50	50	50	50
5. Capital	1000	1050	1100	1150	1200	1250	1300/0
6. Rate of return[a]		5.00	4.76	4.55	4.35	4.17	4.00
7. Income[b]		44.697	46.694	48.782	50.962	53.240	55.619
8. Capital[b]	1000	1044.697	1091.392	1140.174	1191.136	1244.376	1300.00/0
9. External rate of return[a]		4.0	5.0	6.0	5.0	4.0	5.0
10. Income		40.00	52.00	65.52	57.87	48.61	63.20
11. Capital	1000	1040.00	1092.00	1157.52	1215.40	1264.02	1327.22/−27.22/0
12. Income		39.180	50.934	64.176	56.689	47.619	61.904
13. Capital + rent	979.491	1018.671	1069.605	1133.781	1190.470	1238.089	1300.00/0
14. Market value	1000	1030	1070	1120	1180	1260	1300
15. Income		30	40	50	60	80	40
16. Rate of return[a]		3.0	3.88	4.67	5.36	6.78	3.17

[a] Percent per annum; [b] $r = 4.4697$ percent per annum.

(.044697) we find that the capital has grown to just $1300 by the end of the sixth year, and the final payment just extinguishes it. The reader may wish to check that income of each year in line 7, divided by the capital of the previous year, is .044697.

It must be emphasized that the events shown in lines 2 and 3, 4 and 5, 7 and 8, etc., of Table 55 are *accounting events*, all of which can be derived from the *real* events of line 1. They all represent different ways of allocating income over time, and in a sense all are equally arbitrary. Lines 2 and 3 may be called the realized income method, which is frequently followed by accountants—almost universally for short periods of, say, under one year, less and less so as longer periods are taken into account. Lines 4 and 5 may be called *linear allocation*. It is a method rarely, if ever, used in practice outside the special case of calculating depreciation, where the *straight line* method common in the United States involves the linear allocation of the difference between the initial cost and scrap value of an item over the intervening years. Lines 7 and 8 illustrate what may be called *exponential* allocation at a constant internal rate of return. This method is aesthetically very satisfying; in so far as income is a growth of capital, the rate of growth is a highly significant parameter, and when the method of allocation as in line 6 produces a decline in the recorded rate of growth, for which there is nothing to correspond in the real payments series of line 1, we feel intuitively that income is being overallocated to the early years and underallocated to the later years, and that the decline in the rate of return is spurious, owing only to faulty allocation. On the other hand, with a somewhat different aesthetic criterion, one might feel that the rising income under exponential allocation in line 7 is spurious, and that the logical thing to do is to distribute income equally, as in line 4.

A possible resolution of this dilemma would be to allocate income at external rates of interest prevailing at each time in the loan market. This is shown in lines 9, 10, and 11 in Table 55. Here we suppose that in each year there is an external rate of interest, shown in line 9. Income is then found in each year by multiplying the capital of the previous year by this external rate of interest. The justification for this procedure rests on the assumption that the external rate of interest represents an *alternative cost* of capital, and that therefore the income allocated represents, as it were, *income foregone* by having capital tied up in this particular investment rather than in others. This is a method of allocation frequently recommended by economists. Nevertheless there are severe objections to it. The first is that unless the right kind of average of the external rates just happens to equal the internal rate—which is unlikely —then if the average external rate is less than the internal rate, not all the income earned will be allocated. Furthermore, if the average external rate is greater than the internal rate, as in lines 9, 10, and 11 of Table 55, more will be allocated to the various years than is actually earned. Thus in the above case $327.22 is allocated, whereas only $300 is earned. We can regard this deficiency in earnings as a kind of *negative rent,* as an excess of earnings over allocations would be a positive rent. The rent may be added or subtracted at the end of the period. Thus in line 11 we suppose that $27.22 is allocated as negative income or outgo at the end of the period. This is open to the same objections as the allocation in line 2; rent however could be distributed throughout the period, allocated at external rates of interest. Thus in lines 12 and 13, Table 55, we subtract $20.509 from the initial capital on the base date, this being the equivalent, at the given rates of interest of line 9, of the $27.22 rent in year 7. Allocating income at external rates of interest as in lines 12 and 13 now allocates the whole $300, no more and no less, as we end up with a capital value of $1300 just before the final payment which extinguishes it. These procedures are clumsy, and share with all other methods of allocation a certain arbitrariness, but they are necessary if allocation is to be done at external rates of interest.

THE THEORY OF VALUATION

One of the most important applications of the theory of time allocation is to the theory of valuation. This is the problem of how to put a money value on, or find a money equivalent to, an expected series of related economic events stretching into the future. Thus we may wish to value a machine, or a building, or a whole enterprise, or a stock or bond, or even a person, meaning by this that we want to find a sum of "dollars" which is equivalent, at the present moment, to all the future net income to be derived from the thing valued. As we shall see, this problem is essentially the same as the problem of how to allocate income over the whole life of an investment—that is, a complete, related series of a payments record. The problem of how to compute the profit or income accruing to an enterprise or an investment during a particular period, such as a given year, is likewise another aspect of exactly the same problem of income allocation over time.

Consider first the concept of *amount of capital invested* in an investment account as in Table 55, in lines 3, 5, 8, 11, or 13. Here we suppose there is some base date which marks the *birth* of the account, before which there are no events in this particular account. The capital invested by any date is then equal to the total of payments out (expenditures), minus payments in (receipts), plus incomes, positive or negative, allocated to or before the date in question. A payment out is an exchange event (type B2), in which money declines and the capital value of this particular investment rises by an equal amount. Similarly a payment in (receipt) represents an exchange in which capital invested is exchanged for money. An allocation of income is an accounting event of type A1 (income-expansion); net worth and capital invested rise by the amount of income allocated. If the investment is financed in part by borrowed funds, interest accruals on these represent deductions from net worth and capital invested; this, however, we will neglect for the moment. If, then, E_p represents all past expenditures R_p, all past receipts, and Y_p, all past allocations of income up to and including the present date t, the capital invested up to date t is

$$C_t = E_p - R_p + Y_p \tag{1}$$

Consider now a "complete" investment with a final date, t_n, after which there are no economic events relevant to the investment. Any date t between t_0 and t_n divides the total expenditures (E_t) into past expenditures (E_p) (up to and including date t) and future expenditures (E_f) after date t or between date t and t_n. So we have

$$E_t = E_p + E_f \tag{2}$$

Similarly, using like notation,

$$R_t = R_p + R_f \tag{3}$$
$$Y_t = Y_p + Y_f \tag{4}$$

We also have

$$Y_t = R_t - E_t \tag{5}$$

That is, the total of income to be allocated is equal to the excess of receipts over expenditures, for this represents the gross addition to net worth of the owner over the whole life of the investment. Then from equations (2) to (5) we get

$$Y_p + Y_f = R_p + R_f - E_p - E_f, \text{ or}$$
$$E_p - R_p + Y_p = R_f - E_f - Y_f = V_t \tag{6}$$

The left-hand side of equation (6) we have already identified as the amount of capital invested up to the date t. The right-hand side is the sum of future receipts, less future expenditures and future income allocated; this is known as the *present value* of the investment at date t, V_t. We have therefore, from equation (6),

$$C_t = V_t \tag{7}$$

That is, if all income is allocated, the amount of capital invested up to any date is equal to the present value of the investment. Capital invested is a backward-looking concept, summarizing the history of the investment to date; present value is a forward-looking concept, summarizing the future.

An apparent paradox is contained in equation (7). The past is known and certain; the future is unknown and uncertain. How then can a value derived from the past (C_t) be equal to one derived from expectations of the future (V_t)? Suppose, for instance, that we revise our expectations of the future, so that we now expect higher receipts, R'_f, than before; will not the present value of the investment rise? The answer to this question depends on whether we allocate any of the expected increase in total income to the past; if we do not, then the rise in R_f is exactly offset by the rise in Y_f, income allocated to the future, and neither capital invested nor present value will change. If however we decide to allocate some of this rise in expected total income to the past or present, then both C_t and V_t will rise in equal amount. If dR_f is the expected rise in future receipts, this is also equal to the expected rise in total income (expenditures assumed constant), which is divided between the increase in income allocated to the past or present, dY_p, and the increase in income allocated to the future, dY_f. If then dC_t is the change in the capital invested and dV_t the change in present value,

$$dC_t = dY_p \tag{8}$$
$$dV_t = dR_f - dY_f = dY_p + dY_f - dY_f = dY_p \tag{9}$$

The identity of capital invested with present value therefore remains, no matter how we allocate expected changes in future income.[1]

Calculation of Profit

From equation (1) it is easy to show the relation between the expenditures, receipts, incomes, and valuations pertaining to any given year or accounting period. Thus, let R be the receipts, E, the expenditure, and Y, the allocated income or profit in any one year. Let R_p, E_p, Y_p be the sums of all receipts, expenditures, and incomes or profits allocated previous to that date. Let V be the capital invested (or present value of the investment) at the beginning and V', at the end of the year. Then,

[1] If we conceive the *present* as a mere mathematical point of time, all expenditures and receipts must lie on one side of it or the other. If, however, the present is an appreciable period we must adopt some convention in the definition of the amount of capital invested and of the present value of the investment. We shall assume that the present (as it shares with the past the property of being known, whereas the future is uncertain) will be included with the *past*.

$$V' = E_p + E - R_p - R + Y_p + Y$$
$$= V + E - R + Y$$

or
$$Y = (V' - V) + (R - E) \tag{10}$$

That is, the profit or income in any one year is equal to the increase in the value of the investment in that year, plus receipts and minus expenditures. This is the basis of the profit-and-loss statement of Table 24, page 341.

Various Methods of Valuation

All the various methods of valuation, whether used by accountants or not, are based on various methods of allocating profit. The difficulties and uncertainties of valuation also depend on this fact, for the total sum of profit which it is necessary to allocate between the past and the future is itself uncertain until the very date of liquidation of the enterprise. No matter what our *method* of allocating profit, therefore, as long as the method allocates any to past years the results of our valuation will be uncertain. A possible method of avoiding this uncertainty is the method of valuing *at cost*. By this method no attempt is made to allocate profit to past years, but it is all assumed to accrue at some future date or at the end of the process. In this case, therefore, the amount of capital invested is calculated by adding up the past outlays and subtracting any past revenues, without taking any *profit* items into account. Although this method has the virtue of avoiding uncertainty, it also avoids the main problem which the accountant has to solve. For the allocation of profit among various accounting periods is the principal task of the accountant —otherwise accountancy would be mere arithmetic.

Valuation at Market Rates of Interest

Another possible method of valuation is to allocate profit according to the prevailing market rates of interest, as in Table 55, lines 9 to 11. In this case again, to avoid uncertainty we must assume that the *rent* is all allocated to future dates, for the rent is an item whose magnitude can only be estimated. Again, this method avoids the main task of the accountant, which should be to allocate rent just as much as to allocate profit. The value at any date is equal to the *compounded* sum of past outlays and revenues. This must be equal to the *discounted* sum of expected future outlays and revenues—including rent. As the expected future outlays are uncertain, the sum of rent is also uncertain.

Valuation at Internal Rates of Interest

Where the accountant is practically certain of the course of future payments in an investment, he may perform the valuation according to the "constant rate of profit" or *exponential* method. Suppose, for instance, that he has to value a bond. Here he knows the past payments, and with almost equal certainty the future payments. He knows, therefore, the rate of profit on the bond over its whole lifetime. Hence he can calculate its value either by compounding the past payments (C_t) or by discounting the future payments (V_t), as in Table 55, lines 7 and 8. If the rate of profit at which calculations are made is the correct *internal* value, the compounded sum of past payments should, of course, equal the discounted sum of future payments.

Capital Loss and Gain

Yet another method is to allocate the expected profit according to some principle and then to make corrections as it appears that the anticipation was too favorable or too adverse. Suppose we had allocated income exponentially in Table 55, lines 7 and 8 up to date 5, and then discovered that the payment at date 6 was not going to be $1300 as we expected but only $1250. We have already allocated $244.38, so now there is only $5.62 left to allocate to the last year. We can recognize this situation by taking a capital loss in year 5. If we want to continue allocation at the old rate of return (4.4697 percent per annum) we take a capital loss equal to the discounted value of the deficiency of $50 at date 6, or $50/1.044697 = 47.860. Capital value in year 5 (line 8) is then reduced to $1196.516; this gives an income next year of $53.481, which makes the capital value $1196.52 + $53.48 or $1250, as required. The only real point in this procedure however is consistency of habit, as .044697 no longer represents the true internal rate of return. In a sense a more logical procedure would be to calculate the new overall rate of return and discount the capital loss at that rate. All these devices, however, merely boil down to stating that too much has been allocated to previous years, and the capital loss corrects for this by allocating a negative income equal to the excess allocations. Similarly a capital gain is recognition that too little has been allocated to previous years, so that it represents an extra income allocated to the year of this recognition to correct for this deficiency. Capital loss and gain then must be distinguished from the mere capital increase or decrease which occurs when revenues and expenditures are paid in or out, or normal incomes are allocated.

Valuation at Market Price

Another possible method of valuation, not much used in practice, is valuation at market price. Suppose that the investment of Table 55, line 1, was a common form of obligation or bond, which was bought and sold at all "ages," so that, at date 1, or at any other date, for instance, the holder could sell it in the market. Then we might value the investment at any date by the market value of the corresponding security, or document (bond) which entitles its owner to the payments of Table 55. Thus suppose the market value of the bond which represents the investment of Table 37 is shown in Table 55, line 14. The corresponding incomes are shown in line 15, and the annual rate of return in line 16. It is clear that this method is equivalent to valuation at market rates of interest, the market rate in any year being defined as the rate of return earned by buying the investment (bond) at the beginning of the year and selling it at the end. In this case we may note that the market value must converge on the end date value, since at the end of the 6th year, when the final $1300 is to be paid, nobody would buy it for more or sell it for less than $1300. This means that there is no economic rent when market rates of return are computed in this way, as all the income is allocated. No matter what the values at the intermediate dates, the sum of incomes must be $300.

Valuation at Cost or Market

A common rule in accountancy is to value objects at *cost or market, whichever is the lower*. Although this is an arbitrary rule, it has a certain basis in principle. In allocating an *uncertain* future profit or rent to present or to past years, it is better to be as conservative as possible. It is pleasanter for an investor to discover that he has a positive rent when a process is liquidated than to discover that his rent is negative and that profit which has been cheerfully allocated—and perhaps enjoyed—at past dates has not, in fact, been earned. If the market valuation is below cost, it is an indication that the market expects the process ultimately to be unprofitable. It is perhaps better, therefore, to allocate expected losses than to allocate expected profits. The cost or market rule, in effect, achieves this end, for by making cost the maximum it has the result of allocating *no* profits to past dates at all, as we have seen; and by valuing at market when market value is below cost, the result is to allocate anticipated losses to past dates.

DEPRECIATION AS A SPECIAL CASE OF VALUATION

Depreciation is the process of allocating the cost of durable goods to periods over the life of the goods rather than concentrating this cost in the period in which the goods are purchased. Thus, suppose we buy a machine for $1000, use it for four years, and then sell it for $200. The decline in the value of the machine from $1000 to $200 over the four years is depreciation. There are a number of different methods in use for computing the value in each year, the commonest of which is the straight-line method, in which the value diminishes by a fixed amount each year until it is exhausted.

The various methods are illustrated in Table 56. Here we suppose that the income or rent from the machine is $300 a year. In lines 1 and 2

TABLE 56.   DEPRECIATION

		Year				
	0	*1*	*2*	*3*	*4*	*Total*
1. Receipts		300	300	300	300+200	1400
2. Expenditure	1000					1000
3. Value	1000	0	0	0	200/0	
4. Income		−700	300	300	500	400
5. Value	1000	800	600	400	200/0	
6. Income		100	100	100	100	400
7. Value	1000	668.7	447.2	299.0	200	
8. Income		− 31.3	78.5	151.8	201.0	400
9. Value	1000	837	652	441	200	
10. Income		137	115	89	60	400

we show the record of receipts and expenditure, the income from the machine being counted as a receipt. In lines 3 and 4 we show the results of a failure to change any depreciation, the whole cost of the machine being charged as cost to the first year and the scrap value as income, to the last. We see in line 4 that this results in a sharp failure to allocate the income earned to the various years, with a gross underestimate in the first year and an overestimate in subsequent years. In lines 5 and 6 we show the results of straight-line depreciation, with an equal decline in value ($200) recorded each year. If the receipts are constant in each year this results in linear allocation of income. The rate of return on the value of the machine rises, of course, as the value declines, just as in Table 55, line 6, the rate of return falls under linear allocation as capital rises. This however, is a minor defect, if it is one at all. Lines 7 and 8 show a method of computing depreciation, still occasionally practiced, known as the reducing balance method, in which the value of the machine is reduced by a constant proportion each year; in this case the proportion has to be .6687 to reduce the value of the machine to $200 by year 4. If the receipts from the machine are constant this results in an underestimate of income in the early years and an overestimate in later years. If we want to show the same rate of return, or ratio of income to capital in each year this can be done as in lines 9 and 10. Here we calculate the internal rate of return on the payments table of lines 1 and 2, which is about 13.7 percent per annum. Then we allocate income to each year as 13.7 percent of the previous year's capital value. This is equivalent to yet another method of depreciation accounting, sometimes used, called the *annuity* method, though only when the internal rate of return is used as the rate of interest.

We must not confuse depreciation, as such, with another concept, which is the possible decline in the receipts from the machine with the passage of time as a result of its wearing out. Depreciation does not measure the wearing out of the machine, but merely its decline in value due to the allocation of the income from it evenly over the years. Even with the "one-hoss shay" of Holmes' poem,[2] which did not decline at all in services rendered until the last fatal moment, depreciation accounting would lead to a decline in its value. If the receipts from a machine decline with age, then if income is distributed evenly over the years the value of the machine will decline more sharply in early years. This is illustrated in Table 57. Here again we suppose a machine purchased for $1000 and

TABLE 57. DEPRECIATION WITH DECLINING INCOME

	0	1	2	3	4	Total
			Year			
1. Receipts		450	350	300	100+200	1400
2. Expenditure	1000					1000
3. Value	1000	650	400	200	200	
4. Income		100	100	100	100	400

sold after four years for $200; now, however, we suppose the machine declines in quality during the four years as in line 1. We note that, when the receipts from the machine are just equal to the income allocated, the machine ceases to depreciate, as in year 4. The other methods of depreciation of Table 56 could also be applied to this case.

THE VALUATION OF PUBLIC UTILITIES

Our analysis of profit and valuation throws a certain amount of light on the problem of the regulation of public utilities discussed in Chapter 23. We can put the problem in this form: How great a *sum* of profit can a monopoly be allowed to earn in a given year in order to give it a normal *rate* of profit? We see clearly that the answer to this question depends upon the valuation placed on the property of the monopoly at the be-

[2] Oliver Wendell Holmes, "The Deacon's Masterpiece"; or "The Wonderful One-Hoss Shay," *Collected Works*, vol. XII.

ginning and at the end of the year. The smaller these values, the smaller will be the *sum* of profit which is equivalent to a given *rate* of profit. If, for instance, the value at the beginning of the year is $1,000,000 and the allowed rate of profit is 5 percent per annum, the corporation will be allowed to earn $50,000. If, however, the valuation is $2,000,000, the corporation will be allowed to earn $100,000. Clearly, a regulated corporation will want to have itself assessed at a high rather than a low value for purposes of regulation. For purposes of taxation, of course the reverse may be the case.

Original and Reproduction Cost

Two methods of valuation are important in this connection. One is the method of valuation by *original* cost. Strictly, this method implies that no profits are allocated to past dates. It will therefore give a value which is low from the point of view of the corporation. The other method is valuation at *reproduction* cost.[3] That is, the property is valued not at what it originally cost but at what it would cost to reproduce at present prices of input. If prices have been rising, the reproduction cost is likely to be greater than the original cost, and is therefore likely to be favored by the corporation. But if prices have been falling, the original cost is likely to be greater and will be preferred by the corporation as a basis for rate making.

The Ideal Valuation

Probably the ideal valuation method for purposes of rate making is that of allocating profit to past dates according to the *normal* rates of profit at those dates, i.e., according to the method in Table 55, lines 9, 10, 11. The amount of capital invested up to the present should be reckoned by taking the sum of *all* past expenditure, whether for capital account or not, less the sum of *all* past receipts, plus all profits allocated to the past. This valuation ensures that the enterprise has earned normal profits up to the date of regulation. Then profit should be allowed in each year thenceforward at the normal rate. Such a method has one flaw which is present in all schemes for the regulation of monopolies. It assumes that the monopoly has a "right" to earn the normal rate of profit, no matter how poorly it is managed or how small the demand for its services. In perfect competition the rate of profit is itself an indication of the efficiency of management, for an enterprise which is poorly managed or which is producing an unwanted commodity suffers losses. But

---

[3] In both cases, of course, allowance is made for depreciation—i.e., for past income imputed to the equipment in question.

with a regulated monopoly the rate of profit, however defined, is no check on the efficiency of management.

Valuation and the Change in Price Level

One problem raised in an acute form by the regulation of monopoly, but present in any valuation problem, is that of reckoning with changes in the general level of prices. Accounting is usually carried on under the assumption that the value of the dollar remains unchanged, and we have made this assumption all through the present chapter. It is, however, one which is seldom justified in economic history. Consequently, accounting and valuation systems are constantly misleading us as to the "true" or *purchasing power* value of our property and profits. At a time of inflation the dollar value of all goods tends to rise, and hence the dollar value of all property tends to rise. This rise in the dollar value is frequently mistaken for profits, for, as we have seen, profits are the growth of the value of property. Such profits are quite illusory unless they are transformed into cash when prices reach a maximum. But they play an important part in the business cycle, for even the illusion of profits is enough to increase the demand for inputs and therefore to increase employment.

At a time of deflation of prices the value of property falls and the accounting system records losses. These losses may be as illusory as the profits of inflation, and yet they may have an equally potent effect. It is possible that a revision of our accounting systems in the direction of identifying these illusory profits and losses would materially reduce the fluctuations of business.

INVENTORY VALUATION

A difficult problem which can be illuminated in some degree by the above analysis is that of inventory valuation. The problem can best be illustrated with reference to a hypothetical wheat marketer whose experience is illustrated in Table 58. Lines 1, 2, and 3 give the data. It will be observed that we have a complete enterprise—that is, one that starts merely with money and finishes with money. Lines 4 and 5 show the wheat and money stocks on each date, assuming that the enterprise starts with $2000 of money. This grows in the course of the transactions to $4287, which is at a rate of 10 percent per week, or whatever is the unit time period. Exponential growth of the net worth over the whole period is shown in line 6, and the corresponding profit allocation in line 7. Each sum of profit is 10 percent of the preceding period's net worth; each period's net worth is the preceding period's net worth, plus 10 percent.

Line 8 shows the value of the wheat stock on this principle; it is the difference between the net worth (line 6) and the money stock (line 5).

TABLE 58. INVENTORY VALUATION

					Week				
	0	1	2	3	4	5	6	7	8
1. Price of wheat		2.00	2.50	3.00	2.00	3.00	4.00	2.00	2.587
2. Wheat bought (+) or sold (−)		+600	+200	−700	+500	+300	−700	+800	−1000
3. Money paid in (+) or out (−)		−1200	−500	+2100	−1000	−900	+2800	−1600	+2587
4. Wheat stock	0	600	800	100	600	900	200	1000	0
5. Money stock	2000	800	300	2400	1400	500	3300	1700	4287
6. Net worth (exponential)	2000	2200	2420	2662	2928	3221	3543	3897	4287
7. Profit (exponential)		200	220	242	266	293	322	354	390
Value of wheat:									
8. (Exponential)		1400	2120	262	1528	2721	243	2197	0
9. FIFO		1200	1700	250	1250	2150	600	2200	0
10. LIFO		1200	1700	200	1200	2100	400	2000	0
Net worth:									
11. FIFO	2000	2000	2000	2650	2650	2650	3900	3900	4287
12. LIFO	2000	2000	2000	2600	2600	2600	3700	3700	4287
Profit:									
13. FIFO		0	0	650	0	0	1250	0	387
14. LIFO		0	0	600	0	0	1100	0	587
Cost of wheat:									
15. FIFO				1450			1550		2200
16. LIFO				1500			1700		2000

LIFO and FIFO

In lines 9 and 10 we show the value of the wheat stock according to the two most common systems of inventory accounting: FIFO, which stands for "first in first out," and LIFO, which stands for "last in first out." According to the FIFO system (which has been dominant, and is now being challenged by LIFO), when stock is sold it is supposed that the oldest part of the stock is disposed of and hence the cost of the oldest part (first in) is charged against the revenue from the sales. This means that remaining stock is valued at the cost of the newest part—that is, the latest acquired. The alternative system, LIFO, charges the cost of the newest part of the stock against revenues, and hence the remaining stock is valued at the cost of the oldest part (see page 341).

Under both systems purchases of wheat do not affect the net worth, as the wheat is immediately valued at cost, so that the value of the wheat acquired is exactly equal to the money given up. Thus for the first two periods the net worth, as shown in lines 11 and 12, remains constant at 2000; the value of the wheat stock is simply the net worth less the money stock (line 5). In period 3, however, when there is a sale of wheat, a difference reveals itself. On the FIFO principle we suppose that the earliest acquisitions are sold. Of the 700 bushels sold it is supposed that 600 come from period 1, at a cost of $1200, and 100 from period 2, at a cost of $2.50, totaling $1450 (line 15). The remaining 100 bushels in the wheat stock (line 4) are therefore valued as if they had been acquired in period 2—that is, at $2.50 per bushel, or at $250 (line 9). On the LIFO principle, of the 700 bushels sold it is supposed that the latest are charged off—200 from period 2, at $2.50 ($500), and 500 from period 1, at $2 ($1000)—the total cost being $1500, and the value of the 100 bushels remaining in stock being $200, valued at $2, the price of period 1. Similarly, in period 6, on the FIFO principle the cost of the 700 bushels sold is 100 at $2.50 (period 2), 500 at $2 (period 4), and 100 at $3 (period 5), or $1550, the remaining 200 bushels being valued at the price of period 5 ($3)—that is, at $600 (line 9). On the LIFO principle we suppose that of the 900 bushels in stock in period 5, the late acquisitions are sold—300 in period 5 ($900) and 400 in period 4 ($800)—the total cost being $1700 (line 16), and the remaining 200 bushels being valued at the price of periods 4 and 2, that is, at $400 (line 10).

Then the net worth in line 11 is the sum of the value of wheat (line 9) and the money stock (line 5); the net worth in line 12 is the sum of the value of wheat of line 10 and the money stock. The profit figure in line 13 is the increase in net worth in each period from line 11; the profit figure in line 14 is the increase in net worth in each period from line 12.

GRAPHIC ILLUSTRATION. Table 58 is illustrated diagrammatically in Fig. 151. In the left-hand part of the figure time is measured along the horizontal axis, money values on the vertical axis. P_0P_8 shows the growth of net worth by exponential allocation. $P_0H_3L_3H_6I_6H_8P_8$ shows the growth of net worth by the LIFO method (line 12). $P_0H_3F_3K_6F_6K_8P_8$ shows the growth of net worth by the FIFO method. The dotted line shows the money stock; the difference between this line and the net worth line is the value of the wheat stock. In the right-hand side of the figure quantities of wheat are measured horizontally from O', and quantities of money vertically. The path $P'_0P_1P_2, \ldots P_8$ then shows the movement of money and wheat stocks in the course of the transactions. By ordinary accounting methods net worth stays at $O'P'_0$ until period 3, when it jumps to OH_3 (LIFO) or OK_3 (FIFO); it makes another jump in period 6 to OH_8 (LIFO) or OK_8 (FIFO) and another jump in period 8 to OP_8. By exponential allocation, net worth would rise gradually from P'_0 to P_8 following the values of the curve P_0P_8.

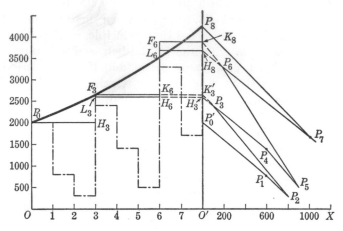

Fig. 151.   Inventory Valuation

Exponential Allocation as a Test

Exponential allocation is not, of course, practical, as it would involve a knowledge of the future which the accountant does not possess. Nevertheless it is a useful theoretical construct by which to test the various practical methods. The weakness of conventional accounting—a weakness which is just as characteristic of the LIFO as the FIFO method—is that it allocates no profits to periods involving purchasing, even though the movements of these periods (e.g., from P'_0 to P_2, or from P_3 to P_5) are absolutely necessary preparation for the subsequent gains. Where the period of turnover is less than the accounting period, however, as it generally is in the case with inventories, this weakness is not serious. Thus in the present example if the accounting period were 3 "weeks," the results given by conventional accounting would not differ sharply from those given by exponential allocation.

The advantage of LIFO over FIFO is that in some degree it solves the problem of the distortion of accounting results due to general inflation and deflation. We see this in the example, where there is a rather steady inflation up to period 6 and then a return to earlier levels. FIFO expresses this inflation in a steadily rising valuation of inventory; LIFO sticks closer to the original price level. Thus the net worth in period 6 is seen to be more inflated by FIFO (F_6) than by LIFO (L_6). Similarly, in a period of deflation FIFO results in unduly low values for inventory and hence unduly low profit figures. Neither LIFO nor FIFO, however, can result in the ideal valuation and allocation that would be possible if the future were known.

QUESTIONS AND EXERCISES

1. With time on the horizontal and dollars on the vertical axis, plot a series of graphs showing how capital grows with time in the various cases in Table 55; assume it increases with each expenditure or income allocated, and decreases with each receipt.

2. "The process of valuation is merely a convention in regard to the allocation of total profit among the accounting periods which an enterprise covers." Discuss.

3. "Call no man happy until he is dead: call no investment profitable until it is liquidated." Discuss.

4. If a process of production took no time, i.e., if there were no time interval between inputs and outputs, would it need any capital? If not, could it have any profits?

5. The following represents a time schedule of the outlays involved in building a bridge:

Year	0	1	2	3	4	5
Outlay ($000)	0	130	200	500	150	25

a. At what sum must the bridge be valued at the end of the fifth year in order to make the investment earn 5 percent per annum (interest reckoned annually)?

b. Suppose that the rate of interest in other investments were 4 percent per annum. What would be the total cost of the bridge, counting this 4 percent as normal profit to be included?

c. Suppose that the following schedule showed the rate of interest in other investments:

Year	1	2	3	4	5
Rate of interest (percent)	10	9	8	7	8

Suppose that the bridge was sold for $1,500,000 at the end of the fifth year. How much rent did the investment earn, reckoning the rent as accruing at the time of sale? What, under these circumstances, is the value of the un-completed bridge at the end of each year? What is the value of the rent at the end of each year? (Use the method in Table 37, lines 9-11, in calculating the values.)

6. The following represents the outlay-revenue series of an enterprise:

Year	1	2	3	4	5	6
Outlay ($000)	500	400	300	200	100	0
Revenue ($000)	0	100	100	344	600	966

Show, in a table like Table 55, that the rate of profit in this investment is 10 percent. Calculate the amount of capital invested and the present value of the investment for each date according to the following methods of allocation of profit: (a) all profit reckoned in the year 6; (b) all profit reckoned in the year 1; (c) linear allocation; (d) exponential allocation at

10 percent per annum. Show that in each case the amount of capital invested is equal to the value of the investment. Assume no interest on cash balances and an initial cash balance just enough to avoid debt.

7. "Valuation is the rock on which all regulation of monopoly splits." Discuss.

8. What problems are raised in the theory of valuation by the fact that the price level changes?

9. On a graph with time measured horizontally and dollars vertically plot the value of the machine in Table 56 according to the various methods of depreciation.

10. Construct a table like Table 56 in which the receipts from the machine decline by a constant percentage each year. Calculate the value of the machine according to the various methods of Table 56 and plot the results. Which method now seems to allocate income most uniformly?

11. The following table shows shifts in holdings of wheat and money of a single marketer in successive periods.

| Wheat stock (bushels) | 0 | 400 | 200 | 300 | 100 | 50 | 150 | 400 | 800 | 600 | 0 |
| Money stock (dollars) | 1000 | 200 | 700 | 400 | 1100 | 1300 | 1000 | 500 | 100 | 400 | 1629 |

Calculate and tabulate, for each period, (a) the quantities of wheat bought and sold, (b) the quantities of money received or spent, (c) the price of wheat. Show that exponential allocation at 5 percent per period will just allocate the total profit. Then calculate the net worth, the profit allocated, the value of the wheat stock, and the cost of wheat sold for each period (a) by the exponential method, (b) by the LIFO method, (c) by the FIFO method. Graph the results, and comment.

APPENDIX

THE MATHEMATICS OF COMPOUNDING AND DISCOUNTING

The most general definition of *compounding* is simply that of finding the sum of all past expenditures, less receipts, and plus profits or income allocated to the past; that is, it is simply the computation of capital invested, C_t, by equation (1), p. 655. Similarly *discounting* is finding the sum of future receipts, less expenditures, and less profits or income allocated to the future—that is, it is computing V_t by equation (6). Suppose now income is allocated exponentially at a constant rate of profit or interest, i, and suppose that net receipts $(R - E)$ in the year t is x_t, with a net receipts series $x_0, x_1 \ldots x_t \ldots x_n$. Then if capital invested in year t is C_t, we have

Year	Net Receipts	Capital Invested	Income Allocated
0	x_0	$- x_0$	
1	x_1	$- (x_0(1 + i) + x_1)$	$- x_0 i$
2	x_2	$- (x_0(1 + i)^2 + x_1(1 + i) + x_2)$	$- (x_0(1 + i)i + x_1 i)$

And by induction,

$$C_t = - [x_0(1 + i)^t + x_1(1 + i)^{t-1} + \ldots + x_{t-1}(1 + i) + x_t] \quad (1)$$

Similarly, if V_t is the present value of the investment, we have

Year	Net Receipts	Present Value	Income Allocated
N	x_n	0	$(V_{n-1})i$
N–1	x_{n-1}	$V_{n-1} = x_n - (V_{n-1})i$, so $V_{n-1} = x_n(1 + i)^{-1}$	$(V_{n-2})i$
N–2	x_{n-2}	$V_{n-2} = x_n + x_{n-1} - x_n (1 + i)^{-1}i - (V_{n-2})i$, so $V_{n-2} = x_n (1 + i)^{-2} + x_{n-1}(1 + i)^{-1}$	$(V_{n-3})i$

Again by induction,

$$V_t = x_n(1 + i)^{-n+t} + x_{n-1}(1 + i)^{-n+t-1} + \ldots + x_{t+1}(1 + i)^{-1} \quad (2)$$

We also have
$$C_n = - x_0(1 + i)^n + x_1(1 + i)^{n-1} \ldots + x_t (1 + i)^{n-t} +$$

$$x_{t+1}(1 + i)^{n-t+1} + \ldots + x_n = 0 \quad (3)$$

as all capital is presumably disinvested by the end of the process. This equation can be solved to give the internal rate of return, i. If it divided by $(1 + i)^{n-t}$ we get immediately, from (1) and (2)

$$C_t - V_t = 0 \quad (4)$$

This is, of course, simply a special case of equation (6), p. 655. The solution of equation (3) is often difficult, and has to be done by successive approximation.

The value of an initial sum, P_0, compounded at a rate of interest i for t years is

$$P_t = P_0(1 + i)^t \qquad (5)$$

This is the process of growth at a constant rate, also known as exponential growth. Suppose now we add the growth to the principal k times a year at a rate i/k per $1/k$ year; we now have

$$P_t = P_0(1 + \frac{i}{k})^{kt} \qquad (6)$$

As k approaches infinity, the expression $(1 + \frac{1}{k})^k$ approaches the exponential number e (approximately 2.718 . . .) and we get the expression for *continuous growth* at a constant rate, i,

$$P_t = P_0 e^{it} \qquad (7)$$

Equations (5) and (7) can also be expressed in the form

$$P_0 = P_t(1 + i)^{-t} \qquad (8)$$

$$P_0 = P_t e^{-it} \qquad (9)$$

P_0 is then called the discounted value of P_t. Under exponential allocation, compounding represents growth, and discounting, decline, at a constant rate.

We can easily see that some customary formulas for calculating the rate of interest in an investment are special cases of equation (3). Thus if we have an investment with one expenditure, P_0 and one receipt P_1 after an interval of one year, we have

$$P_0(1 + i) = P_1 \qquad \text{or} \qquad i = \frac{P_1 - P_0}{P_0} \qquad (10)$$

That is, the rate of interest or rate of return is the ratio of annual income to initial capital. Similarly suppose we have a *perpetuity*—that is, a bond which gives its owner a right to receive a given annual payment of x dollars forever. If this is bought for a sum P, equation (2) gives us

$$P(= V_0) = x(1 + i)^{-1} + x(1 + i)^{-2} + \cdots \text{ to infinity.}$$

Summing the infinite series we have

$$P = \frac{x}{i} \qquad \text{or} \qquad i = \frac{x}{P} \qquad (11)$$

That is, the rate of interest is the ratio of the annual income to the capital value of a perpetuity.

Even in the case of a perpetuity an investor who buys such a bond for P_0 and holds it for one year and sells it again for P_1, receiving one interest payment, x, will earn a rate of interest given by

$$i = \frac{P_1 - P_0 + x}{P_0} \tag{12}$$

Hence we get a paradoxical result that, when the rate of interest is falling, the price of such bonds will rise, and hence the annual rate of return is larger than it otherwise would be.

EXERCISES

1. Calculate the value of $1000, growing at 5 percent per annum interest, at the beginning of each of ten successive years, (a) compounding (adding interest) annually, (b) compounding quarterly, (c) compounding continuously (following equation (7)). Graph the results.

2. An investor buys a perpetuity giving him $5 on each January 1 for all future years. He pays $100. Suppose now the market price rises by $5 a year for five years, after which it remains stable at $125. Calculate the internal rate of return on this investment if he sells the bond (i) after 1 year, (ii) after 2 years, (iii) after 5 years, (iv) after 6 years, (v) after 10 years, (vi) after 25 years.

   (Note: Where equation (3) cannot be solved directly, it may be solved graphically by computing the value of the left-hand side for different values of i, plotting the results, and finding i where the line cuts the axis.)

CHAPTER 30

TIME IN ECONOMIC DECISIONS

Some of the most difficult problems relating to economic decision making center around the fact that the *time* or *date* of an event, relative to others, is an important economic variable. It is not only "what" that is important in economics, but also "when." Thus in production and in consumption we are concerned not only with the magnitude of inputs and outputs, expenditures and receipts, but with the "whens," that is, the dates of these various events. In some processes these dates may be fixed technically, and there is no problem of choice about them. In some processes of production, however, and in all processes of consumption, there is a choice of when—when to cut down a tree, or drink a wine, or slaughter a pig, or take a degree, or save or dissave. We can begin with problems involving production.

THE MATURING OF WINES

Take a simple example. Suppose a man buys new wine and lays it away in a cave, so that the only outlay involved in the process is the initial purchase of wine, say for $1000. Suppose the normal rate of profit is 10 percent per annum.

TOTAL COST. If the wine is kept in the cave for one year, the total cost of the process (in the technical sense of the word cost), i.e., the total outlay plus the normal sum of profit, is $1000 outlay plus $100 normal profit, or $1100. If the wine is kept in the cave for two years, the total cost will be $1000 outlay plus $(100 + 110) normal profit, or $1210, and so on for any number of years. This is shown in line 1 of Table 59. The total cost is therefore equal to the compounded sum of the initial outlay, compounded at the normal rate of interest.

TOTAL REVENUE. Suppose line 2 of Table 59 represents the total value of the wine in each year, if it is sold in that year for consumption.

TABLE 59. TIME EQUILIBRIUM

	Year						
	0	1	2	3	4	5	6
1. Total cost	1000	1100	1210	1331	1464.1	1610.51	1771.56
2. Total revenue	810	1110	1320	1481	1629.1	1775.51	1916.56
3. Net revenue	−190	10	110	150	165 —	165	145
4. Discount factor	1.0	1.1	1.21	1.331	1.464	1.610	1.772
5. Discount net revenue	−190	9.1	90.9	112.7 —	112.7	102.5	81.8
6. Cost differences		100	110	121	133.1	146.41	161.05
7. Revenue differences		300	210	161	148.1	146.41	141.05
8. Rate of cost increase (percent)		10	10	10	10	10	10
9. Rate of revenue increase (percent)		37	18.9	12.2	10	9	7.94
10. Internal rate of return (percent)		11	14.8	14.0	12.8	12.2	11.5

That is to say, if the wine were sold for consumption as soon as it was bought, it would fetch only $810; if it were sold for consumption one year after it was bought, it would fetch $1110, for it would be a better wine; after two years it would fetch $1320; and so on. That is, the figures in this row represent not a present value of a future sale for consumption but what the wine would fetch in a present sale for consumption.

Net Revenue a Maximum Where Marginal Cost of Time Equals Marginal Revenue of Time

The net revenue (line 3) is obtained by subtracting the total cost from the total revenue. It will be seen that the net revenue is a maximum between the fourth and fifth years, where the cost difference (line 6) is equal to the revenue difference (line 7). The cost difference we might call the marginal cost of time, for it is the increase in the total cost which results from a unit increase in the time taken. Similarly, the revenue difference might be called the marginal revenue of time, for it is the increase in the total revenue which results from a unit increase in the time taken.

But We Do Not Want to Maximize Net Revenue. Now, however, arises the question: Do we in fact, in this case, wish to produce so that the net revenue will be a maximum? Might a businessman not prefer a smaller net revenue to the maximum if it accrued to him *earlier?* The answer seems to be, yes, for if the normal rate of profit is, say, 10 percent, then if he received a net revenue of $100 in one year he could put it out to interest and make it turn into $110 by the next year. Obviously, then, if he were confronted with the choice between $100 this year and $100 of the same kind next year, he would prefer the $100 this year, for $100 this year is equivalent to $110 next year.

Maximization of the Discounted Net Revenue

If he wished to compare the net revenues that would accrue in different years, he would have to discount each net revenue back to some convenient date—usually the date of origin. Thus at a rate of 10 percent per annum the $10 net revenue of year 1 in Table 59 is equivalent to $10/1.1, or $9.10 in year 0; the $110 of year 2 is equivalent to $110/1.1^2, or $90.90 in year 0; and so on for all the other net revenues. So we obtain a table of *discounted* net revenues (line 5) by dividing the net revenue in line (3) by the discount factor $(1 + i)^t$ in line (4). Each of the figures in line (5) represents that sum which, put out at interest at the normal rate in the year 0, would grow into a sum equal to the corresponding net revenue. It is evident that the *discounted* net revenue reaches a maximum at a rather earlier date than the net revenue itself; in the table the discounted net revenue reaches a maximum of 112.6+ between the third and fourth years, while the net revenue reaches a maximum between the fourth and fifth years.

Where Rate of Revenue Increase Equals Rate of Cost Increase

Is there any condition, corresponding to the *marginal cost equals marginal revenue* condition, which will tell us when the *discounted* marginal revenue is a maximum? It is not difficult to find such a condition, and it is illustrated in lines 8 and 9 of Table 59. Here we have calculated two quantities named the rate of cost increase (line 8) and the rate of revenue increase (line 9). The rate of cost increase is the rate at which the total cost increases from year to year. It is found by dividing the absolute increase in cost between two dates by the total cost at the earlier date. In this case the rate of cost increase is 10 percent per annum—the rate of interest. The rate of revenue increase is similarly found by dividing the absolute increase in revenue between two dates by the total revenue at the earlier date. Thus between dates 0 and 1 the rate of revenue increase is 300/810, or 37 percent; between 1 and 2 it is 210/1110, or 18.9 percent; between 2 and 3 it is 161/1320, or 12.2 percent; and so on. It will now be observed from the example that the discounted net revenue is at a maximum when the rate or revenue increase is equal to the rate of cost increase. In the present example this point lies between dates 3 and 4. This is a general principle, even with outlays and receipts of many dates. In the above case where the only outlay is at the initial date, it reduces to the proposition that the discounted net revenue is at a maximum when the rate of revenue growth is equal to the normal rate of interest or profit.

GRAPHIC ILLUSTRATION. The graphic proof of the last-mentioned proposition is shown in Fig. 152. Here time is measured in the horizontal,

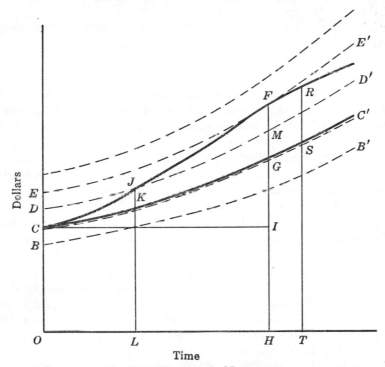

Fig. 152. The Period of Investment

dollars, in the vertical direction. The dashed lines *BB'*, *CC'*, *DD'*, etc., represent a system of growth curves accumulating from various present values, *OB*, *OC*, *OD*, etc. Growth in each case proceeds at any time at the current normal rate of interest. Thus, *LK* is what a sum *OC* would grow into if it were put out at compound interest in the period between time *O* and time *OL*. We do not have to assume a constant rate of growth, i.e., a constant rate of interest; but the rates of growth in all the growth curves at any one date must be the same, and equal to the rate of interest on that date.[1]

Suppose that in a process like the laying down of wines, an outlay

[1] In the figure, continuous growth (compounding) is assumed for the sake of convenience.

of OC is made at the date O. The total cost of the wine at any future date will be given by the growth curve CC'. This is the total cost curve, for the total cost at any date is equal to the initial outlay plus accumulated interest. The interest may be regarded as a *revenue foregone* because of the fact that a sum OC is locked up in the form of wine when it might have been put out to interest. If, for instance, the wine is kept until the date H, the total cost is HG $(HI + IG)$. $HI(= OC)$ represents the original outlay and IG represents the interest which could have been earned on the sum OC if it had not been spent on the wine. We suppose in this example that once the wine has been bought there are no further outlays.

The curve $CJFR$ then represents the total revenue curve. At any time, say T, the ordinate of this curve, TR, represents the total revenue obtained by the sale of the wine originally bought at the time O. If there are selling costs, TR represents the total production revenue. We assume that the total revenue (i.e., the value of the wine) rises as the wine matures, but at an eventually decreasing rate. If the wine were sold at the date L, the total revenue would be LJ, the total cost LK, and the net revenue KJ. The discounted value at the date O of LJ is OD, where JD is a growth curve. The discounted value of LK at date O is OC, for CK is a growth curve. CD, therefore, is the discounted net revenue at date O.

There will be some growth curve, EFE', which will just touch the revenue curve. Let F be the point where it touches, HF the total revenue, HG the total cost, GF the net revenue at that date. The discounted net revenue is CE. CE is the maximum discounted net revenue at date O which can be obtained with the revenue curve $CJFR$.

It can easily be shown that the net revenue (undiscounted) is at a maximum at a later date than H. The rate of growth of the revenue curve at F (the rate of revenue growth) must be equal to the rate of growth of the cost curve at G (the rate of cost growth). But HF is greater than HG. The absolute increase of revenue at F is therefore greater than the absolute increase of cost at G. For example, if the rate of growth at F and at G is 10 percent per annum, and HF is \$1481, the revenue is increasing by an amount equal to \$148.10 per annum. If HG is \$1331 the cost is increasing by an amount equal to \$133.10 per annum. At the date H, then, the revenue is increasing faster than the cost, and the net revenue, GF, is therefore increasing. The maximum net revenue, RS, is found at a date T, where absolute increase of revenue and of cost are equal. The discounted value of RS at date O is clearly less than that of FG, even though RS is greater than FG, for R evidently lies on a lower growth curve than F.

Maximization of the Internal Rate of Return

Another possible criterion of profitability is the internal rate of return in the enterprise. Line 10 of Table 59 shows the internal rate of return for each period of investment; the internal rate of return, i, being given in this case by the formula $C(1 + i)^t = R$. C is the total initial outlay ($1000) in this case; R is the total revenue produced by the sale of the wine; t is the period of investment. Thus after waiting three years we have $1000(1 + i)^3 = 1481$, whence $i = 14.0$ percent. In the table the maximum internal rate of return is 14.8 percent at a period of 2 years.

The diagrammatic solution of the problem of maximizing the internal rate of return is shown in Fig. 153. For convenience in drawing, the costs and revenues are measured on a logarithmic scale, so that curves

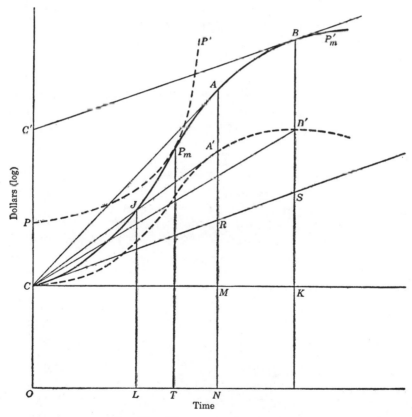

Fig. 153. Time-Production Equilibria

of uniform rate of growth become straight lines. $CJAB$ is the revenue curve showing the growth in the value of output resulting from an initial outlay OC. The internal rate of return at any point J at a time OL is the average rate of growth of capital in the period, which in the logarithmic diagram is equal to the slope of the line CJ. To find the time ON at which the internal rate of return is a maximum, we draw CA to touch the revenue curve at A; the slope of CA clearly represents the highest average rate of growth of capital possible on the given revenue curve. If the normal rate of interest is less than this, the point of maximum internal rate of return is at a shorter period of investment than the point of maximum discounted net revenue, B, for B is the point at which the slope (rate of growth) of the revenue curve is equal to the rate of interest; and if the rate of revenue growth is declining, B will lie further along the revenue curve than A will.

THE OPTIMUM TIME PATTERN

The question of the optimum time pattern of a process admits of no easy answer. We can postulate a formal solution to the problem if we suppose that in Fig. 153 we measure *utility* vertically above the plane of the paper, and have a utility surface in three dimensions, the contours of which would be *time indifference curves* or curves of equal time preference. If one of these, PP_mP' touches the opportunity boundary $CJAB$ at P_m, this is the optimum position. The time indifference curve is plotted by asking the decision maker a series of questions of the type: Would you rather have OP dollars now, or TP_m dollars at a time OT? If he says he would rather have $\$OP$ now, then P is on a higher indifference curve than P_m; if he says he would rather have $\$TP_m$ at the date T, P_m is on a higher indifference curve than P; if he is indifferent, P and P_m are on the same indifference curve. By a series of such questions we could in principle plot the whole preference map of indifference curves. The slope of such an indifference curve at any point (on a log scale) is called the *rate of time preference*: it has the dimensions of a rate of growth or return, say, percent per annum. It is the rate at which values must grow into the future to make the future values psychologically equivalent to the present value. If the rate of time preference is, say, 10 percent per annum, this means that $110 next year is just psychologically equivalent to $100 now. As Irving Fisher[2] pointed out the rate of time preference is a measure of "impatience." The more impatient a man is, the more likely

[2] Irving Fisher, *The Theory of Interest*, New York, Macmillan, 1930.

he is to say, "$P now," in response to the question, whether he would rather have $P now or $P' next year, and the larger must the ratio P'/P be before he will say, "I don't care," at which point his rate of time preference is $(P' - P)/P$.

If now we suppose that the rate of time preference of the decision maker is constant and always equal to the market rate of interest, likewise assumed constant, then the time indifference curves will be parallel straight lines, such as $C'B$, and B will be the optimum position; the position of maximum present value (OC') at market rates of interest is the optimum. This rather heroic assumption may have some plausibility if we suppose that there is a perfect market in loans, so that our decision maker can borrow or lend as much as he likes at the market rate of interest. In such a case, he will expand his borrowings (or lendings) to the point where his rate of time preference is equal to the rate of interest. It can be argued also, however, that it is the maximum internal rate of return, as given by the slope of CA, which determines the decision maker's rate of time preference, for this is the highest rate at which his own capital can grow. In this case CA will be one of a set of parallel indifference curves, and A will be the optimum point, where the rate of revenue growth equals the internal rate of return. In the more general case of the indifference curve PP_mP', the optimum is defined by the condition that the rate of revenue growth should equal the rate of time preference. This is the meaning of the tangency of the curves PP_mP' and CJP_mAB at P_m, but we make no restrictive assumptions about the rate of time preference. Thus, as we have drawn PP_mP', the rate of time preference increased with time—that is, we become more impatient in contemplating more distant futures, which seems not unreasonable.

There is a tricky point involved in the nature of time decisions. If we are deciding at time O when to cut down the tree or broach the cask, our time preference at P_m may be quite high, as in the figure, and our impatience forces a shortening of the period of investment to OT. Once we have arrived at P_m, however, our actual time preference may be no greater than at P; we will change our mind and continue the process to a point such as P'_m, where the rate of revenue growth is equal to a lower rate of time preference such as at P. The problem is complicated by the fact that the rate of time preference at any one moment is affected by the liquidity position and liquidity preference of the decision maker. A decision to "reap" the investment is in effect a decision to exchange nonliquid for liquid assets. If the utility of liquid assets happens to be high, therefore, either because of their scarcity or because, say, a deflation is expected, time preference will also be high—"money now" will look much more attractive than "money then."

Income and the Internal Rate of Return

If the process is continuously repeated then the internal rate of return represents the overall rate of growth of capital invested if withdrawals are not made, or the income per unit of capital, if withdrawals are made. This is shown in Fig. 154. The curve CA_1B_1 is the revenue curve starting from an outlay OC. Suppose now that at the time ON_1, when the selling value of the investment is N_1A_1, the investment is sold and the proceeds are reinvested in the same process. The outlay in the repeated process is N_1A_1, which will grow following the curve A_1WA_2, which is the same

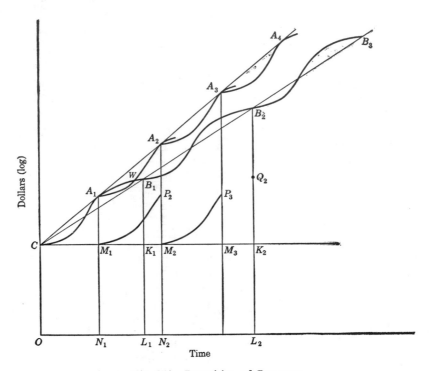

Fig. 154. Repetition of Processes

curve as CA_1, since the vertical axis is drawn on a logarithmic scale. Similarly, at A_2 the investment may be sold, and the proceeds reinvested, growing to A_3; so we get an investment curve $CA_1A_2A_3A_4$, etc., which represents how the total value of the capital will grow if it is continually reinvested after a period of investment equal to ON_1. Similarly, the line $CB_1B_2B_3$ shows how the value of the capital will grow if it is reinvested after a period of investment OL_1. It is evident that continually reinvested capital grows faster when the period of investment is ON_1 than it does for any other period of investment, even though there may be certain intervals, as between A_1 and W, where the value under a longer period of investment is greater.

Maximization of Income Stream

It is not difficult to see from Fig. 154 what period of investment in a repeated process gives the maximum income stream. Suppose that the entrepreneur at the conclusion of each process withdraws the growth in capital from the enterprise and starts each repetition of the process with the amount of capital with which it began. That is to say, if the period of investment is ON_1 in Fig. 154, the entrepreneur will withdraw an amount M_1A_1 from the enterprise at the time N_1 and will start again with an amount of capital N_1M_1, equal to OC. The course of the capital invested then follows the saw-toothed line $CA_1M_1P_2M_2P_3M_3$, . . . etc. M_1A_1, M_2P_2, M_3P_3 represent a succession of income payments at regular intervals each equal to ON_1. The time-rate of income is therefore M_1A_1/CM_1, or the slope of the line CA_1. If the period of investment were CK_1, the income payments would be K_1B_1, K_2Q_2, at intervals equal to CK_1. The rate of income is the slope of the line CB_1, or K_1B_1/CK_1. It is clear that maximizing the internal rate of return at A_1 yields a higher income payments stream than maximizing the discounted net revenue at B_1.[3]

Maximization of Net Income Stream

Even if interest is deducted from the receipts of the enterprise, it can be shown that the maximum net income stream from a repeated investment is given when the internal rate of return is maximized. Thus, in Fig. 153, the interest curve is CRS; this shows the interest cost at each period of investment. The dashed curve $CA'B'$ is the net revenue curve and is derived from the revenue curve CAB by subtracting the interest cost at each point; thus $AA' = RM$, and $BB' = SK$. If now CA touches the curve CAB, it can be shown that CA' likewise touches the curve $CA'B'$.[4] The net income stream of a repeated investment of period CM

---

[3] It should be observed that the above argument is only strictly accurate if the vertical axis is measured on an arithmetic, not a logarithmic, scale. The period of investment which yields the largest income-payment stream is, therefore, somewhat smaller than that which yields the most rapid rate of capital growth. The problem arises because we are measuring growth continuously; if it is measured discontinuously, e.g., every year, and if the period of investment is less than the period of compounding, the two criteria give the same result.

[4] *Let* $OC=c$, $NA=v_1$, $ON=t_1$. Then the equation of the line CA is $v=c+\dfrac{v_1-c}{t_1}t$, v being revenue, t the period of investment. Similarly, if i is the rate of interest, the equation of CA' is $v=c+\dfrac{v_1-c-it_1}{t_1}t$. If n is the net revenue given by the curve $CA'B'$

is therefore $A'M/CM$, or tan $A'CM$. This is clearly the greatest net income stream, as CA' has a greater slope than any other line from C to the curve $CA'B'$, such as CB'.

Rent in an Investment

The economic rent, in an investment of the foregoing type, is that annual charge which will reduce the maximum internal rate of return to the *normal* rate of interest. This is shown in Table 60. Lines 1 and

TABLE 60. RENT AND TIME EQUILIBRIUM

	Year						
	0	*1*	*2*	*3*	*4*	*5*	*6*
1. Total Cost	1000	1100	1210	1331	1464.1	1610.5	1771.6
2. Total Revenue (not repeated)	810	1110	1320	1481	1629.1	1775.5	1916.6
3. Total revenue (repeated in year 2)			1320		1742.4		2300.0
4. Total revenue (repeated in year 3)				1481			2193.4
5. Net revenue (not repeated)		10	110	150	165	165	145
6. Net revenue (rent) per annum		10	55	50	41.2	33	24.2

2 are the same as in Table 59. In line 3 we show what will happen if the wine is sold every second year and the proceeds reinvested in more wine. In two years $1000 grows to $1320; reinvested, therefore, the $1320 will grow to $(1320)^2$ ($= 1742.4$) in another two years; if this is sold and reinvested, it will grow to $(1320)^3$ ($= 2300.0$) in six years; and so on. In line 4 this is compared with what would happen if the wine is allowed to mature for three years, then sold and the proceeds reinvested for another three years. The rate of growth is slower, as we have gone past the maximum internal rate of return, which in this example is at two years. Thus we see that the period of investment for which the discounted net revenue is a maximum is not that which gives the most rapid rate of growth of capital. Line 5 shows the total net revenue for each period of investment—it is the same as line 3 of Table 59. Line 6 shows the net

---

we have $n=v-it$. We have, therefore, $\dfrac{dn}{dt}=\dfrac{dv}{dt}-i$. At the point A the slope of the curve CAB is the same as the slope of the line CA; that is, $\dfrac{v_1-c}{t_1}$. At A', therefore, the slope of the curve $CA'B'$ is $\dfrac{v_1-c}{t_1} - i$, which is the same as the slope of the line CA'. The line CA' is therefore tangent to the curve $CA'B'$.

revenue per annum, obtained by dividing each figure of line 5 by the corresponding number of years. This is the economic rent which corresponds to each period of investment. We see that the maximum economic rent is at year 2, which is also the maximum internal rate of return. If a rent of $55 per annum—or, what is almost the same thing, $110 every two years—is charged against the process the total revenue in year 2 will be $1210 and the internal rate of return (less rent) will be 10 percent, the normal rate of interest. If the investor adopted a three-year period of investment at such a rent, the revenue would be 1481 − (3 × 55) or $1316. This represents a less than 10 percent return on the investment. If therefore the maximum rent is charged, the investor is forced to adopt that period of investment at which the internal rate of return is maximized.

The Rate of Interest and the Period of Investment

The above analysis throws some light on the disputed question of the effect of a change in the market rate of interest on the period of investment. If it is assumed that the optimum period of investment is that at which the present value of future net revenue is a maximum, then, assuming a diminishing rate of value growth with increase in the period of investment, a fall in the rate of interest will lengthen the period of investment. Thus, in Fig. 163, a fall in the rate of interest shows itself in a flattening of the line *C'B*, which will clearly move *B* farther out and will raise the discounted net revenue *CC'*. Here we assume in effect that *C'B* is an indifference curve and that the rate of time preference is equal to the market rate of interest. If, however, the rate of time preference is independent of the market rate of interest, or if we suppose it depends on the internal rate of return rather than on the market rate, then a change in market rates should not affect the period of investment. If the rate of interest exceeds the internal rate of return, of course, the investment will not be made, or will eventually be abandoned. A fall in the rate of interest therefore permits investments to be made which have maximum internal rates of return lower than those now undertaken, and if the period of investment in these investments is not the same as the average period in previous investments, the fall in interest rates will change the average period of investment through the change in the number of investments—an effect somewhat analogous to the industry effect of page 442. There is no reason to suppose, however, that those investments which are now just below the line of profitability at existing rates of interest have either longer or shorter periods of investment than those which are now above the line. A fall in the rate of interest may make more bridge building profitable or it may make more retailing profitable—one with a long, the other with a short, period of investment. It seems impossible to predict, therefore, on a priori grounds, what will be the direction of change of the period of investment under the impact of a fall in interest rates.

More Complex Cases

The case which we have been discussing so far is a very simple one, with a single input and a single output, the value of the output depending on the period of investment. The problem becomes much more complicated when we introduce more inputs and outputs and make the value of inputs as well as of outputs depend on their date of application; and the discontinuities involved make the problem intractable to mathematical analysis. Some indication of the type of problem involved is given in Fig. 155. CQA is a net revenue curve after the deduction of interest, like the curve $CA'B'$ in Fig. 153. Now let us suppose that an outlay of QR at the point Q will result in a new net revenue

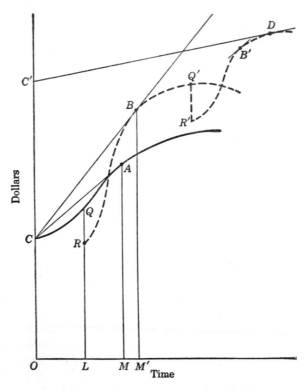

Fig. 155. Complex Time-Production Equilibra

curve *RBQ'*, the net revenue being the market value of the investment less accrued interest on all previous outlays, less the outlays themselves. The curve *CQRB* represents the curve of growth of the *own capital* of the entrepreneur if liquidated at each date at market prices. If now the tangent *CB* has a greater slope than the tangent *CA*, it will be profitable to make the outlay *QR* and to expand the period of investment from *OL* to *OM*, assuming a time preference equal to the internal rate of return. It should be observed, however, that the point *B* does not have to be at a greater period of investment than the point *A;* it would be easy to draw the curve *RB* so that *B* is to the left of *A* instead of to the right. The outlay *Q'R'* is clearly not profitable, as the resultant net revenue or own capital curve never reaches the line *CB*. We may think of the entrepreneur, therefore, standing with his eye at the point *C* looking up at a variety of possible own capital curves of a saw-toothed nature; the most profitable one is that which makes him crane his head farthest —that which has the highest ridge within his range of vision. The problem is complicated by the fact that there may be innumerable possible outlays of various times and sizes and characters, all of which have different effects on the own capital curve. Because of this and because of the discontinuous nature of the curve, it is not possible to make any very simple or secure mathematical generalizations. Nevertheless, it can be seen that the generalizations reached on our simple assumptions are likely to prevail in the more complex case, also. Thus, if there is maximization of discounted net revenue, *CC'* this can be regarded as a raising of the vantage point from which the entrepreneur views the enterprise from *C* to *C';* it is clear that the entrepreneur is now likely to be able to "see further" along his ridges, and will move from *B* to the point *D*, the slope of *C'D* being the market rate of interest. This may not happen, however, as the rise may be insufficient to bring a further ridge into view.

Effects of Rising Costs

With the aid of this analysis we can give some account of the probable effects of rising prices, wages, or other costs on the period of investment. If the price of the product is rising, this means that the own capital or net revenue line, *CQRB* . . . etc., has a generally steeper slope, for the value of the physical capital is here calculated at current market values. If the rise in price is at a constant rate per annum, the effect on the own capital curve is exactly the same as a fall in the rate of interest. There is no reason to suppose any change in the period of investment, for although the own capital curve becomes generally steeper, there is no reason to suppose that further ridges are thereby brought into view; as each ordinate changes by a constant proportion, a mere adjustment in the vertical scale of the diagram would restore it to its former condition. If, however, discounted net revenue is maximized, a rise in the price of the product or a fall in the rate of interest is likely to increase the period of investment, as from the vantage point of C' a rise in the whole range may bring more distant ridges into view.

Consider now the effects of rising prices of input (e.g., wages), other things being equal. The later outlays are now larger than they would have been by the extent of their lateness. The result is to sink the later ridges of the own capital curve more than the earlier; it may easily happen, therefore, that the later ridges sink out of "sight" and the period of investment contracts. Even more difficult to deal with is the situation when the outlays are variable in time position and affect the revenue-growth curves. A shift in relative time values of input —e.g., rising or falling wages—may then upset the whole system of possible own capital curves and we may find that a completely different arrangement of inputs and outputs now yields a maximum rate of return.

How Much Must Previous Analysis Be Modified?

The foregoing discussion raises the question how far the analysis of earlier chapters must be modified in view of our new principles of maximization. We have seen that the maximization of net revenue is not a proper criterion of profitability, and that the internal rate of return may be a better measure. Must we conclude, therefore, that the analysis of the previous chapters must be thrown overboard? Is the maximization of net revenue a useful first approximation, or must it be discarded altogether in favor of more accurate principles?

Fortunately, all is not lost; we do not have to jettison the painfully acquired results of our previous analysis. If the relative dates of the outlays and revenues of a process are *not* variable, the internal rate of return, the discounted net revenue, and the crude net revenue are at a maximum under identical conditions. Happily, a great many—indeed, the majority —of processes fall into this category, where the time structure of production is a fact given to the entrepreneur and is therefore not a matter of choice. Even in the cases of processes like forestry, the maturing of wines and cheeses, the raising of meat animals, etc., where the variability of the period of investment is important, most of the conclusions of the previous analysis are to be modified rather than destroyed.

Suppose, for instance, that we had a time-revenue curve as in Fig. 156. The net revenue, NA, the discounted net revenue CC', the internal

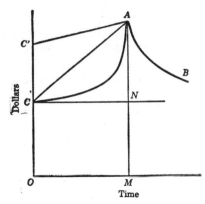

Fig. 156. Technically Determined Investment Period

rate of return $\left(\dfrac{MA}{OC}\right)^{\frac{1}{t}} - 1$, and the annual rent, $\dfrac{NA}{CN}$, are the clearly all maximized at the period of investment, $CN(=t)$. The period of investment in such a case may be said to be technically determined; variations in inputs and outputs, etc., may vary the height of A, AM, but will not vary its date, OM. Any combination of variables, therefore, which maximizes AN automatically maximizes both the discounted net revenue and the internal rate of return. Fortunately for a great many processes this is the case, and we do not need to worry about the problem of the period of investment at all.

Present Values and Time Discounting

Whenever we make an economic decision we have to compare revenues against costs, benefits against disutilities, gains against losses. Frequently these revenues and costs lie in the future—in a literal sense they always do, though some may be in the psychological present. The problem of *discounting* these revenues and costs therefore always tends to arise, for it is the present value equivalent of them which we are really comparing. Thus when we employ a man for a wage it is the present value of his marginal revenue product which is the significant comparison. If his employment results in a revenue of $100 one year from now, we are more likely to employ him at a given wage than if he produces a revenue of $100 ten years from now. Under strict profit maximization we will only employ him if the estimated present value equivalent of his product is greater than or equal to his wage, or more exactly, his present marginal cost to us. Even his marginal cost may include some future elements which must be discounted. Similarly, when we are considering producing a product, it is the present value of the marginal revenue which must be compared with the present value of the marginal cost; with this understood, most of the conclusions of the elementary theory of maximizing behavior still hold. The difficult problem is what determines the rate of discounting: is it some market rate of interest, the internal rate of return, or some personal psychological time preference, or impatience?

Discounting for Uncertainty

Furthermore, we discount not only for simple time elapsing, but also for uncertainty; the present value equivalent of an uncertain $100 next year is likely to be less than the present value equivalent of a certain $100 next year, by an amount which may depend not only on the expected value or average probability but also on the distribution of these probabilities. Thus if p_i is the probability of getting a sum R dollars the expected value is Rp_i. The expected value of (1) a 99 percent chance of getting $101.01 and and a 1 percent chance of getting nothing; (2) a 50 percent chance of getting $101 and a 50 percent chance of getting $99; (3) a 1 percent chance of getting $10,000 and a 99 percent chance of getting nothing; and (4) a 1 percent chance of getting $1,000,000, a 1 percent chance of losing $990,000, and a 98 percent chance of getting nothing are all equal to $100. Nevertheless the present value equivalent in the minds of most people would vary widely. Chance 1 is a sure thing involving some risk; a person with great confidence in his own luck might pay close to $100 for it; on the other hand, those who greatly fear losses might not be willing to pay very much, for fear even of the small chance of losing what they pay. Chance 2 is well hedged; losses as well as gains are small, and anyone will pay at least $99 for it, neglecting time discounting. Chance 3 is a long shot; persons with a sweepstakes mentality are evidently persuaded to pay *more* than the expected value for such an opportunity. Chance 4 is a sort of Russian roulette with a small chance of very big gains or very big losses; the timid will hardly take this at any price, the desperate might stake their all on it.

In any decision, then, the subjective present net value (SPNV) of each alternative can be postulated, and it is certainly reasonable to suppose that the alternative with the highest SPNV will be selected. Thus, we will cut down a tree when the SPNV cut exceeds the SPNV uncut; we will sell a stock when the SPNV of the money received exceeds the SPNV of the stock unsold; we will commit suicide when the SPNV of death exceeds that of life. This is a principle of beautiful generality, and very little content, and we must regard all our specific models as attempts to limit its generality and increase its content.

SCALE AND SUBSTITUTION IN TIME

One such limited but useful model is found in J. R. Hicks's *Value and Capital*.[5] In this the theory of substitution effects and scale effects is carried over to the analysis of the time positions of inputs and outputs by regarding the inputs or output of each date as a *separate item*. We must, for example, regard labor in one year as a different input from labor in another year, even if they are identical kinds of labor. Then the conclusions which we drew from our timeless analysis apply closely to the time analysis. For instance, we concluded that a rise in the price of one input had a substitution effect causing the substitution of the lower-priced input for the higher and a scale effect causing a general reduction of scale. This is true of two or more inputs which differ in *time* as well as of inputs which differ in kind. Suppose that wages are expected to be lower next year. This will cause a substitution effect—a substitution of next year's cheap labor in place of this year's dear labor—and a scale effect—a general increase in the scale of the enterprise. The substitution effect will operate to diminish the quantity of labor bought this year, and the scale effect will operate to increase it.

Quantity of Input Bought Dependent on Anticipated Prices

Thus we reach the important conclusion that the quantity of labor which will be bought this year depends not merely upon the price in this year but upon what employers *think* the price will be next year and in future years. The effect of their anticipation of next year's price upon this year's labor depends on two things: first, on the degree to which this year's labor can be substituted for next year's labor, upon which depends the magnitude of the substitution effect; and second, on the importance of labor in the process, on which depends the scale effect. It will be observed that the substitution effect and the scale effect in the case of a change in expected *future* prices work in opposite directions as far as the effect on the *present* purchases is concerned. Where, therefore, the substitution effect is great, an expected fall in wages will cause a decrease in the purchase of current labor. This is most likely to be the case where the input results in the creation of an easily storable commodity; for then, if labor is expected to be cheaper next year, less labor will be employed this year, inventories will be de-

[5] *Value and Capital*, 2nd ed., New York, Oxford University Press, 1946.

pleted, and the stock will be replaced next year when labor is cheap. If, on the other hand, the substitution effect is small, where next year's input cannot be anticipated by producing for stock this year and where the input in question plays a large part in the business, it is conceivable that the scale effect may outweigh the substitution effect, and an expected decrease in the price of next year's input actually cause an increase in the purchase of this year's as well as of next year's input.

Production of Output Also Dependent on Anticipated Prices

Exactly similar considerations apply to the production and sale of output. If the price of next year's output is expected to be lower than that of this year's output, there will be a substitution effect—output will tend to be concentrated into this high-priced year—and there will be a scale effect—a general reduction in scale. Again the substitution effect will bring about an increase in this year's output, and the scale effect will bring about a decline in this year's as well as next year's output. Which effect will be stronger will again depend on how far the output is storable. If it can easily be stored it will be easy to increase the sales of one year at the expense of another. The substitution effect, therefore, will be strong. If a rise in price is expected, there will be a diminution in the amount which sellers are willing to sell in the present. Similarly, if the process is such that the dates at which output appears can easily be changed, the substitution effect will also be prominent, and the expectation of a rise in price will cause a diminution of current sales. But if the commodity cannot be stored and if the dates of output cannot easily be changed, the scale effect will outweigh the substitution effect. Then an expected rise in price may cause a rise in current output.

Effects of Expected Rise or Fall, Unsymmetrical

It is possible that the effects of an expected rise and of an expected fall in price may not be symmetrical. It is probably easier to transfer sales of output from the present to the future than it is to transfer them from the future to the present. Sales can be postponed by storing or by slowing up the process of production. To some extent they can be transferred to the present from the future by selling out of stock or by speeding up production, but there are obvious limits to these operations. The substitution effect in the case of output, therefore, will be greater when a rise in price is expected than when a fall is expected. The anticipation of a future rise in price will probably lead to lessened sales of output now —sellers "wait for the rise." The anticipation of a future fall in price is rather less likely to lead to increased sales now, as current sales may not be so readily expansible.

THE IMPORTANCE OF EXPECTATIONS

It is difficult to exaggerate the importance of expectations in determining the course of economic life. From the foregoing it is clear that the quantity of any commodity which people are willing to buy or sell depends not merely upon its current price but also on what people believe will be the future course of its price. This fact does not destroy the concept of a demand or supply schedule, of course. It does mean, however, that one of the principal determinants of the position of any given demand or supply schedule is the expected future price of the commodity in question and of other commodities. We draw a demand or supply curve on the assumption that expectations do not change; if they do change, the fact is reflected in a shift in the demand or supply curves. The demand for any commodity depends also upon our expectations of the *results* of the consumption or use of the commodity.

This is particularly true of those commodities which are inputs of a process of production, although, as we have seen, all commodities are really inputs of some process or other. Our demand for ice cream depends on our expectation of satisfaction to be derived from its consumption. Likewise, the demand for labor depends wholly on the expectation of future benefits to be received as a result of the employment of labor. Labor is employed because the present value of its marginal productivity is at least equal to its wage. But the present value of its marginal productivity is not a realized fact; it is an opinion, an idea, an expectation in the mind of the employer. From some pinnacle of the future we may look back on the past and say, that "at this time the present value of the marginal productivity of John Jones was $2 per hour of his labor." But the fact which decides whether John Jones shall be employed at any given time is not this objective marginal productivity but the subjective marginal productivity; i.e., what some employer, who knows John Jones, *thinks* is his marginal productivity. Furthermore, this subjective marginal productivity depends not merely on the expected size of the future outcome, but also, as we have seen, on the distribution of its probabilities, and even also on the ability to estimate these probabilities.

What Determines Expectations?

Thus expectations help to determine prices at any time. But what determines the expectations? This is unfortunately a problem about which we know all too little, and it does not seem possible to make any clear a priori judgments about it. Do people expect past trends to continue? If, for instance, prices have been rising, do they expect them to go on rising? There is some evidence that this is the case, especially in regard to commodities in which there is much speculation. On the other hand, it may be that a past rise in price induces people to believe that prices are now due for a fall. The problem of expectations therefore resolves itself largely into the question, how far people are governed in their expectations of the future by their experience of the past. Obviously, the experience of the past is all we have to draw upon in seeking to foretell the future. But just how we shall interpret that experience is a difficult matter. We may, perhaps, venture upon one proposition: The more regular is past experience, the more likely are we to believe that the future will copy the past. If prices have been stable for a long time, we are likely to believe that they will continue so. Businessmen apparently believe that business will continue to prosper for an indefinite future period even on the eve of a crash. The longer the period of a depression, the more difficult it seems to be to emerge from it; for the more it continues, the more people believe that it will continue; and the more people believe that it will continue, the more it continues!

The Elasticity of Expectations

To provide a convenient term to measure this phenomenon J.R. Hicks has devised the concept of elasticity of expectations. This is defined as "the ratio of the proportional rise in expected future prices (of a commodity) to the proportional rise in its current price."[6] If a rise in prices is expected to continue at the same rate, the elasticity of expectations is unity. If a current rise in prices leads to the prospect of a smaller price rise in the future, the elasticity of expectations is less than unity. If a fall in price is expected in the future because of a rise in price now, elasticity of expectations is negative. This concept unfortunately has not turned out to be operationally very useful; its value is too unstable, and it expresses only the expected value aspect of the future, not the other dimensions of risk.

Potential Surprise

An interesting alternative approach to the problem of uncertainty in expectations has been proposed by G. L. S. Shackle.[7] He rejects the use of the classical probability concept, on the ground that what we are

[6] Hicks, *op. cit.*, p. 205.
[7] G. L. S. Shackle, *Expectation in Economics*, New York, Cambridge University Press, 1949.

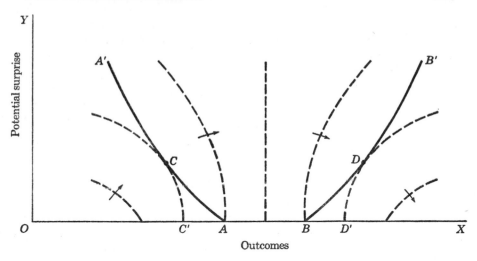

Fig. 157. The Potential Surprise Function

concerned with here is subjective probabilities, not objective probabilities, and he proposes to conceptualize these by the concept of *potential surprise*—that is, how surprised would we be if something happens. Potential surprise clearly has a zero value, of not being surprised at all, and perhaps has a vague upper limit of complete dumbfounderment. If then we plot a series of possible outcomes in Fig. 157 along OX, and potential surprise along OY, we may suppose that between outcomes A and B we would not be surprised at all, but that below A or above B our surprise would increase rapidly. Suppose, for instance, we plotted tomorrow's expected temperature along OX; some range around the usual average, AB, will not surprise us at all, but very high or very low temperatures will surprise us a great deal. Similarly OX could measure tomorrow's wheat price, next year's income, or any economic variable. Then we might postulate indifference curves in this field, like the dashed lines in Fig. 157; the rather peculiar shape of the utility surface of which these are the contours reflects the fact that we like *more* potential surprise for bad outcomes and *less* for good outcomes—outcomes we suppose getting better as we go from O to X. The point D is the most preferred position on the potential surprise curve BB', and C is the *least* preferred position on the potential surprise curve AA'; these Shackle calls the "focus outcomes." The outcomes C' and D' which have the same utility as C and D he calls the "standardised focus outcomes." Whether people actually think this way is a question; however, the approach does have the merit of focusing on two outcomes, good and bad, and this is undoubtedly characteristic of many expectations.

The Consistency of Expectations

An interesting question raised by the concept of expectations is that of the consistency of current expectations. Suppose, for instance, that Mr. A thinks the price of coal next year will be $12 per ton, while Mr. B thinks it will be $10 per ton. Obviously, both these gentlemen cannot be right, and at least one of them *must* be surprised, either favorably or unfavorably. Unless everyone thought alike, therefore, the nonfulfillment of expectations would of necessity be a constant experience of mankind. Even if everyone had the same expectations, there is no guarantee that they would be fulfilled. Indeed, if everyone has the same expectations there is a practical certainty that they will not be fulfilled. Suppose everyone thought that the price of coal next year was going to be very high—say, $25 per ton. As a consequence of this belief people would seek to shift their purchases of coal into the current year, following the principle of substitution. Cellars and bunkers would be filled; mines would work to capacity. The result would be that next year the demand for coal would fall, and the price would fall, probably far below the $25 per ton originally expected.

This whole process, which might be written, expectations—disappointment—revision of expectations, is the key to the learning process in social life. It is a key, however, which is so complex that it is hard to turn the lock, and we are still far from a satisfactory analysis of the processes. We cannot even define accurately those circumstances under which it leads to more realistic images and expectations, and those in which it leads to an increasingly false view of the world and of the future.

Conclusion

We shall go no further in this volume in the analysis of price determination, though much remains to be done, especially in the study of uncertainty. It is clear that when we take time into our consideration in a specific fashion, much of our previous analysis must be modified. The task of reformulating the theory of monopoly, of selling cost, of imperect competition, in terms of expectations, capital, and time is one which remains for the future. Nevertheless, the journey we have made has not been in vain, and the conclusions at which we have arrived, though not the whole truth, are of substantial importance. Those movements in demand, cost, and supply which are due to changes in expectations are ephemeral movements; and though expectations change constantly and seem hopelessly unpredictable, they shift around a base of long-run experience. The longer the period over which we consider our effects, the less importance can we attach to expectations as independent causative forces. In the long run, past and future, expectations and their results are all made one.

QUESTIONS AND EXERCISES

1. "Woodsman, spare that tree." What financial, as apart from sentimental, reasons could you offer in support of this advice?

2. One of the principal criticisms of the concept of a period of production has been that it must be infinite in length, for if we analyze capital goods back into the labor and equipment which made them, and analyze the equipment which made them into further equipment, and so on, there is no place we can stop short of the primordial amoeba. Does this criticism invalidate the proposition that without a period of production there would be no capital?

3. Can the extension of the theory of the firm to include time as an explicit variable be applied also to the theory of the consumer? Does discounting or compounding play any part in the consumer's choice?

4. Under what circumstances will the presence of an elasticity of expectations give rise to fluctuations in economic activity?

5. In what circumstances are expectations likely to be "self-justifying—i.e., when will expectations themselves produce, through their effects on human behavior, the thing expected?

6. If an astronomer foretells the movement of the planets, that movement is quite unaffected by the fact that it has been foretold. If an economist, however, forecasts a movement of prices, the fact that he has made the forecast may itself affect the future of prices. Why? Does this fact raise any question about the objective existence of the subject matter of economics? The astronomical universe is *there,* presumably, whether there are any astronomers or not. Is that true of the economic universe?

7. Sketch the possible potential surprise curves which would correspond to the four cases of uncertain expectations on p. 688. How far is the concept of *focus outcomes* useful in describing these cases? Could we develop a function relating the subjective present net value to the focus outcomes?

APPENDIX

THE LITERATURE OF ECONOMICS

The body of economic analysis presented in this work is the result of a long and often painful process of thought on the part of many minds through the years. The student of economics cannot appreciate adequately the significance of present-day theory unless he has a substantial acquaintance with the great works of the past and with the history of ideas. The study of past errors is a useful discipline against present errors. The study of how the peculiar circumstances of a past time led its thinkers to ascribe general validity to particular institutions serves as a constant warning against ascribing too much general ity to the peculiar circumstances of our own day. Any one author is limited by the scope of his own interests, and the student can never be acquainted with the scope of his subject unless he approaches it through the mediation of many different minds. It is not the purpose of this appendix to outline a systematic history of economic thought, nor an exhaustive bibliography of the literature; rather, is it intended to give some indication to the student of the points of origin of the principal ideas he has encountered in this work, and to guide his interests in further reading. There are several excellent histories of economic thought;[1] and the student would be well advised to read at least one of them, to get the broad historical picture.

Books about great books, however, are no substitute for the great

[1] Alexander Gray, *The Development of Economic Doctrine*, Longmans, Green, 1947; Erich Roll, *A History of Economic Thought*, Prentice-Hall, 1942; Edmund Whittaker, *A History of Economic Ideas*, Longmans, Green, 1940; R. L. Heilbroner, *The Worldly Philosophers*, Simon and Schuster, 1953; T. W. Hutchinson, *A Review of Economic Doctrines*, Oxford University Press, 1953; Joseph A. Schumpeter, *History of Economic Analysis*, Oxford University Press, 1954; Henry W. Spiegel (ed.), *The Development of Economic Thought*, Wiley, 1952.

books themselves, and the serious student should not long delay the study of the classical works of theory. The greatest of these, even after more than a century and a half, is Adam Smith's *Inquiry into the Nature and Causes of the Wealth of Nations* (1776).[2] Lacking virtually all the mathematical and graphic techniques of modern value theory, Adam Smith nevertheless perceived, not always with perfect clarity but always with astonishing insight, the essential relationships that lie at the heart of economic life. What I have called the principle of equal advantage, and the idea of the movement of resources under the stimulus of prices and profits from one occupation to another, which is the central idea of the theory of value and distribution, stems directly from Adam Smith. Chapters 7 and 9 of his Book 1 could be used today with hardly any modification in an accurate elementary text. In his concept of "effective demand" (in modern terminology, the quantity demanded at the normal price) lies the germ of the modern theory of supply and demand. His distinction (unfortunately named, but vital nonetheless) between "productive" labor that was embodied in goods and "unproductive" labor not so embodied was the foundation of the theory of capital. His great defense of free trade against the mercantilists in Book 4 is famous, but it must not be thought that he was a bigoted advocate of "laissez faire." Indeed, almost half the work (Book 5) is a discussion of the proper functions of the state. Then his Book 3 outlines with great insight a theory of economic progress, previously much neglected, but now, with the widespread interest in economic development, worth careful study. It is indeed almost depressing to go back to Adam Smith on economic development and see what little progress we have made on the subject since 1776! Most of all, the *Wealth of Nations* is worth reading for its style and spirit—full of wisdom and the observation of life, universal in the material from which it draws. Of Adam Smith it may often be said that he draws correct conclusions from faulty reasoning, his insight and wide observation affording him conclusions which his imperfect analytical techniques did not enable him to prove. More than any other economist, with the possible exception of P. H. Wicksteed, Adam Smith embodies the liberal tradition of humane letters. The student who learns to love his quiet wit and keen but gentle observation of humanity will never degenerate into a narrow-minded specialist.

A writer of very different character, yet in his own way almost equally important, is David Ricardo. The student should read his

[2] Cannan's edition (Methuen, 1904) is probably the best. This has been republished in the Modern Library.

Principles of Political Economy and Taxation (1817)[3] not for its style, which is arid and humorless, nor for its conclusions, many of which are erroneous, but for its crystalline logic. Ricardo's mind cut through the inconsistencies of Adam Smith and reduced economics to a system in which the conclusions followed inexorably from the axioms. Unfortunately, the axioms were not always correct, and the conclusions suffer accordingly, but the student who follows the argument will have an excellent training in the discipline of economic logic. It is to Ricardo that we owe the first faint beginnings of the marginal analysis, in his statement of the law of diminishing returns and his theory of rent. The modern theory of the economic surplus arising in the case of a less than perfectly elastic supply had its beginnings in the Ricardian theory of rent, though its modern applications are much wider than Ricardo imagined.

In reading the classical economists it must constantly be borne in mind that their system is a special case of our more general modern constructions. The relatively little importance given to demand in their theory of value may be traced to their general (implicit) assumption that supplies are perfectly elastic. In such a case, of course, prices do not in the long run depend on demand at all, but are determined by the level at which the supply is perfectly elastic, which in its turn is determined by "the cost of production." Ricardo was perhaps the first to recognize the possibility of what we now call an imperfectly elastic supply in the case of land, and saw that a rise in demand would raise the price at least of foodstuffs by pushing production on to poorer lands. Even Ricardo, however, assumed implicitly a perfectly elastic supply in the case of labor in his subsistence theory.

Ricardo and Torrens between them developed the theory of comparative advantage in international trade, though it was left to an economist of the next generation (Cairnes) to perceive the generality of this principle. With Ricardo, indeed, "model building" enters economics fairly explicitly, even though it is implicit in Adam Smith, and Ricardo does not go beyond the mathematical equipment of arithmetical examples.

Another writer of Ricardo's time who is worth reading today is the Rev. T. R. Malthus. He is principally famous for his essays on population, the first of which, 1798,[4] is a brilliant essay in moral theology on the theme of the long-run equilibrium of human misery; but it does not carry economics much beyond where Adam Smith left it. In the

---

[3] The magnificent edition of Ricardo's complete works in nine volumes by Piero Sraffa (Cambridge University Press, 1955) is the definitive version. The *Principles* are available in Everyman's Library.

[4] The *Essay on Population* is in Everyman's Library and also in Ann Arbor Books.

light of modern monetary theory, however, his *Principles of Political Economy* (especially Part II) stands out as a work of remarkable insight, which anticipates many of the Keynesian principles and yet was largely neglected for over a century.

Another writer whose true significance did not appear till a later date was A. A. Cournot (1801–1877), whose *Recherches*⁵ (1838) developed, in mathematical form, much of the modern theory of the firm; the concepts, though not the names, of the marginal analysis were first developed by him. He should be read by any student who has some elementary knowledge of the calculus. The mathematical form of his writing, however, prevented him from having much influence on the economists of his own time, and the classical system, especially as expounded by J. S. Mill,⁶ held undisputed sway until about 1870.

Kark Marx (1818–1883) stands in a class by himself. *Das Kapital*⁷ (1867) is a book which has had a profound influence on the world. It represents an early attempt to develop a theory of the economic system as a whole and of its progress in time. In this attempt, however, Marx was greatly handicapped by the inadequate analytical apparatus which he inherited from Smith and Ricardo; consequently, errors which can be generously interpreted as matters of exposition in the classical economists, such as the labor theory of value, are erected into the foundation of a logical but inadequate system of economic reasoning. Although Marx made little contribution to the broad line of development of economic thought, the student should read at least the first volume of *Das Kapital* or, better still, Borchardt's condensation. To study the errors of a great, if wrongheaded, mind is often more valuable than to skim the platitudes of a small one.

The next important group of writers constitute the so-called "marginal utility school." The ideas of this school were developed at about the same time (c. 1870), independently in England by Stanley Jevons, in Austria by Karl Menger and Friedrich von Wieser, and in France by Léon Walras. With this school began the extended use of mathematics in economic analysis, foreshadowed by Cournot; for though many of its exponents expressed their ideas in literary form, their theories were essentially mathematical in structure. Perhaps the great-

---

⁵ *Recherches sur les principes mathématiques de la théorie des richesses,* English trans. by N. T. Bacon, Macmillan, 1897; this contains also a useful bibliography of early mathematical economics.

⁶ *Principles of Political Economy* (1848).

⁷ The translation by Eden and Cedar Paul (Allen and Unwin, London, 1928) is very good; the Modern Library edition, containing Stephen Trask's translation of Borchardt's condensation, together with "The Communist Manifesto," is an excellent introduction.

est work of this whole school is P. H. Wicksteed's *The Common Sense of Political Economy*,[8] even though it appeared forty years after the first formulation of 1870. This is a book which every student of economics should read, in spite of a certain prolixity and an occasionally labored style. It is couched (often at the cost of being cumbersome) in nonmathematical language, and it provides the most consistent and highly developed exposition of the utility analysis as the foundation of both demand and supply, and as a general theory of choice. Perhaps Wicksteed's greatest contribution was his demonstration that economics is not merely a matter of the market place or of financial dealings, but is one aspect of *all* human activity—namely, the aspect of choice, or the balancing of alternatives one against another, where limited means have to be apportioned among competing ends. His delightful discussions of how much family prayers should be shortened to speed a parting guest to the train, or of the value of a mother-in-law in terms of how high a cliff one would drive off to save her, should open the eyes of every student to the great *generality* of economic principles. Wicksteed, more than any other, laid the ghost of that shadowy creation, the "economic man." Wicksteed also made valuable contributions to the generality of economic principles themselves, and showed, for instance, the essentially similar derivation of supply and demand, and the universal character of the "law of diminishing returns." The concept of a homogeneous production function, and the distinction between diminishing returns to various proportions of factors and diminishing (or increasing) returns to scale, also owe much to Wicksteed.

The student whose acquaintance with mathematics extends to the elementary calculus should read Jevons's *The Theory of Political Economy*, in spite of the many errors which it contains. Even the nonmathematical student will find much of interest in this work; its freshness of style, its enthusiasm, the sense of discovery, of the opening up of vast new areas of conquest to the human mind, can hardly fail to be inspiring even if, as Marshall pointed out, Jevons was much less of a revolutionary than he himself thought.[9] Much of what the marginal utility school proclaimed is implicit in the classical economists, and, indeed, almost became explicit in the work of Nassau Senior, a contemporary of Ricardo, and was made quite explicit in the unnoticed work of the tragic Gossen (1854). It was not, however, until the productive 1870's that the dependence of value on scarcity in relation to demand, and of scarcity on cost of production, was made quite clear. Von Wieser,[10] in particular, helped to clarify the rela-

[8] Fourth ed., Macmillan, London, 1910 (reprinted 1924).

[9] See Alfred Marshall, *Principles of Economics*, 8th ed., Macmillan, 1938, appendix I, pp. 813-821.

[10] F. von Wieser, *Social Economics*, trans. by A. Ford Hinrichs; Greenberg, 1927.

tionships between the value of finished goods and of factors of production, and showed how the value of factors of production depended on the value of the goods which they produced.

It remained for Walras,[11] however, to bring together the complex relationships of economic life into a single mathematical system of mutual determination and mutual interaction. Walras is the Laplace of economics; just as Laplace transformed astronomy from a system in which the movement of each heavenly body was attached to its own particular cause to a system in which the mutual interactions of all bodies upon each other determine the behavior of all, so Walras transformed economics from a system in which each value was attached to its own particular cause to a system in which all values, whether of finished goods, intermediate products, or factors of production, are mutually determined by the interaction of the innumerable forces of desire upon the innumerable resistances of scarcity. The student who for want of mathematical ability cannot read Walras suffers under a severe handicap, and no better investment for the future economist could be recommended than the improvement of his mathematical skills to this point.

The marginal utility school is also important for its contributions to the theory of capital, though the exact significance of these contributions is still somewhat a matter of dispute. The basic idea of their theory of capital is that of a "period of production" between inputs and outputs. Because of this period of production inputs of "original factors" are embodied in intermediate products, which are "real capital." The volume of these intermediate products clearly depends on the length of the period of production. Jevons developed these ideas in a somewhat crude form, but their greatest development is due to Eugen von Böhm-Bawerk, whose *Positive Theory of Capital*[12] is essential to the study of this part of the subject. Another important contributor to this part of the subject was Knut Wicksell (1851–1926), whose little book *Über Wert, Kapital und Rente* (Jena, 1893) systematized the ideas of Böhm-Bawerk and by reducing them to mathematical form brought out their underlying assumptions.

The next great writer in point of time is Alfred Marshall, who may not unjustly be regarded as the father of modern Anglo-Saxon economics. Perhaps his greatest contribution is the development of supply and demand curves and of the concept of elasticity of demand and supply. These tools of analysis are so essential to the modern economist that

[11] Léon Walras, *Eléments d'économie politique pure*, 4th ed., Lausanne, 1900, trans. by William Jaffé, *Elements of Pure Economics*, Irwin, 1954.
[12] Trans. by William Smart, Stechert, 1923.

he is apt to forget their relative youth. In his *Principles of Economics*[13] Marshall developed a system not unlike that of Walras in essential principles but written in geometrical rather than algebraic language—losing thereby in generality but gaining in practicality. The basic proposition of the system is that the equilibrium output of a commodity is that at which the supply price and the demand price of the output are equal (Volume I). Marshall showed how the demand curve depended on the underlying utility relationships, and how the supply curve was related to costs. We are indebted to him for the distinction—useful, if dangerous —between short-run and long-run situations. We owe to him also certain developments of the theory of the firm in monopoly, though he did not succeed in integrating the theory of the firm explicitly into the main body of analysis.

Marshall began an era of great proliferation of economic writings in which we still live and in which, therefore, it is difficult to assess enduring values. As far as the tools of analysis are concerned, we have seen the development of the indifference curve, especially by Pareto, whose *Cours* and *Manuale*[14] are essential reading for the advanced student. In the theory of capital and interest the works of Irving Fisher are to be highly recommended.[15] H. J. Davenport is worth reading for his original point of view and his concept of alternative cost.[16] F. H. Knight's *Risk, Uncertainty, and Profit*, 1921, reprinted by the London School of Economics, 1946, is an important if somewhat unclassifiable work.

Perhaps the most important developments of twentieth-century economics lie in four fields. (1) There has been a great advance in what used to be called the theory of money, but now is frequently called "macroeconomics"—i.e., the theory of the broad averages and aggregates of the whole economic system, such as the general level of prices, of output, of wages, of employment, of interest rates, and so on. (2) There has also been an advance in extending the theory of relative values to include cases of imperfect competition and monopoly. We should perhaps include in this area, though the developments are somewhat unrelated, some considerable advances in the theory of the firm, both through the applications of the theory of linear programming and through the development of more dynamic, behavioral theories of the behavior of economic organizations. (3) Especially in the past ten or fifteen years there has been a great

[13] Eighth ed., Macmillan, 1938.

[14] *Cours d'économie politique*, Lausanne, 1896; *Manuale di economia politica*, Milan, 1906.

[15] *The Nature of Capital and Income*, Macmillan, 1906; *The Theory of Interest*, Macmillan, 1930.

[16] *The Economics of Enterprise*, Macmillan, 1913; *Value and Distribution*, University of Chicago Press, 1908.

revival of interest in the study of economic development, with some new theoretical contributions to dynamic economics. (4) The application of mathematical models, and more recently of computer techniques to economics, has made great strides, especially in the direction of handling models with large numbers of variables, for instance, input-output models.

Economists up to and including Marshall had many observations regarding the theory of money, but with the possible exception of Ricardo— whose cost-of-production theory of the value of money, however inadequate, at least fitted in with his general system—the theory of money was never integrated into the general theory of value. Although Adam Smith set out on an "inquiry into the nature and causes of the wealth of nations," the attention of economists in the 19th century became increasingly concentrated on the problem of "value"—i.e., of relative prices. The reawakening of interest in the broader problems of macroeconomics begins perhaps with Wicksell, whose *Geldzins und Guterpreise*[17] should be read by every student, and whose *Lectures on Political Economy*[18] are well worth the attention of the more advanced student. Irving Fisher's *The Purchasing Power of Money* is also a landmark, for it gives the first clear formulation of the "equation of exchange" ($MV = PT$). The modern developments in macroeconomics, however, are most closely associated with the work of J. M. Keynes (the late Lord Keynes). His early *Tract on Monetary Reform* (Harcourt, Brace, 1924) is still worth reading, in spite of some out-of-date material. It is an eloquent plea for the stabilization of prices as the object of monetary policy, and contains, along with D. H. Robertson's little book entitled *Money*, the essence of the "oral tradition" on this subject at Cambridge, England, which flowed from the teaching of Marshall. Keynes's major works are the *Treatise on Money* (Harcourt, Brace, 1931) and the *General Theory of Employment, Interest, and Money* (Harcourt, Brace, 1936). These are not easy to read, and are often confused in thought. Nevertheless, the serious student cannot fail to derive substantial benefit from their study; they open up vistas of intellectual exploration which have by no means been fully covered.

The theory of imperfect competition has been developed in two principal works—E. H. Chamberlin's *The Theory of Monopolistic Competition* (Harvard University Press, 1933) and Joan Robinson's *The Economics of Imperfect Competition* (Macmillan, 1934).[19] The elementary theory of the firm and industry in its modern form, especially as it involves the use of the marginal revenue curve, is to be attributed mainly to

[17] Trans. under the title of *Interest and Prices* by R. F. Kahn, Macmillan, 1930.
[18] Trans. by E. Classen, New York, Macmillan, 1934.
[19] Another important work in the field is Robert Triffin, *Monopolistic Competition and General Equilibrium Theory*, Harvard University Press, 1940.

these writers. The assumption of perfect competition which underlay so much of the classical economics, and even the Marshallian system, was shown by these writers to be a special case of a more general theory.

The theory of economic decision-making has received much attention in recent years. One aspect of this is the development of the theory of games. The student who finds the classic work of J. von Neumann and Oskar Morgenstern[20] heavy going may find a clear exposition in R. O. Luce and H. Raiffa.[21] Another aspect is "operation research," of which the theory of linear programming is a part; a brief résumé of these developments will be found in K. E. Boulding and W. A. Spivey.[22] Another development is in the analysis of dynamic patterns of decision-making and their computer simulation; R. M. Cyert and J. G. March[23] and the group at the Carnegie Institute of Technology have pioneered in this work.

Recent contributions to the theory of economic development are A. O. Hirschman[24] and H. Leibenstein;[25] this field seems almost to be moving out of economics into a general social science with such writers as Everett E. Hagen[26] and David C. McClelland.[27]

In econometrics the great pioneers were Henry Schultz[28] and Ragnar Frisch,[29] and Wesley Mitchell.[30] The name of Wassily Leontief[31] is particularly associated with input-output analysis. G. Tintner[32] and Stephen Valavanis-Vail[33] have written good textbooks.

Among more general works, those of J. A. Schumpeter[34] are important

[20] J. von Neumann and Oskar Morgenstern, *Theory of Games and Economic Behavior*, Princeton University Press, 1944.

[21] R. O. Luce and H. Raiffa, *Games and Decisions*, New York, Wiley, 1957.

[22] K. E. Boulding and W. A. Spivey, eds., *Linear Programming and the Theory of the Firm*, New York, Macmillan, 1960.

[23] R. M. Cyert and J. G. March, *A Behavioral Theory of the Firm*, Englewood Cliffs, N.J., Prentice-Hall, 1963.

[24] A. O. Hirschman, *The Strategy of Economic Development*, Yale University Press, 1958.

[25] H. Leibenstein, *Economic Backwardness and Economic Growth*, New York, Wiley, 1953.

[26] F. E. Hagen, *On the Theory of Social Change*, Homewood, Ill., Dorsey Press, 1962.

[27] D. C. McClelland, *The Achieving Society*, Princeton, N.J., Van Nostrand, 1961.

[28] Henry Schultz, *The Theory and Measurement of Demand*, 2nd ed., University of Chicago Press, 1957.

[29] Ragnar Frisch was the first editor of *Econometrica* (Vol. 1, 1933).

[30] His last work, *What Happens during Business Cycles*, New York, National Bureau of Economic Research, 1951, is probably the best introduction.

[31] W. W. Leontief, *The Structure of American Economy, 1919–1939*, 2nd ed., New York, Oxford University Press, 1951.

[32] G. Tintner, *Econometrics*, New York, Wiley, 1952.

[33] S. Valavanis-Vail, *Econometrics*, New York, McGraw-Hill, 1959.

[34] *The Theory of Economic Development*, trans. by Redvers Ouie, Harvard University Press, 1935; *Business Cycles*, New York, McGraw-Hill, 1939; and *Capitalism, Socialism and Democracy*, New York, Harper & Row, 1942.

for their insight into business cycles and into the whole process of economic development. The student of the dynamic process will find important contributions in J. R. Hicks's *Value and Capital* (2nd ed., Oxford University Press, 1946), as well as an admirable exposition of the static theory of value. Perhaps the most important of modern works is Paul A. Samuelson's *Foundations of Economic Analysis* (Harvard University Press, 1947), though it is not accessible to those without a fair mathematical equipment. It contains a definitive account of the theory of maximization, and the first systematic exposition of dynamic theory using the tool of difference equations. Baumol's *Economic Dynamics* (Macmillan, 1951) is a very useful introduction to this field, as is R. F. Harrod's *Toward a Dynamic Economics* (Macmillan, 1948).

The field of welfare economics has shown great activity in recent years. Pigou's *Economics of Welfare* (4th ed., Macmillan, 1932), though now quite out of date, is still a "classic" work in the field. Students interested in modern welfare economics should read works by Reder,[35] Myint,[36] Little,[37] and Arrow.[38] Arrow's work in particular represents a somewhat new departure in economics, using the apparatus of mathematical logic.

The nearer we get to the present day the more important becomes periodical literature as a source of important contributions. The *Quarterly Journal of Economics,* published in Cambridge, Mass., founded in 1885, is probably the oldest periodical specializing in economic theory. The *Economic Journal,* organ of the Royal Economic Society and published in London, was founded in 1891. The *Journal of Political Economy* (founded in 1892 and published at the University of Chicago) and the *American Economic Review* (organ of the American Economic Association, founded in 1911) often contain important theoretical articles, but tend predominantly in the direction of applied studies. *Economica* (founded in 1921) is the organ of the London School of Economics. The *Review of Economic Studies* (founded in 1933) is a frequent vehicle for the younger theorists and contains many important articles. *Econometrica* (organ of the Econometric Society and founded in 1933) is the principal vehicle for articles in mathematical and statistical economics. The *Review of Economic Statistics* (Harvard University) is also important in this field. There are several "local" journals which from time to time have articles of general interest: the *Canadian Journal of Economics and Political*

[35] Melvin W. Reder, *Studies in the Theory of Welfare Economics,* Columbia University Press, 1947.

[36] Hla Myint, *Theories of Welfare Economics,* Harvard University Press, 1948.

[37] I. M. D. Little, *A Critique of Welfare Economics,* New York, Oxford University Press, 1950.

[38] Kenneth Arrow, *Social Choice and Individual Values,* New York, Wiley, 2nd ed., 1963.

Science, the *Economic Record* (Australia), the *South African Journal of Economics,* *The Manchester School,* are especially to be recommended. The *Zeitschrift für Nationaloekonomie* (Vienna) and the *Giornale degli economisti* (Italy) are also of importance. *Kyklos* (Zurich) is an international journal with articles in several languages. It would be impossible to attempt a bibliography of the important articles in these journals in the small space of this appendix; the student whose interests lie in any special field will soon have to make such a bibliography for himself. The book reviews in these journals (especially in the *American Economic Review*) in themselves form a most valuable bibliography both for general theory and for all the special fields. The American Economic Association now publishes *The Journal of Economic Abstracts,* invaluable in the light of the increasing volume of periodical literature.

In recent years the publications of specialized economic research agencies, such as the Cowles Foundation at Yale University and the National Bureau of Economic Research in New York, and publications of government departments, such as the U.S. Department of Commerce, have become increasingly important, especially on the empirical side of economics.

The volumes of collected articles published by the American Economic Association are a useful introduction to the periodical literature. The *Survey of Contemporary Economics,* Vols. I and II, also published by the American Economic Association, is a useful guide to recent economic thought and bibliography in many fields.

The list might be continued almost indefinitely, and it is not the purpose of this appendix to provide the student with a complete bibliography. It is hoped, however, that the works mentioned above may provide an essential point of departure for further inquiry.

INDEX

711